Mastering Windows Server 2019

Third Edition

The complete guide for system administrators to install, manage, and deploy new capabilities with Windows Server 2019

Jordan Krause

BIRMINGHAM - MUMBAI

Mastering Windows Server 2019

Third Edition

Producers: Caitlin Meadows, Suman Sen
Acquisition Editor – Peer Reviews: Saby D'silva
Project Editor: Rianna Rodrigues
Content Development Editors: Bhavesh Amin
Copy Editor: Safis Editing
Technical Editor: Karan Sonawane
Proofreader: Safis Editing
Indexer: Manju Arasan
Presentation Designer: Ganesh Bhadwalkar

First published: October 2016
Second edition: March 2019
Third edition: July 2021

Production reference: 2280721

Published by Packt Publishing Ltd.
Livery Place
35 Livery Street
Birmingham B3 2PB, UK.

ISBN 978-1-80107-831-3

www.packt.com

Contributors

About the author

Jordan Krause is an IT professional of more than 20 years and has received 9 Microsoft MVP awards for his work with Microsoft server and networking technologies. One of the world's first experts on Microsoft DirectAccess, he has a passion for helping companies find the best ways to enable a remote workforce. Committed to continuous learning, Jordan holds certifications as an MCSE, MCSA, and MCITP Enterprise Administrator and has authored numerous books on Microsoft technologies. Jordan lives in beautiful West Michigan (USA) but works daily with companies around the world.

I would never have the capacity, focus, or drive to work on a writing project like this without the support of my wonderful wife. Thank you for being by my side for all of those 5:00am starts, Laura!

About the reviewer

Luka Manojlović works as an external consultant, architect, and implementer for IT infrastructure solutions. With more than 20 years of experience in storage, networking, virtualization, and servers, Luka still enthusiastically approaches challenges and projects he works on.

First of all, I would like to thank the author, Jordan Krause. It was a pleasure to read the book as it was written. I think it will help the reader to better understand the magical world of Windows Server technologies. I would also like to thank the staff at Packt for their great collaboration.

We'd also like to thank **Aaron Guilmette** and **Dishan Francis** for their feedback on *Chapter 3, Active Directory*.

Table of Contents

Preface

The world is changing. When my wife and I had our first child, I remember numerous people telling us all about how quickly life would fly past now. This is one of those things that everyone hears, but nobody believes until they suddenly realize it has been 5…10…*20* years and suddenly we're looking back wondering, "Where did it go?"

So it is with technology. Computers are ever-changing, ever-improving. My first computer at my first IT job was running Windows 98. Some of you reading this have likely never heard of Windows 98, because you weren't born yet. Ouch.

Entering the technology workforce today is very different than it was back then. Nowadays you're often expected to know everything there is to know about current on-premises infrastructures such as Windows 10, Windows Server 2019, switching and routing, and firewalls, and even have a pretty good bearing on security risks, prevention, and remediation. In addition to current systems, it is extremely helpful to know and have experience with previous versions of these technologies so that you aren't completely lost when you encounter one for the first time. Tack on to that all the quickly escalating cloud options provided by Azure, which seem to change daily, and I imagine it can all feel a bit overwhelming.

While marketing engines around the world are working hard to make everyone believe that on-premises resources are a thing of the past, it simply isn't true. Most businesses, and especially most enterprises, will continue to run on-premises servers, storage, and impressively complex networking for decades to come. What is it that drives the processing power of these physical datacenters for the majority of companies around the world? Windows Server. In fact, even if you have gone all-in for cloud adoption and host 100% of your serving resources in Azure, you are still making use of Windows Server 2019. It is the operating system that underpins Azure!

Over the last few years, we have all become familiar with software-defined computing, using virtualization technology to turn our server workloads into a software layer. Now, Microsoft is expanding on this idea with new terms such as software-defined networking, software-defined storage, and even an entire Software-Defined Data Center. The technologies that make these happen allow us to virtualize and share resources on a grand scale.

To make our workloads more flexible and cloud-ready, Microsoft is taking major steps in shrinking the server compute platform and creating new ways of interfacing with those servers. There is an underlying preference for new Windows Servers to be running the smaller, more efficient, and more secure Server Core interface. Additionally, application containers have made huge advancements over the past few years, and Server 2019 allows us to transition our applications into containers to run them in isolation from each other and on a mass scale. We also have new centralized management tools for administering our servers and networks, namely, the newly updated Windows Admin Center.

We'll take some time to discover together the inner workings of the newest version of this server operating system, which will drive and support so many of our business infrastructures over the coming years. Windows servers have dominated our datacenter rack spaces for more than two decades. Will this newest iteration in the form of Windows Server 2019 continue that trend?

Who this book is for

Anyone interested in Windows Server 2019 or in learning more in general about a Microsoft-centric datacenter will benefit from this book. An important deciding factor when choosing which content was appropriate for such a volume was making sure that anyone who had a baseline in working with computers could pick this up and start making use of it within their own networks. If you are already proficient in Microsoft infrastructure technologies and have worked with prior versions of Windows Server, then there are some focused topics on the aspects and parts that are brand new and only available in Server 2019. On the other hand, if you are currently in a desktop support role, or if you are coming fresh into the IT workforce, care was taken in the pages of this book to ensure that you will receive a rounded understanding, not only of what is brand new in Server 2019, but also what core capabilities it includes as carryovers from previous versions of the operating system, and that are still crucial to be aware of when working in a Microsoft-driven datacenter.

What this book covers

Chapter 1, Getting Started with Windows Server 2019, gives us an introduction to the latest Server operating system and an overview of the new technologies and capabilities that it can provide. We will also spend a little bit of time exploring the updated interface for those who may not be comfortable with it yet.

Chapter 2, Installing and Managing Windows Server 2019, dives right into the very first thing we will have to do when working with Server 2019: install it! While this seems like a simple task, there are a number of versioning and licensing variables that need to be understood before you proceed with your own install. From there, we will start to expand upon Microsoft's centralized management mentality, exploring how we can now manage and interact with our servers without ever having to log into them.

Chapter 3, Active Directory, leads us into the most core and essential role that exists in a Windows Server environment. AD is the central repository for many different types of data inside most corporate infrastructures, and without understanding the tools that exist to interface with this directory you will not be able to do much work with those fancy new servers.

Chapter 4, DNS and DHCP, segues into two other important roles that exist in almost every network. DNS and DHCP are both necessary technologies and concepts to understand for any IT administrator, and both happen to be roles that can be serviced from Windows Server 2019. We'll dig into both.

Chapter 5, Group Policy, showcases a fantastic policy engine that can be used inside any Active Directory environment to create a centralized management location for your users and workstations. Whether you are interested in setting up password policies, configuring lockdowns on your systems, automatically mapping network drives, or even distributing software, Group Policy is a powerful tool that is often underutilized.

Chapter 6, Certificates in Windows Server 2019, jumps into one of the pieces of Windows Server that has existed for many years, and yet most server administrators that I meet are unfamiliar with it. We'll take a closer look at certificates as they become more and more commonly required for new technologies that we roll out. By the end of this chapter, you should be able to spin up your own PKI and start issuing certificates for free!

Chapter 7, Networking with Windows Server 2019, begins with an introduction to that big, scary IPv6, and continues from there into building a toolbox of items that are baked into Windows Server 2019 and can be used in your daily networking tasks. We will also discuss the parts and pieces that make up Software-Defined Networking.

Chapter 8, Remote Access, takes a look at the different remote access technologies that are built into Windows Server 2019. Follow along as we explore the capabilities provided by VPN, DirectAccess, Web Application Proxy, and the new Always On VPN.

Chapter 9, Hardening and Security, gives some insight into security and encryption functions that are built into Windows Server 2019. Security is the primary focus of CIOs everywhere, so we'll explore what protection mechanisms are available to us out of the box.

Chapter 10, Server Core, throws us into the shrinking world of headless servers. Server Core has flown under the radar for many years but is critical to understand as we bring our infrastructures into a more security-conscious mindset. We'll make sure you have the information necessary to make your environment more secure and more efficient, all while lowering the amount of space and resources that are consumed by those servers.

Chapter 11, PowerShell, gets us into the new, blue command-line interface so that we can become comfortable using it and also learn why it is so much more powerful than Command Prompt. PowerShell is quickly becoming an indispensable tool for administering servers, especially in cases where you are adopting a centralized management and administration mindset.

Chapter 12, Redundancy in Windows Server 2019, looks at some platforms in Server 2019 that provide powerful data and computing redundancy. Follow along as we discuss Network Load Balancing, Failover Clustering, Storage Spaces Direct, and build our own instance of Storage Replica.

Chapter 13, Containers and Nano Server, incorporates the terms *open source* and *Linux* into a Microsoft book! Application containers are quickly becoming the new standard for hosting modern, scalable applications. Learn how to start enhancing your DevOps story using tools such as Windows Server containers, Hyper-V containers, Docker, and Kubernetes.

Chapter 14, Hyper-V, covers a topic that every server administrator should be very familiar with. Organizations have been moving their servers over to virtual machines en masse for many years. We'll use this chapter to make sure you understand how that hypervisor works and give you the resources required to build and manage one if and when you have the need.

Chapter 15, Troubleshooting Windows Server 2019, provides information about tools and software included with Windows Server that can be used to troubleshoot common problems. Server 2019 seems to be Microsoft's most stable and reliable server operating system to date, yet as you all know nothing is perfect, and issues are bound to present themselves. Here we discover tools like Resource Manager, Performance Monitor, and System Insights that help to keep our servers tuned and running well.

To get the most out of this book

Each technology that we discuss within the pages of this book is included in, or relates directly to, Windows Server 2019. If you can get your hands on a piece of server hardware and the Server 2019 installer files, you will be equipped to follow along and try these things out for yourself. We will talk about and reference some enterprise-class technologies that come with stiffer infrastructure requirements to make them work fully, and so you may have to put the actual testing of those items on hold until you are working in a more comprehensive test lab or environment, but the concepts are all still included in this book.

We will also discuss some items that are not included in Server 2019 itself, but that are used to extend its the capabilities and features. Some of these items help tie us into an Azure cloud environment, and some are provided by third parties, such as using Docker and Kubernetes on your Server 2019 to interact with application containers. Ultimately, you do not need to use these tools to manage your new Windows Server 2019 environment, but they do facilitate some pretty cool things that I think you will want to explore.

Download the color images

We also provide a PDF file that has color images of the screenshots/diagrams used in this book. You can download it here: `https://static.packt-cdn.com/downloads/9781801078313_ColorImages.pdf`.

Conventions used

There are several text conventions used throughout this book.

`CodeInText`: Indicates code words in text, database table names, folder names, filenames, file extensions, pathnames, dummy URLs, user input, and Twitter handles. For example: "Inside DNS, I am going to create an alias record that redirects `intranet` to `web1`."

Any command-line input or output is written as follows:

```
Uninstall-WindowsFeature -Name Windows-Defender
```

Bold: Indicates a new term, an important word, or words that you see on the screen. For example, words in menus or dialog boxes appear in the text like this. Here is an example: "Simply find the appropriate OU for his account to reside within, right-click on the OU, and navigate to **New** | **User**."

Warnings or important notes appear like this.

 Tips and tricks appear like this.

Get in touch

Feedback from our readers is always welcome.

General feedback: Email feedback@packtpub.com, and mention the book's title in the subject of your message. If you have questions about any aspect of this book, please email us at questions@packtpub.com.

Errata: Although we have taken every care to ensure the accuracy of our content, mistakes do happen. If you have found a mistake in this book we would be grateful if you would report this to us. Please visit, http://www.packtpub.com/submit-errata, selecting your book, clicking on the Errata Submission Form link, and entering the details.

Piracy: If you come across any illegal copies of our works in any form on the Internet, we would be grateful if you would provide us with the location address or website name. Please contact us at copyright@packtpub.com with a link to the material.

If you are interested in becoming an author: If there is a topic that you have expertise in and you are interested in either writing or contributing to a book, please visit http://authors.packtpub.com.

Reviews

Please leave a review. Once you have read and used this book, why not leave a review on the site that you purchased it from? Potential readers can then see and use your unbiased opinion to make purchase decisions, we at Packt can understand what you think about our products, and our authors can see your feedback on their book. Thank you!

For more information about Packt, please visit packtpub.com.

Share your thoughts

Once you've read *Mastering Windows Server 2019, Third Edition*, we'd love to hear your thoughts! Scan the QR code below to go straight to the Amazon review page for this book and share your feedback.

https://packt.link/r/1-801-07831-9

Your review is important to us and the tech community and will help us make sure we're delivering excellent quality content.

1
Getting Started with Windows Server 2019

Many years ago, Microsoft adjusted its operating system release ideology so that the latest Windows Server operating system is always structured very similarly to the latest Windows client operating system. This has been the trend for some time now, with Server 2008 R2 closely reflecting Windows 7, Server 2012 feeling a lot like Windows 8, and many of the same usability features that came with the Windows 8.1 update are also included with Server 2012 R2. This, of course, carried over to Server 2016 as well — giving it the same look and feel as if you were logged into a Windows 10 workstation.

Now that we are all familiar and comfortable with the Windows 10 interface, we typically have no problems jumping right into the Server 2016 interface and giving it a test drive. Windows Server 2019 is once again no exception to this rule, except that the release of client-side operating systems has shifted a little bit. Now, instead of releasing new versions of Windows (11, 12, 13, and so on), we are, for the time being, simply sticking with Windows 10 and giving it sub-version numbers, indicative of the dates when that operating system version was released. For example, Windows 10 version 1703 was released around March of 2017. Windows 10 version 1709 was released in September of 2017.

Then came 1803 and 1809—although 1809 was delayed a little and didn't release until somewhere closer to November, which wasn't the original plan. Follow that up with 1903 and 1909 and you start to see a pattern emerge. Then we moved into the year 2020, and suddenly our spring release of Windows 10 was called 2004. Hmm…2004 sounds fine when you pronounce it twenty-oh-four indicating the year 2020 and the month of April, but when seeing 2004 on paper, most folks started calling it two-thousand four, which sounds quite old and outdated, don't you think? I can't say for sure, but perhaps this is part of the reason that the newest (as of the time of writing) release version of Windows 10 goes by the name 20H2. All in all, you can see that Microsoft's current plan is to continue releasing a new feature release version of the Windows operating system every six months or so. However, expecting IT departments to lift and shift all of their servers just for the purposes of moving to an OS that is six months newer is crazy; sometimes it takes longer than that just to plan a migration.

Anyway, I'm getting ahead of myself a little, as we will be discussing the versioning of Windows Server later in this chapter, in our *Windows Server versions and licensing* section. The point here is that Windows Server 2019 looks and feels like the latest version of the Windows client operating system that was released at about the same time—that OS being Windows 10 1809. Before we get started talking about the features of Windows Server, it is important to establish a baseline for usability and familiarity in the operating system itself before diving deeper into the technologies running under the hood.

Let's spend a few minutes exploring the new graphical interface and options that are available for finding your way around this latest release of Windows Server, with a view to covering the following topics in this chapter:

- The purpose of Windows Server
- It's getting cloudy out there
- Windows Server versions and licensing
- Overview of new and updated features
- Navigating the interface
- Using the newer Settings screen
- Task Manager
- Task View

The purpose of Windows Server

Is asking what is the purpose of Windows Server a silly question? I don't think so. It's a good question to ponder, especially now that the definition for servers and server workloads is changing on a regular basis. The answer to this question for Windows clients is simpler. A Windows client machine is a requester, consumer, and contributor of data.

From where is this data being pushed and pulled? What enables the mechanisms and applications running on the client operating systems to interface with this data? What secures these users and their data? The answers to these questions reveal the purpose of servers in general. They house, protect, and serve up data to be consumed by clients.

Everything revolves around data in business today. Our email, documents, databases, customer lists—everything that we need to do business well is data. That data is critical to us. Servers are what we use to build the fabric upon which we trust our data to reside.

We traditionally think about servers using a client-server interface mentality. A user opens a program on their client computer, this program reaches out to a server in order to retrieve something, and the server responds as needed. This idea can be correctly applied to just about every transaction you may have with a server. When your domain-joined computer needs to authenticate you as a user, it reaches out to Active Directory on the server to validate your credentials and get an authentication token. When you need to contact a resource by name, your computer asks a DNS server how to get there. If you need to open a file, you ask the file server to send it your way.

Servers are designed to be the brains of our operation, and often by doing so transparently. In recent years, large strides have been taken to ensure resources are always available and accessible in ways that don't require training or a large effort on the part of our employees. It used to be true that the general user population knew the name of your server and how to contact it because that was generally required for them to be able to get to the information they needed. If their mapped drives disappeared, it wasn't uncommon that everyone would know how to throw \\server\share into File Explorer to get there via Plan B. It also used to be the case that your average business only ran one single server, enabling this to be true. Today our server landscape is vastly different, with even small businesses running a virtualization host that typically contains a dozen or more virtual servers, and much effort is made so that your workforce doesn't know or care anything about that server infrastructure; they simply expect it to work 100% of the time.

In most organizations, many different servers are needed in order to provide your workforce with the capabilities they require. Each service inside Windows Server is provided as, or as part of, a **role**. When you talk about needing new servers or configuring a new server for any particular task, what you are really referring to is the individual role or roles that are going to be configured on that server to get the work done. A server without any roles installed is useless, though depending on the chassis can make an excellent paperweight. A 3U SAN device could weigh upward of 100 pounds and keep your desk orderly even in the middle of a hurricane!

If you think of roles as the meat and potatoes of a server, then the next bit we will discuss is sort of like adding salt and pepper. Beyond the overhead roles you will install and configure on your servers, Windows also contains many features that can be installed, which sometimes stand alone, but more often complement specific roles in the operating system. Features may complement and add functionality to the base operating system such as **Telnet Client**. Or a feature may be added to a server in order to enhance an existing role, such as adding the **Network Load Balancing** feature to an already equipped remote access or IIS server. The combination of roles and features inside Windows Server is what equips that piece of metal to do work.

This book will, quite obviously, focus on a Microsoft-centric infrastructure. In these environments, the Windows Server operating system is king and is prevalent across all facets of technology. There are alternatives to Windows Server and different products that can provide some of the same functions to an organization, but it is quite rare to find a business environment anywhere that is running without some semblance of a Microsoft infrastructure.

Windows Server contains an incredible amount of technology, all wrapped up in one small installation disk. With Windows Server 2019, Microsoft has got us thinking out of the box about what it means to be a server in the first place and comes with some exciting new capabilities that we will spend some time covering in these pages. Things such as PowerShell, Windows Admin Center, software-defined storage, and software-defined networking are changing the way that we manage and size our computing environments; these are exciting times to be or to become a server administrator!

It's getting cloudy out there

There's this new term out there, you may have even heard of it...*the cloud*. I say this tongue in cheek of course, and if smiley faces were appropriate within published works, I would insert one here. While the word "cloud" has certainly turned into a buzzword that is often misused and spoken of inappropriately, the idea of cloud infrastructure is an incredibly powerful one.

A cloud fabric is one that revolves around virtual resources—virtual machines, virtual disks, and even virtual networks. Being plugged into the cloud typically enables things like the ability to spin up new servers on a whim, or even the ability for particular services themselves to increase or decrease their needed resources automatically, based on utilization.

Think of a simple e-commerce website where a consumer can go to order goods. Perhaps 75% of the year, they can operate this website on a single web server with limited resources, resulting in a fairly low cost of service. But, the other 25% of the year, maybe around the holiday seasons, utilization ramps way up, requiring much more computing power. Prior to the cloud mentality, this would mean that the company would need to size their environment to fit the maximum requirements all the time, in case it was ever needed. They would be paying for more servers and much more computing power than was needed for the majority of the year. With a cloud fabric, giving the website the ability to increase or decrease the number of servers it has at its disposal as needed, the total cost of such a website or service can be drastically decreased. This is a major driving factor of the cloud in business today.

The public cloud

Most of the time, when your neighbor Suzzi Knowitall talks to you about the cloud, she is simply talking about the internet. Well, more accurately, she is talking about some service that she uses, which she connects to by using the internet. For example, Office 365, Google Drive, OneDrive, Dropbox—these are all public cloud resources, as they store your data *in the cloud*. In reality, your data is just sitting on servers that you access via the internet, but you can't see those servers and you don't have to administer and maintain those servers, which is why it feels like magic and is then referred to as the cloud.

To IT departments, the term *cloud* more often means one of the big three cloud hosting providers. Since this is a Microsoft-driven book, and since I truly feel this way anyway, Azure is top-notch in this category. Azure itself is another topic for another book (or many other books) but is a centralized cloud computing architecture that can host your data, your services, or even your entire network of servers.

Moving your datacenter to Azure enables you to stop worrying or caring about server hardware, replacing hard drives, and much more. Rather than purchasing servers, unboxing them, racking them, installing Windows on them, and then setting up the roles you want configured, you simply click a few buttons to spin up new virtual servers that can be resized at any time for growth. You then pay ongoing op-ex costs for these servers—monthly or annual fees for running systems in the cloud—rather than the big cap-ex costs for server hardware in the first place.

Other cloud providers with similar capabilities are numerous, but the big three are Azure, Amazon (AWS), and Google. As far as enterprise is concerned, Azure simply takes the cake and eats it too. I'm not sure that the others will ever be able to catch up with all of the changes and updates that Microsoft constantly makes to the Azure infrastructure.

The private cloud

While most people working in the IT sector these days have a pretty good understanding of what it means to be part of a cloud service, and many are indeed doing so today, a term that is being pushed into enterprises everywhere and is still many times misunderstood is **private cloud**. At first, I took this to be a silly marketing ploy, a gross misuse of the term "cloud" to try and appeal to those hooked by buzzwords. Boy was I wrong. In the early days of private clouds, the technology wasn't quite ready to stand up to what was being advertised.

Today, however, that story has changed. It is now entirely possible to take the same fabric that is running up in the true, public cloud, and install that fabric right inside your datacenter. This enables you to provide your company with cloud benefits such as the ability to spin resources up and down and to run everything virtualized, and to implement all of the neat tips and tricks of cloud environments, with all of the serving power and data storage remaining locally owned and secured by you. Trusting cloud storage companies to keep data safe and secure is absolutely one of the biggest blockers to implementation on the true public cloud, but, by installing your own private cloud, you get the best of both worlds, specifically stretchable compute environments with the security of knowing you still control and own all of your data.

This is not a book about clouds, public or private. I mention this to give a baseline for some of the items we will discuss in later chapters, and also to get your mouth watering a little bit to dig in and do a little reading yourself on cloud technology. You will see the Windows Server 2019 interface in many new ways with the cloud and will notice that so many of the underlying systems available in Server 2019 are similar to, if not the same as, those becoming available in Microsoft Azure.

In these pages, we will not focus on the capabilities of Azure, but rather a more traditional sense of Windows Server that would be utilized on-premise. With the big push toward cloud technologies, it's easy to get caught with blinders on and think that everything and everyone is quickly running to the cloud for all of their technology needs, but it simply isn't true. Most companies will have the need for many on-premise servers for many years to come; in fact, many may never put full trust in the cloud and will forever maintain their own datacenters. These datacenters will have local servers that will require server administrators to manage them. That is where you come in.

Windows Server versions and licensing

Anyone who has worked with the design or installation of a Windows Server in recent years is probably wondering which direction we are taking in this book. You see, there are different capability editions, different technical versions, plus different licensing models of Windows Server. Let's take a few minutes to cover those differences so that you can have a well-rounded knowledge of the different options, and so that we can define which portions we plan to discuss over the course of this book.

Standard versus Datacenter

When installing the Windows Server 2019 operating system onto a piece of hardware, as you will experience in *Chapter 2, Installing and Managing Windows Server 2019*, you will have two different choices of server capability. The first is Server 2019 Standard, which is the default option and one that includes most of your traditional Windows Server roles. While I cannot give you details on pricing because that could potentially be different for every company depending on your agreements with Microsoft, Standard is the cheaper option and is used most commonly for installations of Windows Server 2019.

Datacenter, on the other hand, is the luxury model. There are some roles and features within Windows Server 2019 that only work with the Datacenter version of the operating system, and they are not available in Standard. If ever you are looking for a new piece of Microsoft technology to serve a purpose in your environment, make sure to check the requirements to find out whether you will have to build a Datacenter server. Keep in mind that Datacenter can cost significantly more money than Standard, so you generally only use it in places where it is actually required. For example, if you are interested in hosting shielded VMs or working with Storage Spaces Direct, you will be required to run the Server 2019 Datacenter edition on the servers related to those technologies.

One of the biggest functional differences between Standard and Datacenter that even small businesses may need to consider is the number of **virtual machines** (**VMs**) that they can host. Server 2019 Standard can only run two VMs on it at any given time, which is a pretty limiting factor if you are looking to build out a Hyper-V server. Datacenter allows you to run unlimited numbers of VMs, which makes it a no-brainer when building your virtualization host servers. For running Hyper-V, Datacenter is the way to go.

Running a container infrastructure will also impact your decision making on Windows Server licensing. While your host container server can run an unlimited number of traditional containers whether that host server is Windows Server Standard or Datacenter, if you want to move into the new and enhanced world of Hyper-V-isolated containers, the same rules apply. A container host server running Windows Server Standard is limited to running two Hyper-V containers, but bumping your host to Windows Server Datacenter will bring you back into the unlimited category. An easy way to remember this is that each Hyper-V container is essentially its own VM, and so the limit of two applies in the Standard OS, whether talking about regular VMs or Hyper-V container VMs.

Three different interfaces

Now let's discuss the different footprints and user interfaces that you can run on your Windows Server 2019 machines. There are three variants of Windows Server that can be used, and the correct one for you depends on what capabilities and security you are looking for.

Desktop Experience

This is the most common choice among Windows Servers everywhere. Whether you are building a Windows Server 2019 Standard or Datacenter, you have a choice of running Windows Server with or without a graphical user interface. The traditional look and feel and point-and-click interface is called **Desktop Experience**. This allows things such as RDPing into your servers, having a traditional desktop, being able to use the graphical Server Manager right from your logged-in server, and all in all is the best way to go if you are new to server administration.

If you are familiar with navigating around inside Windows 10, then you should be able to at least make your way around Windows Server 2019 running Desktop Experience. This is the version of Windows Server 2019 that we will be focusing on for the majority of this book, and almost all of the screenshots will be taken from within a Desktop Experience environment.

Server Core

As you will see when we install Windows Server 2019 together, the default option for installation is *not* Desktop Experience. What this means is that choosing the default install path would instead place a headless version of Windows Server onto your machine, most commonly referred to as Server Core. The nature of being headless makes Server Core faster and more efficient than the Desktop version, which makes sense because it doesn't have to run all of that extra code and consume all of those extra resources for launching and displaying a huge graphical interface.

Almost anything that you want to do within Windows Server is possible to do on either Server Core or Desktop Experience, the main differences being the interface and security. To be able to use Server Core, you definitely have to be comfortable with a command-line interface (namely PowerShell), and you also have to consider remote server management to be a reliable way of interacting with your servers. We will talk much more about Server Core in *Chapter 10, Server Core*.

The largest benefit that Server Core brings to the table, other than performance, is security. Most malware that attempts to attack Windows Servers is reliant upon items that exist inside the GUI of Desktop Experience. Since those things aren't even running inside Server Core—alas, you couldn't get to a *desktop* even if you wanted to—attacks against Server Core machines are much, much less successful.

Nano Server – now only for containers

A third platform for Windows Server 2019 does exist, known as **Nano Server**. This is a tiny version of Windows Server, headless like Server Core but running an even smaller footprint. The last time I booted up Nano Server, it consumed less than 500 MB of data for the complete operating system, which is incredible.

It seemed like Nano Server was discussed much more surrounding the release of Server 2016, because at that time Microsoft was pressing forward with plans to include a whole bunch of roles inside Nano Server so that we could start replacing some of our bloated, oversized everyday servers with Nano. It used to be the case that you could use the Windows Server installation media (I suppose you could still make it happen with Server 2016 installation media) to spin out a VHDX file that allowed you to boot into Nano Server and check it out, but that mentality of *Nano Server as an actual server* has since gone by the wayside.

As of Windows Server version 1803 (we'll discuss what *Server 1803* means in the next section of this chapter), Nano Server is married to the use of containers. In fact, the only way to spin up a Nano Server is to download it as a **container base OS image**, and then boot that image on an existing container host server. We will discuss both in more detail in *Chapter 13, Containers and Nano Server*. If you know what containers and modern applications are, and are interested in using them, then you will benefit from learning all there is to know about Nano Server. If you are not in a position to work with containers, you will probably never run into Nano Server in your environment.

Licensing models – SAC and LTSC

Another decision about how to set up your Windows Server is what licensing/ support model and release cadence you would like to follow. There are two different paths that you can take. It is possible to have a mix of these in a single environment if you have a need for both.

Semi-Annual Channel (SAC)

If you opt to run SAC releases of Windows Server, your naming convention for the operating system changes. Rather than calling it *Server 2019*, you are really running Windows Server 1803, 1809, 1903, 1909, and so on. It follows the same mentality and release cadence that Windows 10 does. What that implies is that these new versions of Windows Server SAC are released at much shorter intervals than we have ever seen for servers in the past. The SAC channel is planned to receive two major releases every year — generally in the spring and the fall. Because of the fast release cadence, support for SAC versions of Windows Server lasts for a short 18 months. If you use SAC, you had better get used to always jumping on the latest version shortly after it releases.

If swapping out your server operating systems twice a year sounds daunting, you're not alone. Thankfully, Microsoft recognizes this and realizes that the general server administrator population is not going to use this model for their regular, everyday servers. Rather, SAC versions of Windows Server are only going to be used for running containers and containerized applications. In this new world of flexible application hosting, where applications are being written in ways that the infrastructure resources behind those applications can be spun up or spun down as needed, containers are a very important piece of that DevOps puzzle. If you host or build these kinds of applications, you will almost certainly be using containers — now or in the future. When you find yourself in the position of researching and figuring out containers, you will then probably find that the best way to accomplish a highly performant container environment is by hosting it on SAC server releases.

 It is important to note that SAC versions of Windows Server only come in the Server Core flavor – you'll find no graphical desktop interface here!

Long-Term Servicing Channel (LTSC)

Some of you probably think that LTSC is a typo, as in previous years this model was called **Long-Term Servicing Branch (LTSB)**. While you can go with either and people will generally know what you are talking about, LTSC is now the proper term.

Windows Server 2019 is an LTSC release. Essentially, LTSC releases are what we have always thought of as our traditional Windows Server operating system releases. Server 2008, Server 2008 R2, Server 2012, Server 2012 R2, Server 2016, and now Server 2019 are all LTSC releases. What has changed is that the LTSC releases will now be coming with fewer things that are *wow, that's so awesome and brand new*, because we will be seeing and getting hints about those brand new things as they are created and rolled out in a more short-term fashion through the SAC releases. So, your SAC releases will come out roughly every six months, and then every two to three years we will experience a new LTSC release that rolls up all of those changes into a new full version that also grants you access to the desktop experience graphical interface.

While SAC is generally all about DevOps and containers, LTSC servers are for running pretty much everything else. You wouldn't want to install a domain controller, certificate server, or file server and have to replace that server every six months. So, for any of these scenarios, you will always look to LTSC.

Also keep in mind that most Windows Server administrators still deploy their servers with the Desktop Experience graphical interface, which means you are only interested in LTSC for these server purposes. The SAC versions of Windows Server do NOT include Desktop Experience — SAC is focused only on Server Core, which has no GUI.

With LTSC versions of Windows Server, you continue to get the same support we are used to: five years of mainstream support followed by five years of available extended support.

Throughout this book, we will be working and gaining experience with Windows Server 2019 – LTSC release.

Overview of new and updated features

The newest version of the Windows Server operating system is always an evolution of its predecessor. There are certainly pieces of technology contained inside that are brand new, but there are even more places where existing technologies have been updated to include new features and functionality. Let's spend a few minutes providing an overview of some of the new capabilities that exist in Windows Server 2019.

The Windows 10 experience continued

Historically, a new release of any Microsoft operating system has meant learning a slightly new and changed user interface, or sometimes a drastically new and changed interface like that of Windows 8. Server 2019 is an exception to this rule, and subsequent versions will likely follow suit. The ongoing Windows 10 releases give us first looks into the same graphical platform that will reside on our newest LTSC release of Windows Server. This idea started when Windows Server 2016 was first released. Now that Windows 10 updates are releasing but continuing on with essentially the same desktop interface, the same is true for Server 2019. Logging in and using Windows Server 2019 is, in a lot of ways, the same experience that you have had inside Windows Server 2016. Even so, some reading this book have never experienced logging into a server of any kind before, and so we will certainly be looking over that interface and learning some tips and tricks for navigating around smoothly and efficiently within Server 2019.

Hyper-Converged Infrastructure

When you see the phrase **Hyper-Converged Infrastructure** (**HCI**), it is important to understand that we are not talking about a specific technology that exists within your server environment. Rather, HCI is a culmination of a number of different technologies that can work together and be managed together, all for the purposes of creating the mentality of a **Software-Defined Datacenter** (**SDDC** as it is sometimes referred to). Specifically, HCI in the Microsoft world is most often referred to as the combination of Hyper-V and **Storage Spaces Direct** (**S2D**) on the same cluster of servers. Clustering these services together enables some big speed and reliability benefits over hosting these roles separately, and on their own systems.

Another component that is part of, or related to, a software-defined datacenter is **Software-Defined Networking** (**SDN**). Similar to how compute virtualization platforms (like Hyper-V) completely changed the landscape of what server computing looked like 12 or more years ago, we are now finding ourselves capable of lifting the network layer away from physical hardware and shifting the design and administration of our networks to be virtual and managed by the Windows Server platform.

A newly available tool that helps configure, manage, and maintain clusters as well as HCI clusters is the always-improving **Windows Admin Center** (**WAC**). WAC can be a hub from which to interface with your Hyper-Converged Infrastructure.

Windows Admin Center

Windows Admin Center (WAC) is one of the coolest things I've seen yet that came to us around the same time as the Server 2019 release. This is a free tool, available to anyone, that you can use to start centrally managing your server infrastructure. While not fully capable of replacing all of the traditional PowerShell, **Remote Desktop Protocol (RDP)**, and **Microsoft Management Console (MMC)** administration tools, it enables you to do a lot of normal everyday tasks with your servers, all from a single interface.

WAC has been continually updated and improved since release, and can now be used to manage servers, to build out clusters and HCI environments, and as a centralized administration tool not only for your on-premise servers but for those residing inside Azure as well. Prior to official release and naming, Windows Admin Center was formerly known as Project Honolulu, if you ever encounter a text that still includes that title.

We will take a closer look at Windows Admin Center in *Chapter 2, Installing and Managing Windows Server 2019*.

Windows Defender Advanced Threat Protection

If you haven't done any reading on **Advanced Threat Protection (ATP)**, you may see the words Windows Defender and assume I am simply talking about the antivirus/anti-malware capabilities that are now built into both Windows client operating systems, as well as Windows Server starting with 2016. While it is true that Windows Server 2019 does come out of the box with built-in antivirus, the ATP service and Windows Defender as a whole are becoming much, much more.

We'll discuss it in more depth in *Chapter 9, Hardening and Security*, but the short summary is that Windows Defender Advanced Threat Protection is a cloud-based service that you tap your machines into. The power of ATP is that many thousands, or perhaps even millions, of devices are submitting data and creating an enormous information store that can then be used with some AI and machine learning to generate comprehensive data about new threats, viruses, and intrusions in real time. ATP customers then receive the benefits of protection as those new threats arise. It's almost like crowd-sourced anti-threat capabilities, with Azure handling all of the backend processing.

Banned passwords

Active Directory has stored all of our user account information, including passwords, for many years. The last few releases of the Windows Server operating system have not included many updates or new features within AD, but Microsoft is now working with many customers inside their cloud-based Azure AD environment, and new features are always being worked on in the cloud. Banned passwords are among those things. Natively an Azure AD capability, it can now be synchronized back to your on-premise domain controller servers, giving you the ability to create a list of passwords that cannot be used in any fashion by your users. For example, the word *password*. By banning *password* as a password, you effectively ban any password that includes the word *password*. For example, *P@ssword*, *Password123!*, or anything else of similar bearing that might otherwise pass muster for meeting standard complexity requirements.

Soft restart

The ability to perform a soft restart was actually new with Server 2016, but it had to be manually added into Server 2016 and I don't think anybody really ever started using it. I have never seen a single person initiate a soft restart, so I assume it is not well-known and I will include it here in our list of features. In an effort to speed up reboots, there is an optional reboot switch called **soft restart**, which is now included automatically inside Server 2019. So, what is a soft restart? It is a restart without hardware initialization.

In other words, it restarts the operating system without restarting the whole machine. It is invoked during a restart by adding a special switch to the shutdown command. Interestingly, in Server 2016 you could also invoke a soft restart with the Restart-Computer cmdlet in PowerShell, but that option seems to have fallen away in Server 2019. So, if you want to speed up your reboots, you'll have to turn back to good old Command Prompt. Note the following using the shutdown command:

```
shutdown /r /soft /t 0
```

Here /r is for restart, /soft is for soft restart, and /t 0 is for zero seconds until reboot initiates.

Integration with Linux

Heresy! Under whose authority did I type the word *Linux* inside a book about Windows Server?! Historically, corporate computing environments have run Windows, or they have run Linux, or maybe they have run both but with a very clear separation between the two. Windows Server 2019 blurs that line of separation. We now have the ability to run Linux VMs within our Microsoft Hyper-V and to even interface with them properly. Did you know some Linux operating systems actually know how to interact with a mouse? Before now, you didn't have much chance of that when trying to run a Linux-based VM on top of Windows Server, but we now have some compatibility implemented in Hyper-V.

Linux-based containers can also be run on top of Server 2019, which is a big deal for anyone looking to implement scaling applications via containers.

You can even protect your Linux virtual machines by encrypting them, through the use of shielded virtual machines!

SAC releases are shrinking!

We have already learned that LTSC major releases of Windows Server only happen once every few years at most, but what's new in those bi-annual SAC releases? Most of the enhancements made there revolve around containers, since the SAC versions of Windows Server 2019 are only used for containerized purposes, but there is one common theme that resounds with almost every new release – the container image shrinks!

While this doesn't seem earth-shattering, if you've been around Microsoft Windows products for a long time and have watched new releases, you know that almost every updated release has grown in size, not shrunk. Minimizing the footprint of container images is a priority for Microsoft, because the smaller they are the more you can squeeze onto your server, and the more efficient they will be!

As an example, the base container image for Windows Server 1903 was 5.1 GB on disk, while the image for Windows Server 2004 (again, ouch with the name) is a gigabyte-penny-pinching 3.98 GB.

Enhanced shielded virtual machines

So many companies are running a majority of their servers as virtual machines today. One of the big problems with this is that there are some inherent security loopholes that exist in the virtualization host platforms of today. One of those holes is backdoor access to the hard disk files of your virtual machines. It is quite easy for anyone with administrative rights on the virtual host to be able to see, modify, or break any virtual machine that is running within that host. And, these modifications can be made in almost untraceable ways. Take a look at *Chapter 14, Hyper-V*, to learn how the new capability to create **shielded virtual machines** closes up this security hole by implementing full disk encryption on those VHDX files.

Server 2019 brings some specific benefits to the shielded VM world: we can now protect both Windows-based and Linux-based virtual machines by shielding them, and we are no longer so reliant on communication with the Host Guardian Service when trying to boot protected VMs from our guarded host servers. We will discuss this further in *Chapter 14, Hyper-V*.

Azure Network Adapter

Hybrid cloud — isn't it great when you can take two separate buzzwords, and combine them to make an even larger and more powerful buzzword? Hybrid cloud is a thing of CIOs' dreams. I hope you know I say this in jest; the idea of hybrid cloud is incredibly powerful and is the bridge that is making cloud utilization possible. We can have both on-premise servers, and servers hosted in Azure, and make it all one big happy network where you can access any resource from anywhere.

Now, there is already a myriad of technologies that allow you to tap your local network into your Azure network — namely site-to-site VPNs and Azure ExpressRoute are both technologies that allow you to create full, permanent tunnels between your on-premise datacenter and Azure virtual networks. However, another option never hurts, especially for small companies that don't want the complexity of building a site-to-site VPN, nor the cost of ExpressRoute.

Enter Azure Network Adapter. This new capability allows you to very quickly and easily add a virtual network adapter to a Windows Server (even one as far back as 2012 R2), and then connect that virtual NIC straight to your Azure network! Windows Admin Center is required for this transaction to take place; we will take a closer look in *Chapter 7, Networking with Windows Server 2019*.

Always On VPN

Users hate launching VPN connections. I know this because I hear that kind of feedback every day. Having to manually make a connection to their work network is wasting time that they could otherwise spend doing actual work. In *Chapter 8, Remote Access*, we will discuss the different remote access technologies available in Windows Server 2019. There are actually two different technologies that allow for a fully automatic connection back to the corporate network, where the users don't have to take any manual action to enact those connections. One of those technologies is DirectAccess and has been around since Server 2008 R2. We will detail DirectAccess because it is still a viable and popular connectivity option, and we will also cover the newest version of automated remote connectivity — Always On VPN.

System Insights

As a Windows Server administrator, you may often receive rather ambiguous requests such as *please figure out what is wrong with the server* (when you actually run a shop of 100+ servers) or *server22 puked again this morning, can you fix it?*

These are the types of questions and requests that often show up first thing on a Monday morning, before your coffee has had a chance to do its magic. While *reboot the server!* is still a valid option and oftentimes quells strange issues temporarily, it would be nice to track down the issue further and perhaps have some fair warning in the future of when this behavior might happen next.

To create trends surrounding issues on servers, it makes sense that the storage and analysis of historical data would be necessary. We have event logs, sure, which can sometimes tell a story after a lot of manual searching through them, but with event logs, it is up to the admin to put the puzzle pieces together. Event logs also have a tendency to fill up quickly when an issue is present and will start rolling away the oldest logs in order to keep a certain amount of free space — logs that might be essential to your troubleshooting venture.

New in Windows Server 2019, **System Insights** is a predictive analytics engine that runs locally on our servers, capturing information about the server itself and keeping historical data for up to a year, which can then be translated and manipulated with Windows Admin Center, or PowerShell, to find patterns and trends. We will take a firsthand look at System Insights in *Chapter 15, Troubleshooting Windows Server 2019*.

Windows Server 2019 interface

Unfortunately, Microsoft turned a lot of people off with the introduction of Windows 8 and Server 2012, not because functionality or reliability was lacking, but because the interface was so vastly different than it had been before. It was almost like running two separate operating systems at the same time. You had the normal desktop experience, in which all of us spent 99.9% of our time, but then there were also those few moments where you found yourself needing to visit the full-page **Start** menu. More likely, you stumbled into it without wanting to. However, you ended up there, inside that fullscreen tablet-like interface, for the remaining 0.01% of your Server 2012 experience, you were left confused, disturbed, and wishing you were back in the traditional desktop. I am, of course, speaking purely from experience here. There may be variations in your personal percentages of time spent, but, based on the conversations I have been involved with, I am not alone in these views. And I haven't even mentioned the magical self-appearing **Charms bar**. Some bad memories are better left in the recesses of the brain.

The major update of Windows 8.1 and Server 2012 R2 came with welcome relief to these symptoms. There was an actual **Start** button in the corner again, and you could choose to boot primarily into the normal desktop mode. However, should you ever have the need to click on that **Start** button, you found yourself right back on the full-page Start screen, which I still find almost all server admins trying their best to avoid at all costs.

Well, it turns out that Microsoft listened and brought some much-needed relief in Windows 10 and Windows Server 2016. While not quite back to the traditional **Start** menu that existed back in 2008, we have a good mix of both old ways and new ways of launching the tools that we need to access on our server platforms.

As far as the graphical interface goes, Windows Server 2019 is mostly unchanged from Server 2016, because we have not seen a major interface update on the client operating system. As you already know, each new version of Windows Server has received updates to the point-and-click interface based on what the latest Windows client operating system is at the time, and this is the first time in many years that a new server operating system has been released while the client operating system is still hanging out on the same version—Windows 10. If you are comfortable navigating around in Windows 10, you will be well-suited to Windows Server 2019.

For anyone new to working within Windows or just looking for some tips and tricks to get you rolling, this section is for you.

The updated Start menu

As sub-versions of Windows 10 have been released, there have been small ongoing changes to the **Start** menu. All in all, I consider many of the changes to be backpedaling from the Windows 8 fiasco. We are now back to a real **Start** button that launches a real **Start** menu, one that doesn't take over the entire desktop. To be honest, personally I almost never open the **Start** menu at all, other than to search for the application or feature that I want. We will cover more on that very soon. However, when I do open up the **Start** menu and look at it, there are a few nice things that stand out:

- All of the applications installed on the server are listed here, in alphabetical order. This is very useful for launching an application, or for doing a quick check to find out whether or not a particular app or feature is installed on your server.

- The left side of the **Start** menu includes a few buttons for quick access to items. Probably the most useful buttons here are power controls for shutting down or restarting the server, and the **Settings** gear that launches system settings.

- By default, the right side of the **Start** menu shows some bigger buttons, sometimes called **live tiles**. Pinning items to be shown here gives you an easy-access location for items that you commonly launch on your server, and having the larger buttons is useful when you are controlling your server from a touchscreen laptop or something similar.

You can see all three of these functions in *Figure 1.1*:

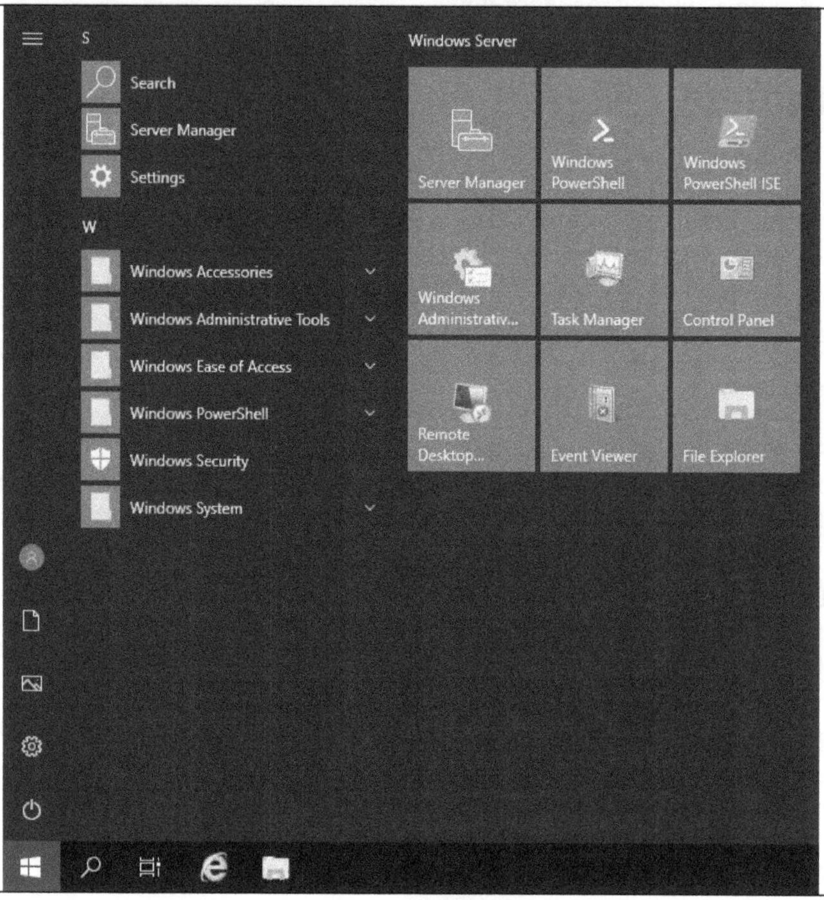

Figure 1.1: The new Start menu

Now that is a breath of fresh air. A simple but useful **Start** menu, and more importantly, one that loads quickly over remote connections such as RDP or Hyper-V consoles.

The Quick Admin Tasks menu

As nice as it is to have a functional **Start** menu, as a server administrator I still very rarely find myself needing to access the traditional menu for my day-to-day functions. This is because many items that I need to access are quickly available to me inside the **Quick Admin Tasks** menu, which opens by simply right-clicking on the **Start** button. This menu has been available to us since the release of Windows 8, but many IT professionals are still unaware of this functionality.

This menu has become an important part of my interaction with Windows Server operating systems, and hopefully, it will be for you as well. Right-clicking on the **Start** button shows us immediate quick links to do things like open **Event Viewer**, view the **System** properties, check **Device Manager**, and even **Shut down** or **Restart** the server. The two most common functions that I call for in this context menu are the **Run** function and using it to quickly launch a PowerShell prompt. Even better is the ability from this menu to open either a regular user context PowerShell prompt or an elevated/administrative PowerShell prompt. Using this menu properly saves many mouse clicks and shortens troubleshooting time:

 Alternatively, this menu can be invoked using the *WinKey + X* keyboard shortcut!

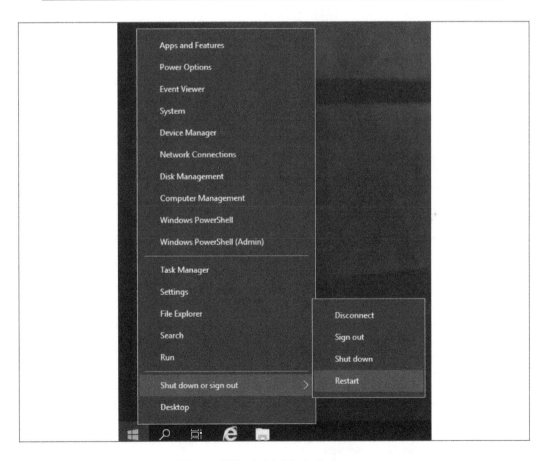

Figure 1.2: The Quick Admin Tasks menu

While I find it extremely beneficial to have PowerShell options listed here in the **Quick Admin Tasks** menu, you may still prefer using Command Prompt over PowerShell. There is an easy way to swap out the PowerShell options in the **Quick Admin Tasks** menu with Command Prompt options – both regular user context as well as admin context. To make that change, take the following steps:

1. Right-click on the taskbar and select **Taskbar settings**.

2. Disable the option (it is enabled by default) to **Replace Command Prompt with Windows PowerShell in the menu when I right-click the start button or press Windows key+X**:

> Replace Command Prompt with Windows PowerShell in the menu when I right-click the start button or press Windows key+X
>
> 🔘 On

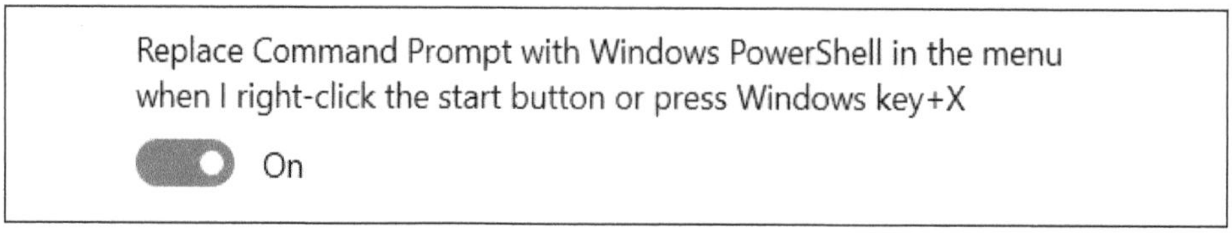

Figure 1.3: Replace Command Prompt with Windows PowerShell in the menu

Using the Search function

While the **Quick Admin Tasks** menu hidden behind the **Start** button is useful for calling common administrative tasks, using the **Search** function inside the **Start** menu is a powerful tool for interfacing with literally anything on your Windows Server. Depending on who installed applications and roles to your servers, you may or may not have shortcuts available to launch them inside the **Start** menu. You also may or may not have desktop shortcuts or links to open these programs from the taskbar. I find that it is often difficult to find specific settings that may need to be tweaked in order to make our servers run like we want them to. **Control Panel** is slowly being replaced by the newer **Settings** menu in newer versions of Windows, and sometimes this results in the discovery of particular settings being difficult. All of these troubles are alleviated with the search bar inside the **Start** menu. By simply clicking on the **Start** button, or even easier by pressing the Windows key (*WinKey*) on your keyboard, you can simply start typing the name of whatever program, setting, or document that you want to open up. The search bar will search everything on your local server, and present options to you for which application, setting, or even document to open.

As a most basic example, press *WinKey* on your keyboard, then type notepad and press the *Enter* key. You will see that good old Notepad opens right up for us. We never had to navigate anywhere in the Programs folder in order to find and open it. In fact, we never even had to touch the mouse, which is music to the ears for someone like me who loves doing everything he possibly can via the keyboard:

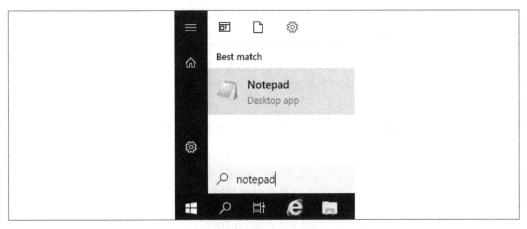

Figure 1.4: Windows Search

An even better example is to pick something that would be buried fairly deep inside **Settings** or the **Control Panel**. How about changing the amount of time before the screen goes to power save and turns itself off? The traditional server admin will open **Control Panel** (if they can find it), probably navigate to the **Appearance and Personalization** section because nothing else looks obviously correct, and still not find what they were looking for. After poking around for a few more minutes, they would start to think that Microsoft forgot to add in this setting altogether. But alas, these power settings are simply moved to a new container and are no longer accessible through **Control Panel** at all. We will discuss the new **Settings** screen momentarily in this chapter, but ultimately for the purposes of this example, you are currently stuck at the point where you cannot find the setting you want to change. What's the quick solution? Press your *WinKey* to open the **Start** menu, and type monitor (or power, or just about anything else that would relate to the setting you are looking for). You'll see in the list of available options showing in the search menu one called **Choose when to turn off the screen**. Click on that, and you have found the setting you were looking for all along:

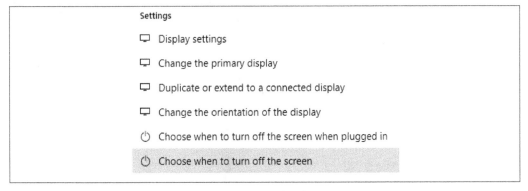

Figure 1.5: Screen-related settings

You will also notice that you have many more options on this **Search** screen than what you were originally searching for. Search has provided me with many different items that I could accomplish, all relating to the word monitor that I typed in. I don't know of a more powerful way to open applications or settings on Windows Server 2019 than using the search bar inside the **Start** menu. Give it a try today!

Pinning programs to the taskbar

While Windows Server 2019 provides great searching capabilities so that launching hard-to-find applications is very easy, sometimes it's easier to have quick shortcuts for commonly used items to be available with a single click, down in the traditional taskbar. Whether you have sought out a particular application by browsing manually through the **Start** menu or have used the **Search** function to pull up the program that you want, you can simply right-click on the program and choose **Pin to taskbar** to stick a permanent shortcut to that application in the taskbar at the bottom of your screen. Once you have done this, during future logins to your session on the server, your favorite and most-used applications will be waiting for you with a single click. As you can see in *Figure 1.6*, you also have the ability to pin programs to the **Start** menu, which of course is another useful place from which to launch them regularly:

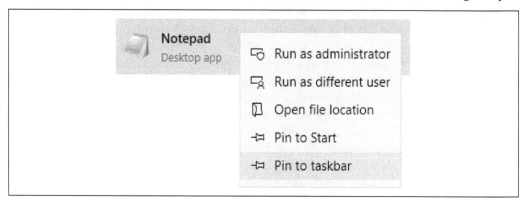

Figure 1.6: Pinning programs to the taskbar

Many readers will already be very familiar with the process of pinning programs to the taskbar, so let's take it one step further to portray an additional function you may not be aware is available to you when you have applications pinned.

The power of right-clicking

We are all pretty familiar with right-clicking in any given area of a Windows operating system in order to do some more advanced functions. Small context menus displayed upon a right-click have existed since the two-button mouse rolled off the assembly line.

We often right-click in order to copy text, copy documents, paste the same, or get into a deeper set of properties for a particular file or folder. Many day-to-day tasks are accomplished with that mouse button. What I want to take a minute to point out is that software makers, Microsoft and otherwise, have been adding even more right-click functionality into application launchers themselves, which makes it even more advantageous to have them close at hand, such as inside the taskbar.

The amount of functionality provided to you when right-clicking on an application in the taskbar differs depending on the application itself. For example, if I were to right-click on Command Prompt, I have options to either open **Command Prompt**, or to **Unpin from taskbar**. Very simple stuff. If I right-click again on the smaller menu option for Command Prompt, I have the ability to perform the same functions, but I could also get further into **Properties**, or **Run as administrator**. So, I get a little more enhanced functionality the deeper I go:

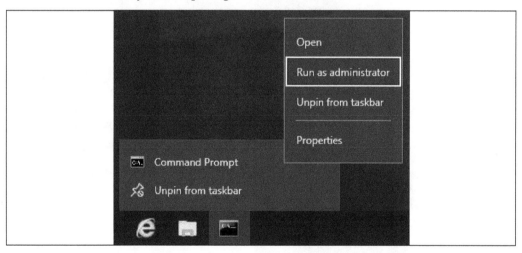

Figure 1.7: Right-click to Run as administrator

With other programs, you may find even more results. And the more you utilize your servers, the more data and options you will start to see in these right-click context menus. Two great examples are Notepad and the Remote Desktop Client. On my server, I have been working in a few text configuration files, and I have been using my server to jump into other servers to perform some remote tasks. I have been doing this using the Remote Desktop Client. Now, when I right-click on Notepad listed in my taskbar, I have quick links to the most recent documents that I have worked on:

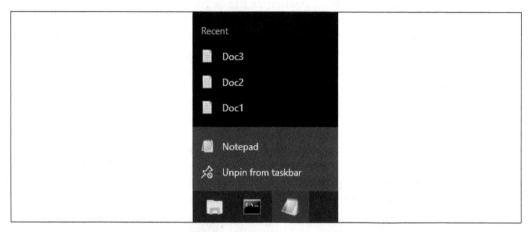

Figure 1.8: Right-clicking reveals recent documents

When right-clicking on my RDP icon, I now have quick links listed right here for the recent servers that I have connected to. I don't know about you, but I RDP into a lot of different servers on a daily basis. Having a link for the Remote Desktop Client in the taskbar automatically keeping track of the most recent servers I have visited definitely saves me time and mouse clicks as I work through my daily tasks:

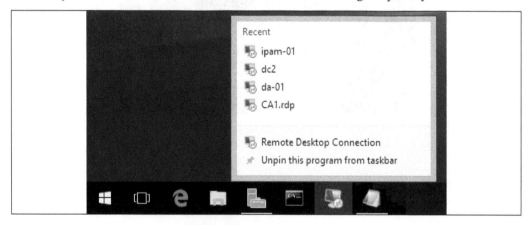

Figure 1.9: Recent RDP connections

These right-click functions have existed for a couple of operating system versions now, so it's not new technology, but it is being expanded upon regularly as new versions of the applications are released. It is also a functionality that I don't witness many server administrators utilizing, but perhaps they should start doing so in order to work more efficiently, which is why we are discussing it here.

Something that is enhanced in the Windows 10 and Server 2019 platforms that is also very useful on a day-to-day basis is the **Quick access** view that is presented by default when you open File Explorer. We all know and use File Explorer and have for a long time, but typically when you want to get to a particular place on the hard drive or to a specific file, you have many mouse clicks to go through in order to reach your destination. Windows Server 2019's **Quick access** view immediately shows us both recent and frequent files and folders that we commonly access from the server. We, as admins, often have to visit the same places on the hard drive and open the same files time and time again. Wouldn't it be great if **File Explorer** would lump all of those common locations and file links in one place? That is exactly what **Quick access** does.

You can see in the following screenshot that opening File Explorer gives you quick links to open both frequently accessed folders as well as links to your recent files. A feature like this can be a real time-saver, and regularly making use of these little bits and pieces available to you in order to increase your efficiency demonstrates to colleagues and those around you that you have a real familiarity and comfort level with this latest round of operating systems:

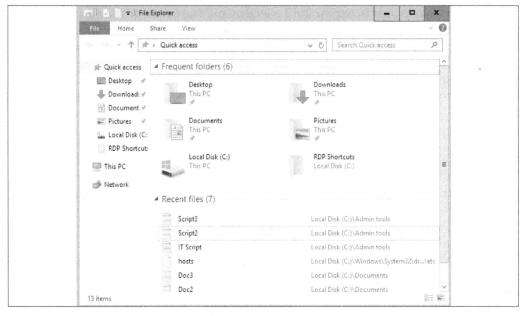

Figure 1.10: Quick access

You'll also notice the small pushpin icons next to some of those **Quick access** locations. You can easily right-click on any folder location via File Explorer and choose **Pin to Quick access**, adding it to your **Quick access** menu, and Windows will maintain that pinned location right here inside the **Quick access** section until you choose to unpin it.

Using the newer Settings screen

If you work in IT and have been using Windows 10 on a client machine for any period of time, it's a sure bet that you have stumbled across the new **Settings** interface — perhaps accidentally, as was the case for me the first time I saw it. I have watched a number of people now bump into the **Settings** interface for the first time when trying to view or configure Windows Updates. You see, **Settings** in Windows Server 2019 is just what the name implies, an interface from which you configure various settings within the operating system. What's so hard or confusing about that? Well, we already have a landing platform for all of the settings contained inside Windows that has been around for a zillion years. It's called **Control Panel**.

The **Settings** menu inside Windows isn't a brand new idea but looks and feels quite new when compared to **Control Panel**. Windows Server 2012 and 2012 R2 had a quasi-presence of settings that as far as I know went largely unused by systems administrators. I believe that to be the effect of poor execution as the **Settings** menu in 2012 was accessed and hidden behind the **Charms bar**, which most folks have decided was a terrible idea. We will not spend too much time on technology of the past, but the **Charms bar** in Server 2012 was a menu that presented itself when you swiped your finger in from the right edge of the screen. Yes, you are correct, servers don't usually have touchscreens. Not any that I have ever worked on, anyway. So, the **Charms bar** was also presented when you hovered the mouse up near the top right of the screen. It was quite difficult to access, yet seemed to show up whenever you didn't want it to, like when you were trying to click on something near the right of the desktop and instead you clicked on something inside the **Charms bar** that suddenly appeared out of nowhere.

I am only giving you this background information in order to segue into this next idea. Much of the user interface in Windows 10, and therefore Windows Server 2016 and 2019, can be considered a small step backward from the realm of finger swipes and touchscreens. Windows 8 and Server 2012 were so focused on big app buttons and finger swipes that a lot of people got lost in the shuffle. It was so different than what we had ever seen before and difficult to use at an administrative level. Because of feedback received from that release, the graphical interface and user controls, including both the **Start** menu and the **Settings** menu in Windows Server 2019, are sort of smack-dab in the middle between Server 2008 and Server 2012. This backward step was the right one to take, and I have heard nothing but praise so far for the new user interface.

So, getting back to the **Settings** menu, if you click on your **Start** button, then click on that little gear button just above the power controls, you will see this new interface:

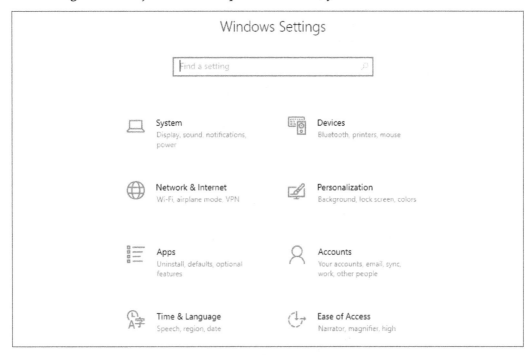

Figure 1.11: Windows Settings

There are many settings and pieces of the operating system that you can configure in this new **Settings** menu. Some settings in Windows now only exist in this interface, but many can still be accessed either here or through the traditional **Control Panel**. The goal seems to be a shift toward all configurations being done through the new menu in future releases, but, for now, we can still administer most setting changes through our traditional methods if we so choose. I mentioned Windows Update earlier, and that is a good example to look over. Traditionally, we would configure our Windows Update settings via the **Control Panel**, but they have now been completely migrated over to the new **Settings** menu in Windows Server 2019. Search **Control Panel** for Windows Update, and the only result is that you can view currently installed updates. But, if you search the new **Settings** menu for Windows Update, you'll find it right away.

 Remember, you can always use the Windows search feature to look for any setting! Hit your *WinKey* and type Windows Update, and you'll be given quick links that take you straight into the appropriate **Settings** menus.

For the moment, you will have to use a combination of **Control Panel** and the **Settings** menu in order to do your work. It gets confusing occasionally. Sometimes, you will even click on something inside the **Settings** menu, and it will launch a **Control Panel** window! Try it out. Open up the **Settings** menu and click on **Network & Internet**. Click on **Ethernet** in the left column. Here, you can see the status of your network cards, but you can't change anything, such as changing an IP address. Then, you notice the link for **Change adapter options**. Oh yeah, that sounds like what I want to do. Click on **Change adapter options**, and you are taken right into the traditional **Network Connections** screen with the **Control Panel** look and feel:

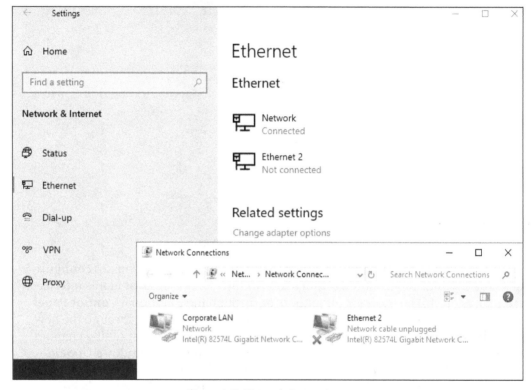

Figure 1.12: Network Connections

Two ways to do the same thing

Potentially confusing as well, until you get used to navigating around in here, is that you can sometimes accomplish the same task in either **Control Panel** or the **Settings** menu, but the process that you take in each interface can have a vastly different look and feel. Let's take a look at that firsthand by trying to create a new user account on our server, once via **Control Panel**, and again via **Settings**.

Creating a new user through Control Panel

You are probably pretty familiar with this. Open **Control Panel** and click on **User Accounts**. Then, click on the **User Accounts** heading. Now, click on the link to **Manage another account**. Inside this screen is your option to **Add a user account**. Click on that and you get the dialog box where you enter a username and password for your new user:

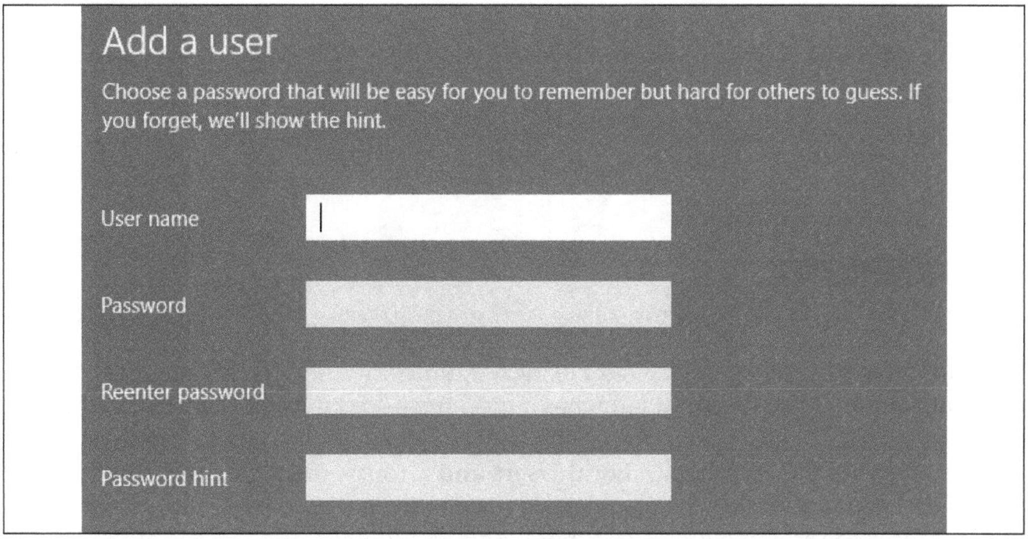

Figure 1.13: Adding a user account via Control Panel

Creating a new user through the Settings menu

Let's take this newer **Settings** interface for a test drive. Open the **Settings** menu and click on **Accounts**. Now, click on **Other users** in the left column. There is an option here to **Add someone else to this PC**; go ahead and click on that:

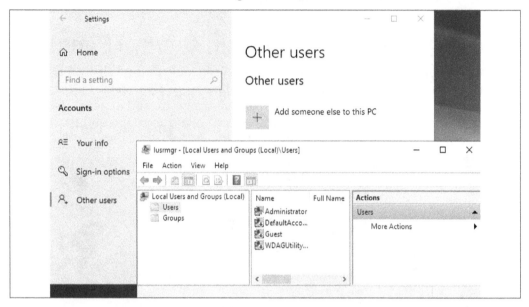

Figure 1.14: Adding a user account via Settings

What in the world is that? Not what I expected, unfortunately. To my surprise, the old **Control Panel** user account launches a nice, fresh-looking interface from which I can create new user accounts. Accessing user accounts via the newer **Settings** console launches me into the old **Local Users and Groups** manager. Technically, from here I could definitely go ahead and create new user accounts, but it seems like there is some sort of a disconnect here. You would naturally think that the new **Settings** would initiate the newer, nicer screen for adding new user accounts, but we found the opposite to be true.

We walked through this simple example of attempting to perform the same function through two different interfaces to showcase that there are some items that can and must be performed within the new **Settings** menu context, but there are many functions within Windows that still need to be accomplished through our traditional interfaces. While **Control Panel** continues to exist, and probably will for a very long time, you should start navigating your way around the **Settings** menu and figure out what is available inside, so that you can start to shape your ideas for the best combination of both worlds in order to manage your servers effectively.

Just one last thing to point out as we start getting comfortable with the way that the new **Settings** menus look: many of the settings that we configure in our servers are on/off types of settings. By that I mean we are setting something to either one option or another. Historically, these kinds of configurations were handled by either drop-down menus or by radio buttons. That is normal; that is expected; that is Windows. Now, you will start to see little swipe bars, or sliders, that allow you to switch settings on or off, like a light switch. Anyone who has used the settings interface of any smartphone knows exactly what I am talking about. This user interface behavior has now made its way into the full Windows operating systems and is probably here to stay. Just to give you an idea of what it looks like inside the context of the new **Settings** menu, here is a screenshot of the current **Windows Update** settings page inside the **Update & Security** settings.

This is a good example of those on/off slider buttons:

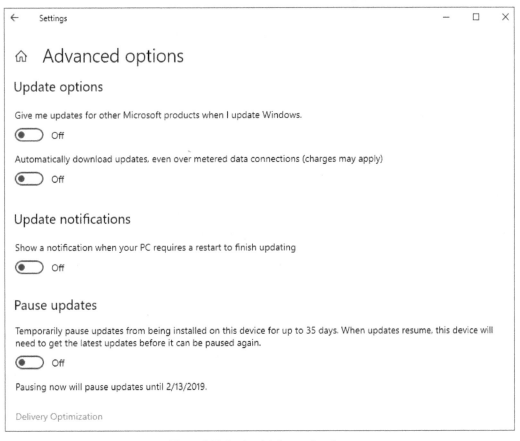

Figure 1.15: Settings' Advanced options

Task Manager

Task Manager is a tool that has existed in all Windows operating systems since the first days of the graphical interface, but it has evolved quite a bit over the years. One of the goals for Windows Server 2019 is to be even more useful and reliable than any previous version of Windows Server has been. So, it only makes sense that we finally remove Task Manager altogether, since it simply won't be needed anymore, right?

I'm kidding, of course! While Server 2019 will hopefully prove itself to indeed be the most stable and least needy operating system we have ever seen from Microsoft, Task Manager still exists and will still be needed by server administrators everywhere. If you haven't taken a close look at Task Manager in a while, it has changed significantly over the past few releases.

Task Manager is still typically invoked by either a *Ctrl + Alt + Del* on your keyboard then clicking on **Task Manager**, or by right-clicking on the taskbar and then choosing **Task Manager**. You can also launch Task Manager with the key combination *Ctrl + Shift + Esc* or typing `taskmgr` inside the **Run** or **Search** dialog boxes. The first thing you'll notice is that very little information exists in this default view, only a simple list of applications that are currently running. This is a useful interface for forcing an application to close that may be hung up, but not for much else. Go ahead and click on the **More details** link, and you will start to see the real information provided in this powerful interface.

We immediately notice that the displayed information is more user-friendly than in previous years, with both **Apps** and **Background processes** being categorized in a more intuitive way and multiple instances of the same application being condensed down for easy viewing. This gives a faster overhead view of what is going on with our system, while still giving the ability to expand each application or process to see what individual components or windows are running within the application, such as in *Figure 1.16*:

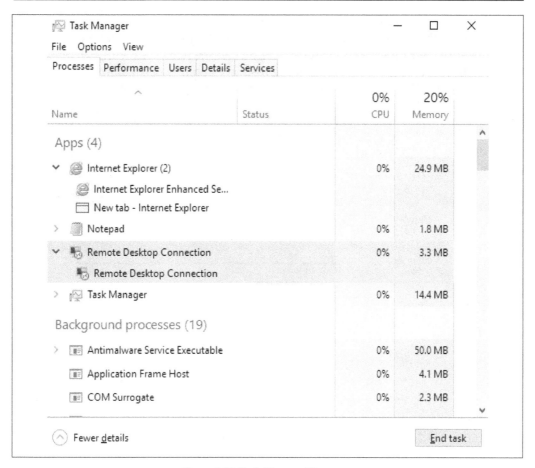

Figure 1.16: Task Manager: Processes

Make sure to check out the other tabs available inside **Task Manager** as well.
Users will show us a list of currently logged-in users and the amounts of hardware
resources that their user sessions are consuming. This is a nice way to identify on
a Remote Desktop Session Host server, for example, an individual who might be
causing a slowdown on the server. The **Details** tab is a little bit more of a traditional
view of the **Processes** tab, splitting out much of the same information but in the older
style we were used to seeing in versions of the operating system long ago. Then, the
Services tab is pretty self-explanatory; it shows you the Windows services currently
installed on the server, their status, and the ability to start or stop these services as
needed, without having to open the **Services** console separately.

The tab that I skipped over so that I could mention it more specifically here is the **Performance** tab. This is a pretty powerful one. Inside, you can quickly monitor CPU, memory, and Ethernet utilization. As you can see in the following screenshot, I haven't done a very good job of planning resources on this particular virtual machine, as my CPU is hardly being touched but I am almost out of system memory:

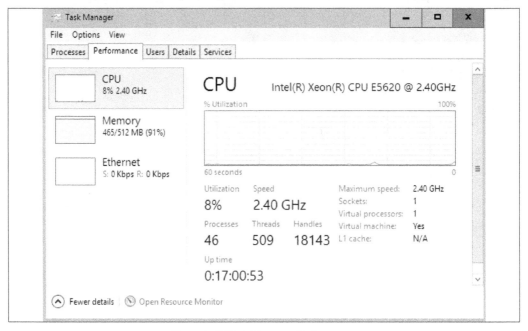

Figure 1.17: Task Manager: Performance

 Another useful piece of information available inside this screen is server uptime. Finding this information can be critical when troubleshooting an issue, and I watch admins time and time again calculating system uptime based on log timestamps. Using **Task Manager** is a much easier way to find that information!

If you are interested in viewing more in-depth data about server performance, there is a link at the bottom of this **Task Manager** window where you can **Open Resource Monitor**. Two technologies provided inside Server 2019 for monitoring system status, particularly for hardware performance, are **Resource Monitor** and **Performance Monitor**. Definitely open up these tools and start testing them out, as they can provide both troubleshooting information and essential baseline data when you spin up a new server. This baseline can then be compared against future testing data so that you can monitor how new applications or services installed on a particular server have affected their resource consumption. We will discuss these additional monitoring tools in *Chapter 15, Troubleshooting Windows Server 2019.*

Moving back to **Task Manager**, there is just one other little neat trick I would like to test. Still inside the **Performance** tab, go ahead and right-click on any particular piece of data that you are interested in. I will right-click on the **CPU** information near the left side of the window. This opens up a dialog box with a few options, of which I am going to click on **Summary view**. This condenses the data that was previously taking up about half of my screen real-estate, into a tiny little window, which I can move to the corner of my screen. This is a nice way to keep hardware utilization data on the screen at all times as you navigate through and work on your server so that you can watch for any spikes or increases in resource consumption when making changes to the system:

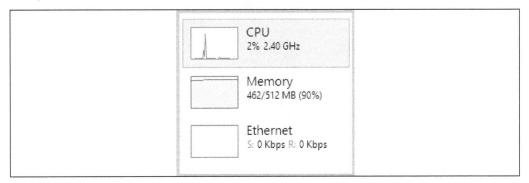

Figure 1.18: Task Manager: Resources

Task View

Task View is a new feature as of Windows 10 and Windows Server 2016, which carries over to Server 2019. It is a similar idea as that of holding down the *Alt* key and then pressing *Tab* in order to cycle through the applications that you currently have running. For anyone who has never tried that, go ahead and hold down those two keys on your keyboard right now. Depending on what version of Windows you are running, your screen might look slightly different than this, but, in effect, it's the same information. You can see all of the programs you currently have open, and you can cycle through them from left to right using additional presses of the *Tab* button. Alternatively, use *Alt + Shift + Tab* in order to cycle through them in reverse order. When you have many windows open, it is perhaps easier to simply use the mouse to jump to any specific window:

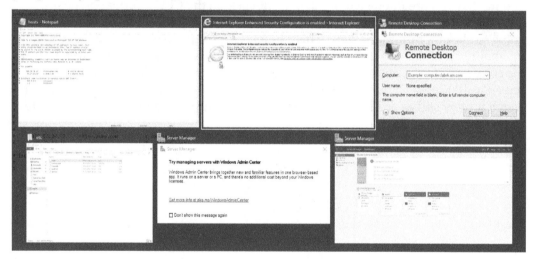

Figure 1.19: Viewing all open windows

Task View is quite a bit more powerful than this, because it adds the capability of managing multiple full-desktops' worth of windows and applications. For example, if you were working on two different projects on the same server, and each project required you to have many different windows open at the same time, you would start to burn a lot of time switching back and forth between all of your different apps and windows in order to find what you were looking for. Using Task View, you could leave all of your open windows for the first project on your first desktop, and open all of the windows dealing with the second project on a second desktop. Then, with two clicks, you can easily switch back and forth between the different desktops, using the **Task View** button. By default, **Task View** is the little button down in the taskbar, immediately to the right of the Search magnifying glass near the **Start** button. Go ahead and click on it now – it looks like this:

Figure 1.20: The Task View button

You now see a listing of your currently open windows; this looks very similar to the *Alt + Tab* functionality we looked at earlier. The difference is the little button near the top-left corner that says **New desktop**. Go ahead and click on that now:

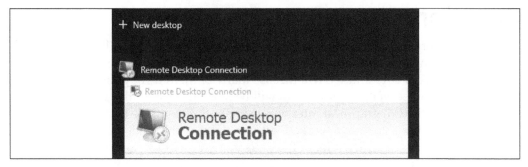

Figure 1.21: Creating a second desktop

Now, you will see **Desktop 1** and **Desktop 2** available for you to use. You can click on **Desktop 2** and open some new programs, or you can even drag and drop existing windows between different desktops, right on this Task View screen:

Figure 1.22: Navigating multiple desktops

Task View is a great way to stay organized and efficient by utilizing multiple desktops on the same server. I suppose it is kind of like running dual monitors, or three or four or more, all from a single physical monitor screen.

 If you want to avoid having to click on the icon for Task View, pressing *WinKey + Tab* on your keyboard does the same thing!

Summary

This first chapter on Windows Server 2019 was all about getting familiar and comfortable with navigating around in the interface. There are various ways to interact with Server 2019 and we will discuss many of them throughout this book, but the majority of server administrators will be interfacing with this new operating system through the full graphical interface, using both the mouse and keyboard to perform their tasks. If you have worked with previous versions of the Windows Server operating system, then a lot of the tools that you will use to drive this new platform will be the same, or at least similar, to the ones that you have used in the past. New operating systems should always be an evolution of their predecessors, and never all new. I think this was a lesson learned with the release of Windows 8 and Server 2012.

With Server 2019, we find a great compromise between the traditional familiarity of the prior versions of Windows and the new benefits that come with rounded edges and touch-friendly screens that will be used more and more often as we move toward the future of Windows-based devices. In the next chapter, we will look into installing and managing Windows Server 2019.

Questions

1. In Windows Server 2019, how can you launch an elevated PowerShell prompt with two mouse clicks?

2. What is the keyboard combination to open the **Quick Admin Tasks** menu?

3. What is the name of Microsoft's cloud service offering?

4. What are the two licensing versions of Windows Server 2019?

5. How many virtual machines can run on top of a Windows Server 2019 Standard host?

6. What installation option for Windows Server 2019 does not have a graphical user interface?

7. Which is the correct verbiage for the latest release of Windows Server 2019, **Long-Term Servicing Branch (LTSB)** or **Long-Term Servicing Channel (LTSC)**?

8. What is the correct tool from which to change configurations on Windows Server 2019, **Windows Settings** or **Control Panel**?

2
Installing and Managing Windows Server 2019

Now that we have taken a look at some of the features inside the graphical interface of Windows Server 2019, I realize that some of you may be sitting back thinking *That's great to read about, but how do I really get started playing around with this for myself?* Reading about technology is never as good as experiencing it for yourself, so we want some rubber to meet the road in this chapter. One of the biggest goals of this book is to make sure we enable you to *use* the product. Rattling off facts about new features and efficiencies is fine and dandy but ultimately worthless if you aren't able to make it work in real life. So, let's make this chunk of raw server metal do some work for us.

In this chapter, we will be covering the following:

- Requirements for installation
- Installing Windows Server 2019
- Installing roles and features
- Centralized management and monitoring
- **Windows Admin Center (WAC)**
- Enabling quick server rollouts with Sysprep

Technical requirements

When planning the build of a new server, many of the decisions that you need to make are licensing-type decisions. *What roles do you intend to install on this server? Can the more common Server 2019 Standard edition handle it, or do we need the Datacenter edition for our purposes? Is Server Core going to be beneficial from a security perspective, or do we need the full Desktop Experience?* In these days of Hyper-V Servers with the ability to spin up virtual machines on a whim, we oftentimes proceed without much consideration of the hardware of a server, but there are certainly still instances where physical equipment will be hosting the Windows Server 2019 operating system. In these cases, you need to be aware of the requirements for this new platform, so let us take a minute to list those specifics. This information is available in longer form on the Microsoft Docs website if you need to double-check any specifics, but here are your summarized minimum system requirements (`https://docs.microsoft.com/en-us/windows-server/get-started-19/sys-reqs-19`):

- **CPU**: 1.4 GHz 64-bit that supports a number of things—NX, DEP, CMPXCHG16b, LAHF/SAHF, PrefetchW, and SLAT.

- **RAM**: 512 MB ECC memory minimum, or a recommended 2 GB minimum for a server running Desktop Experience. I can tell you that it is possible to install and run Desktop Experience with far fewer than 2 GB (such as inside a test lab), but the performance of that server will not be on par with what it could be.

- **Disk**: Server 2019 requires a **PCI Express** (**PCIe**) storage adapter. ATA/PATA/IDE are not allowed for boot drives. The minimum storage space requirement is 32 GB, but Desktop Experience consumes about 4 GB more space than Server Core, so take that into consideration.

Those are sort of the bare minimum specs if you just want to spin up Server 2019 and poke around at it. For production systems, increase these numbers by a lot. There is no magic answer here—the specs you need depend on the workloads you expect to throw at your server. There are additional components that it would be good to look for when building a new system that are required for particular roles and features as well. Things such as UEFI and a TPM chip are quickly becoming mainstream and used by more and more services with every operating system update. In particular, if you are interested in security and protection via BitLocker or working with strong certificates or the new Shielded VMs, you will want to make sure that your systems include TPM 2.0 chips.

Installing Windows Server 2019

In general, the installation process for Microsoft operating systems has improved dramatically over the past 15 years. I assume that a lot of you, as IT professionals, are also the de facto *neighborhood computer guru*, being constantly asked by friends and family to fix or rebuild their computers. If you're anything like me, this means you are still occasionally rebuilding operating systems such as Windows XP. Looking at the bright blue setup screens and finding a keyboard with the *F8* key are imperative to this process. To spend two hours simply installing the base operating system and bringing it up to the highest service pack level is pretty normal. Compared to that timeline, installation of a modern operating system such as Windows Server 2019 is almost unbelievably fast and simple.

It is very likely that the majority of readers have completed this process numerous times already, and, if that is the case, feel free to skip ahead a couple of pages. But for anyone new to the Microsoft world, or new to IT in general, I'd like to take just a couple of quick pages to make sure you have a baseline to get started with. Without earning your **Installing an OS 101** badge on your tool belt, that shiny server will make for an interesting piece of wall art.

Burning that ISO

The first thing you must do is acquire some installation media. The most straightforward way to implement a single new server is to download an `.ISO` file from Microsoft, burn that `.ISO` to a DVD, and slide that DVD in to be used for installation. Since the website links and URLs are subject to change over time, the most trustworthy way to acquire your `.ISO` file to be used for installation is to open a search engine, such as **Bing**, and type `Download Windows Server 2019`. Once you have landed on the official Microsoft downloads page, click on the link to download your `.ISO` file and save it onto the hard drive of your computer.

The trickiest part of getting an `.ISO` file to be a workable DVD used to be the need to download some kind of third-party tool in order to burn it to a disc while making it bootable. If you are running an older client operating system on your computer, this may still be the case for you. I have watched many who are new to this process take the `.ISO` file, drag it over to their disc drive, and start burning the disc. This creates a DVD with the `.ISO` file on it, but that `.ISO` is still packaged up and not bootable in any way, so the disc would be worthless to your new piece of server hardware. Luckily, the newer versions of the Windows client operating systems have built-in functions for dealing with `.ISO` files that make the correct burning process very simple.

Once you have your .ISO file for the Windows Server 2019 installation downloaded onto your computer, insert a fresh DVD into your disc drive and browse to the new file. Simply right-click on the .ISO file, and then choose your menu option for **Burn disc image**. This launches a simple wizard that will extract and burn your new .ISO file the correct way onto the DVD, making it a bootable installation media for your new server, as shown in *Figure 2.1*:

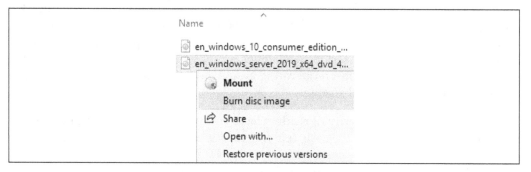

Figure 2.1: Burning your .ISO file onto DVD

It is probable when you attempt to download Windows Server 2019 and use this Windows Disc Image Burner utility with a DVD that you grabbed off your stack of standard blank DVDs, that you will receive the following error message: **The disc image file is too large and will not fit on the recordable disc**.

This should come as no surprise because our operating system installer files have been getting larger and larger over the years. We have now reached the critical tipping point where the standard Server 2019 ISO installer is larger than a standard 4.7 GB DVD disc. To burn this ISO onto a DVD, you will need to hit the store and find some dual-layer discs that can handle more data.

Creating a bootable USB stick

DVDs can be cumbersome and annoying, and now they are also too small for our purposes. Therefore, when installing the newer, larger operating systems it is becoming commonplace to prep a USB stick to use for the installation of the operating system, rather than relying on a DVD.

To do this, all you need is a Windows computer, a USB stick that is at least 8 GB, and access to the internet. You will need to download the same ISO that we discussed earlier, as that contains all of the installation files for Server 2019. Then you will also need to download and install some kind of bootable USB creation tool. There are various free ones available (Rufus is pretty popular), but the one straight from Microsoft is called the **Windows 7 USB/DVD Download Tool**. Why does it have this crazy name that includes the words *Windows 7* right in it? Don't ask me.

But, it works nonetheless and is a quick, easy, and free way to prep your bootable USB sticks for fresh operating system installations. I should point out that this tool has nothing to do with Windows 7. It will take any `.ISO` file and turn it into a bootable USB stick. That ISO can be a Windows 10 or Server 2019 ISO file and it still works just fine. You can also install and run the Windows 7 USB/DVD Download Tool on a Windows 10 workstation without any trouble.

Once the USB DVD Download Tool is installed, launch the application and simply walk through the 4-step wizard.

 This process will erase and format your USB stick. Make sure nothing important is stored there!

You will need to identify the ISO that you want the tool to grab information from, then choose your USB stick from a drop-down list. After that, simply click the **Begin copying** button and this tool will turn your USB stick into a bootable stick capable of installing the entire Windows Server 2019 OS, as shown in *Figure 2.2*:

Figure 2.2: Creating a bootable USB stick

Running the installer

Now go ahead and plug your newly created DVD or bootable USB into the new server hardware. Boot to it, and you will finally see the installation wizard for Windows Server 2019. Now, there really are not that many options for you to choose from within these wizards, so we won't spend a lot of time here. For the most part, you are simply clicking on the **Next** button in order to progress through the screens, but there are a few specific places where you will need to make decisions along the way.

After choosing your installation language, the next screen seems pretty easy. There's just a single button that says **Install now**. Yes, that is what you want to click on, but I want you to notice the text in the lower-left corner of your screen. If you are ever in a position where you have a server that cannot boot and you are trying to run some recovery or diagnostic functions in order to resolve that issue, you can click on **Repair your computer** in order to launch into the recovery console. But for our fresh server installation, go ahead and click on **Install now**, as shown in *Figure 2.3*:

Figure 2.3: Installing Windows Server 2019

You will now be asked to input a product key to activate Windows. If you have your keys already available, go ahead and enter one now. Otherwise, if you are simply installing this to test Server 2019 and want to run in trial mode for a while, you can click on the link that says **I don't have a product key** in order to bypass this screen.

The next screen is an interesting one, and the first place that you really need to start paying attention. You will see four different installation options for Windows Server 2019. There are what seem to be the "regular" installers for both Server 2019 Standard as well as Server 2019 Datacenter, and then a second option for each that includes the words **Desktop Experience**. Typically, in the Microsoft installer world, clicking on **Next** through every option gives you the most typical and common installation path for whatever it is that you are installing. *Not so with this wizard.* If you simply glide by this screen by clicking on **Next**, you will find yourself at the end with an installation of **Server Core**. We will talk more about Server Core in a later chapter of the book, but for now, I will just say that if you are expecting to have a server that looks and feels like what we talked about in *Chapter 1, Getting Started with Windows Server 2019*, this default option is not going to be the one that gets you there. This "Desktop Experience" that the wizard is talking about is the full Windows Server graphical interface, which you are more than likely expecting to see once we are done with our installation. So, for the purposes of our installation here, where we want to interact with the server using full color and a mouse, go ahead and decide whether you want the Standard or Datacenter edition, but make sure you choose the option that includes **Desktop Experience** before clicking on the **Next** button, as shown in *Figure 2.4*:

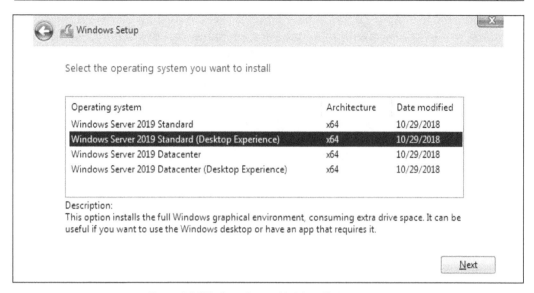

Figure 2.4: Windows Server 2019 installation options

 In some previous versions of Windows Server, we had the ability to migrate back and forth from a full Desktop Experience to Server Core and back again, even after the operating system was installed. This does not work in Windows Server 2019! The ability to transition between the two modes has disappeared, so it is even more important that you plan your servers properly from the beginning.

The next screen details licensing terms to which you need to agree, and then we come to another screen where the top option is most likely *not* the one that you intend to click on. I do understand why the **Upgrade** function is listed first for a consumer-class Windows 10 machine, but it has historically been a pretty rare occurrence that administrators accomplish in-place upgrades to Windows Servers. In a perfect world where everything always works flawlessly following upgrades, this would be a great way to go. You could have many servers all doing their jobs, and every time that a new operating system releases, you simply run the installer and upgrade them. Voila—magic! Unfortunately, it doesn't always work like that, and I almost never see server administrators willing to take the risks in doing an in-place upgrade to an existing production server. It is much more common that we are always building brand new servers alongside the currently running production servers. Once the new server is configured and ready to accept its responsibilities, then, and only then, does the actual workload migrate over to the new server from the old one. In a planned, carefully sculpted migration process, once the migration of duties is finished, then the old server is shut down and taken away.

If we were able to simply upgrade the existing servers to the newest operating system, it would save an awful lot of time and planning. But this is only feasible when you know that the upgrade is actually going to work without hiccups, and most of the time we are not prepared to take that risk. If an upgrade process goes sideways and you end up with a broken server, then you are looking at a costly repair and recovery process on a business-critical production server. You may very well be looking at working through the night or weekend as well. Would you rather spend your time planning a carefully formed cutover, or recovering a critical server with the business breathing down your neck because they cannot work? My money is on the former.

 Microsoft has announced that the Windows Server 2019 installer handles upgrades from Windows Server 2016 much better than any other Windows Server in-place upgrade path in history. Now that I have done a number of them in the wild, I have to say that I agree! Upgrading from any Server version earlier than 2016 is still recommended to be a lift and shift, prepping a brand new server and moving the workload, but if you are already running Server 2016 and are looking to move to Server 2019, in-place upgrades are now a real possibility. However, there are still particular roles that will not accept change like this and would fail following such an upgrade, so as to whether or not in-place upgrades from 2016 to 2019 are a reality in the real world…I guess that's up to you...

Now back to the topic at hand. In the Windows Server world, we rarely touch the **Upgrade** option. So go ahead and choose the **Custom: Install Windows only (advanced)** option, which is where we will get into our options for installing this copy of Windows Server 2019 fresh into a new location on the hard drive, as shown in *Figure 2.5*:

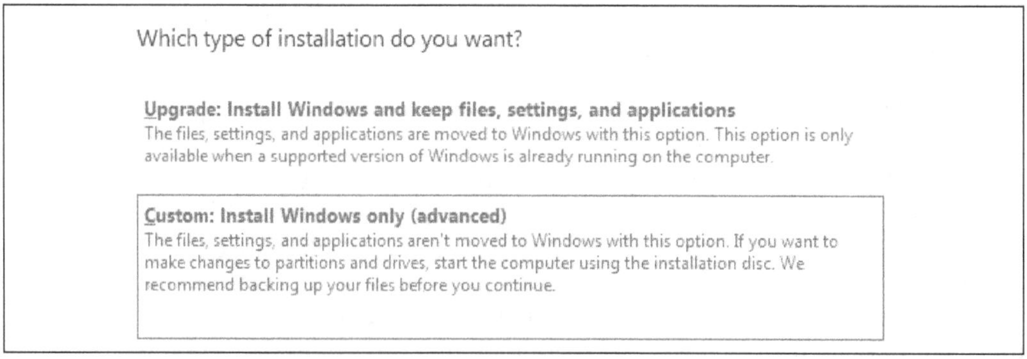

Which type of installation do you want?

Upgrade: Install Windows and keep files, settings, and applications
The files, settings, and applications are moved to Windows with this option. This option is only available when a supported version of Windows is already running on the computer.

Custom: Install Windows only (advanced)
The files, settings, and applications aren't moved to Windows with this option. If you want to make changes to partitions and drives, start the computer using the installation disc. We recommend backing up your files before you continue.

Figure 2.5: In-place upgrade or Custom installation

Now we decide where we want to install our new copy of Windows Server 2019. In many cases, you will simply click on **Next** here, because your server will have just a single hard disk drive, or maybe a single RAID array of disks, and, in either case, you will see a single pool of free space onto which you can install the operating system. If you have multiple hard drives installed on your server and they have not been tied together in any way yet, then you will have multiple choices here of where to install Windows Server. We have just a single hard disk attached here, which has never been used, so I can simply click on **Next** to continue. Note here that if your drives had existing or old data on them, you have the opportunity here, with some disk management tools, to format the disk, or delete individual partitions. If you are using some specialized disks that take specific drivers, there is also a **Load driver** button that you can use to inject these special drivers into the installation wizard in order to view these kinds of disks.

Also, it is important to note on this screen that while there is a button to create a **New** disk partition, you do *not* have to do this in order to continue. Many new admins assume that you must manually create the partition so Windows knows where to install its files. On the contrary, if you have unallocated space selected as I do in *Figure 2.6* and then simply click **Next**, the installer will take care of creating the necessary partitions for you:

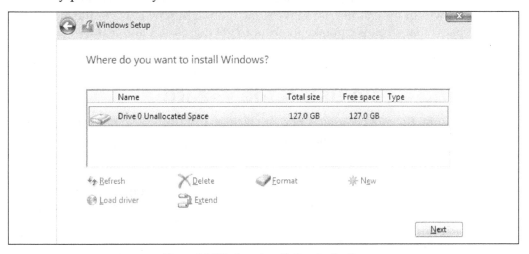

Figure 2.6: Windows installation destination

That's it! You will see the server installer start going to town copying files, installing features, and getting everything ready on the hard drive. This part of the installer runs on its own for a few minutes, and the next time you need to interact with the server it will be within the graphical interface where you get to define the administrator password. Once you have specified a password, you will find yourself on the Windows desktop. Now you are really ready to start making use of your new Windows Server 2019.

Installing roles and features

Installing the operating system gets your foot in the door, so to speak, using your server as a server. However, you can't actually do anything useful with your server at this point. On a client desktop system, the base operating system is generally all that is needed to start working and consuming data. The server's job is to serve up that data in the first place, and, until you tell the server what its purpose is in life, there really isn't anything useful happening in that base operating system. This is where we need to utilize **roles** and **features**. Windows Server 2019 contains many different options for roles. A role is just what the name implies: the installation of a particular role onto a server defines that server's role in the network. In other words, a role gives a server some purpose in life. A feature, on the other hand, is more of a subset of functions that you can install onto a server. Features can complement particular roles or stand on their own. There are pieces of technology available in Windows Server 2019 that are not installed or turned on by default because these features wouldn't be used in all circumstances. Everything in the later chapters of this book revolves around the functionality provided by roles and features. They are the bread and butter of a Windows server, and, without their installation, your servers make good paperweights, but not much else. As we will not be taking the time in each chapter to cover the installation of every particular role or feature that will be used within the chapter, let's take some time right now to cover the most common paths that admins can take in order to get these roles and features installed onto their own servers.

Installing a role using the wizard

Without a doubt, the most common place that roles and features get installed is right inside the graphical wizards available as soon as your operating system has been installed. By default, a tool called **Server Manager** launches automatically every time you log into Windows Server 2019. We will take a closer look at Server Manager itself later in this chapter, but, for our purposes here, we will simply use it as a launching platform in order to get to our wizard, which will guide us through the installation of our first role on this new server we are putting together.

Since you have just logged into this new server, you should be staring at the Server Manager dashboard. Right in the middle of the dashboard, you will see some links available to click on, a quick-start list of action items numbered one through five. If you haven't already done so, put into place any local server configuration that you may need on this machine through the first link, which is called **Configure this local server**.

Items that you will likely want in place are things such as a permanent hostname for the server, IP addressing, and, if you are joining this server to an existing domain (we will discuss domains in *Chapter 3, Active Directory*), you typically handle that process prior to implementing any new roles on the server. But, in our case, we are more specifically interested in the role installation itself, so we will assume that you have already configured these little bits and pieces to have your server identified and routing on your network.

Go ahead and click on step 2, **Add roles and features**. Another way you can launch the same wizard is by clicking on the **Manage** menu from the top bar inside Server Manager and then choosing **Add Roles and Features** from the drop-down list. Selecting either link will bring you into our wizard for installation of the roles, as shown in *Figure 2.7*:

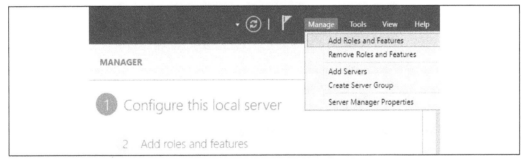

Figure 2.7: Adding roles

You are first taken to a summary screen about installing roles. Go ahead and click on **Next** to bypass this screen. Now we get into our first option, which is an interesting one. We are first asked if we want to continue with a **role-based or feature-based installation**, which is exactly what we have been talking about doing. But the second option here, **Remote Desktop Services installation**, is important to note. Most of us consider the **Remote Desktop Services (RDS)** components of Windows Server to be just another role that we can choose when setting up our server, similar to the installation of any other role. While that is basically true, it is important to note that RDS is so functionally different from the other kinds of roles that the entry path into the installation of any of the RDS components invokes its own wizard, by choosing the second option here. So, if you ever find yourself looking for the option to install RDS, and you have glossed over this screen because you are so used to clicking **Next** through it like I am, remember that you need to head back there to tell the wizard that you want to deal with an RDS component, and the remainder of the screens will adjust accordingly.

At the moment, I am working on building out a new test lab full of Windows Server 2019 boxes, and I am still in need of a **domain controller** (**DC**) to manage Active Directory in my environment. Before installing Active Directory on a server, it is critical that I have a few prerequisites in place, so I have already accomplished those items on my new server. The items that I need to have in place prior to the AD DS role installation are: having a static IP address assigned and making sure that the DNS server setting in my NIC properties points somewhere, even if only to this server's own IP address. I also need to make sure that the hostname of my server is set to its final name, because once you turn it into a domain controller it is not supported to change the hostname. I have already accomplished these items on my server, so I will continue through my role installation wizard here by leaving the option **Role-based or feature-based installation** and clicking on **Next**, as shown in *Figure 2.8*:

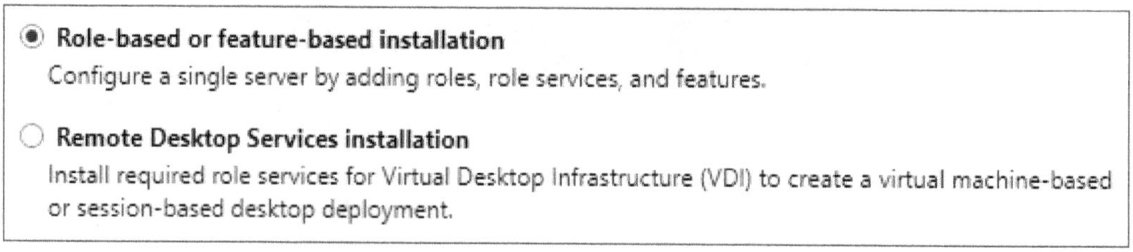

⦿ **Role-based or feature-based installation**

Configure a single server by adding roles, role services, and features.

○ **Remote Desktop Services installation**

Install required role services for Virtual Desktop Infrastructure (VDI) to create a virtual machine-based or session-based desktop deployment.

Figure 2.8: Select Role-based or feature-based installation

Our **Server Selection** screen is a very powerful one. If you've been through this process before, you have likely glossed over this screen, simply clicking on the **Next** button in order to progress through it. But, essentially, what this screen is doing is asking you where you would like to install this new role or feature. By default, each server will only have itself listed on this screen, and so clicking on **Next** to continue is more than likely what you will be doing. But there are a couple of neat options here. First of all, if your Server Manager is aware of other servers in your network and has been configured to monitor them, you will have the option here to install a role or feature remotely onto one of the other servers. We will dig a little deeper into this capability shortly. Another feature on this page, which I haven't seen many people utilize, is the ability to specify that you want to install a role or feature onto a virtual hard disk. Many of us work with mostly virtual servers in this day and age, and you don't even need your virtual server to be running in order to install a role or feature to it! If you have access to the .VHDX file, the hard disk file, from where you are running Server Manager, you can choose this option, which will allow you to inject the new role or feature directly into that hard drive. But, as is the case 99% of the times that you will wander through this screen, we are logged directly into the server where we intend to install the role, and so we simply click on **Next**, as shown in *Figure 2.9*:

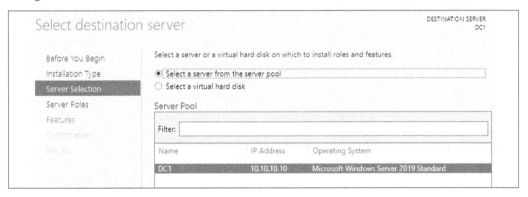

Figure 2.9: Selecting the destination server

Now we have our list of roles that are available to be installed. Clicking on each role will give you a short description of the purpose of that role if you have any questions, and we will also be talking more about the core infrastructural pieces in our next few chapters to give you even more information about what the roles do. All we need to do here in order to install a role onto our new server is check the box and click on **Next**. Since this is going to be a domain controller, I will choose the **Active Directory Domain Services** role, and I will multipurpose this server to also be a **DNS server** and a **DHCP server**. With these roles, there is no need to rerun through this wizard three separate times to install all of these roles; I can simply check them all here and let the wizard run the installers together. Whoops, when I clicked on my first checkbox, I got a pop-up message that the **Active Directory Domain Services** role requires some additional features in order to work properly. This is normal behavior, and you will notice that many of the roles that you install will require some additional components or features to be installed. All you need to do is click on the **Add Features** button, and it will automatically add in these extra pieces for you during the installation process. An example of this is shown in *Figure 2.10*:

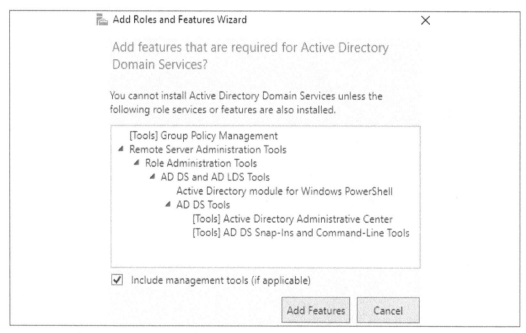

Figure 2.10: Additional features

Now that we have all three of our roles checked, it's time to click on **Next**. And, just to make it clear to all of you readers, I was not required to install all of these roles at the same time; they are not all dependent on each other. It is very common to see these roles all installed onto the same server, but I could split them up onto their own servers if I so desired. In a larger environment, you may have AD DS and DNS installed together, but you might choose to put the DHCP role onto its own server, and that is just fine.

I am configuring this server to support a small lab environment, so, for me, it makes sense to put these core infrastructure services together in the same box, as shown in *Figure 2.11*:

Roles

- [ ] Active Directory Certificate Services
- [x] Active Directory Domain Services
- [ ] Active Directory Federation Services
- [ ] Active Directory Lightweight Directory Services
- [ ] Active Directory Rights Management Services
- [ ] Device Health Attestation
- [x] DHCP Server
- [x] DNS Server
- [ ] Fax Server
- [■] File and Storage Services (1 of 12 installed)
- [ ] Host Guardian Service
- [ ] Hyper-V
- [ ] Network Policy and Access Services
- [ ] Print and Document Services
- [ ] Remote Access
- [ ] Remote Desktop Services
- [ ] Volume Activation Services
- [ ] Web Server (IIS)
- [ ] Windows Deployment Services
- [ ] Windows Server Update Services

Figure 2.11: Role selection

After clicking on **Next**, we have now landed on the page where we can install additional features to Windows Server 2019. In some cases, you may have originally intended only to add a particular feature, and in these cases, you would have bypassed the **Server Roles** screen altogether, and gone immediately to the **Features installation** screen. Just like with the role installation screen, go ahead and check off any features that you would like to install, and click on **Next** again. For our new domain controller, we do not currently require any additional features to be specifically added, so I will just finish out the wizard, which starts the installation of our new roles.

After the installation process has been completed, you may or may not be prompted to restart the server, depending on which roles or features you installed and whether or not they require a restart. Once you have landed back inside Server Manager, you will notice that you are now being prompted near the top with a yellow exclamation mark. Clicking here displays messages about further configurations that may be required in order to complete the setup of your new roles and make them live on the server. The roles for AD DS, DNS, and DHCP are now successfully installed, but there is some additional configuration that is now required for those roles to do their work. For example, to finish turning my server into a domain controller, I need to run through a promotion process to define my domain, or to specify an existing domain that I want to join. There are also some loose ends that I need to tie up before putting DHCP into action:

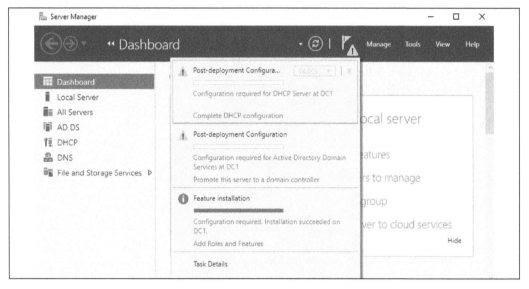

Figure 2.12: Post-deployment Configuration

Installing a feature using PowerShell

Now that you have seen the graphical wizards for installing roles and features, you could certainly always use them to put these components into place on your servers. But Microsoft has put much effort into creating a Windows Server environment where almost anything within the operating system can be manipulated using PowerShell, and the addition of roles and features is included in those capabilities. Let's take a look at the appropriate commands we can use to manipulate roles and features on our server right from a PowerShell prompt. We will view the available list of roles and features, and we will also issue a command to install a quick feature onto our server.

Open up an elevated PowerShell prompt, most easily accomplished via the quick admin tasks menu, accessed by right-clicking on the **Start** button. Then use the following command to view all of the available roles and features that we can install onto our server. It will also show you which ones are currently installed:

```
Get-WindowsFeature
```

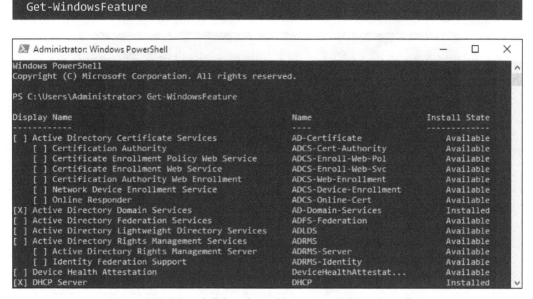

Figure 2.13: A list of all the roles and features available and installed

What I would like to do on this server is install the Telnet Client feature. I use Telnet Client pretty regularly for testing network connections, so it is helpful to have on this machine. Unfortunately, my PowerShell window currently has pages and pages of different roles and features in it, and I'm not sure what the exact name of the Telnet Client feature is in order to install it. So, let's run `Get-WindowsFeature` again, but this time let's use some additional syntax in the command to pare down the amount of information being displayed. I want to see only the features that begin with the letters TEL, as shown in the following examples:

```
Get-WindowsFeature -Name TEL*
```

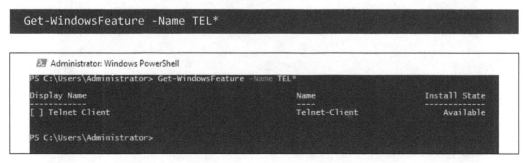

Figure 2.14: A list of features beginning with the letters TEL

There it is! Okay, so now that I know the correct name of the feature, let's run the command to install it, as shown in the following example:

```
Add-WindowsFeature Telnet-Client
```

> Administrator: Windows PowerShell
>
> ```
> PS C:\Users\Administrator>
> PS C:\Users\Administrator> Add-WindowsFeature Telnet-Client
>
> Success Restart Needed Exit Code      Feature Result
> ------- -------------- ---------      --------------
> True    No             Success        {Telnet Client}
>
>
> PS C:\Users\Administrator>
> ```

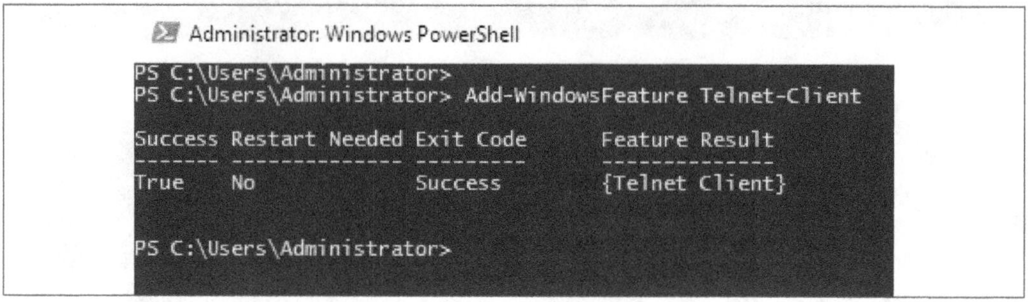

Figure 2.15: Install Telnet Client

One last thing to show you here—there is also a way to manipulate the `Get-WindowsFeature` cmdlet in order to quickly show only the roles and features currently installed on a server. Typing `Get-WindowsFeature | Where Installed` presents us with a list of the currently installed components. If I run that on my domain controller, you can see all the parts and pieces of my roles for AD DS, DNS, and DHCP, as well as my newly installed Telnet Client feature, as shown in *Figure 2.16*:

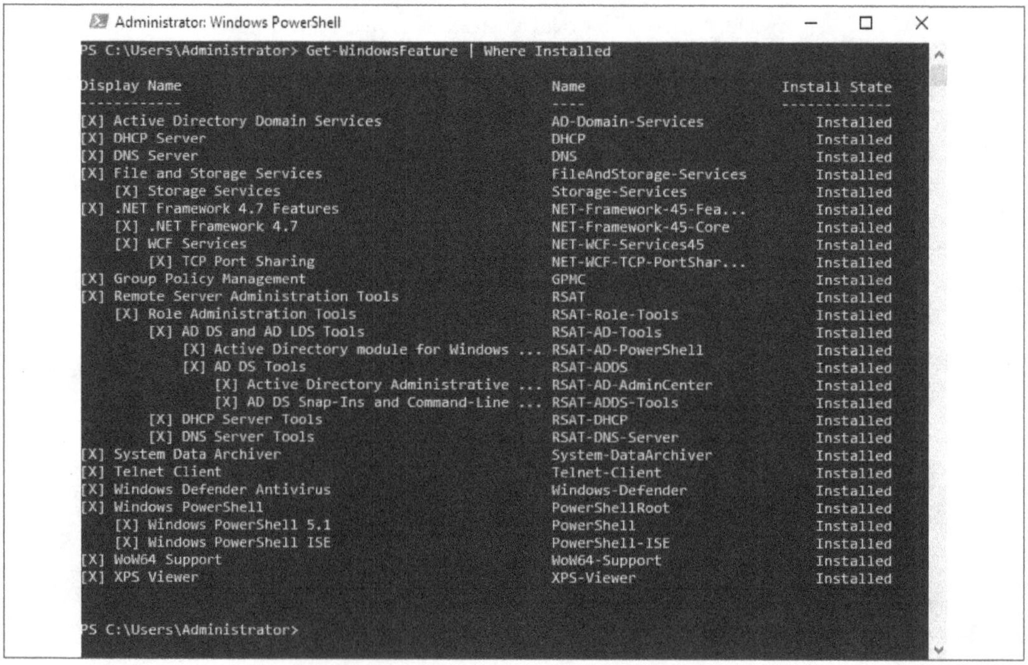

> Administrator: Windows PowerShell   —   □   ×
>
> ```
> PS C:\Users\Administrator> Get-WindowsFeature | Where Installed
>
> Display Name                                        Name                    Install State
> ------------                                        ----                    -------------
> [X] Active Directory Domain Services                AD-Domain-Services         Installed
> [X] DHCP Server                                     DHCP                       Installed
> [X] DNS Server                                      DNS                        Installed
> [X] File and Storage Services                       FileAndStorage-Services    Installed
>     [X] Storage Services                            Storage-Services           Installed
> [X] .NET Framework 4.7 Features                     NET-Framework-45-Fea...    Installed
>     [X] .NET Framework 4.7                          NET-Framework-45-Core      Installed
>     [X] WCF Services                                NET-WCF-Services45         Installed
>         [X] TCP Port Sharing                        NET-WCF-TCP-PortShar...    Installed
> [X] Group Policy Management                         GPMC                       Installed
> [X] Remote Server Administration Tools              RSAT                       Installed
>     [X] Role Administration Tools                   RSAT-Role-Tools            Installed
>         [X] AD DS and AD LDS Tools                  RSAT-AD-Tools              Installed
>             [X] Active Directory module for Windows ... RSAT-AD-PowerShell     Installed
>             [X] AD DS Tools                         RSAT-ADDS                  Installed
>                 [X] Active Directory Administrative ... RSAT-AD-AdminCenter    Installed
>                 [X] AD DS Snap-Ins and Command-Line ... RSAT-ADDS-Tools        Installed
>         [X] DHCP Server Tools                       RSAT-DHCP                  Installed
>         [X] DNS Server Tools                        RSAT-DNS-Server            Installed
> [X] System Data Archiver                            System-DataArchiver        Installed
> [X] Telnet Client                                   Telnet-Client              Installed
> [X] Windows Defender Antivirus                      Windows-Defender           Installed
> [X] Windows PowerShell                              PowerShellRoot             Installed
>     [X] Windows PowerShell 5.1                      PowerShell                 Installed
>     [X] Windows PowerShell ISE                      PowerShell-ISE             Installed
> [X] WoW64 Support                                   WoW64-Support              Installed
> [X] XPS Viewer                                      XPS-Viewer                 Installed
>
>
> PS C:\Users\Administrator>
> ```

Figure 2.16: A list of all installed components

Centralized management and monitoring

Whether you are installing new roles, running backups and maintenance programs, or troubleshooting and repairing a server, it is common sense that the first thing you would do is log directly into the server that you need to work on. Long ago this meant walking up to the server itself and logging on with the keyboard and mouse that were plugged right into that hardware. Then, quite a number of years ago, this became cumbersome and technology advanced to the point where we had the **Remote Desktop Protocol** (**RDP**) available to us. We quickly transitioned over to log into our servers remotely using RDP. Even though it's been around for many years, RDP is still an incredibly powerful and secure protocol, giving us the ability to quickly connect to servers from the comfort of our desk. And, as long as you have proper network topology and routing in place, you can work on a server halfway around the world just as quickly as one sitting in the cubicle next to you. In fact, I recently read that mining rights were being granted in outer space. Talk about a co-location for your datacenter! Maybe someday we will be using RDP to connect to servers in outer space. While this might be a stretch in our lifetimes, I do have the opportunity to work with dozens of new companies every year, and, while there are some other tools available for remotely managing your server infrastructure, RDP is the platform of choice for 99% of us out there.

Why talk about RDP? Because you probably all use it on a daily basis, and I needed to let you know that Windows Server 2019 includes some tools that make it much less necessary to our day-to-day workflow. The idea of centralized management in the server world has been growing through the last few Windows Server operating system rollouts. Most of us have so many servers running that checking in with them all daily would consume way too much time. We need some tools that we can utilize to make our management and monitoring, and even configuration processes, more efficient in order to free up time for more important projects.

Server Manager

If you have worked on Windows Server recently, you are familiar with the idea that logging into any of your servers automatically invokes a large window on top of the desktop. This auto-launching program is **Server Manager**. As the name implies, it's here to help you manage your server. However, in my experience, the majority of server administrators do not utilize Server Manager. Instead, they close it as fast as they can and curse at it under their breath, because it's been popping up and annoying them during every server login for the past 10 years.

Stop doing that! It's here to help, I promise. *Figure 2.17* shows the default view of Server Manager on my new domain controller:

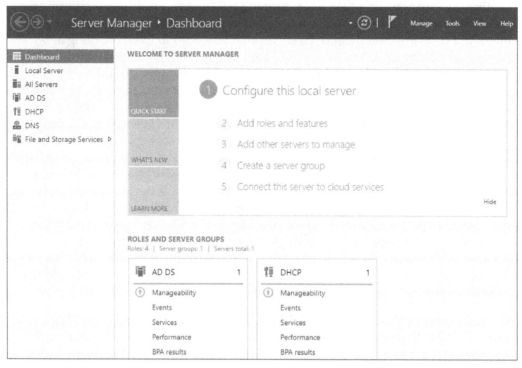

Figure 2.17: Server Manager on my domain controller

What I like about this opening automatically is that it gives me a quick look into what is currently installed on the server. Looking at the column on the left side shows you the list of roles installed and available for management. Clicking on each of these roles brings you into some more particular configuration and options for the role itself. I often find myself hopping back and forth between many different servers while working on a project, and leaving Server Manager open gives me a quick way of double-checking that I am working on the correct server. The **ROLES AND SERVER GROUPS** section at the bottom is also very interesting. You might not be able to see the colors in the picture if you are reading a printed copy of this book, but this gives you a very quick view into whether or not the services running on this server are functioning properly. Right now, both my AD DS and DHCP functions are running normally, I have a nice green bar running through them. But, if anything was amiss with either of these roles, it would be flagged bright red, and I could click on any of the links listed under those role headings in order to track down what the trouble is.

Up near the top-right corner, you see a few menus, the most useful of which, to me, is the **Tools** menu. Click on that, and you see a list of all the available **Administrative Tools** to launch on this server. Yes, this is essentially the same Administrative Tools folder that has existed in each of the previous versions of Windows Server, now stored in a different location. Based on my experience, Server Manager is now the easiest way to access this myriad of tools all from a single location:

Figure 2.18: The Tools menu in Server Manager

So far, the functions inside Server Manager that we have discussed are available on any installation of Windows Server 2019, whether it is standalone or part of a domain. Everything we have been doing is only dealing with the local server that we are logged into. Now, let's explore what options are available to us in Server Manager for the centralization of management across multiple servers. The new mentality of managing many servers from a single server is often referred to as *managing from a single pane of glass*. We will use Server Manager on one of our servers in the network to make connections to additional servers, and after doing that we should have much more information inside Server Manager that we can use to keep tabs on all of those servers.

Front and center inside the **Server Manager** console is the section entitled **Welcome to Server Manager**. Under that, we have a series of steps or links that can be clicked on. The first one lets you configure settings that are specific only to this local server. We have already done some work with the second step when we added a new role to our server. Now we will test out the third step, **Add other servers to manage**.

By the way, this same function can also be called by clicking on the **Manage** menu at the top, and then choosing **Add Servers.**, as shown in *Figure 2.19*:

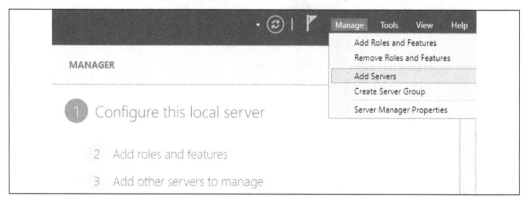

Figure 2.19: Adding servers

Most of you will be working within a domain environment where the servers are all domain-joined, which makes this next part really easy. Simply click on the **Find Now** button, and the machines available within your network will be displayed. From here, you can choose the servers that you want to manage, and move them over to the **Selected** column on the right, as shown in *Figure 2.20*:

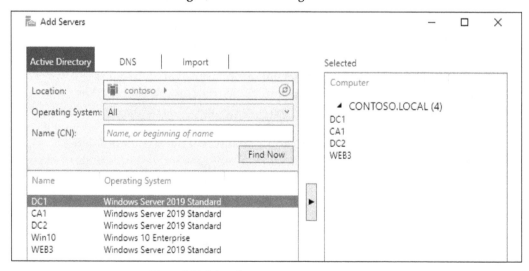

Figure 2.20: Select the servers you want to manage

After clicking **OK**, you will see that Server Manager has transformed in order to give you more information about all of these servers and roles that are installed on them. Now when you log into this single server, you immediately see critical maintenance information about **all** of the systems that you have chosen to add here. You could even use one dedicated server to handle the management of your whole arsenal of servers. For example, I am currently logged into a brand new server called CA1. I do not have any roles installed on this server, so, by default, Server Manager looks pretty basic. As soon as I add other servers (my domain controllers) to be managed, my Server Manager on the CA1 server now contains all of the details about CA1 and my domain controllers, so I can view all facets of my infrastructure from this single pane. As you can see in *Figure 2.21*, I even have some flags here indicating that some services are not running properly within my infrastructure:

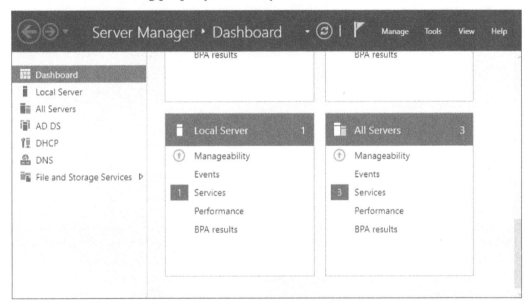

Figure 2.21: Managing servers on Server Manager Dashboard

Clicking on the **All Servers** link, or into one of the specific roles, gives you even more comprehensive information collected from these remote servers. Adding multiple servers into Server Manager is not only useful for monitoring but for future configurations as well. You remember a few pages ago when we added a new role using the wizard? That process has now evolved to become more comprehensive, since we have now *tapped* this server into our other servers in the network.

If I now choose to add a new role from inside Server Manager that is aware of multiple servers in the network, when I get to the screen asking me where I want to install that role, I see that I can choose to install a new role or feature onto one of my other servers, even though I am not working from the console of those servers, as shown in *Figure 2.22*:

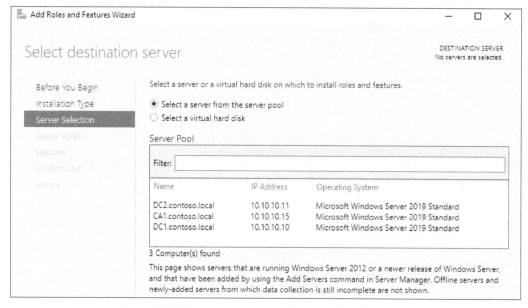

Figure 2.22: Selecting a server to install a new role or feature on

If I wanted to install the AD DS role onto DC2, a server I'm prepping as a second domain controller in my environment, I would *not* have to log into the DC2 server. Right here, from Server Manager running on CA1, I could run through the Add Roles wizard, define DC2 as the server that I want to manipulate, and install the role directly from here.

Remote Server Administration Tools (RSAT)

Using Server Manager on a single server to manage and monitor all of your servers is pretty handy, but what if we could take one more step out of that process? What if I told you that you didn't have to log into *any* of your servers, but could perform all of these tasks from the computer sitting on your desk?

This is possible by installing a toolset from Microsoft called the **Remote Server Administration Tools (RSAT)**. I have a regular Windows 10 client computer online and running in our network, also domain-joined. I am now going to add an optional feature to this Windows 10 computer to give it the RSAT toolset.

Open up **Settings** on the client computer and type the word optional into the search bar. One of the options presented will be **Manage optional features**. Go ahead and click that. Once inside Optional features, click the button to **Add a feature**. This will open a list of many optional features to choose from, including a lot of language options, but if you scroll down in the list you will eventually come to a number of different entries that start with RSAT:. If there were only a select number of the tools that you wanted to use from this Windows 10 client, you could be selective here and only install the admin consoles that you actually need. Since this is a test lab and I want as many options as possible, I am simply going to check the box next to every item that begins with RSAT:, as you can see in *Figure 2.23*:

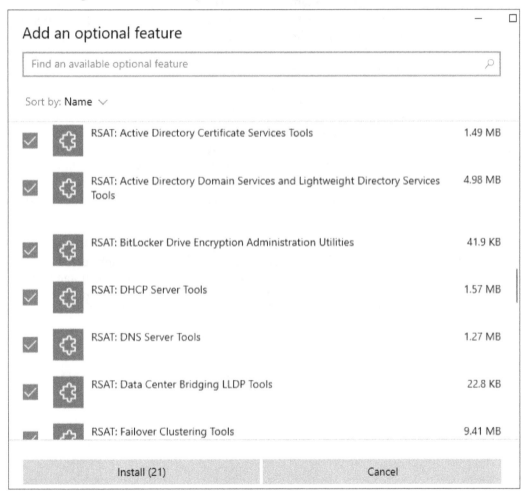

Figure 2.23: Installing RSAT features

If your computer is running a version of Windows 10 that is older than 1809, you won't find these options on your **Settings** screen. Instead, you can download and install the whole RSAT package from the following link: `https://www.microsoft.com/en-us/download/details.aspx?id=45520`.

After walking through the process to get these tools on my Windows 10 client computer, I can't seem to find any program that is called the **Remote Server Administration Tool**. That would be correct. Even though the names of these features we are installing all begin with RSAT, the components that are getting installed onto your system are the actual Windows Server system tools. If you peruse your **Start** menu, you will now find **Server Manager,** just like on a server, along with a folder full of Windows Administrative Tools! This makes sense, except that if you don't realize the name discrepancy, it can take you a few minutes to figure out why you cannot find what you just installed.

So, go ahead and launch Server Manager by finding it in the **Start** menu, or by using the search bar, or even by saying *Hey Cortana, open Server Manager.* Sorry, I couldn't resist. But whatever your method, open up Server Manager on your desktop computer and you will see that it looks and feels just like Server Manager in Windows Server 2019. And, in the same way that you work with and manipulate it within the server operating system, you can take the same steps here in order to add your servers for management.

In *Figure 2.24*, you can see that I have walked through the step to **Add other servers to manage** and selected some of the servers that are within my test network. I now have access, right here from my Windows 10 client computer, to manage and monitor all of the servers in my lab, without even having to log into them:

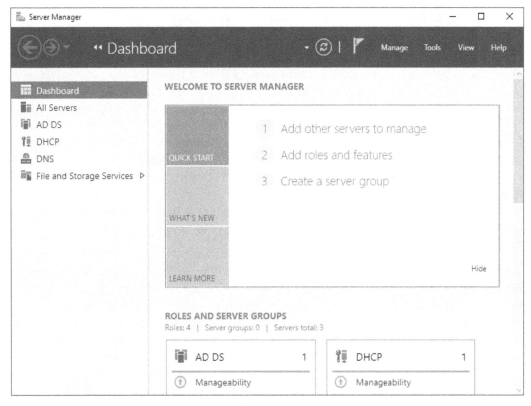

Figure 2.24: Centralized management via Server Manager

Does this mean RDP is dead?

With these new and improved ways to manage the underlying components of your servers without having to log into them directly, does this mean that our age-old friend RDP is going away? Certainly not! We will still have the need to access our servers directly sometimes, even if we go all-in with using the newer management tools. And I also expect that many administrators out there will continue using RDP and full desktop-based access for all management and monitoring of their servers simply because that is what they are more comfortable with, even if newer, more efficient ways now exist to accomplish the same tasks.

Remote Desktop Connection Manager

Since most of us do still utilize RDP occasionally (or often) when bouncing around between our servers, let's take a quick look at a tool that can at least make this task more manageable and centralized. I won't spend a lot of time looking over individual features or capabilities of this tool, since it is a client-side tool and not something that is specific to Windows Server 2019. You can use this to handle RDP connections for any and all of your servers, or even all of the client computers in your network. **Remote Desktop Connection Manager** is an incredibly useful platform for storing all of the different RDP connections that you make within your environment. You can save connections so that you don't have to spend time trying to remember server names, sort servers into categories, and even store credentials so that you don't have to type passwords when connecting to servers. Though a disclaimer should come with that one—your security folks may not be happy if you choose to employ the password storing feature.

Unfortunately, I can no longer provide you with a Microsoft download link for this tool, as the official Microsoft stance is that they are no longer making improvements to Remote Desktop Connection Manager, and that you should instead utilize the built-in MSTSC program or the universal Remote Desktop client application from the Microsoft Store. At this moment in time, these toolsets are limited in capability compared to what RDCM used to offer, and so I will leave it up to you as to which you prefer to pursue. There are still plenty of ways to find the RDCM installer if you seek it out online. You should be aware, however, that the reason it was discontinued and removed from Microsoft's own download pages is that a security vulnerability is present in the RDCM tool. This vulnerability would require an attacker to convince you, the admin, to launch an RDG file on your computer, which would then allow the attacker to extract data from your computer. So the risk is in your hands as to whether you think you could refrain from ever doing that or not. Here is a screenshot of the RDCM tool so you can have an idea of what it looks and feels like:

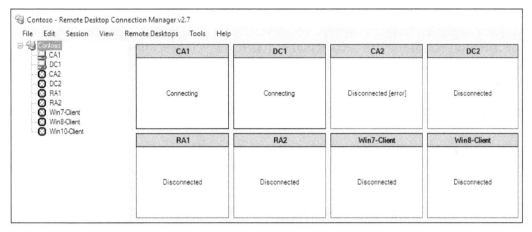

Figure 2.25: The RDCM tool

I almost removed this entire section from the book due to the security vulnerability and the official download no longer being available. In the end, I decided to leave it in place, not to make any official recommendations on what you should do, but to at least pass on the idea that there are options available to you for quick and easy RDP connection management when you are dealing with many different servers. There are plenty of alternative third-party toolsets that can accomplish the same thing, so while the Microsoft-provided Remote Desktop Connection Manager is no longer officially available, there are both free and paid applications that have been written by other companies that can be used to perform the same tasks.

Windows Admin Center (WAC)

Now forget everything I just told you about remote server management and focus here instead. I'm kidding…sort of. All of the tools we have already discussed are still stable, relevant, and great ways to interact with and manage your bunches of Windows servers. However, there's a new kid in town, and Microsoft expects them to be very popular.

Windows Admin Center (WAC) is a server and client management platform that is designed to help you administer your machines in a more efficient manner. This is a browser-based tool, meaning that, once installed, you access WAC from a web browser, which is great. No need to install a management tool or application onto your workstation—simply sit down and tap into it with a URL.

WAC can manage your servers (all the way back to Server 2008 R2), your server clusters, and even has some special functionality for managing hyper-converged infrastructure clusters. You have the ability to manage servers hosted on-premises as well as inside Azure, and you can even manage client machines in the Windows 10 flavor.

 What's the cost for such an amazing, powerful tool? FREE!

Windows Admin Center even has support for third-party vendors to be able to create extensions for the WAC interface, so this tool is going to continue growing. If you have been following along with the test lab configuration in the book so far, you will recognize the words "Windows Admin Center" from a pop-up window that displays itself every time that Server Manager is opened. Microsoft wants administrators to know about WAC so badly that they are reminding you that you should start using it every time that you log into a Server 2019 box, as shown in *Figure 2.26*:

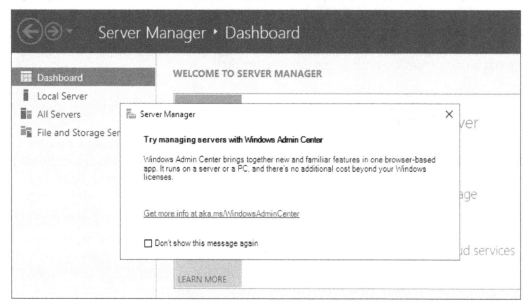

Figure 2.26: Even Server Manager recommends using WAC

Installing Windows Admin Center

Enough talk, let's try it out! First, we need to choose a location to install the components of WAC. True, I did say that one of the benefits was that we didn't need to install a client software component, but what I meant was that once WAC is implemented, then tapping into it is as easy as opening up a browser. That website needs to be installed and running somewhere, right? While you could throw the whole WAC system onto a Windows 10 client, let's take the approach that will be more commonly utilized in the field and install it onto a server in our network. I have a system running called WEB3 that is not yet hosting any roles or websites; it's just an empty server at this point. Sounds like a good place for something like this.

Download WAC from here: https://www.microsoft.com/en-us/windows-server/windows-admin-center.

Once downloaded, simply run the installer on the host machine. There are a few simple decisions you need to make during the wizard, most notable is the screen where you define port and certificate settings. In a production environment, it would be best to run port 443 and provide a valid SSL certificate here so that traffic to and from this website is properly protected via HTTPS, but, for my little test lab, I am going to run 443 with a self-signed certificate, just for testing purposes. Don't use self-signed certificates in production!

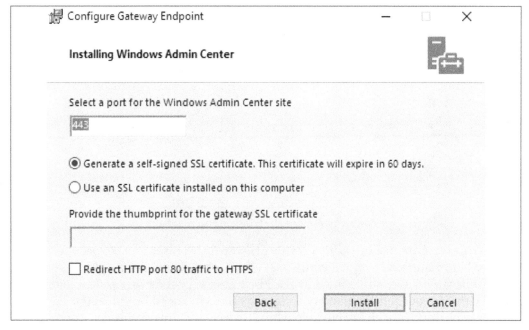

Figure 2.27: Installing WAC

Once the installer is finished, you will now be hosting the Windows Admin Center website on this server. For my particular installation, that new web address is `https://WEB3.contoso.local`.

Launching Windows Admin Center

Now for the fun part, checking this thing out. To tap into Windows Admin Center, you simply open up a supported browser from any machine in your network and browse to the WAC URL. Once again, mine is `https://WEB3.contoso.local`. Interestingly, Internet Explorer is not a supported browser. Microsoft recommends Edge but also works with Chrome. I am logged into my Windows 10 workstation, and will simply open up the Edge browser and try to hit my new site, as shown in *Figure 2.28*:

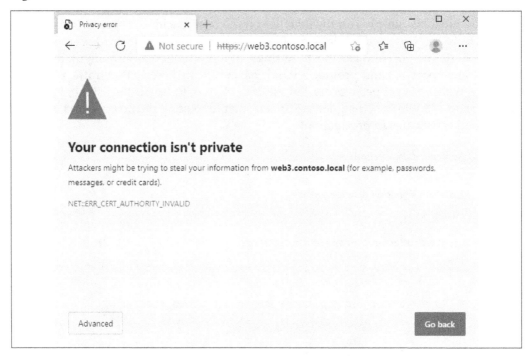

Figure 2.28: Opening a WAC URL in Microsoft Edge

As you can see, I am dealing with a certificate warning. This is to be expected because I am using a self-signed certificate, which, once again, is a bad idea. I only justify it because I'm running in a test lab. Since I am expecting this and am okay with the risk for our purposes today, I can click the **Advanced** button and then click the **Continue to web3.contoso.local** link to proceed. Interestingly, I am now presented with a credentials prompt:

Figure 2.29: Sign in to use WAC

Even though I am logged into a Windows 10 computer that is domain-joined and I am logged in with domain credentials, the WAC website does not automatically try to inject those credentials for its own use but rather pauses to ask who you are. If I simply input my domain credentials here, I am now presented with the Windows Admin Center interface, as shown in *Figure 2.30*:

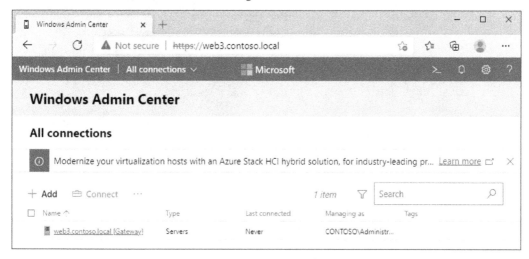

Figure 2.30: WAC interface

Adding more servers to Windows Admin Center

Logging into WAC is great, but not very useful until you add a bunch of machines that you want to manage. To do that, simply click the **+ Add** button that is shown onscreen. You will be presented with choices to add a new server, a new PC, a Windows Server failover cluster, Azure Stack HCI, or even an Azure VM. Make your selection and input the required information. I don't have any clusters in my test lab, not yet anyway, so I am going to add in connections to the standard servers that I have been running in the environment. If I select the option to add Windows servers, I can type out the individual server names, import a list of server names, or even select the option to **Search Active Directory**. I'll go ahead and try that search function to test how well this works. I have already set up a number of different servers in my lab and joined them to my domain (we'll talk more about domains in the next chapter)—but how do I make WAC search for them here? When I click **Search Active Directory**, I still get a field asking me to type in a server name, but there is a note about wildcards being allowed. Aha! If you simply type an asterisk (*) into the search field and click the **Search** button, Windows Admin Center polls your domain and presents a full list of machines that can be added to the console:

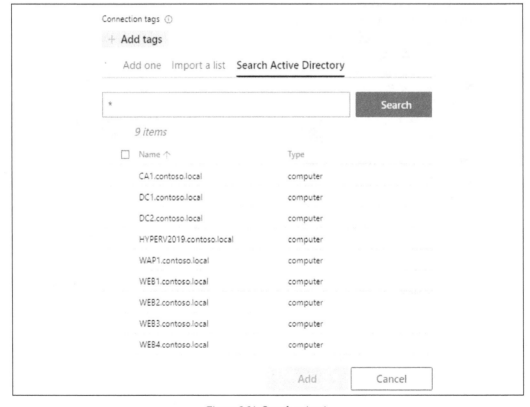

Figure 2.31: Search using *

Now simply select the checkboxes next to each server that you would like to administer via Windows Admin Center and click the **Add** button. You can see in *Figure 2.32* that WAC now contains information about all of the servers in my environment:

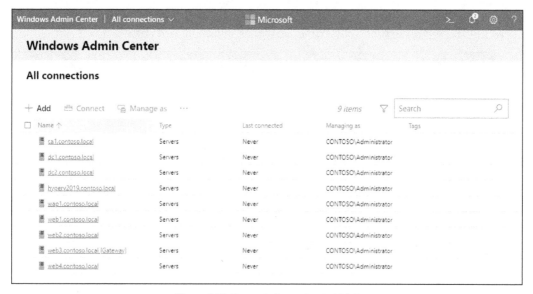

Figure 2.32: Server information in WAC

Managing a server with Windows Admin Center

Beginning the management of a server from within WAC is as simple as clicking on the server name. As you can see in *Figure 2.33*, I have selected my DC1 server, as it is currently the only machine with some real roles installed and running:

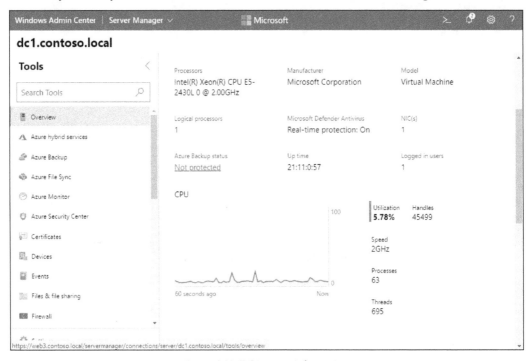

Figure 2.33: DC1 server information

From this interface, I can manage many different aspects of my DC1 server's operating system. There are power control functions, the ability to run backups on my server, I can even view and install certificates from here! You can monitor the performance of the server, view its event logs, manipulate the local Windows Firewall, and launch a remote PowerShell connection to the server. The goal with Windows Admin Center is for it to be your one-stop shop for remotely managing your servers, and I would say it is well on its way to accomplishing that goal.

I don't yet have any Server Core instances running in my lab but rest assured that WAC can be used to manage Server Core instances just as well as servers running Desktop Experience. This makes Windows Admin Center even more potent and intriguing to server administrators. When we get to our chapter on Server Core, we'll make sure to wrap back to this idea and in some way manipulate a Server Core instance through this Windows Admin Center console.

Changes are easy as pie

Monitoring information about your servers from a single place like WAC is great and powerful, but the coolest part about WAC is that you have some serious capabilities to manipulate your servers as well, straight from this web interface. This is yet another place where you can add roles or features onto your servers, create scheduled tasks, start or stop services, or even do things like edit the registry and add Windows Firewall rules. Let's make a quick change to our DC1 server to prove this out. All of my VMs are inside a test lab that is running within Hyper-V, and so interaction with my servers to this point has been directly from Hyper-V console sessions. It is basically like I am walking up to these servers and logging into them from the console, every single time I need to interact with them. At this point, RDP has never been enabled on DC1, but I wonder if there is a way to enable that easily, right from inside our Windows Admin Center?

Scrolling down through my list of tools on the left side of WAC, I suddenly spot one called **Remote Desktop**. Sounds like the right place to be! Clicking on **Remote Desktop** spins for a second as WAC reaches out and queries information from DC1. Then I am presented with a summary that states "Remote desktop connections are not allowed to this computer" with a button that allows me to **Go to settings**. Inside the **Remote Desktop settings** screen, I have here the same options that I would see if I were to log directly into DC1 and edit the Remote Desktop settings from inside the classic advanced System properties screens. You can see in *Figure 2.34* that I have now selected the option **Allow remote connections to this computer** – previously this had not been enabled:

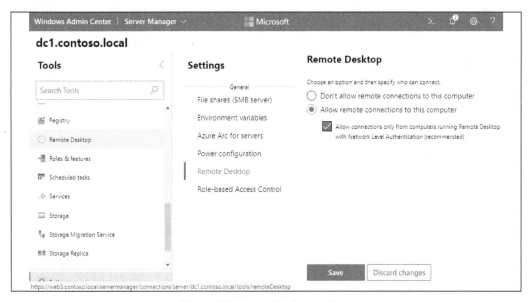

Figure 2.34: Remote Desktop settings

Simply changing the setting here and clicking the **Save** button causes Windows Admin Center to reach out to DC1 and enable this Remote Desktop setting, after which I can immediately connect to it using RDP from my Windows 10 computer. I never needed to log into DC1 to enable remote logins to DC1!

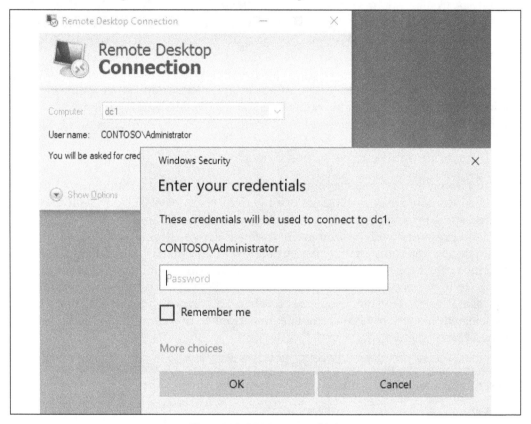

Figure 2.35: RDP is now enabled

Azure integrations

You'll notice inside WAC that there are numerous tools related to Azure. If you have an Azure environment or are thinking about getting started with one, your on-premises Windows Admin Center can be used to administer both on-premises servers as well as Azure servers. WAC can also be used to bind your on-premises environment together with your Azure environment through things like Azure File Sync and Azure Backup. These tools can be a powerful way of creating a hybrid cloud configuration, where you maintain servers in both environments, and can also be used to help ease a transition from a traditional datacenter into a cloud-only mentality.

Enabling quick server rollouts with Sysprep

At the beginning of this chapter, we walked through the process of installing the Windows Server 2019 operating system onto your new server. Whether this was a physical piece of hardware or a virtual machine that we were working with, the installation process was essentially the same. Plugging in the DVD or USB stick, booting to it, and letting the installer run its course is an easy enough thing to do, but what if you need to build out ten new servers instead of just one? This process would soon start to get tedious, and it would seem like you were wasting a lot of time having to do the exact same thing over and over again. You would be correct—this does waste a lot of time, and there is an easier and faster way to roll out new servers as long as you are building them all from a relatively similar hardware platform. If you are building out your servers as virtual machines, which is so often the case these days, then this process works great and can save you quite a bit of time with new server builds.

Now, before I go too far down this road of describing the Sysprep process, I will also note that there are more involved technologies available within the Windows infrastructure that allow automated operating system and server rollouts that can make the new server rollout process even easier than what I am describing here. The problem with some of the automated technologies is that the infrastructure required to make them work properly is more advanced than many folks will have access to if they are just learning the ropes with Windows Server. In other words, to have a fully automated server rollout mechanism isn't very feasible for small environments or test labs, which is where a lot of us live while we are learning these new technologies.

So, anyway, we will not be focusing on an automation kind of approach to server rollouts, but rather we will be doing a few minutes of extra work on our very first server, which then results in saving numerous minutes of setup work on every server that we build afterward. The core of this process is the **Sysprep** tool, which is baked into all versions of Windows, so you can take this same process on any current Windows machine, whether it be a client or a server.

Sysprep is a tool that prepares your system for duplication. Its official name is the **Microsoft System Preparation Tool**, and to sum up what it does in one line, it allows you to create a master *image* of your server that you can reuse as many times as you want in order to roll out additional servers. A key benefit to using Sysprep is that you can put customized settings onto your master server and install things such as Windows Updates prior to Sysprep, and all of these settings and patches will then exist inside your master image.

Using Sysprep saves you time by not having to walk through the operating system installation process, but it saves you even more time by not having to wait for Windows Update to roll all of the current patches down onto every new system that you create.

Now, some of you might be wondering why Sysprep is even necessary. If you wanted to clone your master server, you could simply use a hard disk imaging tool, or, if you were dealing with virtual machines, you could simply copy and paste the .VHDX file itself in order to make a copy of your new server, right? The answer is yes, but the big problem is that the new image or hard drive that you just created would be an exact replica of the original one. The hostname would be the same, and, more importantly, some core identification information inside Windows, such as the operating system's **security identifier (SID)** number, would be exactly the same. If you were to power on both the original master server and a new server based on this exact replica, you would cause conflicts and collisions on the network as these two servers fight for their right to be the one and only server with that unique name and SID. This problem exacerbates itself in domain environments, where it is even more important that each system within your network has a unique SID/GUID—their identifier within Active Directory. If you create exact copies of servers and bring them both online, let's just say neither one is going to be happy about it. If you do this inside a production environment, you can wreak havoc on your network. I know from personal experience what it looks like to help someone recover their domain after a domain controller's hard drive was simply copied, pasted, and turned on as a second server. It's the definition of a bad day.

Sysprep fixes all of these inherent problems with the system duplication process by randomizing the unique identifiers in the operating system. To prepare ourselves to roll out many servers using a master image we create with Sysprep, here is a quick-reference summary of the steps we will be taking:

1. Install Windows Server 2019 onto a new server
2. Configure customizations and updates onto your new server
3. Run Sysprep to prepare and shut down your master server
4. Create your master image of the drive
5. Build new servers using copies of the master image

And now let's cover these steps in a little more detail.

Installing Windows Server 2019 onto a new server

First, just like you have already done, we need to prepare our first server by getting the Windows Server 2019 operating system installed. Refrain from installing any full roles onto the server, because, depending on the role and its unique configuration, the Sysprep process that we run shortly could cause problems for individual role configurations. Install the operating system and make sure device drivers are all squared away, and you're ready for the next step.

Configuring customizations and updates onto your new server

Next, you want to configure customizations and install operating system updates onto your new server. Each setting or installation that you can do now that is universal to your batch of servers will save you from having to take that step on your servers in the future. This portion may be slightly confusing because I just told you a minute ago not to install roles onto the master server. This is because a role installation makes numerous changes in the operating system, and some of the roles that you can install lock themselves down to a particular hostname running on the system. If you were to do something like that to a master server, that role would more than likely break when brought up on a new server. Customizations that you can put into place on the master server are things such as plugging in files and folders that you might want on all of your servers, such as an `Admin Tools` folder or something like that. You could also start or stop services that you may or may not want running on each of your servers, and change settings in the registry if that is part of your normal server prep or hardening process. Whatever changes or customizations you put into place, it's not a bad idea to run a full slew of tests against the first new server that you build from this master image, just to make sure all of your changes made it through the Sysprep process.

Now is also the time to let Windows Update install and to put any patches on this new server that you want to have installed on all of your new servers in the future. There is nothing more frustrating than installing a new operating system in 5 minutes, only to have to sit around and wait 4 hours for all of the current updates and patches to be installed before you can use the new server. By including all of these updates and patches in the master image, you save all of that download and installation time for each new server that you spin up.

Continue to save yourself time and effort by creating new copies of your master images every few months. This way the newest patches are always included in your master image and it continues to save you more and more time throughout the life of Windows Server 2019.

Running Sysprep to prepare and shut down your master server

Now that our master server is prepped how we want, it is time to run the Sysprep tool itself. To do that, open up an administrative Command Prompt and browse to C:\Windows\System32\Sysprep. Now you can make use of the Sysprep.exe utility inside that folder to launch Sysprep itself.

As with many executables that you run from Command Prompt, there are a variety of optional switches that you can tag onto the end of your command to make it do specific tasks. From your Command Prompt window, if you simply run the sysprep. exe command, you will see a graphical interface for Sysprep, where you can choose between the available options, as shown in *Figure 2.36*:

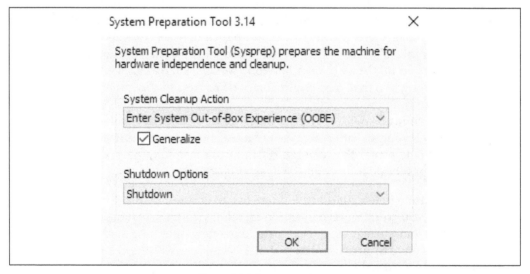

Figure 2.36: Sysprep options

Since I always use the same set of options for Sysprep, I find it easier to simply include all of my optional switches right from the command-line input, therefore bypassing the graphical screen altogether. Here is some information on the different switches that are available to use with sysprep.exe:

- /quiet: This tells Sysprep to run without status messages on the screen.

- /generalize: This specifies that Sysprep is to remove all of the unique system information (SID) from the Windows installation, making the final image usable on multiple machines in your network, because each new one spun up from the image will get a new, unique SID.

- /audit: This restarts the machine into a special audit mode, where you have the option of adding additional drivers into Windows before the final image gets taken.

- /oobe: This tells the machine to launch the mini-setup wizard when Windows next boots.

- /reboot: This restarts when Sysprep is finished.

- /shutdown: This shuts down the system (not a restart) when Sysprep is finished. This is an important one and is one that I typically use.

- /quit: This closes Sysprep after it finishes.

- /unattend: There is a special answerfile that you can create that, when specified, will be used in conjunction with the Sysprep process to further configure your new servers as they come online. For example, you can specify in this answerfile that a particular installer or batch file is to be launched upon the first Windows boot following Sysprep. This can be useful for any kind of cleanup tasks that you might want to perform, for example, if you had a batch file on your system that you used to flush out the log files following the first boot of new servers.

The two that are most important for our purpose of wanting to create a master image file that we can use for quick server rollouts in the future are the /generalize switch and the /shutdown switch. /generalize is very important because it replaces all of the unique identification information, the SID info, in the new copies of Windows that come online. This allows your new servers to co-exist on the network with your original server, and with other new servers that you bring online. The /shutdown switch is also very important because we want this master server to become sysprepped and then immediately shut down so that we can create our master image from it.

 Make sure that your server does NOT boot into Windows again until after you have created your master image or taken your master copy of the .VHDX file. The first time that Windows boots it will inject the new SID information, and you want that only to happen on new servers that you have created based on your new image.

So, rather than simply throwing all of the switches at you and letting you decide, let's take a look at the ones that I typically use. I will make use of /generalize so that I make my new servers unique, and I also like to use /oobe so that the mini-setup wizard launches during the first boot of Windows on any of my new systems. Then, I will of course also use /shutdown, because I need this server to be offline immediately following Sysprep so that I can take a copy of the hard drive to be used as my master image. So, my fully groomed sysprep command is shown in the following code:

```
sysprep.exe /generalize /oobe /shutdown
```

After launching this command, you will see Sysprep moving through some processes within Windows, and after a couple of minutes, your server will shut itself down, as shown in *Figure 2.37*:

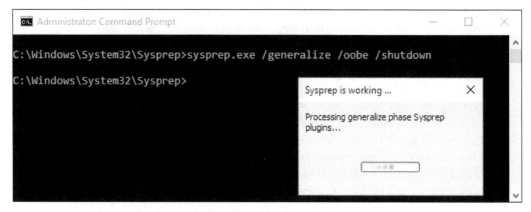

Figure 2.37: Sysprep and shutting down

You are now ready to create your master image from this hard disk.

Creating your master image of the drive

Our master server is now shut down, and we are ready to create our master image from this server. If it is a physical server, you can use any hard disk imaging utility in order to create an image file from the drive. An imaging utility like those from the company Acronis will create a single file from your drive. This file contains an image of the entire disk that you can use to restore down onto fresh hard drives in new servers in the future. On the other hand, most of you are probably dealing with virtual servers most often in your day-to-day work lives and prepping new servers in the virtual world is even easier.

Once our master server has been sysprepped and shut down, you simply create a copy of the `.VHDX` file. Log into your Hyper-V Server, copy and paste the hard disk file, and you're done. This new file can be renamed `WS2019_Master_withUpdates.VHDX`, or whatever you would like it to be named, in order to help you keep track of the current status on this image file. Save this image file or copy of the `.VHDX` file somewhere safe on your network, where you will be able to quickly grab copies of it whenever you have the need to spin up a new Windows Server 2019.

Building new servers using copies of the master image

Now we get to the easy part. When you want to create new servers in the future, you simply copy and paste your master file into a new location for the new server, rename the drive file to be something appropriate for the server you are creating, and boot your new virtual machine from it. Here is where you see the real benefit from the time that Sysprep saves, as you can now spin up many new servers all at the same time, by doing a quick copy and paste of the master image file and booting all of your new servers from these new files. No need to install Windows or pull out that dusty installation DVD!

As the new servers turn on for the first time and boot into Windows, they will run through the out-of-box-experience, mini-setup wizard. Also, in the background, the operating system gives itself a new random and unique hostname and SID information so that you can be sure you do not have conflicts on your network with these new servers.

 New servers created from a sysprepped image file always receive a new hostname when they boot. This often confuses admins who might have named their master server something such as MASTER. After booting your new servers, you can expect to see randomized names on your new servers and you will have to rename them according to their new duties in life.

For example, before running Sysprep and creating my master image, the server that I was working on was named DC1 because I had originally intended to use it as a domain controller in my network. However, because I had not installed the role or configured anything domain-related on it, this server was a perfect candidate for displaying the Sysprep process and so I used it in our text today. I sysprepped it, shut it down, made a copy of its .VHDX file (to be my master image file), and then I started DC1 back up. You can now see inside the system properties that I am back to having a randomized hostname, and so if I still want to use this server as DC1, I will have to rename it again now that it has finished booting through mini-setup, as shown in *Figure 2.38*:

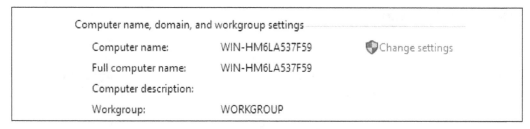

Figure 2.38: System properties

Hopefully, this process is helpful information that can save you time when building out new servers in your own environments. Get out there and give it a try the next time you have a new server to build! You can further benefit yourself with the Sysprep tool by keeping many different master image files. Perhaps you have a handful of different kinds of servers that you prep regularly — there is nothing stopping you from creating a number of different master servers and creating multiple master images from these servers.

Summary

Anyone interested in being a Windows Server administrator needs to be comfortable with installing and managing their servers, and covering those topics establishes an important baseline for moving forward. It is quite common in today's IT world for new operating system releases to be thoroughly tested, both because server hardware resources are so easily available to us through virtualization technologies, and because most business systems are now being designed for 100% uptime. This kind of reliability requires very thorough testing of any platform changes, and, in order to accomplish such testing of the Windows Server 2019 operating system in your environment, you will be burning quite a bit of time spinning through the basic installation processes numerous times. I hope that you can put the suggestions provided in this chapter to good use in saving you precious extra minutes when dealing with these tasks in your Windows Server world.

Years ago, quite a bit of effort was regularly put into figuring out which roles and services could co-exist because the number of servers available to us was limited. With the new virtualization and cloud paradigm shift, many companies have a virtually unlimited number of servers that can be running, and this means we are running much larger quantities of servers to perform the same jobs and functions. Management and administration of these servers then becomes an IT burden and adopting the centralized administration tools and ideas available within Windows Server 2019 will also save you considerable time and effort in your daily workload. In the next chapter, we will start to dive into some of the most commonly used roles and tools in a Windows Server environment, the core infrastructure technologies surrounding Active Directory.

Questions

1. What is the name of the new web-based, centralized server management tool from Microsoft (fun fact, this toolset was formerly known as **Project Honolulu**)?

2. True or False — Windows Server 2019 needs to be installed onto rack-mount server hardware.

3. True or False — By choosing the default installation option for Windows Server 2019, you will end up with a user interface that looks quite like Windows 10.

4. What is the PowerShell cmdlet that displays currently installed roles and features in Windows Server 2019?

5. True or False — Server Manager can be used to manage many different servers at the same time.

6. What is the name of the toolset that can be installed onto a Windows 10 computer, in order to run Server Manager on that client workstation?

7. What are the supported web browsers that can be used to interact with Windows Admin Center?

3

Active Directory

Each of you reading this book will have a different acquired skillset and level of experience with the Windows Server environment. As I mentioned previously, being able to make servers run the operating system is great and a very important first step for doing real work in your environment. But until you know and understand what the purposes behind the main roles available to run on Windows Server 2019 are, the only thing your new server does is consume electricity.

A server is intended to serve data. The kind of data that it serves and to what purpose depends entirely on what roles you determine the server must ... well ... serve. Appropriately, you must install roles within Windows Server 2019 to make it do something. We already know how to get roles installed onto our server but have not talked about any of the purposes behind these roles. Over the next few chapters, we will start looking into what I commonly refer to as the core infrastructural roles available within Windows Server. This involves discussing the role's general purpose, as well as plugging in some particular tasks dealing with those roles that you will be responsible for doing in your daily tasks as a server administrator.

We begin with the single most important role in all of the on-premise Microsoft world, **Active Directory (AD)**, as it is commonly referred to, is a directory service that serves as a kind of database, storing and centralizing various types of information about your organization. User accounts, computer accounts, certificates, policies, and even file replication are all things that you can find hooked into AD.

As we look over the parts and pieces of AD, it will become clearer what information is stored within and why it is so important. If you are new to IT and do not yet have a good grasp of AD, make sure to learn this technology! AD is the hinge upon which almost everything in a Windows Server world revolves. Is it possible to utilize Windows servers without them being connected and joined to Active Directory? Yes. Is it likely you will ever find this scenario at play in the real world? No. In this chapter, we will learn the following:

- What is a domain controller?
- Creating your first domain
- Multiple domain controllers for redundancy
- Active Directory Users and Computers
- Active Directory Domains and Trusts
- Active Directory Sites and Services
- Active Directory Administrative Center
- Read-only domain controllers
- Group Policy

What is a domain controller?

If we are going to discuss the core infrastructure services that you need to piece together your Microsoft-driven network, there is no better place to start than with the domain controller. A **Domain Controller**, commonly referred to as a **DC**, is simply a server that is hosting Active Directory. It is a central point of contact, a central "hub" so to speak, that is accessed prior to almost any communication that takes place between a client and server in your network. Perhaps the easiest way to describe it is as a storage container for all *identification* that happens on the network. Usernames, passwords, computer accounts, groups of computers, servers, groups and collections of servers, security policies, file replication services, and many more things are stored within and managed by DCs. If you are not planning to have a domain controller be one of the first servers in your Microsoft-centric network, you might as well not even start building that network. DCs are essential to the way that our computers and devices communicate with each other and with the server infrastructure inside our companies.

Active Directory Domain Services

If you've stopped reading at this point to install the *Domain Controller* role onto your server, welcome back! There is no role called **Domain Controller**. The role that provides all of these capabilities is called **Active Directory Domain Services**, or **AD DS**. This is the role that you need to install on a server. By installing that role, you will have turned your server into a domain controller. The purpose of running a DC really is to create a directory, or database, of objects in your network. This database is known as **Active Directory**, and is a platform inside which you build a hierarchical structure to store objects, such as usernames, passwords, and computer accounts. You might be thinking, "didn't we just say these same words in a slightly different way?" and you're not wrong. AD is important, and I want to make sure you know it. A career in IT guarantees that you will in some way interface with AD in your work.

Most of the time when you hear anyone talking about "Active Directory" it is likely that what they really mean is a single **domain** within the directory. There is a whole hierarchy within an Active Directory schema, comprised of forests, trees, domains, and organizational units. We will discuss each of these organizational levels of Active Directory as we navigate through the tools that you will be utilizing to interact with AD further along in this chapter.

Once you have created a domain in which you can store accounts, objects, and devices, you can then create user accounts and passwords for your employees to utilize for authentication. You can then also join your other servers and computers to this domain so that they can accept and benefit from those user credentials. Having and joining a domain is the secret sauce that allows you to walk from computer to computer within your company and log on to each of them with your own username and password, even when you have never logged in to that computer before. Even more powerful is the fact that it enables directory-capable applications to authenticate directly against Active Directory when they need authentication information. For example, when I, as a domain user, log in to my computer at work with my username and password, the Windows operating system running on my computer reaches out to a domain controller server and verifies that my password is correct.

Once it confirms that I really am who I say I am, it issues an authentication token back to my computer and I am able to log in. Then, once I am on my desktop and open an application – let's say I open my Outlook to access my email – that email program is designed to reach out to my email server, called an **Exchange Server**, and authenticate against it to make sure that my own mailbox is displayed and not somebody else's. Does this mean I need to re-enter my username and password for Outlook, or for any other application that I open from my computer? Generally not. And the reason I do not have to re-enter my credentials over and over again is that my username, my computer, and the application servers are all part of the same domain.

When this is true, and it is for most networks, my authentication token can be shared among my programs. So, once I log in to the computer itself, my applications can launch and open, and pass my credentials through to the application server, without any further input from me as a user. It would be quite a frustrating experience indeed if we required our users to enter passwords all day, every day as they opened up the programs that they need in order to do their work.

Active Directory itself is a broad enough topic to warrant its own book, and indeed there have been many written on the topic. Now that we have a basic understanding of what it is and why it's critical to have in our Windows Server environment, let's get our hands dirty using some of the tools that get installed onto your domain controller during the AD DS role installation process.

Creating your first domain

I must admit that I have cheated a little bit and have already been working from within a domain for the purpose of taking screenshots for the book up to this point. My test lab already has a DC1 server up and running, and on it I have configured a domain called contoso.local. However, saying "domains are important" and not showing you how to create one would not be helpful to you, the reader, and so we are going to build a brand-new domain now, on a brand-new server.

You probably recognize "Contoso" if you've ever read over Microsoft tutorials or example configuration documentation, because it is one of several fake business names Microsoft uses often in documentation or for the purpose of showing example scenarios. I am using it here as well, but you could name your domain anything you want to. For setting up our second domain, I am going to pull another company name from the Microsoft hat, Fabrikam.

One of the first things that needs to be decided before you can build a domain is the name of the domain. We don't want to discuss DNS in depth here because there's another whole chapter for that, but everyone uses DNS every day whether they realize it or not. Every time that you type any website name – microsoft.com, google.com, bing.com, and so on – you are inputting a name, which DNS is then going to turn into an IP address. You also know that the ending of website names can take on many forms. Most common is .com, but you may visit websites that also end with .org, .biz, .info, .tech, .edu, .mil, and many more.

Let's take `microsoft.com` as an example. If you simply visit `microsoft.com`, you'll see the main website for the company. If you visit `docs.microsoft.com`, you will land on their documentation platform page. Visiting `portal.microsoft.com` takes you to an Office 365 sign-in page, and if you have an Office 365 account you can sign in here and perform many functions. The different addresses you are typing into the web browser are taking you to vastly different web pages and systems, yet the domain names being called for in the browser all end with the same `microsoft.com`. This means that `microsoft.com` is the primary domain name for all of these things, also known as a **domain suffix** or a top-level domain.

Why am I running down this rabbit hole? Because this is important information to understand when you decide on your internal domain name. Just like a domain suffix on the internet, when you build your internal domain and then later join computers and servers to that domain, each of those devices is going to have a true, full name of *computername.domainname.something*. In my current domain, `contoso.local`, a full server name that exists right now is `DC1.Contoso.local`.

Most internal domains that I have encountered in the world end with `.local`. Is it possible to name your internal domain something that ends in one of these internet-based suffixes, like `Contoso.com`? Yes! You can name your internal domain whatever you want, and in fact if you have plans to host email in Office 365, using an internal domain that matches your public domain name used for email carries some advantages. Some of you may be thinking at this point, "I already own contoso.com (insert your own business website name here), so wouldn't it be less confusing overall if I also name my internal domain the same thing? contoso.com?" The answer is yes and no. For certain scenarios that involve cloud resources, like Office 365 and Azure, yes using a `.com` internal domain can make a more seamless transition to the cloud. However, prior to these cloud technologies it was always Microsoft's recommendation to end your internal domain with `.local`. We will talk more about why this is the case in *Chapter 4, DNS and DHCP*, when we discuss something called **split-brain DNS**.

Prep your domain controller

Okay, I have decided to use `fabrikam.local` as my internal domain name. Now, how do I make that a reality? We only need one server to build a domain, the server that you want to be your domain controller. I have a new Windows Server 2019 VM running and plugged into a network, but so far I have not configured anything at all on the server. There are three simple things that need to happen on any server that you plan to turn into a domain controller:

Set a static IP address – Head into your NIC properties and define a static IP address for this server. Even if you already have a DHCP server running in your network to hand out IP addresses, you do not want domain controller servers to ever change IPs. It is possible to do so, but quite challenging. So best practice dictates that whatever IP address you define for your DC, plan on that being its IP address forever.

Set a good hostname – Similar to IP addressing on a domain controller, it is not recommended to ever change the name of a DC server. In fact, this is quite a bit more complicated than IP addressing, and you should definitely plan that whatever name you give your server today will forever be its name on your network until the day you decommission this server entirely.

Set the DNS server address – Head back into your NIC properties and configure the DNS server address that your domain controller is looking for, to be itself. What? Itself? It's not a DNS server! Not yet, but other than pretty rare circumstances, almost every domain controller will also become a DNS server. DNS integrates with Active Directory and there is a lot of benefit to hosting these services together, so most Microsoft environments you encounter will have AD DS and DNS installed together on domain controller servers. Generally, when setting up your first DC, you will always start by pointing the NIC's DNS settings to the server's own IP address.

You can see in *Figure 3.1* that I have now named my new server FAB-DC1, configured a static IP, and pointed DNS to itself:

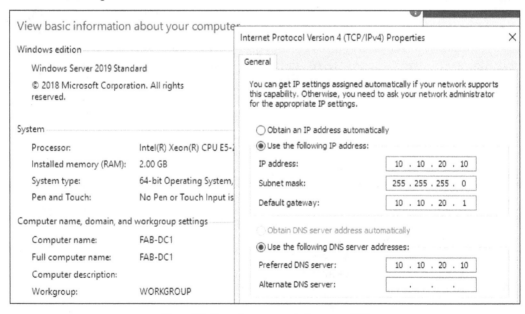

Figure 3.1: Prepping a server to become a DC

Install the AD DS role

Now that the server is prepped to be a domain controller, we install the role! Since you are already familiar with the process of adding roles to servers, we won't step through the whole thing again. Simply utilize Server Manager or PowerShell to install the following components onto your new server:

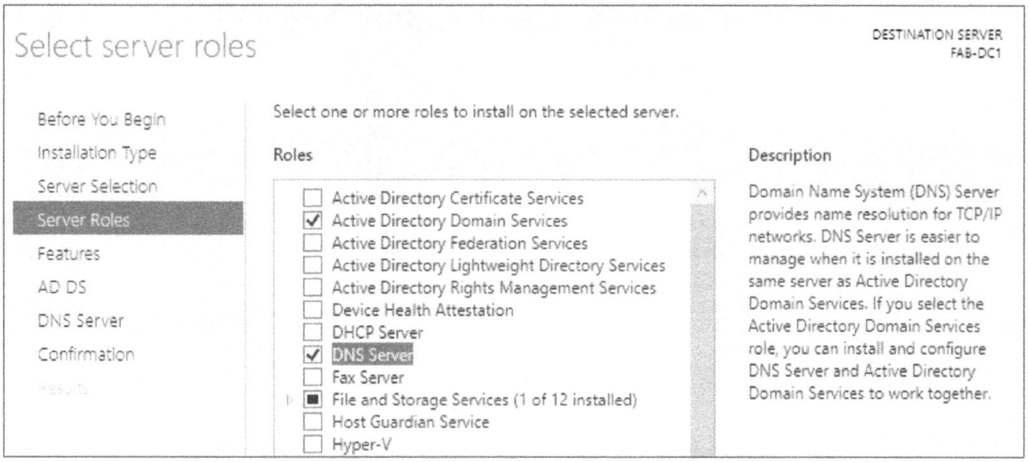

Figure 3.2: Installing Active Directory Domain Services and DNS Server roles

As mentioned, I am going to install **AD DS** for Active Directory, and **DNS Server** so that this domain controller can also serve as a true DNS server for our new business. As you progress through the role installation wizard, you will encounter some informational text that is useful to read over, but there should be no further options that you need to select in order to get both of these roles installed onto your server.

Configure the domain

Following the installation of the roles, you will notice a yellow exclamation mark near the top of Server Manager. Clicking on that icon, you can see text indicating that some configuration is required for the Active Directory Domain Services role:

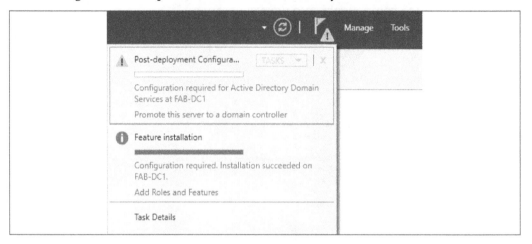

Figure 3.3: Additional configuration is required for the Active Directory Domain Services role

Click on the link that says **Promote this server to a domain controller**. This link will invoke the configuration wizard that is going to walk us through turning the server into a true DC.

Trees, forests, and...domains?

Wait a minute, the first screen we encounter in this promotion wizard where we need to make a decision is talking about shrubbery. What gives? You already know that a domain is like a database, containing information about many kinds of objects, but primarily user accounts and computer accounts that are part of that domain. What we have not really discussed yet is that a domain is not the top tier of its existence, rather a **domain resides within a forest**. These are the two technical terms you will run across when working within Active Directory, domain and forest, and references to a tree are more metaphorical, related to the layout of a forest with domains underneath the forest, with possible child domains underneath. The whole schema when mapped out on paper may resemble the many branches of a tree, thus the term tree.

A forest is the top tier in Active Directory, and you could potentially have many different domains inside the same forest. Why would you want to do that? Most companies don't, and most of the time you will find that any given company has one internal domain, residing within one forest, and that's it.

One reason you may find multiple domains inside the same forest would be if the company had different divisions or business units that needed their authentication and systems to be separated from each other. In a single domain, remember that oftentimes any domain user can authenticate and log in to any domain computer, and perhaps you wanted to ensure that nobody in DivisionA was able to log in to computers that were owned by DivisionB. Creating multiple domains would be one way to accomplish that scenario.

As you walk through the domain configuration wizard that we have just launched on our new server, you will see many different options for what kind of domain controller this server may become. You may be adding a DC to an existing domain, adding a new domain to an existing forest, or creating a new forest altogether. Selecting each of these options in the wizard will present you with different sub-options related to that selection. If you click on **Add a new domain to an existing forest,** you will find that you then have options for creating a new child domain, or a tree domain. A child domain would be a new domain that exists under an existing domain in the hierarchical AD tree, while a tree domain would be a new domain that resides directly under the forest itself and would sit alongside any existing domains. Under the same forest but separated from any existing domains.

Today, we have nothing in this Fabrikam network. No forest, no domains, no child domains. So we are going to choose the third option, **Add a new forest**. All that needs to be decided on this screen is the **Root domain name**, which is where I will enter fabrikam.local, which we decided on earlier:

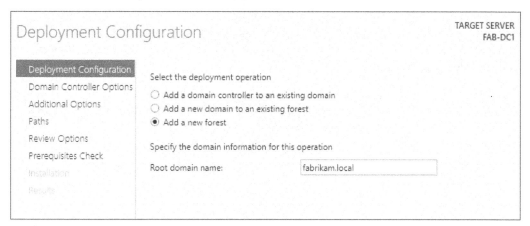

Figure 3.4: Adding a new forest

The remaining screens in this configuration wizard contain a number of options, but not many of them need to be populated if you are unsure of the answers. Especially if you are building out a test lab, the default options are generally sufficient. We'll do a quick summary here of each screen to point out options and what they mean.

Domain controller options

Now that you understand that there are at least two tiers to every Active Directory, at minimum one forest and one domain, it is important to understand that each of those things has its own **functional level**. Forest and domain functional levels are classified by different versions of Windows Server operating system releases. Windows Server 2016 functional level has more features and accessories baked into it than Server 2012 R2 does, for example, and on and on. Something interesting to note is that Windows Server 2019 does not have a new functional level, the newest you can select is Server 2016.

Why does the wizard even ask? Wouldn't it make sense that you would always want to select the newest from this list? In almost all cases, the answer is yes. One reason you may need to select an older functional level for either your forest or domain is if some technology you are planning to implement or some version of device you plan to join to that domain requires an older functional level version. This brings to light another valid scenario that might require a company to build a secondary domain under an existing forest, if a technology that you wanted to implement for the business carried some specific requirements that locked you into a certain version of functional level, but your primary production domain could not meet those requirements for whatever the reason.

For our purposes today, we simply leave both forest and domain functional levels selected on the default Windows Server 2016.

On this screen of the wizard, you also have options to choose whether or not this domain controller will also be a DNS server (usually yes), whether it will be a Global Catalog server (also usually yes), or a read-only domain controller, which we will discuss later in this chapter.

The third option, and the only one that absolutely requires your attention, is to define a Directory Services Restore Mode password. I sincerely hope that you never have to enter Active Directory recovery mode in order to restore information or your directory, but if you do – this password is going to be very important to that process:

Figure 3.5: Domain Controller Options

DNS Options

If you were creating a new domain controller/DNS Server that was going to live inside an existing tree and particularly if your new server is going to play a child role, then you typically want to ensure that the parent's DNS zones have a delegation for this new DNS server you are creating, to ensure that names in your domain can be successfully resolved in the parent domain as well. The creation of that DNS delegation is the only option on this screen, and in cases where we are creating a brand-new forest and domain, there is no existing authoritative parent zone so there is an expected warning message on-screen:

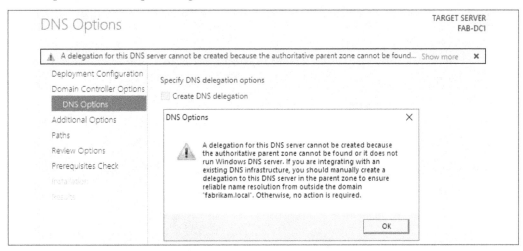

Figure 3.6: Expected warning message regarding no authoritative parent zone

Since we are building a new forest, there is nothing we need to do with this warning message and we simply click **Next** to proceed.

Additional Options

The NetBIOS domain name should self-populate in the wizard and will be the first portion of your domain name. In my example, it has inserted the word FABRIKAM into this field. Many people seem to think that NetBIOS is obsolete, but it is still used by applications to pass traffic around in many cases, so the options for configuring it here are still important. You don't need to do anything on this screen other than to ensure a NetBIOS name populates in the wizard and continue on.

Paths

Active Directory stores quite a bit of very important information on your domain controller server. If desired, here you can specify paths for storing this data if you wanted it to reside in a special location, such as on a dedicated hard drive. The default options are all within the C:\Windows folder, which is generally where everyone leaves it.

Review Options, Prerequisites Check, Installation

That's it! You have now populated all the available options, and you are presented with a screen that allows you to review the selections you have made. Once satisfied that everything looks good on this screen, the wizard will run through a prerequisites check on your server to ensure it is ready to become a domain controller. This is the point where, if you forgot to assign a static IP or to set a DNS server in the NIC properties, the wizard will fail the prereq check and flag you with some warnings. In fact, you will likely see at least one or two warnings even if you have done everything perfectly: one regarding that DNS delegation that we already talked about and another warning about cryptography algorithms. This is normal behavior for configuring a brand new forest/domain on Windows Server 2019.

Assuming you have everything in order, the wizard will continue on to installation, at the end of which your server will reboot, and is now officially a domain controller for your network.

During the first login to your server, which is now a domain controller, you will notice at the login screen that you are now signing in with a domain account, no longer a local account on this server. Domain controllers don't actually have local user accounts anymore; if you were using the built-in administrator account to sign in to your server before, like I was, that account and password have now been converted into the domain administrator account. This account can now be used to log in to any computer or server that is later joined to your domain and will automatically receive administrative rights on that device. Make sure you're using a good domain administrator password, and don't share it with anybody!

Multiple domain controllers for redundancy

Now, having configured our first domain controller, we should jump in and start setting up objects inside Active Directory, right? Not yet! I'm being a little dramatic here, of course you can jump ahead and start using the tools that interface with AD, which we will discuss immediately following this section of our chapter. But if you are setting up a real environment and not just monkeying around in a test lab, it is going to be super critical that you establish redundancy in your domain.

Adding a second domain controller is even easier than spinning up the first one. Simply take the same steps that you did last time, with one exception to the way that the NIC is configured:

1. Spin up a new server.
2. Set a static IP.
3. Configure a good permanent hostname.
4. Deviation from before: Instead of configuring your NIC's DNS server settings to point at the new server itself, point your primary DNS to the existing domain controller's IP address.

Now when you add the AD DS and DNS server roles and walk through the same configuration wizard that we just witnessed a few minutes ago, this time you are going to choose the option **Add a domain controller to an existing domain**. Then all you have to do is select or type the name of the domain and provide administrative credentials on that domain:

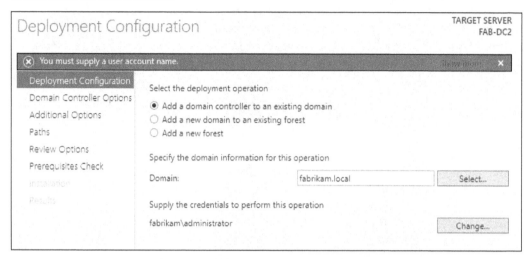

Figure 3.7: Adding a DC to an existing domain

The rest of the wizard is pretty straightforward, but you'll notice that you have a new drop-down menu on the **Domain Controller Options** screen that allows you to select a site name. If you had multiple AD sites, you would select here which site this new DC is being installed into. We will discuss more about Active Directory sites and services in a later section of this chapter. You will also notice that you have to once again create a password for Directory Services Restore Mode. This password is configured per domain controller, so it could potentially be different for each of your DC servers.

If you remember everything we have done so far, you will realize that right now both of our domain controller servers are pointing to FAB-DC1 as their primary DNS server, as defined inside the NIC properties. As long as each DC can contact a DNS server, your domain is going to function properly, but now that we have two DCs created for the purpose of redundancy, your overall solution will be made even better if you ensure that both domain controllers are aware of each other from a DNS perspective.

There are two different ways to go about this, both are considered to be good practice:

- Configure each domain controller to have a primary DNS server address of itself, and the secondary DNS server address to be the other DC. This causes DNS lookups on those servers to happen slightly faster but has the potential drawback that you might have to wait on Active Directory replication to happen between the two servers before newly created DNS records are available on both servers.

- Configure both (or all) of your domain controllers to use a single DNS server as the primary DNS server on your network, with themselves as the secondary DNS server. If all of your DCs are looking to a centralized DNS server, then any updates or additions you make to that DNS server are immediately available on all DCs. However, if that central DNS server goes offline, it will cause all other DCs some grief as they have to realize that they now need to fail over to themselves for name resolution.

Whoops, I said there were two ways to do this, and generally you'll find that either option #1 or option #2 above are the way that DNS is configured in most environments. But, there is a third possibility here that is sort of a mix between the two. You could configure each domain controller's NIC settings so that the primary DNS server is a different DNS server in your environment, and then make the secondary DNS server point back at itself. This causes DNS lookups to always be happening across the network, which generates more traffic than the other options but also ensures that each DC can stand on its own accord if the other one fails. In this third scenario, if there were two DCs in the network, you are basically just pointing them at each other, while using themselves as a backup.

I can't tell you what is best for your own environment, but what I do most of the time is configure each DC to have itself as the primary DNS server, and just realize that whenever I create new DNS records it might take a few minutes for them to replicate between the DCs.

 When you configure a domain controller to point at itself for primary DNS, it is generally recommended to utilize the localhost IP address 127.0.0.1, rather than the DC's actual IPv4 address.

One more important note on the topic of populating DNS server information into the NIC properties of your domain controller servers. NEVER CONFIGURE DCs TO POINT AT PUBLIC DNS SERVERS. Plugging 8.8.8.8 or something similar into a NIC's DNS settings is a common thing to do for internet-connected **home computers**. Not for servers. Do not carry this mentality into your business. Your domain controllers must register special records within Active Directory, and pointing a DC's NIC at a public DNS server will cause that process to fail.

I have actually had to clean up this mess, caused by that exact scenario – a company was having some internet connectivity troubles, and as part of troubleshooting, an IT person decided to replace the actual DNS server information inside the NIC properties of every server in the network with 8.8.8.8. Let's just say that didn't work out very well.

Active Directory Users and Computers

There is not a single tool that is used to manage all facets of Active Directory. Since it is such an expansive technology, our configuration of the directory is spread across a number of different management consoles. Let's take a look at each of them, and a couple of the most common tasks that you will be performing inside these tools. Any of these management consoles can be launched from any of your domain controller servers, and just as we saw in a previous chapter, the easiest way to launch these consoles is right from the **Tools** menu in the upper-right corner of Server Manager.

I'll start with the tool that is alphabetically last in the list of our Active Directory tools, because this is by far the one that the everyday server administrator will use most often. AD Users and Computers is the console from which all of the user accounts and computer accounts are created and managed. Open it up, and you will see the name of your domain listed in the left-hand column. Expand your domain name, and you will see a number of folders listed here. If you are opening this on an existing domain controller in a well-grown network, you may have pages and pages of folders listed here. If this is a new environment, there are only a handful. The most important pieces to point out here are **Computers** and **Users**. As common sense would dictate, these are the default containers in which new computer accounts and user accounts that join the domain will be located.

While this window looks quite a bit like File Explorer with a tree of folders, these *folders* really aren't folders at all. Most of the manila-colored folder icons that you see here are known as **Organizational Units (OUs)**. I say *most of* because there are a few containers that exist out of the box that are legitimate storage containers for holding objects, but they are not official OUs. The ones we pointed out earlier, **Users** and **Computers**, are actually these generic storage containers and are not traditional organizational units. However, any new folders that you create for yourself inside AD are going to be OUs. The difference is depicted in the manila folder icon. You can see in the upcoming screenshots that some of the manila folders have an extra little graphic on top of the folder itself. Only those folders that have the extra little yellow thing are real OUs.

OUs are the structural containers that we use inside Active Directory in order to organize our objects and keep them all in useful places. Just like with folders on a file server, you can create your own hierarchy of organizational units here, in order to sort and manipulate the location inside Active Directory of all your domain-joined network objects and devices. In the following screenshot, you can see that instead of having just a plain **Users** and **Computers** folder, I have created some new OUs including subcategories (more officially known as **nested OUs**) so that as I grow my environment, I will have a more structured and organized directory:

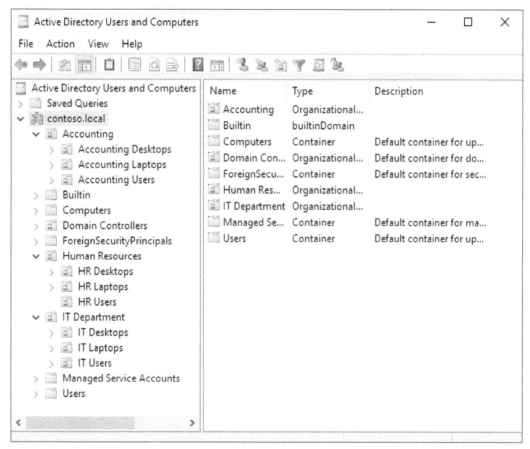

Figure 3.8: Active Directory structure

User accounts

Now that we have some OUs ready to contain our objects, let's create a new user. Say we have a new server administrator coming onboard, and we need to get him an Active Directory login so that he can start his job. Simply find the appropriate OU for his account to reside within, right-click on the OU, and navigate to **New | User**. We are then presented with an information-gathering screen about all the things that AD needs in order to create this new account. Most of the information here is self-explanatory, but if you are new to Active Directory, the one field I will point out is **User logon name**. Whatever information is put in this field is the user's official **username** on the network. Whenever they log in to a computer or server, this is the name they will input as their login.

When finished, our new admin can utilize the new username and password to log in to computers and servers on the network, within the security boundaries we have established on those machines, of course. But that is another topic for another chapter:

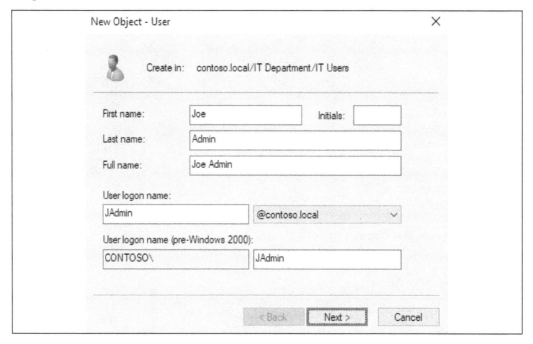

Figure 3.9: Creating a new user

Security groups

Another useful unit of organization inside Active Directory is **security groups**. We can do quite a bit to distinguish between different types and kinds of users and computer accounts using organizational units, but what about when we need a little cross-contamination in this structure? Perhaps we have an employee that handles some HR and some accounting responsibilities. Maybe it is more likely that we have configured file and folder permissions on our file servers so that only people who are part of certain groups have access to read and write into particular folders. Susie from HR needs to have access to the payroll folder, but Jim from HR does not. Both Susie and Jim reside inside the same OU, so at that level, they will have the same permissions and capabilities, but we clearly need a different way to distinguish between them so that only Susie gets access to payroll information. By creating security groups inside Active Directory, we grant ourselves the ability to add and remove specific user accounts, computer accounts, or even other groups so that we can granularly define access to our resources. You create new groups in the same way that you create user accounts, by choosing the OU where you want the new group to reside, and then right-clicking on that OU and navigating to **New | Group**. Once your group has been created, right-click on it and head into **Properties**. You can then click on the **Members** tab; this is where you add in all of the users that you want to be a part of this new group:

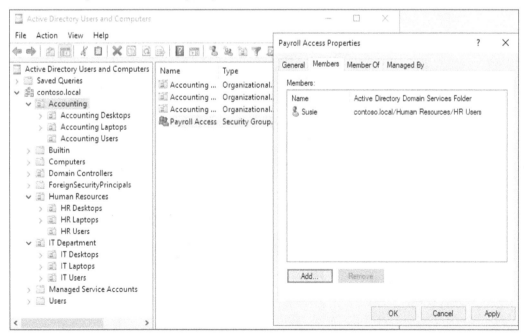

Figure 3.10: Creating a new group

Prestaging computer accounts

It is very common to utilize Active Directory Users and Computers for creating new user accounts because without the manual creation of a user account, that new person is going to be completely unable to log in on your network. It is far less common, however, to think about opening this tool when joining new computers to your domain. This is because most domains are configured so that new computers are allowed to join the domain by actions performed on the computer itself, without any work being done inside Active Directory beforehand. In other words, as long as someone knows a username and password that has administrative rights within the domain, they can sit down at any computer connected to the network and walk through the domain-join process on that local computer. It will successfully join the domain, and Active Directory will create a new computer object for it automatically. These autogenerating computer objects place themselves inside the default **Computers** container, so in many networks, if you click on that Computers folder, you will see a number of different machines listed, and they might even be a mix of both desktop computers and servers that were recently joined to the domain and haven't been moved to an appropriate, more specific OU yet. In my growing lab environment, I recently joined several machines to the domain. I did this without ever opening **Active Directory Users and Computers**, and you can see that my new computer objects are still sitting inside that default **Computers** container:

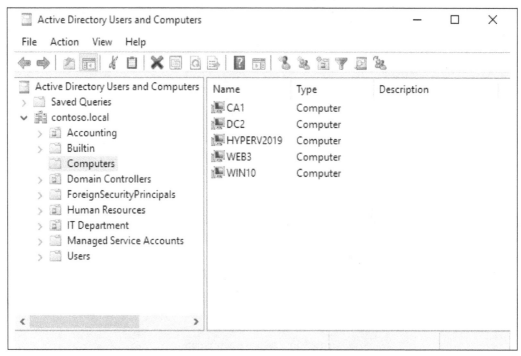

Figure 3.11: Active Directory's default Computers container

Allowing new computer accounts to place themselves inside the default **Computers** container is generally not a big problem for client systems, but if you allow servers to be autogenerated in that folder, it can cause you big issues. Many companies have security policies in place across the network, and these policies are often created in a way that they will be automatically applied to any computer account residing in one of the generalized OUs. Using security policies can be a great way to lock down parts of client machines that the user doesn't need to access or utilize, but if you inadvertently cause these **lockdown** policies to apply to your new servers as soon as they join the domain, you can effectively break the server before you even start configuring it. Trust me, I've done it. And unfortunately, your new server objects that get added to Active Directory will be identified and categorized the same as any client workstation that is added to the domain, so you cannot specify a different default container for servers simply because they are a server and not a regular workstation.

So, what can be done to alleviate this potential problem? The answer is to **prestage** the domain accounts for your new servers. You can even prestage all new computer accounts as a matter of principle, but I typically only see that requirement in large enterprises. Prestaging a computer account is very much like creating a new user account. Prior to joining the computer to the domain, you create the object for it inside Active Directory. By accomplishing the creation of the object before the domain-join process, you get to choose which OU the computer will reside in when it joins the domain. You can then ensure that this is an OU that will or will not receive the security settings and policies that you intend to have in place on this new computer or server. I highly recommend prestaging all computer accounts in Active Directory for any new servers that you bring online. If you make it a practice, even if it's not absolutely required all the time, you will create a good habit that may someday save you from having to rebuild a server that you broke simply by joining it to your domain.

Prestaging a computer object is extremely fast and simple; let's do one together. In the future, I plan to build a Windows Server that hosts the Remote Access role to connect my roaming users into the network from their homes, coffee shops, and so on. Some components in the Remote Access role are finicky when it comes to network security policies, and so I would rather ensure that my new RA1 server will not receive a whole bunch of lockdown settings as soon as I join it to the domain. I have created an OU called **Remote Access Servers**, and I will now prestage a computer object inside that OU for my RA1 server.

Right-click on the **Remote Access Servers OU** and choose **New | Computer**. Then simply populate the **Computer name** field with the name of your server. Even though I have not built this server yet, I plan to name it RA1, so I simply type that into the field:

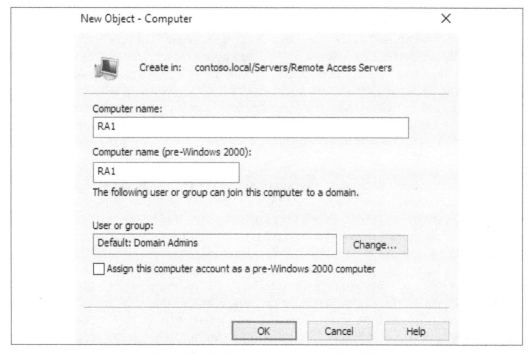

Figure 3.12: Prestaging a computer inside an OU

That's it! With a couple of simple mouse clicks and typing in one server name, I have now prestaged (pre-created) my computer object for the RA1 server. If you look closely at the previous screenshot, you will notice that you could also adjust which users or groups are allowed to join this particular computer to the domain. If you plan to build a new server and want to make sure that you are the only person allowed to join it to the domain, this field is easily updated to accommodate that requirement.

Once I actually get around to building that server, and I go ahead and walk through the steps of joining it to my domain, Active Directory will realize that the name of my new server matches an object already in Active Directory, and will associate my new server with this prestaged RA1 object instead of creating a brand new object inside the generic **Computers** container:

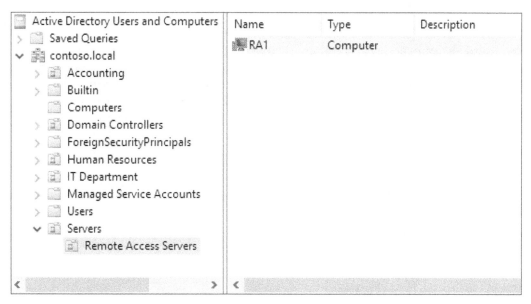

Figure 3.13: RA1's AD object is now prestaged

Active Directory Domains and Trusts

This tool is generally only used in larger environments that have more than one domain within the same network. As we discussed earlier, a company may utilize multiple domain names to segregate resources or services, or for the better organizational structure of their servers and namespaces within the company. You already know the differences between a domain and a forest and how the domain resides within the forest. Another way to think of the forest is as the boundary of your AD structure. If you have multiple domains beneath a single forest, it does not necessarily mean that those domains trust each other. So, users from one domain may or may not have permission to access resources on one of the other domains, based on the level of trust that exists between those domains. When you have a domain and are adding child domains under it, there are trusts placed automatically between those domains, but if you need to merge some domains together in a way other than the default permissions, **Active Directory Domains and Trusts** is the management tool you use to establish and modify those trust relationships.

Growing organizations often find themselves in a position where they need to regularly manage domain trusts as a result of business acquisitions. If Contoso acquires Fabrikam, and both companies have fully functional domain environments, it is often advantageous to work through an extended migration process to bring the Fabrikam employees over to Contoso's Active Directory, rather than suffer all the loss associated with simply turning off Fabrikam's network. So, for a certain period of time, you would want to run both domains simultaneously, and could establish a trust relationship between those domains in order to make that possible.

If you find yourself in a position where a domain migration of any sort is necessary, there is a tool available that you may want to try out. It is called the **Active Directory Migration Tool** (**ADMT**) and can be very useful in situations like the one described earlier. If you are interested in taking a closer look at this tool, you can download it from the following link: `https://www.microsoft.com/en-us/download/details.aspx?id=19188`.

Building a trust

Earlier I mentioned that I already had domain controllers and a whole test lab network built out for `contoso.local`, and in this chapter we built out a new `fabrikam.local` domain. These domains are not associated with each other in any way, they are completely separated forests. As such, a user account in one domain would absolutely not be able to log in to any machine that is joined to the other domain.

Let's change that. We are going to use Active Directory Domains and Trusts to establish a two-way trust relationship between these domains, which will enable exactly that scenario – users from `contoso.local` will be able to log in to computers joined to `fabrikam.local`, and vice versa. It is possible to establish either one-way or two-way trusts. Most commonly in the wild I see two-way trusts because it enables more information to flow between the two domains, and in the case of an acquisition, that is most often what we are looking to accomplish. If there was a need for this trust to only flow in one direction, for example allowing `contoso.local` accounts to log in to `fabrikam.local` machines but not allow Fabrikam employees to sign in to Contoso equipment, that would be possible with a one-way trust.

There are three components to building a successful trust relationship:

- Network connectivity
- Conditional DNS forwarding
- Configuring the trust

Network connectivity

The first one is common sense, those domains need to be able to talk to each other! If you have acquired a company and their servers are in a different physical location, you will likely need to build out some form of site-to-site VPN connectivity between the two physical sites.

In my test lab, I do have Contoso and Fabrikam servers IP addressed into separate subnets, but they are all part of one test lab network, so they already can communicate with each other at a TCP/IP level.

Make sure that you can get packets back and forth between the domain controllers, in both directions, before proceeding with the remaining steps of the trust build.

Conditional DNS forwarding

We haven't done anything in the DNS management console to this point, but it is installed on all of our DCs. Our next chapter is going to cover many more items related to the management of DNS itself, but for now we will need to utilize DNS management and make a change inside each domain. Currently, if I were to log in to a Contoso workstation and `ping fabrikam.local`, or if I signed in to a Fabrikam computer and tried `ping contoso.local` – either of these functions would fail completely, because the two domains have no idea that those DNS namespaces are supposed to resolve to DNS servers in those domains.

To bring name resolution full circle between the two domains, I need to set up conditional forwarding inside each domain.

I log in to DC1, one of my domain controllers for contoso.local, and launch the **DNS Manager** tool from Server Manager's **Tools** menu. Once inside, beneath my server name there is a folder called **Conditional Forwarders**. If I right-click on that folder, I can then select an option to create a **New Conditional Forwarder...**:

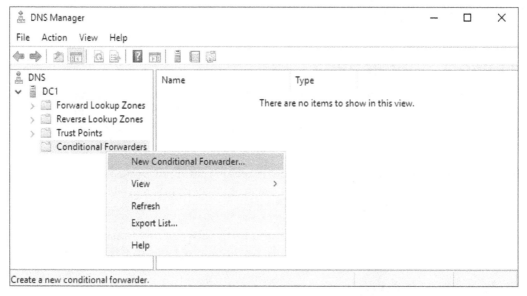

Figure 3.14: Creating a new conditional forwarder

Next, enter the remote domain name that you are trying to contact into the **DNS Domain** field. Then populate the IP addresses of the DNS servers within that other domain. The screen should be able to take your IP address and query the remote server to discover the server FQDN of that server. I also generally select the checkbox to **Store this conditional forwarder in Active Directory**, so that all of my AD-enabled DNS servers can perform this forwarding. Here are the selections I have made within my contoso.local DNS server, which then tells it how to reach out and talk to fabrikam.local:

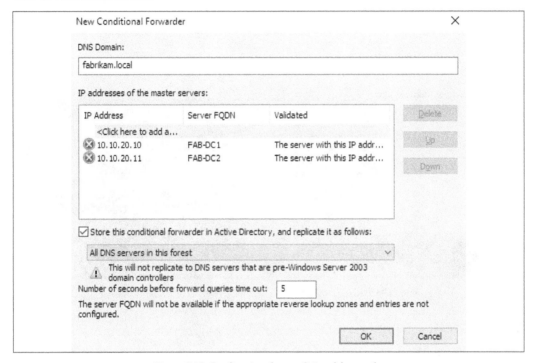

Figure 3.15: Configuring the conditional forwarder

You should now see the new conditional forwarder populate inside DNS Manager, and if you pull up Command Prompt and try to ping the remote domain, fabrikam. local in my case, you can see that name resolution for that remote domain is now successful, where it would have failed prior to our conditional forwarder being created:

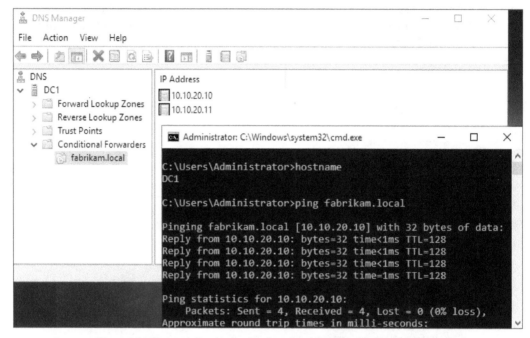

Figure 3.16: Successfully pinging fabrikam.local from a contoso.local server

Do it again!

We have now created a conditional forwarder from contoso.local toward fabrikam. local, but remember that we want to establish a two-way trust, and so we now must configure the same type of forwarder inside the fabrikam.local domain, pointing back at contoso.local's domain controllers. Follow the same steps above to create the second conditional forwarder. Once I complete that step, name resolution is successfully working cross-domain, and I am now ready to configure the trust.

Configuring the trust

VPN or other forms of connectivity between the two domains: Check

Conditional forwarding set up between the two domains: Check

Time to create a trust!

Log in to one of your domain controllers, I am going to use `DC1.contoso.local`, and launch Active Directory Domains and Trusts. Once inside, you should see the name of your domain listed in the left window pane. Right-click on the name of your domain and select **Properties**. Inside **Properties** for your domain, you will see the second tab is called **Trusts**. Go ahead and choose this tab, and at the bottom there is a button to create a **New Trust....** You can see this screen and button in *Figure 3.17*.

There are a few options for naming your trust, but when creating a trust between two forests, as we are today, you want to specify the full DNS name of the remote forest to which you are connecting. In my example, I am creating this trust from inside the `contoso.local` domain, so I am going to specify `fabrikam.local` on this screen, as seen here:

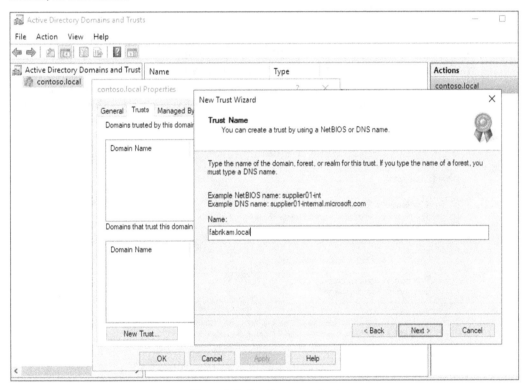

Figure 3.17: Creating a new trust

Now you will encounter a few screens that present various options about how this new trust is to be established. You can create a trust based on domains or forests (**External trust** or **Forest trust**), you can create this as a two-way trust or a one-way trust in either direction, and you can decide to allow authentication to happen forest-wide or to be more selective. There are good descriptions of what each of these options means right inside the wizard interface as you progress, but what I am interested in establishing today is a total two-way transitive trust between `contoso. local` and `fabrikam.local`, so I am selecting the following options:

- **Forest trust.**
- **Two-way.**
- **This domain only.**
- **Forest-wide authentication.**
- **A trust password** – you can specify anything you want as the trust password, the important part is that you remember it because you will have to enter the same trust password again when you move over to your second forest or domain, and walk through these steps again to create the other side of the trust.

Figure 3.18 summarizes the selected settings:

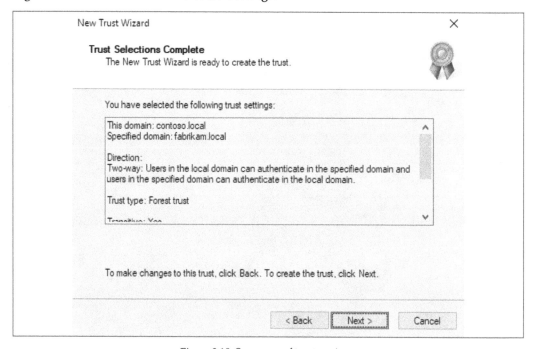

Figure 3.18: Summary of trust settings

The last step of the wizard is whether or not you want to confirm the outgoing trust. Since at this point we have only created one side of the trust, remember we still need to visit `fabrikam.local`'s domain controller and set up the other side of the trust; at this point we do not want to confirm the outgoing trust because the trust setup is not yet complete.

Now that one side of the trust is established in `contoso.local`, log in to a domain controller in `fabrikam.local` and walk through the same setup process. Once complete, you now have a complete, two-way transitive trust configured between your two forests:

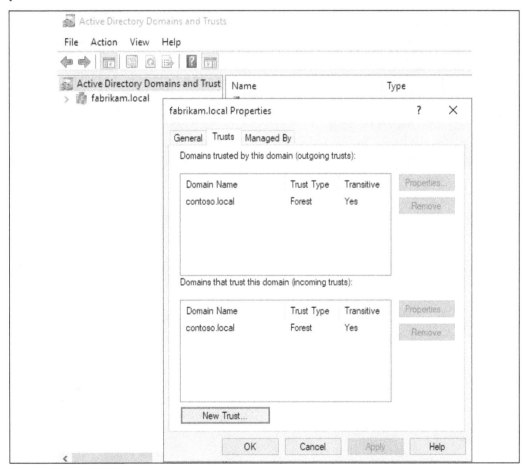

Figure 3.19: Two-way trust completed

Test it out!

We have a trust. Great! Now, what can we do with it? Remember that trusts are all about allowing cross-authentication to happen between domains. You should now be able to hop onto a computer in either domain and log in to it with a user account from the other domain (assuming there is nothing in your network that is restricting logins such as this). Another quick and easy test is to try setting up a file share, which is a very common thing to share back and forth across multiple domains. Set up a folder on any server in one domain and share it as you would with any folder. Now visit the **Security** tab to set some NTFS permissions on this folder. When you click the **Add...** button to include more permissions on this screen, it of course defaults to the domain that this server is joined to. However, if you click on the **Locations...** button you now have the ability, **only because the trust exists**, to specify your remote domain as the location you are searching, and you are then able to add user accounts or groups to your folder share permissions from that remote domain, granting those users access to your shared folder. You can see in *Figure 3.20* that my Share1 folder is now allowing permissions for groups in both the CONTOSO domain and the FABRIKAM domain:

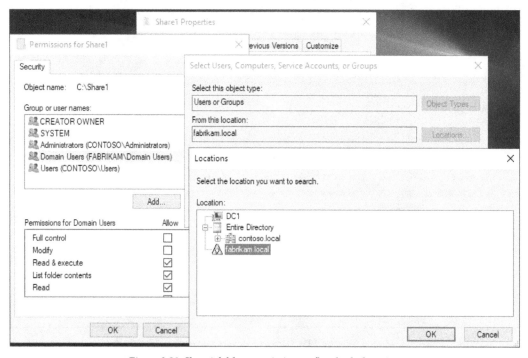

Figure 3.20: Share1 folder permissions reflect both domains

Active Directory Sites and Services

Sites and Services is another tool that is generally only employed by companies with larger Active Directory infrastructures. As is the case with any server, if having one domain controller is good, then having two domain controllers is even better. As your company grows larger, so does your Active Directory infrastructure. Before you know it, you will be looking into setting up servers in a second location, then a third, and so on. In a domain-centric network, having domain controller servers in each significant site is a general practice, and you could soon be looking at dozens of domain controller servers running in your network.

Turning on new domain controllers and joining them to your existing domain so that they start servicing users and computers is pretty easy. The harder part is keeping all of the traffic organized and flowing where you want it to. If you have a primary datacenter where the majority of your servers are located, you probably have multiple DCs onsite in that datacenter. In fact, to make your AD highly available, it is essential that you have at least two domain controllers. But let's pretend you then build a new office that is quite large, where it makes sense to install a local DC server in that office so that the computers in that office aren't reaching over the **Wide Area Network (WAN)** to authenticate all the time. If you were to spin up a server in the new office and turn it into a domain controller for your network, it would immediately start working. The problem is that the client computers aren't always smart enough to know which DC they need to talk to. You may now have computers in the remote office that are still authenticating back to the main datacenter's DCs. Even worse, you probably also have computers in the main office that are now reaching over the WAN to authenticate with the new DC that is in the remote office, even though there are DCs right on the local network with them!

This is the situation where Active Directory Sites and Services become essential. In here, you build out your different physical sites and assign the domain controllers to these sites. Domain-joined users and computers within this network now follow the rules that you have put into place via Sites and Services, so that they are always talking to and authenticating from their local domain controller servers. This saves time, as the connections are faster and more efficient, and it also saves unnecessary bandwidth and data consumption on the WAN, which often saves you dollars.

Here's a look into Active Directory Sites and Services. As you can see, there are multiple sites listed here, and they correspond to network subnet information. This is the way that AD Sites and Services tracks which site is which. When a client computer comes online, it obviously knows what subnet it is part of, based on the IP address it is using. AD Sites and Services then knows, based on that IP address, which site the client now resides in.

That site identification then helps Active Directory to steer authentication requests to the proper domain controllers, and also helps things like Group Policy (which we will talk about shortly) to be able to process site-specific information. There is a good chance you will have to make use of this tool someday if you are part of a growing organization. Adding new objects into AD Sites and Services is about as easy as it gets. Configure all of your sites by simply right-clicking on the **Sites** folder and then choosing **New Site**. You can name your sites anything you like.

Once all sites are placed inside AD Sites and Services, you add your subnets in a similar fashion, by right-clicking on the **Subnets** folder and choosing **New Subnet**. When you create a new subnet, you plug in the identifying network information about that subnet, and the bottom of the screen allows you to select which site the subnet resides within. You can see that process in *Figure 3.21*, as well as a look into my sample AD Sites and Services that is now populated with multiple sites and multiple subnets:

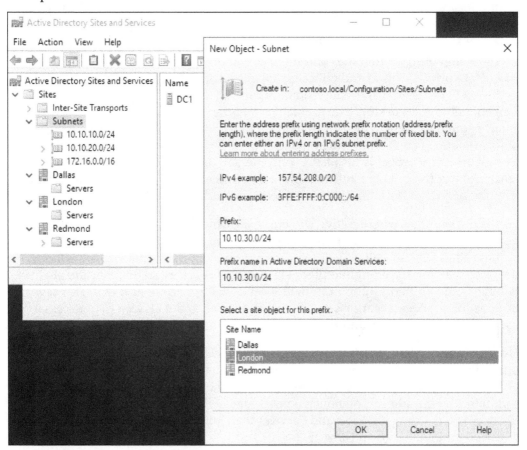

Figure 3.21: Defining subnets in AD Sites and Services

Active Directory Administrative Center

While it is critical to understand and be familiar with the tools we have looked at so far that help us manage Active Directory, you can tell that their aesthetics are a bit dated. The **Active Directory Administrative Center (ADAC)**, on the other hand, has a much more streamlined interface that looks and feels like the newer Server Manager that we are all becoming more and more comfortable with. Many of the functions available within the ADAC accomplish the same things that we can do through the other tools already, but it pulls these functions into a more structured interface that brings some of the most commonly utilized functions up to the surface and makes them easier to run.

One great example is right on the landing page of ADAC. A common helpdesk task in any network is the resetting of passwords for user accounts. Whether the user forgot their password, changed it recently and mistyped it, or you are resetting a password during some other sort of troubleshooting, resetting a password for a user account typically involves numerous mouse clicks inside AD Users and Computers to get the job done. Now, there is a quick link called **RESET PASSWORD**, shown right there on the main page of the Active Directory Administrative Center. Also useful is the **GLOBAL SEARCH** feature right next to it, where you can type anything into the search field, and it will scour your entire directory for results relating to your search. This is another common task in AD that previously required multiple clicks to accomplish:

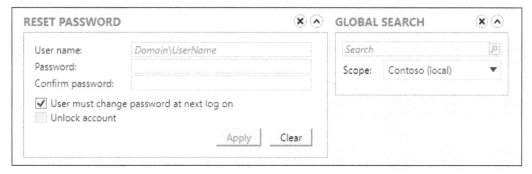

Figure 3.22: Useful tools inside ADAC

If you click on the name of your domain in the left navigational tree, you will dive a little deeper into the capabilities of ADAC. As you can see, the information listed here is being pulled from Active Directory and looks like the same information you would see in AD Users and Computers. That is correct, except instead of having to right-click for every function, such as new user creations or searches, you now have some quick **Tasks** available on the right that can quickly launch you into accomplishing these functions. Also interesting are the links for raising the forest or domain functional level on this screen.

In order to do this using the classic tools, I see that most admins accomplish this by launching AD Domains and Trusts. So, one of the big benefits of the newer ADAC tool is that it is capable of giving you a centralized management window from which you can accomplish tasks that would normally have taken multiple windows and management consoles. Do you sense a common theme throughout Windows Server 2019 with the centralized management of everything?

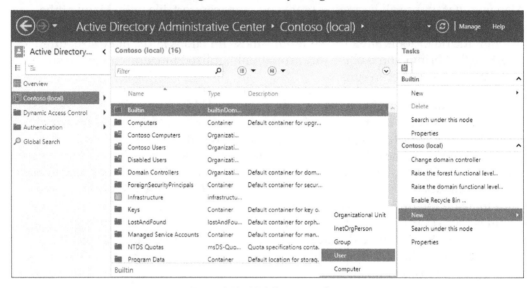

Figure 3.23: ADAC user interface

Dynamic Access Control

In addition to teaching old dogs new tricks, Active Directory Administrative Center also brings some new functionality to the table that is not available anywhere in the classic tools. If you once again take a look at the tree to the left, you will see that the next section in the list is **Dynamic Access Control (DAC)**. This is a technology that is all about the security and governance of your files and the company data that you need to hold onto tightly, making sure it doesn't fall into the wrong hands. DAC gives you the ability to tag files, thereby classifying them for particular groups or uses. Then you can create access control policies that define who has access to these particular tagged files. Another powerful feature of Dynamic Access Control is the reporting functionality. Once DAC is established and running in your environment, you can do reporting and forensics on your files, such as finding a list of the people who have recently accessed a classified document.

DAC can also be used to modify users' permissions based on what kind of device they are currently using. If our user Susie logs in with her company desktop on the network, she should have access to those sensitive HR files. On the other hand, if she brings her personal laptop into the office and connects it to the network, we might not want to allow access to these same files, even when providing her domain user credentials, simply because we do not own the security over that laptop. These kinds of distinctions can be made using the Dynamic Access Control policies.

Fine-Grained Password Policy

Just about anyone who has ever had to use a Windows computer as part of employment at a business is familiar with the requirement to "reset your password every x number of days." In a Microsoft Active Directory environment, there are a few different ways that you can enforce password policies that require a certain password length, set complexity requirements on that password, and defining maximum ages for passwords, which result in users needing to reset their passwords every so often. Many times passwords need to be updated every 30 days or so.

The most common and certainly easiest place to define a password policy is by using Group Policy. We will cover this in more detail as we talk about the Default Domain Policy in *Chapter 5, Group Policy*, but that policy is going to apply one set of password requirements settings to *all* of the users in your domain, bar none. What if your needs are slightly more complex? For example, maybe you require a complex password that needs to be changed every 30 days for all of your office staff, but you manage IT for a manufacturing company that also has some shared computers out on the shop floor. These computers log in with domain accounts so that you can effectively push policies to them and grant permissions at the domain level, but you don't need these shop floor logins to have the same complexity on their passwords, nor do you care about those passwords changing since they are only ever used inside the network.

Enter the **Fine-Grained Password Policy**. Such a policy meets those expanded needs to a "T" by allowing you to configure differing password policies for different groups of people inside Active Directory. We are actually going to build a fine-grained password policy in *Chapter 9, Hardening and Security*, so we'll have to wait on the details until then. The reason I mention it here is that the creation of a fine-grained password policy requires the use of Active Directory Administrative Center, so we will be working within this newer console to create the policy.

Read-only domain controllers

The first domain controller you set up in your network will be a fully writable one, able to accept data from the domain-joined users and computers working within your network. In fact, most DCs in your network will likely be fully functional and writeable. However, it's worth taking a quick minute to point out a limited-scope DC that can be installed called a **Read-Only Domain Controller** (**RODC**). Just like the name implies, an RODC can only have its directory data read from it. Writes that might try to be accomplished to the domain from a user's computer, such as a password change or new user account creation, are impossible with an RODC. Instead, RODCs receive their directory data from other more traditional domain controllers and then utilize that data to verify authentication requests from users and computers. Where would a limited-access domain controller like this be beneficial? Many companies are installing them in smaller branch offices or less secure sites so that the local computers onsite in those smaller offices have quick and easy access to read from and authenticate to the domain without the potential security risk of an unauthorized user gaining access to the physical server and manipulating the entire domain in bad ways. Another valid use-case for an RODC is within a DMZ, a protected network where you would typically never dream of installing a full domain controller because a DMZ network is all about access restriction and keeping internal network information safe.

Configuration of a read-only domain controller is not a totally disparate process, consisting of yet another role or feature, but simply a different option to select when running through the standard installation process of the AD DS role, which we have already worked with a number of times throughout this chapter. In fact, let's set one up right now. I just created a new VM in my environment and have given it an IP address and hostname. After installing the AD DS role as I have done with other domain controllers in my environment already, I am now going to the configuration wizard that helps me promote this server to be a domain controller.

Since I am adding another DC to an existing domain, the first selection is pretty straightforward. It is when we come to the **Domain Controller Options** screen where we make a deviation from the way we have run through this wizard in the past. You see that little checkbox that says **Read only domain controller (RODC)**? Go ahead and check that box:

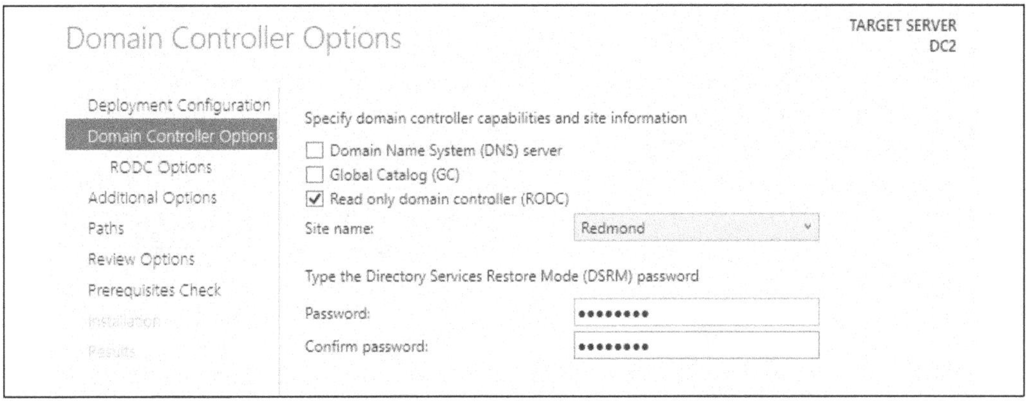

Domain Controller Options

Deployment Configuration
Domain Controller Options
RODC Options
Additional Options
Paths
Review Options
Prerequisites Check
Installation
Results

Specify domain controller capabilities and site information

☐ Domain Name System (DNS) server
☐ Global Catalog (GC)
☑ Read only domain controller (RODC)

Site name: Redmond

Type the Directory Services Restore Mode (DSRM) password

Password: ••••••••

Confirm password: ••••••••

Figure 3.24: Defining a new DC as an RODC

After clicking **Next** on this screen, you are now presented with new options, which
we have never seen before, on a screen entitled **RODC Options**. Most interestingly
here is that fields exist from which we can define which user accounts, or groups
of user accounts, are allowed or denied permission to replicate their passwords to
RODCs. There are objects pre-defined in these fields. Take particular note of two
Active Directory groups called **Allowed RODC Password Replication Group** and
Denied RODC Password Replication Group. Are these brand new groups that
are going to be added into AD when I finish this wizard? No! While there is a good
chance you have never taken notice of these groups before, they already exist inside
Active Directory, but are simply unused if you never roll out an RODC in your
environment:

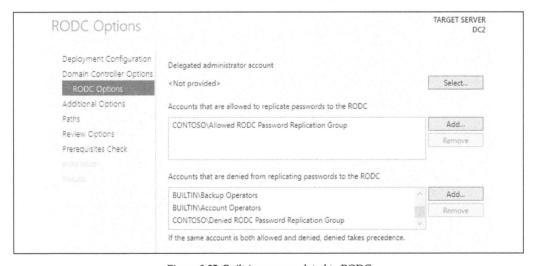

Figure 3.25: Built-in groups related to RODC

The choice is yours on whether to utilize these built-in groups or specify your own groups that are either allowed to replicate passwords to this RODC or denied from being able to do so. RODCs are all about keeping security as tight as possible, so you generally don't want any passwords getting cached on an RODC that won't actually be needed for that local office's authentication. Physical security is yet another advantage of using an RODC instead of a full domain controller. What if someone breaks into your branch office and steals the physical server? If bad guys were to get their hands on a full DC, all usernames and passwords in your domain would be stored on that hard drive. With an RODC, only the accounts that have been allowed to cache are contained on the stolen server.

Each RODC has its own definition of allowances and denials. By default, every RODC that you add into your domain will follow through these same wizard steps, and if you leave all default options in place then all RODCs in your environment will treat those built-in allowed and denied RODC groups as their definitions, meaning that all RODCs in your environment will be caching the same passwords because they all pay attention to the same groups. However, each RODC maintains its own set of users and groups that are allowed or denied caching. This RODC Options screen can be configured differently for every RODC that you establish.

What if you want to make changes to these definitions in the future? Easy enough, you simply need to know where to look for this information to be able to change it. The list of accounts that are allowed or denied caching is generally called the **Password Replication Policy (PRP)** for each RODC. To find an RODC's PRP, simply open up AD Users and Computers and find the object for your read-only domain controller, right-click on that computer object, and visit **Properties**. Inside the properties of your RODC, navigate to the tab called **Password Replication Policy**. Here, you can view and manipulate the password caching policy for each RODC individually:

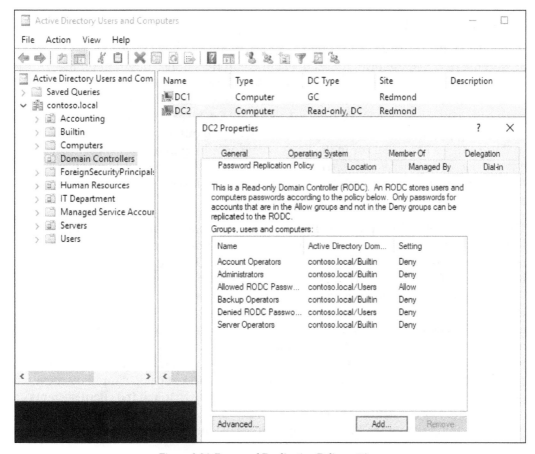

Figure 3.26: Password Replication Policy settings

 Denials always win! In the Microsoft world, a permission denial always takes priority over a permission allowance. The same is true for RODC caching. If a user account is a member of groups that fall inside both the allow RODC caching and deny RODC caching categories, it will be denied caching for that account.

Group Policy

In a network that is based upon Windows Server and Active Directory, it is almost always the case that the primary set of client computers is also based upon the Microsoft Windows operating systems, and that these machines are all domain-joined. Setting everything up this way not only makes sense from an organizational perspective inside Active Directory, but also allows centralized authentication across devices and applications, as we have already talked about. I know that a couple of the examples I gave earlier in the book went something like, *What about when a company has a security policy in place that...* or *Make sure your servers don't get those existing security policies because...* So what are these magical **security policies** anyway, and how do I set one up?

This is the power of Group Policy. It enables you to create **Group Policy Objects (GPOs)** that contain settings and configurations that you want to apply to either computers or users in your Active Directory domain. Once you have created and built out a GPO with a variety of settings, you then have the option to steer that GPO in whatever direction you choose. If you have a policy that you want to apply to all desktop systems, you can point it at the appropriate OU or security group in Active Directory that houses all of your domain-joined desktop computers. Or maybe you created a GPO that only applies to your Windows 7 computers; you can filter it appropriately so that only those systems are receiving the policy. And the real magic is that the issuance of these settings happens automatically, simply by those computers being joined to your domain. You don't have to touch the client systems at all in order to push settings to them via a GPO. You can tweak or lock down almost anything within the Windows operating system by using Group Policy.

Once again, I'm looking in the list of available roles on my Windows Server 2019, and I am just not seeing one called **Group Policy**. Correct again: there isn't one! In fact, if you have been following along with the lab setup in this book, you already have Group Policy fully functional in your network. Everything that Group Policy needs in order to work is part of Active Directory Domain Services. So, if you have a domain controller in your network, then you also have Group Policy on that same server, because all of the information Group Policy uses is stored inside the directory. Since the installation of the AD DS role is all we need to use Group Policy, and we have already done that on our domain controller, we are already prepared to start using Group Policy to send policies and preferences to our computers and users within the domain.

But wait! Group Policy is a large enough topic that it really needs its own chapter, which is exactly what I have decided to do. If you're interested in centralizing administration and policy with this fascinating tool, which you should be, continue reading and we will dive deeper into all things GPO in *Chapter 5, Group Policy*.

Summary

Anyone who has been around Windows Server before knows that Active Directory is nothing new and certainly not something coming to us new in Windows Server 2019. AD has been the authentication underpinning of any Microsoft-centric environment for a very long time and will continue to be far into the future for anyone who hosts an on-premise datacenter. Knowing and understanding AD is entirely critical for the mastery of Windows Server 2019, because without this knowledge your career in server administration won't even make it off the ground.

Some hints were dropped in this chapter about another core infrastructure technology that is often in place alongside Active Directory on all of your domain controller servers, DNS. To effectively manage a Microsoft infrastructure, in my opinion there are three in-the-box server technologies that any admin must be able to work with fluently: Active Directory, DNS, and DHCP. Follow along to *Chapter 4, DNS and DHCP*, as we cover the latter.

Questions

1. Inside Active Directory, a container (folder) that holds computer and user accounts is called a(n)…?

2. What is the term for creating a computer account inside Active Directory prior to that computer being joined to your domain?

3. Which management tool is used to specify that certain physical locations in your network are bound to particular IP subnets?

4. What is the name of a special domain controller that cannot accept new information, only synchronize from an existing domain controller?

5. What tool is needed to create a Fine-Grained Password Policy?

6. What must be configured inside DNS prior to establishing a forest trust?

4
DNS and DHCP

If we consider **Active Directory Domain Services** (**AD DS**) to be the most common and central role in making our Microsoft-centric networks function, then the DNS and DHCP roles slide in at numbers two and three. I am yet to meet an admin who has chosen to deploy a new domain without deploying DNS at the same time, and every network has a need for DHCP whether or not that service is provided by a Windows server. Either of these roles could be served by something other than a traditional server. There are other companies and even appliances that exist to provide DNS within a corporate network, which has some advantages and some disadvantages. Regarding DHCP, there are plenty of options for providing that service outside of the Windows world, as most firewalls and even switches are capable of also being DHCP "servers" in a network. Although the preceding sentences are true, in reality, the majority of internal DNS and DHCP services for companies around the world are provided by Windows servers, and these two roles are very commonly located alongside AD DS on at least some of the **Domain Controller** (**DC**) servers in any given network.

In this chapter, we will cover both DNS and DHCP provided by Windows Server 2019, getting to know their purposes and walking through some common terminology and tasks related to these roles. In this chapter, we will be covering the following:

- The purpose of DNS
- Types of DNS records
- Split-brain DNS
- Types of DNS zones
- IP addressing with DHCP

- Creating a DHCP scope
- DHCP reservations
- DHCP failover
- IPAM

The purpose of DNS

Domain Name System (DNS) is similar to Active Directory in that it is a structured database that is often stored on domain controller servers and distributed automatically around your network to other domain controller/DNS servers. Where an AD database contains information about the domain objects themselves, DNS is responsible for storing and resolving all of the *names* on your network. What do I mean by names? Whenever a user or computer tries to contact any resource by calling for a name, DNS is the platform responsible for turning that name into something else in order to get the traffic to the correct destination. You see, the way that traffic gets from the client to the server is via networking, and typically via the TCP/IP stack, using an IP address to get to its destination. When I open an application on my computer to access some data that resides on a server, I could configure the application so that it communicates directly to my server by using the server's IP address on the network.

If an application on my computer needed to communicate with a server called APP01, and that server was using an IP address of 10.10.10.15 on the network, I could plug 10.10.10.15 into my application configuration, and it would open successfully. If I set up hundreds of different computers this way, all pointing to IP addresses, it would work fine for a while. But the day will come when, for whatever reason, that IP address might need to change. Or perhaps I add a second server to share the load and handle my increased user traffic. What to do now? Re-visit every client computer and update the IP address being used? Certainly not.

This is one of the reasons that DNS is critical to the way that we design and manage our infrastructures. By using DNS, we can employ names instead of IP addresses. With DNS, my application can be configured to talk to APP01 or whatever my server name is, and if I need to change the IP address later, I simply change it inside the DNS console to the updated IP address and immediately all of my client computers will start resolving the APP01 name to the new IP address. Or I can even use a more generic name, such as **intranet**, and have it resolve across multiple different servers. We will discuss that a little bit more shortly.

Any time that a computer makes a call to a server, service, or website, it is using DNS to resolve that name to a more useful piece of information in order to make the network connection happen successfully. The same is true both inside and outside of corporate networks. On my personal laptop right now, if I open Edge and browse to https://www.bing.com/, my internet provider's DNS server is resolving bing.com to an IP address on the internet, which is the address that my laptop communicates with and so that page opens successfully. When we are working inside our own corporate networks, we don't want to rely on or trust a public provider with our internal server name information, and so we build our own DNS servers inside the network. Since DNS records inside a domain network are almost always resolving names to objects that reside inside Active Directory, it makes sense then that DNS and AD DS would be tightly integrated. That rings true in the majority of Microsoft networks, where it is a very common practice to install both the AD DS role, plus the DNS role, on your domain controller servers.

Types of DNS records

Having installed our DNS role on a server in the network, we can start using it to create DNS records, which resolve names to their corresponding IP addresses, or other pieces of information needed in order to route our traffic around the network. Assuming that you are working in a domain network, you may be pleasantly surprised to see that a number of records already exist inside DNS, even though you haven't created any of them. When you are running Active Directory and DNS together, the domain-join process that you take with your computers and servers self-registers a DNS record during that process, which means creating a DNS record for each new server or computer is not something that you need to remember to accomplish.

I have not yet created any DNS records in my new lab environment, not purposefully anyway, and yet when I open the DNS Manager console from inside the **Tools** menu of Server Manager, I can see a handful of records already existing. This is because when I joined each of these machines to the domain, it automatically registered these records for me so that the new servers and clients were immediately resolvable within our domain:

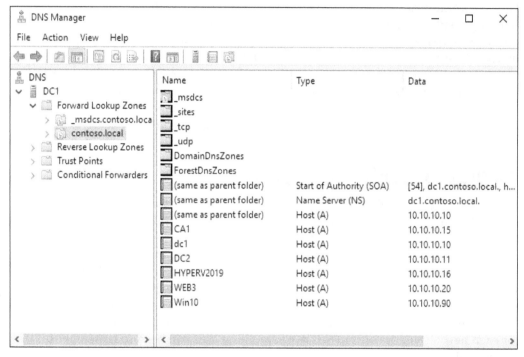

Figure 4.1: DNS Manager

Host record (A or AAAA)

The first kind of DNS record we are looking at is the most common type that you will work with. A **host record** is the one that resolves a particular name to a particular IP address. It's pretty simple, and for most of the devices on your network this will be the only kind of record that exists for them inside DNS. There are two different classes of host records that you should be aware of, even though you will likely only be using one of them for at least a few more years. The two different kinds of host records are called an **A record** and an **AAAA record**, which is pronounced **Quad A**. The difference between the two? A records are for IPv4 addresses and will be used in most companies for years to come. AAAA records serve the exact same purpose of resolving a name to an IP address, but are only for IPv6 addresses, and will only be useful if you use IPv6 in your network.

In *Figure 4.1*, you can see some **Host (A)** records that were self-created when those machines joined our domain. I also have another server running on my network that has not yet been domain joined, and so it has not self-registered into DNS. This server is called RA1, but if I log in to any other system on my network, I fail to contact my RA1 server, since that name is not yet plugged into DNS:

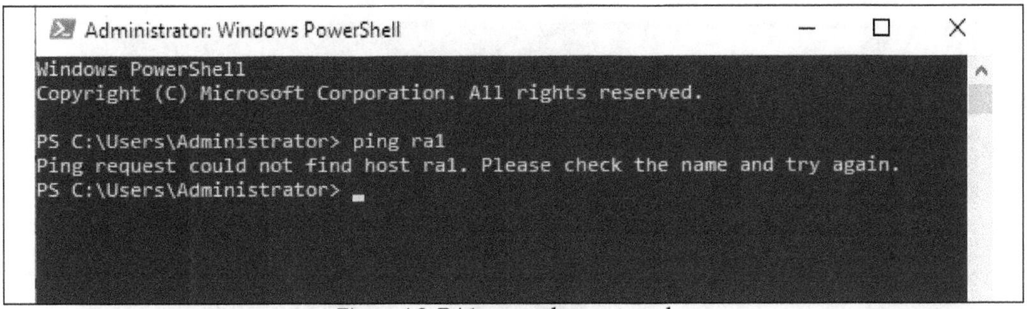

Figure 4.2: RA1 server does not resolve

For now, I am going to choose not to join this server to the domain, so that we can manually create a DNS record for it and make sure that I am able to resolve the name properly after doing that. Back inside DNS Manager on your DNS server, right-click on the name of your domain listed under the **Forward Lookup Zones** folder, and then choose **New Host (A or AAAA)**. Inside the screen to create a new host record, simply enter the name of your server, and the IP address that is configured on its network interface:

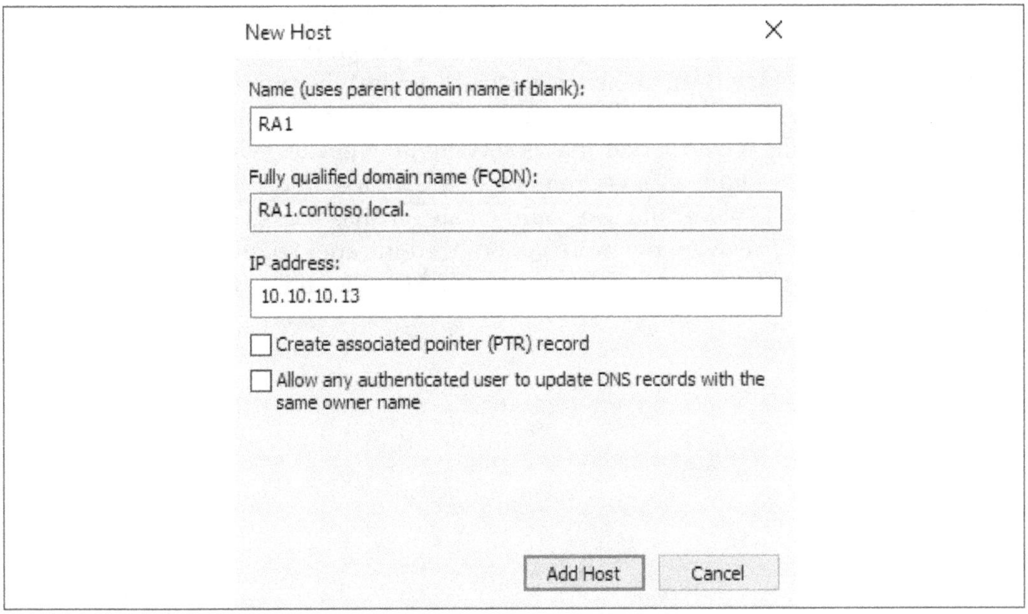

Figure 4.3: Adding a new host record

Now that we have created this new host record, we should immediately be able to start resolving this name inside our domain network. Moving back to the client machine from which I was trying to ping RA1 earlier, I'll try the same command again, and this time it does resolve and reply successfully:

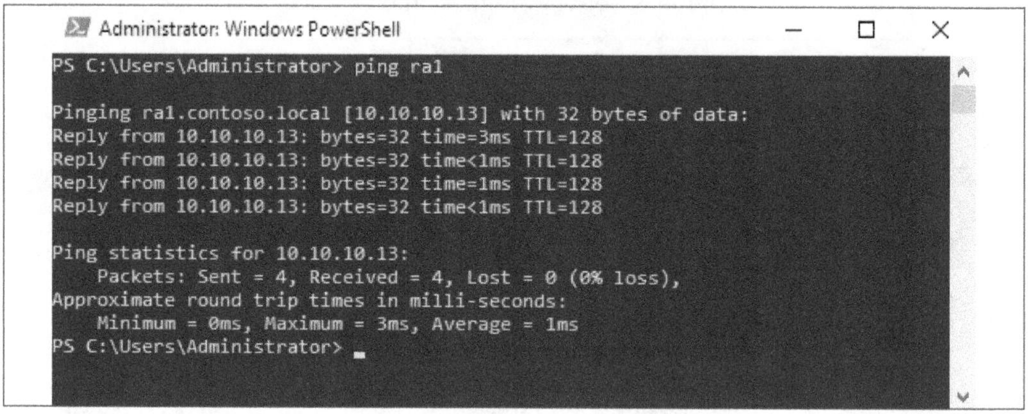

```
Administrator: Windows PowerShell                           —    □    ×
PS C:\Users\Administrator> ping ra1

Pinging ra1.contoso.local [10.10.10.13] with 32 bytes of data:
Reply from 10.10.10.13: bytes=32 time=3ms TTL=128
Reply from 10.10.10.13: bytes=32 time<1ms TTL=128
Reply from 10.10.10.13: bytes=32 time=1ms TTL=128
Reply from 10.10.10.13: bytes=32 time<1ms TTL=128

Ping statistics for 10.10.10.13:
    Packets: Sent = 4, Received = 4, Lost = 0 (0% loss),
Approximate round trip times in milli-seconds:
    Minimum = 0ms, Maximum = 3ms, Average = 1ms
PS C:\Users\Administrator> _
```

Figure 4.4: Successfully pinging RA1

Alias record – CNAME

Another useful type of DNS record is **CNAME**, which more commonly these days is called an **alias record**. This is a record that you can create that takes a name and points it at another name. It sounds a little silly at first glance, because, in the end, you are still going to have to resolve your final name to an IP address by using a host record in order to get the traffic where it needs to go, but the purposes of an alias record can be vast. A good example to portray the usefulness of an alias record is when you are running a web server that is serving up websites within your network. Rather than force all of your users to remember a URL like http://web1.contoso.local in order to access a website, we could create an alias record called **intranet**, and point it at WEB1. This way, the more generalized intranet record can always be utilized by the client computers, which is a much friendlier name for your users to remember.

In addition to creating a happier user experience with this new DNS record, you have, at the same time, created some additional administrative flexibility because you can easily change the server components that are running beneath that record, without having to adjust any settings on the client machines or retrain employees on how to access the page. Need to replace a web server? No problem, just prep the new server alongside the old one and then point the alias record at the new server. Need to add another web server? That's easy too, as we can create multiple alias records, all with the same intranet name, and point them at the different web servers that are in play within the environment. This creates a very simple form of load balancing, as DNS will start to round-robin the traffic among the different web servers, based on that intranet CNAME record.

In fact, rather than continue to talk about this, let's give it a try. I have a website running on exactly that URL in my environment, but currently I can only access it by typing in `http://web1.contoso.local`. Inside DNS, I am going to create an alias record that redirects `intranet` to `WEB1`:

Figure 4.5: Creating a new alias record

Now when I ping intranet, you can see that it resolves to my WEB1 server. And when accessing the web page, I can simply type the word intranet into my address bar inside Internet Explorer in order to launch my page. The website itself is not aware of the name change being made, so I didn't have to make any modifications to the website, only within DNS:

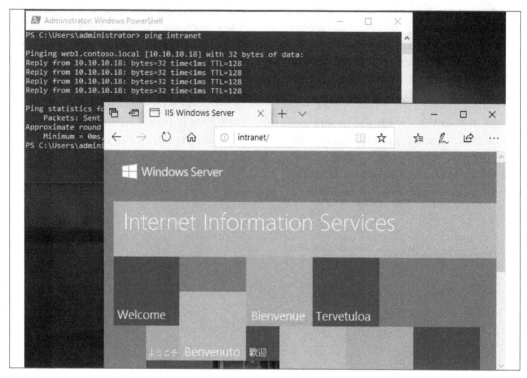

Figure 4.6: Loading WEB1 using the new alias

Mail Exchanger (MX) record

A third type of DNS record is called a **Mail Exchanger** (**MX**) record. In your everyday duties, you will not have to encounter or configure MX records nearly as often as A or CNAME records, but they are important to understand nonetheless. An MX record is all about email services and delivery. Whatever domain name follows the @ in your email address, the DNS servers that are handling that domain name must contain an MX record telling the domain where to point for its mail services. MX records are most commonly used within public DNS, for name resolutions happening over the internet. For companies hosting their own email on local Exchange servers, your public DNS servers will contain an MX record that points at your Exchange environment. For companies hosting their email in a cloud service like Office 365, your public DNS records would need to contain an MX record that directs email traffic toward the cloud provider that is hosting your mailboxes.

Whenever an email is sent outbound, the internet needs to determine how to deliver that email. Public internet DNS is checked for whichever domain the email is destined for, and the MX record contained within that DNS configuration defines where the email is sent. If you don't have an MX record, or if it disappears for some reason, you will receive zero emails to your domain.

TXT record

TXT is simply short for **text** record. TXT records are used within DNS for various purposes, and they can contain just about any kind of information. Sometimes TXT records are placed for actual human reading of some type of info, but more likely you will be asked to create a TXT record at some point as a form of validation.

For example, most websites are protected by SSL certificates, and the process of purchasing an SSL certificate is pretty straightforward. However, you certainly wouldn't want any yahoo with a laptop and internet access to be able to purchase a certificate that can protect a website name that ends in a domain name that your business owns, right? So **certification authorities (CAs)** (the places where you purchase SSL certificates) will require some sort of validation process before allowing you to purchase a certificate for your domain name. Sometimes that validation process is simply sending an email to an address associated with that domain name, or sometimes you will be asked to create a TXT record with a very exact set of characters in your public DNS records. The implication and validation, of course, is that if you really do own that domain name, you will have access to create DNS records within that domain. When the CA sees your newly created TXT record that contains the data they asked you to input, they know you really do own that domain. An attacker trying to spoof your website and acquire an SSL certificate maliciously would not have such access into your domain's DNS settings.

SPF Record

There are a few special kinds of TXT records, a common one being **Sender Policy Framework (SPF)** records. This record pertains to the delivery of emails, but while an MX record identifies which servers email should flow *toward*, an SPF record identifies which locations email is coming *from*. SPF records are part of spam and spoofing calculations, used to identify the locations on the internet from which email from your domain is expected to be flowing. Let's take a look at a couple of example SPF records, which will help you to understand how they are formatted, and also assist in describing why they are necessary:

```
v=spf1 [IP address 1] [IP address 2] [include:<domain>] -<enforcement
rule>
```

The preceding is standard formatting for an SPF TXT record. For simple email systems where all email flows from one public IP address on the internet, or from one hosted email system, your record will be nice and short. A great example is email coming from Office 365. Everyone who hosts email in Office 365 should have an SPF record with the following information inside:

```
v=spf1 include:spf.protection.outlook.com -all
```

SPF record information is used by receiving email servers to validate the mail coming inbound. That mail server will receive the email, discover which domain it came from, and reach back out over the internet to that domain's DNS servers to check for the existence of an SPF record. If it doesn't find such a record, your email has a much higher chance of being flagged as spam. If it does find an SPF record, the mail server then checks the entries in that record, which identifies the safe places that we expect mail to be flowing from, and confirms that the email did, in fact, originate from one of those places. In our preceding Office 365 SPF record, we included the domain spf.protection.outlook.com. All email that flows from Office 365 servers will match this origination, so this simple record is the only thing needed to be in place for safe delivery of email from your Office 365 tenant.

Now pretend that your SPF record is already in place and working with your hosted email, but that you set up an on-premise SMTP relay server so that your copiers on the network have the ability to scan to email. This is a common request by businesses, and something that I find in the wild on a very regular basis. The nature of your SMTP server doesn't really matter; there are various ways to accomplish that. What you'll usually find, though, is that when you send email from your copier, that email may start getting flagged as spam. Sometimes it lands in the recipient's junk mail folder, sometimes it is captured and not delivered to them at all. Why is this? If you have an onsite SMTP relay where the email is coming from, remember the copier just hands email over to the SMTP relay, and that relay is the guy who is shuttling the email over the internet. That relayed email is not coming from spf.protection. outlook.com, but rather email sent from your on-premise server is coming from your ISP outbound public IP address. Your SPF record needs to be adjusted to include this additional safe sender, so that recipients of your email will know that emails coming from your building are legit. Let's build out an SPF record that includes a single IP address:

```
v=spf1 ip4:8.8.8.8 include:spf.protection.outlook.com -all
```

That's it! By simply updating your SPF record to include the public IP address that the copier scans are coming from, your recipient email servers will better trust that incoming mail.

 I'm obviously using **8.8.8.8** as an example in the preceding text; don't plug this into your own SPF records! You will want to identify your actual outbound IP address and use that information instead.

It is also easy to add multiple IP addresses, for example, if your business owns multiple buildings, each with their own ISP connections, and want email traffic to be able to flow from devices (such as copiers) in each location:

```
v=spf1 ip4:8.8.8.8 ip4:4.4.2.2 include:spf.protection.outlook.com -all
```

Enforcement rule -all

What is that `-all` at the end of an SPF record, anyway? I'm glad you asked! The declaration at the end of an SPF is telling the receiving mail server how strictly it should enforce these SPF rules. There are three different ways that you could configure that enforcement rule:

```
-all
```

This is generally the way you always want to set up SPF records. `-all` means "hard fail." It sets the SPF rules as firm, so recipient mail servers will follow these rules.

```
~all
```

Use this alternative if you are unsure that you have all IP addresses listed in your SPF record, for a soft fail scenario. I would only use this as a temporary measure, and honestly I don't know that I have ever encountered an SPF record in a production environment that is configured as such.

```
?all
```

The last option here is neutral. Use it only for testing SPF records, as it will not help mail delivery until you later change it over to `-all`.

Name Server (NS) record

Here is another type of DNS record that you don't have to deal with on a day-to-day basis, but you should still know what it's there for. An NS record is an identifier within a DNS zone that tells it which **name servers** (which are your DNS servers) to use as the authorities for that zone. If you look at the NS records listed in your internal DNS right now, you will recognize that it is calling out the names of your DNS servers on the network. When you add a new DC/DNS server to your domain, a new NS record for this server will be automatically added into your DNS zone:

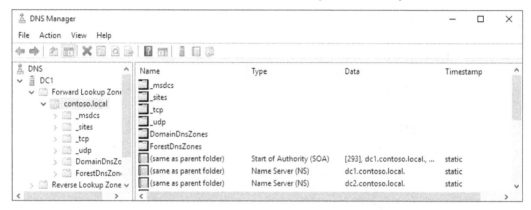

Figure 4.7: Viewing Name Server records in your zone

Public name server records

NS records are critical to understanding when working with public/internet DNS records. I can't tell you how many times I have assisted admins who were trying to create new DNS records for their zone and struggling because it seemed like no matter what they plugged into the DNS settings, their new records would never show up and work on the internet. After a quick look, we discover that their Name Server record for the domain was pointing at a different server or service altogether, which they didn't even realize was part of the DNS equation. Here's an example scenario that helps explain:

You inherit an already established infrastructure as you take over server administration for a company. The previous admin has all passwords documented; things are looking good so far. The director of marketing for the company has their own company credit card, and comes to you on day two to let you know that rather than navigate the proper IT purchasing channels, they just signed up for xyz marketing service that is going to help send out blasts of emails. This marketing company requires things called CNAME records to be created in your public DNS so that your email and their systems can work together. Now it's up to you to put those CNAME records into place.

No big deal, right? You reference the passwords document and find a record labeled "DNS" that has login credentials for GoDaddy. Sounds like the jackpot, and makes sense as GoDaddy is a pretty common platform on the internet for managing DNS zones. You log in to GoDaddy, edit the DNS zone for your domain, and add your new CNAME records. The CNAME records aren't resolving yet, but you know that DNS propagation takes a while to roll around the internet, so you inform Mr. Marketing that his new service should be up and running within 24 hours. You're a hero!

Except…24 hours roll around, and it's still not working. Mr. M is starting to push back, and you're realizing that that quarterly bonus may not be so sure a bet. Unfortunately, you have forgotten one critical piece of the puzzle. Even though you have a GoDaddy account, *and* it is labeled "DNS," *and* you were able to create new DNS records within that account, it is entirely possible that the registrar for your domain is actually pointing Name Server records at a different DNS service entirely! A useful tool in this scenario is the DNS Lookup tool from `MXToolbox.com`. A quick search for that on the internet will find you the current link, you simply type in your domain name to the DNS Lookup tool, and it will spit back at you which name servers are in place, and which service it is that is actually hosting your DNS records on the internet.

Following the previous procedure, you discover that the Name Server records for your domain are actually pointing to Network Solutions, not GoDaddy at all! As it turns out, your IT predecessor wasn't entirely sure how to do a domain transfer, and they got it part-way there but never finished out the process, so while you have GoDaddy available and your domain is even listed inside the GoDaddy console, when any computer on the internet tries to look up DNS info for your domain, the Name Server records are telling that computer to head toward Network Solutions for the domain's DNS servers, not GoDaddy at all. You now have two choices. You can either log in to Network Solutions and add your CNAME records there, and they will work because Network Solutions is currently the service that is doing DNS resolution for your domain, or you can finish out that migration and update your Name Server records so that they point at GoDaddy's DNS servers, instead of Network Solutions.

In summary, this is the flow that happens with a DNS lookup:

Client/server makes a call for DNS >> Name Server records identify which DNS servers are authoritative for the domain you are calling for >> DNS lookups are steered at those name servers >> DNS resolution happens.

ipconfig /flushdns

Just one final note to finish out this section. I have been saying things like *Now when I do this...* or *Immediately following this change...* and if you are creating some of your own records, you may have noticed that it sometimes takes a while for your client computers to recognize these new DNS records. That is normal behavior, and the time that it takes before your change rolls around to the whole network will depend entirely on how large your network is and how Active Directory replication is configured. When you create a new DNS record on one domain controller, your new record needs to replicate itself around to all of the other DCs in your network. This process alone can take upward of a couple of hours if AD is not configured for faster replication. Typically, it only takes a few minutes. And then, once the new record exists on all of your DC servers, your clients may still take a little bit of time to utilize the new record, because client computers in a domain network hold onto a cache of DNS data. This way, they don't have to reach out to the DNS server for every single name resolution request. They can more quickly refer to their local cache in order to see what the information was from the last time they checked in with the DNS server. If you are trying to immediately test out a new DNS record that you just created and it's not working, you may want to try to run the `ipconfig / flushdns` command on your client computer. This forces the client to dump its locally cached copies of DNS resolver records and go grab new information that is current from the DNS server. After flushing your cache, the new record will more than likely start resolving properly.

Split-brain DNS

In all of our lab configurations, screenshots, and examples you will notice that domains we create on the internal network always end with `.local`. This is purposeful and is best practice. Public DNS zones, as you well know, can end in a myriad of ways. Websites or services that live on the internet may end with `.com`, `.org`, `.edu`, `.biz`, `.info`, `.tech`, `.construction` — the list goes on and on. These are known as top-level domains, and the creative use of such DNS suffixes should remain on the internet and away from our internal DNS zones.

Now, many of you may already work in corporate environments where your internal DNS is configured as something other than a `.local`, and so you already realize that internal domains can certainly be configured as one of these other suffixes. For example, `Microsoft.com` is obviously one of the public domains that Microsoft owns, and they could very well also have used `Microsoft.com` as an internal DNS zone too. In fact, it could even be their primary domain name inside Active Directory, and this wouldn't *necessarily* cause any problems, but it certainly increases the *potential* for problems, if you don't know what you are doing.

Whenever a company configures their internal DNS to match their external DNS, this is commonly referred to as **split-brain DNS**. Years ago, there were articles published on the internet by Microsoft warning administrators against doing this, as it caused confusion and problems with some Microsoft roles and technologies that those companies would try to deploy in their environments. As time went on, many people either didn't know or simply ignored this recommendation, and so the world is now awash with networks where split-brain DNS exists. Many of these environments are so populated and complex that they will never be changed at this point, and so Microsoft and the world had no choice but to adapt. Thankfully in today's world, most roles or services that you deploy are written in a way that they accommodate for possible split-brain DNS out of the box, but some still require special considerations.

One example is Microsoft DirectAccess, which we will cover in *Chapter 8, Remote Access*. When deploying DirectAccess, there is a critical piece of client-side technology called the Name Resolution Policy Table that must be populated based on your internal DNS architecture. For companies using a .local domain internally, this configuration is a piece of cake and no special considerations are needed. For anyone with split-brain DNS, this sometimes turns into a convoluted mess and for anyone not well-versed in the intricacies of DirectAccess, simply having split-brain DNS in your environment could very well mean that you are never actually able to get DirectAccess to work in your environment.

At first glance, you would think that administration would be made easier if internal DNS zones matched public DNS zones, but this simply isn't true. The opposite, in fact, is what you will find. Whenever you publish any external service, you will then have to make special considerations with your internal DNS to make that service work as intended from inside the network, because internal DNS zones will typically trump external. Split-brain DNS ends up being more work on a daily basis.

As the saying goes, you can lead a horse to water but can't make him drink. You have now been informed that utilizing the same DNS zone inside your network as what you use on the internet is bound to cause you some headaches. What you decide to do with this information on future builds, well that's up to you...

Types of DNS zones

You are now familiar with creating different types of DNS records, but that information is only going to enable you to create new records inside of an existing DNS zone. At present in our test lab, we have only one DNS zone available to us, contoso.local, which was created automatically when we built the contoso.local domain. As of right now, computers who are using one of my contoso.local domain controllers as their DNS server are only able to look up DNS records that I have plugged into my DNS zone.

With DNS Server provided by Windows Server 2019, you can certainly build out many different DNS zones, to increase name resolution capabilities in your network. There are plenty of different reasons why you might want to create additional DNS zones, and you should understand what types of zones are available to implement. Let's take a minute and discuss the different types of zones available to us.

Active Directory Integrated Zones

This is not a zone "type," per se, but rather an option that can be selected when you create some types of DNS zones. When creating that new zone, you will see a checkbox that states **Store the zone in Active Directory**. When selected, this means that the new zone you are creating is going to be stored inside Active Directory, rather than being stand-alone on the DNS server from which you are creating the zone. Being stored inside AD means that this new zone is capable of being replicated automatically to all domain controller servers in your domain, which means that your DNS zone is highly available and more quickly accessible across your entire network. In general, if the type of zone you are creating allows storage inside Active Directory, do it.

After opening up the DNS Manager tool on your domain controller, you'll notice that any current DNS zones are listed beneath folders entitled **Forward Lookup Zones** and **Reverse Lookup Zones**. What's the difference?

Forward Lookup Zones

Zones configured inside Forward Lookup Zones are your traditional DNS zones. Their purpose is to take an incoming DNS request, such as from a client computer, and turn that DNS name request into an IP address that is handed back to the client computer. Forward Lookup Zones are almost always where DNS administrators will be working from.

Reverse Lookup Zones

If "reverse" is the opposite of "forward," then the same must be true within a DNS context. Reverse Lookup Zones are responsible for mapping IP addresses backward into names. You may not even realize that these happen in your environment, but you can easily test it out anytime. You likely all know how to use the ping command, which is relying on DNS to turn a name into an IP address. That, of course, is being handled by a Forward Lookup Zone, like we see here:

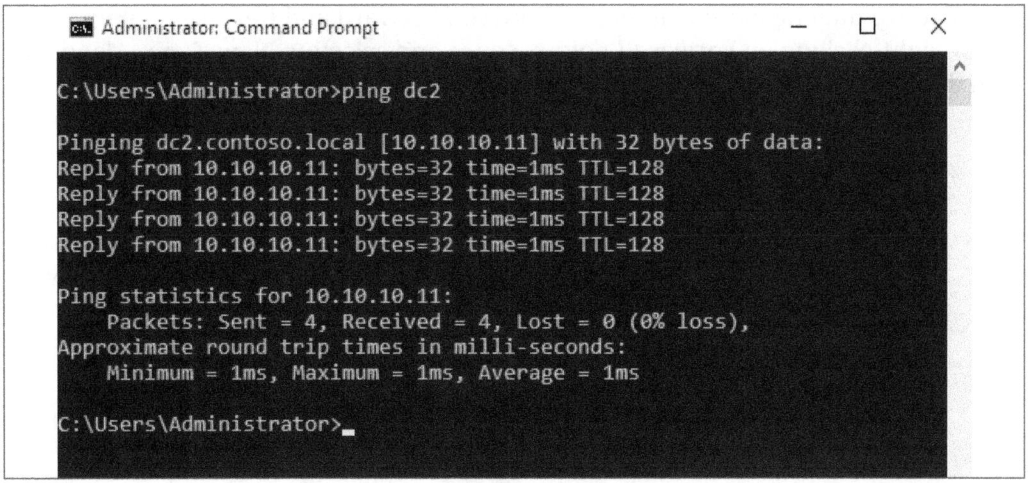

Figure 4.8: Resolving a name to IP

Did you know you can also use the `ping` command to perform the opposite? What if you want to query DNS to find out what hostname the `10.10.10.11` IP address maps back to?

```
ping -a 10.10.10.11
```

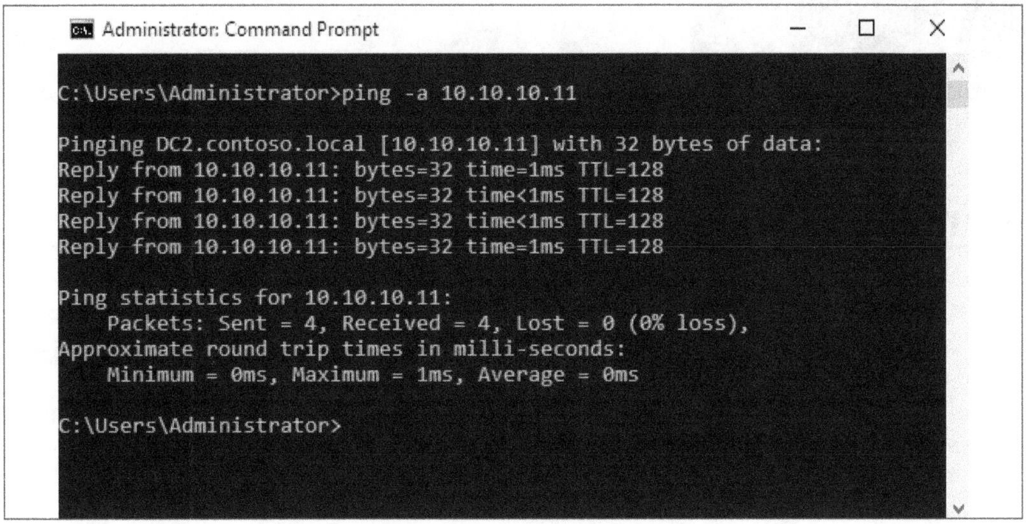

Figure 4.9: Querying DNS to find a hostname from an IP

This reverse lookup, converting IP addresses back to names, has shown us that the IP address `10.10.10.11` has a reverse pointer record mapping back to our `DC2` server. This type of lookup is handled by a Reverse Lookup Zone inside DNS.

Now that we understand the difference between Forward and Reverse Lookup Zones, right-clicking on **Forward Lookup Zones** and selecting **New Zone...** lands us with three choices on which type of zone we would like to create:

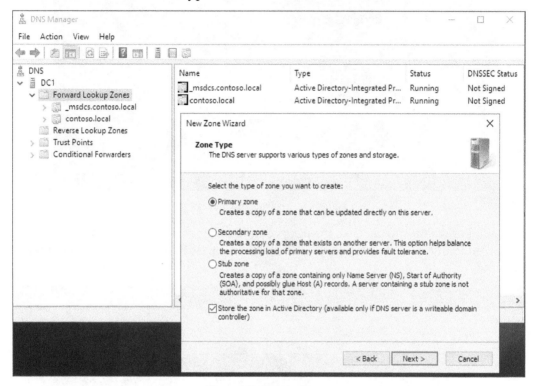

Figure 4.10: Creating zones

Primary Zone

The majority of DNS zones within internal networks are primary zones. This indicates that it is the "parent," so to speak, the master copy of any particular DNS zone is going to be the primary zone for that domain. When changes and updates are made to DNS records, it always happens within the primary zone. We will create a new primary zone together in just a few minutes. You can choose for primary zones to be stored in Active Directory, or not.

Secondary Zone

Based on their names, it would seem secondary zones might be less important than primary zones, and that is generally true. A secondary zone is simply a read-only copy of a primary zone. Because it is read-only, no updates can be made within a secondary zone, it is always syncing from the primary zone. Secondary zones can be used to spread the DNS computing power among multiple servers, taking the load off of the primary zones, but it is important to know that secondary zones are not Active Directory-integrated. When you try selecting the option to create a new secondary zone, you will notice that the AD checkbox grays out.

Inside most networks I have worked with that are based on Microsoft infrastructure, your primary zones all get set up to be Active Directory-integrated, which means they are syncing around to all of your domain controller-based DNS servers anyway. In this case, secondary zones are less likely to be needed. If you deviate from that mentality and create DNS servers that are not also domain controllers (which you can absolutely do) — then you may want to take care that you understand the use cases of secondary zones because it is more likely in this scenario that you would utilize them.

Stub Zone

The third selection on your new zone screen is Stub Zone. Like secondary zones, stub zones are copies of primary zones but only contain certain pieces of information. Namely, stub zones contain resource records that help clients to identify and more quickly get to the full DNS servers for whatever zone they are calling. Stub zones can be AD-integrated if required.

Stub zones are enabling your DNS servers to know how to direct traffic to resolve records inside another domain. Sounds just like a conditional forwarder that we learned about in the previous chapter, right? Similar, yes, but as you know we pointed our conditional forwarder at a specific IP address, telling DNS that requests for the remote domain should always point at a particular server or servers. Stub zones contain NS records for the remote domain, so even if that remote domain makes some internal adjustments and its DNS servers change or are updated, stub zones can more accurately deal with those scenarios.

AD-integrated DNS zones replicate among domain controllers using domain replication, but non-AD-integrated DNS zones have to sync using their own process, known as **zone transfers**. Stub zones can be used to help make the zone transfer process more efficient and create faster name resolution for client computers.

Creating a new zone

We will finish out this section with a quick walk-through on creating a new DNS zone. The process is straightforward, but there are a few options to consider along the way. In most cases when creating new DNS zones, you will be doing so in order to enable internal client computers to resolve names for a new internal namespace (another `.local`, for example), so that you can utilize that internal naming scheme for accessing servers and resources inside the network.

For our example, let's create a new primary zone just like we would for any internal namespace, but we are going to configure the DNS zone with a name that conflicts with a well-known internet namespace. This walk-through will not only portray the options available as we configure a DNS zone, but also give a glimpse into what kind of challenges can present in a split-brain DNS scenario. It also portrays the fact that when clients are inside the network, their internal DNS servers have priority over internet DNS servers.

Inside DNS Manager, right-click on **Forward Lookup Zones** and select **New Zone...**. Now select the options to create a new **Primary Zone**, and I am going to choose to store mine in Active Directory. Refer to *Figure 4.10* if you need a reference point on these options.

We now encounter a screen titled **Active Directory Zone Replication Scope**. This screen and options only present themselves when the **Store inside AD** option is checked, otherwise the wizard would have bypassed this screen. Here you have options for how extensively you would like this new DNS zone to replicate among your domain controllers. You can replicate to all DCs inside the domain, or even the whole forest.

Next, name the zone. The name that you provide the zone here is the namespace for which the zone is going to contain records. The possibilities here are endless, I could even type in `Jordan.local` as my DNS zone, or `Jordan.com`. This is actually a legitimate website that wraps over to `Nike.com`, which I suppose is fair because Michael Jordan is a little bit more popular than I am.

Now, I typed `Jordan.com` just to be silly, but it will actually portray exactly what I was going to show you, so let's stick with it. This is possibly the silliest thing I've ever done inside DNS Manager.

To prove out what is happening here, first from a client computer in my network I have pulled up a web browser and verified that I can successfully get to Jordan. com. If I ping that name, you can see that it resolves to a public IP address, which is expected. This is the public, internet-routable IP address of the web server upon which Jordan.com is hosted:

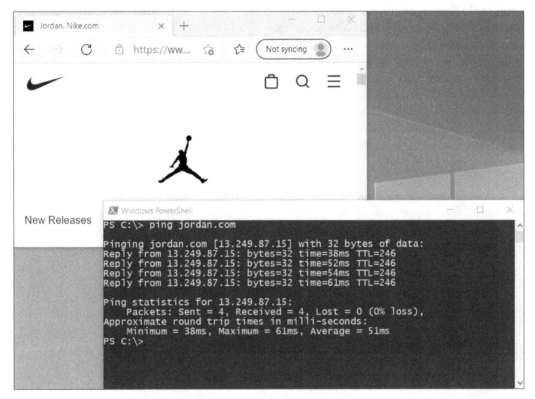

Figure 4.11: Resolving a public DNS zone

This is completely normal behavior, right? Type in a website URL, which is a DNS name; DNS resolves it to the IP address that hosts the website, and your browser takes you there. Next, finish out the creation of our new Jordan.com internal DNS zone, on our internal DNS server.

Walking through the zone creation wizard, I have typed in a zone name of Jordan.com, and the next screen that I have to answer is regarding **Dynamic Update**. Server administrators always have the ability to manually create DNS records inside DNS zones, but if you have hundreds of client computers in your environment, do you really want the creation of DNS records to be a full-time job? Thankfully there is no need to do this, as client computers that are joined to your domain will automatically attempt to register their own hostname and IP address into DNS servers whenever they connect to the network. This process is known as dynamic update, and the settings on this screen show you options regarding these updates. You can allow or disallow dynamic updates for each zone and set some requirements around how secure that updating process needs to be. In most domain environments, configuring the top option is what you will do, only allowing secure updates in your zone. If you have legacy equipment or non-Microsoft products abundant in your network, you may need to select the second option to allow both secure and nonsecure updates:

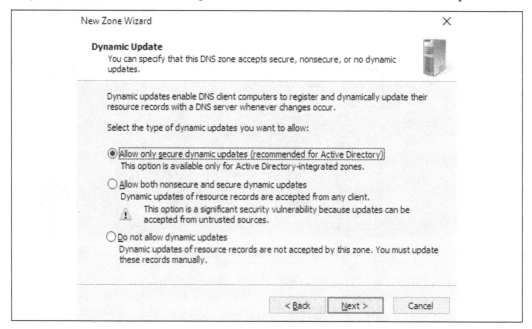

Figure 4.12: Security for DNS updates

That's it! The final screen of the wizard is simply a settings review, and after clicking **Finish**, your new DNS zone is immediately available and working to resolve names in the new Jordan.com namespace, for any client computers who are using this server as their DNS server. As you can see in *Figure 4.13*, the Jordan.com zone is now listed in DNS Manager, and I went ahead and created a couple of A records so that any requests for Jordan.com or www.Jordan.com return an IP address of 10.10.10.23. (See what I did there? Number 23?):

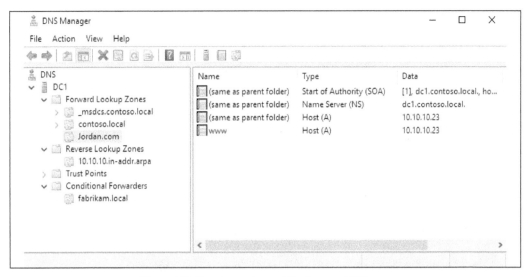

Figure 4.13: Creating an internal Jordan.com DNS zone

Now that our new zone is created inside the network, what has that changed? Let's move back to that client computer in my test network, and try both browsing and pinging Jordan.com again:

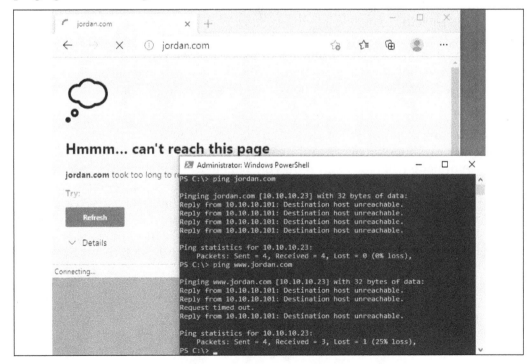

Figure 4.14: Pinging Jordan.com again

Prior to creating this new zone, my client request for Jordan.com was simply forwarded to public internet DNS servers, because my internal DNS servers did not have any of their own definitions for what to do with Jordan.com lookups. After creating an internal DNS zone for Jordan.com, we have now interrupted access to the website, because our own DNS server now has its own ruleset for what to do with these name requests! If I were to build out my own website on a web server and give that server an IP address of 10.10.10.23, my client computer would have successfully loaded my custom website when typing Jordan.com into their browser.

This example had two purposes. First, to walk through the creation of a new DNS zone to review the options available, and to show how easy it is. Second, to make sure you understand that your internal corporate DNS servers have priority over public internet DNS servers. This means you need to take care when creating DNS zones, and when deciding whether or not you want to pursue split-brain DNS by hosting your public namespace inside your network as well, because your internal DNS servers are going to be the primary resolvers for those zones.

IP addressing with DHCP

IP addresses on your network are sort of like home addresses on your street. When you want to send a package to someone, you write their address on the front of the package and set it in the mailbox. In the same way, when your computer wants to send data to a server or another device on a network, each of those devices has an IP address that is used for the delivery of those packets. We know that DNS is responsible for telling the machines which name resolves to which IP address, but how do those IP addresses get put into place on the servers and computers in the first place?

Static addressing is simply the process of configuring IP addresses on your system manually, using your own hands as the configuration tool to plug all of your IP address information into the NIC settings on that device. While this is a quick and easy way to get network traffic flowing between a few endpoints, by giving them each an IP address, it is not scalable. We do often statically address our servers as a way of making sure that those IP addresses are not subject to change, but what about on the client and device side? Even in a small company with 10 employees, each person may have a desktop and a laptop, there are likely going to be printers on the network also needing IP addresses, and you may have a wireless network where employees or even guests can connect phones and other devices in order to gain internet access. Are you going to assign IP addresses by hand to all of these devices? Certainly not.

Our answer to this problem is the **Dynamic Host Configuration Protocol (DHCP)**. This is a protocol that is designed to solve our exact problem by providing the ability for machines and devices to be plugged into your network and automatically obtain IP addressing information. Almost any user on any device in the entire world uses DHCP every day without even realizing it. When you connect your laptop or smartphone to a Wi-Fi router to gain internet access, a DHCP server has given you the ability to route traffic on that Wi-Fi network by assigning you IP addressing information. Often, in the case of public Wi-Fi, your DHCP server is actually running on the router itself, but in our businesses where Windows Server rules the datacenter, our DHCP services are most often hosted on one or more servers across the network.

Creating a DHCP scope

So far in the new Windows Server 2019 lab environment I have been building, I have been statically assigning IP addresses to all of the servers that are being built. This is starting to get old and is hard to keep track of. When the first domain controller was configured, I installed the DHCP role onto it but haven't told it to start doing anything yet. What does a DHCP server need to start handing out IP addresses? It needs to know what IP addresses, subnet mask, default gateway, and DNS server addresses are within your network so that it can package that up and start handing the information out to the computers who request it. This package of information inside the DHCP server is called a **DHCP scope**. Once we define our scope, the DHCP server will start handing out IP addresses from that scope to our new servers and computers that do not already have static addresses defined.

Once again, we need to launch a management tool on our Windows Server 2019, and once again, the easiest way to launch that is by using the **Tools** menu inside Server Manager. Go ahead and launch the **DHCP** console. Inside, you will see the name of your server where the DHCP server is running. Expand that, and you have options for both **IPv4** and **IPv6**. Yes, this means that you can use this DHCP server to hand out both IPv4 addresses as well as IPv6 addresses for those of you who are testing out IPv6, or have plans to in the future. For now, we are sticking with good old IPv4, and so I can right-click on **IPv4** and choose to create a **New Scope**. This launches a **New Scope Wizard** that walks you through the few pieces of information that the DHCP server needs in order to create a scope that is ready to start handing out IP addresses inside your network. I am setting my new scope to hand out IP addresses from `10.10.10.100` through `10.10.10.150`:

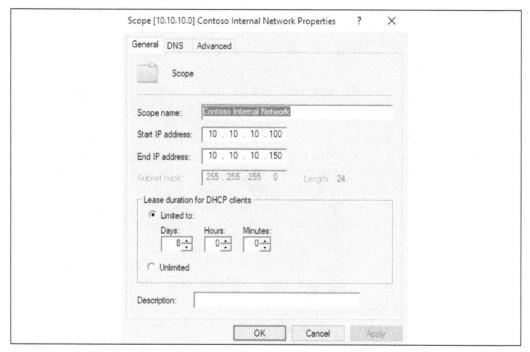

Figure 4.15: Setting up a new DHCP scope

As soon as you finish creating your scope, it is immediately active and any computer in your network whose NIC is configured to grab an address automatically from a DHCP server will start doing so against this new DHCP server.

Now that our new scope has been created, you can expand the scope inside the DHCP console and see some additional information about this scope. By clicking on the **Address Leases** folder, you can see all of the DHCP addresses that have been handed out by this DHCP server.

As you can see in *Figure 4.16*, I have a Windows 10 client computer on the network, which does not have a static address, and so it has grabbed a DHCP address from my DHCP server. It has been given the first IP address that I defined in my scope, `10.10.10.100`. The next machine that reaches in to grab an IP address from this DHCP server will receive `10.10.10.101`, and so on from there:

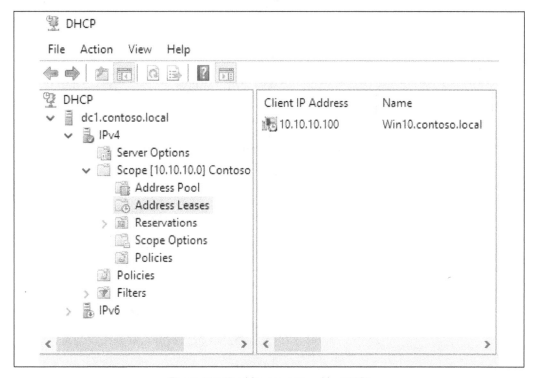

Figure 4.16: IP addresses assigned by DHCP

Scope Options

DHCP scopes can be configured to hand out a very small set of information, like we have configured so far, or when needed DHCP is capable of handing out a lot more. When a client reaches into DHCP to grab information, we are currently handing out an IP address and a subnet mask, because these two pieces of information are critical to making traffic flow on our networks. Most networks, however, are going to require at least a couple of additional pieces of information to be given to DHCP clients, for those devices to really be usable in a traditional corporate network.

Listed under the new scope we just created, you will see a folder titled **Scope Options**. Right-click on **Scope Options**, and then select **Configure Options…**.

Here you will find many, many different checkboxes, all of which are available DHCP scope options. By selecting a checkbox and populating the necessary information for that particular scope option, you are then configuring this DHCP scope to give not only simple IP address and subnet mask information to all clients reaching in, but this additional information as well. Two very common ones are **003 Router** and **006 DNS Servers**. The **003 Router** designation is essentially your default gateway setting on the client NIC. Almost all networks will have a default gateway, typically a firewall or a router, and by selecting this option you can define the default gateway address to be assigned to your DHCP clients.

In *Figure 4.17*, you can see that I have selected **006 DNS Servers**, and configured the IP addresses of the DNS servers in my lab. Now when my client computers pull IP addresses via DHCP, their NICs will also be automatically configured with these two DNS server addresses, which will cause them to be able to resolve DNS names in my environment:

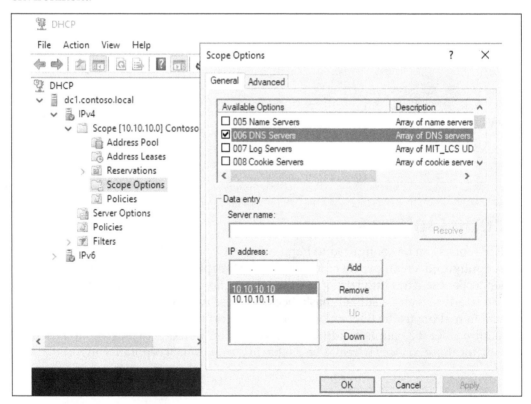

Figure 4.17: Using DHCP options

Another useful DHCP scope option is option **66**. If you have a VoIP phone system and want to set up some automatic provisioning of your physical phones, it is easy to create a DHCP scope just for the phones, and use option **66** to point at your phone system's provisioning link. When phones grab an IP address from the DHCP server, they will be automatically provisioned in the phone system as well!

DHCP reservations

Assigning IP addresses from a big pool of available ones is great, but these address leases are subject to expiry and change. This means that a computer that has `10.10.10.100` today might receive `10.10.10.125` tomorrow. Typically, this is fine from a desktop computer perspective, as they don't generally care what IP address they have. Client computers are usually reaching outward on the network, but other devices are rarely trying to find and contact them. What if you have a more permanent fixture in your network, like a Windows server, but you don't want to have to deal with statically addressing this server? Another great example of such a device is a printer that is connected to your network. Some printers don't even have an interface from which you could assign a static IP address, and once your printer gets a DHCP address you typically want that address to remain the same throughout the printer's life, because you'll be configuring computers to send their print jobs to that IP address. This is where **DHCP reservations** come into play. A reservation is the act of taking a single IP address within your DHCP scope, and reserving it to a particular device. This device will receive the same IP address every time it connects through the DHCP server, and this particular IP address will not be handed out to any other device on your network. By using reservations inside DHCP, you can allow the DHCP server to handle the assigning of IP addresses even to your permanent servers, so that you do not have to manually configure the NICs of those servers, yet still maintain permanent IP addresses on those machines.

You can see the folder called **Reservations** in the DHCP console. Currently, there is nothing listed here, but by right-clicking on **Reservations** and choosing **New Reservation...,** we will create one for ourselves. Let's work once again with that WEB1 server. Right now, I have a static IP address assigned to WEB1, but I will instead create a reservation for it on the IP address 10.10.10.150:

New Reservation   ?   X

Provide information for a reserved client.

Reservation name:	WEB1
IP address:	10 . 10 . 10 . 150
MAC address:	00-15-5D-08-58-08
Description:	WEB1 server

Supported types
- (• Both
- (DHCP
- (BOOTP

Add   Close

Figure 4.18: Setting up a reservation

Whoa, whoa, whoa ... back the train up. Most of the information on this screen makes sense — a quick description of the server name and the IP address itself — but how did I come up with that MAC address? A **MAC address** is a network card's physical address on the network. When your networking equipment tries to send information to a certain IP address, or, in this case, when the DHCP server needs to hand a certain IP address to a particular NIC on a server, it needs a physical identifier for that network card. So, this MAC address is something that is unique to the NIC on my WEB1 server. Every network card on your network has a unique MAC address. By logging in to my WEB1 server, I can run ipconfig /all and see the MAC address listed for my NIC right in that output, that goofy-looking combination of letters and numbers shown as **Physical Address**. That is where I got this information. This is how DHCP decides when to invoke reservations. If a network interface asks it for a DHCP address, and that device's MAC address is listed here in the reservations, then the DHCP server will hand the reserved address back to the device, rather than one from the general pool:

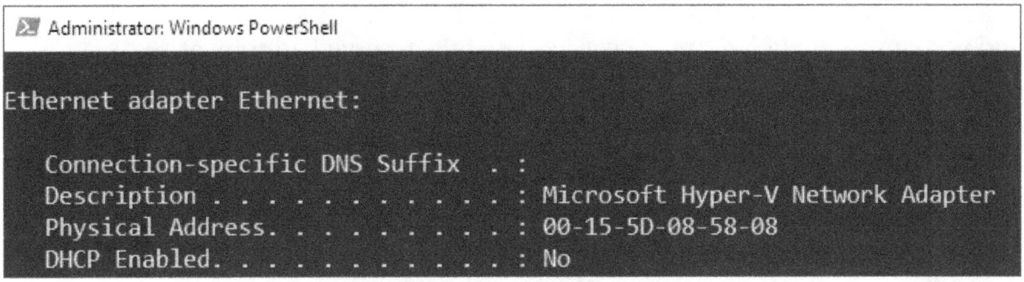

```
Administrator: Windows PowerShell

Ethernet adapter Ethernet:

   Connection-specific DNS Suffix  . :
   Description . . . . . . . . . . . : Microsoft Hyper-V Network Adapter
   Physical Address. . . . . . . . . : 00-15-5D-08-58-08
   DHCP Enabled. . . . . . . . . . . : No
```

Figure 4.19: Finding the MAC address

Now that our DHCP reservation has been created, I will head into the NIC settings on my WEB1 server, and get rid of all the static IP addressing information by choosing the option to **Obtain an IP address automatically**:

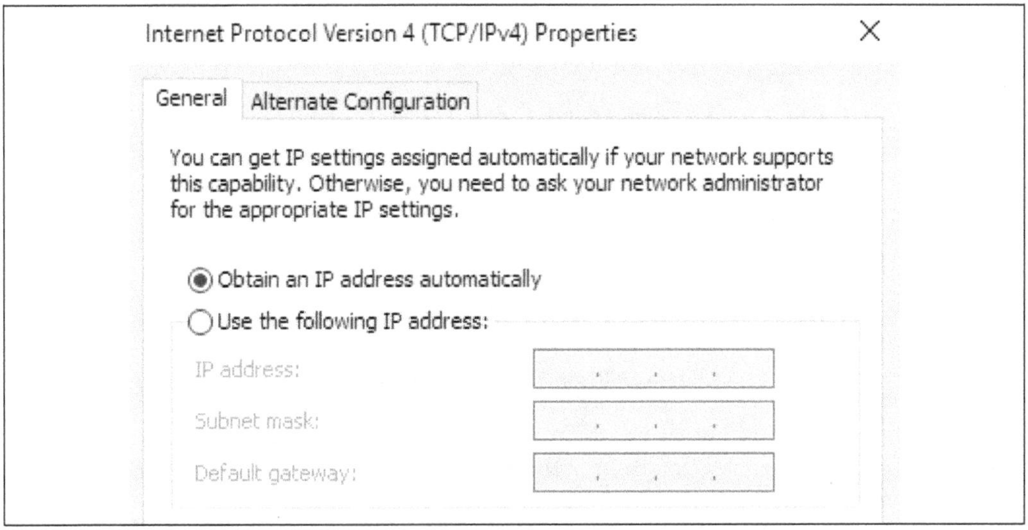

Figure 4.20: Removing the static IP address information

After doing that, WEB1 will reach over to the DHCP server and ask for an address, and you can see that I have now been assigned the reserved address of 10.10.10.150:

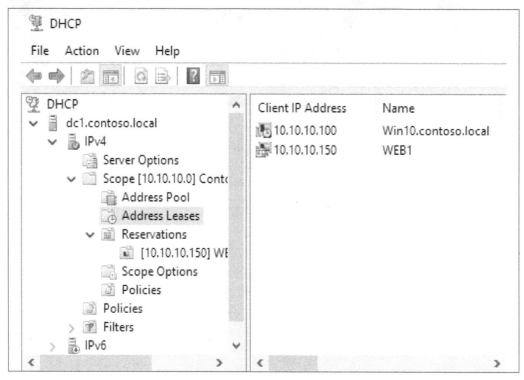

Figure 4.21: Reserving 10.10.10.150 for WEB1

This will always be the IP address of the WEB1 server from this point forward, unless I change my DHCP reservation or somehow change the MAC address of WEB1. This could possibly happen if I were to install a new NIC into WEB1.

You can also create DHCP reservations for objects other than Windows devices in your network. Since all you need is the MAC address of the device (and every device with a network adapter has a MAC address), it is easy to create reservations for devices such as print servers, copy machines, security alarm systems, wireless access points, and more.

DHCP failover

Never too much of a good thing? Just like the creation of multiple domain controller servers creates good redundancy for Active Directory, the DHCP servers in your network can be tied together into a failover pair to create their own form of high availability. While it is true that the DHCP server role often happens to co-exist alongside the AD DS and DNS roles, this is not a requirement. You already know that it is easy to store DNS zones right inside Active Directory so there is automatic replication of zone information, but this mentality is **not** true of DHCP scopes.

DHCP is a useful tool inside domain environments, or outside of domain environments. As such, it is not as tightly integrated a role as DNS. So when we create DHCP failover, we need to take a more manual approach, and whether or not the DHCP role happens to be hosted on top of a domain controller makes no difference.

Two DHCP servers

In a DHCP server failover environment, two DHCP servers can be configured and pointed at each other, and they will then replicate DHCP lease information between themselves, always keeping this information up to date. That way, if one DHCP server goes offline, the other can pick up the slack and continue issuing IPs and renewing the leases of those IPs.

I said "two" DHCP servers above, and this is an important point of clarification. With Windows Server DHCP failover, you can only connect two DHCP servers together. No more. It is also important to note, as we progress into the world of IPv6, that DHCP failover is only intended for use with IPv4 scopes. The failover of DHCP servers wouldn't be necessary in the IPv6 world anyhow, as most IPv6 implementations are stateless, and the only information that DHCP needs to give to IPv6 clients are the options, which could simply be configured on multiple DHCP servers, and the clients care not from which server they pull that option information.

Hot standby mode

There are two different modes of operation that can be employed by DHCP failover: hot standby mode or load sharing mode. Hot standby, as the name indicates, is more of a primary/failover mentality. One DHCP server is primary and is always responsible for an IPv4 scope, unless it becomes unavailable. In that case, the failover DHCP server starts taking over until the primary can be restored.

Hot standby mode is useful for branch offices that are connected back to the primary network via a WAN of some sort. The local branch offices could have their own local DHCP server that handles DHCP primarily, but if that DHCP server were to go offline, DHCP requests would reach over the WAN link and grab a lease from the standby DHCP server sitting in your main site. In this kind of deployment, you could easily configure one single DHCP server in the main site to be the hot standby for multiple branch offices, as it is easy to configure multiple scopes on a DHCP server.

Load sharing mode

Alternatively, indeed much more common, is load sharing mode. This is the default mode of operation for DHCP failover. In load sharing mode, two DHCP servers are configured with the same scope of information and then both service incoming clients. In doing so, they share the load between servers, both responding and also replicating information between themselves, so both are always aware of which IP addresses have been handed out to clients.

In load sharing mode, you want both DHCP servers to be located in the same physical site. They need to have very fast communication between them to keep replication data straight. I have seen DHCP failover configured across sites before, and can tell you definitively that it can cause IP conflicts and similar issues. Keep them in the same site.

Configuring DHCP failover

Now we know about DHCP failover, how do we set it up? You already know that I have DC1 and DC2 in my test lab environment. Both of these servers are already domain controllers and DC1 is also a DNS server, though those facts have no bearing on DHCP configuration. These could be domain controllers, or simply domain-joined servers, or even non-domain-joined servers, and DHCP would have all of the same options for failover. Since I already have these two servers available to me, I am going to use them to create a DHCP scope that is replicated between both. This is an important point to clarify, that DHCP failover is configured on a per-scope basis. You don't necessarily tie DC1 and DC2 together, but rather inside the DHCP scope properties you establish failover between DC1 and DC2 for a particular scope (or scopes). This implies, then, that you have the ability to create DHCP scopes that are running in failover mode, and additionally create DHCP scopes on those same servers that are not doing any form of failover.

Make sure the clocks are in sync! If your DHCP servers are domain-joined, their clocks should always be kept in sync automatically by Active Directory. If your DHCP servers are not domain-joined, you will want to ensure that the system clocks on both servers are using the same time source to always retain continuity.

DC1 already has the DHCP role installed, and I already created a quick scope on it way back when I first set up this test lab, so that my Win10 client computer could grab a DHCP address and communicate with the rest of my network. DC2, however, does not yet have the DHCP role installed, so the first step is to go ahead and add that role.

Whenever creating new DHCP servers in a network, the role must be installed of course, but there is a second critical piece of the puzzle to enable them to be recognized as DHCP servers. It is fairly obvious, but after installing the DHCP role onto a server, Server Manager will prompt you to **Complete DHCP configuration**. This pulls up a small wizard with basically just one step to accomplish — **Authorize** your new DHCP server. This mini-wizard can be called via Server Manager, or if you missed the prompt there and opened up right into the DHCP management tool, you can alternatively authorize a DHCP server by right-clicking on the server name inside the DHCP management tool, and then selecting **Authorize**.

OK, we now have two authorized DHCP servers in our environment, and a scope is already present on DC1. This scope is servicing clients already, handing out IP addresses in our network. Creating failover for this scope is quite easy. Open up DHCP management on DC1, and navigate to find your IPv4 scope. Right-click on the scope itself, and select **Configure Failover...**:

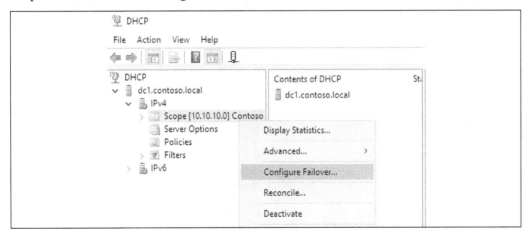

Figure 4.22: Configuring DHCP failover

Next, select which scopes you want to configure into failover. As I mentioned before, DHCP failover configuration is individual per DHCP scope. If your DHCP server has multiple scopes already established, you can select to configure failover on all or only some of them. Then on the second screen, we need to define the failover DHCP server. You can type out the name of the server on this screen, but what I like to do is click that **Add Server** button, which then displays any servers in your environment that are recognized as authorized DHCP servers. By using the button and then selecting the second DHCP server from the list, it gives you one more validation that you have properly authorized the second server, DC2 in my case, in your network. You can see this in *Figure 4.23*:

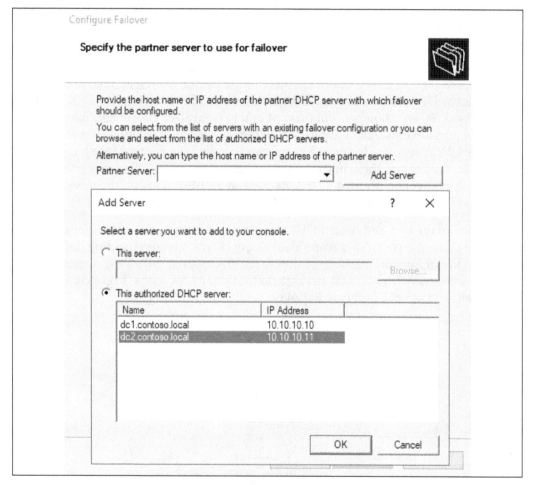

Figure 4.23: Selecting DC2 for DHCP failover

On the following screen of this wizard, we define all of the relationship parameters between the two DHCP servers. As you can see in our next screenshot, this is the screen where you define simple things that don't have too much impact such as **Relationship Name** and creating a **Shared Secret** that the two DHCP servers will use to interact with each other, but this screen is also where you create the definition of which type of failover is happening for this scope. We already talked about **Load balance** mode and **Hot standby** mode, and here is where you would additionally define, in **Load balance** mode, what weights to assign the two servers for establishing that load balancing.

Unless you have a particular reason to deviate, the default settings are generally what you want. Make sure that **Maximum Client Lead Time** remains configured at one hour or more. You may bump that number down smaller for testing failover in your network, but in a production environment one hour is the general recommendation:

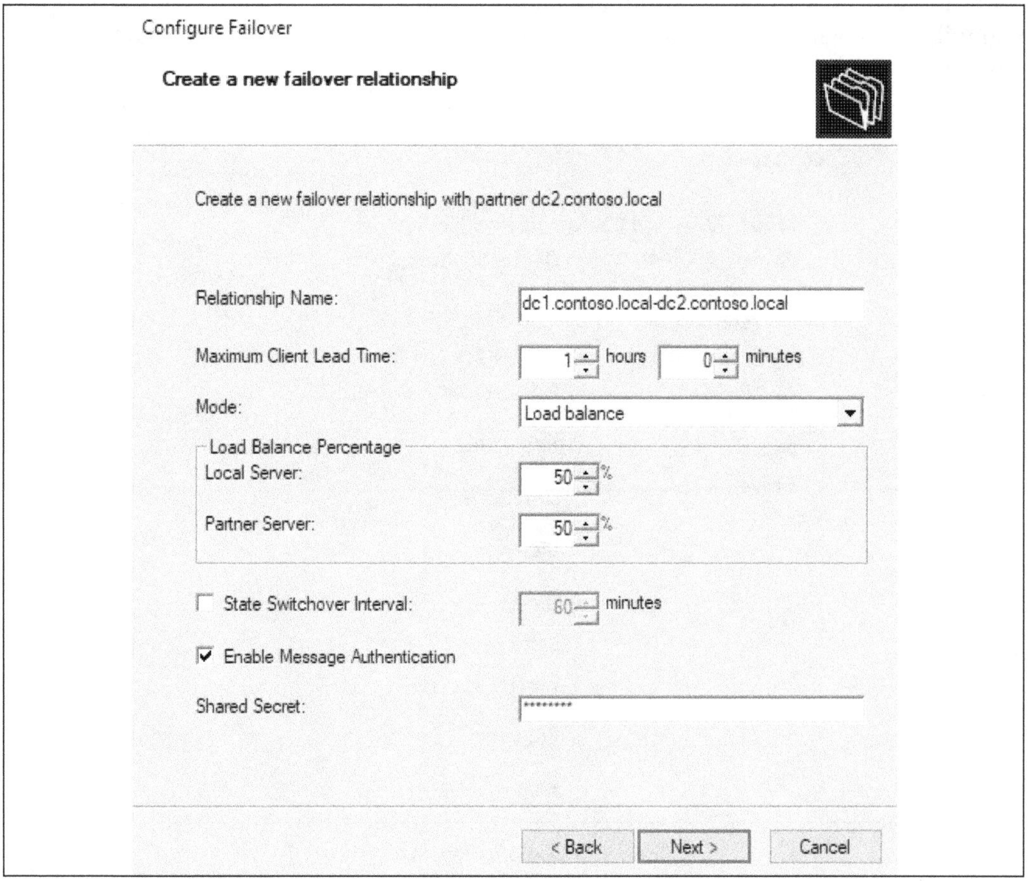

Figure 4.24: Configuring Maximum Client Lead Time to one hour or more

That's it! Click **Next** a couple more times, and your DHCP failover configuration will be pushed out to the second DHCP server. Now, if one of these servers were to go offline or have some kind of issue, DHCP clients coming in fresh or whose DHCP leases are expiring will be able to acquire a lease from either DHCP server setup for failover.

Now that DHCP failover has been established, you would sort of expect something inside the DHCP management console to have changed to visually indicate to us that there is failover configured on the scope, but that is not really the case. Everything in here looks exactly the same as before failover creation. I point this out to let you know that during future visits to this console, or if you are a new admin to an existing infrastructure and want to quickly identify whether or not DHCP failover is established in your environment, you can find this information by right-clicking on the scope. In the menu list that is displayed with that right-click, you will now find an option called **Deconfigure Failover**, which implies that failover is currently configured for this scope. Additionally, if you head into the properties of that scope, you will find a **Failover** tab that displays all pertinent information about DHCP failover:

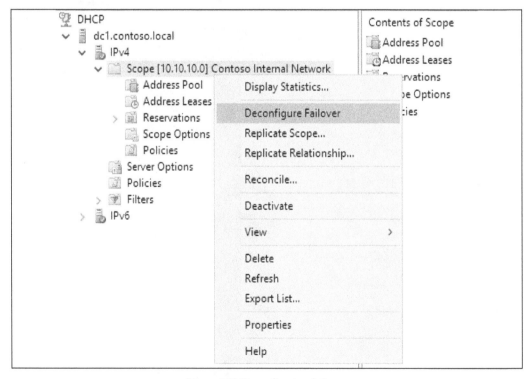

Figure 4.25: Deconfiguring failover

One last verification, let's log into DC2 and see what the DHCP management console looks like now! Remember that previously the only thing I have done on DC2 is to install the DHCP role and to authorize this server. I never even opened up the DHCP management console on that server. If I do so now, you can see that my `10.10.10.0` scope has been replicated over to this server, including the current address lease information!

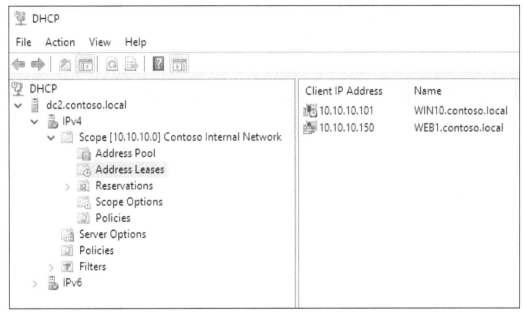

Figure 4.26: Replicating the 10.10.10.0 scope to a DC2

IPAM

The **IP Address Management (IPAM)** feature built into Windows Server 2019 is overlooked by many server administrators because it is a feature and not a full-blown role inside Windows. IPAM is a technology that allows centralized monitoring and management of DHCP and DNS in your environment. If all of your infrastructure is sitting inside one building, it is easy enough to simply use the DNS and DHCP management tools from any server or workstation in your network and have full control over both of those technologies. But how about larger and enterprise-class networks that span many locations, each with its own sets of DNS and DHCP servers? IPAM is useful for gathering up all of those differing namespaces and scopes and providing access to them from one interface.

Let's install the IPAM feature in my lab so you have an idea of where to start, should you choose to employ this feature. Begin by choosing a server upon which you want to install IPAM, and simply walk through the **Add Roles and Features Wizard** to add the feature called **IP Address Management (IPAM) Server**.

 Note: It is not recommended to install IPAM onto a domain controller, or onto a DHCP server as that will hinder its ability to acquire information from these systems.

Now that the feature is installed, launching Server Manager will display a new section in the left window pane called **IPAM**. Go ahead and click on **IPAM**, and you are now presented with a set of six tasks that need to be accomplished in order to use IPAM:

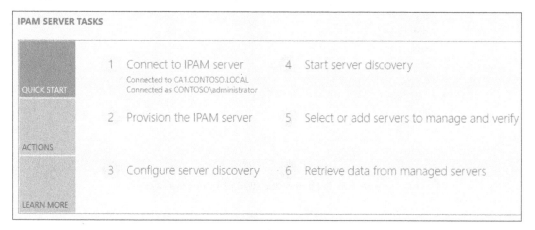

Figure 4.27: IPAM server tasks

The first step is already finished, we are connected to the IPAM server. In my lab, I installed IPAM on my CA1 server, but not for any particular reason. You could dedicate a server to this task or install the feature onto an existing server.

Moving on to *Step 2*, **Provision the IPAM server**, you will have a chance to read over some good descriptive text about how IPAM plans to interact with your servers. You have the option of manually configuring each server (who's going to do that?) but clearly the way Microsoft expects most of us to centrally roll this out is through the use of Group Policy. We discuss Group Policy in the next chapter of this book, but for the purpose of setting up IPAM we can pretty much just flow through these configuration wizards, selecting the default settings, and understand that under the hood this console is establishing GPOs for us, which will then be pushed down to the servers in our network to configure them for reporting into IPAM.

The only selections that need to be made inside *Step 2* are what database for IPAM to utilize, and which provisioning method should be used to send IPAM settings out to your servers. For the database, if you have a SQL server you may certainly use it to store IPAM information, but the default selection is **Windows Internal Database (WID)**, which is a built-in database platform used by many of the Windows Server roles and features. We will utilize WID for this new IPAM server, and as we already mentioned, the rolling out of IPAM settings is easily accomplished via Group Policy. On the screen where you select **Group Policy Based** as the provisioning method, you will also need to define a **GPO name prefix**. When this console creates the GPOs needed for IPAM to work, it will define names for the GPOs and those names cannot be altered, but what Microsoft allows here is for you to assign a prefix to those GPO names, so that when you later look inside the Group Policy management tool, all of the GPO configurations related to IPAM will be listed together, all having the same prefix that you define on this screen:

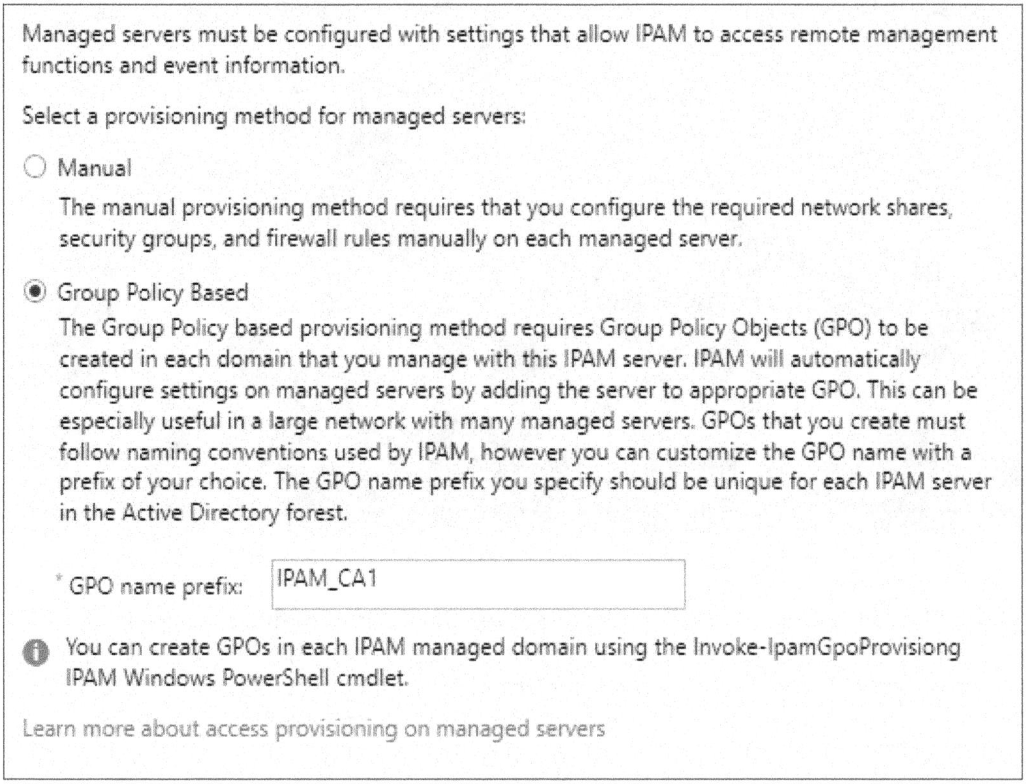

Managed servers must be configured with settings that allow IPAM to access remote management functions and event information.

Select a provisioning method for managed servers:

○ Manual

The manual provisioning method requires that you configure the required network shares, security groups, and firewall rules manually on each managed server.

◉ Group Policy Based

The Group Policy based provisioning method requires Group Policy Objects (GPO) to be created in each domain that you manage with this IPAM server. IPAM will automatically configure settings on managed servers by adding the server to appropriate GPO. This can be especially useful in a large network with many managed servers. GPOs that you create must follow naming conventions used by IPAM, however you can customize the GPO name with a prefix of your choice. The GPO name prefix you specify should be unique for each IPAM server in the Active Directory forest.

* GPO name prefix: IPAM_CA1

ⓘ You can create GPOs in each IPAM managed domain using the Invoke-IpamGpoProvisiong IPAM Windows PowerShell cmdlet.

Learn more about access provisioning on managed servers

Figure 4.28: Selecting a provisioning method

You'll notice a little informational text in *Figure 4.28*, as well as on the summary screen when you finish *Step 2*, regarding a PowerShell cmdlet called `Invoke-IpamGpoProvisioning`. Common sense would tell us that after *Step 2* in the IPAM implementation, you would move on to *Step 3*, right? Actually not in this case. Configuring server discovery (*Step 3*) is a step that we need to take, but at this point the IPAM console is waiting for those GPOs to be created so that they can be used and referenced during the rest of the setup process.

Pause on your work inside the IPAM steps, and open an administrative PowerShell prompt, making sure that you are logged in to your server with a domain admin account. Then simply run `Invoke-IpamGpoProvisioning`. This will ask you to key in the name of your domain, as well as that `GPOPrefixName` you specified during the wizard; be sure to type it in exactly the same!

Figure 4.29: Running Invoke-IpamGpoProvisioning

You will be required to enter *Y* and press *Enter* three times to finish through this command. In reading the warning text that is being displayed, the same text three times in a row, this is asking you for confirmation simply because when these GPOs are being created, their security filtering settings are being modified away from default GPO security filtering behavior. We will explain GPO security filtering soon, but for IPAM's purposes, simply type *Y* and continue through these prompts. Now that `Invoke-IpamGpoProvisioning` has done its work, if we sneak a quick peek into Group Policy Management, you can see that there are three new GPOs now that were not there a minute ago:

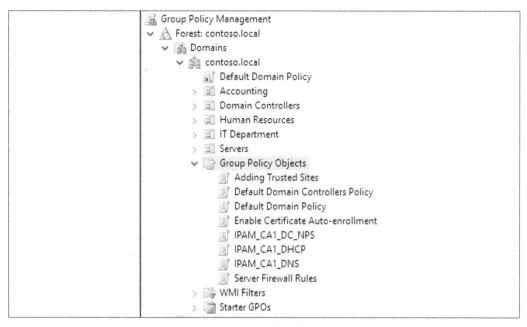

Figure 4.30: Invoke-IpamGpoProvisioning has added three new GPOs

Now back inside IPAM configuration on CA1, we will go ahead and click on *Step 3*, **Configure Server Discovery**. Inside, use the **Get forests** and **Add** buttons to query your domain for infrastructure services that can be monitored by IPAM. Your domain should be listed, with checkboxes selected on the components that the wizard was able to discover about your domain. In my case, I have discovered all three—**Domain controller**, **DHCP server**, and **DNS server**. I will leave all three checked so that IPAM can pull data about all three of these roles and click **OK**:

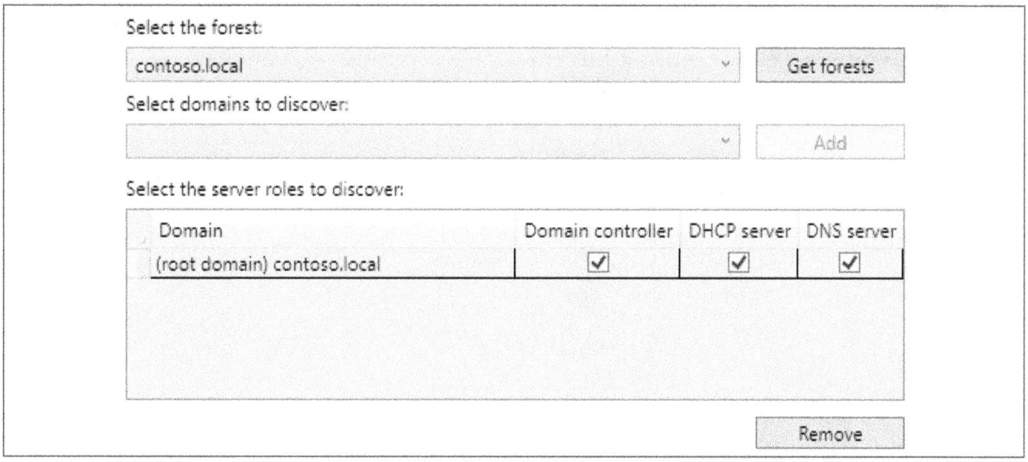

Select the forest:

| contoso.local | | Get forests |

Select domains to discover:

| | | Add |

Select the server roles to discover:

Domain	Domain controller	DHCP server	DNS server
(root domain) contoso.local	☑	☑	☑

| | Remove |

Figure 4.31: Configuring server discovery

Move on to *Step 4*, **Start server discovery**. This launches a scheduled task in the background that is reaching out and finding additional information about your infrastructure. Once finished, click on *Step 5*, **Select or add servers to manage and verify IPAM access**. Here you should see the servers listed that are hosting your AD DS, DNS, and DHCP roles. Right-click on each server that you want to manage, and then select **Edit Server...**. Inside this screen, for each server, change the server's **Manageability status** field to **Managed**:

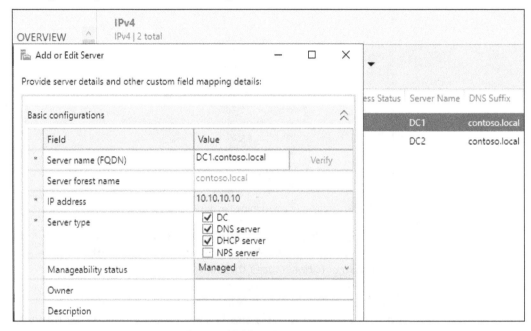

Figure 4.32: Managing your servers

Finally, click on *Step 6*, **Retrieve data from managed servers**, which will set the GPOs into action and start pulling information from those servers into the IPAM database. When finished, you will now have a centralized interface from which you can view information about Active Directory, DNS, and DHCP scopes, as you can see in *Figure 4.33*:

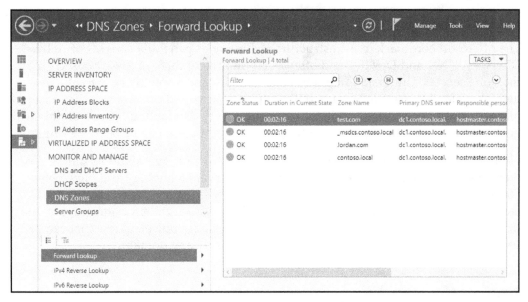

Figure 4.33: IPAM's centralized interface

Management of DHCP from within IPAM is particularly useful, as classic administration of DHCP from within its own management console can get pretty messy in an environment with many different DHCP scopes. IPAM provides an interface from which you can quickly and easily see information about all scopes together, and even run some fun PowerShell cmdlets to quickly gather data that would have otherwise taken manual poking and prodding to discover in the past:

- `Find-IpamFreeSubnet`
- `Add-IpamSubnet`
- `Find-IpamFreeRange` (this one is nice because it helps you to quickly discover a range of available IP addresses)
- `Add-IpamRange`

Summary

The Microsoft core stack of infrastructure technologies generally consists of Active Directory, DNS, and DHCP—and often you will find all three of these housed on the same servers. Understanding these technologies and knowing how to utilize their associated toolsets is an essential part of any server administrator's life. As a manager in an IT company, I will tell you with surety that having a grasp on this will greatly improve your chances of finding that sysadmin role you've been seeking.

I hope these last two chapters have been beneficial to your overall understanding of the ways that companies make use of Windows Server technology and have given you something to help prepare for IT life in a business setting. Next, we turn to another baked-in component of any Active Directory-focused environment, but one that is often underutilized. Group Policy is an amazingly powerful tool that can be used to enhance security and create automation inside any domain.

Questions

1. What kind of DNS record directs email flow?
2. Which type of DNS record resolves a name to an IPv6 address?
3. Which DNS zone type resolves IP addresses backward into hostnames?
4. What DHCP option is often used for VoIP phone provisioning?
5. Which mode of DHCP failover is often used between branch offices and a primary site?
6. What is the standard recommendation and default setting for Maximum Client Lead Time when configuring load balanced DHCP failover?
7. Which Windows Server roles can IPAM tap into?

5
Group Policy

If you find yourself reading this book from front to back, indeed a good and not at all weird way to read a book, you already have a general idea of what Group Policy is and does (because we talked about it for a minute in *Chapter 3, Active Directory*). However, I've been around IT folks long enough to know that reading a book from cover to cover is fairly rare, and attention spans rarely accommodate such a quest. Therefore, any of you hitting up this chapter in a random fashion because the words "Group Policy" drew your attention or you have a specific need that you are hoping to be answered in this chapter, fear not! Let's again summarize the great and glorious power of Group Policy.

It's easy to understand the general use of the word "policy", meaning some kind of ruleset, structure, or standard to which you need something to adhere. In our case, we're talking about Microsoft Windows-based computers (and servers). Applying policies to computers, such as security policies, application policies, or printer policies, sounds like a great idea. If applying policies to a computer is great, applying policies to a group of computers must be even better, hence the term "Group Policy." In a nutshell, Group Policy is a centralized way to issue policies to groups of computers inside your domain network. Here's a quick list of the topics we plan to cover together:

- Group Policy Object
- Building a GPO
- Scoping a GPO
- Computer settings and user settings
- Policy vs preference

- Default Domain Policy
- Administrative Templates
- Central store

Group Policy Object

This is pretty straightforward. The overlying technology we are talking about here is called Group Policy, and an individual instance of a Group Policy is known as a **Group Policy Object**, commonly referred to as a **GPO**. A GPO is a single package that contains one or many policy settings and applies to a domain computer, a domain user, or sometimes many computers and users all at the same time.

GPOs are stored inside Active Directory and are replicated among your domain controller servers. Every time a domain user logs into a domain-joined computer that is connected to your network, the computer reaches out to Active Directory and asks, "Hey, got any GPO settings for me?" Then a whole slew of activity commences as a domain controller hands over all of the GPO settings that it contains, which apply to the computer and/or user logging in. This is a key piece of information. GPOs are scoped upon creation, giving you the power to define to whom each policy is applied. Extremely powerful stuff. These policy settings then plug themselves into place on your computer, forcing certain things to happen (or not happen) at the discretion of your IT department. You can lock down settings, force settings into place, and configure default settings but still allow users to override them. You can throw certain settings at some computers and completely opposite settings at others. You can even apply conflicting GPOs to the same computers and sit back and watch them fight to see who comes out the winner in the end. If you don't understand how Group Policy works, it is very easy to cause huge problems in your network, as it is very, very easy to apply settings to every machine in the domain. A single GPO has the potential to bring your entire network to its knees if misused.

So…*that's* reassuring, right? Trust me, while Group Policy comes with a warning label and *"with great power comes great responsibility"* and all that, you will want to use GPOs more than you are now after seeing all that they can do.

Group Policy background refresh cycle

I mentioned that Group Policy processes on your domain-joined computers every time that a user logs in, and that is true. What is also true is that Group Policy reprocesses itself at intervals throughout the day, even while the user remains logged in. By default, and almost nobody changes it, something called a background refresh happens every 90 minutes. This means that implementing new GPOs during the day generally works fine because those settings will roll into place even without users needing to log off or restart their computers. There are exceptions to this, though, as some GPO settings are unable to process as background cycles and can only take effect during the login process. Some examples of such GPOs are a login script (which can only run during logon or logoff of a computer) or even something like a mapped network drive. Some GPOs will only push themselves into place during the user login process.

Many times I find myself testing GPO settings as I make changes to them, and it would make for a very inefficient workday if I had to wait 90 minutes or restart my test computer after every little tweak or change to a GPO. Thankfully, we have a quick and easy command-line tool that can be used to force Group Policy to reach out and do its thing, any time of any day!

```
gpupdate /force
```

Running this command inside Command Prompt or PowerShell on a domain-joined client computer will cause it to immediately reach out and grab updated GPO settings. Keep in mind, your computer does need to be able to contact a domain controller for Group Policy to process, so this isn't going to work if your work laptop is sitting in your house and not connected via VPN. But for any computers inside the office or in some way connected to your corporate network, you can run gpupdate all the live-long day and continually roll new policies and changes into place.

Building a GPO

There's nothing quite as good as jumping in and getting your hands dirty, so let's get down to business and build a new GPO. Don't worry, we will be careful not to apply this GPO to anything yet and save that for our next section. As with most Microsoft technologies, there is a special management console created just for interacting with Group Policy, appropriately named the **Group Policy Management Console** (**GPMC**). Logging into any of your domain controller servers, you can launch GPMC from inside **Administrative Tools**, inside the **Tools** menu of Server Manager, or by launching GPMC.MSC from Start | Run, Command Prompt, or PowerShell:

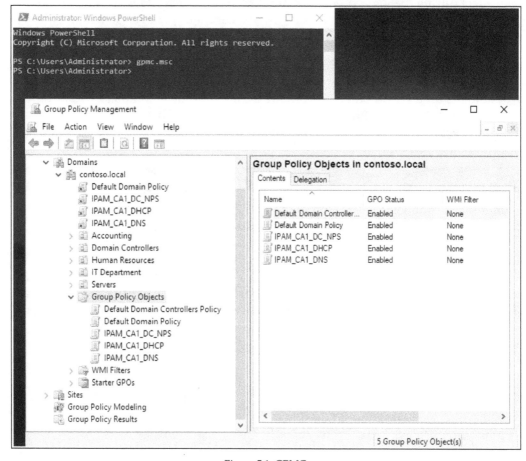

Figure 5.1: GPMC

You'll notice in *Figure 5.1* that there are already some GPOs listed here. They are a combination of default GPOs that always exist when you install Active Directory (we'll talk about the Default Domain Policy a little later in this chapter) and the IPAM GPOs that the IPAM configuration process put into place for us in *Chapter 4, DNS and DHCP*. To create a new GPO in a way that it is not yet applying to any workstations or users, right-click on the **Group Policy Objects** folder and select **New**. Create a name for your new GPO, click **OK**, and you have created a Group Policy Object! So far, your new GPO is void of any settings or configurations, and it is not applying to anything or anybody, so it is precisely pointless. We will soon change that...

Adding Trusted Sites

I named my first GPO "Adding Trusted Sites" because I am going to use this new GPO to apply some URLs to be recognized as trusted sites inside Internet Explorer on my Windows 10 client computer. If you run a web application in your network that needs to run JavaScript or ActiveX controls, or something like that, it may be required that the website is part of the trusted sites list inside Internet Explorer for it to run properly. You could print off an instructions page for the helpdesk on how to do this on each computer and make them spend the time to do it for every user who calls in because they cannot access the application. Or you could simply create a GPO that makes these changes for you automatically on every workstation and save yourself from dealing with all of those phone calls. This is just one tiny example of the power that Group Policy possesses, but it's a good example because it is useful, and it is a setting that is buried way down in the GPO settings, so you can get a feel for just how deep these capabilities go.

Right-click on the new GPO and choose **Edit...**. Now navigate to **Computer Configuration | Policies | Administrative Templates | Windows Components | Internet Explorer | Internet Control Panel | Security Page**. See, I told you it was buried in there!

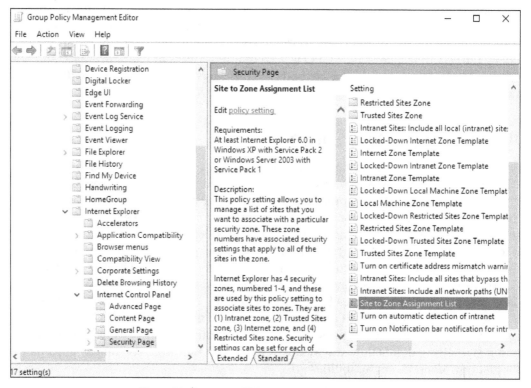

Figure 5.2: Creating a GPO to manage trusted websites

Now double-click on **Site to Zone Assignment List** and set it to **Enabled**. This allows you to click on the **Show...** button, within which you can enter websites and give them zone assignments. Each GPO setting has a nice descriptive text to accompany it, telling you exactly what that particular setting is for and what the options mean. As you can see in the text for this one, in order to set my websites to be trusted sites, I need to give them a zone assignment value of **2**. And, just for fun, I also added a site that I do not want to be accessible to my users and gave it a zone value of **4** so that badsite.contoso.com is a member of the restricted sites zone on all of my desktop computers. Here is my completed list:

Figure 5.3: Assigning websites to different zones

Are we done? Almost. As soon as I click on the **OK** button, these settings are now stored in my Group Policy Object and are ready to be deployed. As you know, we have not assigned this new GPO to apply to anybody yet, so for now the GPO is populated with these settings but still doing nothing. Before we push out these settings, let's build out a couple more common GPOs to make sure our examples here are well-rounded.

Mapping network drives

File servers are some of the most common types of servers that exist because all companies across all industries need to create and maintain documentation to run their businesses. This is not a chapter about how to build a file server, set up shares, restrict permissions, or utilize **Distributed File System** (**DFS**) to improve the overall flexibility and resiliency of your file server infrastructure, although these are all good things to learn. Today, we are going to assume that you already have file servers in place and that there are already shared folders on those file servers. In my test lab, I have shared folders from a few different servers, as identified here:

- `\\DC1\HR`
- `\\DC2\Accounting`
- `\\WEB3\Installers`

The challenge we are trying to solve is how to automate these shared folder locations being available on all of my user's workstations. I could put together a piece of documentation that shows users how to manually get to these locations by using UNC paths plugged into the address bar of File Explorer. Or maybe even take it a step further and show my folks how to map network drives from inside File Explorer so that they end up with drive letters assigned on their computers for ongoing access to these locations. Doing so would work, but it puts an administrative burden on my users, and also leads to the possibility of users having differing drive letters. Grace might use her "R" drive letter to map to the accounting share, while Jackson may decide that "T" is his accounting drive letter of choice.

Obviously, there's a better way to handle this situation. One of the very common chores we task to a GPO is the standardized creation of mapped network drives on client computers. Inside a new GPO we can define UNC paths for shares and assign drive letters to them. We can then assign that GPO to users and computers, and drive letters will magically map when your users log into their computers.

Create a new GPO for this purpose, and edit that GPO, as you already know how to do. This time we are navigating to the following location:

User Configuration | Preferences | Windows Settings | Drive Maps

Right-clicking on **Drive Maps** and choosing **New | Mapped Drive** brings you into the configuration section for a single mapped drive letter. You can see in the screenshot below that I am mapping a drive to \\DC1\HR, and assigning it a drive letter of **H**:

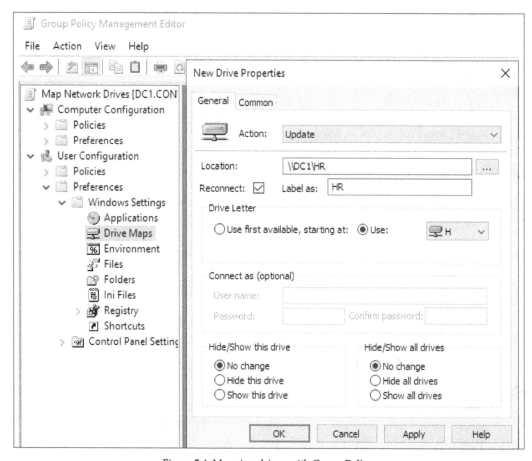

Figure 5.4: Mapping drives with Group Policy

You'll notice the **Action** dropdown menu has four different options: **Create**, **Replace**, **Update**, and **Delete**. This is important to understand as many GPO preference configurations have this same drop-down selection. Here is a quick summary of each available option as it relates to our new drive mapping policy:

- **Create**: Use this action to create the new mapped drive only if it does not already exist. If the H: drive is already in use on a workstation, this new mapping will then be ignored. In our example, if I were to configure this new drive mapping for Create, it would only take an action if the H: drive letter was currently open and available.

- **Replace**: Use this action to remove an existing setting and replace it with a new setting. In our case, it will update whatever mapped drive is using H: to our \\DC1\HR. The Replace option is redundant because of the Update option and is rarely used.

- **Update**: This is the default action for most preference settings and is generally the most useful. If the setting that we are configuring doesn't exist, Update will create it. Additionally, if the setting (mapped drive) is already in place on the workstation, it will now be updated to reflect our new definition inside the GPO. Drive mapping policies almost always use the Update action to push new drive letters into place.

- **Delete**: This removes the specific setting from the client machine. If you are removing a network share and want to ensure that it is removed from all of the computers in your domain, this would be a useful Action to ensure that happens.

Before clicking **OK** on this new drive mapping, go ahead and visit the **Common** tab. This tab and its five options are commonly shown on many preference settings that you plug into a GPO. Most of these are self-explanatory, though we will discuss Item-level targeting more in just a few pages. For our drive mapping GPO, I like to point out the **Run in logged-on user's security context** checkbox. This tells Group Policy to run whatever setting or preference the GPO is putting into place, under the logged-in user's account. For mapped drives, this is particularly useful because you typically want users to interface with their mapped drives in their regular user context. While it is not common to check this box, for drive mapping GPOs I always do:

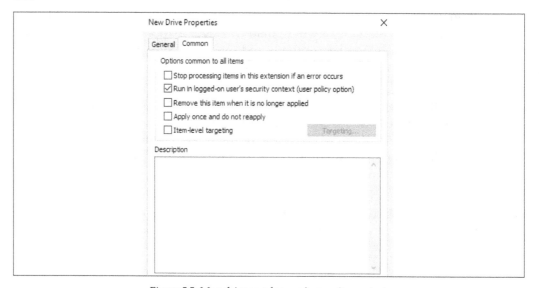

Figure 5.5: Map drives under user's security context

Rinse and repeat for any additional drive letters that you want to include inside your new GPO, and you are now well on your way to automating the mapping of all drive letters across your entire network! I set up drive letter mappings for each of my shared folders and also included a GPO setting to delete the z: drive if it exists. It doesn't in my lab, but this way you can also see an example of what that looks like inside the policy:

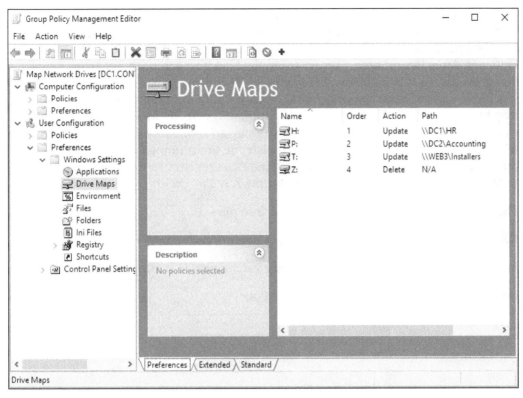

Figure 5.6: Mapped drives via GPO

Once again, this new GPO does not apply to any users yet, but never fear – once we finish creating just one more example GPO, we will move onto scoping GPO settings, which is where we will push the new GPOs into action and verify that settings and mapped drives show up automatically on our client computers.

Installing registry keys

In much the same way that mapped network drives can be pushed to users via GPO, we can implement registry keys and values onto computers automatically as well. This is spectacularly powerful because almost anything within a Windows environment can be manipulated by using registry keys. Create yet another new GPO and this time, navigate to the following location:

User Configuration | Preferences | Windows Settings | Registry

Creating, replacing, updating, or deleting registry keys flows in very much the same fashion as it does for mapping network drives. The tricky bit is making sure that the options are specified properly, or they won't work, particularly the Key Path and Value information. For our example, I am going to push a registry value that prevents users from being able to change their desktop background image and specifies a custom desktop background of my own. In my experience, the easiest way to ensure the GPO configuration is populated correctly inside the configuration window is to actually place the new registry key and/or value that you are working with onto the server or computer from which you are running GPMC. This way you can select the ellipsis button and seek out the exact registry setting, rather than trying to remember how it must be formatted for the Key Path field.

The registry information that I am putting into place is:

HKCU\Software\Microsoft\Windows\CurrentVersion\Policies\System

Inside the System registry key, the registry value name is **Wallpaper**.

Here is my populated entry inside Group Policy:

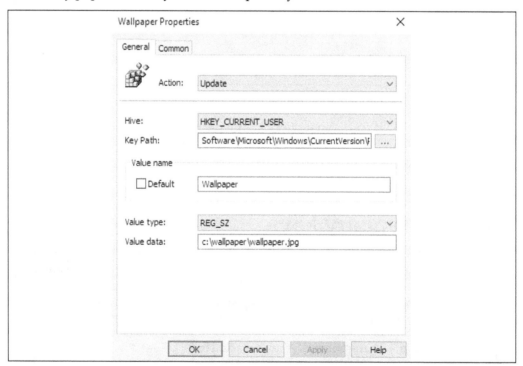

Figure 5.7: Adding registry keys via Group Policy

Because I have selected this registry value to be pushed as an **Update** action, every time that Group Policy processes on this computer, it is going to ensure that this registry key is present, thus continually preventing users from being able to adjust their desktop wallpaper.

I chose this example because it is straightforward and because often in Group Policy you will find that there are multiple ways to accomplish the same thing. Instead of using a registry value to lock down wallpaper settings, I could have alternatively created a GPO that utilized the following GPO setting, and it would have accomplished the same thing without having to touch registry settings:

User Configuration | Policies | Administrative Templates | Desktop | Desktop | Desktop Wallpaper

Scoping a GPO

I briefly mentioned the ability to scope GPOs so that they only apply to machines or users that you desire. This is probably the single most important piece of the Group Policy puzzle to understand. You have already seen a couple of examples of plugging settings into GPOs, and information is abundant on the Internet with useful and exact policy settings and how to put those into place. If there is some particular task you are trying to accomplish on a large scale, turn to search engines and look for that item while including the search word "GPO," and you'll quickly find information about how to set up your new GPO to do that thing. What those articles, Microsoft documents, and blog posts are *not* going to define for you is to what extent you push those settings into your network, and how to ensure your new GPO is not too far-reaching. That decision is yours alone. In this section, we will discuss the different options available within every GPO that allow you to pinpoint very specific details about who should, or should not, receive those GPO settings.

Links

A GPO link is arguably the most important tool in your Group Policy toolbox. Links simply take a GPO and bind it to a location in Active Directory. The GPO that you have now linked will start applying its contained settings to users and devices that are within that location.

We have created multiple GPOs inside Group Policy but have not yet applied them to anything. What this means is that we have not yet linked those GPOs to anything, and when we do, that is when they will be set loose and start doing their work. Before we link one of our new GPOs, let's take a look at which GPOs currently apply to my Windows 10 computer. That way we can check again after creating our link to prove to ourselves that the new GPO is doing something.

GPRESULT

So far, we haven't talked at all about how to check machines to discover what policies may or may not apply to them. Let's take a break from configuration and do that now. Logging into my Windows 10 client machine, I can open either Command Prompt or PowerShell and run the following:

```
Gpresult /r
```

This spits out quite a bit of interesting information, but what we are most interested in here is the section called **Applied Group Policy Objects**. In fact, you may notice that there are two sections to this output and find two instances of Applied Group Policy Objects. One will be listed beneath **COMPUTER SETTINGS**, and the other under **USER SETTINGS**. Shortly, we will describe the differences between computer and user settings within a GPO, but for our example now I want to point out that the output on my test client shows us that no GPOs are being applied at the user settings level, as you can see in *Figure 5.8*:

```
Applied Group Policy Objects
-----------------------------
            N/A
```

Figure 5.8: No GPOs applied to the user

After becoming more familiar with Group Policy, you may often find yourself running `gpresult` and wanting to narrow down the results to either computer or user settings. You can easily do this by adding a switch to your `gpresult` command:

```
Gpresult /r /scope computer
Gpresult /r /scope user
```

Continuing with the link

Back inside the Group Policy Management console, find the location to which you want to **link** your new GPO. I am going to link my Map Network Drives GPO and prove to you that all of my mapped network drives are created automatically during my next login to a workstation. The user account I am logging in with resides inside an OU called **Accounting Users**. Seeking out the **Accounting Users** OU, I right-click on it and choose the **Link an Existing GPO...** option. On the screen that follows, find your newly created GPO and select it. You have now linked the GPO to this specific OU, and this change is immediately in effect in your network. You can see in *Figure 5.9* that my GPO link is displayed under the **Accounting Users** OU:

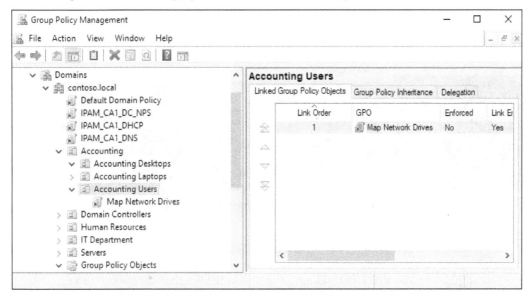

Figure 5.9: Linking a GPO to the Accounting Users OU

The next time users inside this OU log into a domain-joined computer, their network drives should be mapped for them during the login process. Logging into my Windows 10 workstation, I now find that to be true and running `gpresult` again proves that my GPO has successfully been applied!

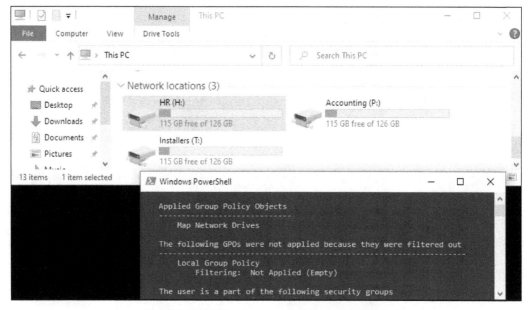

Figure 5.10: GPO has been successfully implemented

 You can link a GPO to more than one OU. Just follow the same process again, this time choosing a different OU to make the link, and that GPO will now apply to both OUs that have active links. You can remove links by right-click on them and deleting them, or by clicking on the Group Policy Object itself to view and modify its link properties.

Group Policy processing order

In the GPO linking example that was just completed, we linked a GPO to a specific OU. You probably noticed in some of the screenshots that there are GPOs linked at different levels too, like right at the root of my `contoso.local` domain. What's that all about? As it turns out, when logging into a computer, there are actually four different levels of Group Policy processing that happens. The location of your links can make a big difference in the proper effect your GPO has on your computers and users. Let's discuss these four levels of GPO processing.

Local Policy

Assuming you have worked in IT for a little while, it is very likely that you have followed a blog post or forum that has led you into a modification via `gpedit.msc`. Running `gpedit.msc` on any Windows system brings you into the **Local Group Policy Editor**. This is the set of policy objects and settings that exist on an individual machine. They can be manipulated manually via `gpedit.msc`, or they can be manipulated and overwritten by GPOs. The key point that I want to make is that when your Windows computer boots and logs in, the very first thing that happens is that settings inside the Local Group Policy Editor are processed. Since Local Policy is first to apply, it means that any levels of Active Directory Group Policy, which we are about to discuss, will take priority over Local Policy. In other words, your computer may have Local Policy settings in place, but milliseconds later during the boot process, those local settings could be overwritten by AD policy settings.

Site-level policies

Remember back in *Chapter 3*, *Active Directory*, when we discussed Active Directory Sites and Services? That comes into play here. If your environment is large enough to contain multiple sites, it is possible to link GPOs at an individual site level, thus enabling Group Policy to issue settings to computers or users based on which site they reside within.

Having GPOs linked to sites is quite a rare occurrence in my experience, but it is something to keep in the back of your mind when troubleshooting GPO applications. Computers and users will only receive site-level policies when they physically reside within those sites, based on the IP addressing scheme and subnets you defined inside AD Sites and Services. If a computer is handed GPO settings based on a site-level link, and these settings contradict what is in Local Group Policy, the site-level policies will override the Local Policy, and these will be the new settings as you continue the login process.

Domain-level policies

Some policies and settings are going to be things that you want to apply to all machines or users in an entire domain, and the appropriate place for those settings are domain-level GPOs. It's important to point out that the GPOs themselves are not different as we talk about all these different policy levels – a GPO is a GPO. The level at which the GPO is *linked* is what we are discussing in relation to these hierarchical levels.

Links created at the root, or top level, of a domain inside Group Policy Management, will by default attempt to apply to any user or computer that is part of the domain. There are many other factors that can filter domain-linked GPOs, but for the most part if you link a GPO to the domain name, you had better be okay with the settings inside that GPO applying to potentially every workstation, every server, every user. If you peek back a few pages at some of the screenshots from inside the Group Policy Management Console, you can see that my IPAM GPOs are all linked directly to `contoso.local`. These are known as domain-level links.

Pretending that we are still flowing through a computer login process with these examples, domain-level policies apply after site-level policies. So any settings that came down to you via site-level policies have now been added to, or potentially overridden by (if there was a conflict), our domain-level policies.

OU-level policies

We started our login journey with Local Group Policy settings, which were then added to or overwritten by site-level GPOs, and those were then added onto again (or overwritten again in the case of conflicts) by domain-level GPOs. You can guess where this is heading. OU-level policies now apply on top of domain-level GPOs.

OUs, as you know, are containing folders for computer and user accounts that are joined to your domain. Most companies take good advantage of using multiple OUs inside Active Directory to differentiate types of machines and users. Servers are separated from workstations, accounting users are different than HR users, and so on. Nesting OUs is a common practice as well. Just like creating folders inside of other folders by using File Explorer, you can use AD Users and Computers to create OUs inside other OUs. This is important to the organization of your domain objects, and it is also important to Group Policy.

Linking GPOs to particular OUs gives us flexibility in handing different settings to different groups of people or machines. When a GPO is linked to a single OU, only computers or users inside that OU, or downstream from it, will be affected by the GPO. You can even have multiple GPOs linked to the same OU.

Nested OUs provide an additional tier to this GPO workflow. Remember the general rule is that Group Policy processes from the top down, so GPOs that are linked to a nested OU will most likely outweigh GPOs that are linked at a higher-level OU.

Security Filtering

Now that you have created a GPO and linked it to particular OU, you have enough information to start using Group Policy in your environment. Using links to determine what machines or users get what policies is the most common method that I see admins use, but there are many circumstances where you might want to take it a step further. What if you had a new GPO and had it linked to an OU that contained all of your desktop computers, but then decided that some of those machines needed the policy and some did not? It would be a headache to have to split those machines up into two separate OUs just for the purpose of this policy that you are building. This is where **GPO Security Filtering** comes into play.

Security Filtering is the ability to filter a GPO down to particular Active Directory objects. On any given GPO in your directory, you can set filters so that the GPO only applies to particular users, particular computers, or even particular groups of users or computers. I find that using groups is especially useful.

For our Map Network Drives GPO, right now I have it linked to my **Accounting Users** OU, but what if I wanted to filter that GPO in a different way? Rather than limit the scope of this GPO to a single OU, I would prefer to make it a little bit further reaching, and I'm going to link the GPO to my contoso.local domain. Yikes, doesn't that mean it's going to apply to everything? Yes, unless you utilize the Security Filtering section to define user accounts or groups of accounts to which it should apply.

 I always make my Security Filtering decisions before creating a link. Links are live as soon as you create them, so building Security Filtering first ensures proper distribution from the start.

Clicking on any GPO inside GPMC will display information about that GPO, and the **Scope** tab displays any links that exist for this GPO, as well as Security Filtering information. All new GPOs will have **Authenticated Users** defined inside **Security Filtering**, which essentially means "all domain users *and* computers". Remember that it means both! In the next screenshot, you can see my Map Network Drives GPO that is linked to the **Accounting Users** OU. It has **Authenticated Users** listed for **Security Filtering**. If I were to simply remove the existing OU link and create a new domain-level link, this GPO would immediately start applying to all user accounts in my whole domain:

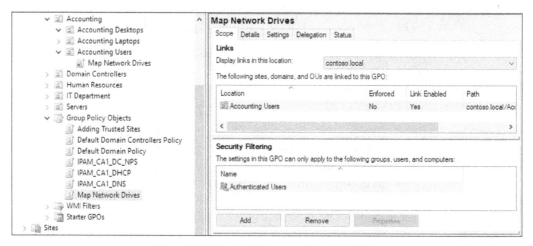

Figure 5.11: Security Filtering settings for GPOs

Instead of doing that, I will adjust my **Security Filtering** settings first. All accounting users are part of a security group called **Acct Group** (I'm so creative!). Adding **Acct Group** to **Security Filtering** for this GPO and **REMOVING Authenticated Users** means that now no matter where I link this GPO, only members of the Acct Group group are going to receive the GPO settings. Now that I have added **Acct Group** to my **Security Filtering**, I can safely link the GPO to the top-level of my domain and remain confident that only members of Acct Group will receive my GPO settings:

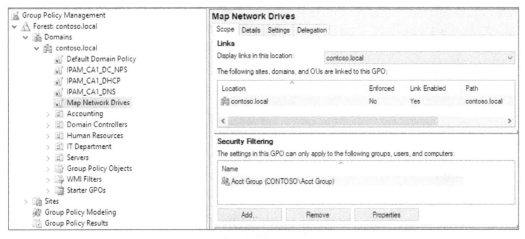

Figure 5.12: Filtering a GPO to the Acct Group

 Another cool feature that is just a click away is the **Settings** tab on this same screen. Click on that tab, and it will display all of the configurations currently set inside your GPO. This is very useful for checking over GPOs that someone else may have created to see what settings are being modified.

WMI Filtering

Using a combination of well-designed links and Security Filtering to narrow the scope of your GPOs, you will likely be able to perfectly plan and apply policy settings 90% of the time. Our next few sub-headings reflect that remaining 10%, as we cover some of the advanced filtering techniques that are available to get even more granular when filtering Group Policy Objects.

WMI Filtering is a genius, although slightly confusing, tool to further define GPO application. WMI filters tap into WMI information that exists on every Windows computer and use that WMI data to further filter GPO settings. WMI filters can be defined to look for operating system version numbers, types of CPU, quantities of RAM, the amount of available disk space, and sometimes even things like BIOS firmware. Once a WMI filter is defined, you can then select that filter for each GPO, in the section titled WMI Filtering that is immediately below Security Filtering inside GPMC.

WMI filters enable you to do things like "only install this huge piece of software if there is at least 5 GB of available disk space" or "only implement these firewall settings on machines running a Windows Server operating system." Another real-world example that uses WMI Filtering to identify whether or not a machine is running mobile hardware, which allows your GPOs to apply only to laptops and tablets, and not desktop computers.

WMI Filtering is drawing information from other components inside the operating system, and therefore causes Group Policy to take a little bit more time and CPU processing power to function. This can cause an increase in system resources on your endpoint computers and also slows logins, as that processing happens in the background.

Building WMI filters is getting in the weeds with Group Policy, and so for further instruction on that, I will point you toward the *Summary* section at the end of this chapter, where I will reference another publication dedicated entirely to Group Policy.

Item-level targeting

Links, Security Filtering, and WMI Filtering are fantastic ways to determine which GPOs apply to which computers and users. But what if you need to take it a step further? What if you have a single GPO that contains multiple settings, and you only want some of those settings to apply to certain users or computers, and other settings in the same policy to apply to different users and computers?

A prime example of this is a Map Network Drives GPO. It is common to place all network drives into a single GPO in the domain and called it "Mapped Drives" or something similar. It is also common that not all users should get all mapped network drives, what is the best way to handle that? For this scenario, you could break your GPO out into many smaller GPOs, creating a separate GPO for each drive letter and then determining with links and filters which users get which drive letters. But then you have a horde of GPOs to deal with.

Enter **Item-level targeting** (ILT). You may not remember, but earlier we glanced at a special **Common** tab that exists inside many GPO settings. One of the five settings inside the **Common** tab is **Item-level targeting**, and this is exactly the clarifying setting we need to make our Map Network Drives GPO dreams come true.

Referencing the same Map Network Drives GPO that I have been working with for many pages now, you know that this policy contains multiple drive letters. Currently, my Acct Group users receive all of those mapped drives. Let's pretend for a minute that I only want the Acct Group to receive one of those drive letter mappings, and not the others. Editing the GPO, I double-click on my P: drive mapping, and then visit the **Common** tab. Here, I check the box for **Item-level targeting** and click on that **Targeting...** button.

Inside the Targeting Editor, choose **New Item** and you will find a large list of criteria that can be utilized for these additional targeting parameters:

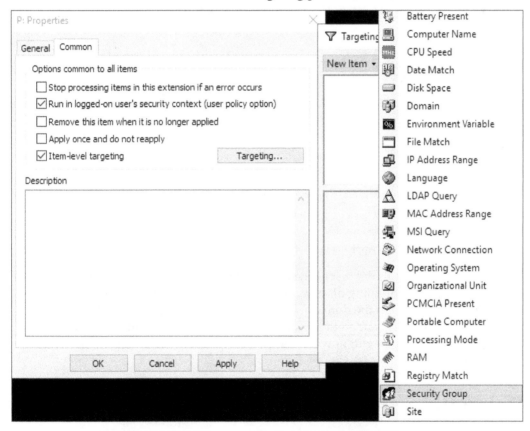

Figure 5.13: Adding a new security group in Targeting Editor

I want to instruct this GPO that the P: drive should only be mapped for users who are part of the Acct Group security group. Choosing to add a new security group to my ILT, I can define the Acct Group and you can see in *Figure 5.14* that my P: drive ILT settings have now been updated so that only if the user is a member of the CONTOSO\Acct Group security group, will that user receive the P: drive mapping when they log in:

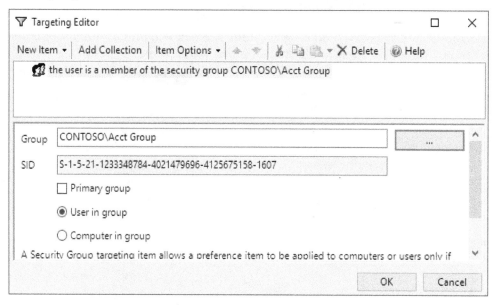

Figure 5.14: Applying the P: drive mapping to CONTOSO\Acct Group

Repeat this process with the rest of the drive letters inside your GPO, and you now have a single GPO containing all drive letter mappings for your entire organization. You can link this GPO to the domain, leave it security filtered to all authenticated users, as it is by default, and yet based on ILT, only drive letters that correspond to their appropriate groups will now be mapped for each user who logs in. ILT is the bomb!

Delegation

Consider this scenario: the executive leadership at your company has asked you to lock down security restrictions on all computers in the domain. Sounds like a job for Group Policy! Except, since they are the leadership and don't want their own systems to hinder their ability to browse Instagram and configure desktop backgrounds of smiling kittens, they have required that these lockdown settings apply to everyone *except* members of the Leadership group in Active Directory.

We know plenty of ways to filter GPOs *to* certain users or groups, but how do we filter GPOs to everything *except* a certain user or group? For this, we visit GPMC, click on the GPO in question, and visit the tab called **Delegation**.

If your GPO has custom Security Filtering applied, you'll notice the names of those users or groups inside the Delegation screen as well. When configuring Security Filtering, what GPMC is really doing is configuring Delegation permissions on the GPO in the background. I have navigated to the **Delegation** tab of my Map Network Drives GPO, which is currently still security filtered to the Acct Group. Inside **Delegation**, clicking on the **Advanced...** button near the bottom-left brings me into the nitty-gritty security details behind delegation and permissions settings on this GPO.

In *Figure 5.15*, you can see that my Acct Group currently has **Read** and **Apply group policy** permissions configured to **Allow**. This is what happened when I added Acct Group to Security Filtering. This is the set of permissions making the magic happen that whenever someone logs into a computer in my domain, they are allowed to both read settings inside this GPO and to apply settings from this GPO:

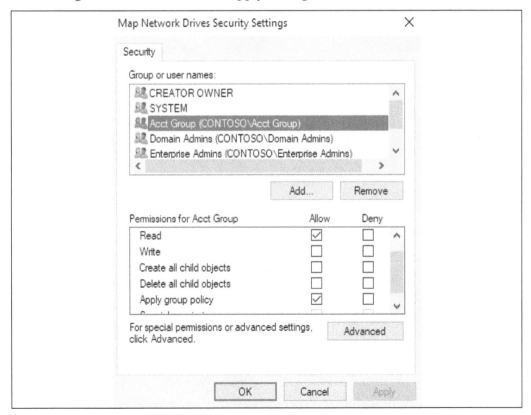

Figure 5.15: Acct Group has read and apply permissions

Circling back to the matter at hand, in the Microsoft world a denial of permission always trumps a permission allowance. If you need to deny a particular user, computer, or group from receiving GPO settings from a particular GPO, you simply add them to the Delegation permissions and check the **Deny** box for **Apply group policy**. Even if they are allowed a Group Policy based on another permission entry in this list, they will now be denied this GPO applying to them. To make this crystal clear with another screenshot, here you can see that my Jordan user account is now denied from applying the Map Network Drives GPO. This means that when Jordan logs in, he will NOT receive network drive mappings from this GPO:

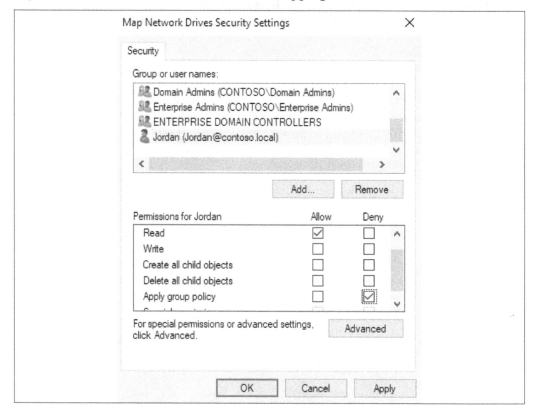

Figure 5.16: Denying a user from receiving this GPO

 Use with caution! Creating GPO denials inside the **Delegation** tab works great, but it is very easy to forget or overlook these settings in the future. I have assisted admins numerous times with troubleshooting a GPO that did not seem to be applying properly, only to find out that a denial permission inside Delegation was causing all the grief.

Computer settings and user settings

After poking around inside GPOs for a few minutes, you are likely to notice that the Group Policy Management Editor is split up into two different sections. When drilling down inside a GPO to find the particular setting that you are about to roll into place, the first choice you need to make is whether you are working on a **Computer Configuration**, or a **User Configuration**. Understanding the differences and always keeping these differences in mind is important not only for finding the setting you are searching for, but also for ensuring that your new GPO is linked to the correct place and applying to the proper type of object. You can see these two sections of any GPO in *Figure 5.17*:

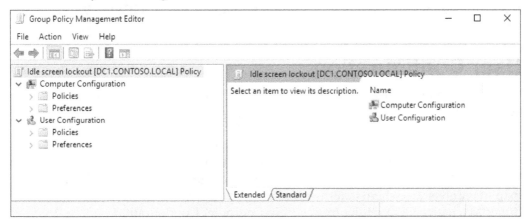

Figure 5.17: Computer Configuration and User Configuration

Computer Configuration

All GPO settings listed beneath Computer Configuration are, of course, settings that can apply to your domain-joined computers. Duh! Aren't all GPO settings applied to computers? No, actually they are not. Many GPO settings do apply to the computer object in Active Directory, and all of these types of GPO settings fall beneath Computer Configuration. Some GPO settings are even things that you can configure at either a computer level or a user level. And other times you might have similar options inside both computer and user configuration that accomplish the task in slightly different ways.

A good example is an idle screen lockout policy. It is a common requirement for companies to require computer screens to lock themselves after a certain number of minutes of inactivity. This way, if a user walks away from their computer and forgets to manually lock the screen, it will self-lock after, say, 15 minutes.

If you are tasked with creating such a policy, you need to decide whether you want this GPO to apply at the computer level, or the user level. This will have to be decided for yourself, based on your normal user activity.

If you determine that the best method for locking the screen is to do so at the computer level, meaning that the screen will lock after 15 minutes no matter who is logged into that computer, then this is the specific configuration that you want to set inside your GPO:

Computer Configuration | Policies | Windows Settings | Security Settings | Local Policies | Security Options

Interactive logon: Machine inactivity limit = Enabled and specified to 900 seconds (15 minutes)

User Configuration

On the other hand, many other GPO settings apply not to the computer account at all, but rather to the domain user who is logging into that computer. User Configuration settings follow the user account around and apply to whichever workstation that user logs into. If you look back to our Map Network Drives GPO, you'll see that the network drive configurations that we created inside that GPO all fall under User Configuration. This means that those drive mappings will attempt to map themselves anywhere that the user logs in. You cannot create mapped network drives as a native GPO setting from within Computer Configuration.

Revisiting our idle screen lockout example, what if you have decided that you want the idle screen to happen for a certain type of users, or perhaps even all users, and that the screen lock would happen for those users no matter which computer they log into? In this case, there is not a specific "screen-lock" policy setting that you can configure inside User Configuration, but what is generally recommended is to get creative with screen saver settings, which are User Configuration settings. If you configure the following four GPO settings, you will effectively create the same behavior as the Computer Config machine inactivity limit timeout setting, but now this policy is taking effect based on user accounts rather than computer accounts:

User Configuration | Policies | Administrative Templates | Control Panel | Personalization

Enable screen saver = Enabled

Force specific screen saver = Use this to define which screen saver you want to run

Screen saver timeout = Enabled and set to 900 seconds

Password protect the screen saver = Enabled

Linking GPOs accordingly

As you seek out GPO configurations to put into place in your environment, sometimes you will find you have no choice between computer or user configuration, as some options will only exist in one location or the other. Other times, you will find that the settings you are putting into place could be configured from either place, and the decision of how to best set the GPO depends upon which level you want the GPO settings to apply.

This decision ties in directly with the location to which you are going to link this GPO! If your GPO contains Computer Configuration settings, those settings can only apply to computer objects and so that GPO would need to be linked to OUs that contain computer objects. Or linked to the domain, of course, which covers all OUs.

Vice versa is also true, if your new GPO contains only User Configuration settings, that GPO is only going to apply to user objects, and any links you create for that GPO should be links to OUs that contain the user objects to which you want the GPO to apply.

You may have already figured this out, but it is generally best practice to create GPOs as either computer-based GPOs, or user-based GPOs. A single GPO can contain a lot of different settings, and if that GPO is linked at a high enough tier, it might indeed be able to apply both user and computer configuration settings all from within a single GPO. But this makes for a higher administrative burden on that single GPO, and it is typically considered best practice for any GPO to contain only Computer Configuration settings, or User Configuration settings.

Group Policy loopback processing

There is a special function inside GPOs that essentially blends computer and user configuration together, to be used in special cases: namely, if you have the requirement to push User Configuration settings to particular computers but want those computers to treat them as if they were Computer Configuration settings, applying the same policy settings to *any* user who was to log into that computer.

Maybe Laura in HR has a certain set of policies on her everyday workstation, but also occasionally logs into a public kiosk workstation sitting in the lobby. You have a set of lockdown restrictions that are applied to that kiosk, but since it is domain-joined normally when Laura logs into the kiosk, Group Policy would treat it just like it was her own workstation and apply all of the same user-based GPO settings. If you create a User Configuration GPO that has loopback policy processing enabled and link the GPO to this kiosk workstation, it will now apply all of those special configurations to Laura, even though she does not receive these GPO settings on her regular computer.

For more detail on loopback processing, I will once again direct you to the *Summary* section at the end of this chapter, where I'll refer you to a great location for learning more on this topic.

Policy vs preference

There is an important distinction that every Group Policy administrator needs to understand about GPO settings. There are two different types of policy settings, and they behave very differently. Now that we understand the differences between Computer Configuration and User Configuration, the next tier you'll notice inside Group Policy Management Editor are sub-folders titled **Policies** and **Preferences**.

Policies

Managed policies, the items listed under the Policies section of both computer and user configurations, generally behave like true gentlemen. These are settings that you put into place and expect results, forcing the setting into place, and nothing the user tries to do can change them. When reversing course and removing a GPO from a system, they happily comply. What do I mean by that? When you plug some policy settings into a GPO and then link that GPO to a location, you expect those settings to be put into place on the machines or users to which you have filtered the GPO. And that indeed works for any GPO setting, whether policy or preference, managed or unmanaged. But what about when that GPO no longer applies to a user or machine? What if you delete the GPO link, or adjust security filtering on the GPO so that it no longer applies to a workstation? Do those settings continue to be applied, or are they actively removed?

The answer to that question depends on whether you are working with a policy or a preference. True policy items will actively remove themselves from a computer when a GPO no longer applies. This is true of most built-in configuration settings inside Group Policy. Technically, under the hood, what is really happening is that Group Policy monitors four special sections of the Windows Registry and reprocesses through all of them during Group Policy refresh cycles. All GPO settings that affect these certain areas of the registry are capable of self-removal. Unmanaged policy settings, even some of those listed beneath the **Policies** folder, could potentially fail to remove their settings when a GPO is unlinked. It just depends on what setting you are talking about and what it is manipulating on the client machines to make the change.

Technically, there are managed policies and unmanaged policies – and both of these things are outside the scope of Group Policy preferences, which we will discuss next.

Preferences

Policies force things to happen, no matter what the user wants. Preferences, on the other hand, are often reversible by the user. Preferences are a good way to configure settings that will make life easier for the user, but you need to ultimately be OK with the fact that those changes and settings could be changed again manually by your users. Some GPO settings exist inside both policies and preferences, and this is your deciding factor – do you want to allow users to manipulate and change the configuration, or always force it into place?

Preferences are also sticky! While most policy settings will self-remove when a GPO stops applying to a computer, preferences do not. This is very important to understand when deleting GPOs or GPO links. Group Policy preferences do not live in those special sections of the registry that we talked about earlier, and so Windows is not actively rescanning those settings to find out whether they should continue to apply. When a GPO puts a preference setting into place, even though the user could adjust that setting if they wanted to, removal of the GPO will NOT revert the computer to its original, default state. The GPO preference setting will hang around and continue to apply to the machine even after the GPO is long gone. To change a preference setting back to defaults, the user will either have to adjust it themselves, or you will need to push out a new GPO that accomplishes that adjustment.

Default Domain Policy

Throughout this chapter, we have bounced in and out of the Group Policy Management Console a number of times, and now that you know what a GPO looks like and how to identify GPO links, you have probably noticed a GPO linked to the root of the domain called **Default Domain Policy**. This GPO comes built-in with Group Policy, every environment has one unless an admin has taken steps to delete it, which I would not recommend.

The Default Domain Policy applies to every user and computer that is part of your domain directory. Since this GPO is completely enabled right off the bat and applies to everyone, it is commonplace for companies to enforce global password policies or security rules that need to apply to everyone. In fact, many who are unfamiliar with Group Policy and uncomfortable with creating, linking, and filtering their own GPOs will just continually throw more and more settings inside Default Domain Policy. All of these settings will apply successfully, of course – to ALL users on ALL machines, including servers in your network. Eventually, this mentality is going to come back and bite hard.

My general rule is to never touch the Default Domain Policy except for one reason – creating global password expiry and complexity requirements within your domain. In fact, in some cases, not even a password policy is appropriate for the Default Domain Policy, for example, if you wanted to create a fine-grained password policy that comes with some additional bells and whistles, such as the ability to require different criteria for passwords on some users compared to others. We will cover fine-grained password policies in *Chapter 9*, *Hardening and Security*, so for the time being let's stick with the idea that we want to create one password policy and apply it to everyone. This seems like a good example to walk through, and remember – if you find yourself heading into the Default Domain Policy to do anything other than password management, you're probably doing it wrong. Just create your own GPO for crying out loud!

With any GPO that you see in the management console, if you right-click on that GPO and then choose **Edit...** you will see a new window open, and this GPO Editor contains all of the internals of that policy. This is where you make any settings or configurations that you want to be a part of that particular GPO. So, go ahead and edit your **Default Domain Policy**, and then navigate to **Computer Configuration | Policies | Windows Settings | Security Settings | Account Policies | Password Policy**:

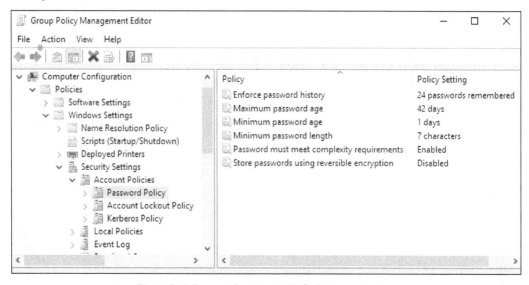

Figure 5.18: Password settings in Default Domain Policy

Here, you can see a list of the different options available to you for configuring the **Password Policy** within your domain. Double-clicking on any of these settings lets you modify them, and that change immediately starts to take effect on all of your domain-joined computers in the network. For example, you can see that the default **Minimum password length** is set to **7 characters**. Many companies have already gone through many discussions about their written policy on the standard length of passwords in the network, and in order to set up your new directory infrastructure to accept your decision, you simply modify this field. Changing the minimum password length to 14 characters here would immediately require the change to be made for all user accounts the next time they reset their passwords.

It's worth repeating: while the Default Domain Policy is a very quick and easy way to get some settings configured and pushed out to everyone, tread carefully when making changes to this default policy. Every time that you make a setting change here, remember that it is going to affect everyone in your domain, including yourself. Many times, you will be creating policies that do not need to apply to everyone. In those cases, it is highly recommended that you stay away from the Default Domain Policy. Instead, set up a new GPO for accomplishing whatever task it is that you are trying to put into place.

Administrative Templates

Go ahead and edit a GPO, any GPO, so that you have the Group Policy Management Editor open in front of you. Expand the **Policies** folder for either **Computer Configuration**, **User Configuration**, or both, and you will notice a folder inside each called **Administrative Templates**. Most of us generally think of Administrative Templates the same as any other GPO configuration setting, simply a collection of items with which you can manipulate users or computers, right? Sort of, but while **Software Settings** and **Windows Settings** are built into Group Policy and are basically the same for any domain environment, Administrative Templates are customizable.

Administrative Templates showcase the flexibility of Group Policy. Each setting within Administrative Templates is being pulled from template files that reside on your domain controller servers. These template files are ADMX files. All of the information needed to display the setting inside Group Policy Management Editor is contained inside these ADMX files. This includes items like which options the setting contains, any drop-down boxes that need to be displayed, and what the description fields will say when an admin double-clicks on the policy setting.

Along with each ADMX file comes an accompanying ADML file. This is a language file that is used to define the language for the settings contained within the ADMX file.

Back with Windows XP (and earlier), these file types did not exist. Settings inside Administrative Templates were based on ADM files instead. Nobody should be running Windows XP anymore, except I know that some of you are, because I still touch Windows XP machines at some of our customers at least once a month. So I figured I would include that info as an FYI. Sidenote: get rid of your Windows XP computers!

Windows 7 and newer know how to work with ADMX/ADML files, so I'm going to assume that your environment is fully up to date, and hopefully doesn't even have too many unsupported Windows 7 machines hanging around.

Implementing ADMX/ADML files

There are two reasons why you might find yourself monkeying around with ADMX files. The first is when moving to a newer version of Windows Server in your environment. Each release of the operating system – 2012, 2012R2, 2016, 2019 – comes with some new and updated Group Policy settings. When you install your first domain controller into the environment that happens to be running a newer platform, the setup process will generally run through a process called ADPrep. This process prepares the Active Directory schema for the new OS and also populates the new Group Policy settings. However, there are times that the first new release OS introduction you are making to the environment is not a domain controller. In this case, Group Policy won't be updated with new settings, but what if you wanted those new settings to be available within Group Policy anyway? Manually copying ADMX/ADML files into place could satisfy that need.

The second and most common reason to be plugging new ADMX/ADML files into place manually is when a software vendor, often Microsoft themselves, releases custom ADMX files. These files, when installed into Active Directory, will provide new settings inside Group Policy that don't exist natively inside Windows Server. Let's try it right now!

Google Chrome (did I just say those words in a Microsoft book???) is one of the most popular web browsers on the planet. The centralized configuration of Chrome is something that many administrators struggle with. What may or may not be news to you is that Google has its own set of ADMX files! You can plug these files into Group Policy and utilize Google-defined settings right from within GPMC to push Chrome-related settings and configurations out to your workforce.

First, we need to download these files. As of writing, this link will do the trick: https://dl.google.com/dl/edgedl/chrome/policy/policy_templates.zip.

If you are unable to use that link, simply perform a web search for `download chrome admx files` and you should be able to find it.

Copy these files to your domain controller and extract them so that you can find the ADMX and ADML files; they should be inside a folder called **windows**. The ADMX files are located right there inside the **windows** folder, and the ADML files will be grouped into folders by language. This matches what we will find inside Group Policy in just a minute. Now that you have the files in hand, go ahead and open the following folder on the domain controller:

`%systemroot%\PolicyDefinitions`

(On most servers this will be `C:\Windows\PolicyDefinitions`.)

In *Figure 5.19*, you can see my Chrome files that have been downloaded, alongside the **PolicyDefinitions** folder. As you can also see, there are already numerous ADMX files inside **PolicyDefinitions**, as to be expected. These ADMX files are the reason that we have any settings currently inside Group Policy, under the **Administrative Templates** folders:

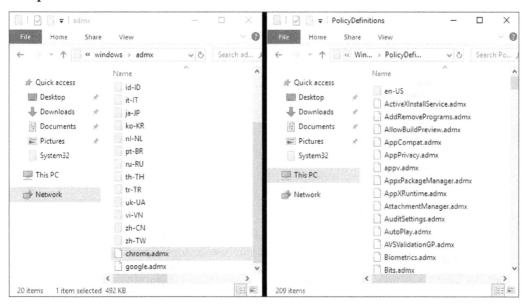

Figure 5.19: Copying new ADMX files to the domain controller

Simply copy your new Chrome ADMX files into **PolicyDefinitions**, and then copy the accompanying language ADML language file from its folder, into the corresponding language folder inside **PolicyDefinitions**. That's it! If you now close and reopen Group Policy Management Console, looking inside **Administrative Templates** displays the new Google Chrome settings, there are tons of them in here from those two little ADMX files:

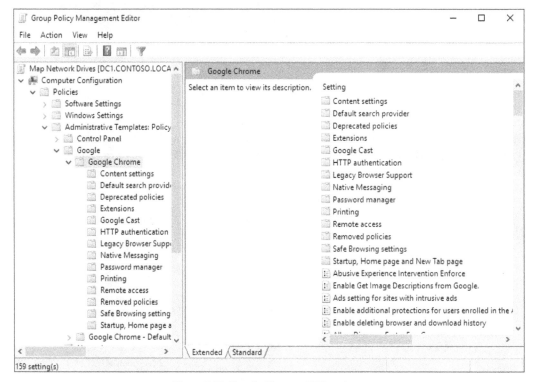

Figure 5.20: Google Chrome GPO settings

 For this particular example, I am working with my test lab and making the assumption that you have a single domain controller in your environment. If you have multiple DCs, you will either have to copy these files into `%systemroot%\PolicyDefinitions` on each of your domain controller servers or continue reading the next section of this chapter to learn more about the Central Store.

Central Store

When opening up the Group Policy Management Console and creating or editing a GPO, the settings available within your console session are settings pulled from ADMX/ADML files that are on the hard drive of the computer or server from which you are using GPMC. When implementing new settings via ADMX files, it would be a huge chore to have to copy those new files into place on every one of your domain controllers, in addition to all of the client computers where you might have the RSAT tools installed. Thankfully, there is a solution to automate this for you!

The Central Store is something that can be enabled in Active Directory that allows the replication of ADMX/ADML files. Once you enable the Central Store, all of your Group Policy management machines, such as domain controllers, will look to the store as its repository for these template files.

Enable the Central Store

All that it takes to enable the Central Store in Active Directory is the creation of two folders inside a special folder called **SYSVOL**. Once created, GPMC will check this location on subsequent launches, and pull in any new ADMX/ADML files that have been added. Log into a domain controller server, and create the following new folder:

`%systemroot%\SYSVOL\sysvol\contoso.local\Policies\PolicyDefinitions`

Create an additional folder within your new **PolicyDefinitions** folder to contain language-specific ADML files. In my case, I need one for English such as the following:

`%systemroot%\SYSVOL\sysvol\contoso.local\Policies\PolicyDefinitions\en-US`

Obviously you'll want to replace `contoso.local` with your own internal domain name, and you're finished! As soon as you have created these two new folders, utilize this location from this point forward to plug in new ADMX and ADML files, and those new settings will show up from wherever you launch GPMC in the future.

Populate the Central Store

You probably didn't have an immediate reason to check inside one of your GPOs and find out what the **Administrative Templates** folder looks like now that we enabled the Central Store, but let's go ahead and do that now. Open up GPMC and edit any of your existing GPOs. Take a look inside one of the **Administrative Templates** folders, and it's empty! You'll also notice that the name of the **Administrative Templates** folder has now changed to reflect the fact that it is looking to the Central Store for this information: **Administrative Templates: Policy definitions (ADMX files) retrieved from the central store**:

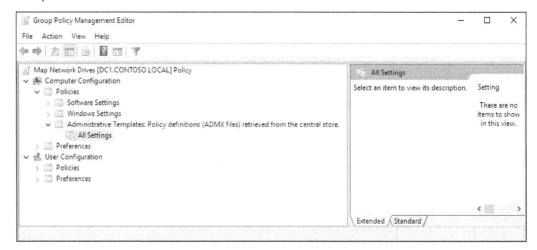

Figure 5.21: The Administrative Templates folder is empty!

Give us our settings back! Thankfully, they are still sitting on the hard drive of your domain controller, in the same location where we added the new Google settings just a few minutes ago. Perform the following file copy jobs, and you should be back in business with all settings now stored inside the Central Store.

Copy %systemroot%\PolicyDefinitions to %systemroot%\SYSVOL\sysvol\contoso.local\Policies\PolicyDefinitions.

Copy `%systemroot%\PolicyDefinitions\en-US` to `%systemroot%\SYSVOL\sysvol\`
`contoso.local\Policies\PolicyDefinitions\en-US` (adjust accordingly for
whichever languages you need):

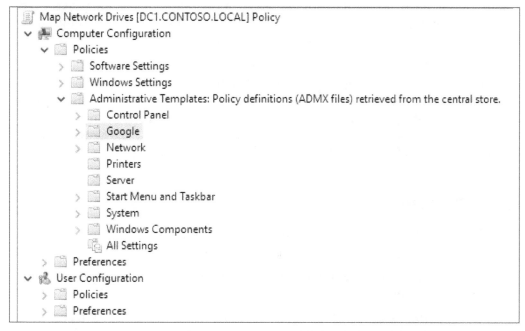

Figure 5.22: The Central Store is now populated with settings

As you can see, the **Administrative Templates** folder is still pulling from the Central
Store, but following our file copies, the Central Store is now populated with ADMX
files and settings to utilize inside a GPO. The Central Store is now available to all
domain controllers in your environment and is being replicated by **SYSVOL**.

Summary

Group Policy is an incredibly powerful tool to have at your disposal when working within a domain environment. Many pre-built configurations and settings exist, and since we can manipulate the registry on client machines, the sky is pretty much the limit on what you can manage on your client computers via GPOs.

As is the case with many topics inside Windows Server, there is so much information related to Group Policy that it warrants a book of its own. Thankfully, I had the opportunity to do exactly that! If you are interested in discovering more about Group Policy and all of the ways that it can be used to secure your infrastructure, check out my title *Mastering Windows Group Policy* (`https://www.packtpub.com/networking-and-servers/mastering-windows-group-policy`).

Questions

1. Are screensaver settings computer or user configuration?
2. Do domain-level or OU-level links process first?
3. What is the special GPO setting that forces user settings to apply to any user on a given computer?
4. What type of GPO filtering do you configure inside the GPO itself, such as with a mapped network drives policy?
5. True or false – It is possible for a user to override a Group Policy preference.
6. What is the default timer between Group Policy background refresh cycles?

6

Certificates in Windows Server 2019

"Ugh, we need to use certificates to make this work."

- Quote from an anonymous admin who just discovered their latest technology purchase requires the use of certificates in their organization

If the quote above sounds familiar, don't scrap that new project just yet! For some reason, the use of certificates seems like a daunting task to many of us, even those who have worked in IT for many years. I think this is probably because there are many different options available on a certificate server, but there is not a lot of common sense or user-friendliness built into the management console for dealing with certificates. This, combined with a general lack of requirements for certificates on servers for so many years, means that, even though this technology has existed for a long time, many server administrators have not had the opportunity to dig in and deploy certificates for themselves. I regularly deploy a couple of technologies that require the broad use of certificates in an organization, often needing to issue them to every workstation or user in the network, and I hear these kinds of concerns all the time. Issuing a certificate to a single business-critical webserver sounds daunting enough if you don't have any experience with the process, let alone issuing hundreds or thousands of certificates all at once.

Another common scenario is one where a company determined certificates to be in their best interests but lacked the on-staff resources to stand it up themselves, and so hired a third party to implement certificates within the network. While this gets certificates rolling, it often leaves a knowledge gap that never gets filled, so you may have a certificate server up and running, but not be at all comfortable modifying or utilizing it.

The broad term for a certificate environment is **public key infrastructure (PKI)**. I call that out specifically because you will probably see PKI listed in documentation or requirements at some point if you haven't already. Your PKI is provided by servers in your network and configuring those servers to issue certificates for you is the purpose of this chapter. The servers that you determine to be your certificate servers are known as **certification authority (CA)** servers, and we will refer to them as CA servers throughout this book.

To get you rolling with certificates in your network, here are the topics that we will cover in this chapter:

- Common certificate types
- Planning your PKI
- Creating a new certificate template
- Issuing your new certificates
- Creating an auto-enrollment policy
- Obtaining a public-authority SSL certificate
- Exporting and importing certificates

Common certificate types

There are a number of different types of certificates that you may find yourself needing to publish. As you will see, when you need a certificate that has a list of particular requirements, you can build a certificate template to whatever specifications you like. So, in a sense, there aren't really certificate *types* at all, but just certificate templates that you scope to contain whatever pieces of information are needed for that certificate to do its job. While this holds true technically, it is generally easier to segment certificates into different groups, making them more distinguishable for the particular job that they are intended to perform.

User certificates

As the name implies, a user certificate is one used for purposes that are specific to the username itself. One of the platforms that are driving more certificate adoption is the network authentication process. Companies that are looking into stronger authentication in their environments often look at certificates as part of that authentication process. Smart cards are one of the mechanisms that can be used for this purpose, specifically, some sort of physical card to be plugged into a computer in order for the user to gain access to that computer.

Smart cards can also be stored virtually within a special place on modern machines called the TPM. But that is a discussion for a different day. The reason we mention smart cards here is that, often, the core functionality of smart-card authentication is provided by a user certificate that has been stored on that smart card. If you find yourself in the middle of a project to deploy smart cards or some form of physical key login, you will probably find yourself in need of a PKI.

Another popular strong authentication form is **one-time passwords** (OTP). This requires the user to enter a randomly generated PIN in addition to their regular login criteria, and in some cases when the user enters their PIN, they are issued a temporary user certificate to be used as part of the authentication chain. Additional places where user certificates are commonly found include when companies employ file-encrypting technologies, such as EFS (short for Encrypting File System), or when building up **virtual private network (VPN)** systems to enable remote users to connect their laptops back to the corporate network. Many companies don't want to rely purely on a username and a password for VPN authentication, so issuing user certificates and requiring that they be present to build that VPN tunnel is commonplace.

Computer certificates

Often referred to as computer certificates or machine certificates, these guys get issued to computers to assist with the interaction between the network and the computer account itself. Technologies, such as SCCM, that interact with and manage the computer systems regardless of which users are logged into those computers make use of computer certificates. These kinds of certificates are also used for encryption processing between systems on the network, for example, if you were interested in using IPsec to encrypt communications between clients and a highly secure file server. Issuing computer or machine certificates to the endpoints within this communication chain would be essential to make that work properly. I often find myself issuing computer certificates to a business' machines to authenticate DirectAccess tunnels, a form of automated remote access. There are many different reasons and technologies you may be interested in that would require the issuance of certificates to the client workstations in your environment.

SSL certificates

If you find yourself in the middle of the certificate road, where you haven't really managed a CA server, but you have at one point issued and installed some kind of certificate, chances are that the certificate you worked with was an SSL certificate. This is by far the most common type of certificate used in today's technology infrastructure, and your company is more than likely using SSL certificates, even if you are not aware of them and do not have a single CA server running inside your network.

SSL certificates are most commonly used to secure website traffic. Any time you visit a website and see HTTPS in the address bar, your browser is using an SSL packet stream to send information back and forth between your computer and the webserver that you are talking to. The webserver has an SSL certificate on it, and your browser has checked over that certificate before allowing you onto the web page, to make sure that the certificate is valid and that the website really is what it says it is. You see, if we did not use SSL certificates on websites, anyone could impersonate our site and gain access to the information being passed to the website.

Let's provide a quick example. Let's say one of your users is at a coffee shop, using the public Wi-Fi. An attacker has figured out a way to manipulate DNS on that Wi-Fi network, and so when your user tries to visit mail.contoso.com in order to access their company's *Outlook on the web* to check email, the attacker has hijacked that traffic and the user is now sitting on a website that looks like their company portal but is actually a website hosted by the attacker. The user types in their username and password, and *bingo*, the attacker now has that user's credentials and can use them to access your real network. What prevents this from happening every day in the real world? **SSL certificates**. When you force your externally facing websites, such as that email login page, to be HTTPS sites, it requires the client browsers to check over the SSL certificate that is presented with the website. That SSL certificate contains information that only you as a company have; it cannot be impersonated. This way, when your user accesses your real login page, the browser checks out the SSL certificate, finds it to be correct, and simply continues on its merry way. The user never even knows they are being protected except for the little lock symbol up near their browser's address bar. On the other hand, if their traffic is being intercepted and redirected to a fake website, the SSL certificate check will fail (because the attacker would not have a valid SSL certificate for your company website name), and the user will be stopped in their tracks, at least to read through a certificate warning page before being able to proceed. At this point, the user should back off and realize that something is wrong and contact IT staff to look into the issue.

SSL certificates used by websites on the internet are almost always provided not by your internal CA server, but by a public certification authority. You have probably heard of many of them, such as Verisign, Entrust, DigiCert, and GoDaddy. Companies generally purchase SSL certificates from these public authorities because those authorities are trusted by default on new computers that users might purchase in the field. When you buy a new computer, even straight from a retail store, if you were to open up the local store of certificates that exists out of the box on that system, you would find a list of trusted root authorities. When you visit a website protected by an SSL certificate issued from one of these public authorities, that certificate, and therefore the website, is automatically trusted by this computer. The public CAs are publicly recognized entities, known for their capacity to securely issue SSL certificates.

When a company acquires an SSL certificate from one of these public authorities, there is an in-depth verification process that the authority goes through to make sure that the person requesting the certificate (you) is really someone with the proper company and authorized to issue these certificates. This is the basis of security in using SSL certificates from a public CA. All new computers know by default to trust certificates that have been issued by these authorities, and you don't have to take any special actions to make your websites function on the internet. On the other hand, it is possible to issue SSL certificates from a CA server that you built yourself and have running inside your network, but it requires a couple of things that make it difficult, because your CA server is obviously not trusted by all computers everywhere, nor should it be. First, if you want to issue your own SSL certificate for use on a public website, you need to externalize at least part of your internal PKI, known as the **certificate revocation list (CRL)**, to the internet. Any time you take a component that is internal to your network and publicize it on the internet, you are introducing a security risk, so unless you absolutely have to do this, it is generally not recommended. The second reason it is difficult to utilize your own SSL certificates on public websites is that only your own company's domain-joined computers will know how to trust this SSL certificate. So, if a user brings their company laptop home and uses it to access their email login page, it will probably work fine. But if a user tries to access the same email login page from their home computer, which is not part of your domain or network, they will get a certificate warning message and have to take special steps in order to gain access to the website. What a pain for the users. You should never encourage users to accept risk and proceed through a certificate warning message—this is a recipe for disaster, even if the certificate they are clicking through is one issued by your own CA. It's a matter of principle never to accept that risk.

These issues can be alleviated by purchasing an SSL certificate from one of those public CAs, and so purchasing these kinds of certificates is the normal and recommended way to make use of SSL on your publicly facing websites. Websites that are completely inside the network are a different story, since they are not facing the internet and their security footprint is much smaller. You can use your internal CA server to issue SSL certificates to your internal websites, and not have to incur the cost associated with purchasing certificates for all of those websites.

There are a few different tiers of SSL certificates that you can purchase from a public CA, information for which is listed on the authority's own websites. Essentially, the idea is that the more you pay, the more secure your certificate is. These tiers are related to the way that the authority validates against the certificate requester, since that is really where the security comes into play with SSL certificates. The authority is guaranteeing that when you access the page secured by their certificate, the certificate was issued to the real company that owns that web page.

Other than the validation tier, which you get to choose when purchasing a certificate, there is another option you have to decide on as well, and this one is much more important to the technical aspect of the way that certificates work. There are different naming conventions available to you when you purchase a certificate, and there is no best answer for which one to choose. Every situation that requires a certificate will be unique and will have to be evaluated individually to decide which naming scheme works best. Let's quickly cover three possibilities for an SSL certificate naming convention.

Single-name certificates

This is the cheapest and most common route to take when purchasing a certificate for an individual website. A single-name certificate protects and contains information about a single DNS name. When you are setting up a new website at `portal.contoso.com` and you want this website to protect some traffic by using HTTPS, you would install an SSL certificate onto the website. When you issue the request to your certification authority for this new certificate, you would input the specific name of `portal.contoso.com` into the **Common name** field of the request form. This single DNS name is the only name that can be protected and validated by this certificate.

Multi-domain or subject alternative name certificates

Multi-domain certificates, sometimes called subject alternative name (SAN) certificates, generally cost a little bit more than single-name certs, because they have more capabilities. When you request a SAN certificate, you have the option of defining multiple DNS names that the certificate can protect. Once issued, the SAN certificate will contain a primary DNS name, which is typically the main name of the website, and, further inside the cert properties, you will find listed the additional DNS names that you specified during your request. This single certificate can be installed on a webserver and used to validate traffic for any of the DNS names that are contained in the certificate. Use-case examples of a SAN certificate are when setting up a Lync (Skype for Business) server, or an Exchange server. Lync uses many different DNS names, but all names are within the same DNS domain. Here is an example list of the names we might include in a single SAN certificate for the purposes of Lync:

- Lync.contoso.com (the primary one)
- Lyncdiscover.contoso.com
- Meet.contoso.com
- Dialin.contoso.com
- Admin.contoso.com

These different websites/services used by Lync are then implemented across one or multiple servers, and you can utilize the same SAN certificate on all of those servers in order to validate traffic that is headed toward any of those DNS names.

Wildcard certificates

Last but certainly not least is the wildcard certificate. This is the luxury model, the one that has the most capabilities, gives you the most flexibility, and at the same time offers the easiest path to implementation on many servers. The name on a wildcard certificate begins with a **star** (*). This star means *any*, as in *anything preceding the DNS domain name* is covered by this certificate. If you own contoso.com and plan to stand up many public DNS records that will flow to many different websites and webservers, you could purchase a single wildcard certificate with the name *.contoso.com, and it may cover all of your certificate needs.

Typically, wildcards can be installed on as many webservers as you need, with no limit on the number of different DNS names that they can validate. I have run across an exception to this once, when a particular customer's agreement with their certification authority specified that they had to report and pay for each instance of their wildcard certificate that was in use. So watch those agreements when you make them with your CA. Most of the time, a wildcard is meant to be a free-for-all within the company so that you can deploy many sites and services across many servers and utilize your wildcard certificate everywhere.

The downside of a wildcard certificate is that it costs more, significantly more. But if you have large certificate needs or big plans for growth, it will make your certificate administration much easier, faster, and cost-effective in the long run.

Planning your PKI

Since we are revolving all of our discussion in this book around Windows Server 2019, this means that your internal CA server can and should be one provided by this latest and greatest of operating systems. As with most capabilities in Server 2019, the creation of a certification authority server in your network is as simple as installing a Windows role. When you go to add the role to a new server, it is the very first role in the list, **Active Directory Certificate Services (AD CS)**. When installing this role, you will be presented with a couple of important options, and you must understand the meaning behind them before you create a solid PKI environment.

 Your server's hostname and domain status cannot be changed after implementing the CA role. Make sure you have set your final hostname and joined this server to the domain (if applicable), prior to installing the AD CS role. You won't be able to change those settings later!

Role services

The first decision you need to make when installing the AD CS role is which role services you would like to install, as you can see in *Figure 6.1*:

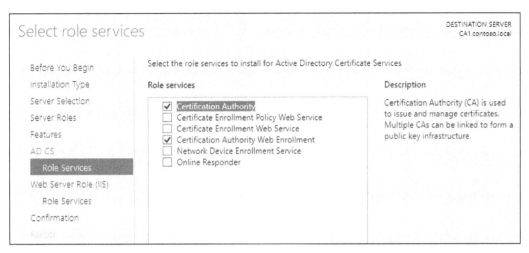

Figure 6.1: Installing the AD CS role

Clicking on each option will give you a description of its capabilities, so you can probably determine which pieces of the role you need by poking around on this screen. Here is a short summary of these options. Note that I am listing them out of order, because of the way that I typically see them configured in the field:

- **Certification Authority**: This is the primary certificate engine that needs to be installed in order for this server to officially become a CA.

- **Certification Authority Web Enrollment**: Often, this one gets installed as well, especially in environments that are small enough to be running a single CA server for the entire environment. The web-enrollment portion will install IIS (webserver) capabilities on this server and launch a small website that is used for the purposes of requesting certificates. We will discuss this further when we walk through issuing certificates from this web interface, later in the chapter.

- **Certificate Enrollment Web Service and Certificate Enrollment Policy Web Service**: Most of the time, we are only concerned with issuing certificates to our company-owned, domain-joined systems. In those cases, these two selections are not necessary. If you plan to issue certificates to non-domain-joined computers from this CA server, you want to select these options.

- **Network Device Enrollment Service**: As the name implies, this piece of the CA role provides the capability to issue certificates to routers and other kinds of networking devices.

- **Online Responder**: This is a special function reserved for larger environments. Inside every certificate is a specification for a CRL. When a client computer utilizes a certificate, it reaches out and checks against this CRL in order to make sure that its certificate has not been revoked. The CRL is an important piece of the certificate security puzzle; in an environment with thousands of clients, your CRL may be very, very busy responding to all of these requests. You can deploy additional CA servers that are running Online Responder to help ease that load.

For the purposes of our lab, and to cover the required capabilities of most small-to-medium businesses out there, I am going to select the two options shown in *Figure 6.1*: **Certification Authority** and **Certification Authority Web Enrollment**.

Enterprise versus Standalone

Following the installation of your AD CS role, Server Manager will notify you that certificate services need some additional configuration, as is common with many role installations. When configuring your CA role for the first time, you will be presented with a big choice. Do you want this CA server to be an **enterprise CA** or a **standalone CA**?

Let's start with the enterprise CA. As the wizard will tell you, an enterprise CA server must be a member of your domain, and these certificate servers typically stay online so that they can issue certificates to computers and users who need them. Wait a minute! Why in the world would we want to turn a certificate server off anyway? We will discuss that in a minute, but if you intend to utilize this CA to issue certificates, it must obviously remain turned on. Most CA servers within a domain environment will be enterprise CAs. When creating an enterprise CA, your templates and some certificate-specific information can store themselves within Active Directory, which makes integration between certificates and the domain tighter and more beneficial. If this is your first interaction with the CA role, I recommend you start with an enterprise CA because this better meets the needs of most organizations.

As you can correctly infer from the preceding text, this means that a standalone CA is less common to see in the wild. Standalones can be members of the domain, or they can remain out of that part of the network and reside on a local workgroup. If you had a security requirement that dictated that your certificate server could not be domain-joined, that might be a reason you would use a standalone CA. Another reason might be because Active Directory simply does not exist in the chosen environment.

In my eyes, it would be extremely rare to find a network where someone was trying to use Windows Server 2019 as their certification authority and at the same time was not running Active Directory Domain Services, but I'm sure there is a corner case somewhere that is doing exactly this. In that case, you would also need to choose standalone. A third example when you would choose standalone is the event we alluded to already, where you might have a reason to turn off your server. When you run this scenario, it is typically referred to as having an **offline root**. We haven't talked about root CAs yet, but we will in a minute. When you run an offline root, you create the top level of your PKI hierarchy as a standalone root CA, and then you build subordinate CAs underneath it. Your subordinate CAs are the ones doing the grunt work issuing certificates — which means that the root can be safely shut down since it doesn't have any ongoing duties. Why would you want to do this? Well, most companies don't, but I have worked with some that have very high-level security policies, and this is why you might visit this topic. If all of a company's CA servers are tied together as enterprise CAs with all of their information being stored inside Active Directory, a compromise to one of the subordinate issuing CAs could spell disaster for your entire PKI. It is possible that the only way to remediate an attack would be to wipe out the whole PKI environment, all of the CA servers, and build them up again. If you had to do this, it would mean not only rebuilding your servers but also re-issuing brand new copies of all your certificates to every user and device that has them.

On the other hand, if you were running a standalone root CA that was offline, it would not have been affected by the attack. In this case, you could tear down your affected certificate servers, but your core root server would have been safely hidden. You could then bring this root back online, rebuild new subordinates from it, and have an easier path to being 100% operational because your root keys that are stored within the CA would not have to be re-issued, as they never would have been compromised in the attack.

As I said, I do not see this very often in the field, but it is a possibility. If you are interested in learning more about offline root CAs and their uses, I highly recommend checking out the TechNet article at http://social.technet.microsoft. com/wiki/contents/articles/2900.offline-root-certification-authority-ca. aspx. If you're thinking about moving forward with an offline root CA only because it seems like it's more secure, but you don't have a specific reason for doing so, I recommend you change gears and go ahead with an online enterprise root CA. While there are some security advantages to the offline root, most companies do not find those advantages to be worth the extra hassle that accompanies using an offline root CA. There are usability trade-offs when going the offline route.

In most cases, you'll want to select **Enterprise CA** and proceed from there.

Root versus subordinate (issuing)

This is the second big choice you need to make when building a new CA. Is your new server going to be a **root CA** or a **subordinate CA**? In some cases, even in a lot of Microsoft documentation, a subordinate CA is more often called an issuing CA. Generally, in a multi-tiered PKI, the subordinate/issuing CAs are the ones that do the issuing of certificates to users and devices in your network.

The difference really is just a matter of what you want your CA hierarchy to look like. In a PKI tree, there is a single high-level certificate, self-signed to itself by the root CA, that everything chains up to. A subordinate CA, on the other hand, is one that resides below a root CA in the tree, and it has been issued a certificate of its own from the root above it.

If your plans are to only run a single CA server, it must be a root. If you are creating a tiered approach to issuing certificates, the first CA in your environment needs to be a root, and you can slide subordinates in underneath it. You are allowed to have multiple roots, and therefore multiple trees, within a network. So your particular PKI can be structured however you see fit. In smaller companies, it is very common to see only a single CA server, an enterprise root. For the sake of simplicity in administration, these customers are willing to take the risk that, if something happens to that server, it won't be that big a deal to build a new one and reissue certificates.

For larger networks, it is more common to see a single root with a couple of subordinates below it. Typically, in this case, the root is only responsible for being the top dog and the holder of important keys, and the subordinate CAs are the ones doing the real work—issuing certificates to the clients.

Naming your CA server

At this point, now that you have installed the role, the hostname of the server itself is set in stone. You already knew this. But as you progress through the wizards to configure your CA for the first time, you will come across a screen called **Specify the name of the CA**. Huh? I thought we already did that when we set the hostname?

Nope, we do have our final hostname and that server name is plugged into Active Directory as my server is joined to the domain, but the actual "CA name" is something else altogether. This is the name that will be identified inside the properties of every certificate that this CA issues. This is also a name that will be configured in various places inside Active Directory, since I am building an Enterprise CA. The wizard identifies a possible name for you to use, which many administrators simply take and use. If you want to configure your own name, this is where you should do it. Once you set the name here, this is the name of the CA forever:

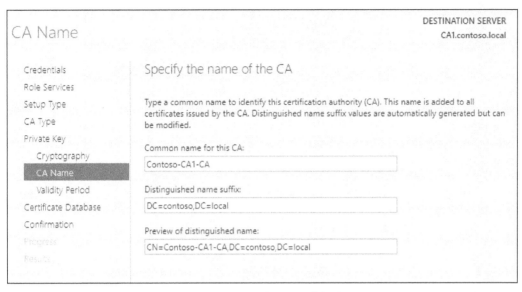

Figure 6.2: Setting the name of the CA

Can I install the CA role onto a domain controller?

Since the role is officially called the **Active Directory Certificate Services** role, does that mean I should install this role onto one of my domain controller servers? No! Unfortunately, I have run across many small-to-medium businesses that have done exactly this, and luckily they don't have too many problems. So technically, it does work. However, it is not a Microsoft-recommended installation path, and you should build your CAs on their own servers; try *not* to co-host them with *any* other roles whenever possible.

Creating a new certificate template

Enough talk. It's time to get some work done. Now that our CA role has been installed, let's make it do something! The purpose of a certificate server is to issue certificates, right? So, shall we do that? Not so fast. When you issue a certificate from a CA server to a device or user, you are not choosing which *certificate* you want to deploy; rather you are choosing which **certificate template** you want to utilize to deploy a certificate based upon the settings configured inside that template. Certificate templates are sort of like recipes for cooking. On the CA server, you build out your templates and include all of the particular ingredients, or settings, that you want to incorporate into your final certificate.

Then, when the users or computers come to request a certificate from the CA server, they are sort of baking a certificate into their system by telling the CA which template recipe to follow when building that certificate. Certificates relating to food? Maybe that's a stretch, but it's getting pretty late at night, and apparently I'm hungry.

When you walk through the steps to configure your first CA server, it comes with some pre-built certificate templates right in the console. In fact, one of those templates, called **Computer**, is typically preconfigured to the point where, if a client computer were to reach out and request a computer certificate from your new CA, it would be able to successfully issue one. However, where is the fun in using prebuilt templates and certificates? I would rather build my own template so that I can specify particular configurations and settings inside that template. This way, I know exactly what settings are contained within my certificates that will ultimately be issued to my computers in the network.

Once again, we need to launch the proper administrative console in order to do our work. Inside the **Tools** menu of **Server Manager**, click on **Certification Authority**. Once inside, you can expand the name of your certification authority and see some folders, including one at the bottom called **Certificate Templates**. If you click on this folder, you will see a list of the templates that are currently built into our CA server. Since we do not want to utilize one of these pre-existing templates, it is common sense that we will try to right-click in here and create a new template, but this is actually not the correct place to build a new template. The reason why new certificate templates are not built right from this screen must be above my pay grade because it seems silly that they aren't. Alas, in order to get into the proper screen for managing and modifying our templates, you need to right-click on the **Certificate Templates** folder, and then choose **Manage**:

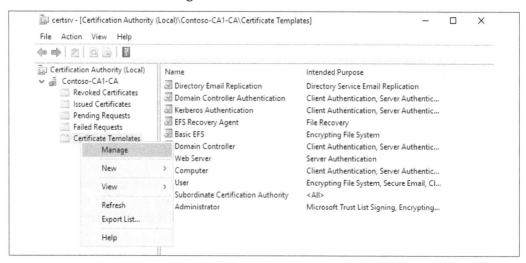

Figure 6.3: Managing certificate templates

Now you see a much more comprehensive list of templates, including a number of them you couldn't view on the first screen. To build a new template, what we want to do is find a pre-existing template that functions similarly to the purpose that we want our new certificate template to serve. Computer templates are becoming commonly issued across many organizations due to more and more technologies requiring these certificates to exist. Yet, we don't want to utilize that baked-in template, which is simply called **Computer**, because we want our template to have a more specific name and we want the flexibility to modify template settings. Perhaps we want the certificate's validity period to be longer than the default settings. Right-click on the built-in **Computer** template and click on **Duplicate Template**. This opens the **Properties** screen for our new template, from which we first want to give our new template a unique name inside the **General** tab.

In an upcoming chapter, we will discuss DirectAccess, the remote access technology that will be used in our environment. A good implementation of DirectAccess includes machine certificates being issued to all mobile client workstations, so we will plan to make use of this new template for those purposes. The **General** tab is also the place where we get to define our validity period for this certificate, which we will set to **2** years:

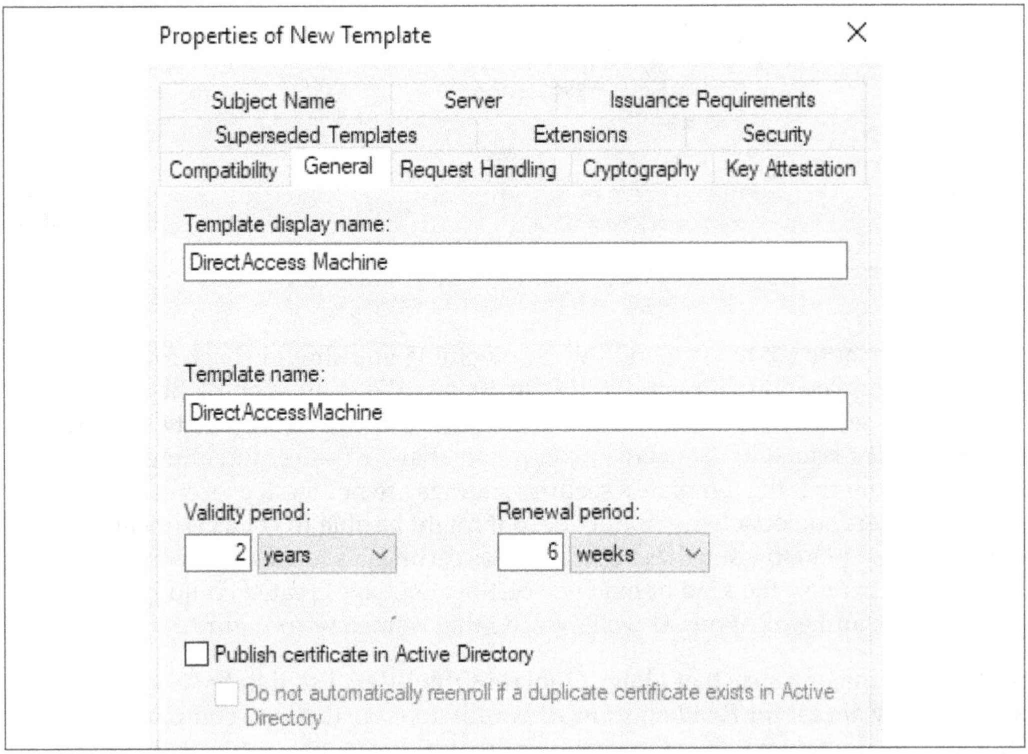

Figure 6.4: The General tab

If the certificates that you want to issue require any additional setting changes, you can flip through the available tabs inside **Properties** and make the necessary adjustments. For our example, another setting I will change is inside the **Subject Name** tab. I want my new certificates to have a subject name that matches the common name of the computer where it is being issued, so I have chosen **Common name** from the drop-down list:

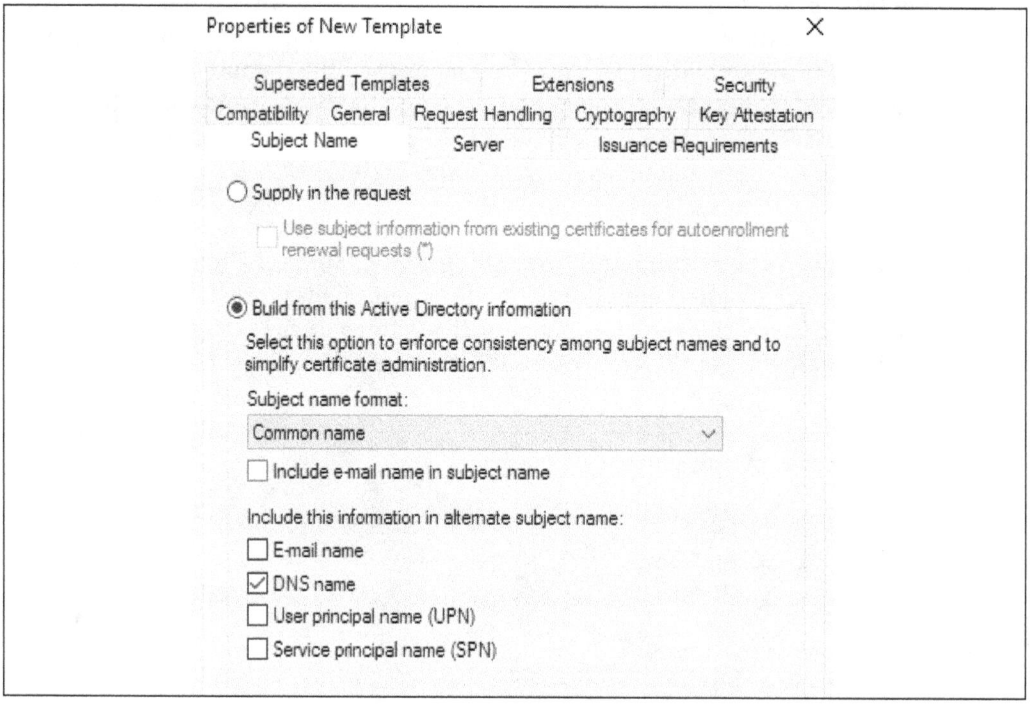

Figure 6.5: The Subject Name tab

We have one more tab to visit, and this is something you should check for every certificate template that you build: the **Security** tab. We want to check here to make sure that the security permissions for this template are set in a way that allows the certificate to be issued to the users or computers that we desire, and at the same time make sure that the template's security settings are not too loose, creating a situation where someone who doesn't need it might be able to get a certificate. For our example, I plan to issue these DirectAccess certificates to all of the computers in the domain, because the kind of machine certificate I have created could be used for general IPsec authentications as well, which I may someday configure.

So, I am just making sure that I have **Domain Computers** listed in the **Security** tab, and that they are set for **Read** and **Enroll** permissions, so that any computer that is joined to my domain will have the option of requesting a new certificate based on my new template:

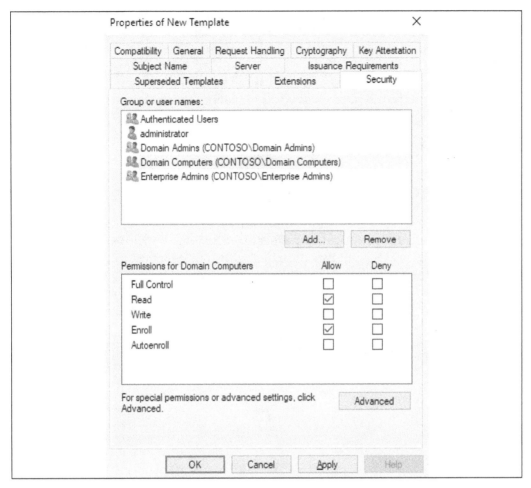

Figure 6.6: Certificate permissions

Since that is everything I need inside my new certificate, I simply click on **OK**, and my new certificate template is now included in the list of templates on my CA server.

Issuing your new certificates

Next comes the part that trips up a lot of people on their first attempt. You now have a brand new template to issue, and we have verified that the permissions within that certificate template are appropriately configured so that any computer that is a member of our domain should be able to request one of these certificates, right? So our logical next step would be to jump onto a client computer and request a certificate, but there is first one additional task that needs to be accomplished in order to make that possible.

Even though the new template has been **created**, it has not yet been **published**. So at the moment, the CA server will not offer our new template as an option to the clients, even though security permissions are configured for it to do so. The process to publish a certificate template is very quick—only a couple of mouse clicks—but unless you know about the need to do this, it can be a very frustrating experience because nothing in the interface gives you a hint about this requirement.

Publishing the template

If your **Certificate Templates Console** is still open (the one where we were managing our templates), close it so you are back at the main certification authority management console. Remember how we noticed that the list of available certificate templates that shows up here is much shorter? This is because only these certificate templates are currently published and available to be issued. In order to add additional templates to the published list, including our new one, we simply right-click on the **Certificate Templates** folder and then navigate to **New | Certificate Template to Issue**:

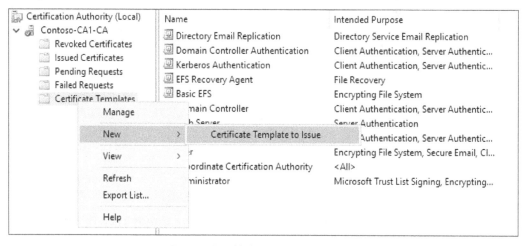

Figure 6.7: Publishing our new template

Now we are presented with a list of the available templates that are not yet issued. All you need to do is choose your new template from the list and click on **OK**. The new template is now included in the list of published certificate templates, and we are ready to request one from a client computer:

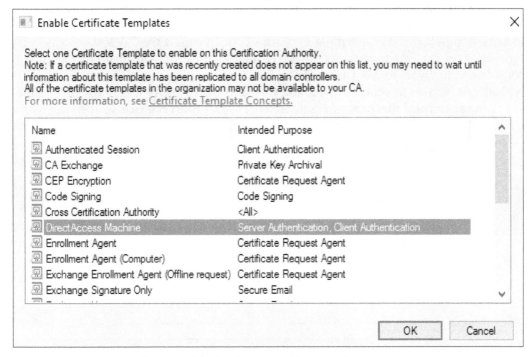

Figure 6.8: Selecting the new certificate template to issue

If you look through this list and do not see your newly created template, you may have to take an additional step. Sometimes simply waiting will resolve this behavior, because occasionally the reason that the new template does not show up in the list is that you are waiting for your domain controllers to finish replicating. At other times, you will find that, even after waiting for a while, your new template is still not in this list. In that case, you probably just need to restart the certification authority service to force it to pull in the new template information. To restart the CA service, you right-click on the CA's name near the top of the **Certification Authority** management console and navigate to **All Tasks | Stop Service**. The stopping of that service typically only takes a second or two, and then you can immediately right-click on the CA name again, and this time navigate to **All Tasks | Start Service**, as seen in *Figure 6.9*. Now, try to publish your new template again, and you should see it in the list:

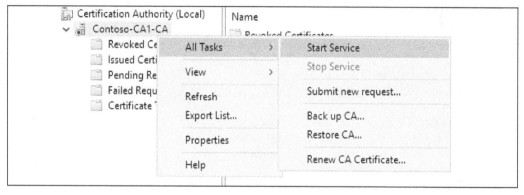

Figure 6.9: Restarting the CA service

Requesting a cert from MMC

Our new certificate template has been created, and we have successfully published it within the CA console, thereby making it officially ready for issuing. It's time to test that out. Go ahead and log into a regular client computer on your network in order to do this. There are a couple of standard ways to request a new certificate on a client computer. The first is by using the good old MMC console. On your client computer, launch MMC and add the snap-in for **Certificates**. When you choose **Certificates** from the list of available snap-ins and click on the **Add** button, you are presented with some additional options for which certificate store you want to open. You get to choose between opening certificates for the **User account**, **Service account**, or **Computer account**. Since we are trying to issue a certificate that will be used by the computer itself, I want to choose **Computer account** from this list, and click on **Finish**:

Figure 6.10: Snapping-in computer certificates

On the next page, click on the **Finish** button again in order to choose the default option, which is **Local computer**. This will snap in the local machine's computer-based certificate store inside MMC.

On more recent operating systems, such as Windows 8 and 10 and with Windows Server 2012, 2012R2, 2016, and 2019, there is an MSC shortcut for opening directly into the local computer's certificate store. Simply type CERTLM.MSC into a **Run** prompt and MMC will automatically launch and create this snap-in for you.

When you are installing certificates onto a computer or server, this is generally the place you want to visit. Inside this certificate store, the specific location that we want to install our certificate into is the **Personal** folder. This is true whether you are installing a machine certificate as we are doing here, or are installing an SSL certificate onto a webserver. The local computer's personal certificate folder is the correct location for both kinds of certificates. If you click on **Personal**, you can see that we do not currently have anything listed in there:

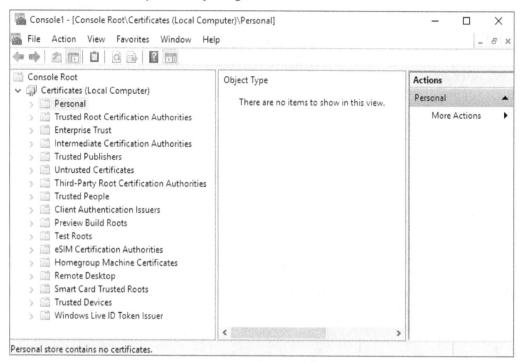

Figure 6.11: Personal is empty

To request a new certificate from our CA server, we simply right-click on the **Personal** folder, and then navigate to **All Tasks | Request New Certificate...**. Doing so opens a wizard; go ahead and click on the **Next** button once.

Now you encounter the screen shown in *Figure 6.12*, which looks like something needs to be done, but in most cases, because we are requesting a certificate on one of our corporate, domain-joined machines, we actually do not need to do anything on the screen presented in the following screenshot. Simply click on **Next** again and the wizard will query Active Directory in order to show all of the certificate templates that are available to be issued:

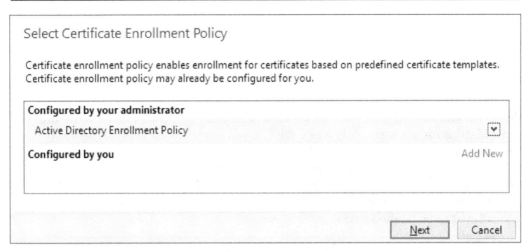

Figure 6.12: Click Next to query Active Directory

Next, the **Request Certificates** screen is shown, which is the list of templates that are available to us. This list is dynamic; it is based on what computer you are logged into and what your user account permissions are. Remember when we set up the security tab of our new certificate template? It is there that we defined who and what could pull down new certificates based on that template, and, if I had defined a more particular group than domain computers, it is possible that my new **DirectAccess Machine** template would not be displayed in this list. However, since I did open up that template to be issuable to any computer within our domain, I can see and select it here:

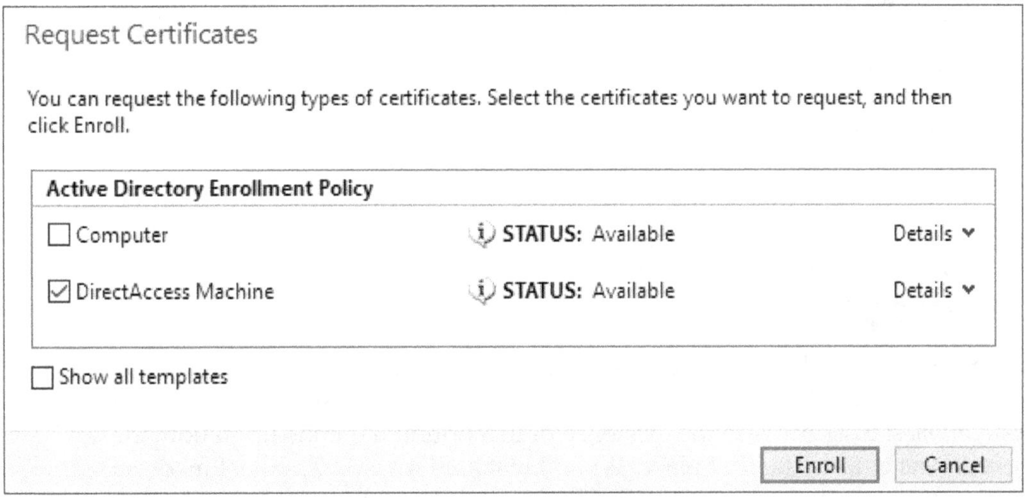

Request Certificates

You can request the following types of certificates. Select the certificates you want to request, and then click Enroll.

Active Directory Enrollment Policy

☐ Computer ⓘ **STATUS:** Available Details ⌄

☑ DirectAccess Machine ⓘ **STATUS:** Available Details ⌄

☐ Show all templates

Enroll Cancel

Figure 6.13: Certificate templates available for issuing

If you do not see your new template in the list, click on the **Show all templates** checkbox. This will give you a full list of all the templates on the CA server, and a description of each one as to the reason that it is currently unavailable for issuing.

Put a checkmark next to any certificates that you want and click **Enroll**. Now the console spins for a few seconds while the CA server processes your request and issues a new certificate that is specific to your computer and the criteria that we placed inside the certificate template. Once finished, you can see that our brand new machine certificate is now inside **Personal | Certificates** in the MMC. If you double-click on the certificate, you can check over its properties to ensure all of the settings you wanted to be pushed into this cert exist:

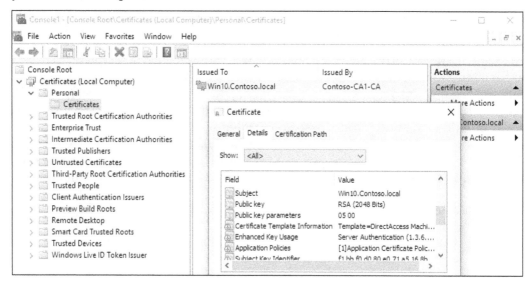

Figure 6.14: Certificate properties

Requesting a certificate from the web interface

I typically use the MMC for requesting certificates whenever possible, but, in most cases, there is another platform from which you can request and issue certificates. I say *in most cases* because the existence of this option depends upon how the CA server was built in the first place. When I installed my AD CS role, I made sure to choose the options for both **Certification Authority** and **Certification Authority Web Enrollment**.

This second option is important for our next section of text. Without the web enrollment piece of the role, we would not have a web interface running on our CA server, and this part would not be available to us. If your CA server does not have web enrollment turned on, you can revisit the role installation page in Server Manager and add it to the existing role:

Figure 6.15: Installing Certification Authority Web Enrollment

Once **Certification Authority Web Enrollment** is installed on your CA, there is a website running on that server that you can access via a browser from inside your network. Having this website is useful if you have the need for users to be able to issue their own certificates for some reason; it would be much easier to give them documentation or train them on the process of requesting a certificate from a website than expecting them to navigate the MMC console. Additionally, if you are trying to request certificates from computers that are not within the same network as the CA server, using MMC can be difficult. For example, if you have the need for a user at home to be able to request a new certificate, without a full VPN tunnel the MMC console is more than likely not going to be able to connect to the CA server in order to pull down that certificate. But since we have this certificate enrollment website running, you could externally publish this website as you do with any other website in your network, using a reverse proxy or firewall in order to keep that traffic safe and present users with the ability to hit this site and request certificates from wherever they are.

To access this website, let's use our regular client computer again. This time, instead of opening MMC, I will simply launch Internet Explorer, or any other browser, and log into the website running at `https://<CASERVER>/certsrv`. For my specific environment, that exact web address is `https://CA1/certsrv`:

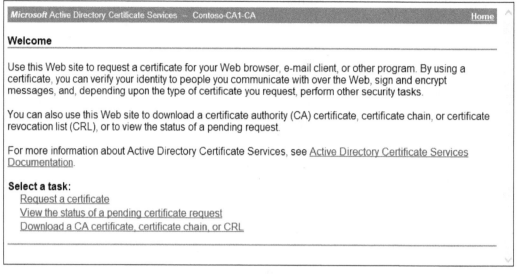

Microsoft Active Directory Certificate Services — Contoso-CA1-CA   Home

Welcome

Use this Web site to request a certificate for your Web browser, e-mail client, or other program. By using a certificate, you can verify your identity to people you communicate with over the Web, sign and encrypt messages, and, depending upon the type of certificate you request, perform other security tasks.

You can also use this Web site to download a certificate authority (CA) certificate, certificate chain, or certificate revocation list (CRL), or to view the status of a pending request.

For more information about Active Directory Certificate Services, see Active Directory Certificate Services Documentation.

Select a task:
Request a certificate
View the status of a pending certificate request
Download a CA certificate, certificate chain, or CRL

Figure 6.16: Viewing the CA web enrollment site

Our URL starts with HTTPS. This website must be configured to run on HTTPS instead of regular HTTP in order to allow the website to request certificates. It does not allow issuing certificates over HTTP because that information would be traveling in cleartext to the client. Enabling the website on the CA server for HTTPS ensures that the certificate issued will be encrypted while it travels.

Clicking on the **Request a certificate** link brings you into our wizard in which we can request a new certificate from the CA server. When you have users driving their own way through this web interface, it is typically for the purpose of a user-based certificate, since we have some pretty easy ways of automatically distributing computer-level certificates without any user interaction. We will discuss that in a moment. However, for this example, since we are asking our users to log in here and request a new **User Certificate**, on the next page, I will choose that link:

Figure 6.17: Selecting a certificate type

 If you were not interested in a user certificate and wanted to use the web interface to request a machine certificate, a webserver certificate, or any other kind of certificate, you could instead choose the link for **advanced certificate request** and follow the prompts to do so.

Next, click the **Submit** button, and, once the certificate has been generated, you will see a link that allows you to **Install this certificate**. Click on that link, and the new certificate that was just created for you will be installed onto your computer. You can see in the following screenshot the response that the website gave me, indicating a successful installation, and you can also see I have opened up the current user certificates inside MMC in order to see and validate that the certificate really exists:

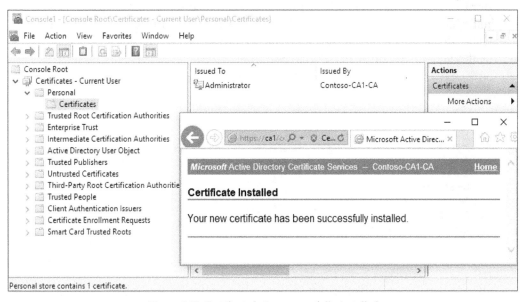

Figure 6.18: Certificate being successfully installed

In this section, we have proven that our CA server is working; follow along with the next few pages as we take certificate issuance to the next level.

Creating an auto-enrollment policy

Our certification authority server is configured and running, and we can successfully issue certificates to the client machines. Great! Now let's pretend we have a new project on our plates, and one of the requirements for this project is that all of the computers in your network need to have a copy of this new machine certificate that we have created. Uh oh, that sounds like a lot of work. Even though the process for requesting one of these certificates is very quick—only a handful of seconds on each workstation—if you had to do that individually on a couple of thousand machines, you'd be talking about a serious period of time needing to be spent on this process. Furthermore, in many cases, the certificates that you issue will only be valid for one year. Does this mean I am facing an extreme amount of administrative work every single year to re-issue these certificates as they expire? Certainly not!

Let's figure out how to utilize Group Policy to create a GPO that will **auto-enroll** our new certificates to all of the machines in the network, and, while we are in there, also configure it so that when a certificate's expiration date comes up, the certificate will auto-renew at the appropriate intervals.

Let's pop into the Certification Authority management console on our CA server and take a look inside the **Issued Certificates** folder. I only want to look here for a minute in order to see how many certificates we have issued so far in our network. It looks like just a handful of them, so hopefully once we are done configuring our policy, if we have done it correctly, and it takes effect automatically, we should see more certificates starting to show up in this list:

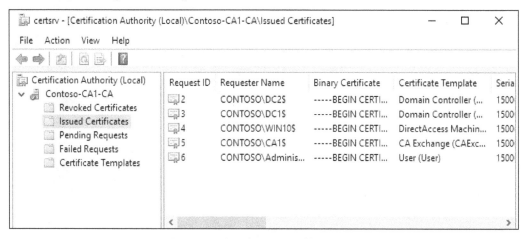

Figure 6.19: Certificates issued by our CA

Log into a domain controller server, and then open up the **Group Policy Management** console. I have created a new GPO called **Enable Certificate Auto-enrollment**, and am now editing that GPO to find the settings I need to configure in order to make this GPO do its work:

Figure 6.20: Editing the new Auto-enrollment GPO

The settings inside this GPO that we want to configure are located at **Computer Configuration | Policies | Windows Settings | Security Settings | Public Key Policies | Certificate Services Client - Auto-Enrollment**.

Double-click on this setting to view its properties. All we need to do is change **Configuration Model** to **Enabled**, and make sure to check the box that says **Renew expired certificates, update pending certificates, and remove revoked certificates**. Also check the box for **Update certificates that use certificate templates**. These settings will ensure that auto-renewal happens automatically when the certificates start running into their expiration dates over the next few years:

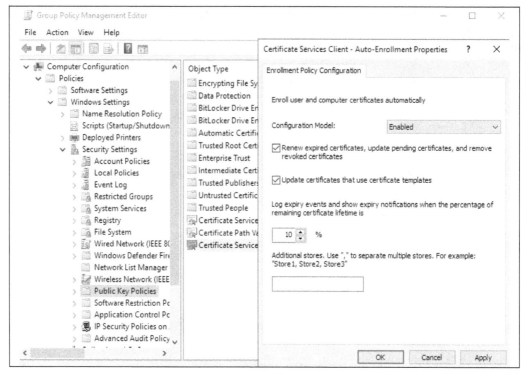

Figure 6.21: Enabling Auto-Enrollment

What is the last thing we need to do on our GPO in order to make it live? Create a link so that it starts applying! For your own environment, you will probably create a more specific link to a particular OU, as we discussed in the last chapter, but, for my lab, I want these certificates to apply to every single machine that is joined to the domain, so I will link my new GPO at the root of the domain so that it applies to all of my clients and servers.

Now that the GPO is created and configured, and we have linked it to the domain, I would think that some new certificates would be issued and there would be more names shown inside my **Issued Certificates** folder inside my certification authority console. But there are not. Wait a minute, in our GPO, we didn't really specify anything particular to my DirectAccess Machine cert template, did we? Could that be the problem? No, there wasn't really an option for specifying which template I wanted to set up for auto-enrollment.

When you enable auto-enrollment in **Group Policy**, you are simply flipping an on/off switch and turning it on for *every* certificate template. So now that we have a policy that is configured to enable auto-enrollment and is linked to the domain, thus making it *live*, auto-enrollment has been enabled on every domain-joined computer, for **every certificate template** that is published on our CA server.

Yet, none of them are issuing themselves to my computers. This is because we need to adjust the security settings on our new DirectAccess Machine template. Currently, we have it configured so that all domain computers have **Enroll** permissions, but if you remember that **Security** tab within the cert template's properties, there was an additional security identifier called **Autoenroll**. Every certificate template has the **Autoenroll** permission identifier, and it is not allowed by default. Now that the light switch has been flipped ON for auto-enrollment in our domain, we need to enable the **Autoenroll** permission on any template that we want to start distributing itself. As soon as we enable that permission, these certificates will start flowing around our network.

Head into the certificate-management section of your CA server and open **Properties** of your new template, then make your way to the **Security** tab and allow **Autoenroll** permissions for the **Domain Computers** group. This should tell the CA to start distributing these certificates accordingly:

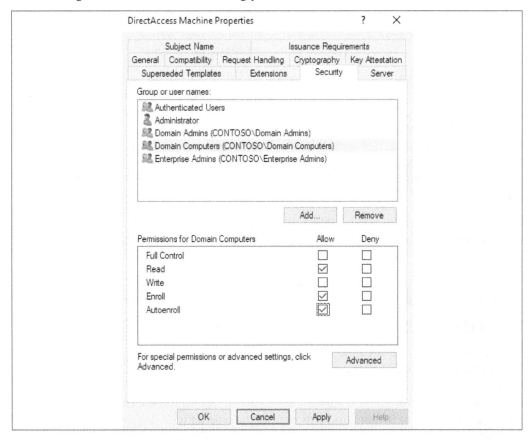

Figure 6.22: Template security for Autoenroll permissions

And sure enough, if I let my environment sit for a little while, giving Active Directory and Group Policy a chance to update on all of my machines, I now see more certificates have been issued from my CA server:

Certification Authority (Local)	Request ID	Requester Name	Binary Certificate	Certificate Template
∨ Contoso-CA1-CA	2	CONTOSO\DC2$	-----BEGIN CERTI...	Domain Controller (...
Revoked Certificates	3	CONTOSO\DC1$	-----BEGIN CERTI...	Domain Controller (...
Issued Certificates	4	CONTOSO\WIN10$	-----BEGIN CERTI...	DirectAccess Machin...
Pending Requests	5	CONTOSO\CA1$	-----BEGIN CERTI...	CA Exchange (CAExc...
Failed Requests	6	CONTOSO\Admin...	-----BEGIN CERTI...	User (User)
Certificate Templates	7	CONTOSO\DC2$	-----BEGIN CERTI...	Directory Email Repli...
	8	CONTOSO\DC2$	-----BEGIN CERTI...	Domain Controller A...
	9	CONTOSO\DC2$	-----BEGIN CERTI...	Kerberos Authenticat...
	10	CONTOSO\DC1$	-----BEGIN CERTI...	Directory Email Repli...
	11	CONTOSO\DC1$	-----BEGIN CERTI...	Domain Controller A...
	12	CONTOSO\DC1$	-----BEGIN CERTI...	Kerberos Authenticat...
	13	CONTOSO\BACK1$	-----BEGIN CERTI...	DirectAccess Machin...
	14	CONTOSO\WEB1$	-----BEGIN CERTI...	DirectAccess Machin...

Figure 6.23: A list of issued certificates on the CA server

To automatically issue certificates from any template you create, simply publish the template and make sure to configure the appropriate auto-enroll permissions on that template. Once the auto-enrollment GPO is in place on those clients, they will reach out to your CA server and ask it for certificates from any template for which they have permissions to receive a certificate. In the future, when that certificate is about to expire and the machine needs a new copy, the auto-enrollment policy will issue a new one prior to the expiration date, based upon the timestamps you defined inside the GPO.

Certificate auto-enrollment can take what would normally be an enormous administrative burden and turn it into a completely automated process!

Obtaining a public-authority SSL certificate

We are now pretty comfortable with grabbing certificates from our own CA server inside our own network, but what about handling those SSL certificates for our webservers that should be acquired from a public certification authority? For many of you, this will be the most common interaction that you have with certificates, and it's very important to understand this side of the coin as well. When you need to acquire an SSL certificate from your public authority of choice, there is a three-step process to do so: create a certificate request, submit the certificate request, and install the resulting certificate.

We are going to use my WEB1 server, on which I have a website running. Currently, the site is only capable of handling HTTP traffic, but when we turn it loose on the internet, we need to enable HTTPS to keep the information that is being submitted to the site encrypted.

To use HTTPS, we need to install an SSL certificate onto the WEB1 server. This webserver is running the Microsoft web services platform, **Internet Information Services (IIS)**. The three-step process we take is the same if you are running a different webserver, such as Apache, but the particular things that you have to do to accomplish these three steps will be different because Apache or any other webserver will have a different user interface than IIS. Since we are working on a Windows Server 2019 webserver, we are utilizing IIS 10.

Public/private key pair

Before we jump into performing those three steps, let's discuss why any of this even matters. You have probably heard of the term **private key** but may not quite understand what that means. When we send traffic across the internet, from our client computers to an HTTPS website, we understand that the traffic is encrypted. This means that the packets are tied up in a nice little package before leaving my laptop so that nobody can see them while they travel and are then unwrapped successfully when those packets reach the webserver. My laptop uses a key to encrypt the traffic, and the server uses a key to decrypt that traffic, but how do they know what keys to use? There are two different kinds of encryption methodology that can be used here:

- **Symmetric encryption**: The simpler method of encryption, symmetric, means that there is a single key, and both sides utilize it. Traffic is packaged up using a key, and the same key is used to unwrap that traffic when it reaches its destination. Since this single key is the all-powerful Oz, you wouldn't want it to get into the wrong hands, which means you will not be presenting it out on the internet. Therefore, symmetric encryption is not generally used for protecting internet website traffic. Rather, it is used more commonly in places where you control both sides of the communication stream, such as VPN traffic.

- **Asymmetric encryption**: This is our focus with HTTPS traffic. Asymmetric encryption utilizes two keys: a public key and a private key. The public key is included inside your SSL certificate, and so anyone on the internet can contact your website and get the public key. Your laptop then uses that public key to encrypt the traffic and sends it over to the webserver. Why is this secure if the public key is broadcast to the entire internet? Because the traffic can only be decrypted by using a corresponding private key, which is securely stored on your webserver. It is very important to maintain security over your private key and your webservers, ensuring the key doesn't fall into anyone else's pocket.

Creating a certificate signing request

If you've already jumped ahead and acquired an SSL certificate from your public CA entity by logging into their website, purchasing a certificate, and immediately downloading it—you've already missed the boat. That certificate obviously would have no way of knowing about a private key that you might have sitting on your webserver, and so that certificate would be effectively useless when installed anywhere.

When you install an SSL certificate onto a webserver, it is very important that the certificate knows about your private key. How do we make sure that happens? This is where the **certificate signing request** (**CSR**) comes into play. The first step in correctly acquiring an SSL certificate is to generate a CSR. When you create that file, the webserver platform creates the private key that is needed and hides it away on your server. The CSR is then created in such a way that it knows exactly how to interact with that private key, and you then utilize the CSR when you log into the CA's website to request the certificate.

> The private key is not *inside* the CSR, and your CA never knows what your private key is. This key is ultra important and is only ever stored on your webserver, inside your organization.

To generate a CSR, open IIS from the **Tools** menu of Server Manager, and then click on the name of the webserver from the navigational tree on the left side of your screen. This will populate a number of different applets into the center of the console. The one we want to work with is called **Server Certificates**. Go ahead and double-click on that:

Figure 6.24: Viewing Server Certificates via IIS

Now, inside the **Server Certificates** screen, you can see any existing certificates that reside on the server listed here. This is where we ultimately need to see our new SSL certificate so that we can utilize it inside our website properties when we are ready to turn on HTTPS. The first step to acquiring our new certificate is creating the certificate request to be used with our CA, and, if you take a look on the right side of your screen, you will see an **Actions** section, under which is listed **Create Certificate Request...**. Go ahead and click on that action:

Figure 6.25: Creating a certificate request

In the resulting wizard, you need to populate the information that will be stored within your SSL certificate. The **Common name** field is the most important piece of information here. It needs to be the DNS name that this certificate is going to protect. So basically, you enter the name of your website here, then continue with filling out the rest of your company-specific information. A couple of special notes here that often seem to trip up admins are that the **Organizational unit** can be anything at all; I usually just enter the word Web. Make sure to spell out the name of your **State**; do not use an abbreviation:

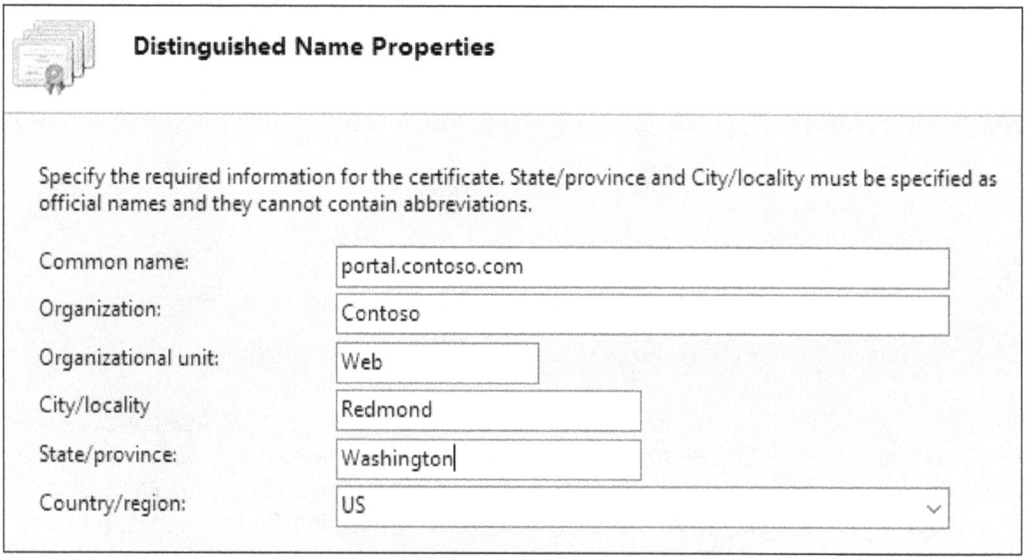

Distinguished Name Properties

Specify the required information for the certificate. State/province and City/locality must be specified as official names and they cannot contain abbreviations.

Common name:	portal.contoso.com
Organization:	Contoso
Organizational unit:	Web
City/locality	Redmond
State/province:	Washington
Country/region:	US

Figure 6.26: Populating information for the certificate

On the **Cryptographic Service Provider Properties** page, you typically want to leave the **Cryptographic service provider** set to its default, unless you have a specialized crypto card in your server and are planning to use it for handling encryption processing for this website. On an IIS server, you will almost always have **Microsoft RSA SChannel Cryptographic Provider** listed here. What you **do** want to change, however, is the **Bit length**. The standard bit length for many years was 1024, and that continues to be the default choice in Windows Server 2019. The general industry for SSL encryption has decided that 1024 is too weak, and the new standard is 2048. When you head onto your CA's website to request a certificate, you will more than likely find that your request needs to have a minimum of 2048 bits. So go ahead and change that drop-down setting to **2048**:

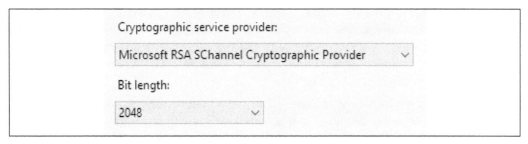

Figure 6.27: Setting the encryption bit length to 2048

The only thing left to do for our CSR is to give it a location and filename. Saving this csr as a text file is the normal way to go and serves our purposes well because all we need to do when we request our certificate is open the file and then copy and paste the contents. You have now created your csr file, and we can utilize this file to request the certificate from our public CA.

Submitting the certificate request

Now, head over to the website for your public certification authority. Again, any of the companies that we mentioned earlier, such as GoDaddy or Verisign, are appropriate for this purpose. Each authority has its own look and feel for its web interface, so I cannot give you the exact steps that need to be taken for this process. Once you have an account and log into the authority's site, you should be able to find an option for purchasing an SSL certificate. For some CAs, the purchasing process and the certificate acquisition process are two different things. For example, you purchase and pay for your new SSL certificate and then you visit a different section of the interface to use the "certificate credit" you just purchased to create a certificate. On the other hand, some CAs walk you through the entire process from start to finish. In any event, once that certificate has been purchased, there will be a process for requesting and deploying that certificate.

Once you have found the interface used for generating the new certificate, you will generally be asked for four pieces of information:

1. **Validity period** – How long should this SSL certificate last? It used to be common that companies would purchase SSL certificates with 1-year, 2-year, or even 3-year validity periods, meaning that the certificate was "good" for that amount of time. Recently, Apple has flexed its muscles in this space and decided that the Safari web browser will only trust certificates that have a validity period of 1 year, more or less. Rather than push back, the industry said "sure, why not?" and so moving forward, SSL certificates will only be valid for 1 year at a time.

2. **Webserver platform** – What type of webserver are you running? The answer to this question impacts what type of file is available to download at the end of this process. When working with Windows Server, your answer will be "IIS" but possible others include Apache, Tomcat, NGINX, and many more Linux-based webserver selections.

3. **Domain ownership validation** – This one is interesting, and if you haven't been through this process before, you likely haven't thought about why it is necessary. What's to stop hacker Joe sitting in an internet café halfway across the world, or the 12-year-old playing video games in his basement, or even your next-door neighbor from creating their own CA login and purchasing an SSL certificate that has *your* company name and website on it? The validation of domain ownership is a process to prove that you really own contoso.com (or whatever your domain is) so that only you are allowed to purchase valid SSL certificates that protect traffic for your domain name. The most common way to validate domain ownership is to select from a list of pre-defined email addresses inside the CA and have it send some flavor of validation email to that email address. For example, you might have a selection of email addresses like the following:

   admin@contoso.com
   administrator@contoso.com
   webmaster@contoso.com
   hostmaster@contoso.com

4. All you need to do is verify that you can receive an email to one of those email addresses, and by selecting this option you will receive an email to that address that usually contains a link and a code. Simply copy the code and paste it into the link, and this is an easy way to validate domain ownership because as the owner of that domain, only YOU would have access to those email addresses. A second form of ownership, if email doesn't pan out, is that the CA may give you a special DNS record that can be put into place in your domain's public DNS. You input the record, the CA sees that record show up on the internet, and they validate you are the domain owner. This process takes much longer to accomplish than email verification, so it is rarely used.

5. **CSR** – The last (and most important) thing you will be asked to provide is the text from inside that CSR file we created a few minutes ago. There will be either an upload function or simply an input box, and all you need to do is copy/paste the entire contents of the CSR into that box. If you open the text file we saved earlier, you will see a big lump of nonsense:

Figure 6.28: The text inside a CSR file

This mess of data contains information about your certificate request and is exactly what the CA needs in order to create your new SSL certificate so that it knows how to interact with your webserver's private key. Only the server that generated the CSR will be able to accept and properly utilize the SSL certificate that is based on this CSR.

Downloading and installing your certificate

Now you sit back and wait. Depending on which authority you are using and on how often your company purchases certificates from this authority, your certificate might be available for download almost immediately, or it could take a few hours before that certificate shows up in the available downloads list. The reason for this is that many of the CAs utilize human approval for new certificates, and you are literally waiting for someone to put eyes on the certificate request and your information to make sure you really work for the company and that you really own this domain name. Remember, the real benefit to a public SSL cert is that the CA is guaranteeing that the user of this certificate is the real deal, so they want to make sure they aren't issuing a certificate for `portal.contoso.com` to someone in the Fabrikam organization by mistake.

Once you are able to download the certificate from the CA website, go ahead and copy it over to the webserver from which we generated the CSR. It is critically important that you install this new certificate onto the **same server**. If you were to install this new certificate onto a different webserver, one that did not generate the CSR this certificate was built from, that certificate would import successfully, but would not be able to function. Once again, this is because the private key that the certificate is planning to interact with would not be present on a different server.

Back inside the IIS management console, we can now use the next action in that list on the right, called **Complete Certificate Request....** This launches a short little wizard in which you point at the newly downloaded certificate file, and the wizard then imports it into our server. Now that the certificate resides on the server, it is ready to be used by your website.

There is one additional item that I always check after installing or importing an SSL certificate. You can now see your new certificate listed inside IIS, and if you double-click on your new certificate, you will see the **Properties** page for the certificate. On the **General** tab of these properties, take a look near the bottom. Your certificate should display a little key icon and the **You have a private key that corresponds to this certificate** text. If you can see this message, your import was successful and the new certificate file matched up with the CSR perfectly. The server and certificate now share that critical private key information, and the SSL certificate will be able to work properly to protect our website. If you do not see this message, something went wrong in the process to request and download our certificate. If you do not see the message here, you need to start over by generating a new CSR, because the certificate file that you got back must not have been keyed appropriately against that CSR, or something along those lines. Without the *You have a private key that corresponds to this certificate* text at the bottom of this screen, your certificate will *not* validate traffic properly.

Here is an example of what it should look like when working correctly:

Figure 6.29: This certificate properly matches up with a private key

Exporting and importing certificates

I often find myself needing to use the same SSL certificate on multiple servers. This might happen in the case where I have more than one IIS server serving up the same website and I am using some form of load balancing to split the traffic between them. This need may also arise when working with any form of hardware load balancer, as you sometimes need to import certificates onto not only the webservers themselves but into the load balancer box. Another example is when using wildcard certificates; when you purchase a wildcard, you typically intend to install it onto multiple servers.

Does this mean that I need to generate a new CSR from each server, and request a new copy of the same certificate multiple times? Definitely not, and in fact doing so could cause you other problems: when a public CA **re-keys** a certificate—in other words, if you have already requested a certificate with a particular name and then come back again later to request another copy of the same certificate—that CA may invalidate the first one as it issues the second copy. This is not always immediately apparent, as there is usually a timer set on the invalidation of the first certificate. If you revisit the CA's web interface and request a new copy of the same certificate using a new CSR for your second webserver, you might discover that everything works fine for a few days, but then suddenly the primary webserver stops validating traffic because its SSL certificate, the original copy, has expired.

When you need to reuse the same SSL certificate on multiple servers, you can simply export it from one and import it on the next. There is no need to contact the CA at all. This process is quite straightforward, and there are two common places where you can do it: inside either the MMC snap-in for certificates or from within IIS itself. It is important to note, though, that the process is slightly different depending on which avenue you take, and you have to be especially aware of what is happening with the private key as you step through these wizards.

Exporting from MMC

Head back into your **Local Computer** certificate store in MMC and navigate to **Personal | Certificates** so that you can see your SSL certificate listed. Right-click on the certificate, and then navigate to **All Tasks | Export....** When you walk through this export wizard, the important part that I wanted to mention happens right away in the wizard steps. The first choice you have to make is whether to export the private key. Again, the private key is the secret sauce that allows the certificate to interact properly with the server on which it is installed. If you export without the private key, that certificate will not work on another server. So it is important here that, if you are exporting this certificate with the intention of installing it onto a second webserver and using it for validating SSL traffic, you select the top option for **Yes, export the private key**:

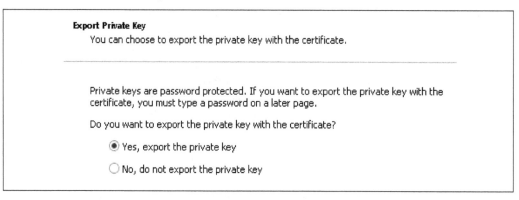

Export Private Key
You can choose to export the private key with the certificate.

Private keys are password protected. If you want to export the private key with the certificate, you must type a password on a later page.

Do you want to export the private key with the certificate?

◉ Yes, export the private key

○ No, do not export the private key

Figure 6.30: Exporting a certificate using MMC

As the wizard sufficiently warns you, when you choose to export a certificate that contains the private key information, you are required to supply a password, which will be used to protect the exported PFX file. It is important to choose a good password. If you forget it, your exported file will be completely useless (which isn't terrible, because you can simply export it again). If you input a password that is very simple or is easy to guess, anyone who gets their hands on this PFX file may be able to use your certificate and private key on their own webservers, which would not be good.

Exporting from IIS

Alternatively, an exported PFX file can be generated from inside the IIS console. Inside the **Server Certificates** applet for IIS, just right-click on the certificate and choose **Export...**. This launches a single-page wizard that simply asks you for a location and password:

Figure 6.31: Exporting a certificate using IIS

We had many more options that we could have chosen or denied when we exported using MMC, so why is this so short? IIS makes assumptions for the rest of the settings in order to speed up the export process. When you are exporting an SSL certificate, the chances are that you also intend to export the private key. Therefore, IIS simply makes that assumption and bypasses the rest of the choices. You are forced to enter a password because you don't have a choice about the private key; it will be included with the certificate export automatically. So, if you had some reason to export a certificate that did *not* contain the private key info, you could not utilize the IIS console for this task. You would need to open up MMC and walk through the more extensive wizard found there.

Importing into a second server

Whichever direction you take for accomplishing the export, once you have the fully fleshed PFX file available, importing into your second server is very easy. From within either console, MMC or IIS, you can right-click and choose the **Import** action. Walking through the steps, you simply choose the PFX file and then input the password that you used to protect the file. The certificate is then imported, and, if you open the **Properties**, you will see that the little key icon and the private key message are displayed properly at the bottom of the certificate properties screen. If you do not see the *you have a private key* message, you did something incorrectly during the export process and you'll need to try it again.

Go ahead and try it yourself; find a server with an SSL certificate and test exporting that cert with and without the private key. When you import into a new server, you will see that importing the certificate file without a private key does not contain this message at the bottom of the properties page, but the exported file that does contain the private key results in the proper message here. To take it a step further, try utilizing both certificates on a non-important website and see what happens. You will find that the certificate lacking the private key will fail to validate SSL traffic.

If you attempt to export an SSL certificate and the option to include the private key is grayed out, this means when the original administrator installed this certificate to the webserver, they chose a special option that blocks the ability for the private key to be exported in the future. In this case, you will not be able to export the certificate with the private key.

Summary

Certificates often get a bad rep, and I believe this is because people think they are a headache to deal with. I see their point. Without knowing how to navigate through the various administrative consoles that deal with your certificate infrastructure, it would be difficult to make even the simplest items function. By walking through the most common certificate-related tasks that any server admin will eventually have to tackle within their own networks, I hope that you have now found some comfort and confidence to progress with those projects that might be currently sitting on hold, waiting for the certificate infrastructure to be built. In the next chapter, we will study networking with Windows Server 2019.

Questions

1. What is the name of the role inside Windows Server 2019 that allows you to issue certificates from your server?

2. What kind of CA server is typically installed first in a domain environment?

3. Should you install the certification authority role onto a domain controller?

4. After creating a new certificate template, what next step needs to be taken before you can issue certificates to your computers or users from that new template?

5. What is the general name of the GPO setting that forces certificates to be issued without manual intervention by an administrator?

6. An SSL certificate will only be able to validate traffic properly if it shares _____ key information with the webserver.

7. What is the primary piece of information that a public certification authority needs in order to issue you a new SSL certificate (hint: you generate this from your webserver)?

7
Networking with Windows Server 2019

As we have been discussing so far in this book, servers are the tree trunks of our networks. They are the backbone infrastructure that enables us to get work done. If servers are the trunks, then the networks themselves must be the roots. Your network is the platform that supports the company infrastructure; it makes up the channels that all devices inside your company use to communicate with each other.

Traditionally, there have been *server admins* and *network admins* in the IT industry, separated roles, and in many places that is still the case. An administrator who primarily works on servers does not generally have enough time in the day to also support the network infrastructure in an organization of any size, and the reverse is also true. Network administrators generally stick to their own equipment and management tools and aren't interested in diving too deeply into the Windows Server world. However, many of us work in smaller companies where many hats must be worn. Some days, the server admin and the network admin hats sit on top of each other, and so we must understand at least a baseline of networking and tools that we can use to troubleshoot connections that are not working. In addition, Windows Server 2019 brings a new networking mindset into focus: the virtualization of your networks. There will always be some semblance of a physical network, using physical switches and routers to move the packets around between different rooms and buildings. But now we are also incorporating the idea of **software-defined networking** (**SDN**) into our Windows servers, which gives us the capability to virtualize some of that configuration. Not only the config itself; we are actually virtualizing the network traffic and building our networks from within a server console, rather than using command-line interfaces to configure our routers, which was always needed in the past.

Hold the phone; I am getting ahead of myself. First, let's talk about some of the new and useful things inside Windows Server 2019 that do involve working with physical networks, or any networks, because these are going to be important for any administrator in today's networking world. Later, we will take a few moments to further explore this new idea of network virtualization.

The following are the topics we plan to discuss in this chapter:

- Introduction to IPv6
- Your networking toolbox
- Building a routing table
- NIC Teaming
- Software-defined networking

Introduction to IPv6

Welcome to the dark side! Unfortunately, that is how many people think of IPv6 for the time being. While IPv6 is by no means a new thing, in my experience it is still something that almost no one has deployed in their networks. While working with hundreds of different companies all over the world over the past few years, I have come across only two organizations that were running IPv6 over their entire production network, and one wasn't even true native IPv6. Instead, they were using a tunneling technology, called ISATAP, over their whole network to make all of the servers and clients talk to each other using IPv6 packets, but these packets were still traversing an IPv4 physical network. Don't get me wrong; I have found plenty of cases where companies are toying around with IPv6 and have some semblance of it configured on a sectioned-off piece of their networks, but using it for the entire production network? Most of us just aren't ready for that big a change yet. Why is it so difficult to put IPv6 into place? Because we have been using IPv4 since basically the beginning of time, it's what we all know and understand, and there really isn't a great need to move to IPv6 inside our networks. Wait a minute; I thought there was some big scare about running out of IPv4 addresses? Yes, that is true for IP addresses on the public internet, but it has nothing to do with our internal networks. You see, even if we run out of public IPv4 addresses tomorrow, the internal networks at our companies are not going to be impacted. We can continue to run IPv4 inside the network for a long time to come, possibly forever and always, as long as we are comfortable using NAT technologies to translate the traffic down into IPv4 as it comes into our network from the internet. We have all been using NAT in one form or another for almost as long as IPv4 has existed, so it is obviously something people are very comfortable with.

Let me be clear: I am not trying to convince you that sticking with IPv4 is the way of the future. I am just laying out the fact that, for most organizations over the next few years, this will simply be the truth. The reason I want to discuss IPv6 here is that, eventually, you will have to deal with it. And once you do, you'll actually get excited about it! There are some huge advantages that IPv6 has over IPv4, namely, the enormous number of IP addresses that you can contain within a single network. Network teams in companies around the world struggle every day with the need to build more and more IPv4 networks and tie them together. Think about it: there are many companies now with employee counts in excess of 10,000. Some have many, many times that number. In today's world, everyone needs almost constant access to their data. Data is the new currency. Most users now have at least two physical devices they utilize for work, sometimes more than that: a laptop and a tablet, or a laptop and a smartphone, or a desktop and a laptop, and a tablet and a smartphone; you get the idea. In the IPv4 world, where you are dealing with comparatively small IP address ranges, you have to get very creative with creating subnets in order to accommodate all of these physical devices. Each needs a unique IP address to communicate on the network. The biggest advantage to IPv6 is that it resolves all of these problems immediately, and by default, by providing the capability to have a huge number of IP addresses within a single network. How many more addresses are we talking about? The following is some comparison data to give you a little perspective:

- An IPv4 address is a 32-bit length address that looks like this: `192.168.1.5`
- An IPv6 address is a 128-bit length address that looks like this:
  `2001:AABB:CCDD:AB00:0123:4567:8901:ABCD`

As you can see, the IPv4 address is much shorter, which obviously means there are fewer possibilities for unique IP addresses. What you don't see is how much longer IPv6 addresses really are. These examples portray IPv4 and IPv6 addresses as we are used to seeing them, in their finished forms. Really though, the IPv4 address is shown in decimal form, and the IPv6 in hexadecimal. IPv6 addresses are shown and used via hex so that the addresses are compressed as much as possible. In reality, if you dig around under the hood, an IPv6 address in its native 128-bit form might look something like this (and indeed, this is how it looks inside the actual packet):

`0001000001000001000011011001100000000000000000001000000000000000`

`0001000000000000000000000001000000000000000000000000000000000001`

That's an impressive set of digits, but not something that is very usable or friendly to the human eye. So rather than show the bits, what about an IPv6 address shown in decimal format, in the same way that IPv4 addresses have always been shown? In that case, an IPv6 address might look something like this:

`192.16.1.2.34.0.0.1.0.0.0.0.0.0.0.1`

Now we fully understand why IPv6 is always used and shown in hexadecimal; the addresses are long even in that compressed format!

Understanding IPv6 IP addresses

When we set up IPv4 networks, subnetting is extremely important because it is what enables us to have more than one collection of IP addresses within the same network. In the most basic form of networking, where you set up some IP addresses and run a /24 subnet (a subnet mask of 255.255.255.0), which is very common on small networks such as inside a house or small business office, you are limited to 254 unique IP addresses. Ouch! Some companies have thousands of different servers, without accounting for all of their client computers and devices that also need to connect to the network. Thankfully, we can build out many different subnets within a single IPv4 network in order to increase our usable IP address scope, but this takes careful planning and calculation of those subnets and address spaces and is the reason that we rely on experienced network administrators to manage this part of the network for us. One invalid subnet configuration in a routing table can tank network traffic flow. The administration of subnets in a large IPv4 network is not for the faint of heart.

When we are talking about IPv6 addressing, the sky almost seems to be the limit. If you were to calculate all of the unique IPv6 addresses available in the preceding 128-bit space, you would find that there are more than 340 undecillion addresses available to create. In other words, 340 trillion, trillion, trillion addresses. This is the number being touted out there about how many available addresses there are on the IPv6 internet, but what does that mean for our internal networks?

To discuss the number of addresses we could have inside a typical internal network that runs IPv6, let's first step back and look at the address itself. The address I showed earlier is just something I made up, but we will break down the parts of it here:

2001:AABB:CCDD:AB00:0123:4567:8901:ABCD

Compared to 192.168.1.5, this thing looks like a monstrosity. That is because we are generally not used to dealing with the hexadecimal format; it is just a different way of looking at data. As we mentioned, this is a 128-bit address. It is broken up into 8 different sections, with each section separated by a colon made up of 16 bits. The first 64 bits (the first half) of the address are routing information, and the latter 64 bits are the unique device ID on the network. Within the first part, we have two different components. The first 48 bits (3 groups of hex) are an organizational prefix that will be the same on all of our devices in the network. Then the fourth set of information, the next 16 bits, can be our subnet ID. This gives us the flexibility of still having many different subnets, if we so desire in the future, by using multiple numbers here as the subnet ID. After dedicating the first half of the address, we now have the latter half to work with, the last 64 bits. These we can leave for device IDs. This part of the address will be different for every device on the network and will define the individual static IPv6 addresses that will be used for communication. Let's lay out our example address into the following parts:

- **Overall IP address**: 2001:AABB:CCDD:AB00:0123:4567:8901:ABCD

- **Organizational prefix**: 2001:AABB:CCDD

- **Subnet ID**: AB00

- **Device ID**: 0123:4567:8901:ABCD is one unique device ID

How many devices can we have in our network with an IP schema such as this? Well, even in our example, where we only allocated one 16-bit section for subnetting, and 64 bits for actual IP addresses, that would provide us with the capability to have more than 65,000 subnets and quintillions of unique device IDs in our IP range. Impressive, isn't it?

If we stick with this and use just a single subnet to contain all of our machines, the first half of our addresses will always be the same, making these long addresses much easier to remember and deal with. It is surprising how quickly you will get used to seeing these large hex numbers in your environment, but even though you will start to recognize them, you still probably are not going to quickly jump into servers or computers in your network anymore by using the static IP addresses. I know a lot of us are still in the habit of saying: I need to quickly jump into my web server; I'll just RDP into 192.168.1.5. Just the time that it takes to type out these IPv6 addresses, even if you do remember them, isn't generally worth it. IPv6 will bring with it a larger reliance on DNS to make it more usable.

Now that we understand what sections of the address are going to be used for what purposes, how do we go about assigning the individual device ID numbers for all of the computers, servers, and other devices on our network? You could start with number 1 and go up from there. Another idea is to calculate out the old IPv4 addresses into hex and use this as the last 32 bits of the address — open up Windows Calculator on your computer, drop down the menu, and change it into Programmer mode. This is a quick and easy tool that you can use to convert decimal into hexadecimal, and vice versa. Let's take the example of my web server that is running on 192.168.1.5. I want to implement IPv6 inside my network, and I want my server's IPv6 addresses to reflect the original IPv4 address in the device ID section of the new address. In my calculator, if I type in 192 and then click on **HEX**, it will show me the corresponding hexadecimal to the decimal of 192, as shown in *Figure 7.1*:

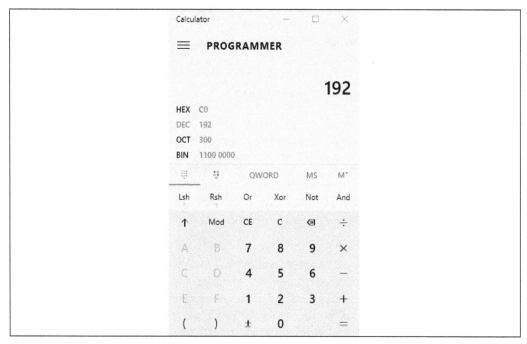

Figure 7.1: Using Windows Calculator to convert decimal to hexadecimal

If we do that with each of the octets in our IPv4 address, we will see the following:

192 = C0

168 = A8

1 = 01

5 = 05

So, my 192.168.1.5 factors out to C0A8:0105. I can now utilize that in combination with my organizational prefix and my subnet ID to create a static IPv6 address for my web server:

2001:AABB:CCDD:0001:0000:0000:C0A8:0105

You'll notice in the preceding IPv6 address that I input the hex for the device ID at the end, but I also made a couple of other changes. Since we are leaving the last 64 bits available for the device ID, but my old IPv4 address only consumes 32 bits, I am left with the 32 bits in the middle. It would be kind of weird to have data in there that didn't mean anything to us, so we will simply make it all zeros to simplify my addressing scheme. In addition to that change, I also adjusted my subnet ID to the number 1, since this is the first subnet in my network.

Our new addressing is starting to look a little cleaner and makes more sense. Now that we see this new address for our web server laid out, I can see that there are some additional clean-up tasks we can perform on the address in order to make it look even better. Right now, the address listed earlier is 100% accurate. I could plug this IP address into the NIC properties of my web server and it would work. However, there are a whole lot of zeros in my address, and I don't need to keep them all. Any time you have unnecessary zeros within a 16-bit segment that are preceding the actual number, they can simply be removed. For example, our subnet ID and the first 32 bits of our device ID have a lot of unnecessary zeros, so I can consolidate the address down to the following:

2001:AABB:CCDD:1:0:0:C0A8:0105

Then, to take it even a step further, any time you have full 16-bit sections that are composed entirely of zeros, they can be fully consolidated into a double colon. So, the first 32 bits of my device ID that are all zeros, I can replace with ::. The following is the full address, and the consolidated address. These numbers look quite different. My consolidated address is much easier on the eye, but from a technological perspective, they are exactly the same number:

2001:AABB:CCDD:0001:0000:0000:C0A8:0105

2001:AABB:CCDD:1::C0A8:0105

In fact, if you are setting up a lab or want to quickly test IPv6, you could use addresses as simple as the following example. The two addresses that I will show you here are precisely the same:

2001:0000:0000:0000:0000:0000:0000:0001

2001::1

It is important to note that you can only use a double-colon **once** within an IP address. If you had two places where it could be applicable within the same address, you can only implement it in one of those places, and you will have to spell out the zeros in the other place. For example, changing `2001:AABB:0000:0000:0001:0000:0` `000:0123` into `2001:AABB::1::123` would cause your computer grief, as it would not know what to do with that double-colon. With the information provided here, you should be able to put together your own semblance of IPv6 and start issuing some IPv6 addresses to computers or servers in your network. There is so much more that could be learned on this subject that an entire book could be written, and indeed there are numerous offerings to choose from.

Your networking toolbox

Whether you are a server administrator, a network administrator, or a combination of the two, there are a number of tools that are useful for testing and monitoring network connections within the Windows Server world. Some of these tools are baked right into the operating system and can be used from the Command Prompt or PowerShell, and others are more expansive graphical interfaces that require installation before running. The following are the built-in Windows network tools that we are going to look at:

- `ping`
- `tracert`
- `pathping`
- `Test-Connection`
- `telnet`
- `Test-NetConnection`

All these tools are free and included out of the box, so you have no excuse to delay getting acquainted with these helpful utilities.

ping

Even the newest IT pros are usually familiar with this one. `ping` is a command that you can utilize from a Command Prompt or PowerShell, and it is simply used to query a DNS name and/or IP address to find out whether it responds. `ping` is, and has always been, our go-to tool for testing network connectivity between two devices on a network. From my Windows 10 client on the LAN, I can open a prompt and `ping <IP_ADDRESS>`. Alternatively, because I am using DNS in my environment, which will resolve names to IP addresses, I can also use `ping <SERVERNAME>`, as shown in *Figure 7.2*. You can see that my server replies to my ping, letting me know that it is online and responding:

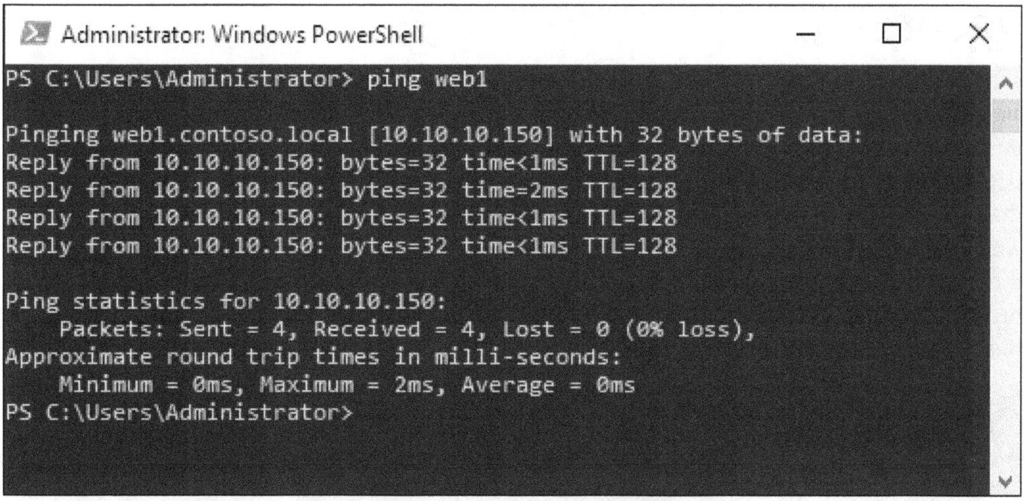

```
Administrator: Windows PowerShell                          —    □    ✕

PS C:\Users\Administrator> ping web1

Pinging web1.contoso.local [10.10.10.150] with 32 bytes of data:
Reply from 10.10.10.150: bytes=32 time<1ms TTL=128
Reply from 10.10.10.150: bytes=32 time=2ms TTL=128
Reply from 10.10.10.150: bytes=32 time<1ms TTL=128
Reply from 10.10.10.150: bytes=32 time<1ms TTL=128

Ping statistics for 10.10.10.150:
    Packets: Sent = 4, Received = 4, Lost = 0 (0% loss),
Approximate round trip times in milli-seconds:
    Minimum = 0ms, Maximum = 2ms, Average = 0ms
PS C:\Users\Administrator>
```

Figure 7.2: Pinging a server

Ping traffic is technically called **ICMP traffic**. This is important because ICMP is blocked by default more and more often these days, with firewalls being turned on by default on so many of our systems and devices. Historically, `ping` was always a tool that we could count on to tell us with a fair degree of certainty whether connectivity was flowing between two devices, but that is no longer the case. If you build a brand new Windows box and plug it into your network, that computer may be communicating with the internet and all of the servers on your network just fine, but if you try to ping that new computer from another machine on your network, the ping will probably fail. Why would that happen? Because Windows has some security measures built into it by default, including the blocking of ICMP traffic in Windows Defender Firewall. In that case, you would need to either turn off the Windows firewall, or provide it with an access rule that allows ICMP traffic. Once such a rule is enabled, pings will start replying from this new computer. Keep in mind whenever building new systems or servers in your network that `ping` is not always the most trustworthy tool to depend upon in today's networking world.

It's easy to allow ICMP responses by plugging a rule into Windows Defender Firewall with Advanced Security, though you still wouldn't want to have to remember to do this manually on every new system you introduce into a network. Thankfully, you already know how to utilize Group Policy to build a GPO and push it out to all machines on your network, and yes, you can absolutely place firewall rules inside that GPO. This is a common way to allow or block ICMP throughout an entire organization, by issuing a firewall rule via Group Policy.

tracert

tracert, which is pronounced **Trace Route**, is a tool used to trace a network packet as it traverses your network. What it really does is watch all of the places the packet bumps into before hitting its destination. These bumps in the road that a network packet needs to get through are called **hops**. Trace route shows you all of the hops that your traffic is taking as it moves toward the destination server or whatever it is trying to contact. My test lab network is very flat and boring, so doing a tracert there wouldn't show us much of anything. However, if I open up a PowerShell prompt from an internet-connected machine and tracert to a web service, such as Bing, we get some interesting results:

```
PS C:\WINDOWS\system32> tracert www.bing.com

Tracing route to any.edge.bing.com [204.79.197.200]
over a maximum of 30 hops:

  1    <1 ms    <1 ms    <1 ms  192.168.8.1
  2     1 ms    <1 ms    <1 ms  192.168.128.1
  3     8 ms     7 ms     5 ms  172.17.224.1
  4    11 ms     9 ms    15 ms  172.19.253.1
  5    10 ms     9 ms    11 ms  172.31.255.1
  6    20 ms     9 ms    13 ms  ht1-max1-1.iserv.net [206.114.55.1]
  7    15 ms    12 ms     8 ms  69.87.144.9
  8    23 ms    18 ms    19 ms  888-2.iserv.net [206.114.40.2]
  9    23 ms    20 ms    15 ms  g5-0-0.core3.grr.iserv.net [206.114.51.20]
 10    19 ms    11 ms    19 ms  g5-0-0.core1.grr.iserv.net [206.114.51.2]
 11    21 ms    28 ms    19 ms  GigabitEthernet4-1.GW5.DET5.ALTER.NET [152.179.10.81]
 12    25 ms    28 ms    28 ms  0.ae1.XL3.CHI13.ALTER.NET [140.222.225.179]
 13    27 ms    37 ms    54 ms  TenGigE0-6-0-1.GW2.CHI13.ALTER.NET [152.63.65.133]
 14    36 ms    34 ms    34 ms  microsoft-gw.customer.alter.net [152.179.105.130]
 15    58 ms    50 ms    46 ms  104.44.81.58
 16    34 ms    33 ms    36 ms  10.201.194.219
 17    26 ms    29 ms    29 ms  a-0001.a-msedge.net [204.79.197.200]

Trace complete.
PS C:\WINDOWS\system32>
```

Figure 7.3: Using tracert

 If you utilize tracert but are not interested in seeing all of the DNS information provided in the output, use tracert -d to focus only on the IP addresses.

This information can be extremely useful when trying to diagnose a connection that is not working. If your traffic is moving through multiple hops, such as routers and firewalls, before it gets to the destination, `tracert` can be essential in figuring out where in the connection stream things are going wrong. Given that the preceding screenshot shows a successful trace route to Bing, now let's see what it looks like when things are broken. I will unplug my internet modem and run the same `tracert` `www.bing.com` again, and now we can see that I am still able to communicate with my local router, but not beyond:

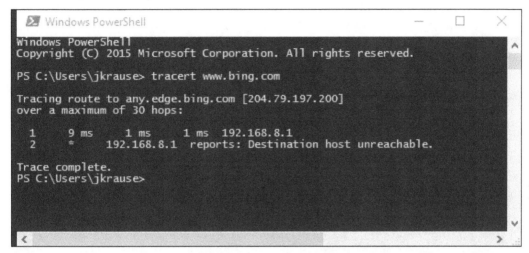

Figure 7.4: Tracing the route to a website when disconnected from the internet

pathping

`tracert` is useful and seems to be the *de facto* standard for tracing packets around your network, but this next command is even more powerful in my opinion. `pathping` essentially does the same thing as `tracert`, except that it provides one additional piece of crucial information. Most of the time, with either of these commands, you are only interested in figuring out where in the chain of hops something is broken, but often, when I'm setting up servers for networking purposes, I am working with servers and hardware that have many different network cards. When dealing with multiple NICs in a system, the local routing table is just as important as the external routers and switches, and I often want to check out the path of a network packet in order to see which local NIC it is flowing out of. This is where `pathping` becomes more powerful than `tracert`. The first piece of information that `tracert` shows you is the first hop away from the local server that you are traversing. However, `pathping` also shows you which local network interface your packets are flowing out of.

Let me give you an example: I often set up remote access servers with multiple NICs, and during this process, we create many routes on the local server so that it knows what traffic needs to be sent in which direction, such as what traffic needs to go out the internal NIC, and what traffic needs to go out the external NIC. After completing all of our routing statements for the internal NIC, we test them by pinging a server inside the network. Perhaps that ping fails, and we aren't sure why. I can try a tracert command, but it's not going to provide me with anything helpful because it simply cannot see the first hop; it just times out. However, if I try a pathping command instead, the first hop will still time out, but I can now see that my traffic is attempting to flow out of my *EXTERNAL NIC*. Whoops! We must have set something up incorrectly with our static route on this server. So, then I know that I need to delete that route and recreate it to make this traffic flow through the internal NIC instead.

The following is the same PowerShell prompt from the same computer that I used in my tracert screenshot. You can see that a pathping command shows me the local IP address on my laptop where the traffic is attempting to leave the system, whereas the tracert command did not show this information:

```
PS C:\Users\jkrause> pathping www.bing.com

Tracing route to any.edge.bing.com [204.79.197.200]
over a maximum of 30 hops:
  0  IVO-PC-328 [192.168.8.113]
  1  192.168.8.1
  2  192.168.128.1
  3     *       192.168.8.1  reports: Destination host unreachable.

Computing statistics for 75 seconds...
                  Source to Here   This Node/Link
Hop  RTT      Lost/Sent = Pct   Lost/Sent = Pct  Address
  0                                                IVO-PC-328 [192.168.8.113]
                                 0/ 100 =   0%   |
  1    1ms     0/ 100 =   0%     0/ 100 =   0%   192.168.8.1
                                 100/ 100 =100%  |
  2   ---      100/ 100 =100%    0/ 100 =   0%   192.168.128.1
                                 0/ 100 =   0%   |
  3   ---      100/ 100 =100%    0/ 100 =   0%   IVO-PC-328 [0.0.0.0]

Trace complete.
PS C:\Users\jkrause>
```

Figure 7.5: pathping shows the initial outbound hop

Test-Connection

The commands we have discussed so far can be run from either the Command Prompt or PowerShell, but now it's time to dive into a newer one that can only be run from the PowerShell prompt: a cmdlet called `Test-Connection`; it is sort of like `ping` on steroids. If we open up a PowerShell prompt in the lab and run `Test-Connection WEB1`, we see output that is very similar to what we'd get with a regular ping, but the information is laid out in a way that I think is a little easier on the eyes. There is also an unexpected column of data here called `Source`:

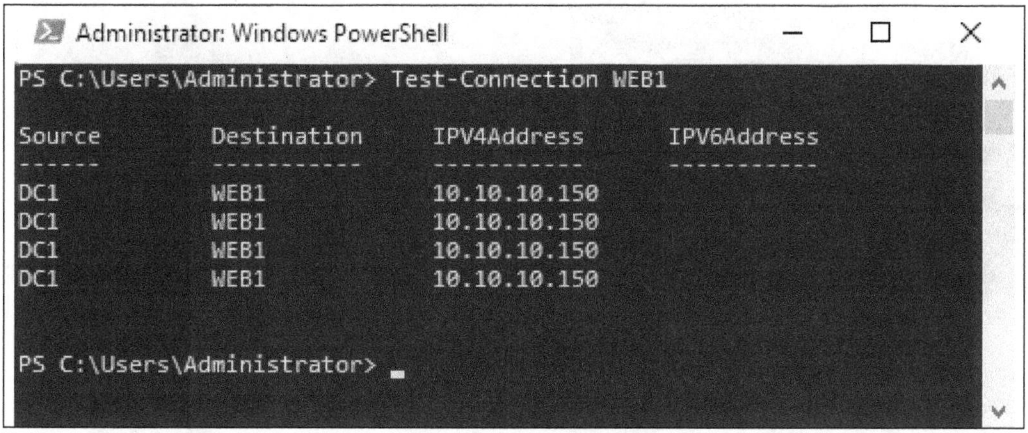

```
PS C:\Users\Administrator> Test-Connection WEB1

Source         Destination     IPV4Address        IPV6Address
------         -----------     -----------        -----------
DC1            WEB1            10.10.10.150
DC1            WEB1            10.10.10.150
DC1            WEB1            10.10.10.150
DC1            WEB1            10.10.10.150


PS C:\Users\Administrator>
```

Figure 7.6: Using Test-Connection

That is interesting. I was logged into my DC1 server when I ran this command, so my source computer for this command was DC1. But does this mean that I can manipulate the source computer for the `Test-Connection` cmdlet? Yes, this is exactly what it means. As with everything in Windows Server 2019 management, the need to be logged in to a local server is decoupled. Specific to the `Test-Connection` cmdlet, this means you can open a PowerShell prompt anywhere on your network and test connections between two different endpoints, even if you are not logged in to either of them. Let's test that out.

I am still logged in to my DC1 server, but I am going to use a `Test-Connection` cmdlet to test connections between a number of my servers in the network. You see, not only can you specify a different source computer than the one you are currently logged in to, you can take it a step further and specify multiple sources and destinations with this powerful cmdlet. So, if I want to test connections from a couple of different source machines to a couple of different destinations, that is easily done with the following command:

```
Test-Connection -Source DC1, DC2 -ComputerName WEB1, BACK1
```

You can see in *Figure 7.7* that I have ping statistics from both DC1 and DC2, to each of the WEB1 and BACK1 servers in my network. Test-Connection has the potential to be a very powerful monitoring tool:

```
Administrator: Windows PowerShell                                              —    □    ×

Windows PowerShell
Copyright (C) 2015 Microsoft Corporation. All rights reserved.

PS C:\Users\Administrator> Test-Connection -Source DC1, DC2 -ComputerName WEB1, BACK1

Source      Destination     IPV4Address      IPV6Address                    Bytes   Time(ms)
------      -----------     -----------      -----------                    -----   --------
DC1         WEB1            10.0.0.150                                      32      1
DC1         WEB1            10.0.0.150                                      32      0
DC1         WEB1            10.0.0.150                                      32      4
DC1         WEB1            10.0.0.150                                      32      1
DC1         BACK1           10.0.0.10                                       32      0
DC1         BACK1           10.0.0.10                                       32      4
DC1         BACK1           10.0.0.10                                       32      2
DC1         BACK1           10.0.0.10                                       32      1
DC2         WEB1            10.0.0.150                                      32      0
DC2         WEB1            10.0.0.150                                      32      2
DC2         WEB1            10.0.0.150                                      32      1
DC2         WEB1            10.0.0.150                                      32      0
DC2         BACK1           10.0.0.10                                       32      1
DC2         BACK1           10.0.0.10                                       32      1
DC2         BACK1           10.0.0.10                                       32      1
DC2         BACK1           10.0.0.10                                       32      1

PS C:\Users\Administrator> _
```

Figure 7.7: Multiple sources and destinations using Test-Connection

One more useful function to point out is that you can clean up the output of the command pretty easily by using the -Quiet switch. By adding -Quiet to a Test-Connection command, it sanitizes the output and only shows you a simple True or False for whether the connection was successful, instead of showing you each individual ICMP packet that was sent. Unfortunately, you cannot combine both the -Source switch and the -Quiet switch, but if you are using Test-Connection from the original source computer that you are logged in to, like most of us will be doing anyway, -Quiet works great. Most of the time, all we really care about is Yes or No as to whether these connections are working, and don't necessarily want to see all four attempts. By using -Quiet, we get exactly that:

```
Test-Connection -Quiet -ComputerName WEB1, BACK1, DC2, CA1
```

If I were to use `Test-Connection` in the standard way to try to contact all of the servers in my network, that would turn into a whole lot of output. But by using the `-Quiet` switch, I get back a simple `True` or `False` on whether each individual server could be contacted:

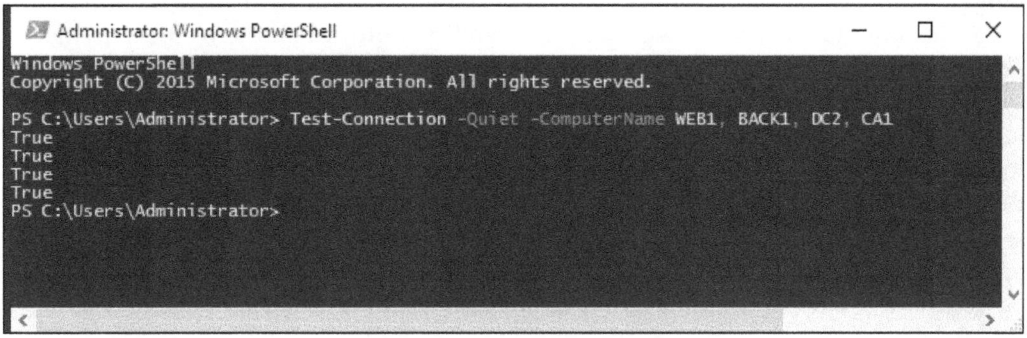

```
Administrator: Windows PowerShell                              —    □    ×
Windows PowerShell
Copyright (C) 2015 Microsoft Corporation. All rights reserved.

PS C:\Users\Administrator> Test-Connection -Quiet -ComputerName WEB1, BACK1, DC2, CA1
True
True
True
True
PS C:\Users\Administrator>
```

Figure 7.8: Using the -Quiet switch

Telnet

`telnet` provides quite a bit of remote management capability; it essentially offers the ability to make a connection between two computers to manipulate the remote machine through a virtual terminal connection. Surprisingly, we are not here to discuss any of the actual functionality that `telnet` provides, because with regard to networking, I find it is quite useful as a simple connection-testing tool, without knowing anything about what functionality the `telnet` command itself actually provides.

When we discussed `ping`, we talked about the downside to ICMP: it is easily blocked, and it is becoming more common in today's networks not to allow pings to be successful. This is unfortunate since `ping` has always been the most common form of network-connection testing, but the reality is that, if `ping` makes our lives easier, it also makes the lives of hackers easier. If we cannot rely on `ping` to tell us with certainty whether we can contact a remote system, what do we use instead? Another case that I see often is where a server itself might be responding correctly, but a particular service running on that server has a problem and is not responding. A simple `ping` may show the server to be online, but it can't tell us anything about the service specifically. By using the **Telnet Client** commands, we can easily query a server remotely. Even more importantly, we can opt to query an individual service on that server, to make sure it is listening as it is designed to do. Let me give you an example that I use all the time.

I often set up new internet-facing web servers. After installing a new web server, it makes sense that I would want to test access to it from the internet to make sure it's responding, right? But maybe the website itself isn't online and functional yet, so I can't browse to it with Edge or any other browser. It is quite likely that we disabled pings on this server or at the firewall level because blocking ICMP over the internet is very common to lower the security vulnerability footprint on the web. So my new server is running, and we think we have the networking all squared away, but I cannot test pinging my new server because, by design, it fails to reply. What can I use to test this? telnet. By issuing a simple telnet command, I can tell my computer to query a specific port on my new web server and find out whether it connects to that port. Doing this establishes a socket connection to the port on that server, which is much more akin to real user traffic than a ping would be. If a telnet command connects successfully, you know your traffic is making its way to the server, and the server service running on the port we queried seems to be responding properly.

The ability to use telnet is not installed by default in Windows Server 2019, or any other Windows operating system, so we first need to head into Server Manager and then **Add Roles and Features** to install the feature called **Telnet Client**:

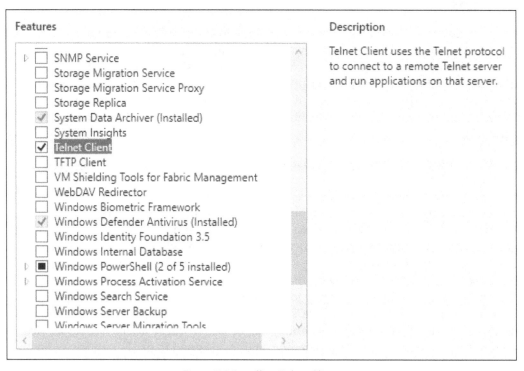

Figure 7.9: Installing Telnet Client

You only need to install **Telnet Client** on the machine from which you want to do command-line testing. You do not have to do anything on the remote server that you are connecting to.

Now that the Telnet Client feature has been installed, we can utilize it from a Command Prompt or PowerShell to do work for us by attempting to make socket connections from our computer to the remote service. All we need to do is tell it what server and port to query. Then `telnet` will simply connect or time out, and based on that result, we can see whether that particular service on the server is responding. Let's try it with our own web server. For our example, I have turned off the website inside IIS, so we are now in the position where the server is online but the website is dead. If I ping WEB1, I can still see it happily responding. You can see where server-monitoring tools that rely on ICMP would be showing false positives, indicating that the server was online and running, even though our website is inaccessible. Just below the successful ping in *Figure 7.10*, you can see that I also tried querying port 80 on the WEB1 server. The command that I used for that is `telnet web1 80`. That timed out. This shows us that the website, which is running on port 80, is not responding:

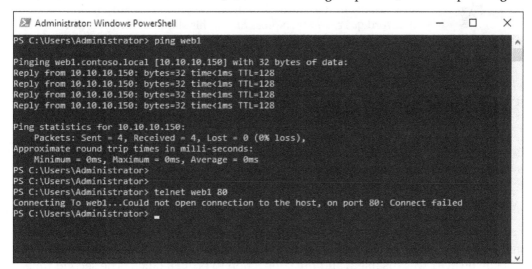

Figure 7.10: Failed connection on port 80

If I turn the website back on, we can try `telnet web1 80` again, and this time I do not get a timeout message. This time, my PowerShell prompt wipes itself clean and sits waiting on a flashing cursor at the top. While it doesn't tell me *yay, I'm connected!*, this flashing cursor indicates that a successful socket connection has been made to port 80 on my web server, indicating the website is online and responding:

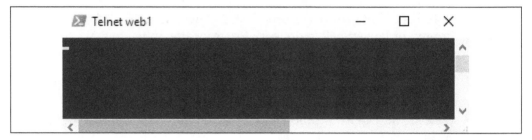

Figure 7.11: A flashing cursor signals a successful connection

After creating a successful `telnet` socket connection, you may be wondering how to get back to the regular PowerShell interface. Press the *Ctrl +]* keys together (that second one is a closed bracket key, usually next to the backslash key on your keyboard), type the word `quit`, and then press *Enter*. This should return you to a regular prompt. Or simply close the PowerShell prompt and open a fresh one.

Test-NetConnection

If `ping` has an equivalent and improved PowerShell cmdlet called `Test-Connection`, does PowerShell also contain an improved tool that works similarly to `telnet` for testing socket connections to resources? It sure does. `Test-NetConnection` is another way to query particular ports or services on a remote system, and the displayed output is friendlier than that of `telnet`.

Let's walk through the same tests, once again querying port 80 on WEB1. You can see in the following screenshot that I have run the command twice. The first time the website on WEB1 was disabled, and my connection to port 80 failed. The second time, I re-enabled the website, and I now see a successful connection:

```
Test-NetConnection WEB1 -Port 80
```

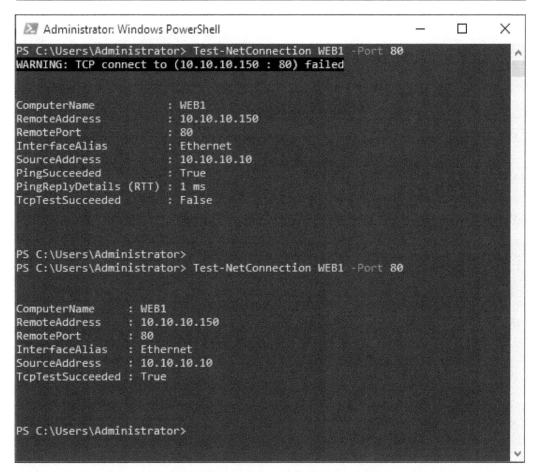

Figure 7.12: Using Test-NetConnection to test individual port connections

Packet tracing with Wireshark

Eventually, you might need to look a little deeper into your network packets. Now we are entering territory where your network team may also be involved, but if you are familiar with these tools, you may be able to solve the problem before needing to call for assistance. Making use of command-line tools to check on the status of servers and services is very useful, but occasionally it may not be enough. For example, you have a client application that is not connecting to the application server, but you don't know why. Utilities such as ping and even telnet might be able to connect successfully, indicating that network routing is set up properly, yet the application fails to connect when it opens. If the application's own event logs don't help you troubleshoot what is going on, you might want to take a deeper look inside the network packets that the application is trying to push toward the server.

This is where the **Wireshark** application comes in handy. Microsoft used to supply and support a couple of self-developed tools called NetMon and Message Analyzer that served similar functions, but both have now been officially retired. Probably because Wireshark is great, and it's free! This tool captures network traffic as it leaves from, or arrives at, a system, and captures the information that is *inside* the packets so that you can take a deeper look into what is going on. In our example of an application that cannot connect, you could run Wireshark on the client computer to watch outgoing traffic, and also on the application server to watch for incoming traffic from the client.

There is a whole lot of functionality inside Wireshark, and we don't have the space to cover all of it here, so I will leave you with a link from which to grab this tool so you can start testing it out for yourself: `https://www.wireshark.org/download.html`.

TCPView

The tools that we have discussed so far are great and can be used daily for poking and prodding individual resources that you want to test, but sometimes, there are situations where you need to step back and figure out what it is you are looking for in the first place. Maybe you are working with an application on a computer and are not sure what server it is talking to. Or perhaps you suspect a machine of having a virus and trying to *phone home* to somewhere on the internet, and you would like to identify the location that it is trying to talk to or the process that is making the call. In these situations, it would be helpful if there was a tool that you could launch on the local computer that shows you all of the network traffic streams that are active on this computer or server clearly and concisely. That is exactly what **TCPView** does. TCPView is a tool created by Sysinternals; you may have heard of some of their other tools, such as ProcMon and FileMon. Running TCPView on a machine displays all of the active TCP and UDP connections happening on that computer in real time. Also important is the fact that you do not need to install anything to make TCPView work; it is a standalone executable, making it extremely easy to use and clear off a machine when you are finished with it.

You can download TCPView from `https://technet.microsoft.com/en-us/sysinternals/tcpview.aspx`.

Simply copy the file onto a computer or server that you want to monitor and double-click on it. *Figure 7.13* shows the TCPView interface running on my local computer, showing all of the connections that Windows and my applications are currently making. You can pause this output to take a closer look, and you can also set filters to pare down the data and find what you are really looking for. Filters get rid of the *noise*, so to speak, and enable you to look more closely at a particular destination or a specific process ID:

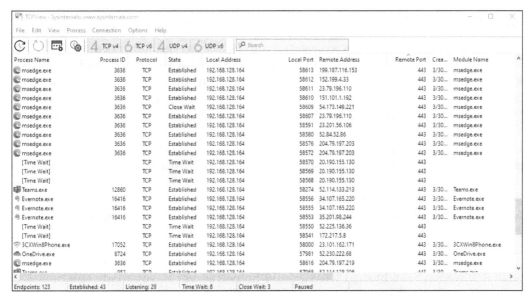

Figure 7.13: TCPView interface

Now that we have discovered and tested some tools that are useful for testing connections, let's move onto a new topic where we begin to manipulate the flow of network traffic from our servers. Follow along as we learn about the Windows routing table.

Building a routing table

When you hear the term **routing table**, it is easy to pass that off as something the network folks need to deal with, something that is configured within the network routers and firewalls. It doesn't apply to the server admins, right? Networking servers together has been made pretty easy for us by only requiring an IP address, subnet mask, and default gateway, and we can instantly communicate with everything inside the rest of our network. While there is indeed a lot of networking magic going on under the hood that has been provided to us by networking equipment and network administrators, it is important to understand how routing inside Windows works because there will be some cases when you need to modify or build out a routing table right on a Windows Server itself.

Multi-homed servers

Running multi-homed servers is a case where you would certainly need to understand and work with a local Windows routing table, so let's start here. If you think this doesn't apply to you because you've never heard of "multi-homed" before, think again. Multi-homed is just a funny-looking word meaning your server has more than one NIC. This could certainly be the case for you, even if you are a small shop that doesn't have a lot of servers. Often, Small Business or Essentials Servers have multiple network interfaces, separating internal LAN traffic from internet traffic. Another instance of a multi-homed server would be a remote access server that provides DirectAccess, VPN, or proxy capabilities at the edge of your network. Yet another reason to be interested and understand multi-homing is Hyper-V servers. It is very common for Hyper-V servers to have multiple NICs, because the VMs that are running on that server might need to tap into different physical networks within your organization.

Now that we have established what a multi-homed server is, you might still be wondering why we are discussing this. If I have more than one NIC, don't I simply configure each NIC individually inside Windows, giving each one an IP address, just like I would for any NIC on any server? Yes and no. Yes, you configure an IP address on each NIC, because it needs that for the identification and transport of packets on the network. No, you do not set up all of the NICs on your server in the same way. There is one critical item that you need to keep in mind and adhere to in order to make traffic flow properly on your multi-homed server.

Only one default gateway

This is the golden ticket. When you multi-home a server by having multiple NICs, you can only have one default gateway. One for your entire server. This means you will have one NIC with a default gateway, and one or many NICs that do *NOT* have a default gateway inside their TCP/IP settings. This is extremely important. The purpose of a default gateway is to be the *path of last resort*. When Windows wants to send a packet to a destination, it browses over the local routing table—yes, there is a routing table even if you haven't configured it or ever looked at it—and checks to see whether a specific, static route exists for the destination subnet where this packet needs to go. If a route exists, it shoots the packet out of that route and network interface to the destination. If no static route exists in the routing table, it falls back onto using the default gateway, and sends the traffic to that default gateway address. On all single NIC servers, the default gateway is a router that is designated with all of the routing information for your network, and so the server simply hands it to the router, and the router does the rest of the work.

When we have multiple NICs on a Windows Server, we cannot give each one a default gateway because it will confuse traffic flow from your server. It will be a crapshoot as to which default gateway traffic flows toward with every network transmission. I have helped many people troubleshoot servers in the field with exactly this problem. They needed to use their server as a bridge between two networks, or to have the server plugged into multiple different networks for whatever reason, and were struggling because sometimes the traffic seemed to work, and sometimes it didn't. We start looking through the NIC properties only to discover that every NIC has its own default gateway address in the TCP/IP properties. Bingo, that's our problem. The system is completely confused when it tries to send out traffic because it doesn't know which gateway it needs to use at what times.

If you have ever tried adding default gateways to more than one NIC on the same server, you are probably familiar with the warning prompt that is displayed when you do this. Let's give it a try. I have added another NIC to one of my servers and have IP settings configured on just one of the NICs. Now I will add a new IP address, subnet mask, and default gateway onto my second NIC. When I click on the **OK** button to save those changes, I am presented with the following popup:

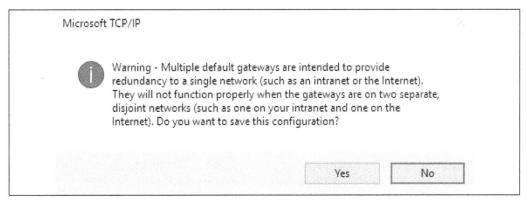

Figure 7.14: Warning message when configuring multiple default gateways

This is one of those warnings that is easy to misread because of its slightly cryptic nature, but you get the essence of it: proceed at your own risk! And then what do most admins do at this point? Simply click through it and save the changes anyway. Then the routing problems start. Maybe not today, but perhaps the next time you reboot that server, or maybe three weeks down the road, but at some point, your server will start to send packets to the wrong destinations and cause you trouble.

Building a route

So what is our answer to all of this? Building a static routing table. When you have multiple NICs on a server, thereby making it multi-homed, you must tell Windows which NIC to use for what traffic inside the routing table. This way, when network traffic needs to leave the server for a particular destination, the routing table is aware of the different directions and paths that the traffic will need to take in order to get there and will send it out accordingly. You will still be relying on routers to take the traffic the rest of the way, but getting the packets to the correct router by sending them out via the proper physical NIC is key to making sure that traffic flows quickly and appropriately from your multi-homed server.

Now that we understand why the routing table is important and conceptually how we need to use it, let's dig in and add a couple of routes on my dual-NIC server. We will add a route using the Command Prompt, and we will also add one using PowerShell, since you can accomplish this task from either platform, but the syntax used is different depending on which you prefer.

Adding a route with the Command Prompt

Before we can plan our new route, we need to get the lay of the land for the current networking configuration on this server. It has two NICs: one is plugged into my internal network and one is plugged into my DMZ that faces the internet. Since I can only have one default gateway address, it goes onto the DMZ NIC because there is no way that I could add routes for every subnet that might need to be contacted over the internet. By putting the default gateway on my DMZ NIC, the internal NIC does not have a default gateway and is very limited in what it can contact at the moment. The internal subnet that I am physically plugged into is `10.10.10.0/24`, so I can currently contact anything in this small network from `10.10.10.1` through `10.10.10.254`. This is known as an **on-link** route; since I am plugged directly into this subnet, my server automatically knows how to route traffic inside this subnet. However, I cannot contact anything else at the moment through my internal NIC because the routing table knows nothing about the other subnets that I have inside my internal network. For example, I have an additional subnet, `192.168.16.0/24`, and there are some servers running within this subnet that I need to be able to contact from this new server. If I were to try to contact one of those servers right now, the packets would shoot out from my DMZ NIC because the routing table on my server has no idea how to deal with `192.168` traffic, and so it would send it toward the default gateway. The following is the general syntax of the route statement we need to follow in order to make this traffic flow from our server into the new subnet:

```
Route add -p <SUBNET_ID> mask <SUBNET_MASK> <GATEWAY> IF <INTERFACE_ID>
```

Before we can type out our unique route statement for adding the 192.168 network, we need to do a little detective work and figure out what we are going to use in these fields. The following is a breakdown of the parts and pieces that are required to build a route statement:

- -p: This makes the command persistent. If you forget to put -p in the route add statement, this new route will disappear the next time you reboot the server. Not good.

- SUBNET_ID: This is the subnet we are adding; in our case, it is 192.168.16.0.

- SUBNET_MASK: This is the subnet mask number for the new route, 255.255.255.0.

- GATEWAY: This one is a little confusing. It is very common to think it means you need to enter the gateway address for the new subnet, but that would be incorrect. What you are actually defining here is the first hop that the server needs to hit in order to send out this traffic. Or, in other words, if you *had* configured a default gateway address on your internal NIC, what would that address be? For our network, it is 10.10.10.1. This effectively instructs the server, "any traffic destined for this route (192.168.16.0/24), shoot those packets at 10.10.10.1 and that guy will figure out what to do."

- INTERFACE_ID: Specifying an interface ID number is not entirely necessary to create a route, but if you do not specify it, there is a chance that your route could bind itself to the wrong NIC and send traffic out in the wrong direction. I have seen it happen before, so I always specify a NIC interface ID number. This is typically a one- or two-digit number that is the Windows identifier for the internal NIC itself. We can figure out what the interface ID number is by looking at the route print command:

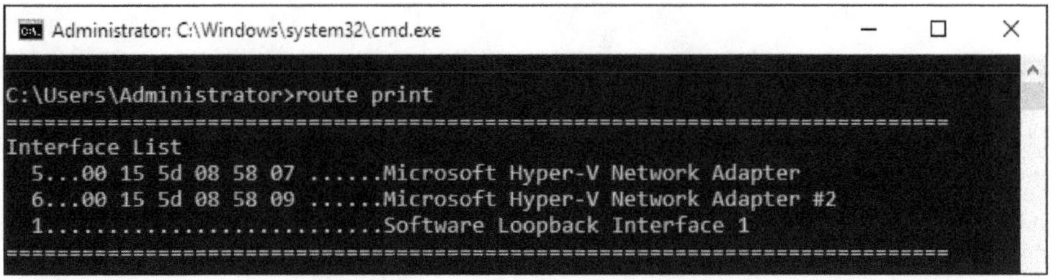

Figure 7.15: Acquiring the interface ID number

At the top of route print, you see all of the NICs in a system listed. In our case, the internal NIC is the top one in the list. I identified it by looking at the MAC address for this NIC from the output of an ipconfig /all command. As you can see, my internal NIC's interface ID number is 5. So in my route add statement, I am going to use IF 5 at the end of my statement to make sure my new route binds itself to that internal physical NIC.

The following is our completed `route add` statement:

```
route add -p 192.168.16.0 mask 255.255.255.0 10.10.10.1 if 5
```

```
Administrator: C:\Windows\system32\cmd.exe                          —    □    ✕

C:\>route add -p 192.168.16.0 mask 255.255.255.0 10.10.10.1 if 5
 OK!

C:\>_
```

Figure 7.16: Running the complete route statement

If you now run a `route print` command, you can see our new `192.168.16.0` route listed in the `Persistent Routes` section of the routing table, and we can now send packets into that subnet from this new server. Whenever our server has traffic that needs to go into the `192.168.16.x` subnet, it will send that traffic out via the *internal* NIC, toward the router running on `10.10.10.1`. The router then picks up the traffic from there and brings it into the `192.168.16.0` subnet:

```
===============================================================================

Persistent Routes:
  Network Address          Netmask  Gateway Address  Metric
          0.0.0.0          0.0.0.0      10.10.10.1  Default
     192.168.16.0    255.255.255.0      10.10.10.1        1
===============================================================================
```

Figure 7.17: Sending traffic to the 192.168.16.0 subnet

Deleting a route

Occasionally, you may key in a route statement incorrectly. The best way to handle this is to simply delete the bad route and then rerun your `route add` statement with the correct syntax. There are possibly other reasons why you might need to delete routes every now and then, so you'll want to be familiar with this command. Deleting routes is much simpler than adding new ones. All you need to know is the subnet ID for the route that you want to remove and then simply `route delete <SUBNET_ID>`. For example, to get rid of our `192.168.16.0` route that we created while we were working inside the Command Prompt, I would simply issue this command:

```
route delete 192.168.16.0
```

Adding a route with PowerShell

Since PowerShell is king when it comes to most command-line-oriented tasks inside Windows Server, we should accomplish the same mission from this interface as well. You can utilize the same route add command from inside the PowerShell prompt and that will work just fine, but there is also a specialized cmdlet that we can use. Let's utilize New-NetRoute to add yet another subnet to our routing table. This time, we are going to add 192.168.17.0. The following is a command we can utilize:

```
New-NetRoute -DestinationPrefix "192.168.17.0/24" -InterfaceIndex 5
-NextHop 10.10.10.1
```

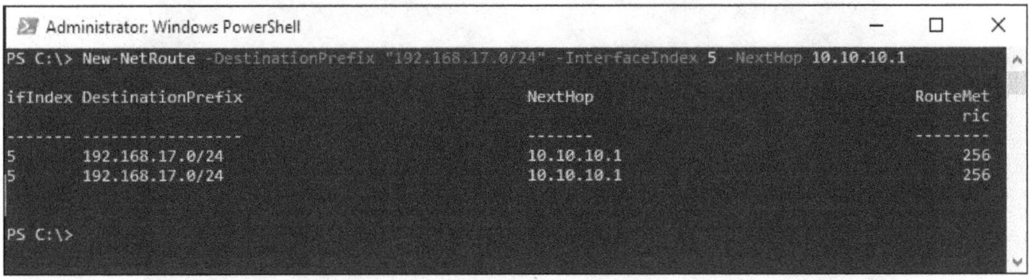

Figure 7.18: Adding another subnet to our routing table

You can see that the structure is similar, but a little bit friendlier. Instead of having to type the word mask and specify the whole subnet mask number, you can use the *slash* method to identify the subnet and mask within the same identifier. Also, where before we were specifying the *gateway*, which is always a little confusing, with the New-NetRoute cmdlet, we instead specify what is called the NextHop. This makes a little bit more sense to me.

Where we previously utilized route print to see our full routing table, the
PowerShell cmdlet to display that table for us is simply Get-NetRoute:

```
Administrator: Windows PowerShell

PS C:\> Get-NetRoute

ifIndex DestinationPrefix                         NextHop
------- -----------------                         -------
6       255.255.255.255/32                        0.0.0.0
5       255.255.255.255/32                        0.0.0.0
1       255.255.255.255/32                        0.0.0.0
6       224.0.0.0/4                               0.0.0.0
5       224.0.0.0/4                               0.0.0.0
1       224.0.0.0/4                               0.0.0.0
5       192.168.17.0/24                           10.10.10.1
1       127.255.255.255/32                        0.0.0.0
1       127.0.0.1/32                              0.0.0.0
1       127.0.0.0/8                               0.0.0.0
5       10.10.10.255/32                           0.0.0.0
5       10.10.10.13/32                            0.0.0.0
5       10.10.10.0/24                             0.0.0.0
6       0.0.0.0/0                                 1.1.1.1
6       ff00::/8                                  ::
5       ff00::/8                                  ::
1       ff00::/8                                  ::
6       fe80::1c58:5bf4:8b46:3559/128             ::
5       fe80::402:a7ae:81ac:e95b/128              ::
6       fe80::/64                                 ::
5       fe80::/64                                 ::
1       ::1/128                                   ::


PS C:\> _
```

Figure 7.19: Displaying our full routing table

Building routing tables is essential knowledge for any server admin who encounters
a server with multiple network interfaces that are connected to different networks.
Now, let's discuss another use case where you may find multiple network cards on
the same server, but this time connected to the same network.

NIC Teaming

Moving on to another network topic that is becoming more and more popular on
server hardware, let's walk through the steps to create NIC Teaming. The ability to
team NICs together essentially consists of binding two or more physical network
interfaces together so that they behave as if they were a single network interface
within Windows. This allows you to plug in two physical cables to two different
switch ports, all using the same settings. That way, if one NIC port or switch port
or patch cable goes bad, the server continues working and communicating without
hesitation, because the teaming allows the NIC that is still working to handle the
network traffic.

NIC Teaming itself is nothing new. It has been around for 10 years or more inside the Windows Server operating system. However, early versions were problematic, and in the field, I find that Server 2016 is the earliest server operating system most IT personnel consider to be stable enough to use NIC Teaming in production. So, based on that, it is still relatively new to the wild.

To begin teaming together your NICs, you need to make sure that you have multiple network cards on your server. I currently have four NIC ports on this machine. I have plans to create two teams: my first and second NICs will bind together to become an **Internal Network Team**, and my third and fourth NICs will become a **DMZ Network Team**. This way, I have network card redundancy on both sides of my network flow on this server.

The first thing I want to do is clear out any IP addressing settings that might exist on my NICs. You see, once you tie together multiple NICs into a team, you will configure IP addressing settings on the team—you will no longer dive into individual NIC properties to assign IP addresses. So open up the properties of each NIC and make sure they are clear of static IP information, like so:

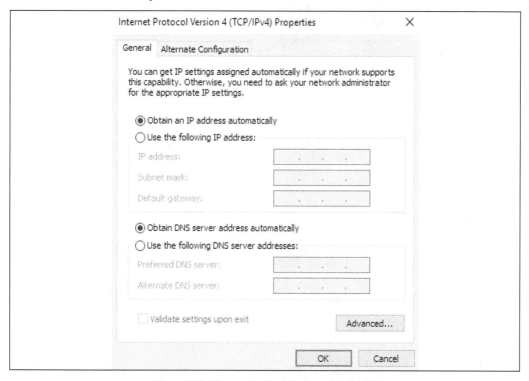

Figure 7.20: Clear static IP addresses of each NIC

Now open up Server Manager and click on **Local Server**. Looking inside the properties information for your server, you will see listings for each of your NICs, as well as an option called **NIC Teaming**, which is currently set to **Disabled**:

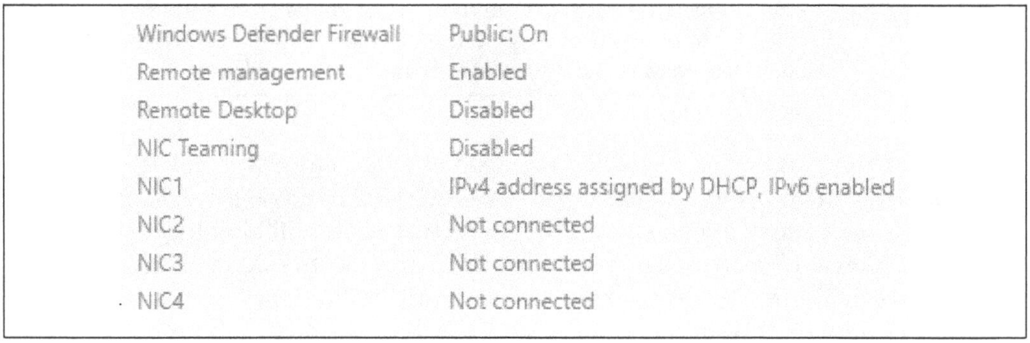

Windows Defender Firewall
Public: On
Remote management
Enabled
Remote Desktop
Disabled
NIC Teaming
Disabled
NIC1
IPv4 address assigned by DHCP, IPv6 enabled
NIC2
Not connected
NIC3
Not connected
NIC4
Not connected

Figure 7.21: NIC Teaming is initially disabled

Go ahead and click on the word **Disabled**, and now look for a section entitled **Teams**. Click on the **Tasks** button and choose to create a **New team**.

Give your new team an appropriate name and select the NICs that you want to be part of this team. Once finished, you can walk through the same steps as many times as you need to create additional teams with your remaining NICs:

NIC Teaming
New team
Team name:
Internal Network Team
Member adapters:
In Team
Adapter
Speed
State
Reason
NIC1
10 Gbps
NIC2
Disconnected
NIC3
Disconnected
NIC4
Disconnected

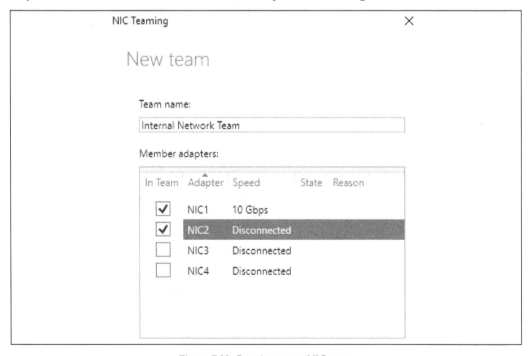

Figure 7.22: Creating a new NIC team

Once finished, you will see your teams listed inside Server Manager, and if you open up the **Network Connections** screen inside Windows, you can see in *Figure 7.23* that, in addition to the four physical NICs, I now have two new entries listed here, which are the configuration locations for our new teams. From here, I can right-click on each of my network teams and configure IP addressing information just like I would have done on a single NIC. IPs input into the team properties will be in effect on all NICs that are part of the team:

Figure 7.23: Additional NIC Teaming options under Network Connections

The items we have discussed so far in this chapter are useful for any environment utilizing Windows Server 2019, and can also be applied to many previous versions of the Windows Server operating system. Next, we will move into a topic that some of you may already be living within, but many others may never need to interface with – software-defined networking.

Software-defined networking

The flexibility and elasticity of cloud computing cannot be denied, and most technology executives are currently exploring their options for utilizing cloud technologies. One of the big stumbling blocks to adaptation is trust. Cloud services provide enormous computing power, all immediately accessible at the press of a button. In order for companies to store their data on these systems, the level of trust that your organization has in that cloud provider must be very high. After all, you don't own any of the hardware or networking infrastructure that your data is sitting on when it's in the cloud, and so your control of those resources is limited at best. Seeing this hurdle, Microsoft has made many efforts in recent updates to bring cloud-like technology into the local data center. Introducing server elasticity into our data centers means virtualization. We have been virtualizing servers for many years now, although the capabilities there are being continually improved. Now that we have the ability to spin up new servers so easily through virtualization technologies, it makes sense that the next hurdle will be our ability to easily move these virtual servers around whenever and wherever we need to.

Do you have a server that you want to move into a data center across the country? Are you thinking of migrating an entire data center into a new colocation across town? Maybe you have recently acquired a new company and need to bring its infrastructure into your network but have overlapping network configurations. Have you bought into some space at a cloud service provider and are now trying to wade through the mess of planning the migration of all your servers into the cloud? These are all questions that require an answer, and that answer is SDN.

SDN is a broad, general term that umbrellas many technologies working together to make this idea possible. Its purpose is to extend your network boundaries whenever and wherever you need. Let's take a look at some of the parts and pieces available in Windows Server 2019 that work in tandem to create a virtual networking environment, the first step in adopting our software-defined networking ideology.

Hyper-V Network Virtualization

The biggest component being focused on right now that brings the ability to pick up your networks and slide them around on a layer of virtualization lies within Hyper-V. This makes sense, because this is the same place you are touching and accessing to virtualize your servers. With Hyper-V Network Virtualization, we are creating a separation between the virtual networks and the physical networks. You no longer need to accommodate IP scheme limitations on the physical network when you set up new virtual networks, because the latter can ride on top of the physical network, even if the configurations of the two networks would normally be incompatible.

This concept is a little bit difficult to wrap your head around if this is the first time you are hearing about it, so let's discuss some real-world situations that would benefit from this kind of separation.

Private clouds

Private clouds are steamrolling through data centers around the world because they make a tremendous amount of sense. Anyone interested in bringing the big benefits of the cloud into their environments, while at the same time staying away from cloud negatives, can benefit from this. Building a private cloud gives you the ability to have dynamically expanding and shrinking compute resources and the ability to host multiple tenants or divisions within the same compute infrastructure. It provides management interfaces directly to those divisions so that the nitty-gritty setup and configuration work can be done by the tenant and you don't have to expend time and resources on the infrastructure-provider level, making small, detailed configurations.

Private clouds enable all of these capabilities while staying away from the big scare of your data being hosted in a cloud service provider's data center that you have no real control over, and all of the privacy concerns surrounding that.

In order to provide a private cloud inside your infrastructure, particularly one where you want to provide access to multiple tenants, the benefits of network virtualization become apparent, and even a requirement. Let's say you provide computing resources to two divisions of a company, and they each have their own needs for hosting some web servers. No big deal, but these two divisions both have administrative teams who want to use IP schemes that are within 10.0.0.0. They both need to be able to use the same IP addresses, on the same core network that you are providing, yet you need to keep all of their traffic completely segregated and separated. These requirements would have been impossible on a traditional physical network, but by employing the power of network virtualization, you can easily grant IP subnets and address schemes of whatever caliber each division chooses. They can run servers on whatever subnets and IP addresses they like, and all of the traffic is encapsulated uniquely so that it remains separated, completely unaware of the other traffic running around on the same physical core network that runs beneath the virtualization layer. This scenario also plays out well with corporate acquisitions. Two companies who are joining forces at the IT level often have conflicts with domains and network subnetting. With network virtualization, you can allow the existing infrastructure and servers to continue running with their current network config, but bring them within the same physical network by employing Hyper-V Network Virtualization.

Another simpler example is one where you simply want to move a server within a corporate network. Maybe you have a legacy line-of-business server that many employees still need access to, because their daily workload includes the LOB application to be working at all times. The problem with moving the server is that the LOB application on the client computers has a static IPv4 address configured by which it communicates with the server. When the user opens their app, it does something such as *talk to the server at* 10.10.10.10. Traditionally, that could turn into a dealbreaker for moving the server, because moving that server from its current data center into a new location would mean changing the IP address of the server, and that would break everyone's ability to connect to it. With virtual networks, this is not an issue. With the ability to ride network traffic and IP subnets on the virtualization layer, that server can move from New York to San Diego and retain all of its IP address settings because the physical network running underneath doesn't matter at all. All of the traffic is encapsulated before it is sent over the physical network, so the IP address of the legacy server can remain at 10.10.10.10, and it can be picked up and moved anywhere in your environment without interruption.

Hybrid clouds

While adding flexibility to your corporate networks is already a huge benefit, the capabilities provided by virtualizing your networks expand exponentially when you do finally decide to start delving into real cloud resources. If and when you make the decision to move some resources to be hosted by a public cloud service provider, you will likely run a hybrid cloud environment. This means that you will build some services in the cloud, but you will also retain some servers and services on-site. I foresee most companies staying in a hybrid cloud scenario for the rest of eternity, as a 100% movement to the cloud is simply not possible given the ways that many of our companies do business. So now that you want to set up a hybrid cloud, we are again looking at all kinds of headaches associated with the movement of resources between our physical and cloud networks. When I want to move a server from on-site into the cloud, I need to adjust everything so that the networking configuration is compatible with the cloud infrastructure, right? Won't I have to reconfigure the NIC on my server to match the subnet that is running in my cloud network? Nope, not if you have your network virtualization infrastructure up and running. Once again, software-defined networking saves the day, giving us the ability to retain the existing IP address information on our servers that are moving, and simply run them with those IP addresses in the cloud. Again, since all of the traffic is encapsulated before being transported, the physical network that is being provided by the cloud does not have to be compatible with, or distinct from, our virtual network, and this gives us the ability to seamlessly shuttle servers back and forth from on-premises to the cloud without having to make special accommodations for networking.

How does it work?

So far, it all sounds like a little bit of magic; how does this actually work and what pieces need to fit together in order to make network virtualization a reality in our organization? Something this comprehensive surely has many moving parts and cannot be turned on by simply flipping a switch. There are various technologies and components running within a network that has been enabled for network virtualization. Let's do a little explaining here so that you have a better understanding of the technologies and terminology that you will be dealing with once you start your work with software-defined networking.

System Center Virtual Machine Manager

Microsoft System Center is a key piece of the puzzle for creating your software-defined networking model, particularly the **Virtual Machine Manager (VMM)** component of System Center. The ability to pick up IP addresses and move them to other locations around the world requires some coordination of your networking devices, and VMM is here to help. This is the component that you interface with as your central management point to define and configure your virtual networks. System Center is an enormous topic with many options and data points that won't fit in this book, so I will leave you with a link as a starting point on VMM learning: https://docs.microsoft.com/en-us/system-center/vmm/?view=sc-vmm-2019.

Network Controller

Microsoft's Network Controller is a role that was initially introduced in Windows Server 2016, and as the name implies, it is used for control over network resources inside your organization. In most cases, it will be working side by side with VMM in order to make network configurations as centralized and seamless as possible. Network Controller is a standalone role and can be installed onto Server 2016 or 2019 and then accessed directly, without VMM, but I don't foresee many deployments leaving it at that. Interfacing with Network Controller directly is possible by tapping into its APIs with PowerShell, but is made even better by adding on a graphical interface from which you configure new networks, monitor existing networks and devices, or troubleshoot problems within the virtual networking model. The graphical interface that can be used is System Center VMM.

Network Controller can be used to configure many different aspects of your virtual and physical networks. You can configure IP subnets and addresses, configurations, and VLANs on Hyper-V switches, and you can even use it to configure NICs on your VMs. Network Controller also allows you to create and manage **Access Control List (ACL)** type rules within the Hyper-V switch so that you can build your own firewalling solution at this level, without needing to configure local firewalls on the VMs themselves or having dedicated firewall hardware. Network Controller can even be used to configure load balancing and provide VPN access through RRAS servers.

Generic Routing Encapsulation

Generic Routing Encapsulation (GRE) is just a tunneling protocol, but it's imperative in terms of making network virtualization happen successfully. Earlier, when we talked about moving IP subnets around and about how you can sit virtual networks on top of physical networks without regard for making sure that their IP configurations are compatible, we should add that all of that functionality is provided at the core by GRE. When your physical network is running `192.168.0.x` but you want to host some VMs on a subnet in that data center, you can create a virtual network of `10.10.10.x` without a problem, but that traffic needs to be able to traverse the physical `192.168` network for anything to work. This is where routing encapsulation comes into play. All of the packets from the `10.10.10.x` network are encapsulated before being transported across the physical `192.168.0.x` network. The `192.168.0.x` network sees these packets as `192.168.0.x` packets, but they are actually carrying payloads for the `10.10.10.x` network.

There are two different specific routing-encapsulation protocols that are supported in our Microsoft Hyper-V Network Virtualization environment. In previous versions of the Windows Server operating system, we could only focus on **Network Virtualization Generic Routing Encapsulation (NVGRE)**, since this was the only protocol that was supported by the Windows flavor of network virtualization. However, there is another protocol, called **Virtual Extensible Local Area Network (VXLAN)**, that has existed for quite some time, and many of the network switches — particularly Cisco — that you have in your environment are more likely to support VXLAN than they are NVGRE. So, for the new network-virtualization platforms provided within Windows Server 2016+, we are now able to support either NVGRE or VXLAN, whichever best fits the needs of your company.

You don't necessarily have to understand how these GRE protocols work in order to make them do work for you, since they will be configured for you by the management tools that exist in this Hyper-V Network Virtualization stack. But it is important to understand in the overall concept of this virtual networking environment that GRE exists, and that it is the secret to making all of this work.

Microsoft Azure Virtual Network

Once you have Hyper-V Network Virtualization running inside your corporate network and get comfortable with the mentality of separating the physical and virtual networks, you will more than likely want to explore the possibilities around interacting with cloud service provider networks. When you utilize Microsoft Azure as your cloud service provider, you have the ability to build a hybrid cloud environment that bridges your on-premises physical networks with remote virtual networks hosted in Azure. Azure's virtual network is the component within Azure that allows you to bring your own IP addresses and subnets into the cloud. You can get more info (and even sign up for a free trial of Azure virtual network) here: https://azure.microsoft.com/en-us/services/virtual-network/.

RAS Gateway/SDN Gateway

When you are working with physical networks, virtual networks, and virtual networks that are stored in cloud environments, you need some component to bridge those gaps, enabling the networks to interact and communicate with each other. This is where a RAS Gateway (also called an **SDN Gateway**) comes into play. This role has enjoyed a few different names over the years; you may also see these servers referenced as a Windows Server Gateway or even the Hyper-V Network Virtualization Gateway in some documentation. A RAS Gateway's purpose is pretty simple: to be the connection between a virtual network and some other network, most often, a gateway between a virtual network and a physical network. These virtual networks can be hosted in your local environment, or in the cloud. In either case, when you want to connect networks, you will need to employ a gateway. When you are creating a bridge between on-premises and the cloud, your cloud service provider will utilize a gateway on their side, which you would tap into from the physical network via a VPN tunnel.

A RAS Gateway is generally a virtual machine, and is integrated with Hyper-V Network Virtualization. A single gateway can be used to route traffic for many different customers, tenants, or divisions. Even though these different customers have separated networks that need to retain separation from traffic of the other customers, cloud providers—public or private—can still utilize a single gateway to manage this traffic, because the gateways retain complete isolation between those traffic streams.

The Windows Server Gateway functionality existed in Server 2016, but once it was put into practice, some performance limitations that restricted network traffic throughput were discovered. Those overheads have now been increased dramatically in Windows Server 2019, meaning that you can flow more traffic and additional tenants through a single gateway than was previously possible.

Virtual network encryption

Security teams are continually concerned with the encryption of data. Whether that data is stored or on the move, making sure that it is properly secured and safe from tampering is essential. Prior to Server 2019, getting inner-network traffic encrypted while it was moving was generally the responsibility of the software application itself, not a network's job. If your software can encrypt traffic while it is flowing between the client and server, or between the application server and the database server, great! If your application does not have native encryption capabilities, it is likely that the communications from that application are flowing in cleartext between the client and server. Even for applications that do encrypt, encryption ciphers and algorithms are sometimes cracked and compromised, and in the future, as new vulnerabilities are discovered, hopefully the way that your application encrypts its traffic can be updated in order to support newer and better encryption methods.

Fortunately, Windows Server 2019 brings us a new capability within the boundaries of software-defined networking. This capability is called **virtual network encryption**, and it does just what the name implies. When traffic moves between virtual machines and between Hyper-V servers (within the same network), entire subnets can be flagged for encryption, which means that all traffic flowing around those subnets is automatically encrypted at the virtual networking level. The VM servers and your applications that are running on those servers don't have to be configured or changed in any way to take advantage of this encryption, as it happens within the network itself, automatically encrypting all traffic that flows on that network.

With Server 2019 SDN, any subnet in a virtual network can be flagged for encryption by specifying a certificate to use for that encryption. If the future happens to bring the scenario where the current encryption standards are out of date or insecure, the SDN fabric can be updated to new encryption standards, and those subnets will continue to be encrypted using the new methods, once again without having to make changes to your VMs or applications. If you are using SDN and virtual networks in your environments, enabling encryption on those subnets is a no-brainer!

Bridging the gap to Azure

Most companies that host servers in Microsoft Azure still have physical, on-premises networks, and one of the big questions that always needs to be answered is *How are we going to connect our physical data center to our Azure data center?* Usually, companies will establish one of two different methods to make this happen. You can deploy gateway servers on the edges of both your on-site and Azure networks, and connect them using a site-to-site VPN. This establishes a continuous tunnel between the two networks that is managed by you, on your own servers or appliances. Alternatively, Microsoft provides a service called **Azure ExpressRoute** that effectively does the same thing; it creates a permanent tunnel between your physical network and that of your Azure virtual networks, although with ExpressRoute, you only need to supply equipment on your end of the connection, and you pay Microsoft to take care of the Azure side. Either of these methods works great once configured, but these solutions might be considered overkill by small organizations that only have a few on-premises servers that need to be connected to the Azure Cloud.

Azure Network Adapter

In the event that you have an on-premises server that you need to quickly connect to your Azure environment (and you don't already have a permanent connection established between your physical and Azure sites), there is a hybrid cloud capability called **Azure Network Adapter** that can be attached to your Windows Servers. In order to use one of these new network adapters, you must be utilizing the new Windows Admin Center to manage your servers.

Using Windows Admin Center, you can quickly add an Azure Network Adapter to an on-premises server, which connects it straight to your Azure network using a point-to-site VPN connection. Cool! This capability could be helpful for small businesses who have cloud resources and want to connect just a single on-premises server into Azure, or even for a branch office scenario at a larger company. Rather than creating site-to-site connections between your primary data center and each branch office, if your primary data center was already permanently connected to Azure, you could then connect branch office servers directly to Azure using Azure Network Adapters.

What Azure Network Adapter really does is configure point-to-site VPN for you on that server, connecting the server to Azure via a VPN tunnel. As you know, a VPN tunnel requires both client configuration and a VPN concentrator or gateway on the receiving side, which is exactly what Azure Network Adapter does. It configures the P2S client VPN on the server and spins up a virtual network gateway inside Azure to receive that connection.

Even better, this capability has been back-ported so that you can add one of these adapters not only to Server 2019 machines, but also to Server 2016 and Server 2012 R2 machines as well.

To make this happen, there are a few requirements that need to be in place. You must have an active Azure subscription, and you need to have at least one Azure virtual network configured.

Next, you need to register your Windows Admin Center with Azure. This is accomplished by opening up **Windows Admin Center** and visiting **Settings**. Once inside, navigate to **GATEWAY | Azure** and walk through the registration process:

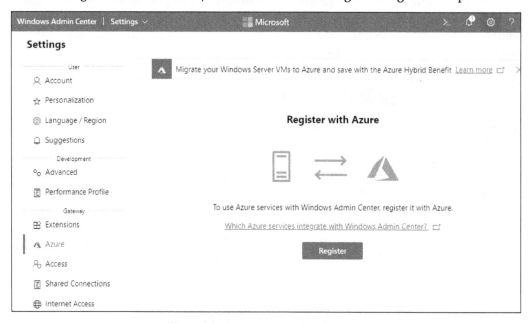

Figure 7.24: Registering WAC with Azure

Now that your WAC is registered with Azure, open up the server that you are managing from inside WAC and head over to the **Networks** section. You will see listed here any NICs that are present on your server, and near the top of the window is an ellipsis that can be selected to show additional options. Inside, click on **Add Azure Network Adapter (Preview)**:

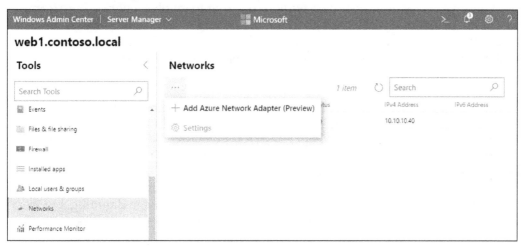

Figure 7.25: Adding an Azure Network Adaptor

You will find that all of the values that Azure needs in order to make this connection are auto-populated for you, based on your Azure network and subscription. If you don't already have an Azure virtual network, this wizard can even create one for you. You also get the opportunity to specify your own certificate for authenticating this connection, and doing so would be a good practice if you plan for this to be a long-term connection to Azure; otherwise, you can proceed without any input by allowing WAC/Azure to generate a self-signed certificate and simply click on the **Create** button. Windows Admin Center will go ahead and create a connection between your on-premises server and the Azure virtual network. That was only a couple of mouse clicks! This is an ingenious way of creating ad hoc connections between your servers and Azure very quickly and without complications.

If you later need to disconnect this server from the Azure network, you can open up **Network Connections** on that on-premises server, just like you would when trying to modify NIC properties on your server, and you will find that what WAC has done under the hood is configure a point-to-site VPN connection, which is listed inside **Network Connections**. You can simply right-click on that Azure VPN connection and disconnect it.

Summary

Server administration and network administration used to be segregated pretty clearly in most organizations, but over time those lines have blurred. There are numerous networking configurations and tasks that now need to be accomplished by Windows Server administrators without needing to involve a networking team, so it is important that you have a good understanding of how your infrastructure connects together. Familiarity with the tools laid out in this chapter will provide you with the ability to configure, monitor, and troubleshoot the majority of Microsoft-centric networks.

Our introduction to software-defined networking may be a partially confusing section if you have never encountered this idea before, but hopefully it will prompt you to dig a little deeper and prepare yourself for dealing with this in the future. Ready or not, the cloud is here to stay. Microsoft on-premises networks now have numerous ways you can interact with Microsoft Azure, and it will soon be imperative that IT staff are familiar with these concepts. The idea of SDN will grow in popularity over the coming years. At the moment, it may seem daunting, but in 5 years, we may all look back and wonder how we ever made things work without virtual networks. There is much more information both on Microsoft Docs and in published books about Hyper-V Virtual Networking and System Center Virtual Machine Manager if you are interested in setting this up for yourself. For now, continue on with our next chapter, where we discuss the componentry in Windows Server 2019 that is going to enable our employees to work remotely, which is particularly interesting content in this new work-from-home world we are living in.

Questions

1. How many bits in length is an IPv6 address?

2. Re-write the following IPv6 address in condensed form:
   `2001:ABCD:0001:0002:0000:0000:0000:0001`.

3. What is the name of the command that is similar to trace route, but displays the local NIC that traffic is flowing out of?

4. True or False—On a server with multiple NICs, you can input a default gateway address onto each of those NICs.

5. What is the PowerShell cmdlet that can be used to create new routes on a Windows Server?

6. Which Windows Server operating systems can be used with an Azure Network Adapter in order to connect them straight to Azure virtual networks?

8
Remote Access

Giving employees the ability to remotely access corporate resources used to be a big benefit to most companies, but not necessarily a requirement. That mindset has changed significantly over the past year, where many of us are now forced to work from home because our governments have put orders in place preventing us from going into the office due to COVID-19. Most companies and employees now expect to get their work done from wherever they happen to be. Cell phones are a big part of this equation but are limited by the scope of what can be done with small screens and restricted operating systems. To grant remote workers the ability to do their jobs from home, coffee shops, or hotels, we have traditionally used Virtual Private Networks (VPNs).

Most VPNs in today's businesses are provided by products from companies other than Microsoft. The Remote Access role in Windows Server 2019 is here to change that. With many improvements having been made to the VPN components right in Windows Server, it is now a feasible and secure platform for providing access to corporate resources from remote computers. In addition to VPN connectivity, we have a couple of newer technologies baked into Windows Server 2019 that are also designed to provide remote access to corporate resources in a different way than a traditional VPN. The topics that we will cover in this chapter are the following:

- Always On VPN
- DirectAccess
- Remote Access Management Console
- DA, VPN, or AOVPN? Which is best?
- Web Application Proxy

- Requirements for WAP
- Latest improvements to WAP

Always On VPN

Giving a user access to a VPN connection traditionally means providing them with a special network connection link that they can launch and enter credentials to pass authentication to connect to their work environment's network to communicate with company resources. After launching a VPN, users can open their email, find documents, launch their line-of-business applications, or otherwise work in the same ways that they can when physically sitting in their office. Also, when connected via a VPN, management of their laptop is possible, enabling successful communication flow for systems such as Group Policy and SCCM. VPN connections offer great connectivity back to your network, but (remember, we are talking about traditional, regular VPN connections here) they only work when the user manually launches them and tells them to work. Anytime that a user has not connected to their VPN, they are navigating the internet with no connectivity back to the company datacenter. This also means that a traditional VPN connection has no form of connectivity on the Windows login screen, because, until they get logged into the computer and find their way to the Windows desktop, users have no way of launching that VPN tunnel. This means that anything that might attempt to happen at the login screen, such as live authentication lookups, or during the login process, such as Group Policy processing or logon scripts, will not function via a traditional VPN.

Always On VPN (AOVPN), just as you have probably guessed based on the name, is simply the idea of making a VPN connection continuous and automatically connected. In other words, any time that the user has their laptop outside the office walls and is connected to the internet, a VPN tunnel back to the corporate network is automatically established, ideally with zero user input to the process. This enables users to forget about the VPN altogether, as it is simply always connected and ready for them to use. They can log into their machines, launch their applications, and start working. It also means that IT management functions such as security policies, updates, and installer packages can push out to client machines a greater percentage of the time, since we no longer wait for the user to decide when they want to connect back to work; it happens automatically and pretty much all the time.

There are actually three different ways in which Always On VPN can be triggered on the client machine, and none of them involve the user having to launch a VPN connection:

- AOVPN can be configured to truly be Always On, meaning that as soon as internet access is available, it will always attempt to connect.

- Another option is **application triggering**, which means that you can configure AOVPN to launch itself only when specific applications are opened on the workstation.

- The third option is DNS name-based triggering. This calls the VPN connection into action when particular DNS names are called for, which generally happens when users launch specific applications.

Since you don't need Always On VPN to be connected and working when your laptop is sitting *inside* the corporate network, we should also discuss the fact that AOVPN is smart enough to turn itself off when the user walks through those glass doors. AOVPN-enabled computers will automatically decide when they are inside the network, therefore disabling VPN components, and when they are outside the network and need to launch the VPN tunnel connection. This detection process is known as **Trusted Network Detection**. When configured properly, Always On VPN components know what your company's internal DNS suffix is, and then it monitors your NIC and firewall profile settings to establish whether or not that same suffix has been assigned to those components. When it sees a match, it knows you are inside the network and then disables AOVPN.

Types of AOVPN tunnels

Before we get started on the particulars of the client and server components required to make AOVPN happen, there is an important core topic that needs to be understood to make appropriate decisions about how you want to utilize AOVPN in your company. There are two very different kinds of VPN tunnels that can be used with Always On VPN: a **user tunnel** and a **device tunnel**. As you will learn later in this chapter, the ability to have two different kinds of tunnels is something included with AOVPN to bring it closer to feature parity with **DirectAccess** (**DA**), which also has this dual-tunnel mentality. Let's take a minute and explore the purposes behind the two tunnels.

User tunnels

The most common way of doing AOVPN in the wild (so far) involves a user tunnel being authenticated on the user level. User certificates are issued from an internal PKI to your computers, and these certificates are then used as part of the authentication process during connection. User tunnels carry all of the machine and user traffic, but it is very important to note that user tunnels cannot be established while the computer is sitting on the login screen because user authentication has not happened at that point. So, a user tunnel will only launch itself once a user has successfully logged into the computer. With only a user tunnel at play, the computer will not have connectivity back to the corporate network for management functions until someone has logged into the computer, and this also means that you will be relying on cached credentials in order to pass through the login prompt.

Device tunnels

A device tunnel is intended to fill the gaps left by only running a user tunnel. A device tunnel is authenticated via a machine certificate, also issued from your internal PKI. This means that the device tunnel can establish itself even prior to user authentication. In other words, it works even while sitting on the Windows login screen. This enables management tools such as Group Policy and SCCM to work regardless of user input, and it also enables real-time authentication against domain controllers, enabling users to log into the workstation who have never logged into it before. This also enables real-time password expiry resets.

Device tunnel requirements

A user tunnel can work with pretty much any Windows 10 machine, but there are some firm requirements to be able to make use of a device tunnel. In order to roll out a device tunnel, you need to meet the following requirements:

- The client must be **domain-joined**.
- The client must be issued a **machine certificate**.
- The client must be running **Windows 10 1709 or newer**.
- **The client must be running Windows 10 Enterprise** or **Education** SKUs.
- A device tunnel can only be **IKEv2**. This is not necessarily a requirement, but it is important to understand once we get around to discussing what IKEv2 is and why it may or may not be the best connectivity method for your clients.

AOVPN client requirements

It is important to understand that the *Always On* part of Always On VPN is really client-side functionality. You can utilize AOVPN on a client computer to connect to many different kinds of VPN infrastructure on the backend. We will talk about that shortly, in the *AOVPN server components* section.

While creating regular, manual VPN connections has been possible on Windows client operating systems for 15 or 20 years, Always On VPN is quite new. Your workforce will need to be running Windows 10 to make this happen. Specifically, they will need to be running Windows 10 version 1607 or a more recent version.

The following are the supported SKUs:

- Windows 10 1607+
- Windows 10 1709+
- Windows 10 1803+

Wait a minute — that doesn't make any sense. Why list those three items separately if they are inclusive of one another? Because, while technically Always On VPN was officially introduced in Windows 10 1607, it has had some improvements along the way. Let's list those again, with a brief summary of what has changed over the years:

- **Windows 10 1607**: The original capability to auto-launch a VPN connection, thus enabling Always On VPN.

- **Windows 10 1709**: Updates and changes included the addition of device tunnels. If you intend to run a device tunnel for computer management purposes (and most enterprises will), then consider 1709 to be your minimum OS requirement.

- **Windows 10 1803**: Includes some major fixes that were discovered in 1709. In reality, what this means is that I never see anyone implementing Always On VPN unless they are running 1803. Thankfully, the Windows 10 update platform is much improved, meaning that many more companies are rolling out newer versions of Win10 on an ongoing basis, and 1803 is now mostly in the dust, having long ago been replaced by even newer versions.

Whether you are running 1607, 1709, 1803, 1809, or whatever the latest and greatest is, the particular SKU within those platforms does not matter. Well, it hardly matters. Always On VPN works with Windows 10 Home, Pro, Enterprise, and all of the other flavors. That is, the user tunnel works with all of those.

It is important enough to point out once again: if you want to utilize a device tunnel with Always On VPN, using domain-joined, Windows 10 Enterprise or Education SKUs is a firm requirement.

Domain-joined

As we have already established, when you're interested in using the AOVPN device tunnel, your client computers must be domain-joined. However, if you are okay with only running the user tunnel for AOVPN access, then there are no domain-membership requirements. Clients still need to be running Windows 10 1607 or newer, but they could be any SKU and could even be home computers that are joined to simple workgroups; no domain is required.

This is emphasized specifically in Microsoft documentation in many places, because it enables Always On VPN to be utilized (somewhat) with the **Bring Your Own Device (BYOD)** crowd. While this is interesting, I don't foresee it being at all common that companies would allow employees' personal computers to be connected to their VPN. Most organizations are trying to cater in a small way to the BYOD market by providing access to some resources via the cloud, such as Office 365 for email and documents. But connecting those personal computers and devices back to your network with a full-scale layer 3 VPN tunnel? I don't think so. That is the stuff of security administrators' nightmares.

Rolling out the settings

Let's say you have all of the server-side parts and pieces ready to roll for VPN connectivity, and in fact, you have successfully established the fact that you can create ad hoc traditional VPN connections to your infrastructure with no problems. Great! Looks like you are ready from the infrastructural side. Now, what is necessary to get clients to start doing Always On connections?

This is currently a bit of a stiff requirement for some businesses. The configuration itself of the Always On VPN policy settings isn't terribly hard; you just have to be familiar with the different options that are available, decide on which ones are important to your deployment, and put together the configuration file/script. While we don't have space here to cover all of those options in detail, the method for putting those settings together is generally to build a manual-launch VPN connection, tweak it to the security and authentication settings you want for your workforce, and then run a utility that exports that configuration out to some configuration files. These VPN profile settings come in XML and PS1 (PowerShell script) flavors, and you may need one or both of these files in order to roll the settings around to your workforce. The following is a great starting point for working with these configurations: `https://docs.microsoft.com/en-us/windows-server/remote/remote-access/vpn/always-on-vpn/deploy/vpn-deploy-client-vpn-connections`.

Once you have created your configuration files, you then face the task of pushing that configuration out to the clients. You ideally need to have a **mobile device management (MDM)** solution of some kind in order to roll the settings out to your workforce. While many technologies in the wild could be considered MDMs, the two that Microsoft is focused on are **System Center Configuration Manager (SCCM)** and **Microsoft Intune**.

If you have SCCM on-premises, great! You can easily configure and roll out PowerShell-based configuration settings to your client computers and enable them for Always On VPN.

Perhaps you don't have SCCM, but you are cloud-focused, and you have all of your computers tapped into Intune? Wonderful! You could alternatively use Intune to roll out those AOVPN settings via XML configuration. One of the benefits of taking the Intune route is that Intune can manage non-domain-joined computers, so you could theoretically include users' home and personal computers in your Intune-managed infrastructure and set them up to connect.

SCCM and Intune are great, but not everybody is running them. There is a third option for rolling out Always On VPN settings via PowerShell scripting. While this is *plan B* from Microsoft (they would really prefer you to roll out AOVPN via an MDM), I'm afraid that PowerShell will be the reality for many SMB customers who want to utilize AOVPN. The biggest downside to using PowerShell to put AOVPN settings in place is that PowerShell needs to be run in elevated mode, meaning that it's difficult to automate because the logged-on user (which is where you need to establish the VPN connection) needs to be a local administrator for the script to run properly.

I am hopefully and anxiously waiting for the day that they announce a Group Policy template for rolling out Always On VPN settings, but so far, there is no word on whether or not that will ever be an option. Everyone has Group Policy; not everyone has MDM. You will read in a few moments that the rollout of Microsoft DirectAccess connectivity settings (an alternative to AOVPN) is done via Group Policy, which is incredibly easy to understand and manage. As far as I'm concerned, at the time of writing, DirectAccess holds a major advantage over AOVPN in the way that it handles the client-side rollout of settings. But, make sure you check out Microsoft Docs online to find the latest information on this topic, as AOVPN is being continuously improved and there will likely be some changes coming to this area of the technology.

AOVPN server components

Now that we understand what is needed on the client side to make Always On VPN work, what parts and pieces are necessary on the server/infrastructure side in order to allow these connections to happen? Interestingly, the *Always On* component of AOVPN has nothing to do with server infrastructure; the Always On part is handled completely on the client side. Therefore, all we need to do on the server side is make sure that we can receive incoming VPN connections. If you currently have a workforce who are making successful VPN connections, then there is a good chance that you already have the server infrastructure necessary for bringing AOVPN into your environment.

Remote Access server

Obviously, you need a VPN server to host VPN connections, right? Well, not so obviously. In Windows Server, the role that hosts VPN, AOVPN, and DirectAccess connections is called the **Remote Access** role, but you can actually get Always On VPN working without Windows Server as your Remote Access server. Since the *Always On* part is client-side functionality, this enables VPN server-side infrastructures to be hosted by third-party vendors. Even though that is technically accurate, it's not really what Microsoft expects; nor is it what I find in the field. In reality, those of us interested in using Microsoft Always On VPN will be using Microsoft Windows Server to host the Remote Access role, which will be the inbound system that our remote clients connect to.

A lot of people automatically assume that AOVPN is married to Windows Server 2019 because it's a brand-new technology and Server 2019 was just released, but that is actually not the case at all. You can host your VPN infrastructure (the Remote Access role) on Server 2019, Server 2016, or even Server 2012 R2. It works the same on the backend, giving clients a place to tap into with their VPN connections.

After installing the Remote Access role on your new Windows Server, you will find that the majority of the VPN configuration happens from the **Routing and Remote Access** (**RRAS**) console. While configuring your VPN, you will find that there are multiple protocols that can be used to establish a VPN connection between client and server, and you should have at least a brief understanding of what those different protocols are. I'll list them here in order of *strongest and most secure*, all the way down to **don't touch this one!**

IKEv2

The newest, strongest, and all-in-all best way to connect your client computers via VPN or AOVPN, IKEv2 is the only way to connect the AOVPN device tunnel. IKEv2 requires machine certificates to be issued to your client computers in order to authenticate. This generally means that if you want clients to connect via IKEv2, those clients will be domain-joined. It is very important to note that IKEv2 uses UDP ports 500 and 4500 to make its connection, which is sometimes a hindrance and blocked by firewalls.

SSTP

Considered to be the *fallback method* for connecting AOVPN connections, SSTP uses an SSL stream to connect. Because of this, it requires an SSL certificate to be installed on the Remote Access server but does not require machine certificates on the client computers. SSTP uses TCP port 443, and so it is able to connect even from inside very restrictive networks where IKEv2 may fail (because of IKEv2's reliance on UDP).

L2TP

Not generally used for AOVPN deployments, L2TP is able to establish VPN connections by using certificates or a pre-shared key. Since you already have two better protocols at your disposal, you shouldn't be using this one.

PPTP

While still a valid configuration option inside RRAS, stay away from this guy! PPTP is no longer a secure method of tunneling, and if you are still running VPN connections based on PPTP, you essentially need to consider those traffic streams to be unencrypted and clear-text over the internet.

Certification Authority (CA)

Machine certificates, user certificates, SSL certificates... Oh, my! Clearly, you need to be familiar with working with and deploying certificates to make use of Always On VPN. This is becoming more and more common with newer, well-secured technologies of any flavor. The major requirement here is that you will need to have PKI inside your environment and at least one Windows CA server to issue the necessary certificates. The following is a list of the places in which certificates could be used by an AOVPN infrastructure:

- **User certificates**: These are the certificates issued to your VPN users from an internal CA, used for authentication of the user tunnel

- **Machine certificates**: These are certificates issued to your workstations (mostly laptops) from an internal CA, used for authentication of the device tunnel

- **SSL certificate**: Installed on your Remote Access server to validate the incoming traffic for SSTP VPN connections

- **VPN and NPS machine certificates**: Your Remote Access server, as well as your NPS servers, which we will talk about in just a minute, require machine certificates issued from your internal CA

Network Policy Server (NPS)

NPS is basically the authentication method for VPN connections. When a VPN connection request comes in, the Remote Access server hands that authentication request over to an NPS server to validate who that user is and also to verify that the user has permissions to log in via the VPN.

Most commonly when working with Microsoft VPN connections, we configure NPS so that it allows only users who are part of a certain Active Directory Security Group. For example, if you create a group called **VPN Users** and then point NPS to that group, it will only allow users whom you have placed inside that group to make successful VPN connections.

NPS is another Windows Server role that can be hosted on its own system or spread across multiple servers for redundancy. As with the Remote Access role, there is no Server 2019 requirement for NPS. You could easily deploy it on previous versions of Windows Server just as well.

In small environments that have just a single Remote Access server, it is common to co-host the NPS role right on the same server that is providing VPN connectivity.

DirectAccess

Throughout our discussion about Always On VPN, I mentioned Microsoft DirectAccess a couple of times. DirectAccess is another form of automatic VPN-like connectivity, but it takes a different approach than that of Always On VPN. Where AOVPN simply uses expected, well-known VPN protocols and does some crafty magic to automatically launch those otherwise traditional VPN tunnels, DirectAccess tunnels are quite proprietary. Tunnels are protected by IPsec and are essentially impenetrable and also unable to be impersonated. I find that security teams love the protections and complexity surrounding DA tunnels because it is a connection platform that attackers have no idea how to tamper with or how to replicate.

In my experience, at this point in the game, Microsoft DirectAccess is the most common reason that administrators deploy the Remote Access role on a Windows Server instance. As stated, the easiest way to think about DirectAccess is to think of it as an automatic VPN. Similar to a VPN, its purpose is to connect users' computers to the corporate network when they are outside the office. Different from a VPN, however, is the method that employees use in order to make this connection possible. DirectAccess is not a software component; it is a series of components that are already baked into the Windows operating system, working in tandem to provide completely seamless access for the user. What do I mean by seamless? In the same way that AOVPN connects without user interaction, there is nothing the user needs to do to make DirectAccess connect. It does that all by itself. As soon as the mobile computer receives an internet connection, whether that connection is home Wi-Fi, public internet at a coffee shop, or a cell phone hotspot connection, DirectAccess tunnels automatically build themselves using whatever internet connection is available, without any user input.

Whether using Always On VPN or DirectAccess, when your computer connects automatically it saves you time and money. Time is saved because the user no longer has to launch a VPN connection. Money is saved because time equals money, but also because having an *always-on* connection means that patching, security policies, and the management of those remote computers always happens, even when the user is working remotely. You no longer have to wait for users to get back into the office or for them to choose to launch their manual VPN connection in order to push new settings and policies down to their computers; it all happens wherever they are, as long as they have internet access. Clearly, with the advent of two different remote access technologies that are both focused on automatic connectivity for remote users, Microsoft is clearing the way for a more productive workforce. The terms **user-friendly** and **VPN** have never gone hand-in-hand before, but in the latest versions of the Windows operating systems, that is exactly the goal.

DirectAccess has actually been around since the release of Windows Server 2008 R2, and yet I regularly bump into people who have never heard of it. In the early days, it was quite difficult to deploy and came with a lot of awkward requirements, but much has changed over the past few years and DirectAccess is now easier than ever to deploy, and more beneficial than ever to have running in your environment.

The truth about DirectAccess and IPv6

One of the awkward requirements I mentioned *used* to be the need for IPv6 inside your network. With the first version of DirectAccess, this was an unfortunate requirement. I say unfortunate because even today almost nobody is running IPv6 inside their corporate networks, let alone years ago when this technology was released—a lot of admins didn't even know what IPv6 was. Fortunately, the requirement for IPv6 inside your networks is no more. I repeat, just in case anybody wasn't paying attention or is reading old, outdated TechNet documents—*you do not need IPv6 to use DirectAccess!* I have seen too many cases where DirectAccess was considered by a company, but the project was tossed aside because reading on TechNet made them believe that IPv6 was a requirement, and they discarded DirectAccess as something that wouldn't work. You absolutely do not have to be running IPv6 in your network to make DirectAccess function, but it is important to understand how DirectAccess uses IPv6, because you will start to encounter traces of it once your deployment gets underway.

When I am sitting at home, working on my company laptop, DirectAccess connects me to the corporate network. My internal network at work has absolutely no IPv6 running inside of it; we are a completely IPv4 network at the moment. This is true for most companies today. However, when I open Command Prompt and ping one of my servers from my DirectAccess laptop, this is what I see—apologies for the sanitized output of the screenshot:

```
Pinging     -vdt-02.    .local [fd63:c3   :4b8:7777::c0a8:   10]
ta:
Reply from fd63:c3   :4b8:7777::c0a8:   10: time=133ms
Reply from fd63:c3   :4b8:7777::c0a8:   10: time=59ms
Reply from fd63:c3   :4b8:7777::c0a8:   10: time=74ms
Reply from fd63:c3   :4b8:7777::c0a8:   10: time=54ms
```

Figure 8.1: Pinging an internal server from a DirectAccess laptop

What in the world is that? Looks like IPv6 to me. This is where IPv6 comes into play with DirectAccess. All of the traffic that moves over the internet part of the connection, between my laptop and the DirectAccess server that is sitting in my datacenter, is IPv6 traffic. My internal network is IPv4, and my DirectAccess server only has IPv4 addresses on it, and yet my DirectAccess tunnel is carrying my traffic using IPv6. This is the core of how DirectAccess works and cannot be changed. Your DA laptop sends IPsec-encrypted IPv6 packets over the internet to the DA server, and when the DA server receives those packets, it has the capability to spin them down into IPv4 in order to send them to the destination server inside the corporate network. For example, when I open my Outlook and it tries to connect to my Exchange server, my Outlook packets flow over the DirectAccess tunnel as IPv6. Once these packets hit my DirectAccess server, that DA server reaches out to internal DNS to figure out whether my Exchange server is IPv4 or IPv6.

If you are actually running IPv6 inside the network and the Exchange server is available via IPv6, the DA server will simply send the IPv6 packets along to the Exchange server. Connection complete! If, on the other hand, you are running IPv4 inside your network, the DA server will only see a single host record in DNS, meaning that the Exchange server is IPv4 – only. The DirectAccess server will then manipulate the IPv6 packet, changing it down into IPv4, and then send it on its way to the Exchange server. The two technologies that handle this manipulation of packets are **DNS64** and **NAT64**, which you have probably seen in some of the documentation if you have read anything about DirectAccess online. The purposes of these technologies are to change the incoming IPv6 packet stream into IPv4 for networks where it is required, which is pretty much every network at the moment, and spin the return traffic from IPv4 back up into IPv6 so that it can make its way back to the DirectAccess client computer over the IPv6-based IPsec tunnel that is connecting the DA client to the DA server over the internet.

It is important to understand that DirectAccess uses IPv6 in this capacity, because any security policies that you might have in place that squash IPv6 on the client computers by default will stop DirectAccess from working properly in your environment. You will have to reverse these policies to allow the clients to push out IPv6 packets and get their traffic across the internet. However, it is also very important to understand that you do *not* need any semblance of IPv6 running *inside* the corporate network to make this work, as the DirectAccess server can spin all of the traffic down into IPv4 before it hits that internal network, and most DA implementations that are active today run in exactly this fashion.

Prerequisites for DirectAccess

DirectAccess has a lot of moving parts, and there are many different ways in which you can set it up. However, not all of these ways are good ideas. So, in this section, we are going to discuss some of the big decisions that you will have to make when designing your own DirectAccess environment.

Domain-joined

The first big requirement is that the systems involved with DirectAccess need to be domain-joined. Your DA server, or servers, all need to be joined to your domain, and all of the client computers that you want to be DA-connected need to be joined to a domain as well. Domain membership is required for authentication purposes, and also because the DirectAccess client settings that need to be applied to mobile computers come down to these computers via Group Policy.

I always like to point out this requirement early in the planning process, because it means that users who purchase their own laptops at a retail location are typically not going to be able to utilize DirectAccess—unless you are somehow okay with adding home computers to your domain—and so DA is really a technology that is designed for managing and connecting your corporate assets that you can join to the domain. It is also important to understand this requirement from a security perspective, since your DirectAccess server or servers will typically be facing the edge of your network. It is common for the external NIC on a DA server to sit inside a DMZ, but they also have to be domain-joined, which may not be something you are used to doing with systems in a perimeter network.

Supported client operating systems

Not all Windows client operating systems contain the components that are necessary to make a DirectAccess connection work. Enterprise does, which covers the majority of larger businesses who own Microsoft operating systems, but that certainly does not include everyone. I still see many small businesses using professional or even home SKUs on their client machines, and these versions do not include DirectAccess components. The following is a list of the operating systems that do support DirectAccess. During your planning, you will need to make sure that your mobile computers are running one of these:

- Windows 10 Enterprise
- Windows 10 Education
- Windows 8.0 or 8.1 Enterprise
- Windows 7 Enterprise
- Windows 7 Ultimate

DirectAccess servers – one or two NICs?

One big question that needs to be answered even prior to installing the Remote Access role on your new server is: How many NICs are needed on this server? There are two supported methods for implementing DirectAccess.

Single NIC mode

Your DirectAccess server can be installed with only a single NIC. In this case, you would typically plug that network connection directly into your internal network so that it had access to all of the internal resources that the client computers are going to need to contact during the user's DA sessions. In order to get traffic from the internet to your DirectAccess server, you would need to establish a **Network Address Translation** (**NAT**) from a public IP address into whatever internal IP address you have assigned to the DA server.

Many network security administrators do not like this method because it means creating a NAT that brings traffic straight into the corporate network without flowing through any kind of DMZ.

I can also tell you from experience that the single NIC mode does not always work properly. It does a fine job of spinning up a quick test lab or proof of concept, but I have seen too many problems in the field with people trying to run production DirectAccess environments on a single NIC. The ability to use only a single network card is something that was added to DirectAccess in more recent versions, so it was not originally designed to run like this. Therefore, I strongly recommend that, for your production DA install, you do it the right way and go with...

Dual NICs

Here, we have two network cards in the DirectAccess server. The internal NIC typically gets plugged right into the corporate network, and the external NIC's physical placement can vary depending on the organization. We will discuss the pros and cons of where to place the external NIC immediately after this section of the chapter. Edge mode with two NICs is the way that DirectAccess works best. As you may recall from earlier in the book, implementing a Windows Server instance with multiple NICs means that you will be multihoming this server, and you need to set up the network settings accordingly. With a Remote Access server, your external NIC is always the one that receives the default gateway settings, so you need to make sure you follow this rule and *do not configure a default gateway on the internal NIC*. On the other hand, you do want to configure DNS server addresses into the internal NIC properties, but you do *not* want to configure DNS servers for the external NIC. Since this server is multihomed, you will likely need to create some route statements to add your corporate subnets into the Windows routing table of this server before it can successfully send and receive traffic. The only networks that would not need to accommodate adding static routes would be small networks, where all of your internal devices are on a single subnet. If this is the case, then you do not need to input static routes. But most corporate networks span multiple subnets, and in this case, you should refer back to *Chapter 7, Networking with Windows Server 2019*, where we discussed multihoming and how to build out those route statements.

More than two NICs

Nope, don't go there. If you are familiar with configuring routers or firewalls, you know that you have the potential to install many different NICs on a server and plug them all into different subnets. While there are many reasons why splitting up network access like this on a Remote Access server might be beneficial, it won't work how you want it to. The DirectAccess configuration itself is only capable of managing two different network interfaces.

As you can see in *Figure 8.2*, in the course of the setup wizards, you will have to define one NIC as **External**, and the other as **Internal**. Any more NICs that exist in that server will not be used by DirectAccess, unfortunately. Maybe this is something that will change in future versions!

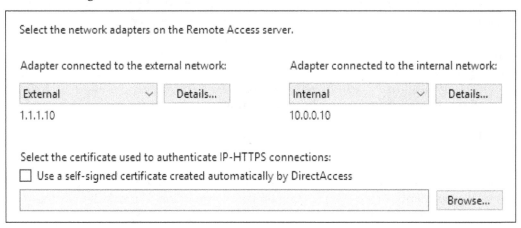

Figure 8.2: Defining NICs during DirectAccess configuration

To NAT or not to NAT?

Now that you have decided to roll with two NICs in your DirectAccess server, where do we plug in the external NIC? There are two common places that this external network interface can be connected to, but depending on which you choose, the outcome of your DirectAccess environment can be vastly different. Before we talk about the actual placement of the NIC, I would like to define a couple of protocols that are important to understand, because they pertain very much to answering this question about NIC placement. When your DirectAccess laptop makes a connection to the DirectAccess server, it will do so using one of the three IPv6 transition tunneling protocols. These protocols are **6to4**, **Teredo**, and **IP-HTTPS**. When the DA client connects its DA tunnels, it will automatically choose which of these protocols is best to use, depending on the user's current internet connection. All three protocols perform the same function for a DirectAccess connection: their job is to take the IPv6 packet stream coming out of the laptop and encapsulate it inside IPv4 so that the traffic can make its way successfully across the IPv4 internet. When the packets get to the DirectAccess server, they are decapped so that the DA server can process these IPv6 packets.

6to4

DA clients will only attempt to connect using 6to4 when a remote laptop has a true public internet IP address. This hardly ever happens these days, with the shortage of available internet IPv4 addresses, and so 6to4 is typically not used by any DirectAccess client computers. In fact, it can present its own set of challenges when users are connecting with cell phone cards in their laptops, and so it is common practice to disable the 6to4 adapter on client computers as a DirectAccess best-practice setting.

Teredo

When DA clients are connected to the internet using a private IP address, such as behind a home router or a public Wi-Fi router, they will attempt to connect using the Teredo protocol. Teredo uses a UDP stream to encapsulate DA packets, and so, as long as the user's internet connection allows outbound UDP 3544, Teredo will generally connect and is the transition protocol of choice for that DirectAccess connection.

IP-HTTPS

If Teredo fails to connect, such as in the case where the user is sitting in a network that blocks outbound UDP, then the DirectAccess connection will fall back to using IP-HTTPS, pronounced *IP over HTTPS*. This protocol encapsulates the IPv6 packets inside IPv4 headers, but then wraps them up inside an HTTP header and encrypts them with TLS/SSL, before sending the packet out over the internet. This effectively makes the DirectAccess connection an SSL stream, just like when you browse an HTTPS website.

Installing on the true edge – on the internet

When you plug your DirectAccess server's external NIC directly into the internet, you grant yourself the ability to put true public IP addresses on that NIC. In doing this, you enable all three of the preceding transition tunneling protocols, so that DirectAccess client computers can choose between them for the best form of connectivity. When installing via the true edge method, you would put not only one but two public IP addresses on that external NIC. Make sure that the public IP addresses are consecutive as this is a requirement for Teredo. When your DirectAccess server has two consecutive public IP addresses assigned to the external NIC, it will enable the Teredo protocol to be available for connections.

The NIC does not necessarily have to be plugged directly into the internet for this to work. Depending on your firewall capabilities, you might have the option to establish a *Bridged DMZ* where no NATing is taking place. You need to check with your firewall vendor to find out whether or not that is an option for your organization. In this scenario, you are still able to configure true public IP addresses on the external NIC, but the traffic flows through a firewall first, in order to protect and manage that traffic.

Installing behind a NAT

It is much more common for the networking team to want to place the external NIC of your DirectAccess server behind a firewall, inside a DMZ. This typically means creating a NAT to bring this traffic into the server. While this is entirely possible and better protects the DirectAccess server itself from the internet, it does come with a big downside. When you install a DA server behind a NAT, Teredo no longer works. In fact, the DirectAccess configuration wizards will recognize when you have a private IP address listed on the external NIC and will not even turn on Teredo.

When Teredo is not available, all of your DirectAccess clients will connect using IP-HTTPS. So why does it even matter if Teredo is unavailable? Because it is a more efficient protocol than IP-HTTPS. When Teredo tunnels packets, it simply encapsulates IPv6 inside IPv4. The DirectAccess traffic stream is already and always IPsec-encrypted, so there is no need for the Teredo tunnel to do any additional encryption. On the other hand, when IP-HTTPS tunnels packets, it takes the already-encrypted IPsec traffic stream and encrypts it a second time using SSL. This means all of the packets that come and go are subject to double encryption, which increases processing and CPU cycles, and makes for a slower connection. It also creates additional hardware load on the DirectAccess server itself, because it is handling twice the amount of encryption processing.

This is a particularly apparent problem when you are running Windows 7 on client computers, as double encryption processing will cause a noticeably slower connection for users. DirectAccess still works fine, but if you sit a Teredo-connected laptop next to an IP-HTTPS-connected laptop, you will notice the speed difference between the two.

Thankfully, in Windows 8 and Windows 10, there have been some countermeasures added to help with this speed discrepancy. These newer client operating systems are now smart enough that they can negotiate the SSL part of the IP-HTTPS tunnel by using the NULL encryption algorithm, meaning that IP-HTTPS is not doing a second encryption and IP-HTTPS performance is now essentially on par with Teredo.

However, this only works for the newer client operating systems (Win7 will always double encrypt with IP-HTTPS), and it still doesn't work in some cases. For example, when you enable your DirectAccess server to also provide VPN connectivity, or if you choose to employ a **One-Time-Password** (OTP) system alongside DirectAccess, then the NULL algorithm will be disabled because it is a security risk in these situations, and so even your Windows 8 and Windows 10 computers will perform double encryption when they connect via IP-HTTPS. You can see where it would be beneficial to have Teredo enabled and available so that any computers that can connect via Teredo will do so.

To summarize, you can certainly install your DirectAccess server's external NIC behind a NAT, but be aware that all DA client computers will connect using the IP-HTTPS protocol, and it is important to understand the potential side-effect of implementing it in this way.

Network Location Server

This major component in a DirectAccess infrastructure is something that does not even exist on the DA server itself, or at least it shouldn't if you are setting things up properly. The **Network Location Server** (**NLS**) is simply a website that runs inside the corporate network. This website does not need to be available for access over the internet; in fact, it should not be. The NLS is used as part of the inside/outside detection mechanism on DirectAccess client computers, similar to the way that Trusted Network Detection works for Always On VPN. Every time a DA client gets a network connection, it starts looking for the NLS website. If it can see the site, then it knows that you are inside the corporate network, and DirectAccess is not required, so it turns itself off. However, if your NLS website cannot be contacted, it means you are outside the corporate network, and DirectAccess components will start turning themselves on.

This prerequisite is easily met; all you need to do is spin up a VM and install IIS on it to host this new website, or you can even add a new website to an existing web server in your network. There are only two things to watch out for when setting up your NLS website. The first is that it must be an HTTPS site, and so it requires an SSL certificate. We will discuss the certificates used in DA, including this one, in the next section of this chapter. In addition to making sure that the website is accessible via HTTPS, you must also make sure that the DNS name you are using to contact this website is unique. You want to do this because, whatever name you choose for the NLS website, that name will not be resolvable when client computers are outside the corporate network. This is by design, because you obviously don't want your DA clients to be able to successfully contact the NLS website when they are working remotely, as that would then disable their DirectAccess connection.

The reason I bring up the unique DNS name is that I often see new DirectAccess admins utilizing an existing internal website as their NLS website. For example, if you have `https://intranet` running as a SharePoint site, you could simply use this in the DA config as the NLS server definition. However, once you set it up this way, you will quickly realize that nobody who is working remotely can access the `https://intranet` website. This is by design, because the DA environment now considers your intranet website to be the NLS server, and you cannot resolve it while you are mobile. The solution to this problem? Make sure that you choose a new DNS name to use for this NLS website. Something like `https://nls.contoso.local` is appropriate.

The most important part about the Network Location Server that I want to stress is that you should absolutely implement this website on a server in your network that is *not* the DirectAccess server itself. When you are running through the DA config wizards, you will see on the screen where we define NLS that it is recommended to deploy NLS on a remote web server, but it also gives you the option to self-host the NLS website right on the DirectAccess server itself. Don't do it! There are many things that can go wrong when you co-host NLS on the DA server. Running NLS on your DA server also limits your DirectAccess potential in the future, because some of the advanced DA configurations require you to remove NLS from the DA server anyway, so you might as well do it correctly the first time you set it up. Changing your NLS website after you are running DA in production can be very tricky, and often goes sideways. I have helped numerous companies move their NLS website after realizing that they cannot co-host NLS on the DA server if and when they want to add a second DirectAccess server for growth or redundancy. The following is a screenshot of the section in the DA config wizard where you choose the location of NLS. Make sure you stick with the top box!

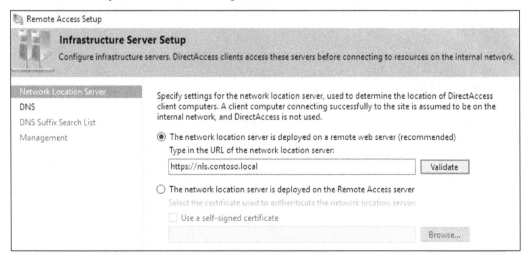

Figure 8.3: Defining the network location server

Certificates used with DirectAccess

Aside from reading and misunderstanding how DirectAccess uses IPv6, here is the next biggest "turn off" for administrators who are interested in giving DirectAccess a try. Once you start to read about how DA works, you will quickly come to realize that certificates are required in a few different places. While VPNs generally also require the use of certificates, it is admittedly difficult to distinguish which certificates need to go where when you are wading through Microsoft DirectAccess documentation, so this section clears up any confusion that exists about DirectAccess certificates. It really is not very complicated, once you know what does and does not need to be done.

The core prerequisite is that you have a Windows CA server somewhere in your network. The stature of your PKI implementation is not that important to DirectAccess. We simply need the ability to issue certificates to our DA server and clients. There are only three places that certificates are used in DirectAccess, and two of them are SSL certificates.

SSL certificate on the NLS web server

As mentioned previously, your NLS website needs to be running HTTPS. This means that you will require an SSL certificate to be installed on the server that is hosting your NLS website. Assuming that you have an internal CA server, this certificate can be easily acquired from that internal CA, so there are no costs associated with this certificate. You do not need to purchase one from a public CA, because this certificate is only going to be accessed and verified from your domain-joined machines, the DirectAccess clients. Since domain-joined computers automatically trust the CA servers in your network, this certificate can simply be issued from your internal CA, and it will do exactly what we need it to do for the purposes of DirectAccess.

SSL certificate on the DirectAccess server

An SSL certificate is also required to be installed on the DirectAccess server itself, but this one should be purchased from your public certification authority. This certificate will be used to validate IP-HTTPS traffic streams coming in from the client computers, because that is SSL traffic and so we need an SSL certificate to validate it. Since the IP-HTTPS listener is facing the public internet, it is definitely recommended that you use a certificate from a public CA, rather than trying to use a cert from your internal PKI.

 If your company already has a wildcard SSL certificate, use it here to save costs!

Machine certificates on the DA server and all DA clients

The last and most complicated part of the DirectAccess certificate puzzle is machine certificates. Once you know what is required though, it's really not hard at all. We simply require that a computer or machine certificate be installed on the DirectAccess server, as well as each of the DirectAccess client machines. This machine certificate is used as part of the authentication process for IPsec tunnels. It is a big part of the way in which DirectAccess verifies that you really are who you say you are when your computer makes that DA connection happen.

The best way to go about issuing these machine certificates is to log into your CA server and create a new certificate template that is duplicated from the built-in "Computer" template. When setting up your new certificate template, just make sure that it meets the following criteria:

- The **Common Name** (subject) of the certificate should match the FQDN of the computer.
- The **Subject Alternative Name (SAN)** of the certificate should equal the DNS Name of the computer.
- The certificate should serve the intended purposes (Enhanced Key Usage) of both Client Authentication and Server Authentication.

I should note here, though I don't really want to, that issuing these certificates is not absolutely necessary to make DirectAccess work. If you are running Windows 8 or higher on the client side, then it is possible to get DA working without machine certificates. It is possible for client computers running without machine certificates to instead utilize something called **Kerberos Proxy** for their computer authentication when the IPsec tunnels are being built, but I highly recommend sticking with certificates. Using certificates as part of the authentication process makes the connection more stable and more secure. Additionally, as with the placement of NLS, if you want to perform any advanced functions with DirectAccess, such as load balancing or multisite, or even if you simply want to make some Windows 7 computers connect through DA, then you will be required to issue certificates anyway. So, stick with the best practice in the first place and issue these certificates before you even get started with testing DirectAccess.

Do not use the Getting Started Wizard (GSW)!

After making the necessary design decisions and implementing the prerequisites we have talked about so far, it is finally time to install the Remote Access role on your new DirectAccess server! After you have finished installing the role, similarly to many roles in Windows Server 2019, you will be shown a message informing you that additional configuration is required to use this role. If you follow the yellow exclamation mark inside Server Manager, the only option that you are presented with is **Open the Getting Started Wizard**. Ugh! This is *not* what you want to click on:

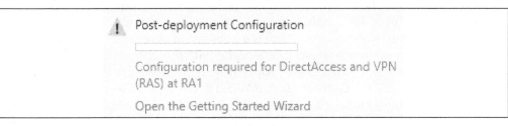

Figure 8.4: Do not click on this!

 Don't do it!

Your home for DirectAccess configurations is the **Remote Access Management Console**, which is available from inside the **Tools** menu of Server Manager now that our Remote Access role has been installed. Go ahead and launch that, and now we are presented with a choice:

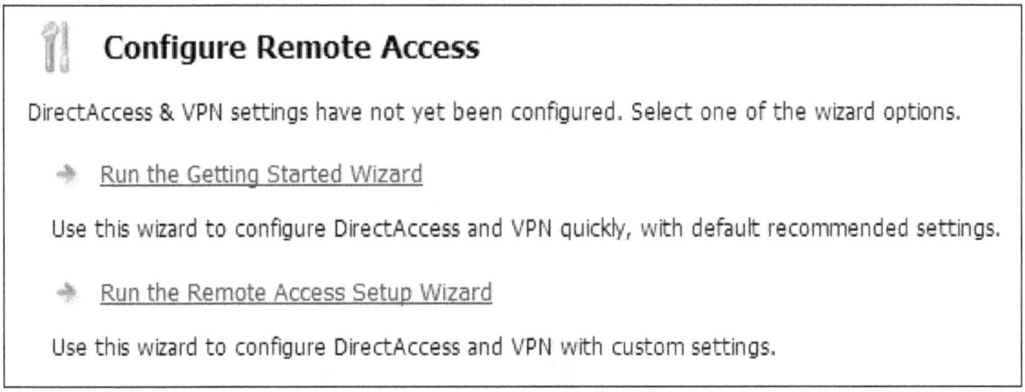

 Configure Remote Access

DirectAccess & VPN settings have not yet been configured. Select one of the wizard options.

➔ Run the Getting Started Wizard

Use this wizard to configure DirectAccess and VPN quickly, with default recommended settings.

➔ Run the Remote Access Setup Wizard

Use this wizard to configure DirectAccess and VPN with custom settings.

Figure 8.5: Configuring Remote Access

Do *not* click on **Run the Getting Started Wizard**! The GSW is a shortcut method for implementing DirectAccess, designed only for getting DA up and running as quickly as possible, perhaps for a quick proof of concept. Under no circumstances should you trust the GSW for your production DA environment, because in an effort to make configuration quick and easy, many configuration decisions are made for you that are not best practices.

You want to make sure you click on **Run the Remote Access Setup Wizard** when you are first prompted in the console; this will invoke the full set of DirectAccess configuration screens. DA setup consists of a series of four different steps, each containing a handful of screens that you will navigate through to choose your appropriate configuration options. There is a good amount of detail on these screens as to what each one of them means and what your options are, so don't be afraid to dive in and set this up in the proper way. If you have already configured DirectAccess and used the **Getting Started Wizard**, DA may be working for you, but it will not be running as efficiently or securely as it could be. The following is a quick list of the reasons why the **Getting Started Wizard** is not in your best interests. These are the things that it does that go directly against a best-practice DirectAccess install, with accompanying *peanut gallery* commentary from yours truly:

- GSW co-hosts the NLS website on the DA server — *bad*
- GSW applies the DA client GPO settings to Domain Computers — *this is a terrible idea*
- GSW utilizes self-signed certificates — *a "Security 101 level" no-no*
- GSW automatically disables Teredo — *inefficient*
- GSW does not walk you through any of the advanced options for DirectAccess, probably because the way that it sets everything up invalidates your ability to even use the advanced functions — *lame*

Remote Access Management Console

You are well on your way to giving users remote access capabilities on this new server. As with many networking devices, once you have established all of your configurations on a Remote Access server, it is pretty common for admins to walk away and let it run. There is no need for a lot of ongoing maintenance or changes to that configuration once you have it running well. However, Remote Access Management Console in Windows Server 2019 is useful not only for the configuration of remote access parts and pieces but for monitoring and reporting as well.

When working with DirectAccess, this is your home for pretty much everything: configuration, management, monitoring, and troubleshooting. On the VPN/AOVPN side of the remote access toolset, you will be making many of the VPN configuration decisions inside RRAS, but RAMC is the place to go when checking over server-side monitoring, client-connection monitoring, and reporting statistics. Whether you use DA, VPN, or a combination of the two, RAMC is a tool you need to be comfortable with.

Let's take a look inside this console so that you are familiar with the different screens you will be interacting with:

Figure 8.6: Remote Access Dashboard

Configuration

The configuration screen is pretty self-explanatory; this is where you create your initial remote access configuration, and where you update any settings in the future. As you can see in the *Figure 8.6*, you can configure **DirectAccess** and **VPN**, and even **Web Application Proxy**, right from this **Remote Access Management Console**.

Do not follow my lead with this screenshot. I have installed the DA/VPN portion of the Remote Access role alongside the Web Application Proxy portion of the same role, but it is not recommended to run both DA/VPN and WAP together on the same server. I did it simply for the purpose of creating screenshots in my test lab.

There is not a lot to configure as far as the VPN goes; you really only have one screen of options where you define what kinds of IP addresses are handed down to the VPN clients connecting in, and how to handle VPN authentication. It is not immediately obvious where this screen is, so I wanted to point it out. Inside the **DirectAccess and VPN** configuration section, if you click on **Edit...** under **Step 2**, this will launch the **Step 2** mini-wizard. The last screen in this mini-wizard is called **VPN Configuration**. This is the screen where you can configure these IP addresses and authentication settings for your VPN connections. The remainder of your VPN configuration duties will fall within the traditional VPN configuration console, called RRAS. However, everything about DirectAccess connections is configured right from inside **Remote Access Management Console** and those four mini-wizards:

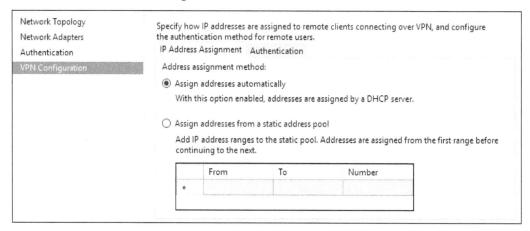

Figure 8.7: VPN Configuration

Dashboard

Remote Access Dashboard gives you a 30,000-foot view of the Remote Access server status. You can view a quick status of the components running on the server, whether or not the latest configuration changes have been rolled out, and some summary numbers near the bottom about how many DirectAccess and VPN connections are ongoing:

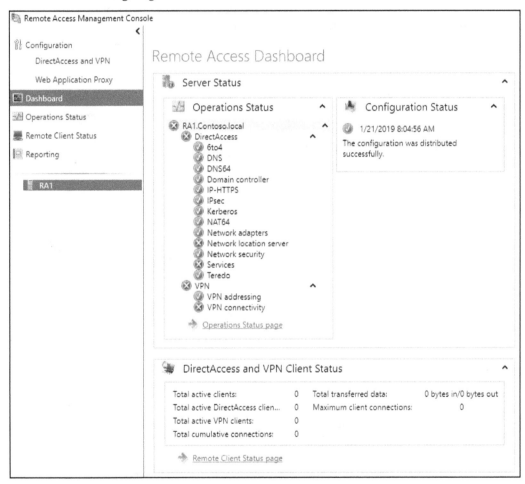

Figure 8.8: Summary stats on Remote Access Dashboard

Operations Status

If you want to drill down further into what is happening on the server side of the connections, that is what the **Operations Status** page is all about. Here, you can see more details on each of the components that are running under the hood to make your DA and VPN connections happen. If any of them have an issue, you can click on the specific component to get a little more information. For example, as a test, I have turned off the NLS web server in my lab network, and I can now see on the **Operations Status** page that NLS is flagged with an error:

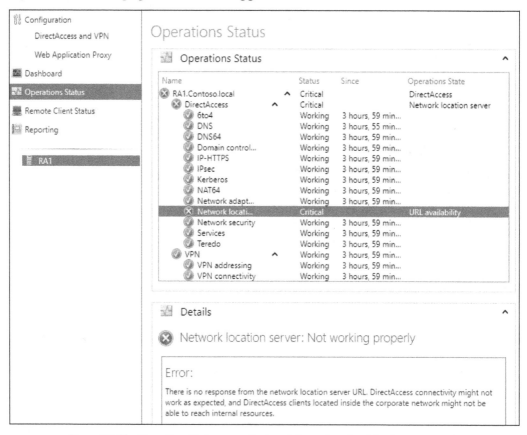

Figure 8.9: The Operations Status page displays information about server components

Remote Client Status

Next up is the **Remote Client Status** screen. As indicated, this is the screen where we can monitor client computers that are connected. It will show us both DirectAccess and VPN connections here. We will be able to see computer names, usernames, and even the resources that they are utilizing during their connections. The information on this screen can be filtered by simply putting any criteria into the **Search** bar at the top of the window.

It is important to note that the **Remote Client Status** screen only shows live, active connections. There is no historical information stored here.

Reporting

You guessed it: this is the window you need to visit if you want to see historical remote access information. This screen is almost exactly the same as the **Remote Client Status** screen, except that you have the ability to generate reports for historical data pulled from date ranges of your choosing. Once the data is displayed, you have the same search and filtering capabilities that you had on the **Remote Client Status** screen.

Reporting is disabled by default, but you simply need to navigate to the **Reporting** page and click on **Configure Accounting**. Once that is enabled, you will be presented with options about storing the historical information. You can choose to store the data in the local WID or on a remote RADIUS server.

You also have options here for how long to store logging data and a mechanism that can be used to clear out old data:

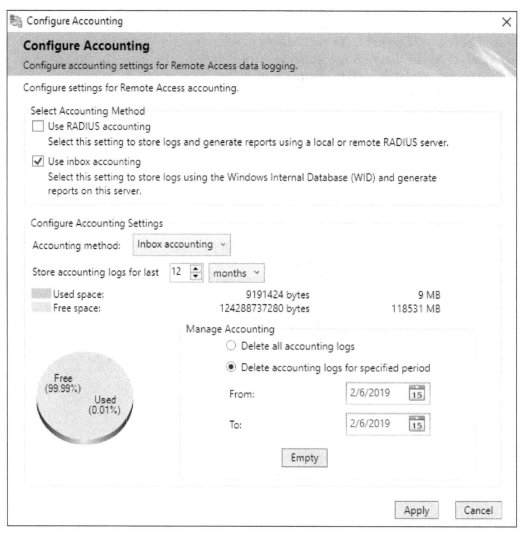

Figure 8.10: Configuring account (reporting) settings

Tasks

The last window pane in **Remote Access Management Console** that I want to point out is the **Tasks** bar on the right-hand side of your screen. The actions and options that are displayed in this taskbar change depending on what part of the console you are navigating through. Make sure you keep an eye on this side of your screen to set up some more advanced functions. Some examples of available tasks are creating usage reports, refreshing the screen, enabling or disabling VPNs, and configuring network load balancing or multisite configurations if you are running multiple Remote Access servers.

DA, VPN, or AOVPN? Which is best?

VPN has been around for a very long time, making it a pretty familiar idea to anyone working in IT. Always On VPN certainly brings its share of new capabilities, but under the hood what AOVPN is doing is launching a traditionally configured VPN connection, so the connection flow is similar to what we have always known. In this chapter, we have also discussed quite a bit about DirectAccess in order to bring you up to speed on this alternative method of automatically connecting your remote clients back to the datacenter. Now that you know there are two great connectivity platforms built into Windows Server 2019 for enabling your mobile workforce, which one is better?

You don't have to choose! You can run both of these technologies side by side, even on the same Remote Access server. Each technology has its pros and cons, and the ways that you use each, or both, will depend upon many variables. Your users, your client computers, and your organization's individual needs will need to be factored into your decision-making process. Let's discuss some of the differences between DirectAccess and VPN so that you can make intelligent decisions on which connectivity platforms fit into your organization.

Domain-joined or not?

One of the biggest requirements for a DirectAccess client computer is that it must be domain-joined. While this requirement in and of itself doesn't seem so major, what it implies can have huge implications. Trusting a computer enough to be joined to your domain more than likely means that the laptop is owned by the company. It also probably means that this laptop was initially built and prepped by the IT team. Companies that are in the habit of allowing employees to purchase their own computers to be used for work purposes may not find that DirectAccess fits well with that model. DA is also not ideal for situations where employees use their existing home computers to connect to work remotely.

In these kinds of situations, such as home and personally owned computers, VPN may be better suited to the task. You can connect to a VPN (including Always On VPN) from a non-domain-joined Windows 10 machine, and you can even establish VPN connections (manual connections) from many non-Microsoft devices. iOS, Android, Windows phones, and Mac—all these platforms have a VPN client built into them that can be used to tap into a VPN listener on a Windows Server 2019 Remote Access server. If your only remote access solution was DirectAccess, you would not be able to provide non-domain-joined devices with a connectivity platform.

Keep in mind that, while the Always On VPN user tunnel is more flexible than DirectAccess in this regard, if you intend to use the AOVPN *device tunnel*, then your machines will still need to be domain-joined.

Auto or manual launch

There are multiple different ways to look at this one. When discussing whether DirectAccess or a traditional VPN is better, DirectAccess is the clear winner. Nobody wants to make their users open a connection and manually launch it to establish VPN connectivity when an automated platform is available to use.

Always On VPN, however, brings automated and seamless connectivity to the VPN world. AOVPN is almost as seamless as DirectAccess in this regard. I say *almost* because, at the time of writing, it's fairly difficult to make a device tunnel work well. This means that most companies rolling out AOVPN are only using the user tunnel. In the user tunnel scenario, the VPN does launch automatically, but not until the user has already passed the login screen. That means in these situations, DirectAccess still holds an advantage over AOVPN because DA connects seamlessly *at* the login screen. This enables password resets and new domain users to log into DA-connected machines. I hope that future improvements will enable AOVPN device and user tunnels to co-exist in a stable way, which will give true always-on connectivity to AOVPN clients.

Software versus built-in

I'm a fan of Ikea furniture. They do a great job of supplying quality products at a low cost, including packaging them up in incredibly small boxes. After you pay for the product, unbox it, put it together, and then test it to make sure it works—it's great. If you can't see where this is going, I'll give you a hint: it's an analogy for traditional, third-party VPNs. As in, you typically pay a vendor for their VPN product, unbox it, implement it at more expense, then test the product. That VPN software then has the potential to break and need reinstallation or reconfiguration, and will certainly come with software updates that need to be accomplished down the road. Maintenance, maintenance, maintenance.

Maybe I have been watching too many home improvement shows lately, but I am a fan of houses with built-ins. Built-ins are essentially furniture that is permanent to the house, built right into the walls, corners, or wherever it happens to be. It adds value, and it integrates into the overall house much better than furniture that was pieced together separately and then stuck against the wall in the corner.

DirectAccess and Always On VPN are like built-ins. They live inside the operating system. There is no software to install, no software to update, no software to reinstall when it breaks. Everything that DA and AOVPN need is already in Windows today, you just aren't using it. Oh, and it's free! Well, built into the cost of your Windows license anyway. There are no user CALs, and no ongoing licensing costs related to implementing one of Microsoft's remote access solutions.

If your workforce consists of Windows 10 machines, Microsoft DirectAccess or Microsoft Always On VPN are clear winners when compared to any third-party VPN connectivity solution.

Password and login issues with traditional VPNs

If you have ever worked on the helpdesk for a company that uses a VPN, you know what I'm talking about. There are a series of common troubleshooting calls that happen in the VPN world related to passwords. Sometimes, the user forgets their password. Perhaps their password has expired and needs to be changed — ugh! VPN doesn't handle this scenario very well either. Or perhaps the employee changed their expired password on their desktop before they left work for the day, but are now trying to log in remotely from their laptop and it isn't working.

What is the solution to password problems with VPN? Reset the user's password, and then make the user come into the office in order to make it work on their laptop. Yup, this kind of phone call still happens every day. This is unfortunate, but a real potential problem with old-school VPNs.

What's the good news? New Microsoft remote access solutions don't have these kinds of problems! Since DA and AOVPN are part of the operating system, they have the capability to be connected anytime that Windows is online. This includes the login screen! Even if I am sitting on the login or lock screen, and the system is waiting for me to input my username and password, as long as I have internet access, I also have a DirectAccess tunnel or an Always On VPN device tunnel. This means that I can actively do password management tasks. If my password expires and I need to update it, it works. If I forgot my password and I can't get into my laptop, I can call the helpdesk and simply ask them to reset my password. I can then immediately log in to my DA or AOVPN laptop with the new password, right from my house.

Another cool function that this seamlessness enables is the ability to log in with new user accounts. Have you ever logged into your laptop as a different user account in order to test something? Yup, that works over DA and AOVPN as well. For example, I am sitting at home and I need to help one of the sales guys troubleshoot some sort of file permission problem. I suspect it's got something to do with his user account, so I want to log in to my laptop as him in order to test it. The problem is that his user account has never logged into my laptop before. With VPN, not a chance; this would never work. With DirectAccess, piece of cake! I simply log off, type in his username and password, and bingo. I'm logged in, while still sitting at home in my pajamas.

 It is important to note that you can run both DirectAccess and VPN connections on the same Windows Server 2019 Remote Access server. This enables you to host clients who are connected via DA, via AOVPN, and also via traditional VPN connections if you have non-Win10 machines that need to connect. If any of these connectivity technologies have capabilities that you could benefit from, use them all!

Port-restricted firewalls

One of the other common VPN-related helpdesk calls has always been *My VPN won't connect from this hotel*. Unfortunately, most protocols that VPNs use to connect are not firewall-friendly. Chances are that your router at home allows all outbound traffic, and so from your home internet connection everything is fine and dandy when connecting with a VPN protocol. But take that same laptop and connection over to a public coffee shop, or a hotel, or an airport, and suddenly the VPN fails to connect, with a strange error. This is usually caused by that public internet connection flowing its traffic through a port-restricting firewall. These firewalls restrict outbound access, oftentimes blocking things such as ICMP and UDP, which can interfere with VPN connections. In the most severe cases, these firewalls may only allow two outbound ports: TCP 80 for HTTP and TCP 443 for HTTPS website traffic. Then they block everything else.

In the event that you are sitting behind a port-restricted firewall, how do these newer remote access technologies handle connectivity?

DirectAccess is built to handle this scenario out of the box. Remember those three different protocols that DA can use to connect? The *fallback* option is called IP-HTTPS, and it flows its traffic inside TCP 443. So, even while sitting behind the most severe firewalls, DA will generally connect automatically and without hesitation.

Always On VPN is generally deployed (as it should be) with best practices in mind, which includes prioritizing IKEv2 as the VPN connectivity protocol. In fact, some companies deploy AOVPN with only IKEv2. For these folks, a port-restricting firewall would be detrimental to that user's VPN connection, as IKEv2 uses UDP ports to connect. It wouldn't work. So, hopefully, the main point you take from this is that, when setting up AOVPN, make sure that you take the necessary steps to also enable SSTP VPN connectivity as a fallback method. SSTP flows traffic inside TCP 443, which can connect even through hardcore firewalls.

 Super important: The AOVPN device tunnel can only use IKEv2. If you are behind a port-restricting firewall and are relying on a device tunnel for connectivity, it's not going to work. The AOVPN user tunnel is the only one capable of doing SSTP fallback.

In fact, I recently worked on this exact scenario with someone who was trying to decide whether they wanted to set up DirectAccess or Always On VPN for their remote machines. This was a company that manages computers for numerous hospitals and doctors' offices, and they did not have WAN links into those offices. The offices did have internet access though, and so we needed the ability to keep those computers automatically connected back to the main datacenter at all times. So far in the scenario, either DirectAccess or Always On VPN would fit the bill. Then, during testing, we discovered that many hospital networks restrict outbound internet access. The only way that DA would connect was via IP-HTTPS, and the only way that AOVPN would connect was via SSTP. Not a problem, right? Except that it was. You see, these remote workstations are often treated as kiosk, walk-up machines, where dozens of different employees could walk up at any moment and log into them. Oftentimes, this means that users are logging into these machines who have never logged into them before, so they don't have cached credentials on those computers.

If you haven't figured it out already, we had no choice but to go with DirectAccess in this scenario. DA is always connected at the login screen, even when using its *fallback* IP-HTTPS method. Always On VPN, however, can only do IKEv2 at the login screen, because the device tunnel requires IKEv2. This uses UDP and was blocked by the firewall, so the only way that AOVPN would connect was by using SSTP, but that wasn't available until the user tunnel could launch, which was only after the user had logged into the machine. It was an extremely interesting real-world use case that helped shed some light on the decision-making process you may need to take for your own environments.

Manual disconnect

If you aren't already convinced that old-school, traditional VPNs are yesterday's news, let's throw another point at you. When you use VPNs that require the user to manually launch the connection, you are relying on the user themselves to keep that machine managed, patched, and up to date. Sure, you may have automated systems that do these things for you, such as WSUS, SCCM, and Group Policy. But when the laptop is out and about, roaming around away from the LAN, those management systems can only do their jobs when the user decides to establish a VPN connection. It's very possible that a laptop could spend weeks completely outside the corporate network, connecting to dozens of insecure hotspots while that employee works their way around the Caribbean on a cruise ship. After weeks of partying and Netflix, they then connect back into the LAN or via VPN to do some work, and wouldn't you know it, that machine has been offline for so long that it's picked up all kinds of fun and creative new software that you now have to deal with.

Not so with the Microsoft remote access tools! Providing an automatic connectivity option such as Always On VPN or DirectAccess means that the laptop would have been connected and receiving all of its security policies and patches during that entire vacation.

In fact, to take it one step further, on a DirectAccess-connected machine, the user cannot disable their DA tunnels even if they want to. You do have the ability to provide them with a **Disconnect** button, but that basically just fakes out the connection from the user's perspective to make it feel to them like DA is offline. In reality, the IPsec tunnels are still flowing in the background, always allowing management-style tasks to happen.

Native load-balancing capabilities

Long story short, DirectAccess is the winner here. Remote Access Management Console in Windows Server 2019 has built-in capabilities for configuring and managing arrays of DA servers. You can stack multiple DA servers on top of each other, tie them together in load-balanced arrays, and provide redundancy and resiliency right from inside the console, without any extra hardware or traditional load-balancer consideration. You can even configure something called **DirectAccess Multisite**, where you can configure DirectAccess servers that reside in different geographical locations together in arrays, giving cross-site resiliency. Almost every company that runs DirectAccess configures a redundant environment, providing either inner-site load balancing or multisite, or sometimes both, because these capabilities are built in and easy to configure.

Unfortunately, these capabilities are not (not yet, anyway) ported over into the Microsoft VPN world. Whether you are connecting Windows 7 clients via traditional VPN connectivity or getting Windows 10 clients to connect using Always On VPN, the backend infrastructure of RRAS VPN is the same, and has no built-in accommodation for multiple servers or sites. It is certainly possible to do so, making that VPN system redundant, but that would require you to set it up on your own by using external load balancers and, oftentimes, would require the use of global site/ server load balancers to make that traffic flow properly.

Anyone who has set up load-balanced VPNs of any flavor in the past may be well aware of this process and be able to configure that easily, and that is great. But this is definitely a limiting factor for small business customers who have a limited number of servers, network equipment, and IT experience. All in all, the extra capabilities built into the console related to DirectAccess put it a step ahead of any VPN solution in terms of building up your remote access infrastructure to be resilient to failure.

Distribution of client configurations

The last primary consideration that you need to take into account when deciding which direction you want to go in for remote access is the method by which client-side settings get pushed down to their respective computers:

- **Third-party VPN**: We have already discussed the downsides to dealing with software applications for third-party VPN vendors. If you can use something baked into the Windows operating system instead, that seems like a no-brainer.

- **Always On VPN**: The recommended way to roll out AOVPN settings to client computers is through the use of an MDM solution, namely either SCCM or Intune. If you have one of these systems, rolling out AOVPN settings to your workforce is a breeze. If you do not have one of those systems, it is still possible, but not a straightforward process.

- **DirectAccess**: I think DA's approach to client settings distribution is definitely the easiest to work with, and the most flexible. You have to keep in mind that DirectAccess is only for your domain-joined systems. Given that you can expect all clients to be domain-joined, you have access to rolling DirectAccess connectivity settings out via Group Policy, which exists inside any Microsoft-driven infrastructure.

I genuinely hope that we will see a Group Policy distribution option added in the future for Always On VPN configuration rollouts. If such a capability were introduced, I am completely confident that it would immediately become the most popular way to roll out AOVPN settings.

To summarize this whole topic, when comparing DirectAccess against traditional, manual-launch VPNs, DA cleanly takes first prize. There really is no comparison. Now that we have Always On VPN at our disposal, the benefits of one over the other (DA or AOVPN) are quite fuzzy. They both accomplish a lot of the same things, but in different ways. The primary deciding factors for most customers so far seem to be client-side rollout capabilities, whether or not they have access to an MDM solution, and how important device tunnel connectivity is to them. Microsoft's goal is for AOVPN to have feature parity with DirectAccess, and it's getting close. Always On VPN also has some advanced authentication features that DirectAccess does not have, such as integration with Windows Hello for Business or Azure MFA.

Web Application Proxy

DirectAccess and VPN are both great remote access technologies, and combining the two of them together can provide a complete remote access solution for your organization, without having to pay for or work with a third-party solution. Better still, in Windows Server 2019, there is yet another component of the RemoteAccess role available to use. This third piece of the remote access story is **Web Application Proxy (WAP)**. This is essentially a reverse-proxy mechanism, giving you the ability to take some HTTP and HTTPS applications that are hosted inside your corporate network and publish them securely to the internet. Any of you who have been working with Microsoft technologies in the perimeter networking space over the last decade will probably recognize a product called Forefront **Unified Access Gateway (UAG)**, which accomplished similar functionality. UAG was a comprehensive SSLVPN solution, also designed for publishing internal applications on the internet via SSL. It was considerably more powerful than a simple reverse-proxy, including components such as pre-authentication, SSTP VPN, and RDS gateway; DirectAccess itself could even be run through UAG.

If all of your mobile workers have access to launching either DirectAccess or VPN, then you probably don't have any use for WAP. However, with the growing cloud mentality, it is quite common for users to expect that they can open up a web browser from any computer, anywhere, and gain access to some of their applications. Document access is now often provided by web services such as SharePoint. Email access can be had remotely, from any computer, by tapping into Outlook Web Access. This is very easy to accomplish when using cloud services such as Azure and Microsoft 365, but many don't realize that this can also be true of on-premises Exchange and SharePoint services.

So many applications and so much data can be accessed through only a web browser, and this enables employees to access this data without needing to establish a full-blown corporate tunnel such as a VPN. So what is the real-world use case for WAP? Home computers that you do not want to be VPN-connected. This way, you don't have to worry as much about the health and status of the home or user-owned computers, since the only interaction they have with your company is through the web browser. This limits the potential for sinister activity to flow into your network from these computers. As you can see, a technology such as WAP does certainly have its place in the remote access market.

I have hopes that, over time, WAP will continue to be improved, and that will enable it to be a true replacement for UAG. UAG ran on Windows Server 2008 R2 and has now been officially discontinued as a Microsoft product. The closest solution Microsoft now has to UAG is the WAP role. It is not yet nearly as comprehensive, but they are working on improving it. Currently, WAP is useful for publishing access to simple web applications. You can also publish access to rich clients that use basic HTTP authentication, such as Exchange ActiveSync. Also included is the ability to publish data to clients that use MSOFBA, such as when users try to pull down corporate data from their Word or Excel applications running on the local computer.

WAP can be used to reverse-proxy (publish) remote access to things such as Exchange and SharePoint environments. This is no small thing, as these are technologies that almost everyone uses, so it can certainly be beneficial to your company to implement WAP for publishing secure access to these resources; it's certainly better than NATing directly to your Exchange server.

WAP as AD FS Proxy

Another useful way in which you can utilize a WAP server is when setting up **Active Directory Federation Services** (**AD FS**) in your network (this is perhaps the most common use for WAP right now). AD FS is a technology designed to enable single sign-on for users and federation with other companies, and so it involves taking traffic coming in from the internet into your internal network. In the past, there was a Windows Server role component that accompanied AD FS, called the **AD FS Proxy**. In the latest versions of AD FS, this separate role no longer exists and has been replaced by the Web Application Proxy component of the Remote Access role. This better unifies the remote access solution, bringing your inbound AD FS traffic through the official Remote Access server, rather than needing a separate AD FS Proxy server. Anyone implementing outward-facing AD FS in their environments will likely find themselves required to deploy WAP at some point.

Requirements for WAP

Unfortunately, the ability to make use of Web Application Proxy comes with a pretty awkward requirement: you must have AD FS installed in your environment to be able to use it—even to test it, because the WAP configuration is stored inside AD FS. None of the WAP configuration information is stored on the Remote Access server itself, which makes for a lightweight server that can be easily moved, changed, or added to. The downside to this is that you must have AD FS running in your environment so that WAP can have a place to store that configuration information.

While a tight integration with AD FS does mean that we have better authentication options, and users can take advantage of AD FS single-sign-on to their applications that are published through WAP, so far this has proven to be a roadblock to implementation for smaller businesses. Many folks are not yet running AD FS, and if the only reason they are looking into implementing AD FS is so that they can use WAP to publish a few web applications to the internet, they may not choose to invest the time and effort just to make that happen.

One thing to keep in mind if you are interested in using WAP and are therefore looking at the requirement for AD FS is that AD FS can certainly be used for other functions. In fact, one of its most common uses at present is integration with Office 365. If you are planning to incorporate, or thinking of incorporating, Office 365 into your environment, AD FS is a great tool that can enhance authentication capabilities for that traffic.

Latest improvements to WAP

Web Application Proxy was introduced in Server 2012 R2 and had many improvements when Windows Server 2016 was released. There have been no major modifications since that time, but it is still important to point out the latest benefits that have been rolled into this feature, to show that it is still learning to do new things. The following are some of the improvements that have been made if you haven't taken a look at WAP since its first iteration.

Preauthentication for HTTP Basic

There are two different ways that users can authenticate to applications that are being published by Web Application Proxy—preauthentication or pass-thru authentication. When publishing an application with preauthentication, this means that users will have to stop by the AD FS interface to authenticate themselves before they are allowed through to the web application itself.

In my eyes, preauthentication is a critical component to any reverse-proxy and I would have to be stuck between a rock and a hard place to externally publish an application that did not require preauthentication. However, the second option is to do pass-thru authentication, and it does exactly that. When you publish access to an application and choose pass-thru authentication, all WAP is doing is shuttling the packets from the internet to the application server. Users are able to get to the web application without authentication, so in theory, anyone can hit the web frontend of your application. From there, the application itself will likely require the user to authenticate, but there is no man-in-the-middle protection happening; that web application is available for the public to view. As you can tell, I do not recommend taking this route.

We already know that WAP can preauthenticate web applications, but the original version could not do any form of preauthentication on HTTP Basic applications, such as when a company wanted to publish access to Exchange ActiveSync. This inability leaves ActiveSync a little bit too exposed to the outside world and is a security risk. Thankfully, this changed in Windows Server 2016—you can now preauthenticate traffic streams that are using HTTP Basic.

HTTP to HTTPS redirection

Users don't like going out of their way or wasting time by having to remember that they need to enter HTTPS:// in front of the URL when they access applications. They would rather just remember email.contoso.com. The inability of WAP to do HTTP to HTTPS redirection was an annoyance and a hindrance to adoption, but that has since changed. Web Application Proxy now includes the capability for WAP itself to handle HTTP to HTTPS redirection, meaning that users do not need to type HTTPS into their browser address bar any longer; they can simply type in the DNS name of the site and let WAP handle the translations.

Client IP addresses forwarded to applications

In the reverse-proxy and SSLVPN world, we occasionally run across applications that require knowing what the client's local IP address is. While this requirement doesn't happen very often and is typically segregated to what we would call legacy applications, it does still happen. When the backend application needs to know what the client's IP address is, this presents a big challenge with reverse-proxy solutions. When the user's traffic flows through WAP or any other reverse-proxy, it is similar to a NAT, where the source IP address information in these packets changes. The backend application server is unable to determine the client's own IP address, and trouble ensues. Web Application Proxy now has the ability to propagate the client-side IP address through to the backend application server, alleviating this problem.

Publishing Remote Desktop Gateway

One of the items that UAG was commonly used for was publishing access to Remote Desktop Services. UAG was essentially its own Remote Desktop Gateway, which gave you the ability to publish access to RDSH servers, individual RDP connections to desktop computers, such as in a VDI implementation, and even access to RemoteApp applications. Unfortunately, WAP cannot do any of this, even in the new version, but the fact that they have added a little bit of functionality here means movement in the right direction is happening.

What has been improved regarding WAP and Remote Desktop is that you can now use WAP to publish access to the Remote Desktop Gateway server itself. Traditionally, a Remote Desktop Gateway sits on the edge of the network and connects external users through to internal Remote Desktop servers. Placing WAP in front of the RD Gateway allows stronger preauthentication for Remote Desktop services and creates a bigger separation between the internal and external networks.

All of my fingers are crossed that we will continue to see improvements in this area and that WAP can be expanded to handle traffic like Remote Desktop natively, without even needing a Remote Desktop Gateway in the mix.

Improved administrative console

The original version of WAP inside Windows Server 2012 R2 was best served using PowerShell to implement it. You can certainly still use PowerShell to create your publishing rules if you so choose, but Remote Access Management Console has now been improved in terms of how it relates to Web Application Proxy. Before you see WAP in the RAMC, you need to make sure that the appropriate box was checked during the Remote Access role installation. If you did not select **Web Application Proxy** when you first installed that role, revisit the add/remove Roles function inside Server Manager in order to add WAP to this server:

Select the role services to install for Remote Access

Role services

- [ ] DirectAccess and VPN (RAS)
- [ ] Routing
- [x] Web Application Proxy

Description

Web Application Proxy enables the publishing of selected HTTP- and HTTPS-based applications from your corporate network to client devices outside of the corporate network. It can use AD FS to ensure that users are authenticated before they gain access to published applications. Web Application Proxy also provides proxy functionality for your AD FS servers.

Figure 8.11: Adding WAP to a server

Note that, while Web Application Proxy is a component of the same Remote Access role that houses DirectAccess and VPN, it is not recommended to run WAP alongside DA and VPN on the same server. As you already know, you can co-host DA and VPN connections together, simultaneously on a single Remote Access server. But once you make the foray into WAP, this should be a standalone component. Do not run WAP on a DA/VPN server, and do not run DA/VPN on a WAP server.

Now that we have added **Web Application Proxy** to our server, you can open up the **Remote Access Management Console** and see it listed inside the **Configuration** section. From here, you launch the **Web Application Proxy Configuration Wizard** and start walking through the steps to define your AD FS server, the certificates you are planning to use, and other criteria needed for the role:

Figure 8.12: Configuring WAP from Remote Access Management Console

Summary

The nature of the world today demands that most companies enable their employees to work from wherever they are. Working from home has become normal over the past handful of years, and specifically in this last year, with a worldwide pandemic, we have seen staggering increases in the percentage of employees who work outside of an office building. Companies need a secure, stable, and efficient way to provide access to corporate data and applications for these mobile workers. The Remote Access role in Windows Server 2019 is designed to do exactly that. With three different ways of providing remote access to corporate resources, IT departments have never had so much remote access technology available at their fingertips, built right into the Windows operating system that they already own. If you are still supporting a third-party or legacy VPN system, you should explore the new capabilities provided here and discover how much they could save your business.

DirectAccess and Always On VPN are particularly impressive and compelling connectivity options—a fresh way of looking at remote access. Automatic connectivity means your machines are constantly patched and updated because they are always connected to your management servers. You can improve user productivity and network security at the same time. These two things are usually oxymorons in the IT world, but with the Microsoft remote access stack, they hold hands and sing songs together.

Next, we are going to take a look at some of the security functions built into your Windows Server 2019 operating systems, and at some of the ways that your servers can be hardened to provide even better security than what comes out of the box.

Questions

1. What does AOVPN stand for?
2. What are the two primary protocols used for connecting AOVPN clients?
3. In which version of Windows 10 was AOVPN released?
4. In what special instance would an AOVPN client be required to be joined to your domain?
5. Does DirectAccess require your corporate internal network to be running IPv6?
6. What is the name of the internal website that DirectAccess clients check in with in order to determine when they are inside the corporate network?
7. What role does a Web Application Proxy server hold in a federation environment?

9
Hardening and Security

8.19 million dollars. For anyone who read that in the voice of Dr. Evil, my hat goes off to you. For anyone who has no idea what I'm talking about, you may have had a sheltered childhood. Joking aside, that number is significant to IT security. Why? Because 8.19 million dollars is the average cost to a business when they are the victim of a data breach. I originally heard this and other scary statistics at a Microsoft conference in Redmond, and the numbers have continued to climb year on year. How about looking at another statistic that can be used to get approval for an increase in your security budget? Depending on which study you read, the average number of days of **dwell time** an attacker has in your network (the time they spend hanging around inside your files and infrastructure before they are detected and eradicated) is around 200. Think about that—200 days! That is the better part of a year that they're camping out for before you discover them! What are they typically doing during those 200 days? Siphoning all of your data bit by bit out of the back door. Another number is 76% — as in the percentage of network intrusions that happen as a result of compromised user credentials. Furthermore, it is becoming more and more difficult to identify these attacks in the first place because attackers are using legitimate IT tools to grab what they want. For instance, an attacker could socially engineer their way into the trust of a single employee and leverage that trust to get a remote access connectivity tool installed onto the user's work computer. Why use malware when you can use something that is *trusted* and is going to fly under the radar of intrusion detection systems? Makes sense to me.

Data security, network security, credential and identity security — these things are all becoming harder to accomplish, but there are always new tools and technologies coming out that can help you fight off the bad guys. Windows Server 2019 is the most secure server OS that Microsoft has produced; in this chapter, let's discuss some of the functionality included that makes that statement true:

- Windows Defender Antivirus
- Windows Defender Firewall – no laughing matter
- Encryption technologies
- Azure AD Password Protection
- Fine-grained password policy
- Advanced Threat Analytics – end of support
- General security best practices

Windows Defender Antivirus

The term Windows Defender has been around for many years, but its terminology and capabilities have evolved numerous times with new OS releases. Defender existed even as far back as 2005, at the time providing very simple antimalware protection. The Windows 8 era introduced a fairly staggering change for Windows users, including Windows Defender in the operating system free out of the box. Although this sounds great on paper, Defender's capabilities were not taken too seriously by the IT population. Fast forward to today, however, and what is now known as Windows Defender Antivirus is a much improved antimalware/antivirus that is running on millions of Windows 10 client computers as well as, you guessed it, current versions of Windows Server. Defender Antivirus exists in the OS and is enabled by default, and as a result has a level of integration and responsiveness that is hard for third-party vendors to match. I can't tell you how many times I have tracked memory leaks and random server reboots back to a poorly functioning third-party antivirus software, which is unacceptable in today's server world. Some still consider the antivirus capabilities provided by Defender to be lackluster, perhaps only because it is free, but it does certainly carry some advantages over third-party AV. I have yet to see a Windows Defender product tank a client or server.

You have likely also seen and heard references to Windows Defender **Advanced Threat Protection** (**ATP**), recently renamed to Microsoft Defender Advanced Threat Protection. This is a family of products and systems that work together to protect your Windows machines. Antivirus/antimalware is only one of those capabilities, and built-in antivirus is a relatively new idea when talking about the Windows Server family of OSes.

The first server OS that we found with built-in Defender for antivirus was Server 2016. Many servers running in production for companies around the world are still Server 2012 R2 at this point (I know because I work on them every day), and so the improved existence of the Defender toolset in Server 2019 is yet another reason to start planning your migration today.

We simply do not have enough page space to dive into every aspect of Windows Defender ATP, and it is being continually improved upon. What we will do is explore some of the interfaces, make sure you know how to use the most common components that don't require policy-level manipulation or centralized administration, and expand your knowledge of some of the more advanced features that are available for further learning and digging.

Installing Windows Defender Antivirus

You're done! Windows Defender Antivirus is installed by default in Windows Server 2019. In fact, unless you have somehow changed it, not only is Defender AV installed, it is automatically protecting your system as soon as the OS is installed. But don't take my word for it: if you open up Server Manager and choose **Add roles and features**, click ahead to the **Select features** page and you should find a checkbox already selected next to **Windows Defender Antivirus**:

Figure 9.1: Windows Defender Antivirus is preinstalled

If it's not already checked for some reason, then this is exactly the place to visit in order to get it installed and working.

Exploring the user interface

The interface for the Windows Defender toolset is the same as within the latest versions of Windows 10, but if you haven't explored that yet, we will take a quick look at it here. Go ahead and launch **Settings** from inside the **Start** menu, then click on **Update & Security**.

Once inside that section, you will see **Windows Security** listed on the left. Here you get an overhead view of the different Defender components that are working together to protect your system.

Remember, you have done nothing to enable any of this functionality; these are all out-of-the-box capabilities:

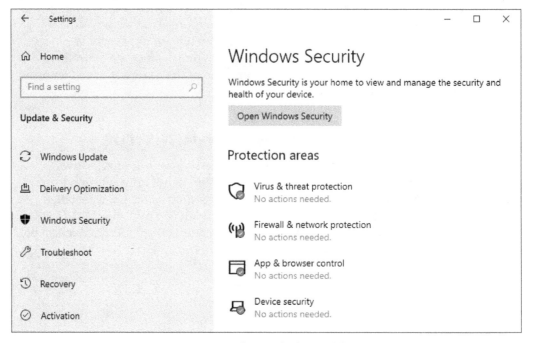

Figure 9.2: Windows Defender capabilities

Clicking further into any of these **Protection areas** will bring you more detailed descriptions of each capability, as well as many options for enabling or disabling particular protections that exist. For example, if you were to click on **Virus & threat protection**, you would see summary information about Defender AV, when its definition files were updated, what it's scanning, and so on. Then clicking further into a link called **Manage settings** will give you options for disabling Defender AV if you ever have the need, as well as numerous other options that can be selected or deselected. *Figure 9.3* shows you a few of the settings available inside Defender AV. I chose to display these three because they are important to another topic we will cover shortly, when we discuss the ATP portion of Defender ATP:

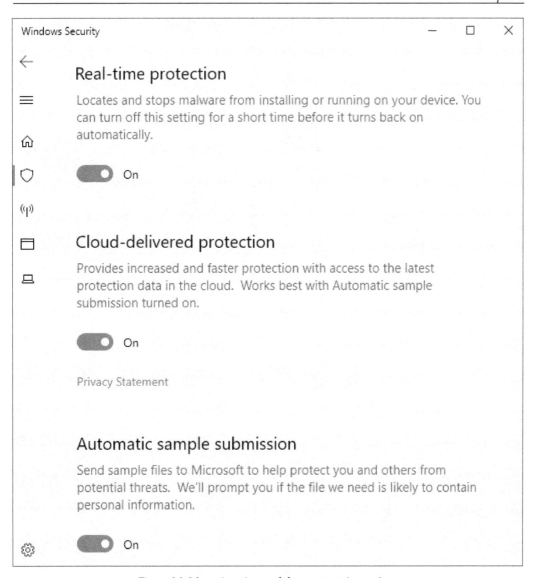

Figure 9.3: Managing virus and threat protection options

Disabling Windows Defender Antivirus

You already know that Defender AV is enabled by default, as are many other components that make up the Windows Defender family of products. By flipping the radio option shown in *Figure 9.3*, you can temporarily disable AV. Taking it a step further, if you are absolutely sure that you do not want to use Defender AV because you have your own AV software that you have already paid for, you have two different avenues that could be taken.

First, Defender AV is designed to automatically step down in the event that another AV is installed. More than likely, all you need to do is install your other third-party antivirus tool, and after the server finishes restarting, Defender AV will stand down and allow the third-party product to run, so that they don't conflict with each other. This is important because a fact that even many computer technicians don't realize is that multiple AV programs running on a single system is generally a terrible idea. They often cause conflicts with each other, have memory allocation errors, and cause otherwise slow and strange behavior on the system.

If you are planning to utilize your own AV and want to make sure Defender is *completely* removed, it is possible to uninstall the Defender feature from your server. This is most easily done via PowerShell, with the following command:

```
Uninstall-WindowsFeature -Name Windows-Defender
```

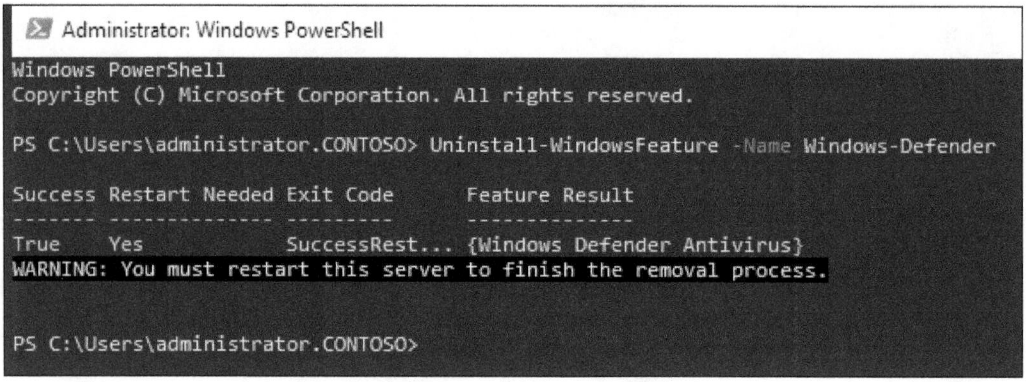

Figure 9.4: Uninstalling Defender

What is ATP, anyway?

It's hard to define what exactly ATP means because it is a culmination of Windows Defender parts, pieces, and security mechanisms working together in order to protect clients and servers from bad stuff: AV, firewalling capabilities, hardware protections, and even specific resistance against ransomware.

The combination of capabilities inside the *Windows Security* section of Windows 10 and Server 2019 work together to become ATP.

Something that should be incredibly intriguing to all of us is the smart way that Microsoft is now utilizing cloud connectivity and computing to improve Defender AV on a daily basis. Whether we realize it or not, most of the internet-connected Windows machines in the world are now continuously helping each other out by reporting newly discovered vulnerabilities and malicious activity to Microsoft. This information is then parsed and investigated via machine learning, and the resulting information can be immediately used by the rest of the Windows machines around the globe.

While this sounds a little *Big Brother* and full of privacy concerns, I believe we as a community will soon get over that fear and realize that the benefits outweigh the potential fears. Millions of users now flow their email through Office 365; you may not even realize it, but Office 365 does this kind of data handling as well to identify and block exploits. For example, if an email address within a company is suddenly sending emails to a large group of people, and that email contains a macro-enabled Word document, which is something that a user does not typically do, Office 365 can very quickly take that document offline into a secure zone, open it (or launch it if the attachment happened to be an executable), and discover whether or not this file is actually malware of some kind. If it is, Office 365 will immediately start blocking that file, thereby stopping the spread of this potentially disastrous behavior. All of this happens without input from the user or the company's IT staff. This is not even inner-company specific. If one of my users' emails is the first to receive a new virus and it is identified by Microsoft, that discovery will help to block the new virus for any other customers who also host their email in Microsoft's cloud. This is pretty incredible stuff!

This same idea holds true for Defender AV when you choose to allow it to communicate with and submit information to Microsoft's cloud resources. Earlier, I pasted in a screenshot of some Defender AV capabilities called **cloud-delivered protection and automatic sample submission** — it is these pieces of Defender AV that allow this cloud-based magic to happen and benefit the entire computer population.

Windows Defender ATP Exploit Guard

Once again, we are taking a look at what seems to be a long title for a technology that must have a very specific purpose, right? Nope. The new Exploit Guard is not *a* new capability but rather a whole *set* of new capabilities baked into the Windows Defender family. Specifically, these new protections are designed to help detect and prevent some of the common behaviors that are used in current malware attacks.

Here are the four primary components of the Defender ATP Exploit Guard:

- **Attack Surface Reduction (ASR)**: ASR is a series of controls that block certain types of files from being run. This can help mitigate malware installed by users clicking on email attachments, or from opening certain kinds of Office files. We are quickly learning as a computer society that we should never click on files in an email that appear to be executables, but often a standard computer user won't know the difference between an executable and any other kind of file. ASR can help to block the running of any executable or scripting file from inside an email.

- **Network protection**: This enables Windows Defender SmartScreen, which can block potential malware from phoning home, communicating back to the attacker's servers to siphon or transfer company data outside of your company. Websites on the internet have reputation ratings, deeming sites or IP addresses to be trusted or not trusted, depending on the types of traffic that have headed to that IP address in the past. SmartScreen taps into those reputation databases to block outbound traffic from reaching bad destinations.

- **Controlled folder access**: Ransomware protection! This one is intriguing because ransomware is a top concern for any IT security professional. If you're not familiar with the concept, ransomware is a type of malware that installs an application onto your computer that then encrypts files on your computer. Once encrypted, you can't open or repair those files without the encryption key, which the attackers will (most of the time) happily hand over to you for lots of money. Every year, many companies end up paying that ransom (and therefore engaging in passive criminal behavior themselves) because they do not have good protections or good backups from which to restore their information. Controlled folder access helps to protect against ransomware by blocking untrusted processes from grabbing onto areas of your hard drive that have been deemed protected.

- **Exploit protection**: Generalized protection against many kinds of exploits that might take place on a computer. The exploit protection function of Defender ATP is a rollup of capabilities from something called the **Enhanced Mitigation Experience Toolkit (EMET)**, which was previously available but reached its end of life in mid-2018. Exploit protection watches and protects system processes as well as application executables.

These controls, particularly exploit protection controls, can be managed in many different ways. They can be rolled out in a centralized fashion via Intune, Group Policy, or the Microsoft Endpoint Configuration Manager. Additionally, they can be configured on a per-machine basis by using PowerShell or the Windows Security app that is built into every current Windows version.

Let's take a peek at the settings on an individual instance of Windows Server 2019. Open up **Windows Settings | Update & Security**. Inside, in the left navigation pane, you will see a shield icon that says **Windows Security**. Go ahead and click on that. Now into **App & browser control**. At this screen, you have options for configuring **Windows Defender SmartScreen**, which we discussed, and also a section for **Exploit protection**. Clicking on **Exploit protection settings**, now we get into the nitty gritty of these protection mechanisms. There are many different pieces of exploit protection that can be globally enabled or disabled (many are enabled by default), and clicking on **Program settings** allows you to get granular, defining to what extent exploit protection handles individual programs, as you can see in *Figure 9.5*:

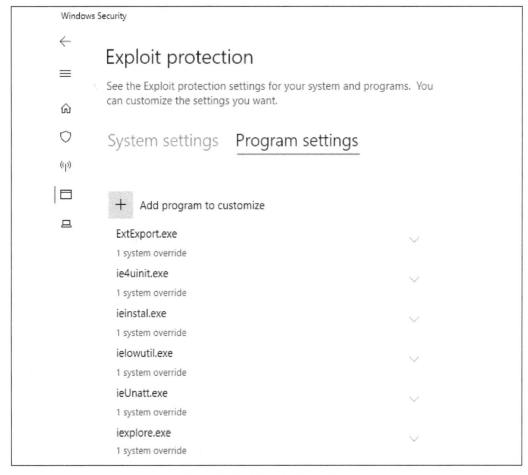

Figure 9.5: Exploit protection settings

Windows Defender Firewall – no laughing matter

Let's play a word association game. I will say something, and you say the first word that comes to mind.

Network security.

Did you say *firewall*? I think I would have. When we think of securing our devices at the network level, we think of perimeters. Those perimeters are defined and protected by firewalls, mostly at a hardware level, with specialized networking devices made to handle that particular task in our networks. Today, we are here to talk about another layer of firewalling that you can and should be utilizing in your environments. Yes, we are talking about Windows Firewall. Stop laughing, it's rude!

It is easy to poke fun at Windows Firewall based on its history. In the days of Windows XP and Server 2003, it was pretty useless and caused way more headaches than it solved. These feelings were so common that I still today find many companies who completely disable Windows Firewall on all of their domain-joined systems as a matter of default policy. If you ask them, there is usually no specific reason they are doing this—*it's always been this way* or *it's in our written security policy* are standard replies. This is a problem because the **Windows Defender Firewall with Advanced Security (WFAS)** that exists in the Windows OSes of today is much more robust and advanced than ever before and can absolutely be used to enhance your security architecture. I would go as far as to say that it is entirely silly to disable WFAS on a current OS, unless you have a very good, very specific reason to do so.

Three Windows Firewall administrative consoles

First, it is important to know that there are three different consoles from which you can configure Windows Firewall settings. Two of these consoles make each other redundant, and the third is much more capable than the others. Let's take a quick look at each one.

Windows Defender Firewall (Control Panel)

When trying to launch any application or setting in Windows Server 2019, it is usually most efficient to simply click on the **Start** button and then type a word relating to the task you are trying to accomplish. In my case, I clicked on **Start** and typed the word firewall. The best match option that was provided first in my search results was **Windows Defender Firewall**, so I went ahead and clicked on that.

Interestingly, this link opens the Windows Firewall configuration console from inside **Control Panel**, the old-school way of doing system settings. This console is still online and fully capable of manipulating basic firewalling functions, such as enabling or disabling the Windows Firewall, but since this tool resides inside **Control Panel**, we have to assume that this is actually not the tool that Microsoft intends for us to utilize. Remember, all new configuration capabilities have been migrated to the **Windows Settings** screens, rather than the old **Control Panel**:

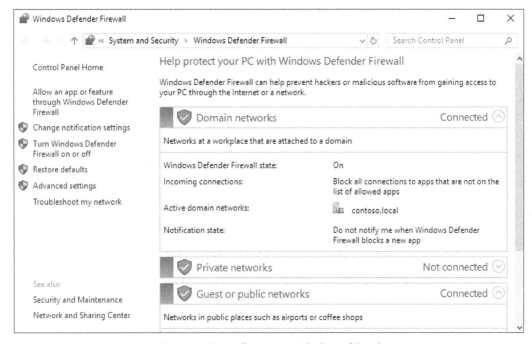

Figure 9.6: Firewall settings inside Control Panel

Firewall & network protection (Windows Security Settings)

While the **Control Panel**-based tools were always the proper place to make these changes in past versions of the OS, we already know that there are many Windows Defender options stored inside **Windows Settings**. Could it be the case that there are also Windows Defender Firewall configuration settings stored inside the **Windows Security** section of **Settings**?

Yes, there definitely are. Open up **Windows Settings** and click on **Update & Security**, then on **Windows Security**. You've been here before—this is the screen that gives a quick summary of the Windows Defender components. Sure enough, there is one here called **Firewall & network protection**.

Click on that button, and you will be taken into a new configuration platform for the Windows Firewall functions that did not exist in earlier versions of Windows Server:

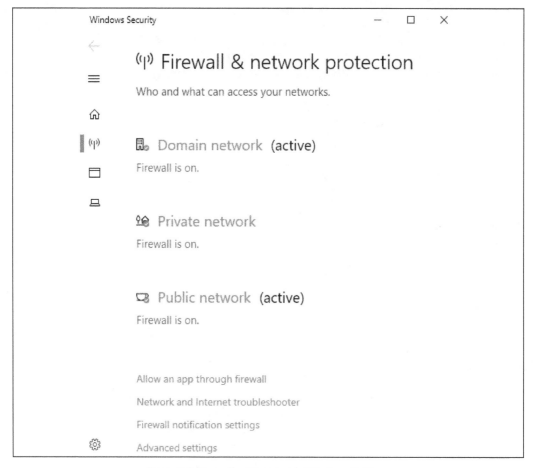

Figure 9.7: Firewall settings inside Windows Settings

Clicking on any of the links provided here will open additional configuration options. For example, if you wanted to quickly enable or disable particular firewall profiles (we will learn about those shortly), you could click on the profile you want to configure, such as the **Domain network** profile, and from there easily turn off the firewall for this networking profile. Many companies disable the domain network profile on their machines so that the firewall is not protecting traffic that happens inside a corporate LAN network.

While disabling the firewall is generally a bad idea, sometimes it is required to fit your business model:

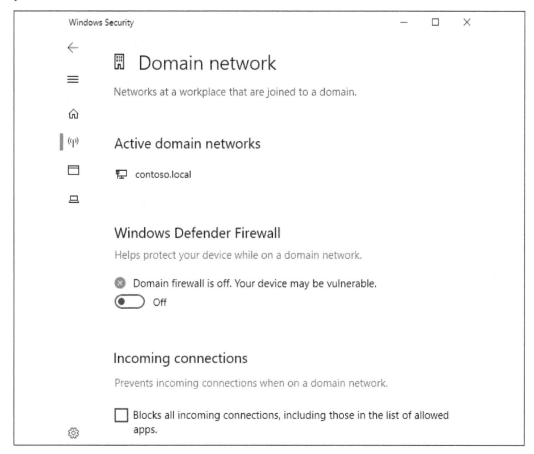

Figure 9.8: Disabling the Windows Firewall while on Domain network

The firewall configuration screen available inside **Windows Settings** is a good place to make simple, overhead decisions about the Windows Defender Firewall, but this interface is limited in capabilities. For any real utilization of firewall functionality or configuration...

Windows Defender Firewall with Advanced Security (WFAS)

If you are anything like me, you won't be satisfied with the firewall information provided inside **Windows Settings**, and you will want to see what is going on under the hood, and so you will want a little more information than the basic Windows Firewall tools alone can give you. You can either click on one of the **Advanced settings** links shown in previous screenshots or simply open Command Prompt or a **Start | Run** prompt and type wf.msc. Either of these functions will launch the full **WFAS** administration console:

Figure 9.9: Windows Defender Firewall with Advanced Security

Here you can see much more in-depth information about the activity and rules that are in play with Windows Firewall and make more acute adjustments in your allowances and blocks. There is also a **Monitoring** section where you can view actively engaged rules, including **Connection Security Rules**. This is an important section because it highlights the fact that WFAS does much more than block network traffic. It is not only a firewall; it is also a connectivity platform. If you plan to utilize IPsec for encryption of network traffic, whether it be native IPsec inside your network or through the remote access technology DirectAccess, you will see rules populated in this section that are the definitions of those IPsec tunnels.

Believe it or not, Windows Firewall is actually responsible for making those encrypted connections and tunnels happen. This is way more advanced than the Windows Firewall of yesteryear.

Three different firewall profiles

When any NIC on a computer or server is connected to a network, Windows Firewall will assign that connection one of the three different profiles. You have probably interfaced with this decision-making process before without even realizing it. When you connect your laptop to the Wi-Fi at your local coffee shop, did Windows ask you whether you were connecting to a home, work, or public network? Or in more recent versions of Windows, it asks you a question more along the lines of "would you like to allow your computer to be discoverable on this network, yes or no?" This is your Windows Firewall asking you which profile you would like to assign to the new network connection. The reason that you can assign NICs and network connections to different firewall profiles is that you can assign different access rules and criteria for what is or is not allowed over those different profiles. Effectively, it is asking you *how much do you trust this network?* For example, when your laptop is connected to the corporate network you can probably be a little bit more lax than when that same laptop is connected at a hotel across the country. By assigning more intense firewall rules to the profile that is active when you are in the hotel, you build bigger walls for attackers to face when you are out working on that public internet. Let's take a look at the three different types of profiles that are available, with a quick description of each:

- **Domain Profile**: This is the only one that you cannot choose to assign. The Domain Profile is only active when you are on a domain-joined computer that is currently connected to a network where a domain controller for your domain is accessible. So, for any corporate machine inside the corporate network, you can expect that the Domain Profile will be active.

- **Private Profile**: When connecting to a new network and you are prompted to choose where you are connected, if you choose either **Home** or **Work**, that connection will be assigned the Private Profile.

- **Public Profile**: When prompted, if you choose **Public**, then of course you are assigned the public firewall profile. Also, if you are not prompted for some reason, or if you do not choose an option at all and simply close the window that is asking you what to assign to your new connection, this Public Profile will be the default profile that is given to any connections that do not have a different profile already assigned.

In the more recent versions of Windows (particularly in Win10), you don't usually get the prompt asking what kind of network it is; instead, you get that prompt asking whether or not you want to allow your computer to communicate with other devices on the new network. Effectively, this is still the same prompt, and the decision you make at that prompt will assign your connection to either the public or private firewall profile.

Each network connection gets assigned its own profile definition. You could certainly have more than one firewall profile active at the same time on the same system. For example, my RA1 server is connected to both the corporate network as well as the public internet. Inside WFAS, you can see that both the Domain Profile and Public Profile are active:

Figure 9.10: Multiple NICs can mean multiple firewall profiles

Alternatively, if you open up **Network and Sharing Center** on this server, we can also see the profiles listed here, and you can easily tell which NIC is using which profile:

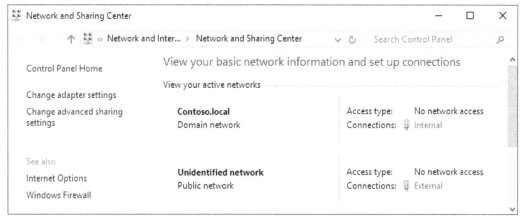

Figure 9.11: Firewall profiles assigned to each NIC

Building a new inbound firewall rule

Now that we know that the real meat and potatoes of Windows Firewall is inside the WFAS console, let's use WFAS to build ourselves a new rule. On this RA1 server, I have enabled RDP access so that I can more easily manage this server from my desk. However, by turning on RDP I have now allowed RDP access from all of the networks on this server. That means I can RDP into RA1 from inside the network, but I can also RDP into RA1 from the internet, since this is a remote access server and happens to be connected straight to the internet. This is a big problem, because now any yahoo on the internet could potentially find my server, find the RDP login prompt, and try to brute force their way into RA1.

To alleviate this problem, I want to squash RDP only on my external NIC. I want it to remain active on the inside so that I can continue to access the server from my desk, but is there an easy way inside WFAS to create a firewall rule that blocks RDP access only from the outside? Yes, there certainly is.

Open up wf.msc to launch Windows Defender Firewall with Advanced Security, navigate to the **Inbound Rules** section and you will see all of the existing inbound firewall rules that exist on this server (there are many rules listed here even if you have never visited this console before, these rules are installed with the OS). Right-click on **Inbound Rules** and choose **New Rule...**. This launches a wizard from which we will create our new firewall rule. The first screen is where we identify what kind of a rule we want to create. You can create a rule that modifies traffic for a particular program, or you can look through a list of **Predefined** protocols.

However, I like knowing exactly what my rule is doing because of the way that *I* defined it, not because of a pre-existing protocol definition, and I know that RDP runs over TCP port 3389. So, I am going to choose **port** on this screen, and after I click on **Next**, I will define 3389 as the specific port that I want to modify:

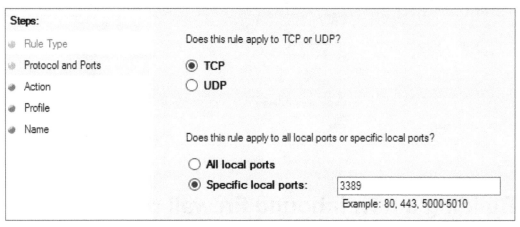

Figure 9.12: This firewall rule is going to manipulate port 3389 (RDP) traffic

Our third step is to decide whether we want to allow or block this particular port. There is a third option listed about only allowing the connection if it is authenticated by IPsec, which is a powerful option, but necessitates having IPsec established in our network already. Because of that requirement, this option doesn't apply to most people. For our example, we already have RDP working, but we want to block it on one of the NICs, so I am going to choose **Block the connection**:

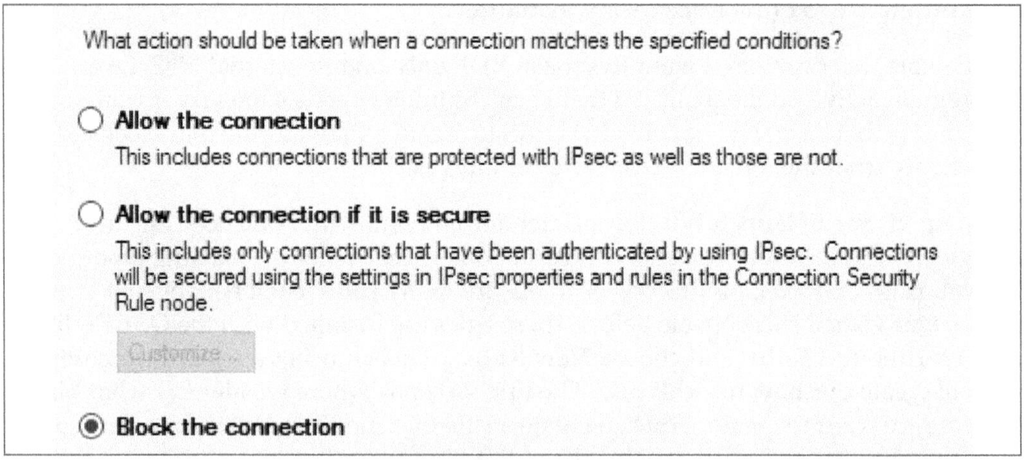

What action should be taken when a connection matches the specified conditions?

○ **Allow the connection**
This includes connections that are protected with IPsec as well as those are not.

○ **Allow the connection if it is secure**
This includes only connections that have been authenticated by using IPsec. Connections will be secured using the settings in IPsec properties and rules in the Connection Security Rule node.

Customize...

◉ **Block the connection**

Figure 9.13: Blocking a connection

We don't want to block RDP for *all* of the NICs, though, so this next screen is very important. Here we need to reference back to our knowledge about those firewall profiles we talked about. Remember that internal NICs connected to our domain network will have the Domain Profile assigned to them. But any NICs that are not connected to an internal network where a domain controller resides will have either Public or Private Profiles active. That is the knowledge we need to employ on this screen. If we want to disable RDP only on the external NIC, we need this rule to be active for only the Private Profile and Public Profile. In fact, in looking back at the screenshots we already saw, we can see that the external NIC is assigned the Public Profile specifically, and so we could check only the **Public** checkbox here and RDP would then be blocked on the external NIC. But in case we add more NICs to this server in the future for which we want to make sure RDP access is not possible, we will leave both **Public** and **Private** checked, to ensure better security for the future. Make sure that you **uncheck** the **Domain** profile! Otherwise, you will block RDP access completely, and if you are currently using RDP to connect to this server, you will kick yourself out of it and be unable to reconnect:

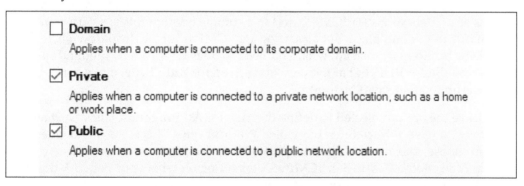

Figure 9.14: Blocking a connection for different profiles

And now we simply create a name for our new rule, and we are done! Our ability to RDP into this server from the internet has immediately been disabled, and we can rest much easier tonight.

Creating a rule to allow pings (ICMP)

Very often I find myself needing to create either an allow or a block rule for ICMP. In other words, I often find myself needing to adjust the firewall on servers in order to enable or disable their ability to reply to ping requests. You probably noticed with newer server OSes that it is pretty normal for the firewall to automatically block pings (ICMP) out of the box.

This is a problem for environments where ping is the standard method for testing whether an IP address is consumed or available. You may be laughing, but trust me, there are still plenty of IT administrators out there that don't keep track of which IP addresses they have used inside their networks, and when faced with the need to set up a new server and decide what IP address to give it, they simply start pinging IP addresses in their network until they find one that times out! I have seen this so many times. While this is obviously not a good way to manage IP addresses, it happens. Unfortunately, this method encounters big problems, because most new Windows installations are designed to block ICMP responses out of the box, which means that you may ping an IP address and receive a timeout, but there could actually be another server or PC running on that IP address.

So, getting back to the point. You may have a need to enable ICMP on your new server, so that it responds when someone tries to ping it. When we need to create a new rule that allows pings to happen, we set up a rule just like we did for RDP, but there is one big catch. On that very first **Rule Type** screen when creating the new rule, where you have to identify what kind of rule you are creating, there are no options or predefinitions for ICMP. I find this strange because this is a very common type of rule to put into place, but alas, choosing ICMP from the drop-down list would just be too easy. Instead, what you need to do is create a new inbound rule just like we did for RDP, but at the very first screen for **Rule Type**, make sure you select the option that says **Custom**.

Next, leave the option selected to define this rule for **All programs**. Click **Next** again, and now you have a drop-down box called **Protocol type**. This is the menu where you can choose your new rule to manipulate ICMP traffic. As you can see in *Figure 9.15*, you can choose **ICMPv4** or **ICMPv6**, depending on what your network traffic looks like. My test lab is IPv4-only, so I am going to choose **ICMPv4**:

Steps:
Rule Type
Program
Protocol and Ports
Scope
Action
Profile
Name
To which ports and protocols does this rule apply?
Protocol type:
ICMPv4
Protocol number:
Local port:
Remote port:
Internet Control Message (ICMP) settings:
Any
Custom
HOPOPT
ICMPv4
IGMP
TCP
UDP
IPv6
IPv6-Route
IPv6-Frag
GRE
ICMPv6
IPv6-NoNxt
IPv6-Opts
VRRP
PGM
L2TP

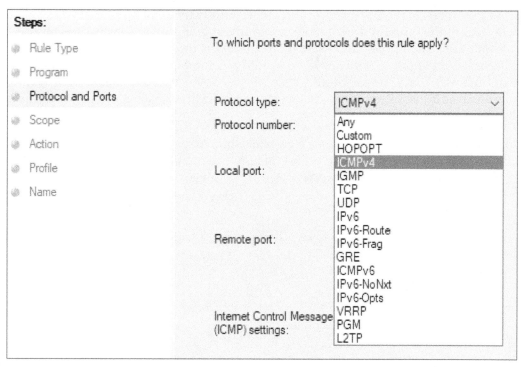

Figure 9.15: Applying the rules to specific protocols

For the rest of the ICMP rule creation, follow the same procedures outlined when we created the RDP rule, choosing to either allow or block this traffic, and for which firewall profiles. Once finished, your new ICMPv4 rule is immediately enacted, and if you have configured an Allow rule, your new server will now successfully respond to ping requests:

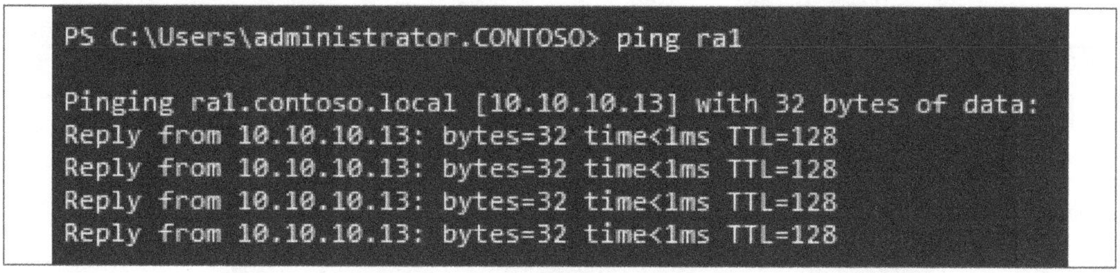

PS C:\Users\administrator.CONTOSO> ping ra1
Pinging ra1.contoso.local [10.10.10.13] with 32 bytes of data:
Reply from 10.10.10.13: bytes=32 time<1ms TTL=128
Reply from 10.10.10.13: bytes=32 time<1ms TTL=128
Reply from 10.10.10.13: bytes=32 time<1ms TTL=128
Reply from 10.10.10.13: bytes=32 time<1ms TTL=128

Figure 9.16: Pinging your server and now receiving an ICMP response

If ever you need to modify a rule or dig into more advanced properties of a firewall rule, back at the **Inbound Rules** screen you can right-click on any individual firewall rule and head into **Properties**. Inside these tabs exists the opportunity to modify any criteria about the rule. For example, you could accommodate additional ports, you could modify which firewall profiles it applies to, or you could even restrict which specific IP addresses this rule applies to by use of the **Scope** tab.

This enables you to apply your firewall rule only to traffic coming or going from a specific portion of your network, or a certain subset of machines. For example, here I have modified my **Scope** tab to reflect that I only want this firewall rule to apply to traffic that is coming in from the 192.168.0.0/16 subnet:

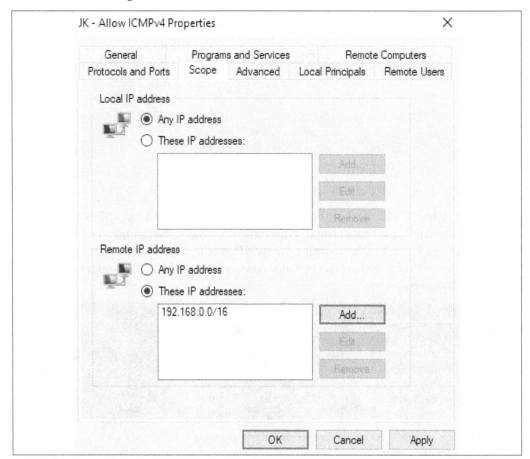

Figure 9.17: Applying the firewall rule to specific IP addresses or subnets

Managing WFAS with Group Policy

Managing firewall rules on your servers and clients can be a huge step toward a more secure environment for your company. The best part? This technology is enterprise class and free to use since it's already built into the OSes that you use. The only cost you have associated with firewalling at this level is the time it takes to put all of these rules in place, which would be an administrative nightmare if you had to implement your entire list of allows and blocks on every machine individually.

Thank goodness for **Group Policy**. As with most settings and functions inside the Microsoft Windows platform, setting up a firewall policy that applies to everyone is a breeze for your domain-joined machines. You can even break it up into multiple sets of policies, creating one GPO that applies firewall rules to your clients and a separate GPO that applies firewall rules to your servers, however you see fit. The point is that you can group many machines together into categories, create a GPO ruleset for each category, and automatically apply it to every machine by making use of Group Policy's powerful distribution capabilities.

You are already familiar with creating GPOs, so go ahead and make one now that will contain some firewall settings for us to play with. Link and filter the GPO accordingly so that only the machines you want to have the settings will actually get them. Perhaps a good place to start is a testing OU, so that you can make sure all the rules you are about to place inside the GPO work well together and with all of your other existing policies, before rolling the new policy out to your production workforce.

Once your new GPO is created, right-click on it from inside **Group Policy Management Console** and click on **Edit...**:

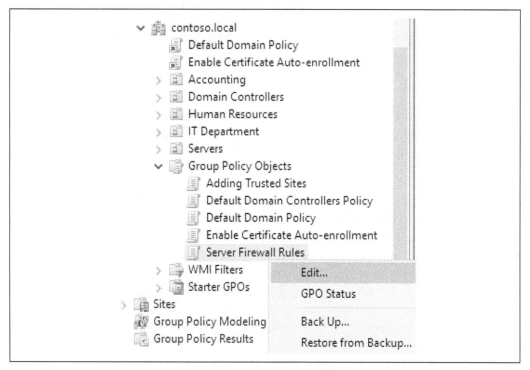

Figure 9.18: Using Group Policy to centrally manage Windows Firewall rules

Now that we are looking at the insides of this new GPO, we just need to figure out where the correct location is for us to create some new firewall rules. When you are looking inside the rules on the local machine itself, everything is listed under a **Windows Defender Firewall with Advanced Security** heading, and that is located at **Computer Configuration | Policies | Windows Settings | Security Settings | Windows Defender Firewall with Advanced Security | Windows Defender Firewall with Advanced Security**:

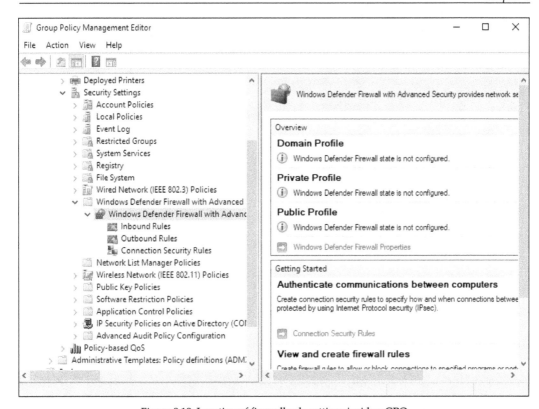

Figure 9.19: Location of firewall rule settings inside a GPO

As you can see, this is also the place to go when you want to make sure that particular firewall profiles, or Windows Firewall as a whole, are specifically turned on or off. So, this is the same place that you would go if you wanted to disable Windows Firewall for everyone.

By clicking on the **Windows Defender Firewall Properties** link shown in *Figure 9.19*, you can determine the status of each firewall profile individually:

Figure 9.20: Separate tabs to modify each firewall profile's behavior

Once you are finished setting your profiles according to your needs, click on **OK**, and you find yourself back at the WFAS part of the GPO. Just like inside the local WFAS console, you have categories for **Inbound Rules** and **Outbound Rules**. Simply right-click on **Inbound Rules** and click on **New Rule...** to get started with building a rule right into this GPO. Walk through the same wizard that you are already familiar with from creating a rule in the local WFAS console, and when you are finished, your new inbound firewall rule is shown inside the GPO:

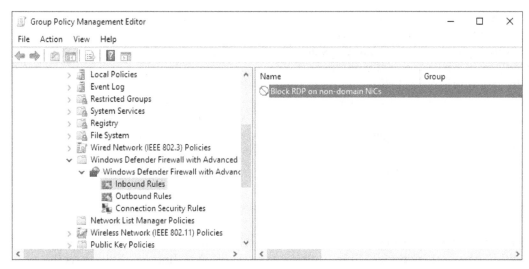

Figure 9.21: A successfully implemented firewall rule

Faster than you can say Jack Robinson, this new firewall rule is already making its way around Active Directory and installing itself onto those computers and servers that you defined in the policy's links and filtering criteria.

Encryption technologies

An idea that has taken a fast step from *something the big organizations are playing around with* to *everybody needs it* is the use of encryption. Most of us have been encrypting our website traffic for many years by using HTTPS websites, but even in that realm there are surprising exceptions, with a lot of the cheap web-hosting companies still providing login pages that transmit traffic in clear text. This is terrible, because with anything that you submit over the internet now using regular HTTP or an unencrypted email, you *have to assume* that it is being read by someone else. Chances are you are being paranoid and nobody is actually intercepting and reading your traffic, but you need to know that if you are accessing a website that says HTTP in the address bar, or if you are sending an email from any of the free email services, any data that is being entered on that web page or in that email can easily be stolen by someone halfway around the world. Data encryption is an absolute requirement for corporate information that needs to traverse the internet; though at the same time that I say that, the back of my mind is telling me that the vast majority of companies are still not using any kind of encryption technology on their email system, and so that is still a potential disaster waiting to happen for many.

While we are getting better and better at protecting internet browser traffic, we traditionally are still not paying a lot of attention to data that is *safe* within the walls of our organization. The bad guys aren't dumb, though, and they have a very large toolbox of tricks to socially engineer their way into our networks. Once inside, what do they find? In most cases, it's a big free-for-all. Get a hold of one user account or one computer and you've got keys to a large part of the kingdom. Fortunately, there are several technologies built into Windows Server 2019 that are designed to combat these intrusions and protect your data even while it sits within the four walls of your datacenter. Let's look at some information on them so that you can explore the possibility of using these encryption technologies to further protect your data.

BitLocker and the virtual TPM

BitLocker is a technology that has become pretty familiar to see on our client systems within corporate networks. It is a full-drive encryption technology, giving us the advantage of making sure our data is fully protected on laptops or computers that might be stolen. If a thief gets their hands on a company laptop, claws out the hard drive, and plugs it into their computer...sorry Charlie, no access. The entire volume is encrypted. This makes all kinds of sense for mobile hardware that could be easily lost or stolen. But in the beginning stages of this technology, there was never real consideration of using BitLocker to protect our servers.

With the escalated adoption of cloud computing resources, suddenly it makes much more sense to want BitLocker on our servers. More particularly when talking about the cloud, what we really want is BitLocker on our **Virtual Machines (VMs)**, whether they be client or server OSes. Whether you are storing your VMs in a true cloud environment provided by a public cloud service provider or you are hosting your own private cloud where tenants reach in to create and manage their own VMs, without the possibility of encrypting those virtual hard drives—the VHD and VHDX files—your data is absolutely **not** secure. Why not? Because anyone with administrative rights to the virtualization host platform can easily gain access to any data sitting on your server's hard drives, even without any kind of access to your network or user account on your domain. All they have to do is take a copy of your VHDX file (the entire hard drive contents of your server), copy it to a USB stick, bring it home, mount this virtual hard disk on their own system, and bingo—they have access to your server hard drive and your data. This is a big problem for data security compliance.

Why has it historically not been feasible to encrypt VMs? Because BitLocker comes with an interesting requirement. The hard drive is encrypted, which means that it can't boot without the encryption being unlocked. How do we unlock the hard drive so that our machine can boot? One of two ways.

The best method is to store the **unlock keys** inside a **Trusted Platform Module (TPM)**. This is a physical microchip that is built right into most computers that you purchase today. Storing the BitLocker unlock key on this chip means that you do not have to connect anything physically to your computer to make it boot, you simply enter a pin to gain access to the TPM, and then the TPM unlocks BitLocker. On the other hand, if you choose to deploy BitLocker without the presence of a TPM, to unlock a BitLocker volume and make it bootable you need to plug in a physical USB stick that contains the BitLocker unlock keys. Do you see the problem with either of these installation paths in a VM scenario? VMs cannot have a physical TPM chip, and you also have no easy way of plugging in a USB stick! So, how do we encrypt those VMs so that prying eyes at the cloud hosting company can't see all our stuff?

Enter the **virtual TPM**. This capability came to us brand new in Windows Server 2016; we now have the ability to give our virtual servers a virtual TPM that can be used for storing these keys! This is incredible news and means that we can finally encrypt our servers, whether they are hosted on physical Hyper-V servers in our datacenter or sitting in the Azure cloud.

Shielded VMs

Using BitLocker and virtual TPMs to encrypt and protect virtual hard drive files produces something called **Shielded VMs**. Shielded VMs are a capability first introduced in Windows Server 2016 and have been improved in Server 2019. I know this is just a tiny taste and preview of this amazing new technology, but I wanted to mention it here because it definitely relates to the overall security posture of our server environments.

We will cover much more detail on Shielded VMs in *Chapter 14, Hyper-V*.

Encrypted virtual networks

Wouldn't it be great if we could configure, control, and govern our networks from a graphical administrative interface, rather than looking at router CLIs all day? Would we not benefit from networking flexibility to move servers and workloads from one subnet to another, without having to change IP addressing or routing on those servers? Couldn't we find some way to automatically encrypt all of the traffic that is flowing between our servers, without having to configure that encryption on the servers themselves?

Yes, yes, and yes! Through the use of **Software Defined Networking (SDN)** and a new capability called **encrypted virtual networks,** we can accomplish all of these things. This section of text is really just a reference point, a place to steer you back toward *Chapter 7, Networking with Windows Server 2019,* if you skipped over it and landed here instead. We have already discussed SDN and its new capability to create and automatically encrypt virtual networks that flow between Hyper-V VMs and Hyper-V host servers, so if this idea intrigues you, make sure to head back and revisit that chapter.

Encrypting File System

Encrypting File System (EFS) is a component of Microsoft Windows that has existed on both client and server OSes for many years. Whereas BitLocker is responsible for securing an entire volume or disk, EFS is a little more particular. When you want to encrypt only certain documents or folders, this is the place you turn to. When you choose to encrypt files using EFS, it is important to understand that Windows needs to utilize a user certificate as part of the encrypt/decrypt process, and so the availability of an internal PKI is key to a successful deployment. Also important to note is that authentication keys are tied to the user's password, so a fully compromised user account could negate the benefits provided by EFS.

I think that many companies don't employ EFS because you leave the decision on what documents to encrypt up to the user. This also means that you depend on them to remember to do the encryption in the first place, which means they will have to understand the importance of it to make it worthy of their time. I wanted to mention EFS because it is still alive and is still a valid platform for which you can encrypt data, but most administrators are landing on BitLocker as a better solution. The lack of responsibility on the user's part and a good centralized management platform do put BitLocker a solid step ahead of EFS. Both technologies could certainly co-exist, though, keeping data safe at two different tiers instead of relying on only one of the data encryption technologies available to you.

IPsec

A lot of the encryption technology built into OSes revolves around data at rest. But what about our data on the move? We talked about using SSL on HTTPS websites as a way of encrypting web browser data that is on the move across the internet, but what about data that is not flowing through a web browser?

And what if I'm not even concerned about the internet; what if I am interested in protecting traffic that could even be flowing from point to point *inside* my corporate network? Is there anything that can help with these kinds of requirements? Certainly.

IPsec is a protocol suite that can be used for authenticating and encrypting the packets that happen during network communication. IPsec is not a technology that is particular to the Microsoft world, but there are various ways in Windows Server 2019 that IPsec can be utilized in order to secure data that you are shuttling back and forth between machines.

The most common place where IPsec interaction shows up on Windows Server is when using the Remote Access role. When configuring VPN on your RA server, you will have a number of different connection protocols that the VPN clients can use to connect to the VPN server. Included in this list of possible connection platforms are IPsec (IKEv2) tunnels. The second remote access technology that uses IPsec is DirectAccess. When you establish DirectAccess in your network, every time that a client computer creates a DirectAccess tunnel over the internet to the DirectAccess server, that tunnel is protected by IPsec. Thankfully the Remote Access Management Console that you use to deploy both VPN and DirectAccess is smart enough to know everything that is needed to make IPsec authentication and encryption work, and you don't need to know a single thing about IPsec in order to make these remote access technologies work for you!

The big missing factor with IPsec provided by the Remote Access role is traffic *inside* your network. When you are talking about VPN or DirectAccess, you are talking about traffic that moves over the internet. But what if you simply want to encrypt traffic that moves between two different servers inside the same network? Or the traffic that is flowing from your client computers inside the office to their local servers, also located in the office? This is where some knowledge of the IPsec policy settings comes in handy because we can specify that we want traffic moving around inside our corporate networks to be encrypted using IPsec. Making that happen is a matter of putting the right policies in place.

Configuring IPsec

There are two different places that IPsec settings can be configured in a Microsoft Windows environment. Both old and new systems can be supplied with IPsec configurations through the traditional **IPsec Security Policy snap-in**. If you are running all systems that are newer, such as Windows 7 and Server 2008 and above, then you can alternatively employ **Windows Defender Firewall with Advanced Security** for setting up your IPsec policies. WFAS is the most flexible solution but isn't always an option depending on the status of legacy systems in your environment.

First, let's take a glance at the older IPsec policy console. We will start here because the different options available will help to build a baseline for us to start wrapping our minds around the way that IPsec interaction works between two endpoints. There are three different classifications of IPsec policy that can be assigned to your machines that we will encounter in this console. Let's take a minute to explain each one, because the policy names can be a little bit misleading. Understanding these options will put you a step ahead for understanding how the settings inside WFAS work as well.

Server policy

The Server policy should probably be renamed to the *Requestor* policy because that is really what this one does. When a computer or server makes a network request outbound to another computer or server, it is requesting to establish a network connection. On these requesting computers—the ones initiating the traffic—this is where we tell the IPsec Server policy to apply. Once applied, the Server policy tells that computer or server to request IPsec encryption for the communication session between the initiating machine and the remote computer. If the remote system supports IPsec, then the IPsec tunnel is created in order to protect the traffic flowing between the two machines. The Server policy is pretty lenient, though, and if the remote computer does not support IPsec, then the network connection is still successful but remains unencrypted.

Secure Server policy

The difference here is that the Secure Server policy *requires* IPsec encryption to allow the network communication to happen. The regular Server policy that we talked about earlier will encrypt with IPsec when possible, but if not possible it will continue to flow the traffic unencrypted. The Secure Server policy, on the other hand, will fail to establish the connection at all if IPsec cannot be negotiated between the two machines.

Client policy

The Client policy needs to be renamed to *Response* policy, because this one is on the other end of the connection. The Client policy does not care about requesting an IPsec session; it only cares about **receiving** one. When a computer makes a network request to a server, and that computer has the Server or Secure Server policy so it is requesting IPsec, then the server to which that computer is trying to connect would need to have the Client policy assigned to it in order to accept and build that IPsec tunnel. The Client policy responds by allowing the encryption to happen on that session.

IPsec Security Policy snap-in

The original console for manipulating IPsec settings is accessed via MMC. Open that up, and add the **IP Security Policy Management** snap-in. Interestingly, when adding this snap-in you will notice that you can view either the local IPsec policy of the machine that you are currently logged in to, or you can open the IPsec policy for the domain. If you are interested in configuring a domain-wide IPsec implementation, this would be your landing zone for working on those settings. But for the purposes of just sticking our head in here to poke around a little, you can choose **Local computer** to take a look at the console:

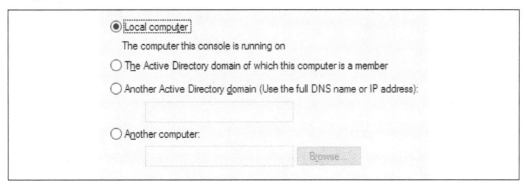

Figure 9.22: Exploring the IPsec configuration for our local server

Once inside, you can see any existing IPsec policies that might be in place, or you can start creating your own by using the **Create IP Security Policy...** action available when right-clicking on **IP Security Policies**. Doing this will invoke a wizard that will walk through the configuration of your own IPsec policy:

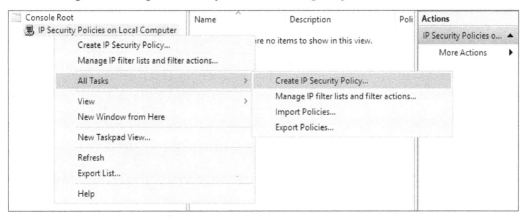

Figure 9.23: Creating an IP security policy

Using WFAS instead

The newer platform used for establishing IPsec connection rules is **Windows Defender Firewall with Advanced Security**. Go ahead and open that up, as you are already familiar with doing. Once inside, navigate to the **Connection Security Rules** section, which is listed immediately below **Inbound Rules** and **Outbound Rules**. **Connection Security Rules** is where you define IPsec connection rules. If you right-click on **Connection Security Rules** and choose **New Rule...**, you will then walk through a wizard that is similar to the one for creating a firewall rule:

Figure 9.24: WFAS can also be used to create IPsec policy rules

Once inside the wizard to create your new rule, you start to see that the options available to you are quite different from the ones shown when creating a new firewall rule. This is the platform from which you will establish IPsec connection security rules that define what the IPsec tunnels look like, and on which machines or IP addresses they need to be active:

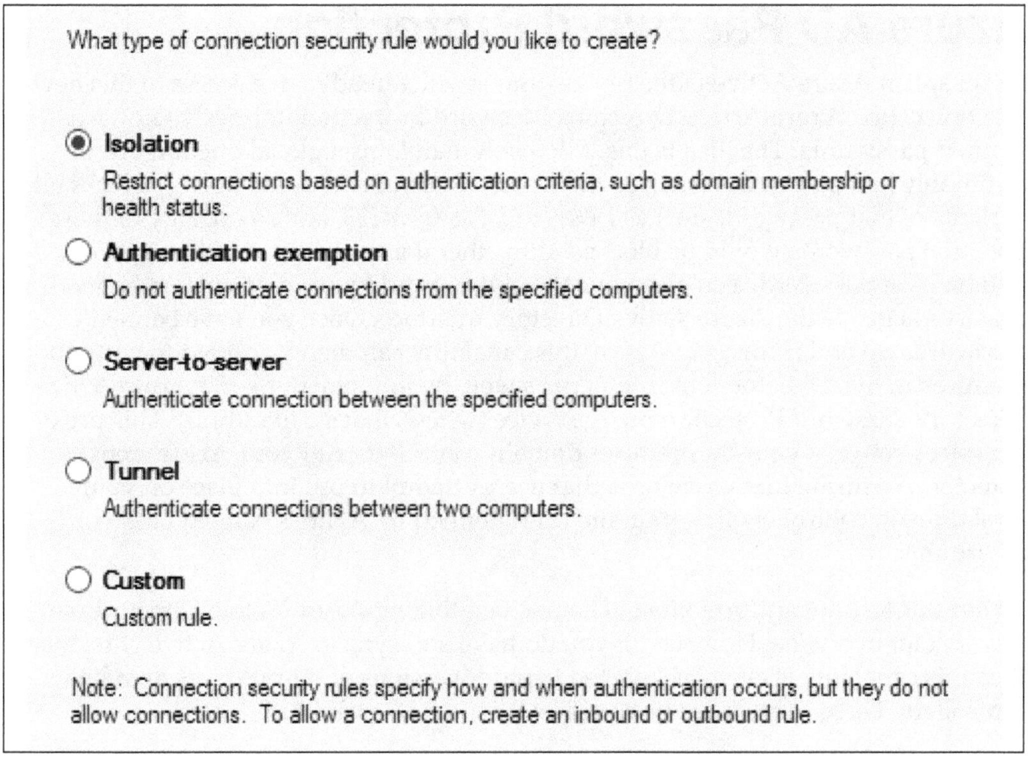

What type of connection security rule would you like to create?

◉ **Isolation**

Restrict connections based on authentication criteria, such as domain membership or health status.

○ **Authentication exemption**

Do not authenticate connections from the specified computers.

○ **Server-to-server**

Authenticate connection between the specified computers.

○ **Tunnel**

Authenticate connections between two computers.

○ **Custom**

Custom rule.

Note: Connection security rules specify how and when authentication occurs, but they do not allow connections. To allow a connection, create an inbound or outbound rule.

Figure 9.25: Types of connection security rules

We do not have space here to cover all of the available options in this wizard, but I definitely recommend picking up from here and taking it a step further with the following Microsoft Docs article: `https://docs.microsoft.com/en-us/previous-versions/windows/it-pro/windows-server-2012-R2-and-2012/hh831807(v=ws.11)`.

Azure AD Password Protection

If you are an Azure Active Directory customer, you already have access to this new function called **Azure Active Directory Password Protection**, formerly known as **banned passwords**. The idea is this: Microsoft maintains a global ongoing list of commonly bad passwords (such as the word *password*) and automatically blocks all variants of that password, such as *P@ssword*, *Password123*, and so on. Any of these potential passwords would be blocked altogether if a user ever tried to create one as their own password. You also have the ability to add your own custom banned passwords inside the Azure Active Directory interface. Once you have banned passwords up and running in Azure, this capability can then be ported to your on-premises Active Directory environment as well, by implementing the Azure Active Directory Password Protection proxy service (whew, that's a mouthful). This proxy interfaces between your on-premises domain controllers and your Azure Active Directory, ensuring that passwords that users attempt to put into place on your local domain controllers fit within the rules defined by Azure's banned password algorithms.

To use this technology, you must of course be utilizing Azure Active Directory, so this isn't for everyone. However, if you do have and sync to Azure Active Directory, then this capability is even backported to older versions of on-premises domain controllers. These servers can be as old as Windows Server 2012.

Here is a link to further information on banned passwords: `https://docs.microsoft.com/en-us/azure/active-directory/authentication/concept-password-ban-bad-on-premises`.

Fine-grained password policy

As promised way back during our discussion of domain-level password policy, we are here to walk through the build of a fine-grained password policy. Most organizations do require specific password complexity for their users, but almost always by way of the default domain policy GPO, which means that the password complexity and expiration settings are exactly the same for everyone within the domain.

What if you have requirements to enable complexity on some user accounts but not on others? Perhaps you have sales personnel who travel constantly and requiring very strong and complex passwords makes a lot of sense for them. But let's say you also have a machine shop where users have to log into computers every day, but those computers never leave the office and the users never type in their credentials into any systems other than those physically secure devices.

Is it really necessary for those machine shop users to have the same level of password complexity as the traveling sales personnel? Should they also be required to update their password every 30 days simply because you also ask it of your sales folks?

Starting with Windows Server 2012, log into any domain controller server and launch Server Manager, and at the very top of your Tools list you will see something called **Active Directory Administrative Center** (**ADAC**). This ADAC tool can be used to manipulate many things within Active Directory, but most importantly for our purposes today, this new tool is the mechanism that enables you to create a **fine-grained password policy** (**FGPP**). An FGPP enables the scenario we alluded to a paragraph ago, the ability to create multiple password policies and assign those policies to different classes of users and user accounts.

Log into a domain controller as a domain admin and open ADAC. In the left navigation pane, expand the name of your internal domain, then **System | Password Settings Container**. In my lab environment, I am clicking on **contoso (local) | System | Password Settings Container**. Currently, the Password Settings Container is empty, but using the **New | Password Settings** task will get things rolling:

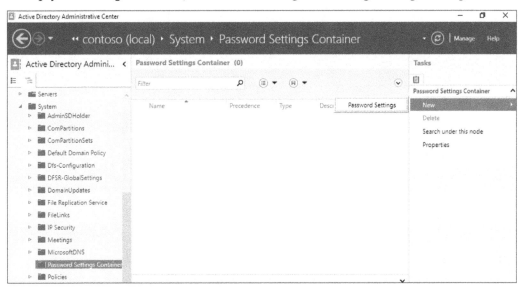

Figure 9.26: Fine-grained password policies are configured inside ADAC

The **Password Settings** screen is fairly self-explanatory. Here you define the same types of password complexity, length, and expiration criteria that you would normally configure inside the default domain policy GPO. You can see in *Figure 9.27* that I have created a Password Settings policy called **Sales Users**, with a number of specific criteria.

I was able to configure password settings as well as account lockout settings (another security setting commonly done globally via GPO) and filtered this password policy so that it only applies to users that are inside my AD group called **Sales Users**:

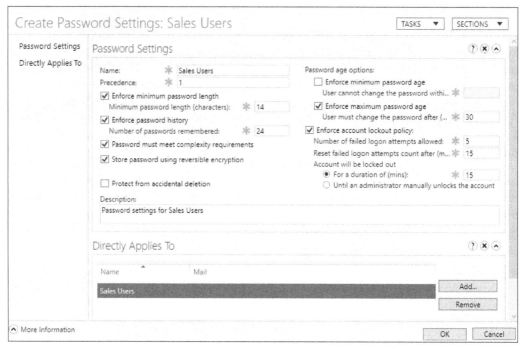

Figure 9.27: Creating new Password Settings policies

Now I'm going to repeat the process a couple more times, after which you can see that I have three separate Password Settings policies inside my ADAC container:

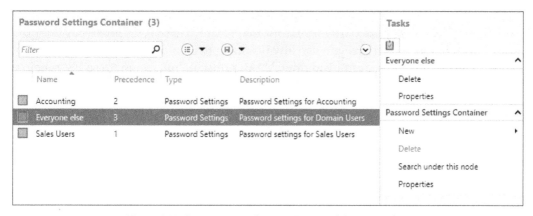

Figure 9.28: Creating more than one Password Settings policy

 Something that is important to note here is that each Password Setting policy has a **Precedence** declaration. Since we apply these password settings to groups, it is certainly possible that a particular user could be part of multiple groups that would give them multiple password policies. The **Precedence** number helps FGPPs to distinguish which settings should apply.

That's it! As soon as you have defined a fine-grained password policy inside ADAC, these new password settings will now take priority over settings inside the default domain policy GPO. Rather than pushing password settings via Group Policy, using a fine-grained password policy utilizes its own objects inside Active Directory to do its work. These objects are called **Password Settings Objects (PSOs)**. If you want to see a little bit further under the hood of a PSO, now that you have created an FGPP inside ADAC, head over to Active Directory Users and Computers and enable **Advanced Features** under the **View** menu. Once **Advanced Features** is enabled, you can navigate to **Domain | System | Password Settings Container** and see the new PSOs that you created a minute ago.

Double-clicking on any of these objects and then visiting the **Attribute Editor** tab will display details on password criteria for that object. There is no *need* to visit these objects from inside ADUC, as you can always make tweaks and changes to your fine-grained password policy from inside the ADAC console, but seeing these PSOs helps us to understand how Active Directory is storing and processing these policies:

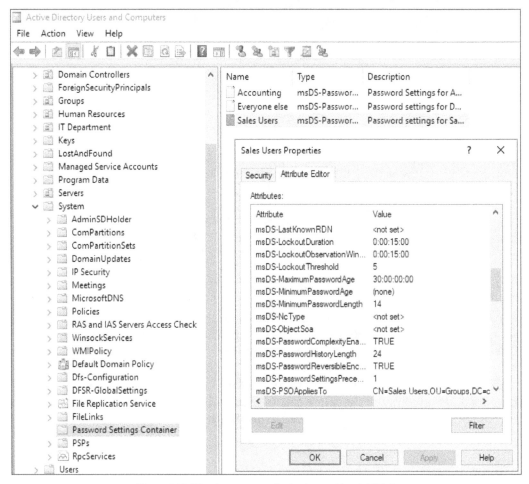

Figure 9.29: Viewing password criteria outside of ADAC

Advanced Threat Analytics – end of support

In my opinion, one of the coolest security features to have come out of Microsoft over the past handful of years is **Advanced Threat Analytics (ATA)**, and yet I have hardly heard anyone talking about it. Perhaps because they never went so far as to add it as a native feature built into the Windows Server OS. ATA is an on-premises software that rides on top of Windows to produce some amazing functionality. Essentially, what ATA does is monitor all of your Active Directory traffic and warn you of dangerous or unusual behavior in real time, immediately as it is happening.

Unfortunately, ATA reached the end of its mainstream support in January 2021. Extended support continues for five more years, however, and so I am choosing to retain information in this latest book edition because this is still a valid technology and will continue to exist in environments where it is installed for years to come. There is additional information at the end of this section regarding the ATA roadmap.

What is (was) ATA?

The idea of ATA is pretty simple to understand and makes so much sense that we are all going to wonder why it took so many years for someone to come up with this idea. Active Directory has been around for a very long time, and attacks against your environment utilizing user accounts for just as long. Discovering and troubleshooting attacks within the directory is complicated and messy; there is so much information being logged all the time inside AD that it is almost impossible to catch or track bad guys as they do their worst. Following some form of attack, you can certainly pore over log data from multiple domain controllers and piece together some semblance of what happened, but being able to identify that happening *as it is happening* is just a pipe dream. Or is it…?

ATA is an advanced form of Active Directory monitoring that uses machine learning. This is the coolest part of ATA. You configure your network so that all of the traffic flowing in or out of your domain controllers also lands in the ATA system. The most secure way to accomplish this is at the networking level, establishing port mirroring so that all of the domain controller packets also make their way to ATA, but at a level that an attacker would not be able to see.

This way, even if someone nefarious is inside your network and is on the lookout for some kind of protections working against them, ATA remains invisible to their prying eyes. However, port mirroring that traffic is something that smaller companies may not be able to do or may be too complex for an initial setup, and so a second option exists to install an ATA lightweight agent right onto the domain controllers themselves. This agent then sends the necessary information over to the ATA processing servers.

In either case, those ATA processing servers receive all of this data and start finding patterns. If Betty uses a desktop computer called **BETTY-PC** and a tablet called **BETTY-TABLET**, ATA will see that pattern and associate her user account with those devices. It also watches for her normal traffic patterns. Betty usually logs in around 8 a.m. and her traffic usually stops somewhere around 5 p.m. She typically accesses a few file servers and a SharePoint server. After a week or so of collecting and monitoring data, ATA has a pretty good idea of Betty's standard MO.

Now, one night, something happens. ATA sees a bunch of password failures against Betty's account. That in itself might not be something to get too excited about, but then all of a sudden Betty logs into a terminal server that she doesn't typically access. From there, her credentials are used to access a domain controller. Uh oh, this clearly sounds like an attack to me. With the tools built into Active Directory that we currently have at our disposal, what do we know? Nothing, really. We might see the password failures if we dig into the event logs, and based on that we could try poking around other servers' event logs in order to find out what that account was accessing, but we really wouldn't have any reason to suspect anything, nor any prompts or warnings that anything was happening whatsoever. This could be the beginning of a very large breach, and we would never see it. Thankfully, ATA knows better.

The management interface for ATA is like a social media feed, updated almost in real time. During the events I have just laid out, if we had been looking at the ATA media feed, we would have seen all of these items happen, as they happened, and it would be immediately obvious that someone compromised Betty's account and used it to gain access to a domain controller. There has never been a technology that watches Active Directory traffic so intensely, and there has certainly never been anything that learns patterns and behavioral diversions like this. It is truly an amazing technology, and I don't say that only because I happen to know the guys who built it. But since I do, I can tell you that they are brilliant, which is already pretty obvious since Microsoft scooped them up.

Even though this technology is now being morphed into something at the cloud level, let's take a few minutes and review a couple of screenshots from the ATA interface so you have an idea of what this social media-style feed looks like. This screenshot was taken from a Microsoft demo where they purposefully stole the Kerberos ticket from a user, and then utilized it on another computer in order to access some confidential files that only Demi Albuz should have been able to access. While ATA did not stop this activity, it immediately — and I mean within seconds — alerted inside this feed to show the **Pass-the-Ticket Attack**:

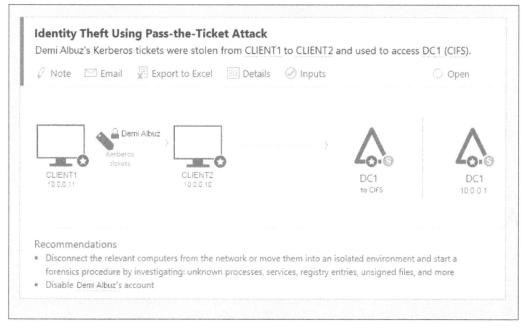

Figure 9.30: ATA identifying a pass-the-ticket attack

Here's another example where a user named Almeta Whitfield suddenly accessed 16 computers that she does not usually access, another big red flag that something is going on with her user account:

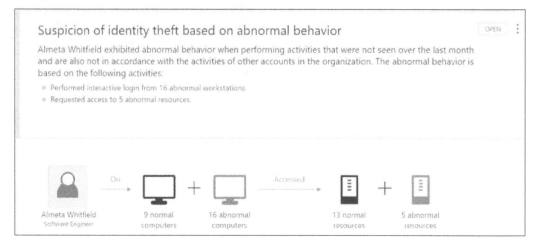

Figure 9.31: ATA alerts on abnormal behavior

Azure ATP

While ATA is an on-premises solution, its replacement lives in the cloud. **Azure Advanced Threat Protection** is Microsoft's recommended replacement for ATA, though that announcement seems to have caused many grumblings among ATA users. The primary catch is licensing—Azure ATP is only available so far with Microsoft 365 E5 licenses, which carry a hefty price tag.

Documentation is still online for ATA, and further learning materials can be found here: `https://docs.microsoft.com/en-us/advanced-threat-analytics/what-is-ata`.

For more information on the new Azure ATP, the following link is a good starting point: `https://techcommunity.microsoft.com/t5/security-compliance-identity/introducing-azure-advanced-threat-protection/ba-p/250332`.

General security best practices

Sometimes we need only to rely on ourselves, and not necessarily on functionality provided by the OS, to secure our systems. There are many common-sense approaches to administratorship (it's kind of fun being behind this keyboard: I get to make up new words all day long) that are easy to accomplish but are rarely used in the field.

The following are a few tips and tricks that I have learned over the years and have helped companies implement. Hopefully, you as the reader have even more to add to this list as to what works well for you, but if nothing else this section is intended to jog your thinking into finding creative ways with which you can limit administrative capability and vulnerability within your network.

Getting rid of perpetual administrators

Do all of your IT staff have domain admin rights the day they are hired? Do any of your IT staff have access to the built-in domain administrator account password? Do you have regular users whose logins have administrative privileges on their own computers? You know where I'm going with this—these are all terrible ideas!

Unfortunately, that was all the status quo for many years in almost every network, and the trend continues today. I still regularly watch engineers use the **administrator** domain account for many tasks when setting up new servers. This means they not only have access to potentially the most important account in your network and are using it for daily tasks, but it also means that anything that is set up with this user account is not accountable. What do I mean by that? When I set up a new server or make changes to an existing server using the general administrator account, and I end up causing some kind of big problem, nobody can prove that I did it. Using generalized user accounts is a sure way to thwart responsibility in the event that something goes wrong. I'm not trying to imply that you are always on the lookout for "who dunnit," but if I mess something up on an application server that I don't normally administer, it would be nice if the guys trying to fix it could easily figure out that it was me and come ask me what I did so that they can reverse it. There are many reasons that using the built-in administrator account should be off-limits for all of us.

To address the client side, do your users really need administrative rights on their computers? *Really*? I think you could probably find ways around it. Bringing regular users down to user or even power user rights on their systems can make a huge impact on the security of those computers. It gives viruses a much harder time installing themselves if the user needs to walk through a prompt asking for admin privileges before they can proceed with the install. It also keeps all of your machines in a much more consistent behavioral pattern, without new and unknown applications and settings being introduced by the user.

Using distinct accounts for administrative access

This idea piggybacks off the last one and is something that I have started employing even on all of the home computers that I install for friends and family members. It really boils down to this: utilize two different user accounts. One with administrative access and one without. When you are logged in for daily tasks and chores, make sure that you are logged in with your regular user account that does not have administrative privileges, either on the local computer or on the domain. That way, if you attempt to install anything, or if something attempts to install itself, you will be prompted by the **User Account Control** (**UAC**) box, asking you to enter an administrative username and password before the installer is allowed to do anything. I can tell you that this works, as I have stopped a number of viruses and/or bloatware software on my own computer from installing themselves as I'm browsing around the internet trying to do research for one project or another. If I get a UAC prompt asking me for an admin password and I haven't clicked on an installer file, I know it's something I don't want. All I have to do is click on **No**, and that installer will not get a hold of my computer. On the other hand, if it is something that I am intending to install, then it is a minor inconvenience to simply enter the password of my administrative account and allow the installer to continue.

Maintaining two separate accounts allows you to work your way through most daily tasks while putting your mind at ease that you do not have the rights to inadvertently do something bad to your system. This mindset also naturally limits the amount of activity or changes performed on any given computer by an administrative account, meaning that logging and tracking of changes by those accounts becomes easier. This results in greater accountability and better change management processes.

Using a different computer to accomplish administrative tasks

If you want to progress even further on the idea of separate user accounts, you could make your computing experience even more secure by utilizing a separate computer altogether when accomplishing administrative-level tasks. One computer for regular knowledge worker tasks and another computer for administration. This would certainly help to keep your administrative system secure, as well as the remote systems that it has access to. And while it does seem cumbersome to have two physical computers at your desk, remember that with most SKUs in Windows 10, we can run Hyper-V right on our desktop computers.

I do exactly this with my own computer. I have my computer that is running Windows 10, and then inside that computer I am running a virtual machine via Hyper-V from which I do all administrative tasks on the sensitive servers. This way, a compromise of my day-to-day OS doesn't necessitate a compromise of the entire environment.

You could also employ this idea in reverse. When needing to test some new software, functionality, or link, you could spin up a VM in Hyper-V on your workstation, keep it fully disconnected from any networks so that it is sandboxed away, and test out whatever new or sketchy thing it is that you need to test. If it bombs your VM, no big deal. Just delete it and create a new one.

Whether you choose to split up administrative access at the user account level or the computer level, remember this simple rule: **never administer Active Directory from the same place that you browse Facebook**. I think that pretty well sums this one up.

Never browse the internet from servers

Seems like a no brainer, but everyone does it. We spend all day working on servers and very often have to reach out and check something from a web browser. Since Internet Explorer exists on Windows servers, sometimes it is just quicker and easier to check whatever it is that we need to check from the server console where we are working, rather than walk back over to our desks. Sometimes (perhaps oftentimes) we even go the extra step, consciously installing a different, better browser onto servers just so it's there if ever we need it. Resist the temptation! It is so easy to pick up bad things from the internet, especially on servers because if any machines in our network are running without antivirus protection, it is probably on the server side. The same is true for internet filters. We always make sure that client traffic is flowing through our corporate proxy (if we have one) or other protection mechanisms, but we don't always care whether or not the server traffic is moving outward the same way.

Don't even do it for websites that you trust. A man-in-the-middle attack or a compromise of the website itself can easily corrupt your server, or worse give someone access to it and therefore the rest of your network. It's much easier to rebuild a client computer than it is a server.

Role-Based Access Control (RBAC)

The phrase **Role-Based Access Control** (**RBAC**) is not one that is limited to Microsoft environments. It also is not a particular technology that can be utilized inside Windows Server 2019, but rather it is an ideology that is all about separating job roles and duties.

When we think about separating our employees' job roles from an IT perspective, we traditionally think in terms of Active Directory groups. While adding user accounts to groups does solve many problems about splitting up levels of permissions and access, it can be complicated to grow in this mentality, and ultimately AD groups still empower administrators with full access to the groups themselves. RBAC technologies divide up roles at a different level, caring about more than permissions. RBAC focuses more on employee job descriptions than access restrictions. There are a number of different technologies that take advantage of RBAC tools integrated into them, and there are even third-party RBAC solutions that ride on top of all your existing infrastructure, making it widely accessible across your entire organization and not restricted to working in the confines of a single domain or forest.

Just Enough Administration (JEA)

A great example of an RBAC technology that is included in Windows Server 2019 is **Just Enough Administration (JEA)**, which is part of PowerShell. JEA provides you with a way to grant special privileged access for people, without needing to give them administrative rights, which would have been required to accomplish the same duties in the past. The necessity to add someone to the administrators group on a server so that they can do their job is quite common, but JEA is a first step away from that necessity.

In our old way of thinking, it might be easy to think of JEA as doing something like allowing users to have administrative access within PowerShell even when they don't have administrative access to the OS itself, but it's even more powerful than that. The design of JEA is such that you can permit users to have access only to run particular PowerShell commands and cmdlets at an administrative level, leaving other commands that they do not need access to in the dark.

In fact, if a user is working within a JEA context of PowerShell and they try to invoke a cmdlet that is not part of their **allowed** cmdlets, PowerShell pretends as though it doesn't even recognize that cmdlet. It doesn't say, *sorry, you can't do this* – it just ignores the command! This definitely helps to keep prying fingers out of the cookie jar, unless you want to let them in.

Here's an example scenario that helps portray JEA capability. Maybe you are a DNS administrator, and you might occasionally need to restart DNS services. Since we are adopting the JEA/RBAC mentality, you are not going to have administrative rights on the OS of that DNS server, but you will have JEA-based rights within PowerShell so that you can run the tools that you need in order to do your work.

Restarting the DNS service requires access to use the `Restart-Service` cmdlet, right? But doesn't that mean I would be able to restart any service on that server and could potentially do all sorts of things that I don't need to do? JEA is even powerful enough to deal with this scenario. When setting up the level of access that the user needs to get, you can dive into particular cmdlets and divide up permissions. In our example, you could provide the user with access to the `Restart-Service` cmdlet, but only give permissions to restart particular services, such as those pertaining to DNS. If the user tried to `Restart-Service` on WINrm, they would be denied.

Disable external RDP...NOW

We all know how to RDP into servers, and indeed I bet 99% of anyone reading this RDPs into servers most days of the week. Doing so from inside the corporate network is a fast and easy way to interact with servers, and it makes a lot of sense that we employ this technology. Have you ever thought about the possibility of allowing RDP access over the internet? Wouldn't it be nice if you could simply open up MSTSC on your home computer and hop right into your servers without having to first establish a cumbersome VPN? Have you done it? Do you have servers who right now have NAT rules configured in your firewall so that you can hit a certain port using RDP from anywhere in the world and RDP directly into your server?

STOP IT RIGHT NOW!

Shut down the port, delete the NAT rule, do not pass Go, do not collect $200.

This is the absolute worst idea, and yet I discover NAT rules just like this on a very regular basis. I often work with new companies, supporting various parts of their infrastructure, and during the discovery of these client networks, we always check over firewall rules. It is truly amazing how many places in the world have RDP access to servers open to the entire internet.

Now, perhaps you're saying to yourself, "Of course I don't do that! Well, I do, but I am tricky and use ambiguous port numbers for this access. You certainly won't find RDP port 3389 open on my firewall because I set up my NAT rules so that you have to connect to crazy things like port 33343 and 5896; nobody will ever find those."

You. Are. Wrong.

It makes no difference whether your external ports are 3389 or 12345 or anything else. You might have gotten even sneakier and changed the port your servers are using to listen for RDP connections, so that 3389 is not involved either in the external or the internal part of the communication. That still makes no difference. Attackers have port scanners that can easily seek out any open RDP channels; the port those RDP channels use makes no difference to them.

What's the risk? Everything. Ransomware. Your entire network going down. That is the risk. How do I know? Because I have helped multiple companies through restoring everything from backup, all of their servers, because of one NAT rule that allowed RDP access into a server from the internet. Just one little rule to one little server and the entire infrastructure was locked down with ransomware overnight.

If you allow RDP connections to flow into your network from a NAT rule that allows communication from the internet, it is literally only a matter of time before someone bad is inside your network. It will happen. The fact that it has not happened yet is simply luck.

Delete the firewall rules and lock it down immediately, and then look into a better way of providing RDP access remotely. This could mean launching a VPN from your client, or it could mean setting up an RD Gateway server in your environment. RD Gateways are secure, and I am in no way saying that your RD Gateway servers are risks because they allow RDP access to internal machines from the internet. That is their purpose, and they have mechanisms to make that kind of communication secure.

Summary

The number-one agenda item for many CIOs is security. Security for your client machines, security for your networks, security for your cloud resources, and most importantly security for your data. There is no single solution to secure your infrastructure; it requires many moving parts and many different technologies all working together to provide safety for your resources. The purpose of this chapter was to provide examples of security measures and technologies that can be utilized in anyone's environments, as well as to reprioritize the importance that security has in today's IT world. Concerns about privacy and security need to be discussed for any and every technology solution that we put into place. Too many times do I find new applications being implemented inside organizations without any regard to how secure that application platform is. Applications that transmit or store data unencrypted need to be modified or dumped. Protection of information is essential to the longevity of our businesses.

We cannot complete a discussion about security in Windows Server 2019 without discussing the default OS installation option that we have thus far ignored throughout this book. In the next chapter, we'll dive into Server Core, our headless and less vulnerable version of Windows Server.

Questions

1. What is the name of the antimalware product built into Windows Server 2019?

2. When a domain-joined computer is sitting inside the corporate LAN, which Windows Defender Firewall profile should be active?

3. Other than the Domain Profile, what are the other two possible firewall profiles inside Windows Defender Firewall?

4. When creating a firewall rule to allow IPv4 ping replies, what protocol type must you specify inside your inbound rule?

5. What is the easiest way to push standardized Windows Defender Firewall rules to your entire workforce?

6. A virtual machine whose virtual hard disk file is encrypted is called a...?

7. What is the name of the Microsoft technology that parses domain controller information in order to identify pass-the-hash and pass-the-ticket attacks?

10
Server Core

Honey, I shrunk the server! Another chapter, another outdated movie reference. Over the past 20 years or so, we have seen nothing but growth from Microsoft operating systems. Growth can be good; new features and enhancements make our lives easier. But growth can also be bad, such as bloated file structures and memory-hogging graphical interfaces. If you were to chronologically graph the Windows and Windows Server operating systems in terms of their footprints based on factors such as disk space consumption and memory requirements, it would show a steady upward slope. Every new release requires just a little more processing power and just a little more hard drive space than the previous version. That was the case until, I'm guesstimating a little bit here, maybe Windows 8 and Server 2012. We saw some surprising steps taken with lowering these threshold numbers, a welcome change, but the change wasn't too dramatic. I mean, what can you glean from the fact that a new Windows Server 2019 box contains all kinds of core items still running inside C:\Windows\System32? We're not even going to talk about what's in the registry. Clearly, more cutbacks could be made, and at some level, new operating systems are still just being built and patched on top of the old ones.

Until now, perhaps. Here, we are going to talk about an alternative way to use Windows Server 2019 on a much, much smaller scale. Server Core has been around for quite some time now, but I'm hard-pressed to find people who actually use it. This miniaturized version of Server 2019 has been built to provide you with a smaller, more efficient, and more secure server platform.

We will cover the following topics in this chapter:

- Why use Server Core?
- Interfacing with Server Core
- Windows Admin Center for managing Server Core
- The Sconfig utility
- Roles available in Server Core
- Building a Server Core domain controller
- What happened to Nano Server?

Why use Server Core?

Why am I even talking about Server Core? Hasn't it been around since 2008? Yes, that is exactly why I *am* talking about it. The Server Core variant of the Windows Server operating system has been around for quite some time, but it seems like many admins are scared to trust it. I work with many different companies from many different industries. They all have one big thing in common: they use a lot of Windows Servers, and all of these Windows Servers are running the full GUI (Desktop Experience). Have they heard of Server Core? Sure. Have they tested it out in a lab? Sometimes. Everyone seems to have a slightly different experience level with Core, but it's quite rare to find one in production. Maybe I'm just talking to the wrong people, but I have to assume that there is a majority of us out there, myself included, who need to start using Server Core on a more regular basis.

Why do we need to start using Server Core? Because GUI-less servers are the future, says Microsoft. Would you believe that early in the previews for Windows Server 2016, the Desktop Experience option didn't even exist? You couldn't run a full GUI desktop shell on Server 2016 even if you wanted to (which everyone did), other than a mini-shell that could be plopped on top of Server Core. Microsoft received so much flack about this that the full Desktop Experience was added back during one of the Technical Preview rollouts. Even so, since that time, you have probably noticed that Server Core is the default option when installing any Windows Server operating system. Remember, back at the beginning of our book, where we did a quick review of the actual Server 2019 installation? The default option for installation is not Desktop Experience; rather, that top option in *Figure 10.1* is the option for installing the command-line-driven Server Core:

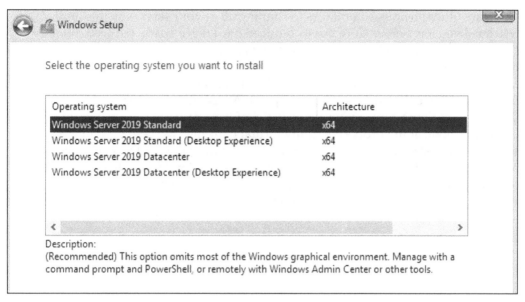

Figure 10.1: The default installation option is Server Core

One of the reasons for a move away from the graphical interface is increased capabilities for automation and scalability. When all of our servers are built similarly, it means that we can do more cloud-like functions with them. Automatic spinning up and down of resources as they are needed, rolling out dozens of servers at the flip of a switch—this kind of automation and sizing is possible in the cloud, but is only possible because the infrastructure is set up in a way that it is so standardized. Cloud hardware resources need to be so streamlined that the operations and automation tools can make them do what is needed, without worrying about all of the variables that would be present in a user-tweaked graphical interface.

There are other obvious advantages to running all of your servers as this limited, restricted version. Server Core boasts reduced hard drive space, reduced memory consumption, and a reduced attack surface when compared to a traditional, full-blown server experience. Now you can see why I made the hefty statements a minute ago about how we all need to start becoming more comfortable with Server Core! In fact, let's take a look at that reduced footprint. A base Server 2019 Standard running Desktop Experience consumes around 10 GB of hard drive space; I just verified this by taking a look at the properties of my virtual hard disk file being used by my CA1 server. CA1 is a standard Windows Server 2019 running the full Desktop Experience. Now, I have just finished running through the installation for my first Server Core operating system, and we can see in *Figure 10.2* that the VHDX file being used by this new VM is only 5.8 GB, a 40% reduction in space:

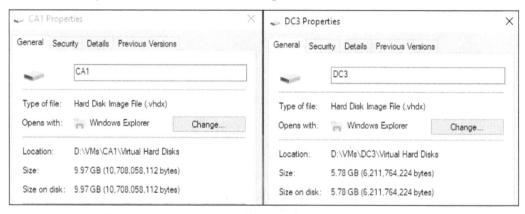

Figure 10.2: Server Core takes up less space than Server 2019 Standard

No more switching back and forth

There is a very important note that I wanted to make here: those of you who have worked with Server Core in Windows Server 2012 R2 know that we had the option of changing a server *on the fly*. What I mean is that if you created a new server as the full Desktop Experience, you could later change it to be Server Core. The opposite approach was equally possible; you could take Server Core and flip it over to a full Desktop Experience. While this capability existed, it actually enabled more people to use Server Core because it meant that even if you knew nothing about interfacing with Server Core, you could build a new server in a graphical way like you would with any other server, install roles and get them configured, and when you were all finished, switch it to be a Server Core, effectively disabling the graphical interface.

Not any more! This capability to move servers back and forth between platforms has been removed. I repeat, *this is no longer possible*. So, plan carefully from here on out when installing these operating systems. If you implement a server as Server Core, that guy is going to remain a Server Core for its lifetime.

Interfacing with Server Core

After running through your first installation of Server Core, you will be presented with the following lock screen:

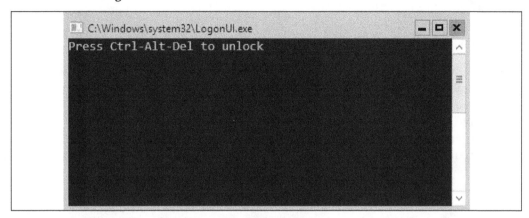

Figure 10.3: Server Core lock screen

Is that really a Command Prompt window that says **Press Ctrl-Alt-Del to unlock**? Yes, yes it is. This usually gets a few chuckles when an admin sees it for the first time. I know it did for me, anyway. It reminded me a little of when we used to code if/then games on our TI-83 calculators during high school math class. Press *Ctrl + Alt + Del*, and you will be prompted to change your administrator password for the first time, which is the same task that must always be performed first inside GUI versions of Windows Server. Except, of course, that you do it all from within the Command Prompt window using only your keyboard. Once you are officially logged in to the server, you will find yourself sitting at a traditional C:\Windows\system32\cmd.exe prompt, with a flashing cursor awaiting instructions:

Figure 10.4: Server Core user interface

Interestingly, the Command Prompt window isn't consuming the full screen; it is clear that there is a black background that cmd.exe is riding on top of. I only find this interesting because you can tell that the Core operating system itself is something other than Command Prompt, and that cmd.exe is just an application that autolaunches upon login. You can even utilize the mouse here and resize or move that Command Prompt window around. I do wonder if and when this will be replaced with a PowerShell prompt as the default interface.

Even more interesting and good to know is that you can launch some GUI-like applications from this prompt. For example, you can open up Notepad and utilize it with both a keyboard and mouse, just like you would from any version of Windows. If you have Notepad open, create a note and then save it; you can see that there is a real file structure and a set of relatively normal-looking system folders. So, rather than some form of black magic, Server Core is actually the real Windows Server operating system, wrapped up in a smaller and more secure package:

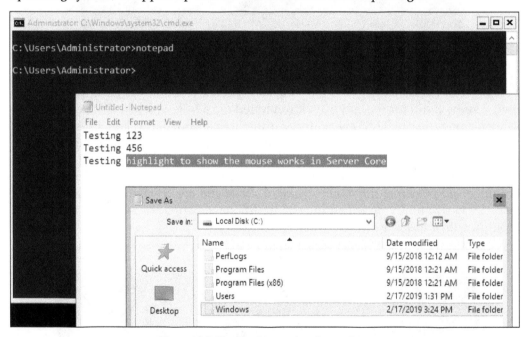

Figure 10.5: Opening Notepad on Server Core

PowerShell

So, as far as managing Server Core, you can obviously work straight from the console and use Command Prompt, which appears to be the default interface presented by the operating system. In reality, though, the commands and functions available from inside Command Prompt are going to be limited. If you are working from the console of a Windows Server Core box, it makes much more sense to use Command Prompt for just one purpose: to invoke PowerShell, and then use it to accomplish whatever tasks you need to do on that server. The quickest way I know to move into PowerShell from the basic Command Prompt is to simply type the word powershell and press *Enter*. This will bring the PowerShell capabilities right into your existing Command Prompt window so that you can start interfacing with the PowerShell commands and cmdlets that you need in order to really manipulate this server:

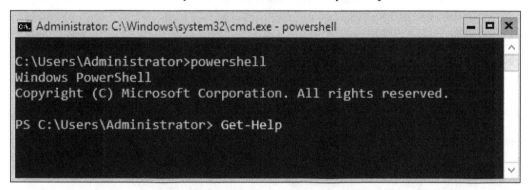

Figure 10.6: Loading PowerShell inside Server Core

What is the first thing we typically do on new servers? Give them IP addresses, of course. Without network connectivity, there isn't much that we can do on this server. You can assign IP address information to NICs using PowerShell on any newer Windows Server, but most of us are not in the habit of doing so. Since we can't just open up **Control Panel** and get into the Network and Sharing Center like we can from inside the Desktop Experience GUI of Windows Server, where do we begin with getting network connectivity on this new Server Core?

Using cmdlets to manage IP addresses

There are cmdlets that you can use to view and manipulate IP address settings from within PowerShell. Again, these same cmdlets can be used in the full GUI version of Windows Server or from within Server Core.

Currently, working from Server Core, where we only have command-line interfacing available to us, these cmdlets are essential for getting network connectivity flowing on our new server:

- `Get-NetIPConfiguration`: This displays the current networking configuration.
- `Get-NetIPAddress`: This displays the current IP addresses.
- `Get-NetIPInterface`: This shows a list of NICs and their interface ID numbers. This number is going to be important when setting an IP address because we want to make sure we tell PowerShell to configure the right IP on the right NIC.
- `New-NetIPAddress`: This is used to configure a new IP address.
- `Set-DNSClientServerAddress`: This is used to configure DNS server settings in the NIC properties.

Let's quickly walk through the setup of a static IP address on a new Server Core instance to make sure this all makes sense. I want to assign the `10.10.10.12` IP address to this new server, but first, we need to find out which NIC interface ID number it needs to be assigned to. The output of `Get-NetIPInterface` tells us that the `ifIndex` for my Ethernet NIC is number 4:

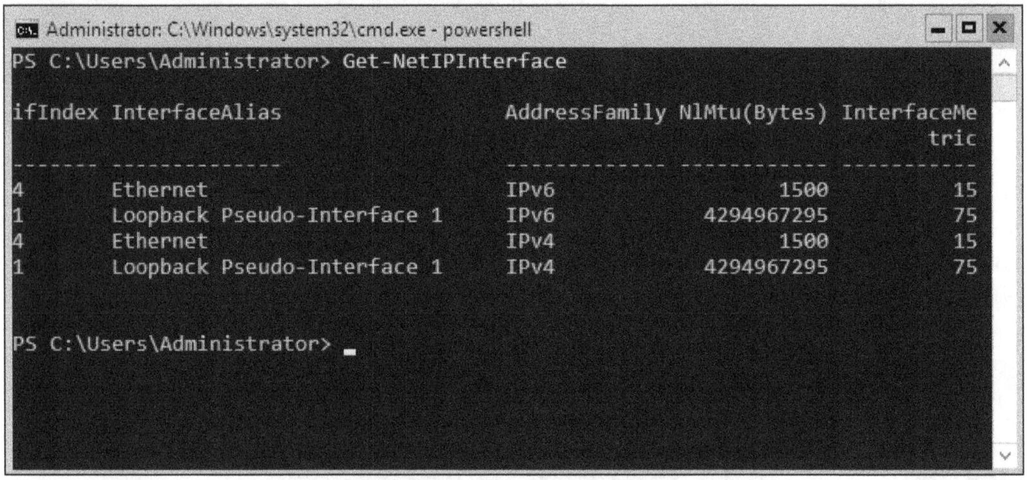

```
PS C:\Users\Administrator> Get-NetIPInterface

ifIndex InterfaceAlias                 AddressFamily NlMtu(Bytes) InterfaceMe
                                                                          tric
------- --------------                 ------------- ------------ -----------
4       Ethernet                       IPv6                  1500          15
1       Loopback Pseudo-Interface 1    IPv6            4294967295          75
4       Ethernet                       IPv4                  1500          15
1       Loopback Pseudo-Interface 1    IPv4            4294967295          75


PS C:\Users\Administrator> _
```

Figure 10.7: Finding the interface ID number for your NIC

Alternatively, or as a double-check, you could also run `route print` and verify your interface ID number near the top of that output. You can see in *Figure 10.8* that my Hyper-V NIC on this Server Core VM is interface 4 (shown at the left of the output):

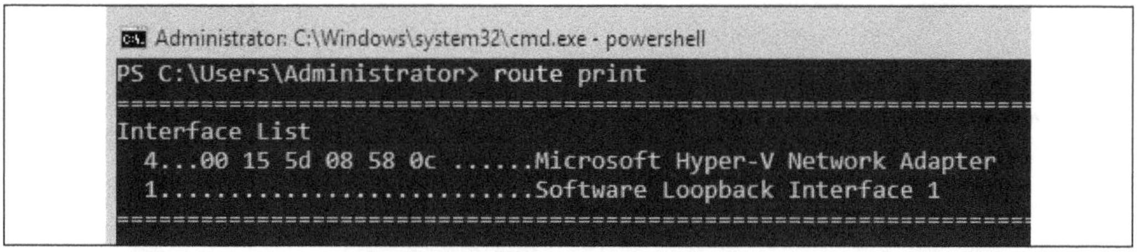

Figure 10.8: Displaying your interface list

Now that we know the interface number, let's build the commands that are going to assign the new IP address settings to the NIC. I am going to use one command to assign the IP address, subnet mask prefix, and default gateway. I will use a second command to assign DNS server addresses:

```
New-NetIPAddress -InterfaceIndex 4 -IPAddress 10.10.10.12 -PrefixLength
24 -DefaultGateway 10.10.10.1

Set-DNSClientServerAddress -InterfaceIndex 4 -ServerAddresses
10.10.10.10,10.10.10.11
```

Figure 10.9 shows us the resulting output:

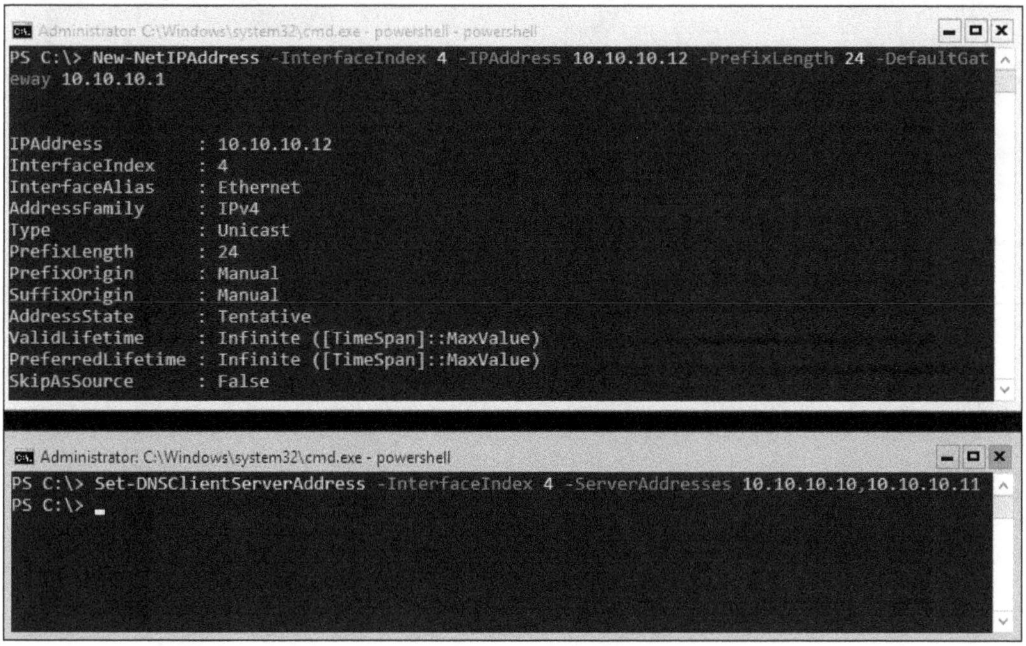

Figure 10.9: Assigning the IP and DNS server addresses

Hold the phone! How did I get *two* PowerShell prompts open at the same time within the Server Core interface? Make sure to read the *Accidentally closing Command Prompt* section later in this chapter to discover how you can launch multiple windows and tools inside the Server Core console.

Now, all of these IP settings should be in place on the NIC. Let's double-check that with a Get-NetIPConfiguration command, seen in *Figure 10.10*. Alternatively, you could use good old ipconfig to check these settings, but where's the fun in that?

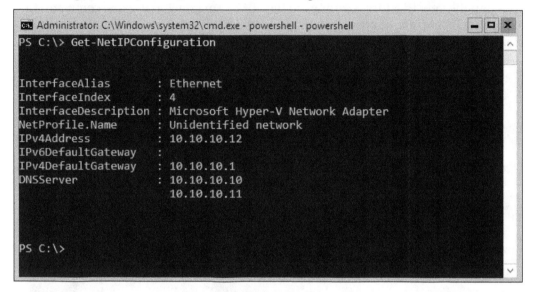

Figure 10.10: Checking the IP settings

Remember, you can always utilize DHCP reservations to make this a little bit easier. If you were to run a simple ipconfig /all from your Server Core and jot down the MAC address of your NIC, you could use this address to create a reservation in DHCP and assign a specific IP address to the new server that way.

Setting the server hostname

Now that we have network connectivity, a good next step is setting the hostname of our server and joining it to the domain. First things first, let's see what the current name of the server is, and change it to something that fits our standards. When you freshly install Windows, it self-assigns a random hostname to the server. You can view the current hostname by simply typing hostname and pressing *Enter*:

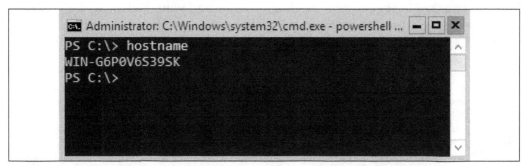

Figure 10.11: Checking the current hostname

To change the hostname of your server, we need to use PowerShell. Bring yourself into a PowerShell prompt if not already there, and all we need to do is use the Rename-Computer cmdlet to set our new hostname. I have decided to name this new server WEB4 because later we will install the Web Services role onto it and host a website. Remember, after renaming your computer just like in the GUI version of Windows Server, a system restart is necessary to put that change into action. So, following your Rename-Computer command, you can issue a Restart-Computer command to reboot the VM:

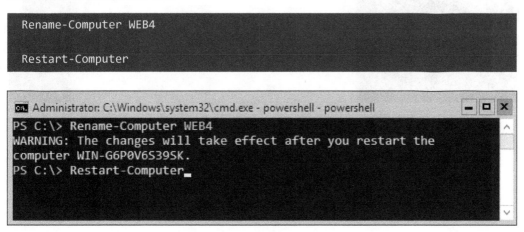

Figure 10.12: Changing the hostname and restarting your system

Joining your domain

The next logical step is, of course, joining your domain. These are the standard functions that we would perform on any new server in our environment but done in a way that you may have never encountered before since we are doing all of this strictly from the Command Prompt and PowerShell interfaces. To join a Server Core to your domain, head into PowerShell and then use the Add-Computer cmdlet. You will be asked to specify both the domain name and your credentials for joining the domain—the same information you would have to specify if you were joining a Windows Server 2019 in Desktop Experience mode to a domain. First, you must specify credentials that will be used to accomplish this domain join:

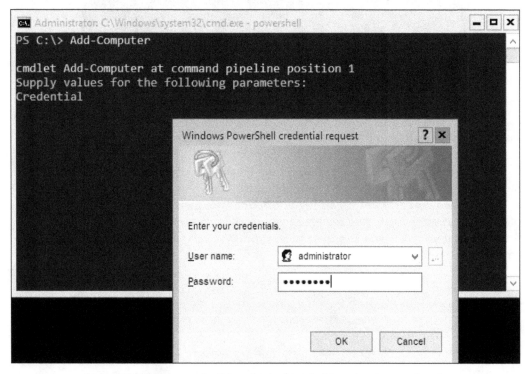

Figure 10.13: Entering credentials authorized to join this system to your domain

Then you tell it what domain you would like to join:

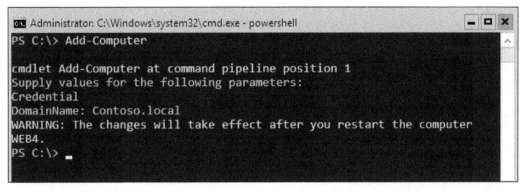

Figure 10.14: Specifying the domain to join

Alternatively, you could utilize the -DomainName parameter in combination with the original Add-Computer cmdlet to specify the name of the domain as part of the original command. And of course, after joining the domain, you need to Restart-Computer once again to finalize this change.

Remote PowerShell

Once the new server is IP-addressed, named, and domain-joined, we can start doing some real administration on this new Server Core instance. You could certainly continue to log in and interface directly with the console, but as with managing any other server in your environment, there must be ways to handle this remotely, right? One of the ways that you can manipulate Server Core without having to sit in front of it is by using a remote PowerShell connection.

We will cover the process for using remote PowerShell to manipulate servers (both GUI and headless) in more detail in *Chapter 11, PowerShell*, but here is a glimpse of the commands necessary and the capabilities present when you are able to achieve a remote session from a PowerShell prompt on a workstation inside a domain-joined environment.

Open up PowerShell from another system—this can be a server or even a client operating system. This PowerShell window is obviously open within the context of whatever machine you are currently logged in to, and any commands you issue via PowerShell will elicit a response from the local system. To tap PowerShell into the WEB4 Server Core instance, I will issue the following command. After running this, I am prompted for a password corresponding to the administrator account, and will then be able to issue remote PowerShell commands against our Server Core:

```
Enter-PSSession -ComputerName WEB4 -Credential administrator
```

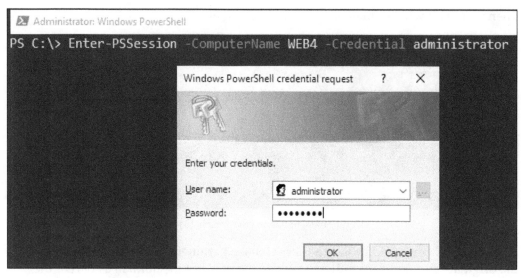

Figure 10.15: Using Enter-PSSession to remotely connect to WEB4

Now we are sitting at a PowerShell prompt, remotely connected to the WEB4 Server Core box. You can see this by [WEB4] being listed to the left of our prompt. Perhaps you don't trust that little identifier, and want to make sure that this PowerShell window is now accessing and manipulating the remote WEB4 server? Let's issue a couple of quick commands, such as hostname and ipconfig, to prove that the information being given to us in this PowerShell session is really coming from the new WEB4 server:

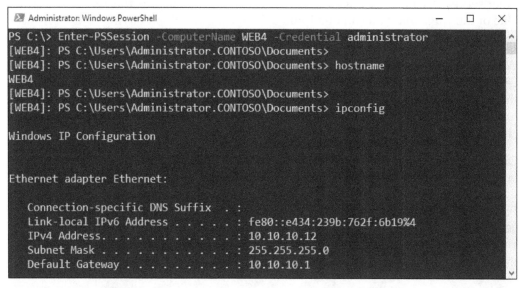

Figure 10.16: PowerShell now responds as if I was logged in to WEB4

Now that we have a remote PowerShell connection to this new Server Core, we can do pretty much whatever we want to that server, right from this console. Commands and cmdlets issued inside this remote PowerShell session will manipulate WEB4, rather than our local workstation.

Server Manager

While the initial configuration of your server will be handled to a degree from the command-line interfaces available at the console, once your server has been established on the network, it will likely be more advantageous for you to expand your horizons a little. You could probably find PowerShell cmdlets that allow you to manage and manipulate anything in your new server, but that is still a pretty new mentality for most of us—we are generally more accustomed to using graphical tools such as Server Manager. You already know that Server Manager can be used to manage multiple servers, local and remote, and is a piece of the Microsoft *centralized management* puzzle. This remote management capability in Server Manager that we explored earlier in the book allows you to tap into not only GUI-based Windows Servers but Server Core instances as well.

I want to install a role on my new WEB4 server. I could do that with PowerShell right on the server console, but instead let's try adding WEB4 into Server Manager, which is running on another one of my servers. I am going to log in to WEB3 and use Server Manager from there. Just like we have already seen, I can add a new server into Server Manager using the **Manage** menu and choosing **Add Servers**:

Figure 10.17: Adding new servers to be managed inside Server Manager

Add the new WEB4 server into our list of managed machines and it is now manageable from inside this instance of Server Manager. Getting back to what my original intentions were, I want to install the Web Server (IIS) role on WEB4. If I use the **Add roles and features** function inside Server Manager, I can now choose to manipulate the WEB4 server:

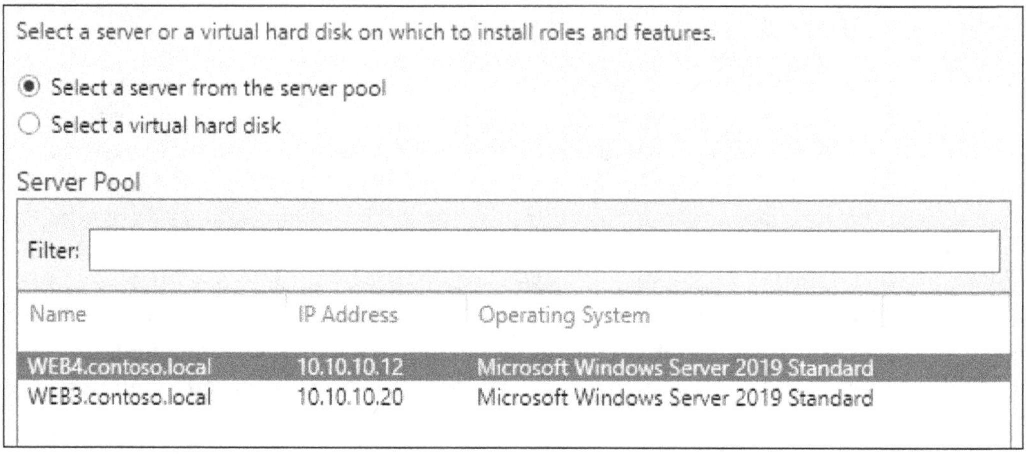

Select a server or a virtual hard disk on which to install roles and features.

◉ Select a server from the server pool
◯ Select a virtual hard disk

Server Pool

| Filter: | | |

Name	IP Address	Operating System
WEB4.contoso.local	10.10.10.12	Microsoft Windows Server 2019 Standard
WEB3.contoso.local	10.10.10.20	Microsoft Windows Server 2019 Standard

Figure 10.18: Modifying WEB4 from WEB3's Server Manager

Just like with any server running the full Desktop Experience version of Windows Server, we can now finish walking through the role installation wizard, and the Web Server role will be installed on WEB4.

Remote Server Administration Tools

Also true is the fact that you can manage Server Core instances with the **Remote Server Administration Tools (RSAT)** in Windows 10. RSAT is essentially just a copy of Server Manager and accompanying administrative tools that are designed to run on the client operating system. In our case, I already have a Windows 10 machine on which I installed RSAT earlier in the book, so I will test by logging in to that guy and adding WEB4 to the interface. I just finished installing the IIS role on WEB4 in our previous task, so I should be able to see that listed inside RSAT when I connect it to WEB4.

If you haven't used RSAT before and haven't read over that section of our text, it is important to know that there is no application called **Remote Server Administration Tools**. Instead, after the RSAT installation has been completed, take a look inside your **Start** menu for the application called **Server Manager**. This is how you utilize a Windows 10 client to remotely manage Windows Server 2019 instances:

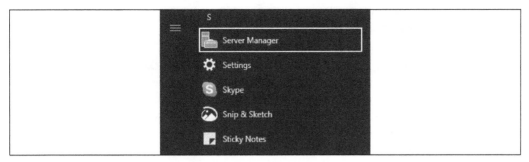

Figure 10.19: Server Manager inside Windows 10, courtesy of RSAT

Precisely as you would do from a Server Manager interface of Windows Server 2019, go ahead and walk through the wizard to add other servers to manage. Once I have added WEB4 as a managed server in my Win10's Server Manager, I can see **IIS** listed inside my **Dashboard**. This indicates that my IIS service running on WEB4 is visible, accessible, and configurable right from my Windows 10 desktop computer. For the majority of the tasks that I need to accomplish on WEB4, I will never have to worry about logging in to the console of that server.

If I right-click on the WEB4 server name from within this RSAT console, you can see that I have many features available to me that I can use to manage this remote Server Core instance:

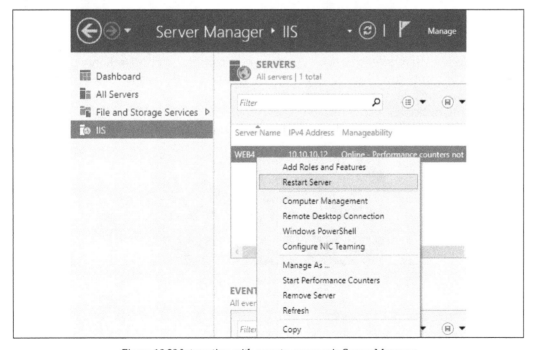

Figure 10.20 Interacting with remote servers via Server Manager

So, you can see that there are ways to use the GUI tools to manage our GUI-less instances of Windows Server. It's just a matter of putting your mind into a place where you are thinking of servers as headless, and that tools such as PowerShell or Server Manager really don't care at all whether the server they are changing is local or remote. The processes and tools are the same either way. You can see in the previous screenshot that I could even click from here to launch a remote PowerShell connection to WEB4. Clicking on this button immediately launches a PowerShell prompt that is remotely tied to the WEB4 server, even though I am currently only logged in to my Windows 10 workstation. This is even easier than issuing the Enter-PSSession cmdlet from inside PowerShell.

Accidentally closing Command Prompt

Let's now take a look at one more thing directly from the Server Core console; this is a common hurdle to overcome if you haven't utilized Server Core much. We tend to close windows and applications that are no longer being used, and so you might unconsciously close the Command Prompt window that is serving your entire administrative existence within a Server Core console session. Now you're sitting at a large blank screen, with seemingly no interface and nowhere to go from here.

How do you get back to work on this server? Do we have to turn the server off and back on to reset it? That would interrupt any roles or traffic that this server might be serving up to users, so obviously isn't the ideal approach.

There is a simple way to get Command Prompt back, and that is by using **Task Manager** to launch a new instance of Command Prompt. After mistakenly closing your current Command Prompt window, when sitting at the empty black screen of a Server Core console, you can press *Ctrl + Alt + Del* and you will be presented with the following options:

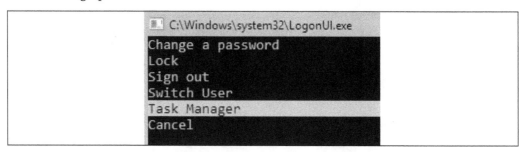

Figure 10.21: Ctrl+Alt+Del works inside Server Core

There are a few different functions you can perform here, which is pretty neat. But to get our Command Prompt window back, arrow-down to **Task Manager** and press *Enter*. This will launch the **Task Manager** application that we are all familiar with. Now, click on **More details** to expand Task Manager's screens. Drop down the **File** menu, and then click on **Run new task**:

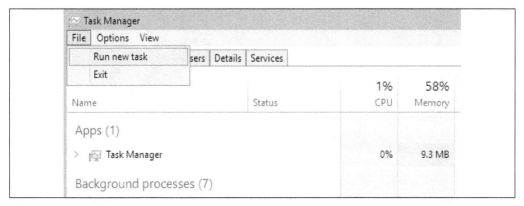

Figure 10.22: Running a new task via Task Manager

In the **Create new task** box, type cmd and then click **OK**:

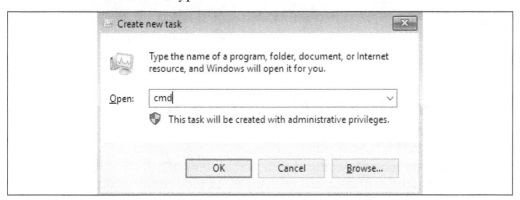

Figure 10.23: Opening Command Prompt

Alternatively, you could specify to launch any application directly from this **Create new task** prompt. If you were interested in moving straight into PowerShell, instead of typing cmd, you could instead simply type powershell into that prompt, and it would open directly:

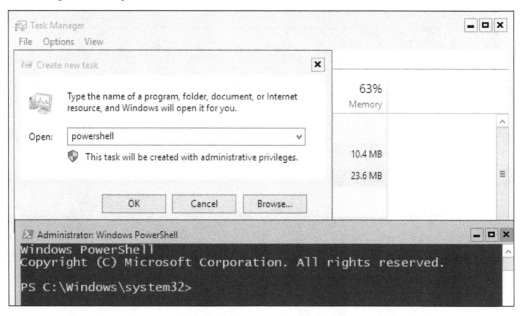

Figure 10.24: Opening PowerShell in Server Core

Windows Admin Center for managing Server Core

While Command Prompt from the console, remote PowerShell connections, remote Server Manager administration, and even the RSAT tools running on a Windows 10 workstation are all valid and powerful tools for administering our Server Core instances, they have all now been upstaged by the release of Windows Admin Center. You have already learned what Windows Admin Center can do for centrally managing your entire server infrastructure, but what we need to point out here is that WAC can be used for servers both with and without graphical interfaces.

I have spoken with many Windows Server administrators about the topic of Server Core, and one of the biggest blocks to implementing these more efficient and secure server platforms is an apprehension that, once configured, ongoing administration and maintenance of these servers will be more difficult to handle. Admins who are familiar and comfortable working within the Windows Server Desktop Experience know exactly what needs to be done to accomplish their daily tasks, but remove that point-and-click interface and suddenly the workday gets a lot more complicated.

Thankfully, you don't have to memorize the PowerShell handbook to use Server Core! Windows Admin Center treats Server Core instances in the same way that it does a server running Desktop Experience. It just works!

We already have WAC installed on a server in our test lab, so let's open it up and add in my new WEB4 server to be administered and take a look at what options are available for ongoing maintenance of this server.

When we first connect to WEB4 via the WAC console, there is nothing in here that even indicates this is a Server Core instance. We have all of the WAC tools and utilities available to click on:

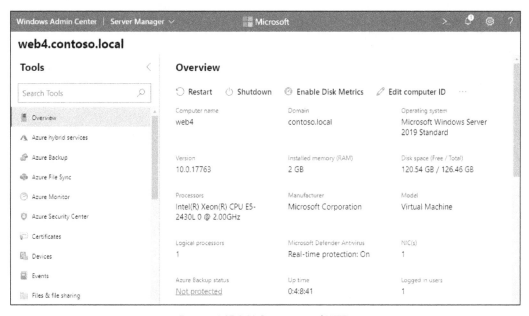

Figure 10.25: WAC overview of WEB4

Let's try a couple of things from Windows Admin Center. You have power controls right near the top of the screen from which you could easily shut down or restart the server. That is much easier and faster than having to establish a remote PowerShell connection from which you can issue commands to accomplish the same actions. There are also performance metrics on the home screen (if you scroll down), showing your consumed **CPU**, **Memory**, and **Networking** resources. Without WAC, you would need to log in to WEB4 and launch **Task Manager** to see these statistics:

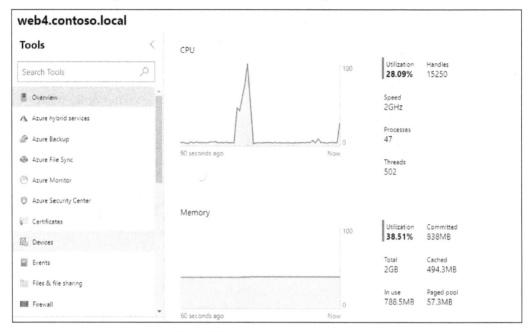

Figure 10.26: Server performance metrics

Moving away from the home screen, useful as it is, try clicking on one of the tools listed along the left side of the screen, such as **Events**. Without WAC, if you wanted to troubleshoot an issue on a Server Core, it would make sense to look into the Windows Event Logs on that server, but how would you go about doing that from a command-line interface? I suppose you could have logged on to the Server Core console and used **Task Manager** to launch EventVwr, but opening up WAC and simply clicking on **Events** is much easier:

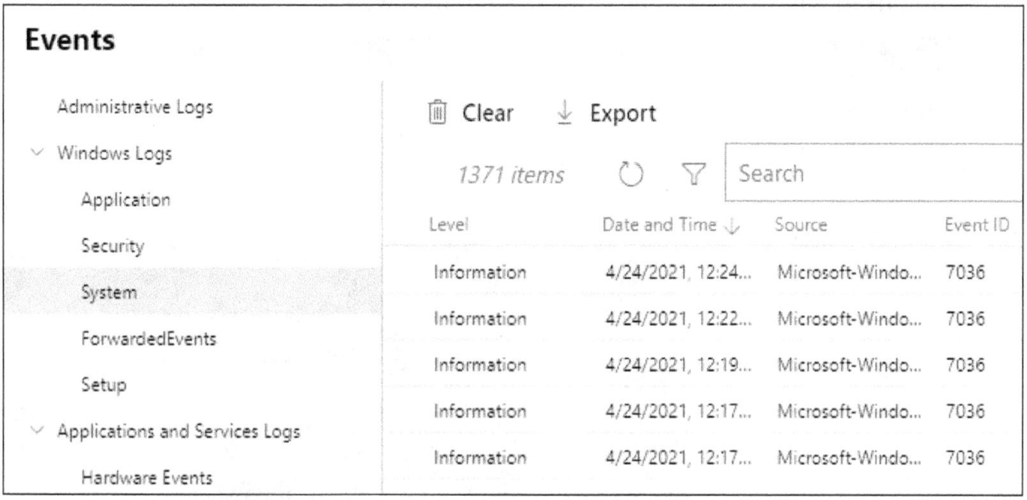

Figure 10.27: System event logs

Other examples of useful functions inside WAC, particularly when working with a Server Core instance, would be using **Files & file sharing** to navigate the file and folder structure of the hard drive of WEB4, or using the **Firewall** function here to create or remove Windows Firewall rules on WEB4. There is also a **Networks** tool, from which you can manipulate IP addressing configurations.

While many more tools exist inside the Windows Admin Center, the last one I want to point out is that, once again, we have a **PowerShell** option (similar to what we can launch from inside Server Manager). This **PowerShell** button will invoke and display for us a remote PowerShell connection to the WEB4 Server Core instance if ever we can't find a function that is needed inside WAC and need to dive a little further under the hood to accomplish something from a command interface. And the best part is that you never actually had to launch PowerShell! This is still all happening from within your internet browser window:

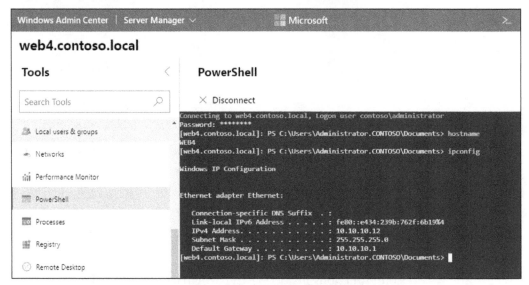

Figure 10.28: Using PowerShell in WAC

There is so much more that can be accomplished from inside the Windows Admin Center. Editing **Registry**, adding **Roles & Features**, checking the status of your **Services**, even interfacing with Windows Update. If you aren't already using WAC, you're missing the boat!

The Sconfig utility

Now we will take a step backward and check out a tool that is available inside Server Core, but one that is generally only useful when working on the console of your server. As you have seen, any time that you boot Server Core, you land inside a Command Prompt window from which you can flip over into PowerShell and then use traditional Windows cmdlets to configure your new Server Core instance.

Alternatively, you may employ the **Sconfig** utility. This is a set of tools, kind of like command-line shortcuts, for implementing the basic items needed to bring your new server online and get it connected to the network. The purpose of Sconfig is to be step 1 after installing the operating system, taking care of the initial configurations on the new server so that you can then jump over to using one of the more robust administrative interfaces, such as Server Manager or Windows Admin Center.

Immediately after spinning up a Server Core instance, you find yourself at Command Prompt, awaiting input. Inside this screen, simply type Sconfig and press *Enter*. You should experience a quick change from black to blue and see the following screen:

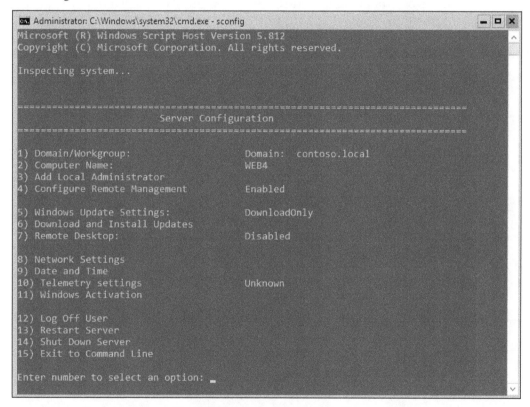

Figure 10.29: Server configuration utility

The options available inside Sconfig are fairly self-explanatory, but we'll cover the common tasks performed here. Again, these are all things that you could instead accomplish via PowerShell cmdlets, but I find it easier to take the Sconfig approach. The most common uses of this interface are to configure initial networking settings by pressing *8* or to configure the server hostname and domain membership by using options *2* and *1*.

I will go ahead and press *2* on my keyboard and then press *Enter*, and I am immediately presented with a prompt asking me to specify a new computer name. This is an extremely fast way to configure the hostname of new Server Core servers. Since I don't actually want to rename WEB4, I will leave the selection blank and press *Enter* to return to the main screen.

Now I want to check out the networking settings. Pressing *8* and then *Enter* brings me into Network Settings, where I can see that my current IP address on WEB4's NIC is 10.10.10.12. This is correct, but let's change that address for the sake of walking through a real Sconfig setting change.

I first selected my network adapter index, which was number one. I am now shown additional information about what is already configured on this NIC and have options to change this information. Selecting option one again will allow me to set the network adapter address:

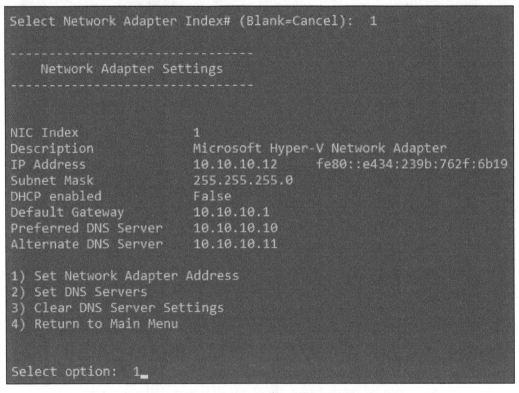

Figure 10.30: Configuring an IP address with Sconfig

Input the letter *S*, which tells Sconfig that you want to enter a static IP address, and then input the new IP address that you want configured on this NIC. I will change WEB4 to be 10.10.10.30, just to prove that this works. After inputting the IP address, I must also define a new subnet mask and gateway address:

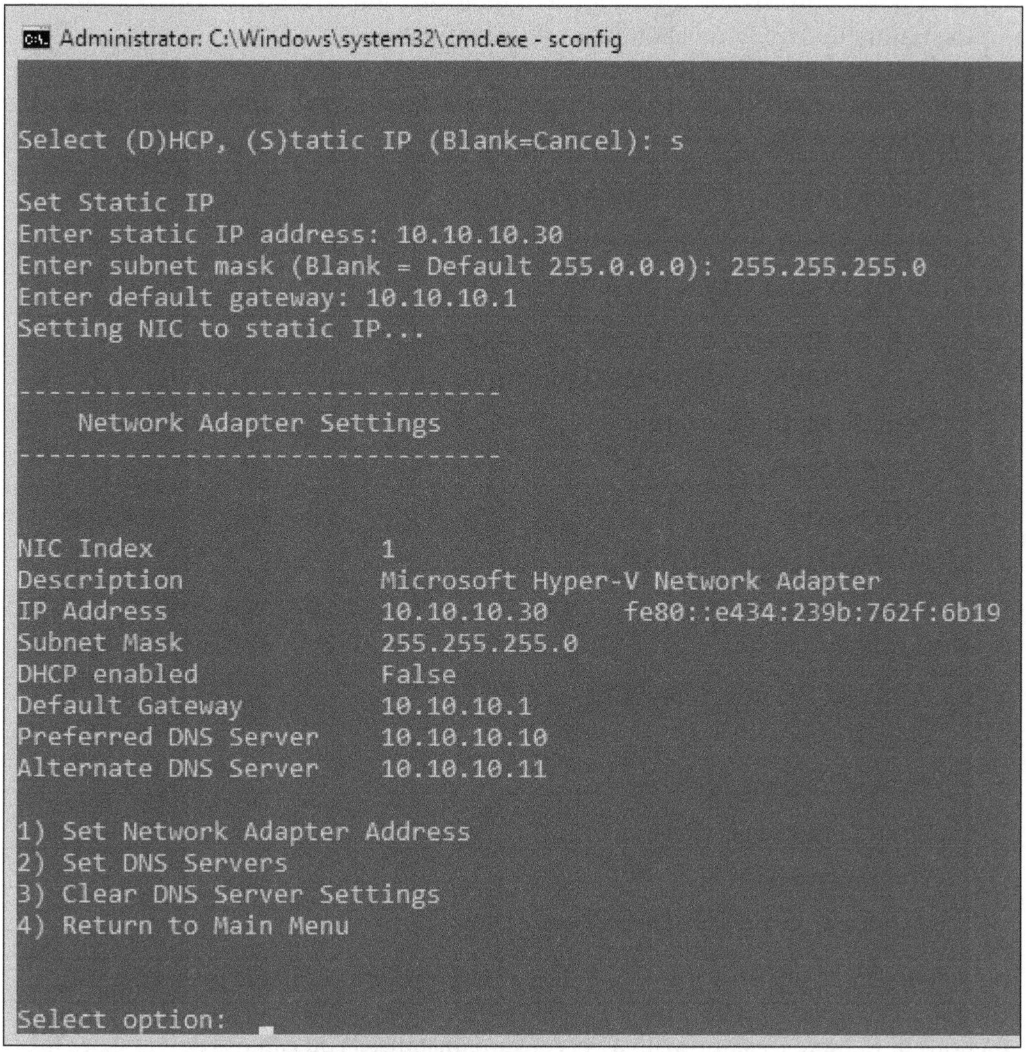

```
Administrator: C:\Windows\system32\cmd.exe - sconfig


Select (D)HCP, (S)tatic IP (Blank=Cancel): s

Set Static IP
Enter static IP address: 10.10.10.30
Enter subnet mask (Blank = Default 255.0.0.0): 255.255.255.0
Enter default gateway: 10.10.10.1
Setting NIC to static IP...


- - - - - - - - - - - - - - - - - - - - - - - - - - -
    Network Adapter Settings
- - - - - - - - - - - - - - - - - - - - - - - - - - -



NIC Index              1
Description            Microsoft Hyper-V Network Adapter
IP Address             10.10.10.30      fe80::e434:239b:762f:6b19
Subnet Mask            255.255.255.0
DHCP enabled           False
Default Gateway        10.10.10.1
Preferred DNS Server   10.10.10.10
Alternate DNS Server   10.10.10.11

1) Set Network Adapter Address
2) Set DNS Servers
3) Clear DNS Server Settings
4) Return to Main Menu


Select option: _
```

Figure 10.31: Setting the subnet mask and default gateway

The NIC of WEB4 has been immediately updated to a new IP address of 10.10.10.30, as seen in the resulting output. While it may not be a common occurrence to visit the Sconfig tool after the initial configuration of a Server Core instance, this tool can be a real timesaver when used for the initial configuration of network and naming settings of any new Server Core instance.

Roles available in Server Core

Server Core is obviously a restricted form of the operating system, and some of the roles inside Windows Server are just not designed to work properly within that limited context. Fortunately for us, most of them are, which enables Server 2019 administrators to deploy most of their critical infrastructure via the more secure Server Core platform. Here is a list of the roles that are currently supported to run on a Windows Server 2019 Server Core instance, and I marked the ones in bold that I see most often used within the businesses I work with:

- Active Directory Certificate Services
- **Active Directory Domain Services**
- Active Directory Federation Services
- Active Directory Lightweight Directory Services
- Active Directory Rights Management Services
- Device Health Attestation
- **DHCP Server**
- **DNS Server**
- **File and Storage Services**
- Host Guardian Service
- **Hyper-V**
- Print and Document Services
- Remote Access
- Remote Desktop Services*
- Volume Activation Services
- **Web Server (IIS)**
- Windows Server Update Services

You'll notice that I placed a * next to Remote Desktop Services in the preceding list. While you can install the RDS role on a Server Core, you cannot perform *all* the functions of Remote Desktop with a Server Core instance. You can use Server Core to be your RDS Connection Broker or RDS Licensing server, but you cannot use Server Core as a Remote Desktop Session Host. Similar limitations exist for other roles as well.

For an always-updated, comprehensive list of what parts and pieces of which roles and features are supported on Server Core, check out the following Microsoft document: https://docs.microsoft.com/en-us/windows-server/administration/ server-core/server-core-roles-and-services.

Building a Server Core domain controller

You are now equipped to spin up Server Core instances, configure them with hostnames, IP addresses, and domain memberships, and administer these new servers using various administrative toolsets. One of the most frequent uses of Server Core that I have seen in production environments is as a secondary domain controller. Let's walk through the process of setting one up so that you have exact steps if ever this situation applies to you.

Begin by prepping the new server. You already know all of this, but here is the basic outline of steps that you want to accomplish before thinking about turning this server into a domain controller:

1. Spin up the new server and install Server Core.

2. Use Sconfig or PowerShell from the console to configure a static IP address and a permanent hostname. Remember, once you turn this server into a domain controller, it is not supported to change the name, and not easy to change the IP – so choose wisely. I have named mine DC3 since I already have a DC1 and a DC2 in my lab.

    *   Make sure to specify an existing domain controller as the NIC's DNS server address.

3. Use Sconfig or PowerShell to join this new server to your existing domain.

4. At this point, your server is online and communicable on the network but has no roles installed. You could proceed from here with the installation of any role to serve any purpose.

Install the AD DS role

There are numerous ways in which this step could be accomplished. Using Windows Admin Center or remotely manipulating the new server via Server Manager on another machine would be valid ways of installing the new role. You should already be familiar with those processes based on what we have covered in this chapter so far.

Instead, let's stick to pure PowerShell for converting this new Server Core into a headless domain controller. From the console of DC3, make sure that you are logged in to a Domain Admin account. Then, use the powershell command to change my Command Prompt into a PowerShell prompt. Then, run the following command to install the AD DS role onto the new server:

```
Install-WindowsFeature -Name AD-Domain-Services -IncludeManagementTools
```

If you also want this server to respond to DNS lookups (as most domain controllers do), also install the DNS role with the following command:

```
Install-WindowsFeature DNS
```

```
Administrator: C:\Windows\system32\cmd.exe - powershell

C:\Users\administrator.CONTOSO>powershell
Windows PowerShell
Copyright (C) Microsoft Corporation. All rights reserved.

PS C:\Users\administrator.CONTOSO> Install-WindowsFeature -Name AD-Domain-Services -IncludeManagementTools

Success Restart Needed Exit Code    Feature Result
------- -------------- ---------    --------------
True    No             Success      {Active Directory Domain Services, Group P...

PS C:\Users\administrator.CONTOSO> Install-WindowsFeature DNS

Success Restart Needed Exit Code    Feature Result
------- -------------- ---------    --------------
True    No             Success      {DNS Server}

PS C:\Users\administrator.CONTOSO> _
```

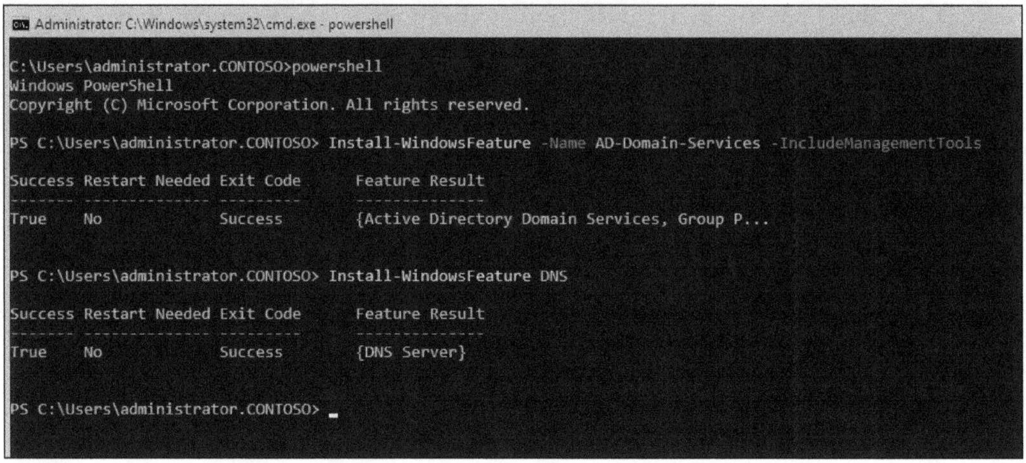

Figure 10.32: Installing AD DS and DNS roles onto a Server Core

Promote this server to a domain controller

With roles installed, we are now ready to promote this server to a domain controller. The old dcpromo command still exists and could be used to perform this function, or we could, of course, utilize one of the graphical administrative tools to handle this remotely as well. Since we started with PowerShell, though, we'll finish out the process using the same:

```
Install-ADDSDomainController -InstallDns -DomainName "contoso.local"
```

(replace contoso.local with your own domain name, of course.)

As this command runs, you will be asked to input required information, such as the AD SafeMode password and administrative credentials with permission to create a new domain controller:

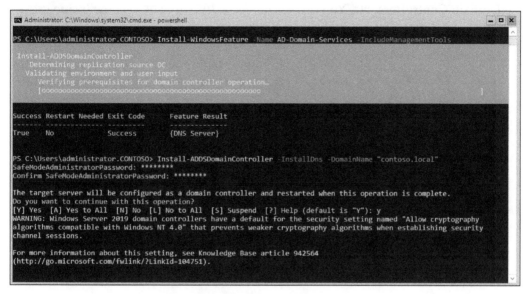

Figure 10.33: Creating your first Server Core DC

Once finished, the server will restart automatically and your new Server Core is now a headless domain controller in your environment!

Verify that it worked

I know you trust me implicitly, but just for the sake of argument, what if we wanted to verify that those simple PowerShell commands really did what they said they did? Let's verify that DC3 really is a domain controller through a couple of different methods.

All domain controllers in an environment automatically get their computer object moved into the "Domain Controllers" OU inside Active Directory. Logging in to any DC in your network, open Active Directory Users and Computers, and navigate to the **Domain Controllers** OU. You can see in *Figure 10.34* that DC3 is now inside this container, indicating that it is a DC for my domain:

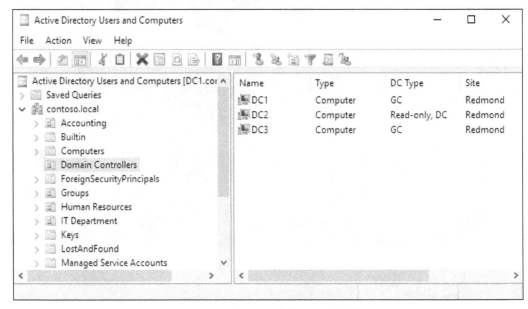

Figure 10.34: A successfully created DC3

To verify the DNS side of things, you can now open up the DNS Management console from inside your network and go into **Properties** of your primary internal DNS zone. In my case, that is contoso.local. Opening up those properties, I can see that my **Name Servers** tab now displays DC3 as a name server for this zone:

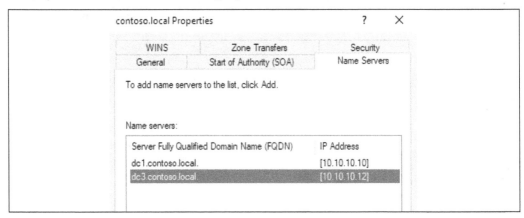

Figure 10.35: DC3 is a confirmed DNS server

One final test and verification. Let's use a command that queries and displays the replication status between domain controller servers in our environment. Open Command Prompt or PowerShell on any DC and run the following command:

```
Repadmin /showrepl
```

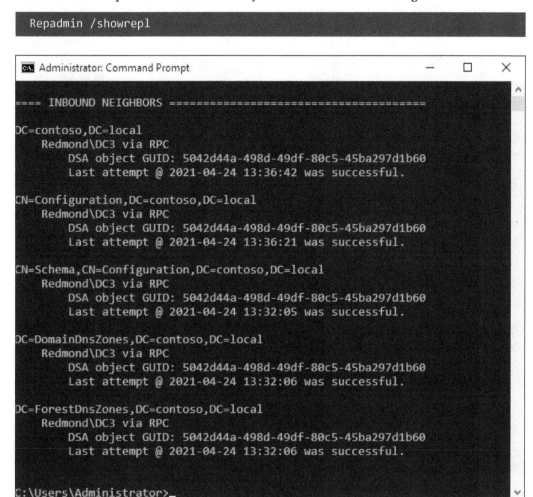

Figure 10.36: Verifying the DC3 connection

There you go! Proof in three different flavors that our DC3 Server Core instance really is a domain controller and DNS server in our domain. How cool is that?!

What happened to Nano Server?

This story about small-footprint Windows Server platforms didn't used to end with Server Core. Anyone who kept tabs on the new features coming out with Server 2016 is aware that there was another installation option for the Server 2016 operating system, called Nano Server. The premise of Nano Server was an even smaller, more secure, more efficient, super-tiny operating system that could run a limited set of roles. Though limited, it was still capable of being installed on a physical or virtual server platform, run as a true server operating system, and could still host traditional workloads on it.

Unfortunately for Nano Server enthusiasts, and especially for anyone who has already done the work of installing and using it, the story behind Nano Server has flipped around completely over the last few years. To cut a long story short, you can no longer use Nano Server for anything that a traditional server can do. You cannot install it on physical hardware; you cannot even install Nano on a VM. Additionally, management functionalities, such as PowerShell and WinRM, have been removed from Nano Server, and you cannot install any of the Microsoft infrastructural roles onto it.

With all of this functionality having been ripped out of Nano Server's scope, what is left? Is it dead? Can Nano Server do *ANYTHING*?

The answer is **containers**. If you are interested in utilizing containers to build and host cloud-ready and scalable applications, this is where Nano is now focused. We will cover more information about containers and the fact that Nano Server is completely married to them in *Chapter 13, Containers and Nano Server*, but suffice to say that downloading container images from Microsoft will now be the *only* place where you will find Nano Server.

Summary

I have to be honest with you — writing this chapter has been exactly the kick in the pants that I needed to start thinking about shrinking my own servers. I am in the same boat as many of you: I know what Server Core is and have played around with it but have never taken the steps to really use it in the production environments that I support. Now that tools such as Sconfig and the new Windows Admin Center are available to us, I have officially run out of excuses as to why I shouldn't be deploying new roles onto Server Core boxes. In fact, as I was building out the new DC3 server, I realized just how much faster it is to get a Server Core instance off the ground compared to the full graphical interface. Reboots are faster and using Sconfig to set the IP address, hostname, and domain membership all took me about 2 minutes in total.

While it never hurts to learn something new, using Server Core no longer comes with the requirement that you must be fluent in PowerShell. The early days of Server Core came with a requirement to be really good with PowerShell, as this was the only reliable way to configure and interface with your tiny servers, but these new tools allow us to utilize the smaller platform and administer it without memorizing a bunch of new cmdlets.

Security is the primary reason that we should all be considering Server Core as our new standard. The Windows graphical interface adds a lot of code and grants a lot of ability to those logged in to the servers, such as the ability to browse the internet. This opens up all kinds of doors to vulnerabilities that simply don't exist in Server Core.

Questions

1. True or False—Server Core is the default installation option for Windows Server 2019.

2. True or False—You can utilize PowerShell to change a Server 2019 from *Server Core* mode to *Desktop Experience* mode.

3. When sitting at the console of a freshly booted Windows Server 2019 Server Core instance, what application do you see on the screen?

4. What cmdlet can be used to view the current networking configuration on a Server Core?

5. Which PowerShell cmdlet can be used to configure the hostname of a Server Core?

6. Name some of the management tools that can be used to remotely interface with a Server Core.

7. What is the name of the utility built into Server Core that can be launched to provide quick task links for configuring IP addresses, hostnames, and domain membership?

11
PowerShell

Let's be honest, many of us are still using Command Prompt on a daily basis. If you have cut over and are using the newer PowerShell prompt as a total replacement for Command Prompt, I applaud you! I, however, still tend to open up cmd.exe as a matter of habit, though with the most recent releases of Windows 10 and Windows Server 2019, I am definitely making a more conscious effort to use the newer, bluer, prettier, and more powerful interface that is PowerShell. In this chapter, we are going to explore some of the reasons that you should do so too. Other than the fact that Microsoft seems to have shrunk the default text size in Command Prompt to deter us from using it, which I find pretty funny, we are going to take a look at some of the technical reasons that PowerShell is far and away more useful and powerful than Command Prompt could ever dream of being.

In this chapter, we will cover the following topics:

- Why move to PowerShell?
- Working within PowerShell
- Using a pipeline
- PowerShell Integrated Scripting Environment
- Remotely managing a server
- Desired State Configuration

Why move to PowerShell?

I don't think there is any question in people's minds that PowerShell is indeed the evolution of Command Prompt, but the reason that many of us still default to the old interface is that it still contains all of the functionality required to accomplish what we historically have needed to do on our servers. What Command Prompt really contains is the ability to do the same things that we have always done from Command Prompt, and nothing else. Without realizing it, there are a lot of functions that you use the GUI to accomplish that cannot be done well from within a Command Prompt window.

The limitations within Command Prompt that force you into using your mouse to interface with the GUI do not exist with PowerShell. It is fully comprehensive and capable of modifying almost any aspect of the Windows operating system. How did PowerShell become so much more powerful than Command Prompt? It differs from any classic I/O shell in that it is built on top of .NET and runs much more like a programming language than simple input and output commands.

Cmdlets

Most of the functionality that a traditional server admin will use within PowerShell comes in the form of **cmdlets** (pronounced *command-lets*). These are commands that you run from within the PowerShell prompt, but you can think of them as tools rather than simple commands. Cmdlets can be used to both get information from a server and to set information and parameters on a server. Many cmdlets have intuitive names that begin with get or set, and similar to the way that most command-line interfaces work, each cmdlet has various switches or variables that can be configured and flagged at the end of the cmdlet, to make it do special things. It is helpful to understand that cmdlets are always built using a verb-noun syntax. You specify the action you want to accomplish, such as get or set, and then your noun is the piece inside Windows that you are trying to manipulate. Here are a few simple examples of cmdlets in PowerShell to give you an idea of what they look like and how they are named in a fairly simple way:

- `Get-NetIPAddress`: With this cmdlet, we can see the IP addresses on our system
- `Set-NetIPAddress`: We can use this guy to modify an existing IP address
- `New-NetIPAddress`: This cmdlet allows us to create a new IP address on the computer
- `Rename-Computer`: As we saw earlier in the book, `Rename-Computer` is a quick and easy way to set the computer hostname of a system

If you're ever struggling to come up with the name or syntax of a particular command, Microsoft's online Docs website (formerly and sometimes still called TechNet) has a full page of information dedicated to each cmdlet inside PowerShell. That can be incredibly useful, but sometimes you don't want to take the time to pop onto the internet just to find the name of a command that you are simply failing to remember at the moment. One of the most useful cmdlets in PowerShell shows you a list of all the available cmdlets. Memorizing the names of cmdlets isn't critically important, as long as you commit this one to permanent memory, Get-Command:

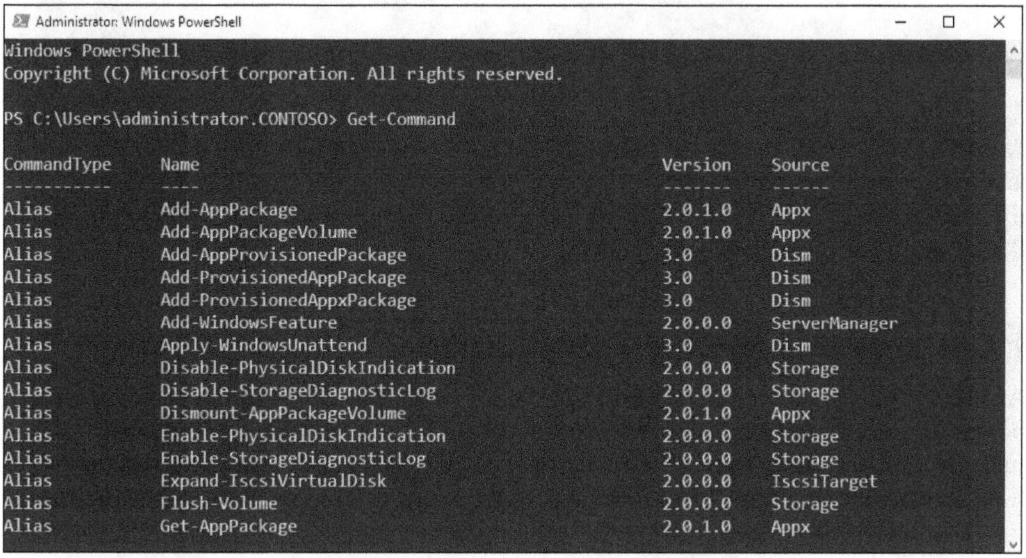

```
Administrator: Windows PowerShell                                          —    □    ×

Windows PowerShell
Copyright (C) Microsoft Corporation. All rights reserved.

PS C:\Users\administrator.CONTOSO> Get-Command

CommandType     Name                              Version     Source
-----------     ----                              -------     ------
Alias           Add-AppPackage                    2.0.1.0     Appx
Alias           Add-AppPackageVolume              2.0.1.0     Appx
Alias           Add-AppProvisionedPackage         3.0         Dism
Alias           Add-ProvisionedAppPackage         3.0         Dism
Alias           Add-ProvisionedAppxPackage        3.0         Dism
Alias           Add-WindowsFeature                2.0.0.0     ServerManager
Alias           Apply-WindowsUnattend             3.0         Dism
Alias           Disable-PhysicalDiskIndication    2.0.0.0     Storage
Alias           Disable-StorageDiagnosticLog      2.0.0.0     Storage
Alias           Dismount-AppPackageVolume         2.0.1.0     Appx
Alias           Enable-PhysicalDiskIndication     2.0.0.0     Storage
Alias           Enable-StorageDiagnosticLog       2.0.0.0     Storage
Alias           Expand-IscsiVirtualDisk           2.0.0.0     IscsiTarget
Alias           Flush-Volume                      2.0.0.0     Storage
Alias           Get-AppPackage                    2.0.1.0     Appx
```

Figure 11.1: Results of Get-Command

Whoa, there are pages and pages and pages of cmdlets! Rather than scrolling through the entire list to find the one you are looking for, it is easy to filter this list down based on any criteria that you would like. If we were interested in seeing only the commands that deal with IP addressing, we could give this a try:

```
Get-Command -Name *IPAddress*
```

The Get-Command cmdlet combined with the -Name parameter allows you to selectively search for useful items in PowerShell that relate to any name or portion of a name:

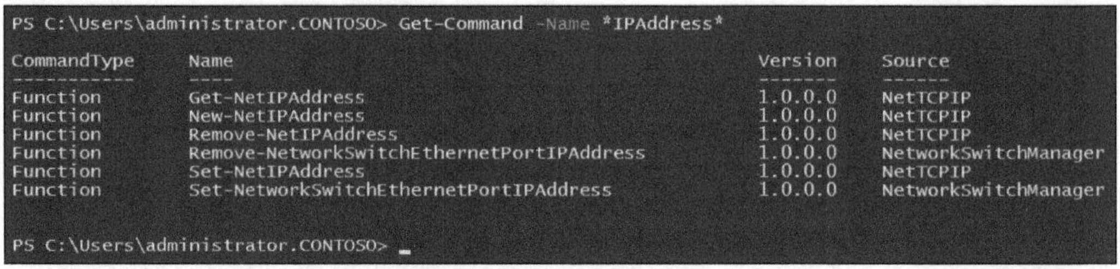

```
PS C:\Users\administrator.CONTOSO> Get-Command -Name *IPAddress*

CommandType     Name                                         Version    Source
-----------     ----                                         -------    ------
Function        Get-NetIPAddress                             1.0.0.0    NetTCPIP
Function        New-NetIPAddress                             1.0.0.0    NetTCPIP
Function        Remove-NetIPAddress                          1.0.0.0    NetTCPIP
Function        Remove-NetworkSwitchEthernetPortIPAddress    1.0.0.0    NetworkSwitchManager
Function        Set-NetIPAddress                             1.0.0.0    NetTCPIP
Function        Set-NetworkSwitchEthernetPortIPAddress       1.0.0.0    NetworkSwitchManager


PS C:\Users\administrator.CONTOSO> _
```

Figure 11.2: Searching with Get-Command

As with many toolsets, PowerShell utilizes * as a wildcard indicator. In the search we just accomplished, and in truth for almost any cmdlet search that I ever run, using the * wildcard on both ends of the term I am searching helps to display any results that contain the term I am searching for.

PowerShell is the backbone

As you will discover in this chapter, interfacing with PowerShell puts all kinds of power at your fingertips. What we sometimes find, though, is that admins don't fully trust PowerShell because they are used to taking these actions and making these changes from a graphical interface. After running a single PowerShell cmdlet to set a configuration that would have taken you a dozen different mouse clicks to accomplish the same thing, it is easy to think that it must not have actually done anything. That was too easy, and it processed my command way too quickly, right? I'd better go into that graphical interface anyway, just to double-check that PowerShell actually did the job.

When I started using PowerShell, I was tempted to do exactly that all the time. But the more I used it, and the more I started digging into those graphical interfaces themselves, the more I realized that I'm not the only one using PowerShell. A lot of the administrative tool GUIs use PowerShell too! Without even realizing it, you use PowerShell for quite a few graphically driven tasks inside the Windows Server operating system. When you open up that management console for whatever you happen to be changing on the server, make your configurations, and then click on the **Go** or **Finish** button, how does that graphical console put your configuration into place? PowerShell. Under the hood, in the background, the console is taking the information that you input, plugging that information into PowerShell cmdlets, and running them to do the actual configuration work.

Many of the administrative tools that we run from inside Server Manager take this approach, accepting changes and configurations from you and then formulating those settings into PowerShell commands that run in the background to push the changes into action.

So, if you're hesitant to start using PowerShell because it just feels different, or you don't trust the process to be uniform with the way that it would have worked in the GUI, forget all of that. Because often, when you are using mouse clicks to change settings on your server, you are actually invoking PowerShell cmdlets to do the work.

Scripting

The more you use PowerShell, the more powerful it becomes. In addition to running ad hoc single commands and cmdlets, you can build extensive scripts that can accomplish all sorts of different things. I mentioned that PowerShell has similarities to a regular programming language, and scripting is where we start to navigate into that territory. PowerShell provides the ability to create script files, which we will do for ourselves shortly, saving scripts for easy running of those same scripts time and time again. You can also use variables, like in other forms of coding, so that you can provide variable input and objects that scripts can use to make them more flexible and squeeze even more functionality out of them.

Server Core

If there were any one area where I think we as server admins could do a better job of using the technology at our disposal, it is using PowerShell to fulfill the Microsoft model of centralized management. When we have a task that needs to be accomplished on a server, it is our default tendency to log into that server (usually via RDP), then use our mouse to start clicking around and doing the work. Logging into the server is becoming more and more unnecessary, and we could save a lot of time by using the central management tools that are available to us. PowerShell is one of these tools. Rather than RDPing into that server, simply use the PowerShell prompt on your local machine to reach out and change that setting on the remote server.

This kind of remote management becomes not only efficient but necessary as we start dealing more with headless servers. I hope to see increased utilization of Server Core in our organizations in the coming years, and interacting with these servers is going to require a shift in your administrative mindset. By becoming familiar with accomplishing daily tasks from inside PowerShell now, you will better equip yourself for the future administration of these headless machines, which will require you to interface with them differently than you are comfortable doing today.

Working within PowerShell

The first step to doing real work with PowerShell is getting comfortable interfacing with the platform and becoming familiar with the daily routines of working from this command-line interface, rather than relying on your mouse pointer. Here, we will explore some of the most common ways that I have seen server administrators make use of PowerShell to enhance their daily workflow.

We will be working throughout this chapter inside the version of PowerShell that comes out of the box with Windows Server 2019, PowerShell 5.1. You may have heard the news of PowerShell 7's release. If you are familiar with this and already utilizing it, everything that we discuss will work perfectly well on that updated platform. To administer a Windows Server instance, the differences between versions won't have much of a bearing. Installing PowerShell 7 will not update PowerShell 5.1, but rather they will run side by side.

PowerShell 7 is open-source and comes with the ability to work cross-platform, with Windows, macOS, and Linux. It also includes some additional support for working with Docker containers. If you seek out and install PowerShell 7, keep in mind that the two versions are different executable files:

- PowerShell 5.1 = `powershell.exe`
- PowerShell 7 = `pwsh.exe`

Launching PowerShell

The first thing we need to do is get PowerShell opened up to start using it. The PowerShell console is installed by default in all recent versions of Windows, so you can run it from the **Start** menu, pin it to the Desktop, or access it in any way that you normally open any application.

Since I tend to prefer using my keyboard for everything, the way that I normally open PowerShell is to hold down the *WinKey* and press *R* to open a **Run** prompt, type the word `powershell`, and press *Enter*:

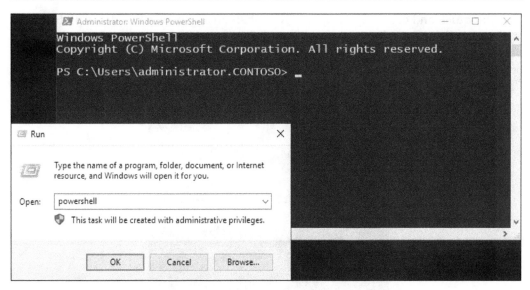

Figure 11.3: Launching PowerShell with only your keyboard

As you can see, since I am logged in to an administrative account on my server, my PowerShell prompt has been opened with elevated permissions. The word **Administrator** is listed in the top toolbar of the PowerShell window. It is important to note that, just like Command Prompt, you can open a PowerShell prompt with either regular user permissions or elevated administrator privileges. It is generally safer to work from within a regular PowerShell session that does not have elevated rights unless the task that you are trying to accomplish requires those extra permissions.

Another quick and easy way to open PowerShell on any newer Windows platform is by right-clicking on the **Start** button and selecting it right from the quick-tasks list that is presented. As you can see in *Figure 11.4*, I have right-clicked on the **Start** button of one of my new Server 2019 machines and can choose from here to open PowerShell or even an elevated (administrative) PowerShell prompt:

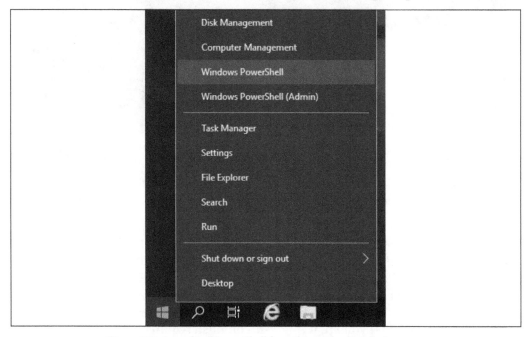

Figure 11.4: Launching PowerShell from the quick admin tasks menu

If you right-click on your **Start** button and do not find options for PowerShell but rather for opening Command Prompt, do not be dismayed. This is a configurable option; you can show either Command Prompt or PowerShell options in the quick admin tasks menu. If you right-click on your taskbar and select **Taskbar settings**, you will find an option that is called **Replace Command Prompt with Windows PowerShell in the menu when I right-click the start button or press Windows key+X**. Toggling this option will swing your quick admin menu back and forth between the two command-line interfaces.

You also have the option of entering into a PowerShell prompt from inside an existing Command Prompt window. Normally, when you are working from Command Prompt, you cannot make use of any PowerShell cmdlets. Let's go ahead and give this a shot. Open an administrative Command Prompt window and try to type in the name of one of the cmdlets we mentioned earlier. Perhaps type Get-NetIPAddress to show us what IP addresses reside on this system. Whoops—that failed because Command Prompt doesn't recognize the Get-NetIPAddress cmdlet.

Now type the word powershell and press *Enter*. Instead of opening a separate PowerShell window, your prompt changes, but the application window itself remains the same. You have now entered the PowerShell shell from inside the black and white Command Prompt window, and you can start utilizing cmdlets as you wish. Running Get-NetIPAddress again now produces some information:

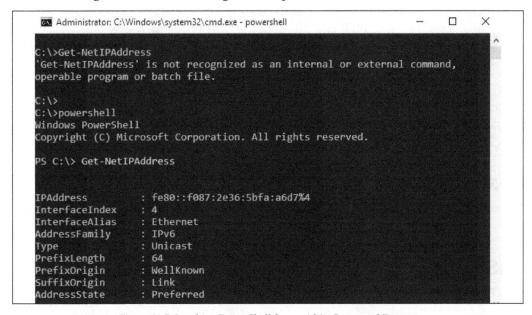

Figure 11.5: Invoking PowerShell from within Command Prompt

You can move from PowerShell mode back to regular Command Prompt mode by typing exit.

Default execution policy

When you are working with the PowerShell command-line interface directly, you can simply open up PowerShell, start typing cmdlets, and start getting work done. However, one of the big advantages of using PowerShell comes when you start playing around with creating, saving, and running scripts. If you open up PowerShell, create a script, and then try to run it, you will sometimes find that it fails with a big messy error message, such as this one:

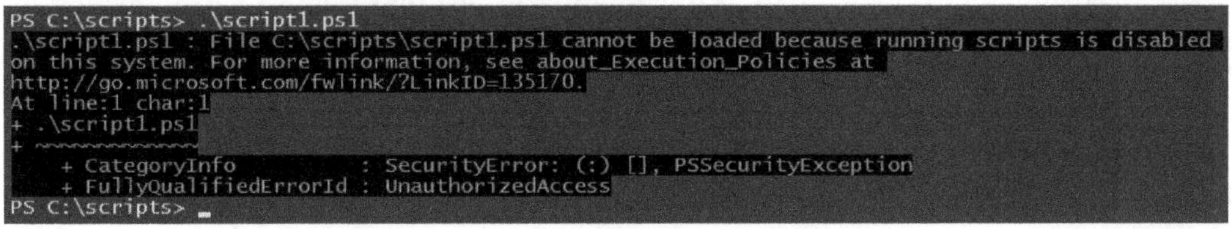

Figure 11.6: A common PowerShell script execution error

This shouldn't happen on a fresh instance of Windows Server 2019 but could if you have any GPOs being applied to your new server or if you are using a different operating system and are trying to run some PowerShell scripts; you might find yourself stuck at one of these error messages right out of the gate. While the nature of some versions of Windows to block the running of scripts by default is a security enhancement, it can be a nuisance to work around when you are trying to get something done. Thankfully, if you do encounter this problem, the resolution is easy: you simply need to adjust the **Default Execution Policy** (**DEP**) inside PowerShell so that it allows the execution of scripts to happen properly.

This is not a simple ON/OFF switch. There are five different levels within the DEP, and it is important to understand each one so that you can set your DEP accordingly, based on the security that you want in place on your servers. Here are descriptions of each level, in order of most to least secure.

Restricted

The Restricted policy allows individual commands and cmdlets to be run but stops the running of scripts altogether.

AllSigned

This requires that any script being run needs to be signed by a trusted publisher. When set to AllSigned, even scripts that you write yourself will have to be put through that validation process and signed before they will be allowed to run.

RemoteSigned

RemoteSigned is the default policy in Windows Server 2019. For scripts that have been downloaded from the internet, it requires that these scripts are signed with a digital signature from a publisher that you trust. However, if you choose to create your own scripts, it will allow these local scripts to run without requiring that digital signature.

Unrestricted

Scripts are allowed to run, signed or unsigned. You do still receive a warning prompt when running scripts that have been downloaded from the internet.

Bypass mode

In Bypass mode, nothing is blocked and no warnings are given when you run scripts. In other words, you're on your own.

Sometimes a single execution policy doesn't meet all of your needs, depending on how you utilize PowerShell scripts. DEPs can be further enhanced by setting an Execution Policy Scope that allows you to set different execution policies to different aspects of the system. For example, the three scopes that you can manipulate are Process, CurrentUser, and LocalMachine. By default, the DEP affects LocalMachine so that any scripts running adhere to the DEP. But if you need to modify this behavior so that different DEPs are set for CurrentUser or even an individual process, you have the ability to do that.

If you are unsure about the current status of your DEP or suspect that someone may have changed it, you can easily view the currently assigned execution policy with a simple cmdlet called Get-ExecutionPolicy. As you can see in *Figure 11.7*, mine is set to Restricted, which explains my earlier error message when I tried running a script:

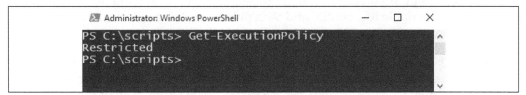

Figure 11.7: ExecutionPolicy is currently set to Restricted

Once you have decided on the level of DEP that you want on your server or workstation, you can set it accordingly with a quick cmdlet. For example, since this is a test lab and I want scripts to be able to run, and I am not really concerned about security since I am isolated, I am going to change mine to Unrestricted. Here is my command for doing just that:

```
Set-ExecutionPolicy Unrestricted
```

```
PS C:\scripts> Set-ExecutionPolicy Unrestricted

Execution Policy Change
The execution policy helps protect you from scripts that you do not trust.
Changing the execution policy might expose you to the security risks
described in the about_Execution_Policies help topic at
http://go.microsoft.com/fwlink/?LinkID=135170. Do you want to change the
execution policy?
[Y] Yes  [A] Yes to All  [N] No  [L] No to All  [S] Suspend  [?] Help
(default is "N"):y
PS C:\scripts>
```

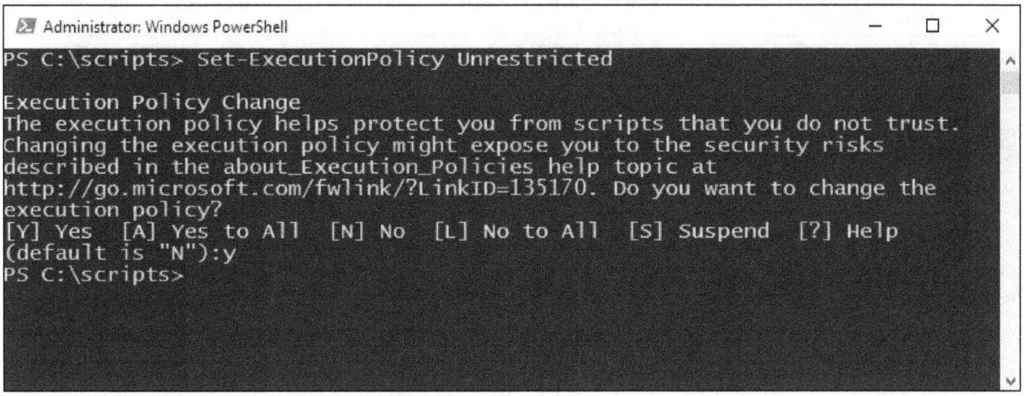

Figure 11.8: Setting ExecutionPolicy to Unrestricted

Remember, right now, we are running PowerShell on this local system (I happen to be logged in to my WEB3 server), so the only execution policy I am setting is the local one for my WEB3 system. If I wanted to change this setting globally or for a group of machines at the same time, I could utilize Group Policy for that change. The location inside Group Policy for configuring PowerShell script execution policy is **Computer Configuration | Policies | Administrative Templates | Windows Components | Windows PowerShell | Turn on script execution**.

Using the Tab key

Before we get started navigating inside PowerShell, there is one important thing I want to point out: get used to pressing the *Tab* key when you are inside the PowerShell prompt! If you type the first few letters of any command or cmdlet or even an added variable to a cmdlet and then press *Tab*, the remainder of the cmdlet name will be automatically populated on the screen.

If we type get-co and then press *Tab*, the prompt automatically populates the full Get-Command cmdlet. Since there are multiple cmdlets that started with get-co, if you press *Tab* numerous times, you can see that it cycles through all of the available cmdlets that start with those letters.

Tab also works with file and folder names. For example, I downloaded a hotfix that needs to be installed onto a server. I want to launch this hotfix using the PowerShell prompt that I already have open, but I don't want to spend an entire minute or more trying to type out the huge filename of this hotfix. I have already navigated to the folder where my hotfix resides, and now if I simply type the first few letters of the filename and press the *Tab* key, PowerShell will populate the remainder of the filename. From there, all we need to do is press *Enter* to launch that installer:

Figure 11.9: The tab key auto-fills file or command names

Useful cmdlets for daily tasks

When I started incorporating PowerShell into my daily workflow, I found it useful to keep a list of commonly used commands and cmdlets handy. Until you get to the point where they become memorized and second nature, if you don't have a quick and easy way to recall those commands, chances are you aren't going to use them and will revert to the old method of configuring your servers.

Here is a list of some of the items I use regularly when I'm building servers. Some are traditional commands that would also work from Command Prompt and some are cmdlets, but they are all useful when working inside a PowerShell window:

- `Get-Command`: This is useful for finding additional commands or cmdlets that you may want to run or research.

- `Get-Command -Name *example*`: Enhances the usefulness of `Get-Command` by adding the `-Name` switch to the end of it, so that you can filter results to whatever types of cmdlets you are searching for.

- `GCM`: This is simply a short alias for `Get-Command`. I only wanted to point this one out because many of the PowerShell cmdlets have aliases, such as `gcm`, that allow you to launch these commonly used cmdlets with fewer keystrokes.

- `Get-Alias`: Since we just mentioned the GCM alias for `Get-Command`, you may be wondering what other aliases are available inside PowerShell. To see a complete list, simply plug in the `Get-Alias` cmdlet. Using aliases rather than full cmdlet names can greatly reduce the number of characters you type inside PowerShell.

- `Rename-Computer`: This allows you to set a new hostname for the server.

- `Add-Computer`: Use the `Add-Computer` cmdlet to join servers or computers to a domain.

- `hostname`: This displays the name of the system you are currently working on. I use `hostname` all the time to make sure that I really am working on the server that I think I am. Have you ever rebooted the wrong server? I have. By running a quick `hostname` command, you can get peace of mind that the function you are about to perform is really happening on the correct system.

- `$env:computername`: This presents you with the hostname of the system you are working on, but I'm calling it out to show that PowerShell can easily tap into your environment variables in order to pull out information. The simpler `hostname` command is useful when you are logged into a local system and are simply trying to verify its name, but the ability to pull information from a variable, such as `$env:computername`, will be much more useful when creating scripts or trying to perform a function against a remote system.

- `Logoff`: The name is self-explanatory; `Logoff` just logs you out of the system. Rather than trying to find the **Sign out** function by clicking around inside your server's **Start** menu, you can throw a quick `Logoff` command into either a Command Prompt or PowerShell window, and you will be immediately logged out of that server. I use this one all the time when closing out RDP connections.

- `Install-WindowsFeature`: Use PowerShell to simplify the addition of new roles or features on your servers.

Both shutdown and Restart-Computer are useful for shutting down or restarting a server. On my own computer, these commands are most commonly preceded by the hostname command. When rebooting a server, you want to take special care that you restart the correct machine, so I find it best to open a PowerShell prompt, do a quick hostname check and then run a Restart command from that same prompt. This ensures that I am restarting the server that was returned in the hostname output:

```
shutdown /r /t 0
```

If you run a simple shutdown command, the system will shut down in one minute. I'm not sure why this is the default, as I have never found any IT administrator who actually wanted to wait that extra minute before shutting down their system. Instead, it is more efficient to set a time limit before that shutdown commences. In the preceding command, I have told the shutdown command that I want to restart instead of shutting down; that is what /r does. I have also told it to wait zero seconds before performing this restart. This way, it happens immediately; I don't have to wait for that default 60-second timer.

Query user or quser

Most useful in RDS environments, the quser command will display all of the users that are currently logged in to a server, including statistics about whether they are logged in locally or remotely, and how long their session has been active. I commonly use quser to discover RDS sessions that have been sitting around idle for a long time, so that I can end those sessions and free up resources on the server:

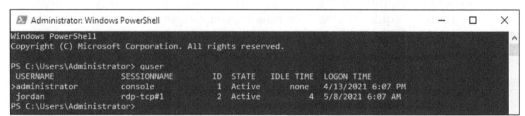

Figure 11.10: The quser command displays logged-in sessions

```
quser /server:WEB1
```

Using quser in combination with the /server switch allows you to see the currently logged-in users on a remote system. This way, you can remain logged in to a single server in your RDS farm but can check on the user sessions for all of your systems without having to log into them. You could even write a script that runs this command against each of your session host servers and outputs the data to a file. This output could then be run on a schedule and used as a reporting mechanism for keeping track of which users were logged in to which RDS session host servers at any given time.

IP addressing cmdlets

When we built a Server Core instance together earlier in this book, we utilized the Sconfig tool to define IP addressing for that server. While that was a quick and easy way to accomplish such a task, let's define the PowerShell cmdlets that are used for the configuration of IP addressing information on a server NIC:

```
New-NetIPAddress -InterfaceIndex 12 -IPAddress 10.10.10.40
-PrefixLength 24 -DefaultGateway 10.10.10.1
```

The above is just an example command with some sample numbers; the point here is that we can use `New-NetIPAddress` to assign IP addresses to NICs on your servers.

Often used in combination with `New-NetIPAddress`, use the following command to set the DNS server addresses in your NIC properties:

```
Set-DnsClientServerAddress -InterfaceIndex 12 -ServerAddresses
10.10.10.2,10.10.10.3
```

Using Get-Help

How many hundreds of times have you used the /? switch in Command Prompt to pull some extra information about a command that you want to run? The extra information provided by this help function can sometimes mean the difference between a command being useful or completely useless. PowerShell cmdlets have a similar function, but you cannot simply /? at the end of a PowerShell cmdlet because a space following a cmdlet in PowerShell indicates that you are about to specify a parameter to be used with that cmdlet. For example, if we try to use /? with the `Restart-Computer` cmdlet to find more information about how to use `Restart-Computer`, it will fail to recognize the question mark as a valid parameter, and our output will be as follows:

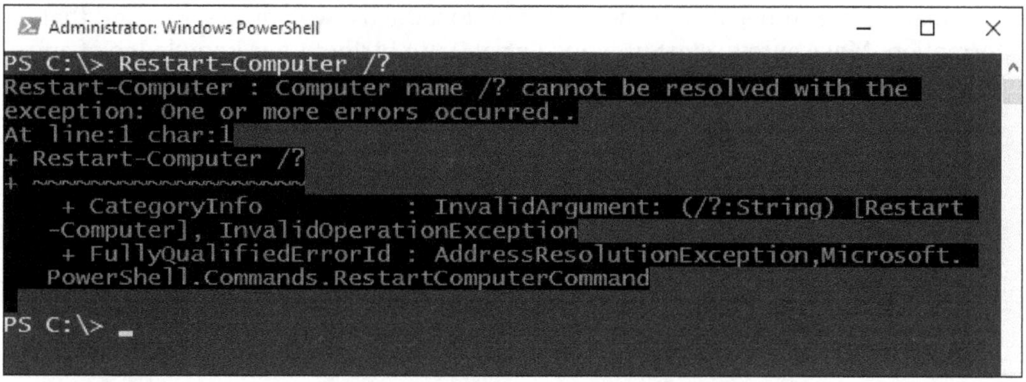

Figure 11.11: PowerShell cmdlets do not work with /?

Instead, there is an even more powerful help function inside PowerShell. `Get-Help` is a cmdlet itself, and like any cmdlet, we need to use information following the cmdlet to specify and pull the information that we are looking for. So instead of using `Get-Help` at the end of a command, like we used to do with the question mark, we use it as its own entity.

Running `Get-Help` by itself only gives us more information about the `Get-Help` command, which may be useful to look over, but right now we are more interested in finding out how we can use `Get-Help` to give us additional information for a cmdlet we want to run, such as the `Restart-Computer` function. What we need to do is use `Get-Help` as a cmdlet, and then specify the other cmdlet as a parameter to pass to `Get-Help`, by placing a space between them:

```
Get-Help Restart-Computer
```

```
Administrator: Windows PowerShell                                    —    □    ✕
PS C:\> Get-Help Restart-Computer

NAME
    Restart-Computer

SYNTAX
    Restart-Computer [[-ComputerName] <string[]>] [[-Credential]
    <pscredential>] [-DcomAuthentication <AuthenticationLevel>
    {Default | None | Connect | Call | Packet | PacketIntegrity |
    PacketPrivacy | Unchanged}] [-Impersonation
    <ImpersonationLevel> {Default | Anonymous | Identify |
    Impersonate | Delegate}] [-WsmanAuthentication <string>
    {Default | Basic | Negotiate | CredSSP | Digest | Kerberos}]
```

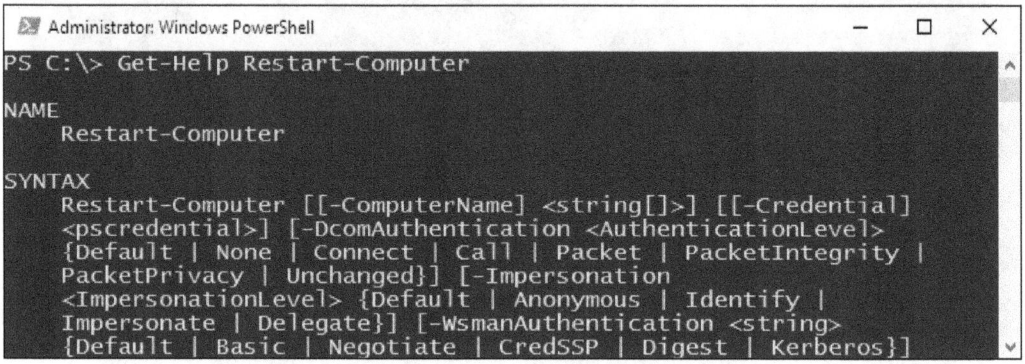

Figure 11.12: Displaying help information for any cmdlet

The information provided by `Get-Help` is very comprehensive; in some cases, it has all of the same information that you can find on Microsoft Docs. Using `Get-Help` is a quick way of finding example syntax for commands and cmdlets that you may be unfamiliar with, and negates the need for you to launch a web browser to find that information. Make sure to start utilizing `Get-Help` to further your knowledge of any cmdlet in PowerShell!

 When using PowerShell on a fresh system, or one that you haven't worked on in a while, take a minute to run a command called `Update-Help`. This will cause PowerShell to reach out to Microsoft and download the latest versions of help files, so that you know you are viewing the most up-to-date information when using `Get-Help`.

Formatting the output

When searching for information in PowerShell, I often encounter the case where so much information is provided to me that it's difficult to sort through. Are you trying to find useful cmdlets from Get-Command, or maybe track down a particular alias with Get-Alias? The output from these cmdlets can be staggeringly long. While we have discussed some parameters you can use to whittle down this output, such as specifying particular -Name parameters, there are a couple of formatting parameters that can also be appended to cmdlets, in order to modify the data output.

Format-Table

The purpose of Format-Table is pretty simple: it takes the data output from a command and puts it into a table format. This generally makes the information much easier to read and work with. Let's look at an example. We have used Get-NetIPAddress a couple of times, but, let's be honest, its output is a little messy. Running the cmdlet by itself on my virtual server, which only has a single NIC assigned to it, results in four pages of data inside my PowerShell window, with all kinds of informational fields that are either empty or not important for finding the IP addresses assigned to my server:

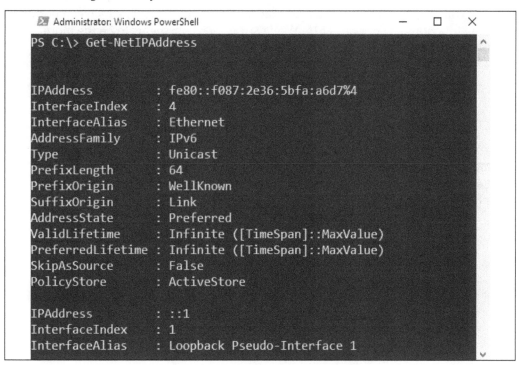

Figure 11.13: Default output from Get-NetIPAddress

If we simply add `Format-Table` to the end of my `Get-NetIPAddress` cmdlet, the generated data is much easier on the eyes, while still giving me the important information that I am really looking for: the IP addresses being used on the system:

```
Get-NetIPAddress | Format-Table
```

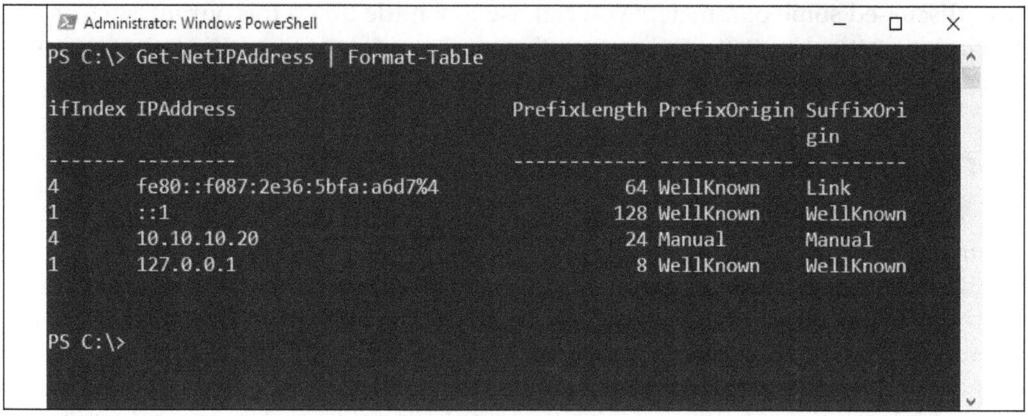

Figure 11.14: Formatted output of Get-NetIPAddress

Some of you may be familiar with a cmdlet called `Select-Object`, which can perform the same functions as `Format-Table`. While `Select-Object` seems to be the more widely known cmdlet, in my experience, it is actually less powerful than `Format-Table`, and so I suggest you spend some time playing around with the one we have discussed here.

Format-List

Similar to the way that `Format-Table` works, you can utilize `Format-List` to display command output as a list of properties. Let's give it a quick try. We already know that `Get-Command` gives us the available cmdlets within PowerShell, and by default, it gives them to us in a table format.

If we wanted to view that output in a list instead, with more information being provided about each cmdlet, we could tell `Get-Command` to output its data in list format, with the following command:

```
Get-Command | Format-List
```

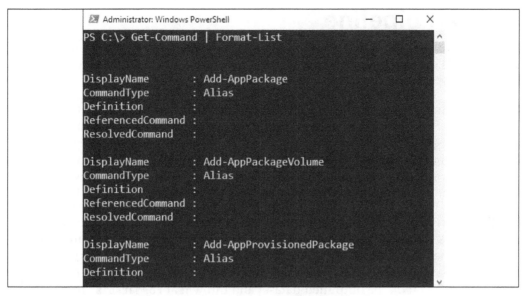

Figure 11.15: Using Format-List to modify cmdlet output

This results in a tremendously long output of information, so long in fact that my PowerShell window had a problem displaying it all. Maybe we need to whittle that info down a little bit by narrowing our focus. Let's search for all of the cmdlets that include the word Restart while displaying them in list format:

```
Get-Command -Name *Restart* | Format-List
```

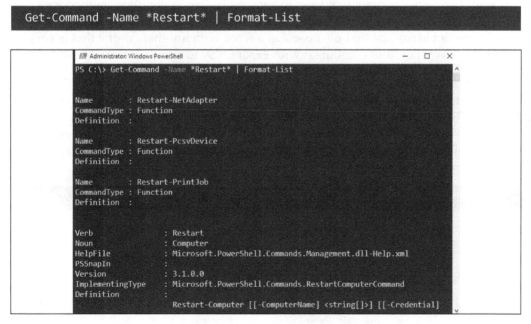

Figure 11.16: List format information about Restart-related cmdlets

Using a pipeline

Following the last couple of example cmdlets that we ran, you may be thinking to yourself, "I see that he is using that vertical line on the key above *Enter* on my keyboard, but why?"

Great question. In Command Prompt, we generally issue one command at a time. The same is often true for PowerShell when we are manually interacting with it, but in PowerShell, we have the potential for so much more power. One of those items of power is the ability to create a pipeline of commands. In other words, you can connect, or chain, commands together. This is commonly referred to as *piping* information from one cmdlet to another cmdlet and is done by using that little |.

Cmdlets often output data. If you then want to utilize that set of data against another cmdlet, this is where the pipe comes in handy. In our last example command, we told PowerShell to gather all of the commands that included the word Restart by performing Get-Command -Name *Restart*. Then we **piped** that output to Format-List. PowerShell took the outputted dataset and threw it at Format-List to display a different set of output. The pipe is used very often in PowerShell commands.

Export to CSV

One common way to use a pipe is when grabbing information via PowerShell that you want to retain, document, or send to somebody else. A common method for storing output data is within CSV files, a popular enough request that Microsoft has baked a cmdlet in for just that purpose. Let's work with another cmdlet that is very useful, Get-EventLog, and combine it with Export-CSV to show off this capability.

Event logs are essential information in a Windows Server environment. Troubleshooting issues on a server almost always involves a step of reviewing the Windows event logs. There is, of course, a graphical interface from which to accomplish this, but filtering and searching within that GUI is not as useful as it should be. Instead, we can use PowerShell to output event log information, such as the following:

```
Get-EventLog System
```

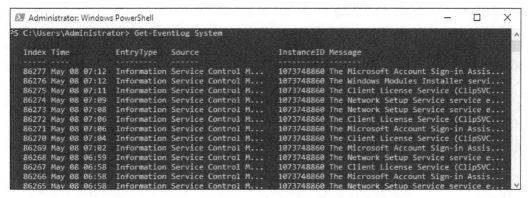

Figure 11.17: Viewing the system event logs in PowerShell

As you can see, the system event logs on this server contain a lot of information, and reading through it all within the PowerShell window could take the next three years. Filtering and searching is key to making this data useful, so let's see what this does instead:

```
Get-EventLog System | Export-CSV C:\Logs\SysLog.csv
```

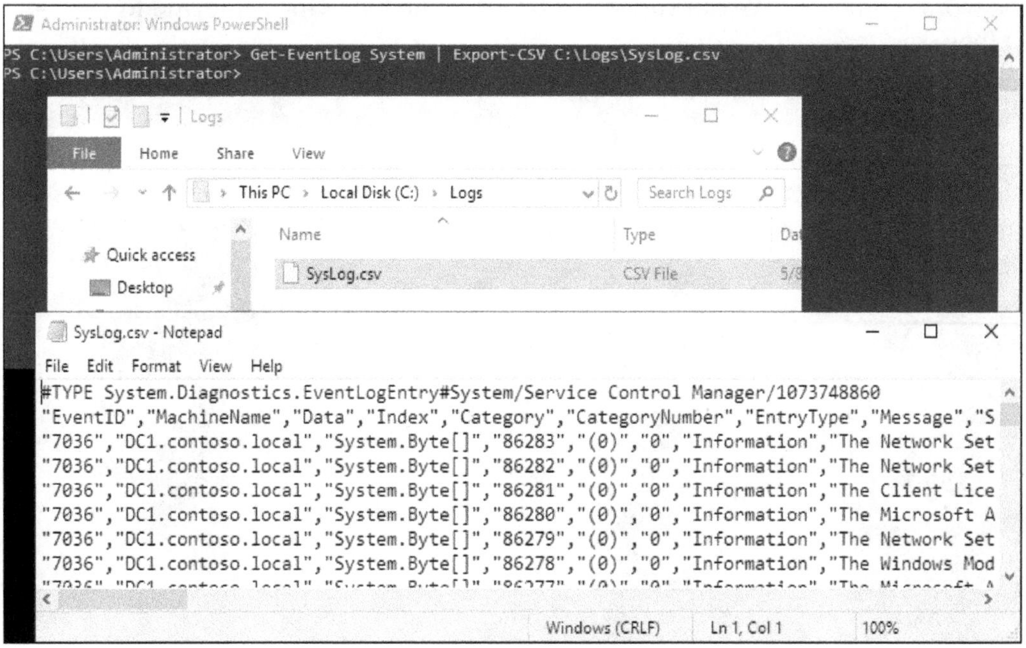

Figure 11.18: Piping output to a CSV file

PowerShell grabbed all of the information from system event logs and spit that info into a CSV file for us. We can now take that CSV file, open it inside a program like Microsoft Excel, and easily sort, filter, or search on these events in a much easier way than we could do from within the default Windows Event Viewer.

> You can also export to XML, HTML, or even pipe output directly to a printer!

Pipes can invoke action

So far, we have only seen pipes modify outputted data. This is very useful, but I don't want you to walk away from this thinking that pipes are only useful for generating information. They can also take the output from one command and throw it at another command, but perhaps a command that actually causes a change or action to be performed. A good example is stopping a process or service. Let's pretend that for some reason you want to have a way to immediately stop all of the Hyper-V services on a server. Those services all have a `DisplayName` that begins with the word "Hyper-V." We can verify that by using the following command to view all of those services:

```
Get-Service -DisplayName hyper*
```

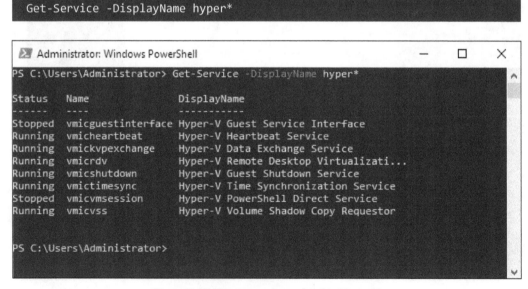

Figure 11.19: Viewing services related to Hyper-V

We can take the output of this `Get-Service` cmdlet and pipe it to `Stop-Service`, and the resulting command will immediately stop all services that begin with the word "Hyper":

```
Get-Service -DisplayName hyper* | Stop-Service
```

PowerShell Integrated Scripting Environment

Most server administrators are familiar with the concept of creating batch files for use in the Command Prompt world. Have a series of commands that you want to run in sequence? Need to run this sequence of commands multiple times across different servers or over and over again in the future? Throwing multiple commands inside a text document and then saving it with the `.BAT` file extension will result in a batch file that can be run on any Windows computer, issuing those commands in sequence, which saves you the time and effort of having to plunk out these commands over and over inside the command-line interface.

Scripting in PowerShell is the same idea but is much more powerful. Commands in Command Prompt are useful, but limited, while PowerShell cmdlets have the ability to manipulate anything within the operating system. With PowerShell, we can reference items from inside environment variables or the registry, we can easily issue commands to remote systems, and we can even utilize variables inside a PowerShell script, just like you would do with any full programming language.

Let's explore a couple of different ways that can be used to start creating your first PowerShell scripts.

PS1 files

Creating a simple `.PS1` file (a PowerShell script file) is almost exactly the same idea as creating a `.BAT` file. Simply open up a text document using your favorite editor, throw in a series of commands or cmdlets, and then save the file as `FILENAME.PS1`. As long as your PowerShell environment allows the running of scripts – see earlier in the chapter about the DEP – you now have the ability to double-click on that `.PS1` file, or launch it from any PowerShell prompt, to run the series of cmdlets inside that script. Let's give it a try and prove that we can get a simple script up and operational.

Since you are only going to create scripts that serve a purpose, let's think of a real-world example. I work with terminal servers quite a bit – pardon me, RDS servers – and a common request from customers is a log of what users logged in to which servers.

A simple way to gather this information is to create a logon script that records information about the user session to a file as they are logging in. To do this, I need to create a script that I can configure to run during the logon process. To make the script a little bit more interesting and flexible down the road, I am going to utilize some variables for my username, the current date and time, and record the name of the RDS server being logged in to. That way, I can look at the collective set of logs down the road, and easily determine which users were on which servers. I am going to use Notepad to create this script. I have opened up a new instance of Notepad, entered in the following commands, and am now saving this as `C:\Scripts\UserReporting.ps1`:

```
$User = $env:username
$RDSH = $env:computername
$Date = Get-Date

echo $User,$Date,$RDSH | Out-File C:\Scripts\UserReporting.txt -append
```

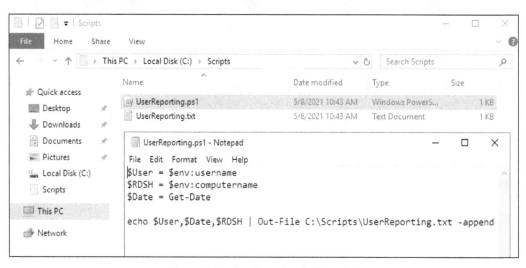

Figure 11.20: Creating a simple PS1 script

You can probably already tell what this script is doing, but let's walk through it anyway. First, we are defining three variables. I am telling the script that $User needs to equal the environment variable username. This will give me the username of the person who is signing in. $RDSH is going to be the name of the server where the user is logging in, also pulled by accessing the server's environment variables. The third variable defined is $Date, which simply pulls the current system date by calling a PowerShell cmdlet named Get-Date.

After pulling all of the information into the PowerShell variables, I am then outputting these three items into a text file that is sitting on my server's hard drive.

If I run this script a few times, I can open up my `UserReporting.txt` file and see that every time the script is run, it successfully logs my specified variables into this report file:

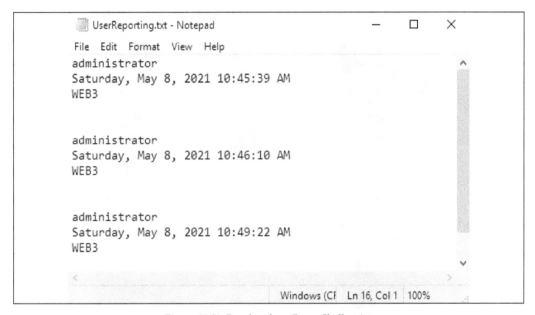

Figure 11.21: Results of our PowerShell script

Working with PowerShell ISE

If I'm being honest, putting together that simple script we just ran took some trial and error. I didn't have a copy of it readily available to work from, and I needed to test a couple of the lines individually in PowerShell before I was confident they would work in my script. I also first tried to pull the username without using the environment variable, and it didn't work. Why did I have so much trouble putting together just a few simple lines of code? Because as I type those lines in Notepad, I have absolutely no idea whether they are going to work when I save and attempt to run that script. All of the text is just black with a white background, and I am fully trusting my own knowledge and scripting abilities to put together something that actually works.

Thankfully, we have access to the **PowerShell Integrated Scripting Environment** (**ISE**). This is a program that is installed by default in Windows Server 2019; it is a scripting shell that allows you to write PowerShell scripts and provides help along the way. Let's go ahead and open it up. If you have any PS1 PowerShell script files, you can simply right-click on one of them and choose **Edit**. Otherwise, by right-clicking on the PowerShell application icon (from the taskbar, for example), you will find an option to launch **Windows PowerShell ISE** right from that menu:

Figure 11.22: Launching PowerShell ISE

Now, if we start typing in the same script information that I used in Notepad a few minutes ago, you can see that even as we type, we get popups and prompts that help us decide which cmdlets or variables we want to utilize. Similar to the way that autocomplete keyboards on our smartphones work, ISE will give suggestions about what you are starting to type, so that you don't necessarily have to remember what the cmdlets or parameters are called; you can take an educated guess on what letter it starts with and then choose one from the list that is presented. There is also a list off to the right of all the commands available, and it is searchable! That is a great feature that really helps to get these scripts rolling:

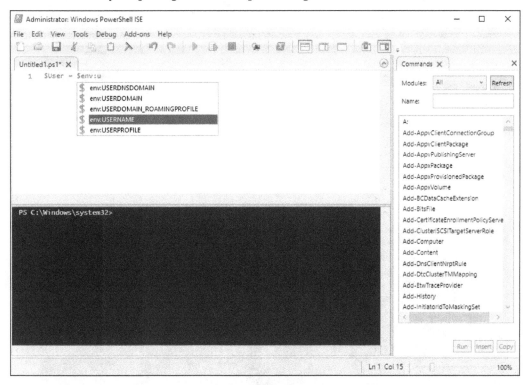

Figure 11.23: ISE provides suggestions for cmdlets and variables

Also useful is the blue PowerShell mini screen that consumes the bottom half of the development window inside ISE. Basically, when you type in some commands, ISE helps to make sure they are all going to work by color-coding the cmdlets and parameters for easy identification, and then you can click on the green arrow button in the taskbar that is labeled **Run Script (F5)**. Even if you haven't saved your script anywhere yet, ISE launches through your commands and presents the output in the following PowerShell prompt window. This allows you to test your script, or test changes that you are making to an existing script, without having to save the file and then launch it separately from a traditional PowerShell window:

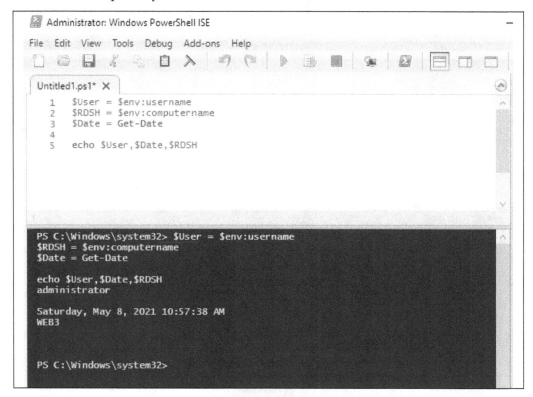

Figure 11.24: Testing the script inside ISE

What's even better is that you can highlight particular sections of your script and choose to run only isolated pieces of the code. This allows you to test certain sections of a script, or do something creative, such as keep one big PS1 script file that is full of common PowerShell commands that you might use on a daily basis. When you have the need to run just one of them, you can simply highlight the text that you want to run and click on the **Run Selection (F8)** button. By highlighting text before running the script from within ISE, only the selected cmdlet(s) will be put into action. In the following screenshot, you can see that I have numerous cmdlets listed inside my script file, but only the one that is highlighted has been run when I pressed *F8*:

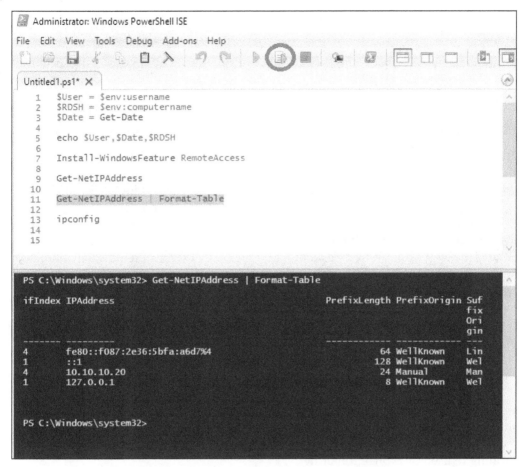

Figure 11.25: Running only highlighted commands in ISE

Remotely managing a server

Now that we have worked a little bit in the local instance of PowerShell and have explored a couple of methods that can be used to start creating scripts, it is time to take a closer look at how PowerShell fits into your centralized administration needs. If you start using PowerShell for server administration but are still RDPing into the servers and then opening PowerShell from there, you're doing it wrong. We already know that you can tap remote servers into Server Manager so that they can be managed centrally. We also know that the tools inside Server Manager are, for the most part, just issuing a series of PowerShell cmdlets when you click on the buttons. Combine those two pieces of information, and you can surmise that PowerShell commands and cmdlets can be easily run against remote systems, including ones that you are not currently logged in to.

Taking this idea and running with it, we are going to look over the criteria necessary to make this happen in our own environment. We are going to make sure that one of our servers is ready to accept remote PowerShell connections, and then use a PowerShell prompt on a different machine to pull information from and make changes to that remote server.

Preparing the remote server

There are just a couple of items that need to be running and enabled on your remote servers for PowerShell to be able to tap into them from a different machine. If all of your servers are Windows Server 2019 (in fact, if they are all Windows Server 2012 or higher), then PowerShell remoting is enabled by default, and you may be able to skip the next couple of sections. However, if you try to use PowerShell remoting and it's not working for you, it is important that you understand how it works under the hood. This way, you can troubleshoot it and manually establish remote capabilities in the event that you run into problems or are running some older operating systems where these steps may be necessary. It is also possible that you have pre-existing security policies that are disabling components used by the remote connection capabilities of PowerShell, so if you find your remote access to be blocked, these are the items to look into on those systems.

The WinRM service

One piece of the remote-management puzzle is the WinRM service. Simply make sure that this service is running. If you have stopped it as some sort of hardening or security benefit, you will need to reverse that change and get the service back up and running to use PowerShell remoting.

You can check the status of the WinRM service from `services.msc`, of course, or since we are using PowerShell in this chapter, you could check it with the following command:

```
Get-Service WinRM
```

Figure 11.26: Ensuring that the WinRM service is running

Enable-PSRemoting

Typically, the only other thing that needs to be accomplished on your remote server is to run a single, simple cmdlet. Well, the server needs to have network access, of course, or you won't be able to see it on the network at all. But other than making sure network connectivity and flow are working directly from the console of your new server, you are then ready to issue the PowerShell command that enables this server to be able to accept incoming, remote PowerShell connections:

```
Enable-PSRemoting -Force
```

Using -Force at the end of the Enable-PSRemoting command causes the command to roll without asking you for confirmations. There are a few different things that Enable-PSRemoting is doing in the background here. First, it is attempting to start the WinRM service. Why did I already specify that you should check it manually? Because if you have it disabled as part of a lockdown strategy, you will interfere with this process. Checking WinRM before using Enable-PSRemoting increases your chances of success when running the Enable-PSRemoting cmdlet. There are two other things that this command is doing: starting the listener for remote connections and creating a firewall rule on the system to allow this traffic to pass successfully.

If you intend to use PowerShell remoting on a large scale, it is daunting to think about logging in to every single server and running this command. Thankfully, you don't have to! As with most functions in the Windows world, we can use Group Policy to make this change for us automatically. Create a new GPO, link and filter it appropriately so that it only applies to those servers that you want to be centrally managed, and then configure this setting: **Computer Configuration | Policies | Administrative Templates | Windows Components | Windows Remote Management (WinRM) | WinRM Service**.

Set **Allow remote server management through WinRM** to **Enabled**, as follows:

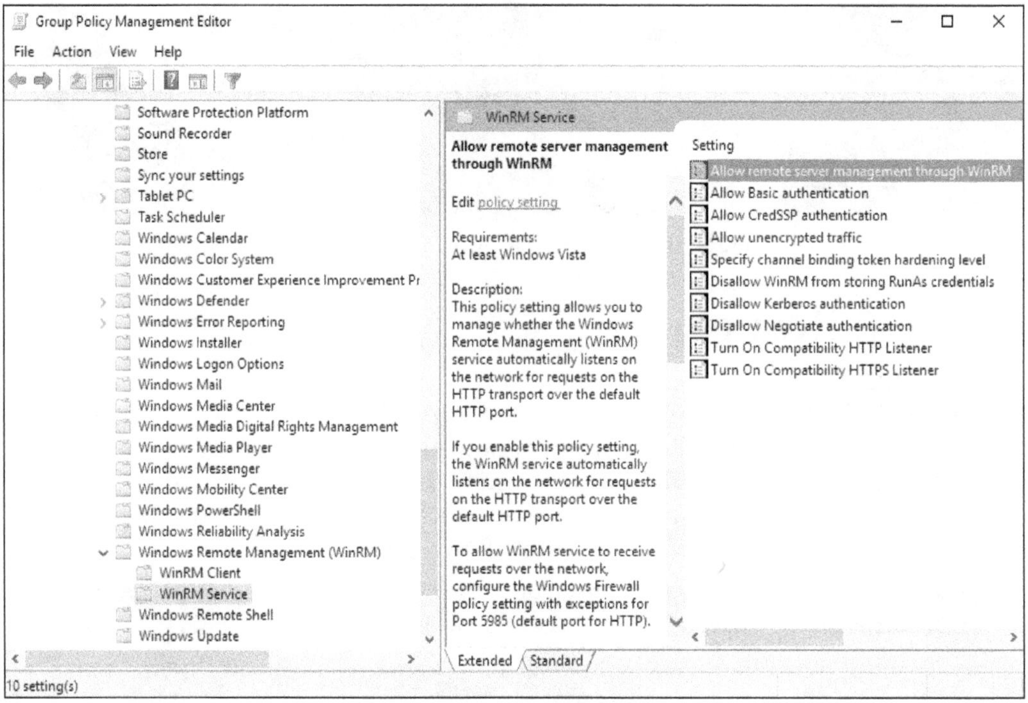

Figure 11.27: Enabling remote management via GPO

Allowing machines from other domains or workgroups

If you are working with servers that are all part of the same corporate domain, which will most often be the case, then authentication between machines is easy to accomplish. They automatically trust each other at this level. However, on the server you are prepping to accept remote connections, if you expect those remote computers will be members of a different domain that is not trusted – or even members of a workgroup – then you will have to issue another command to manually trust the individual computers that are going to be connecting in. For example, if I am planning to manage all of my servers from a client computer called Win10Client that is not trusted by the servers, I would need to run the following command on these servers:

```
Set-Item wsman:\localhost\client\trustedhosts Win10Client
```

If you wanted to allow *any* machine to connect remotely, you could replace the individual computer name with a *, but in general, this wouldn't be a good practice, as you may be inviting trouble by allowing *any* machine to connect to your server in this way.

Connecting to the remote server

I typically see administrators utilize remote PowerShelling in two different ways. You can perform some commands against remote systems on an ad hoc basis while your PowerShell prompt is still running in a local context, or you can launch a full-blown remote PowerShell session to make your PowerShell prompt behave as if it is running directly on that remote system. Let's take a look at both options.

Using -ComputerName

Many of the cmdlets available in PowerShell, particularly ones that begin with Get-, can be used with the -ComputerName parameter. This specifies that the command you are about to run needs to execute against the remote system that you specify in the -ComputerName section. For our remote PowerShell examples, I will be using a PowerShell prompt on my Windows 10 client computer to access information on some of my servers in the network. I want to query the WinRM service, to make sure that it is up and running. For the sake of proving to you that I am remotely communicating with WEB3, you will see in the output that I have first queried my local WinRM service, which I happened to disable on my Win10 workstation.

You see in *Figure 11.28* that my local WinRM service shows as Stopped, but when I issue the same command specifying to query -ComputerName of WEB3, it reaches out and reports back to me that the WinRM service is indeed Running successfully on the WEB3 server:

```
Hostname
Get-Service WinRM
Get-Service WinRM -ComputerName WEB3
```

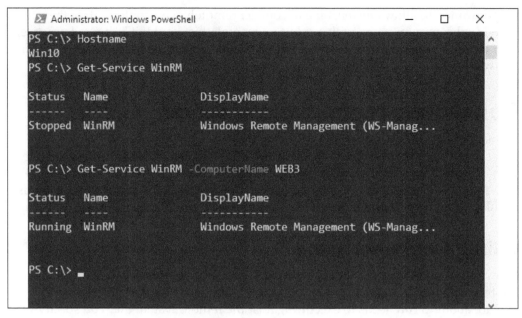

Figure 11.28: Using -ComputerName to query a remote system

Alternatively, perhaps I want to query the new Server Core instance we set up a little while ago and check which roles are currently installed on WEB4:

```
Get-WindowsFeature -ComputerName WEB4 | Where Installed
```

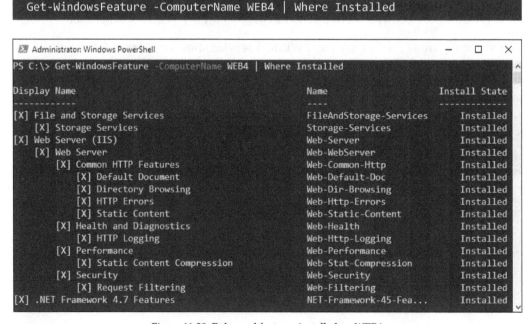

Figure 11.29: Roles and features installed on WEB4

The -`ComputerName` parameter can even accept multiple server names at the same time. If I wanted to check the status of the WinRM service on a few of my servers, by using a single command, I could do something such as this:

```
Get-Service WinRM -ComputerName WEB1,WEB2,DC1
```

```
Administrator: Windows PowerShell                                    —    □    ✕
PS C:\> Get-Service WinRM -ComputerName WEB1,WEB2,DC1

Status    Name              DisplayName
------    ----              -----------
Running   WinRM             Windows Remote Management (WS-Manag...
Running   WinRM             Windows Remote Management (WS-Manag...
Running   WinRM             Windows Remote Management (WS-Manag...


PS C:\>
```

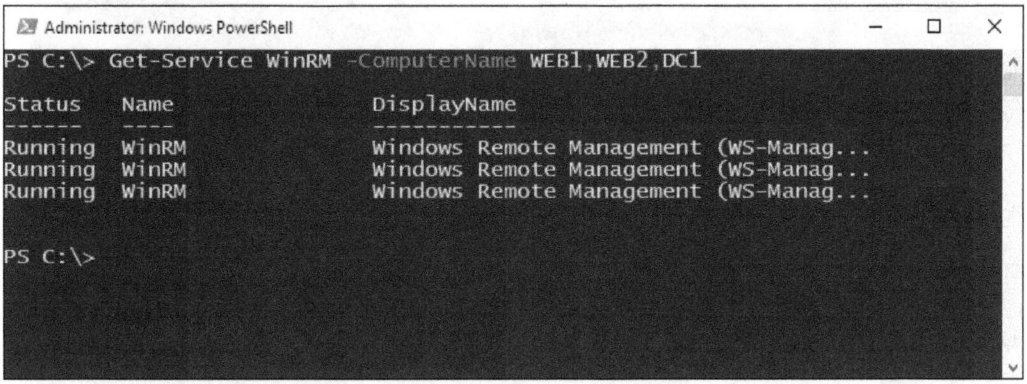

Figure 11.30: Remote PowerShell running against multiple machines

Using Enter-PSSession

On the other hand, sometimes you have many different cmdlets that you want to run against a particular server. In this case, it makes more sense to invoke the fully capable, fully remote PowerShell instance to that remote server. If you open up PowerShell on your local system and utilize the `Enter-PSSession` cmdlet, your PowerShell prompt will be a full remote representation of PowerShell on that remote server. You are then able to issue commands in that prompt, and they will execute as if you were sitting at a PowerShell prompt from the console of that server. Once again, I am logged in to my Windows 10 client computer and have opened up PowerShell. I then use the following command to remotely connect to my WEB4 server:

```
Enter-PSSession -ComputerName WEB4
```

You will see the prompt change, indicating that I am now working in the context of the WEB4 server.

 If your user account does not have access to the server, you can specify alternative credentials to be used when creating this remote connection. Simply append your `Enter-PSSession` cmdlet with -`Credential USERNAME` to specify a different user account.

Commands that I issue from this point forward will be executed against WEB4. Let's verify this. If I check a simple $env:computername, you can see that it presents me with the WEB4 hostname:

```
Administrator: Windows PowerShell                              —    □    ✕
PS C:\> Enter-PSSession -ComputerName WEB4
[WEB4]: PS C:\Users\Administrator.CONTOSO\Documents> $env:computername
WEB4
[WEB4]: PS C:\Users\Administrator.CONTOSO\Documents>
```

Figure 11.31: PowerShell is remotely connected to WEB4

And to further verify this, if I check the installed Windows roles and features, you can see that I have the Web Server role installed, as we accomplished when we initially configured this Server Core to be a web server. Clearly, I do not have the Web Server role installed on my Windows 10 workstation; PowerShell is pulling this data from the WEB4 server:

```
Get-WindowsFeature | Where Installed
```

```
Administrator: Windows PowerShell                                              —    □    ✕
[WEB4]: PS C:\Users\Administrator.CONTOSO\Documents> Get-WindowsFeature | Where Installed

Display Name                              Name                      Install State
------------                              ----                      -------------
[X] File and Storage Services             FileAndStorage-Services      Installed
    [X] Storage Services                  Storage-Services             Installed
[X] Web Server (IIS)                       Web-Server                   Installed
    [X] Web Server                         Web-WebServer                Installed
        [X] Common HTTP Features           Web-Common-Http              Installed
            [X] Default Document           Web-Default-Doc              Installed
            [X] Directory Browsing         Web-Dir-Browsing             Installed
            [X] HTTP Errors                Web-Http-Errors              Installed
            [X] Static Content             Web-Static-Content           Installed
        [X] Health and Diagnostics         Web-Health                   Installed
            [X] HTTP Logging               Web-Http-Logging             Installed
        [X] Performance                    Web-Performance              Installed
            [X] Static Content Compression Web-Stat-Compression         Installed
        [X] Security                       Web-Security                 Installed
```

Figure 11.32: Roles and features installed on WEB4

This is pretty powerful stuff. We are sitting at our local desktop computer, have a remote PowerShell session running to the WEB4 server, and are now able to pull all kinds of information from WEB4 because it is as if we are working from PowerShell right on that server. Let's take it one step further, and try to make a configuration change on WEB4, just to verify that we can. Maybe we can install a new feature on this server. I use Telnet Client quite a bit for network connectivity testing but can see that it is currently not installed on WEB4:

```
Get-WindowsFeature -Name *telnet*
```

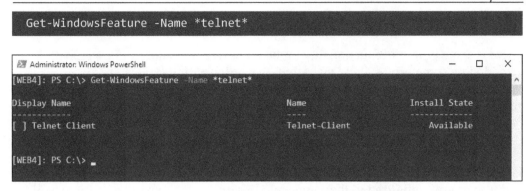

Figure 11.33: Telnet Client is currently not installed on WEB4

By using the `Add-WindowsFeature` cmdlet, I should be able to make quick work of installing that feature:

```
Add-WindowsFeature Telnet-Client
```

Figure 11.34: Installing Telnet Client on WEB4 via remote PowerShell

There is a ton of potential in utilizing remote PowerShell daily, not only for your servers running the full-blown Desktop Experience graphical interface but also for interacting with your security-focused Server Core deployments. Becoming familiar with working in remote PowerShell sessions will be essential to a successful deployment of Server Core in your infrastructure.

Desired State Configuration

There is some powerful functionality in the more recent versions of PowerShell, provided by something called **Desired State Configuration (DSC)**. DSC is a management platform plugged into PowerShell, which provides some new functions and cmdlets that you can take advantage of in your scripts to enable some really cool features. As the name implies, it allows you to build **configurations** inside PowerShell that will provide a *desired state*. What do I mean by that? Well, in a basic sense, DSC makes sure that the PowerShell scripts you build will always work the same way across all of the servers where you apply them by making sure the servers themselves are configured in the same way. It is quite easy to build a script in a way that means it will work correctly on the server you are currently working on. But, if you try to roll that same script out to a different server that might reside in a different **organizational unit (OU)**, or have different items installed on it to begin with, then the script could produce different results than what it was originally intended to do. DSC was built to counteract these differences.

In building your DSC configuration, you identify particular roles, settings, functions, accounts, variables, and so on that you want to retain in your specific desired state. Once you identify and configure these variables, DSC will work to ensure they stay where you have them set, and that they remain uniform according to your DSC configuration policy, which means they are uniform against the other servers where you have run this script.

DSC also helps to prevent unwanted changes on servers. If your DSC-enabled script has identified that a particular service should be running all the time on your servers, and that service stops for some reason, DSC can be there to help spin it back up so that you don't experience an outage. Alternatively, perhaps you have a script that configures a server to a particular set of standards, and another person in IT comes along and adjusts a configuration on the server — perhaps they log in and stop a service purposefully for some reason. Normally, this could result in an outage for that server, but DSC will get that service running again to maintain your originally configured *desired state* for this server. DSC is your *scripting nanny*, so to speak. It helps to build configurations that will remain uniform across multiple platforms and will then work to ensure these configurations are always true. You can then be confident that your servers are always running within the context of your specified desired state.

After building a configuration that identifies the items you want to be installed or monitored, an engine called the **Local Configuration Manager (LCM)** works to ensure the resources remain within the configuration specifications. LCM polls the system regularly, watching for irregularities and changes, and takes action when needed to bring your servers back into the DSC.

The ultimate goal of DSC is to keep everything constant and consistent across your servers and services. DSC's capabilities and access to reach more and more places in the operating system grows constantly, as roles are rewritten to accept DSC parameters and monitoring. This technology helps to ensure that servers are always working with your defined standards, helping to maintain your 99.999% uptime status.

There is a lot to learn about DSC, and I encourage you to explore this topic more once you are familiar with creating and using PowerShell scripts. Here are some great starting points for learning more about DSC:

- https://docs.microsoft.com/en-us/powershell/scripting/dsc/getting-started/wingettingstarted?view=powershell-7.1
- https://docs.microsoft.com/en-us/powershell/scripting/dsc/configurations/write-compile-apply-configuration?view=powershell-7.1
- https://mva.microsoft.com/en-US/training-courses/getting-started-with-powershell-desired-state-configuration-dsc--8672?l=ZwHuc1G1_2504984382

Summary

In Windows Server 2019, we see in multiple places that administration via PowerShell is the recommended path for interacting with our servers. Because the management GUIs are now just shells running PowerShell scripts and the default installation option for Windows Server is Server Core, we can assume that headless, command line-oriented servers are expected to be our servers of the future. Even though PowerShell has been at the core of our operating system functionality since Server 2012, I believe that so far PowerShell has been viewed by most admins as simply an alternative way of managing servers. "Yeah, I know it exists and that I should start using it, and the scripting looks pretty cool, but I can still do anything I want to with the old Command Prompt or my mouse button." That old mentality is quickly changing.

Now that we are experiencing an onset of new technologies, such as DSC, we can see that PowerShell is starting to develop functionality that simply does not exist anywhere else in the operating system. This, combined with the remote management accessibility provided by the standardized PowerShell platform that can be used across all of your current Windows devices (even against servers sitting inside Azure!), means that we will definitely be seeing more and more PowerShell in subsequent Microsoft operating systems and services.

Questions

1. What is the fastest way to get from Command Prompt into PowerShell?

2. What is the cmdlet that will display all available PowerShell cmdlets?

3. What PowerShell cmdlet can be used to connect your PowerShell prompt to a remote computer?

4. What file extension does a PowerShell scripting file have?

5. To which setting is the DEP configured on a fresh Windows Server 2019 instance?

6. What key on your keyboard can be used to auto-populate the remainder of a cmdlet or filename when working in a PowerShell prompt?

7. Which service must be running on a system before it can be connected to by a remote PowerShell connection?

12
Redundancy in Windows Server 2019

Multiply that by two. This is a phrase I hear all the time when planning server deployments for work. I'm sure you have as well. Any time you are rolling out new technology, you want to plan that rollout very carefully. Figure out what servers you need, where they need to be placed, and how the networking needs to be configured for those guys. Once the planning is done, order two of everything, in case one breaks. We live in a world of always-on technology. Services going down is unacceptable, particularly if we are hosting cloud or private cloud services. Any application or service that our users depend on to get their work done is mission-critical and needs 100% uptime, or darn close to it. The problem with redundancy is that it's much easier to *talk the talk* than to *walk the walk*. Maybe one day we will be blessed with a magic *Press here to make this server redundant* button – but today is not that day. We need to understand the technologies that are available to us that enable us to provide redundancy on our systems. This chapter will introduce us to some of those technologies. This book is focused on Server 2019 used on-premises, so the technologies we cover are ones that you can utilize in your local datacenters on real (physical or virtual) servers that you are responsible for building, configuring, and maintaining. Yes, the cloud can provide us with some magical scalability and redundancy options, but those are easy, and often we don't even need to understand how they work. When we use our servers within our own walls, *how can we add some increased reliability to our systems?*

We will cover the following topics in this chapter:

- **Network Load Balancing (NLB)**
- Configuring a load-balanced website
- Failover clustering
- Clustering tiers
- Setting up a failover cluster
- Clustering improvements in Windows Server 2019
- **Storage Spaces Direct (S2D)**

Network Load Balancing (NLB)

Often, when I hear people discussing redundancy on their servers, the conversation includes many instances of the word *cluster*, such as, *"If we set up a cluster to provide redundancy for those servers..."* or *"Our main website is running on a cluster..."* While it is great that there is some form of resiliency being used on the systems to which these conversations pertain, it is often the case that clustering is not actually involved anywhere. When we boil down the particulars of how their systems are configured, we discover that it is NLB doing this work for them. We will discuss real clustering further along in this chapter, but first I wanted to start with the more common approach to making many services redundant. NLB distributes traffic at the TCP/IP level, meaning that the server operating systems themselves are not completely aware of or relying on each other, with redundancy instead being provided at the network layer. This can be particularly confusing—NLB versus clustering—because sometimes Microsoft refers to something as a cluster when in fact it is using NLB to make those connections happen. A prime example is **DirectAccess**. When you have two or more DA servers together in an array, there are TechNet documents and even places inside the console where it is referred to as a cluster. But there is no failover clustering going on here; the technology under the hood that is making connections flow to both nodes is actually Windows NLB.

You've probably heard some of the names in the hardware load balancer market— **F5**, **Cisco**, **Kemp**, **Barracuda**, and many more. These companies provide dedicated hardware or virtual appliances that can take traffic headed toward a particular name or destination, and split that traffic between two or more application servers. While this is generally the most robust way that you can establish NLB, it is also the most expensive and makes the overall environment more complex. One feature these guys offer that the built-in Windows NLB cannot provide is SSL termination, or SSL offloading, as we often call it.

These specialized appliances are capable of receiving SSL website traffic from user computers and decrypting the packets before sending them on their way to the appropriate web server. This way, the web server itself is doing less work, since it doesn't have to spend CPU cycles encrypting and decrypting packets. However, today we are not going to talk about hardware load balancers at all, but rather the NLB capabilities that are provided right inside Windows Server 2019.

Not the same as round-robin DNS

I have discovered, over the years, that some people's idea of NLB is really round-robin DNS. Let me give an example of that: say you have an intranet website that all of your users access daily. It makes sense that you would want to provide some redundancy to this system, and so you set up two web servers, in case one goes down. However, in the case that one does go down, you don't want to require manual cutover steps to fail over to the extra server; you want it to happen automatically. In DNS, it is possible to create two host A records that have the same name but point to different IP addresses. If Server01 is running on 10.10.10.5 and Server02 is running on 10.10.10.6, you could create two DNS records both called **INTRANET**, pointing one host record at 10.10.10.5 and the other host record at 10.10.10.6. This would provide round-robin DNS, but not any real load balancing. Essentially, what happens here is that when the client computers reach out to INTRANET, DNS will hand them one or the other IP address to connect. DNS doesn't care whether that website is actually running, it simply responds with an IP address. So even though you might set this up and it appears to be working flawlessly because you can see that clients are connecting to both Server01 and Server02, be forewarned. In the event of a server failure, you will have many clients who still work, and many clients who are suddenly getting **Page cannot be displayed** when DNS decides to send them to the IP address of the server that is now offline.

NLB is much more intelligent than this. When a node in an NLB array goes down, traffic moving to the shared IP address will only be directed to the node that is still online. We'll get to see this for ourselves shortly when we set up NLB on an intranet website of our own.

What roles can use NLB?

NLB is primarily designed for *stateless* applications, in other words, applications that do not require a long-term memory state or connection status. In a stateless application, each request made from the application could be picked up by Server01 for a while, then swing over to Server02 without interrupting the application. Some applications handle this very well (such as websites), and some do not.

Web services (IIS) definitely benefit the most from the redundancy provided by NLB. NLB is pretty easy to configure and provides full redundancy for websites that you have running on your Windows Servers, without incurring any additional cost. NLB can additionally be used to enhance FTP, firewall, and proxy servers.

Another role that commonly interacts with NLB is the remote access role. Specifically, DirectAccess can use the built-in Windows NLB to provide your remote access environment with redundant entry-point servers. When setting up DirectAccess to make use of load balancing, it is not immediately obvious that you are using the NLB feature built into the operating system because you configure the load-balancing settings from inside the Remote Access Management console, rather than the NLB console. When you walk through the Remote Access Management wizards to establish load balancing, that Remote Access console is actually reaching into the NLB mechanism within the operating system and configuring it, so that its algorithms and transport mechanisms are the pieces being used by DirectAccess in order to split traffic between multiple servers.

One of the best parts about using NLB is that you can make changes to the environment without affecting the existing nodes. *Want to add a new server into an existing NLB array?* No problem. Slide it in without any downtime. *Need to remove a server for maintenance?* No issues here either. NLB can be stopped on a particular node, allowing another node in the array to pick up the slack. In fact, NLB is actually NIC-particular, so you can run different NLB modes on different NICs within the same server. You can tell NLB to stop on a particular NIC, removing that server from the array for the time being. Even better, if you have a little bit of time before you need to take the server offline, you can issue a `drainstop` command instead of an immediate stop. This allows the existing network sessions that are currently live on that server to finish cleanly. No new sessions will flow to the NIC that you have drain-stopped, and old sessions will evaporate naturally over time. Once all sessions have been dropped from that server, you can then yank it and bring it down for maintenance with zero user interruption.

Virtual and dedicated IP addresses

It is important to understand how NLB utilizes IP addresses on your servers. First of all, any NIC on a server that is going to be part of a load-balanced array must have a static IP address assigned to it. NLB does not work with DHCP addressing. In the NLB world, a static IP address on a NIC is referred to as a **Dedicated IP Address (DIP)**. These DIPs are unique per NIC, obviously meaning that each server has its own DIP. For example, in my environment, WEB1 is running a DIP address of 10.10.10.40, and my WEB2 server is running a DIP of 10.10.10.41.

Each server is hosting the same website on their own respective DIP addresses. It's important to understand that when establishing NLB between these two servers, I need to retain the individual DIPs on the boxes, but I will also be creating a new IP address that will be shared between the two servers. This shared IP is called the **Virtual IP Address** (**VIP**). When we walk through the NLB setup shortly, I will be using the IP address of 10.10.10.42 as my VIP, which is so far unused in my network. Here is a quick layout of the IP addresses that are going to be used when setting up my network load-balanced website:

```
WEB1 DIP = 10.10.10.40
WEB2 DIP = 10.10.10.41
Shared VIP = 10.10.10.42
```

When establishing my DNS record for intranet.contoso.local, which is the name of my website. I will be creating just a single host A record, and it will point at my 10.10.10.42 VIP.

NLB modes

Shortly, we will find ourselves in the actual configuration of our load balancing and will have a few decisions to make inside that interface. One of the big decisions is what NLB mode we want to use. Unicast is chosen by default and is the way that I see most companies set up their NLB, perhaps because it is the default option and they've never thought about changing it. Let's take a minute to discuss each of the available options, to make sure you can choose the one that is most appropriate for your networking needs.

Unicast

Here, we start to get into the heart of how NLB distributes packets among the different hosts. Since we don't have a physical load balancer that is receiving the traffic first and then deciding where to send it, *how do the load-balanced servers decide who gets to take which packet streams?*

To answer that question, we need to back up a little bit and discuss how traffic flows inside your network. When you open up a web browser on your computer and visit HTTP://WEB1, DNS resolves that IP address to 10.10.10.40, for example. When the traffic hits your switches and needs to be directed somewhere, the switches need to decide where the 10.10.10.40 traffic needs to go. You might be familiar with the idea of MAC addresses.

Each NIC has a MAC address, and when you assign an IP address to a NIC, it registers its own MAC address and IP with the networking equipment. These MAC addresses are stored inside an ARP table, which is a table that resides inside most switches, routers, and firewalls. When my WEB1 server was assigned the 10.10.10.40 IP address, it registered its MAC address corresponding to 10.10.10.40. When traffic needs to flow to WEB1, the switches realize that traffic destined for 10.10.10.40 needs to go to that specific NIC's MAC address and shoots it off accordingly.

So in the NLB world, when you are sending traffic to a single IP address that is split between multiple NICs, *how does that get processed at the MAC level?* The answer with unicast NLB is that the physical NIC's MAC address gets replaced with a virtual MAC address, and this MAC is assigned to all of the NICs within the NLB array. This causes packets flowing to that MAC address to be delivered to all of the NICs, therefore all of the servers, in that array. If you think that sounds like a lot of unnecessary network traffic is moving around the switches, you would be correct. Unicast NLB means that when packets are destined for the virtual MAC address of an array, that traffic is basically bounced through all ports on the switch (or at least on the VLAN) before finding and landing on their destinations.

The best part about unicast is that it works without having to make any special configurations on the switches or networking equipment in most cases. You set up the NLB configuration from inside the Windows Server tools, and it handles the rest. A downside to unicast is that, because the same MAC address exists on all the nodes, it causes some intra-node communication problems. In other words, the servers that are enabled for NLB will have trouble communicating with each other's IP addresses. Often, this doesn't really matter, because WEB1 would rarely have reason to communicate directly with WEB2. But if you really need those web servers to be able to talk with each other consistently and reliably, the easiest solution is to install a separate NIC on each of those servers and use that NIC for those intra-array communications, while leaving the primary NICs configured for NLB traffic.

The other downside to unicast is that it can create some switch flooding. The switches are unable to learn a permanent route for the virtual MAC address because we need it to be delivered to all of the nodes in our array. Since every packet moving to the virtual MAC is being sent down all avenues of a switch so that it can hit all of the NICs where it needs to be delivered, it has the potential to overwhelm the switches with this flood of network packets. If you are concerned about that or are getting complaints from your networking people about switch flooding, you might want to check out one of the multicast modes for your NLB cluster.

An alternative method for controlling unicast switch flooding is to get creative with VLANs on your switches. If you plan an NLB server array and want to ensure that the switch traffic being generated by this array will not affect other systems in your network, you could certainly create a small VLAN on your switches and plug only your NLB-enabled NICs into that VLAN. This way, when the planned flood happens, it only hits that small number of ports inside your VLAN, rather than segmenting its way across the entire switch.

Multicast

Choosing multicast as your NLB mode comes with some upsides and some headaches. The positive is that it adds an extra MAC address to each NIC. Every NLB member then has two MAC addresses: the original and the one created by the NLB mechanism. This gives the switches and networking equipment an easier job of learning the routes and sending traffic to its correct destinations, without an overwhelming packet flood. To do this, you need to tell the switches which MAC addresses need to receive this NLB traffic; otherwise, you will cause switch flooding, just like with unicast. Telling the switches which MACs need to be contacted is done by logging into your switches and creating some static ARP entries to accommodate this. For any company with a dedicated networking professional, usually proficient in Cisco equipment, this will be no sweat. If you are not familiar with modifying ARP tables and adding static routes, it can be a bit of a nuisance to get it right. In the end, multicast is generally better than unicast, but it can be more of an administrative headache. My personal preference still tends to be unicast, especially in smaller businesses. I have seen it used in many different networks without any issues, and going with unicast means we can leave the switch programming alone.

Multicast IGMP

Better yet, but not always an option, is multicast with **Internet Group Management Protocol (IGMP)**. Multicast IGMP really helps to mitigate switch flooding, but it only works if your switches support IGMP snooping. This means that the switch has the capability to look inside multicast packets to determine where exactly they should go. So where unicast creates some amount of switch flooding by design, multicast can help to lower that amount, and IGMP can get rid of it completely.

The NLB mode that you choose will depend quite a bit upon the capabilities of your networking equipment. If your servers have only a single NIC, try to use multicast or you will have intra-array problems. On the other hand, if your switches and routers don't support multicast, you don't have a choice—unicast will be your only option for configuring Windows NLB.

Configuring a load-balanced website

Enough talk; it's time to set this up for ourselves and give it a try. I have two web servers running on my lab network, WEB1 and WEB2. They both use IIS to host an intranet website. My goal is to provide my users with a single DNS record for them to communicate with but have all of that traffic be split between the two servers with some real load balancing. Follow along with the steps on making this possible.

Enabling NLB

First things first, we need to make sure that WEB1 and WEB2 are prepared to do NLB, because it is not installed by default. NLB is a feature available in Windows Server 2019, and you add it just like any other role or feature, by running through the **Add roles and features** wizard. Add this feature on all of the servers that you want to be part of the NLB array:

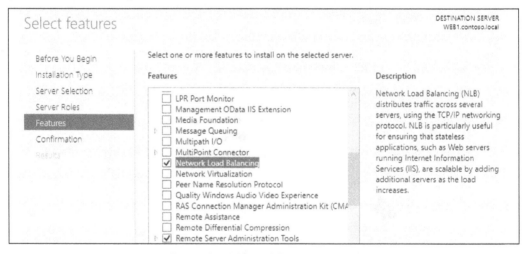

Figure 12.1: Adding NLB to your servers

Enabling MAC address spoofing on VMs

Remember when we talked about unicast NLB and how the physical MAC address of the NIC gets replaced with a virtual MAC address that is used for NLB array communications? Yeah, virtual machines don't like that. If you are load balancing physical servers with physical NICs, you can skip this section. But many of you will be running web servers that are VMs. Whether they are hosted with Hyper-V, VMware, or some other virtualization technology, there is an extra option in the configuration of the virtual machine that you will have to choose so that your VM will happily comply with this MAC addressing change.

The name of this setting will be something along the lines of **Enable MAC address spoofing**, though the specific name of the function could be different depending on what virtualization technology you use. The setting should be a simple checkbox that you have to enable in order to make MAC spoofing work properly. Make sure to do this for *all* of your virtual NICs upon which you plan to utilize NLB. Keep in mind, this is a per-NIC setting, not a per-VM setting. If you have multiple NICs on a VM, you may have to check the box for each NIC, if you plan to use them all with load balancing.

The VM needs to be shut down to make this change, so I have shut down my WEB1 and WEB2 servers. Now find the checkbox and enable it. Since everything that I use is based on Microsoft technology, I am of course using Hyper-V as the platform for my virtual machines here in the lab. Within Hyper-V, if I right-click on my WEB1 server and head into the VM's settings, I can then click on my network adapter to see the various pieces that are changeable on WEB1's virtual NIC. In the latest versions of Hyper-V, this setting is listed underneath the NIC properties, inside the section titled **Advanced Features**. And there it is, my **Enable MAC address spoofing** checkbox. Simply click on that to enable it, and you're all set:

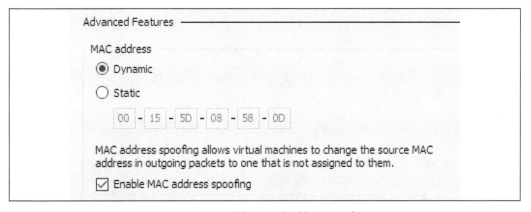

Figure 12.2: Enabling MAC address spoofing

If **Enable MAC address spoofing** is grayed out, remember that the virtual machine must be completely shut down before the option appears. Shut it down, then open **Settings** and take another look. The option should now be available to select.

Configuring NLB

Let's summarize where we are at this point. I have two web servers, WEB1 and WEB2, and they each currently have a single IP address. Each server has IIS installed, which is hosting a single website. I have enabled MAC address spoofing on each (because these servers are virtual machines), and I just finished installing the NLB feature onto each web server. We now have all of the parts and pieces in place to be able to configure NLB and get that web traffic split between both servers.

I will be working from WEB1 for the initial configuration of NLB. Log into this, and you will see that we have a new tool in the list of tools that are available inside Server Manager, called **Network Load Balancing Manager**. Go ahead and open up that console. Once you have NLB Manager open, right-click on **Network Load Balancing Clusters** and choose **New Cluster**, as shown in *Figure 12.3*:

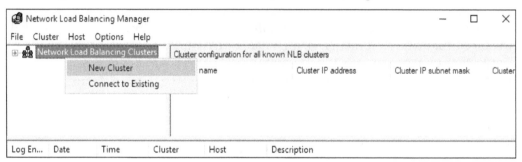

Figure 12.3: Creating a new NLB cluster

When you create a new cluster, it is important to note that currently there are zero machines in this cluster. Even the server where we are running this console is not automatically added to the cluster, and we must remember to manually place it into this screen. So first, I am going to type in the name of my WEB1 server and click on **Connect**. After doing that, the NLB Manager will query WEB1 for NICs and will give me a list of available NICs upon which I could potentially set up NLB:

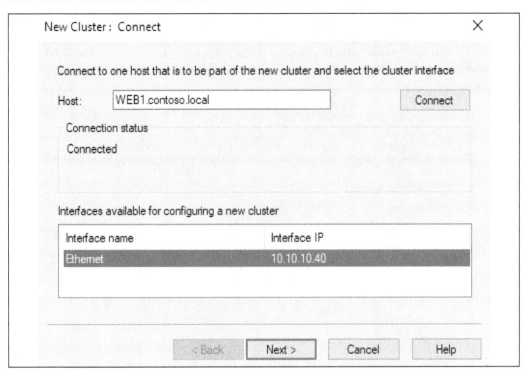

Figure 12.4: Choosing a NIC to set up the NLB

Since I only have one NIC on this server, I simply leave it selected and click on **Next**. The following screenshot gives you the opportunity to input additional IP addresses on WEB1, but since we are only running one IP address, I will leave this screen as is, and click on **Next** again.

Now we have moved on to a window asking us to input cluster IP addresses. These are the VIPs that we intend to use to communicate with this NLB cluster. As stated earlier, my VIP for this website is going to be `10.10.10.42`, so I click on the **Add...** button and input that IPv4 address along with its corresponding subnet mask:

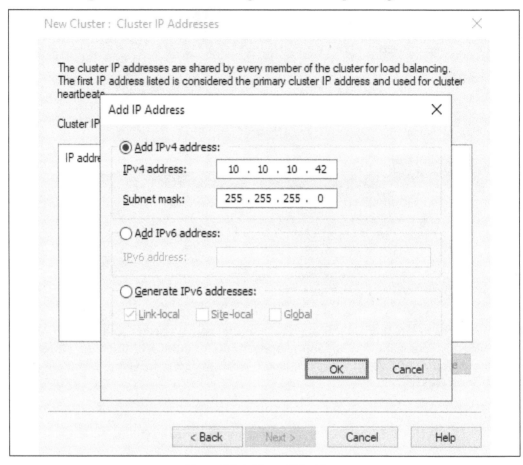

Figure 12.5: Adding a VIP address

One more click of the **Next** button, and we can now see our option for which **Cluster operation mode** we want to run. Depending on your network configuration, choose between **Unicast**, **Multicast**, and **IGMP multicast**:

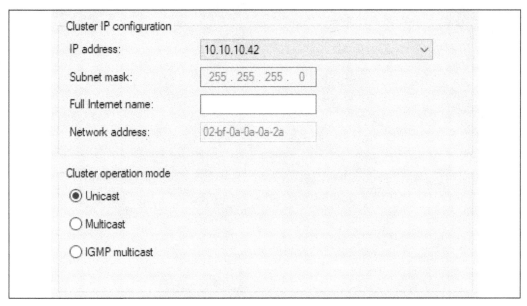

Figure 12.6: Choosing a cluster operation mode

The following screenshot of our NLB wizard allows you to configure port rules. By default, there is a single rule that tells NLB to load balance any traffic coming in on any port, but you can change this if you want. I don't see a lot of people in the field specifying rules here to distribute specific ports to specific destinations, but one neat feature in this screenshot is the ability to disable certain ranges of ports.

That function could be very useful if you want to block unnecessary traffic at the NLB layer. For example, *Figure 12.7* shows a configuration that would block ports 81 and higher from being passed through the NLB mechanism:

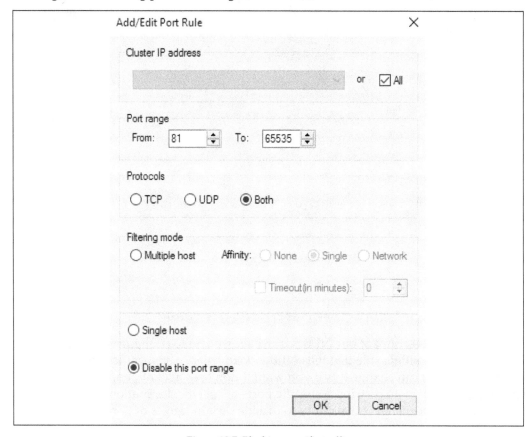

Figure 12.7: Blocking specific traffic

Finish that wizard, and you have now created an NLB cluster! However, at this point, we have only specified information about the VIP, and about the WEB1 server. We have not established anything about WEB2. We are running an NLB array, but currently, that array has just a single node inside of it, so traffic to the array is all landing on WEB1. Right-click on the new cluster and select **Add Host To Cluster**:

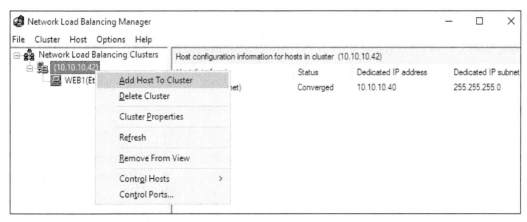

Figure 12.8: Adding a host to the new cluster

Input the name of our WEB2 server, click on **Connect**, and walk through the wizard to add the secondary NLB node of WEB2 into the cluster. Once both nodes are added to the cluster, our NLB array, or cluster, is online and ready to use. (See, I told you that the word *cluster* is used in a lot of places, even though this is not talking about a failover cluster at all!)

If you take a look inside the NIC properties of our web servers and click on the **Advanced** button inside the TCP/IPv4 properties, you can see that our new cluster IP address of 10.0.0.42 has been added to the NICs. Each NIC will now contain both the DIP address assigned to it, as well as the VIP address shared in the array:

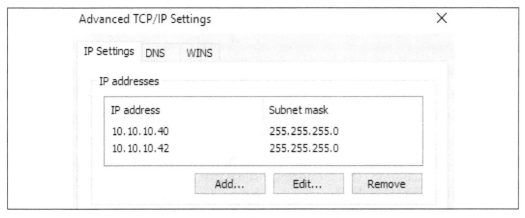

Figure 12.9: Updated IP addresses on the NIC

The traffic that is destined for the 10.10.10.42 IP address is now starting to be split between the two nodes, but right now the websites that are running on the WEB1 and WEB2 servers are configured to only be running on the dedicated 10.10.10.40 and 10.10.10.41 IP addresses, so we need to make sure to adjust that next.

Configuring IIS and DNS

Just a quick step within IIS on each of our web servers should get the website responding on the appropriate VIP address. Now that the NLB configuration has been established and we confirmed that the new 10.10.10.42 VIP address has been added to the NICs, we can use that IP address as a website binding. Open up the IIS management console and expand the **Sites** folder so that you can see the properties of your website. Right-click on the site name, and choose **Edit Bindings...**:

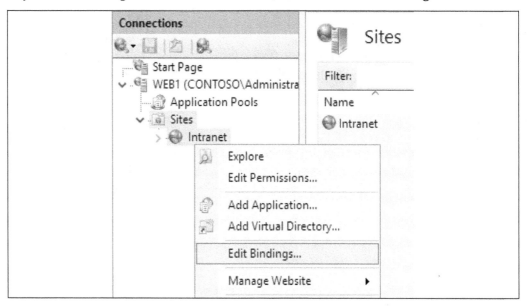

Figure 12.10: Editing website bindings

Once inside **Site Bindings**, choose the binding that you want to manipulate, and click on the **Edit...** button. This intranet website is just a simple HTTP site, so I am going to choose my HTTP binding for this change. The binding is currently set to 10.10.10.40 on WEB1, and 10.10.10.41 on WEB2. This means that the website is only responding to traffic that comes in on these IP addresses. All I have to do is change that **IP address** drop-down menu to the new VIP, which is 10.10.10.42. After making this change (on both servers) and clicking **OK**, the website is immediately responding to traffic coming in through the 10.10.10.42 IP address:

Figure 12.11: Updating your binding so the website runs on your new VIP

Now we come to the last piece of the puzzle: DNS. Remember, we want users to have the ability to simply enter `http://intranet` into their web browsers to browse this new NLB website, so we need to configure a DNS host A record accordingly. That process is exactly the same as any other DNS host record; simply create one and point `intranet.contoso.local` to `10.10.10.42`:

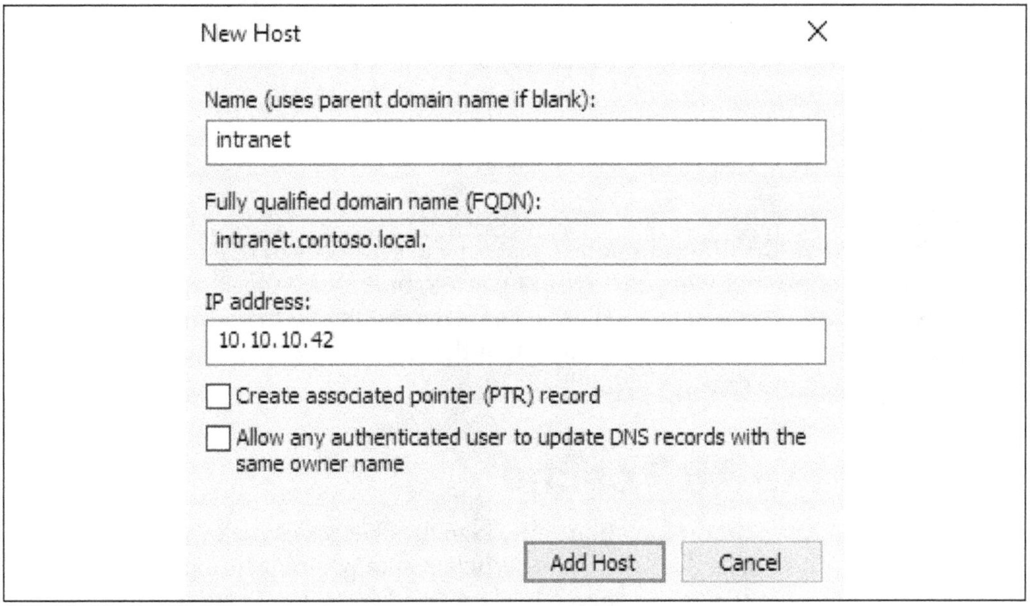

Figure 12.12: Configuring the DNS record

Testing it out

NLB configured? Check.

IIS bindings updated? Check.

DNS record created? Check.

We are ready to test this thing out. If I open up an internet browser on a client computer and browse to http://intranet, I can see the website:

Figure 12.13: Site 1 running on the WEB1 server

But *how can we determine that load balancing is really working?* If I continue refreshing the page, or browse from another client, I continue accessing http://intranet, and eventually the NLB mechanism will decide that a new request should be sent over to WEB2, instead of WEB1. When this happens, I am presented with this page instead:

Figure 12.14: Site 2 running on the WEB2 server

As you can see, I modified the content between WEB1 and WEB2 so that I could distinguish between the different nodes, just for the purposes of this test. If this were a real production intranet website, I would want to make sure that the content of both sites was exactly the same, so that users were completely unaware of the NLB even happening. All they need to know is that the website is going to be available and working, all of the time.

Flushing the ARP cache

Earlier, we had a little discussion about how switches keep a cache of ARP information, which lessens the time those switches take when deciding where packets should flow. When you assign a NIC an IP address, the MAC address of that NIC gets associated with the IP address inside the ARP table of certain pieces of networking equipment.

Switches, routers, firewalls – these tools commonly have what we refer to as an ARP table, and therefore they have a set of data in that table that is known as the ARP cache.

When configuring NLB, particularly unicast, the NIC's MAC address gets replaced with a new, virtual MAC address. Sometimes the switches and networking equipment are very quick to catch on to this change, and they associate the new MAC address with the new IP address, and everything works just fine. However, I find that when configuring NLB, the following is generally true: *The smarter and more expensive your networking equipment is, the dumber it gets when configuring NLB.* What I mean is that your networking equipment might continue to hold onto the old MAC address information that is stored in its ARP table, and doesn't get updated to reflect the new MAC addressing.

What does this look like in real life? Network traffic will stop flowing to or from those NICs. Sometimes when you establish NLB and it turns itself on, all network traffic will suddenly stop cold to or from those network interfaces. *What do you need to do to fix this situation?* Sometimes you can wait it out, and within a few minutes, hours, or even a few days the switches will drop the old ARP info and allow the new virtual MACs to register themselves in that table. *What can you do to speed up this process?* Flush the ARP cache.

The procedure for doing this will be different depending on what kind of networking equipment you are working on – whether it is a switch or router, what brand it is, what model it is, and so on. But each of these guys should have this capability, and it should be named something along the lines of *flushing the ARP cache*. When you run this function on your equipment, it cleans out that ARP table, getting rid of the old information that is causing you problems and allowing the new MAC addresses to register themselves appropriately in the fresh table.

I only wanted to point this out in the event that you configure NLB, only to see traffic flow cease on your server. More than likely, you are dealing with the ARP cache being stuck on one or more pieces of network equipment that is trying to shuttle the traffic to and from your server.

Failover clustering

We have established that NLB is a great solution for stateless applications, with a prime example being websites that you want to make highly available. *What about other server roles or functions that you want to make redundant?* Well, the opposite of stateless is stateful, so *how about giving high availability to stateful pieces of technology?*

Failover clustering provides this level of capability and can be used in cases where the nodes within the cluster are accessing shared data. This is a key factor in the way failover clustering is designed. The storage used by the cluster nodes must be shared and accessible by each node that needs it. There are many different roles and services that can take advantage of failover clustering, but there are four specific technologies that seem to make up the majority of clusters running in datacenters today: Hyper-V, file services, Exchange, and SQL. If you are working with any of these technologies – and chances are that you work with all of them – you need to look into the high-availability capabilities that can be provided for your infrastructure by the use of failover clustering.

While failover clustering provided by Windows Server is Microsoft-built and has the capacity to work very well out of the box with many Microsoft roles and services, it is important to note that you can establish failover clustering for non-Microsoft applications as well. Third-party applications that run on Windows Server in your environment, or even homegrown applications that have been built in-house, can also take advantage of failover clustering. As long as that application uses shared storage and you can specify the tasks that it needs to be able to perform against those applications for the clustering administration tools – how to start the service, how to stop the service, how to monitor the service health, and so on – you can interface these custom services and applications with failover clustering and provide some major redundancy for just about any type of application.

Clustering Hyper-V hosts

One of the most powerful examples of failover clustering is displayed when combining clustering with Hyper-V. It is possible to build out two or more Hyper-V servers, cluster them together, and give them the capability to each host all of the virtual machines that are stored in that virtual environment. By giving all of the Hyper-V host servers access to the same shared storage where the virtual hard disks are stored, and configuring failover clustering between the nodes, you can create an incredibly powerful and redundant virtualization solution for your company. When a Hyper-V Server goes down, the VMs that were running on that Hyper-V host will fail over to another Hyper-V host server and spin themselves up there instead.

After minimal service interruption while the VMs spin up, everything is back online automatically, without any administrative input. Even better, *how about when you need to patch or otherwise take a Hyper-V host server offline for maintenance?* You can easily force the VMs to run on a different member server in the cluster; they are live-migrated over to that server so there is zero downtime, and then you are free to remove the node for maintenance and finish working on it before reintroducing it to the cluster. We use virtual machines and servers for all kinds of workloads, so *wouldn't it be great if you could get rid of any single point of failure within that virtualization environment?* That is exactly what failover clustering can provide.

Virtual machine load balancing

In fact, not only does a Hyper-V cluster have the ability to quickly self-recover in the event of a Hyper-V server node going offline, but we now have some smart load-balancing logic working along with these clustered services. If your Hyper-V cluster is becoming overloaded with virtual machines, it makes sense that you would add another node to that cluster, giving the cluster more capability and computing power. But once the node is added, *how much work is involved in sliding some of the VMs over to this new cluster node?*

None! As long as you have VM load-balancing enabled, the cluster's weights will be evaluated automatically, and VM workloads will be live-migrated, without downtime, on the fly, in order to better distribute the work among all cluster nodes, including the new host server. VM load-balancing can be run and evaluated on demand, whenever you deem fit, or can be configured to run automatically, taking a look at the environment every 30 minutes, automatically deciding whether any workloads should be moved around.

Clustering for file servers

Clustering for file servers has been available for quite a while; this was one of the original intentions behind the release of clustering. Originally, file-server clustering was only useful for document and traditional file utilization; in other words, when knowledge-worker types of users need to access files and folders daily, and you want those files to be highly available. To this day, this general-purpose file-server clustering works in an active-passive scenario. When multiple file servers are clustered together for general-purpose file access, only one of those file-server nodes is active and presented to the users at a time. Only in the event of downtime on that node does the role get flipped over to one of the other cluster members.

Scale-out file server

While general file-server clustering is great for ad hoc access of files and folders, it isn't comprehensive enough to handle files that are continuously open or being changed. A prime example of these files is virtual hard disk files used by Hyper-V virtual machines.

There is a need for virtual hard disk files to be redundant; losing these files would be detrimental to our businesses. Thankfully, hosting application-data workloads such as this is exactly what **Scale-Out File Server (SOFS)** does. If you plan to host virtual machines using Hyper-V, you will definitely want to check out the failover clustering capabilities that are available to use with Hyper-V services. Furthermore, if you intend to use clustered Hyper-V hosts, you should check out SOFS as an infrastructure technology to support that highly available Hyper-V environment.

SOFS helps support failover clustering by providing file servers with the capability to have multiple nodes online (active-active) that remain persistent between each other constantly. This way, if one storage server goes down, the others are immediately available to pick up the slack without a cutover process that involves downtime. This is important when looking at the difference between storing static data, such as documents, and storing virtual hard disk files being accessed by VMs. The VMs can stay online during a file-server outage with SOFS, which is pretty incredible!

Clustering tiers

An overhead concept to failover clustering that is important to understand is the different tiers at which clustering can benefit you. There are two levels upon which you can use clustering: you can take an either/or approach and use just one of these levels of failover clustering, or you can combine both to really impress your high-availability friends.

Application-layer clustering

Clustering at the application level typically involves installing failover clustering onto VMs. Using VMs is not a firm requirement but is the most common installation path. You can mix and match VMs with physical servers in a clustering environment, as long as each server meets the installation criteria. This application mode of clustering is useful when you have a particular service or role running within the operating system that you want to make redundant. Think of this as more of a microclustering capability, where you are really digging in and making one specific component of the operating system redundant with another server node that is capable of picking up the slack in the event that your primary server goes down.

Host-layer clustering

If application clustering is micro, clustering at the host layer is more macro. The best example I can give of this is the one that gets most admins started with failover clustering in the first place: Hyper-V. Let's say you have two physical servers that are both hosting virtual machines in your environment. You want to cluster these servers together so that all of the VMs being hosted on these Hyper-V servers can be redundant between the two physical servers. If a whole Hyper-V server goes down, the second one can spin up the VMs that had been running on the primary node. And after a minimal interruption of service, your VMs that are hosting the actual workloads in your environment will be back up and running, available for users and their applications to tap into.

A combination of both

These two modes of using failover clustering mentioned earlier can certainly be combined together for an even better and more comprehensive high-availability story. Let's let this example speak for itself: you have two Hyper-V Servers, each one prepared to run a series of virtual machines. You are using host clustering between these servers, so if one physical box goes down, the other picks up the slack. That in itself is great, but you use SQL a lot, and you want to make sure that SQL is also highly available. You can run two virtual machines, each one a SQL server, and configure application-layer failover clustering between those two VMs for the SQL services specifically. This way, if something happens to a single virtual machine, you don't have to fail over to the backup Hyper-V Server, rather your issue can be resolved by the second SQL node taking over. There was no need for a full-scale Hyper-V takeover by the second physical server, yet you utilized failover clustering to ensure that SQL was always online. This is a prime example of clustering on top of clustering, and by thinking along those lines, you can start to get pretty creative with all of the different ways that you can make use of clustering in your network.

How does failover work?

Once you have configured failover clustering, the multiple nodes remain in constant communication with each other. This way, when one goes down, they are immediately aware and can flip services over to another node to bring them back online. Failover clustering uses the registry to keep track of many per-node settings. These identifiers are kept synced across the nodes, and then when one goes down, those necessary settings are blasted around to the other servers and the next node in the cluster is told to spin up whatever applications, VMs, or workloads were being hosted on the primary box that went offline. There can be a slight delay in services as the components spin up on the new node, but this process is all automated and hands-off, keeping downtime to an absolute minimum.

When you need to cut services from one node to another as a planned event, such as for patching or maintenance, there is an even better story here. Through a process known as **live migration**, you can flip responsibilities over to a secondary node with zero downtime. This way, you can take nodes out of the cluster for maintenance or security patching, or whatever reason, without affecting the users or system uptime in any way. Live migration is particularly useful for Hyper-V clusters, where you will often have the need to manually decide which node your VMs are being hosted on so that you can accomplish work on the other node or nodes.

In many clusters, there is an idea of **quorum**. This means that if a cluster is split, for example, if a node goes offline or if there are multiple nodes that are suddenly unavailable through a network disconnect of some kind, then quorum logic takes over to determine which segment of the cluster is the one that is still online. If you have a large cluster that spans multiple subnets inside a network, and something happens at the network layer that breaks cluster nodes away from each other, all the two sides of the cluster know is that they can no longer communicate with the other cluster members, and so both sides of the cluster would automatically assume that they should now take responsibility for the cluster workloads.

Quorum settings tell the cluster how many node failures can happen before action is necessary. By the entire cluster knowing the quorum configuration, it can help provide answers to those questions about which section of the cluster is to be primary in the event that the cluster is split. In many cases, clusters provide quorum by relying on a third party, known as a **witness**. As the name implies, this witness watches the status of the cluster and helps to make decisions about when and where failover becomes necessary. I mention this here as a precursor to our discussion on new clustering capabilities baked into Server 2019, one of which is an improvement in the way that witnesses work in small environments.

There is a lot more information to be gained and understood if you intend to create clusters large enough for quorum and witness settings. If you're interested in learning more, check out `https://docs.microsoft.com/en-us/windows-server/ storage/storage-spaces/understand-quorum`.

Setting up a failover cluster

We are going to take a few minutes to set up a small cluster of servers so that you can see the management tools and the places that have to be visited to accomplish this. I have now backed out all of the NLB config on my WEB1 and WEB2 servers that we set up earlier so that they are just simple web servers at the moment, once again with no redundancy between them. Let's set up our first failover cluster and add both of these servers into that cluster.

Building the servers

We have two servers already running with Windows Server 2019 installed. Nothing special has been configured on these servers, but I have added the **File Server** role to both of them because, eventually, I will utilize these as a cluster of file servers. The key point here is that you should have the servers as identical as possible, with the roles already installed that you intend to make use of within the cluster.

One other note during the building phase: if possible, it is a best practice with clustering that member servers belonging to the same cluster reside within the same **organizational unit** (**OU**) in **Active Directory** (**AD**). The reason for this is twofold: first, it ensures that the same GPOs are being applied to the set of servers, in an effort to make their configurations as identical as possible. Second, during cluster creation, some new objects will be auto-generated and created in AD, and when the member servers reside in the same OU, these new objects will be created in that OU as well. It is very common with a running cluster to see all of the relevant objects in AD be part of the same OU, and for that OU to be dedicated to this cluster:

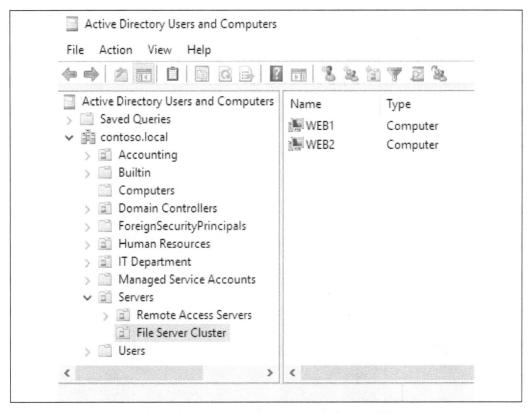

Figure 12.15: Cluster servers are stored in the same OU

Installing the feature

Now that our servers are online and running, we want to install the clustering capabilities on each of them. **Failover Clustering** is a feature inside Windows Server, so open up the **Add roles and features** wizard and add it to all of your cluster nodes:

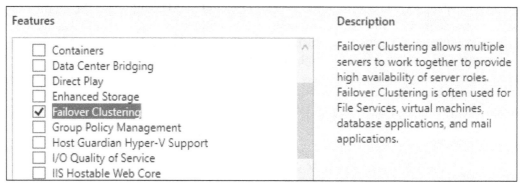

Figure 12.16: Adding Failover Clustering to your cluster nodes

Running Failover Cluster Manager

As is the case with most roles or features that can be installed on Windows Server 2019, once implemented, you will find a management console for it inside the **Tools** menu of Server Manager. If I look inside there on WEB1 now, I can see that a new listing for **Failover Cluster Manager** is available for me to click on. I am going to open that tool, and start working on the configuration of my first cluster from this management interface:

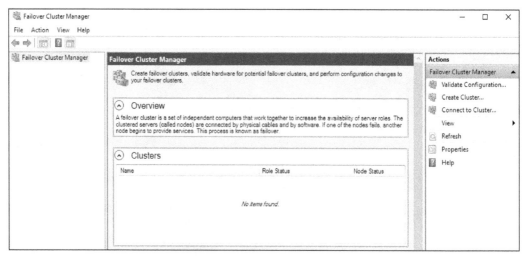

Figure 12.17: Configuring a cluster

Running cluster validation

Now that we are inside Failover Cluster Manager, you will notice a list of tasks available to launch under the **Management** section of the console, near the middle of your screen:

 Management

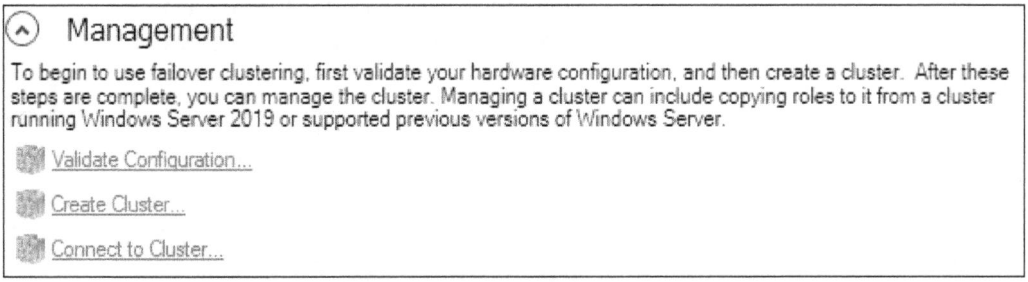

To begin to use failover clustering, first validate your hardware configuration, and then create a cluster. After these steps are complete, you can manage the cluster. Managing a cluster can include copying roles to it from a cluster running Windows Server 2019 or supported previous versions of Windows Server.

 Validate Configuration...

 Create Cluster...

 Connect to Cluster...

Figure 12.18: Cluster configuration tasks

Before we can configure the cluster itself or add any server nodes to it, we must first validate our hardware configuration. Failover clustering is a pretty complex set of technologies, and there are many places where misconfigurations or inconsistencies could set the whole cluster askew. Your intentions behind setting up a cluster are obviously for reliable redundancy, but even a simple mistake in the configuration of your member servers could cause problems large enough that a node failure would not result in automated recovery, which defeats the purpose of the cluster in the first place. To make sure that all of our T's are crossed and I's dotted, there are some comprehensive validation checks built into Failover Cluster Manager, sort of like a built-in best practices analyzer. These checks can be run at any time – before the cluster is built or after it has been running in production for years. In fact, if you ever have to open a support case with Microsoft, it is likely that the first thing they will ask you to do is run the Validate Configuration tools and allow them to look over the output.

To start the validation process, click on the **Validate Configuration...** link. We are now launched into a wizard that allows us to select which pieces of the cluster technology we would like to validate. Once again, we must put on our Microsoft *centralized management theology* thinking caps and realize that this wizard doesn't know or care that it is running on one of the member servers that we intend to be part of the cluster. We must identify each of the server nodes that we want to scan for validation checks, so in my case, I am going to tell it that I want to validate the WEB1 and WEB2 servers:

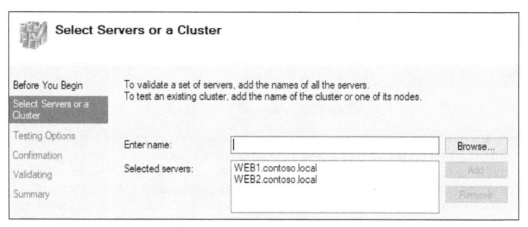

Figure 12.19: Selecting server nodes for cluster validation checks

The **Testing Options** screen allows you to choose the **Run only tests I select** radio button and you will then be able to run only particular validation tests. Generally, when setting up a new cluster, you want to run *all* of the tests so that you can ensure everything measures up correctly. On a production system, however, you may choose to limit the number of tests that run. This is particularly true with respect to tests against **Storage**, as those can actually take the cluster offline temporarily while the tests are being run, and you wouldn't want to interfere with your online production services if you are not working within a planned maintenance window:

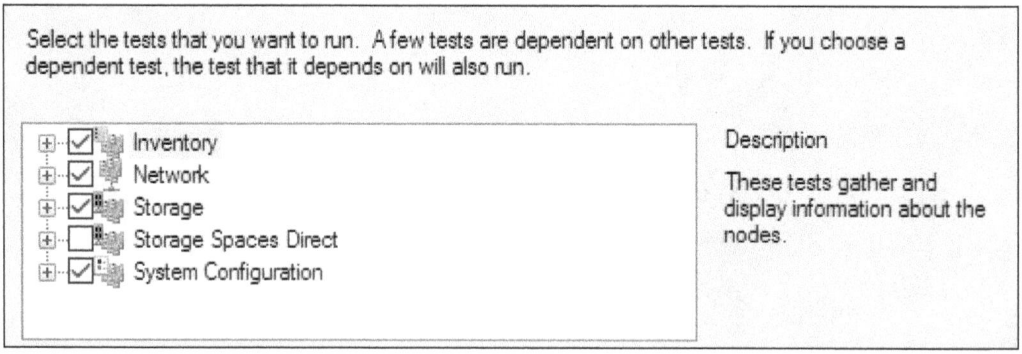

Select the tests that you want to run. A few tests are dependent on other tests. If you choose a dependent test, the test that it depends on will also run.

- ☑ Inventory
- ☑ Network
- ☑ Storage
- ☐ Storage Spaces Direct
- ☑ System Configuration

Description

These tests gather and display information about the nodes.

Figure 12.20: Selecting the validation tests to run

Since I am setting up a new cluster, I am going to let all of the tests run. So I will leave the recommended option selected, **Run all tests (recommended)**, and continue:

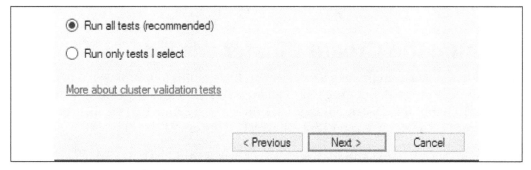

Figure 12.21: Running all tests

Once the tests have completed, you will see a summary output of their results. You can click on the **View Report...** button to see a lot of detail on everything that was run. Keep in mind that there are three tiers of pass/fail. Green is *good* and red is *bad*, but yellow is more like *it'll work, but you're not running best practices*. For example, I only have one NIC in each of my servers; the wizard recognizes that, and for my setup to be truly redundant in all aspects, I should have at least two. It'll let this slide and continue to work, but it is warning me that I could make this cluster even better by adding a second NIC to each of my nodes.

If you ever need to reopen this report or grab a copy of it off the server for safekeeping, it is located on the server where you ran the tests, inside C:\Windows\ Cluster\Reports:

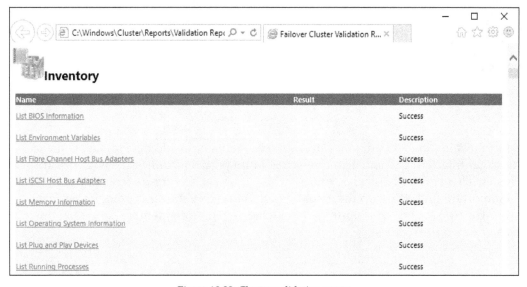

Figure 12.22: Cluster validation report

Remember, you can rerun the validation processes at any time to test your configuration using the **Validate Configuration...** task inside Failover Cluster Manager.

Running the Create Cluster wizard

The validation phase might take a while if you have multiple results that need fixing before you can proceed. But once your validation check comes back clean, you are ready to build out the cluster. For this, click on the next action that we have available in our Failover Cluster Manager console: **Create Cluster....**

Once again, we must first specify which servers we want to be part of this new cluster, so I am going to input my WEB1 and WEB2 servers. After this, we don't have a whole lot of information to input about setting up the cluster, but one very key piece of information is on the **Access Point for Administering the Cluster** screen. This is where you identify the unique name that will be used by the cluster and shared among the member servers. This is known as a **Cluster Name Object** (**CNO**), and after completing your cluster configuration, you will see this name show up as an object inside AD:

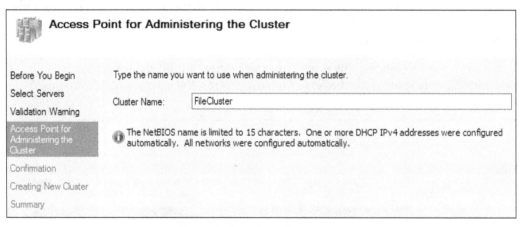

Figure 12.23: Setting a cluster name

After finishing the wizard, you can see the new cluster inside the Failover Cluster Manager interface and can drill down into more particular functions within that cluster. There are additional actions for things such as **Configure Role...**, which will be important for setting up the actual function that this cluster is going to perform, and **Add Node...**, which is your spot to include even more member servers in this cluster down the road:

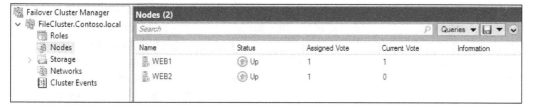

Figure 12.24: Viewing nodes in our first cluster

Clustering improvements in Windows Server 2019

The clustering feature has been around for a while but is continually being improved. There have been some big changes and additions to failover clustering in the two latest LTSC releases, Server 2016 and Server 2019. Some of the changes that we will discuss were originally introduced in 2016, so they are not brand new, but are still relevant to the way that we handle clusters in Server 2019 so they are worth mentioning here.

True two-node clusters with USB witnesses

When configuring quorum for a failover cluster, prior to Server 2019, a two-node cluster required three servers, because the witness for quorum needed to reside on a witness share of some kind, usually a separate file server.

Starting in 2019, that witness can now be a simple USB drive, and it doesn't even have to be plugged into a Windows Server! There are many pieces of networking equipment (switches, routers, and so on) that can accept USB-based file storage media, and a USB stick plugged into such a networking device is now sufficient to meet the requirements for a cluster witness. This is a win for enhanced clustering in small environments.

Higher security for clusters

A number of security improvements have been made to failover clustering in Windows Server 2019. Previous versions relied on **New Technology LAN Manager (NTLM)** for authentication of intra-cluster traffic, but many companies are taking proactive steps to disable the use of NTLM (at least the early versions) within their networks. Failover clustering can now do intra-cluster communication using Kerberos and certificates for validation of that networking traffic, removing the requirement for NTLM.

Another security/stability check that has been implemented when establishing a failover cluster file share witness is the blocking of witnesses stored inside DFS. Creating a witness inside a DFS share has never been supported, but the console previously allowed you to do so, which meant that some companies did exactly this, and paid the price for it as this can cause cluster stability issues. The cluster-management tools have been updated to check for the existence of a DFS namespace when creating a witness and will no longer allow it to happen.

Multi-site clustering

Can I configure failover clustering across subnets? In other words, if I have a primary datacenter and I also rent space from a CoLo down the road, or I have another datacenter across the country, *are there options for me to set up clustering between nodes that are physically separate?* There's a quick, easy answer here: yes, failover clustering doesn't care! Just as easily as if those server nodes were sitting right next to each other, clustering can take advantage of multiple sites that each host their own clustered nodes and move services back and forth across these sites.

Cross-domain or workgroup clustering

Historically, we were only able to establish failover clustering between nodes that were joined to the same domain. Windows Server 2016 brought the ability to move outside of this limitation, and we can even build a cluster without Active Directory being in the mix at all. In Server 2016 and 2019, you can, of course, still create clusters where all nodes are joined to the same domain, and we expect this will be the majority of installations out there. However, if you have servers that are joined to different domains, you can now establish clustering between those nodes. Furthermore, member servers in a cluster can now be members of a workgroup and don't need to be joined to a domain at all.

While this expands the available capabilities of failover clustering, it also comes with a couple of limitations. When using multi-domain or workgroup clusters, you will be limited to PowerShell as your cluster-management interface. If you are accustomed to interacting with your clusters from one of the GUI tools, you will need to adjust your thinking cap on this. You will also need to create a local user account that can be used by clustering and provision it to each of the cluster nodes, and this user account needs to have administrative rights on those servers.

Migrating cross-domain clusters

Although establishing clusters across multiple domains has been possible for a few years, migrating clusters from one AD domain to another was not an option. Starting with Server 2019, this has changed. We have more flexibility in multi-domain clustering, including the ability to migrate clusters between those domains. This capability will help administrators navigate company acquisitions and domain-consolidation projects.

Cluster operating system rolling upgrades

This new capability given to us in 2016 has a strange name but is a really cool feature. It's something designed to help those who have been using failover clustering for a while be able to improve their environment. If you are running a cluster currently, and that cluster is Windows Server 2012 R2, this is definitely something to look into. Cluster Operating System Rolling Upgrade enables you to upgrade the operating systems of your cluster nodes from Server 2012 R2 to Server 2016, and then to Server 2019, *without downtime*. There's no need to stop any of the services on your Hyper-V or SOFS workloads that are using clustering; you simply utilize this rolling upgrade process and all of your cluster nodes will run the newer version of Windows Server. The cluster is still online and active, and nobody knows that it even happened. Except you, of course.

This is vastly different from the previous upgrade process, where in order to bring your cluster up to Server 2012 R2, you needed to take the cluster offline, introduce new server nodes running 2012 R2, and then re-establish the cluster. There was plenty of downtime and plenty of headaches in making sure that it went as smoothly as possible.

The trick that makes this seamless upgrade possible is that the cluster itself remains running at the 2012 R2 functional level until you issue a command to flip it over to the Server 2016 functional level. Until you issue that command, clustering runs on the older functional level, even on the new nodes that you introduce, which are running the Server 2016 operating system. As you upgrade your nodes one at a time, the other nodes that are still active in the cluster remain online and continue servicing the users and applications, so all systems are running as normal from a workload perspective. As you introduce new Server 2016 boxes into the cluster, they start servicing workloads like the 2012 R2 servers, doing so at a 2012 R2 functional level. This is referred to as **mixed mode**. This enables you to take down even that very last 2012 R2 box, change it over to 2016, and reintroduce it, all without anybody knowing. Then, once all of the OS upgrades are complete, issue the Update-ClusterFunctionalLevel PowerShell command to flip over the functional level, and you have a Windows Server 2016 cluster that has been seamlessly upgraded with zero downtime.

Virtual machine resiliency

As you can successfully infer from the name, **virtual machine resiliency** is an improvement in clustering that specifically benefits Hyper-V server clusters. In the clustering days of Server 2012 R2, it wasn't uncommon to have some intra-array, or intra-cluster, communication problems. These sometimes represented themselves as transient failures, meaning that the cluster thought a node was going offline when it actually wasn't, and would set into motion a failover that sometimes caused more downtime than if the recognition patterns for a real failure would have simply been a little bit better in the first place. For the most part, clustering and the failover of cluster nodes worked successfully, but there is always room for improvement. That is what virtual machine resiliency is all about. You can now configure options for resiliency, giving you the ability to more specifically define what behavior your nodes will take during cluster-node failures. You can define things such as **resiliency level**, which tells the cluster how to handle failures. You also set your own **resiliency period**, which is the amount of time that VMs are allowed to run in an isolated state.

Another change is that unhealthy cluster nodes are now placed into quarantine for an admin-defined amount of time. They are not allowed to rejoin the cluster until they have been identified as healthy and have waited out their time period, preventing situations such as a node that was stuck in a reboot cycle inadvertently rejoining the cluster and causing continuous problems as it cycles up and down.

Storage Replica (SR)

SR is a new way to synchronize data between servers. It is a data-replication technology that provides the ability for block-level data replication between servers, even across different physical sites. SR is a type of redundancy that we hadn't seen in a Microsoft platform prior to Windows Server 2016; in the past, we had to rely on third-party tools for this kind of capability. SR is also important to discuss on the heels of failover clustering because SR is the secret sauce that enables multi-site failover clustering to happen. When you want to host cluster nodes in multiple physical locations, you need a way to make sure that the data used by those cluster nodes is synced continuously, so that a failover is actually possible. This data flow is provided by SR.

One of the neat data points about SR is that it finally allows a single-vendor solution, that vendor being Microsoft of course, to provide the end-to-end technology and software for storage and clustering. It is also hardware-agnostic, giving you the ability to utilize your own preference for storage media.

SR is meant to be tightly integrated and one of the supporting technologies of a solid failover clustering environment. In fact, the graphical management interface for SR is located inside the Failover Cluster Manager software – but is of course also configurable through PowerShell – so make sure that you take a look into failover clustering and Storage Replica as a *better together* story for your environment.

Storage Replica is now available inside Server 2019 Standard edition! (Previously, it required Datacenter edition, which was prohibitive to some implementations.) Administration of SR is also now available inside the new **Windows Admin Center (WAC)**. Let's put together a Storage Replica environment, so you can see how quick and easy it is to create storage redundancy.

Configuring Storage Replica

I have created two new servers in my lab, with the intention of turning them into redundant file servers via SR. These servers are called FS01 and FS02 and are joined to my domain, and there are a few important things I have done with them:

- Attached a new disk to be used for data storage. Windows is running on a normal virtual disk on my server, but I added a second one that will be dedicated to storage. The important part here is that the data disk must be initialized with GPT.

- Created a volume to contain data. This volume in Windows is labeled as the S: drive, and once again I am just making sure that this data volume resides on a GPT-initialized disk.

- Created a separate volume to contain SR logging data. When creating the SR replication set shortly, we will need to define a location for keeping SR logs, and it is easiest to do so on its own drive letter. I have called mine the L: drive. It also resides on my GPT-initialized data disk. The volume used for logs must be a minimum of 9GB.

- Installed the **Storage Replica** feature inside Windows, on both servers.

Initializing disks as GPT

If you're not familiar with the process stated above to initialize your new data disk as GPT, let's cover that for a minute. After attaching a new disk to your server, right-click on the **Start** Button and head into **Disk Management**. This tool should automatically recognize the new disk and ask whether you want to initialize it using MBR or GPT. Make sure to select **GPT** here:

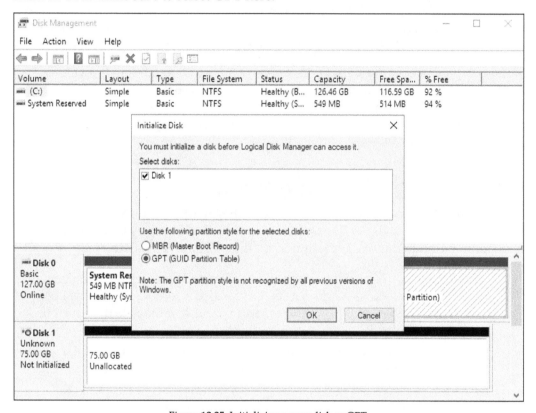

Figure 12.25: Initializing a new disk as GPT

Testing preparedness for Storage Replica

We now have two file servers, each with a new GPT data disk that contains two new volumes. One will be used for SR data storage, and the other for SR logs. Here's a quick look at the volumes I have. They are set up exactly the same on both servers:

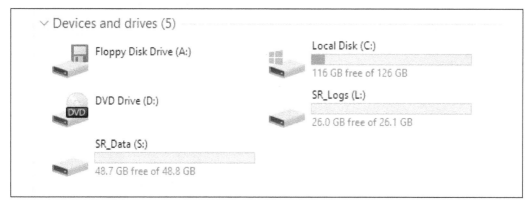

Figure 12.26: Volumes created on the servers

At this point, we could plow forward with creating the Storage Replica environment, and since these are brand new servers with identical configurations, it would most likely work. However, you will often be configuring SR on servers that have already been running in production for a while, or at least the primary file server where your source data is going to be located. Knowing whether or not SR is going to be successful would be comforting knowledge.

Thankfully, there is a testing process that SR can run before putting your configurations into place. Using PowerShell, let's issue a big long command from our primary FS01 server. The following is the command I am running. You will, of course, have to adjust it to accommodate your own server names and volume letters. As you can see at the end of the command, I specify for the output to be placed inside the C:\SR_TEST folder, so make sure that folder exists on your server:

```
Test-SRTopology -SourceComputerName FS01 -SourceVolumeName
S: -SourceLogVolumeName L: -DestinationComputerName FS02
-DestinationVolumeName S: -DestinationLogVolumeName L:
-DurationInMinutes 10 -ResultPath C:\SR_TEST\
```

This test will gather information about the servers and volumes and run some sample data transfers in the background for 10 minutes (as specified in the command). After completion, you will find a results file inside C:\SR_TEST that should launch in a web browser to show you all kinds of resulting information. Any issues with the environment that may hinder SR's ability to work will be detailed here so that you can go resolve those issues:

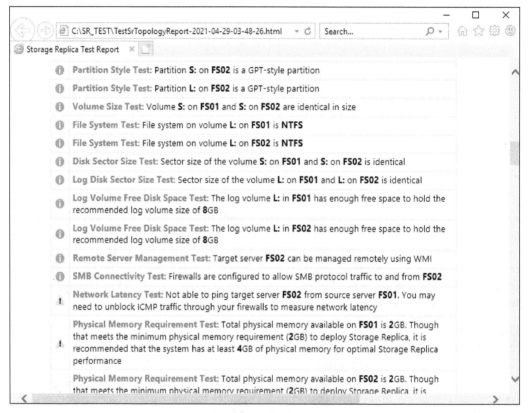

Figure 12.27: Storage Replica test report

You'll notice in *Figure 12.27* that I do have some warnings in my lab, which I did intentionally so that you had a visual of what the warnings look like. I never opened up ICMP traffic between these servers, so I received a warning about not being able to perform the network latency test. Also shown are some physical memory warnings. In a Storage Replica group, each server needs to have 2GB of RAM for SR to work properly, which is what I assigned to my VMs. While 2GB is required, 4GB is recommended, and the warnings are simply letting me know. In a production environment, you would never run a file server with even as little as 4GB of RAM, so you will likely not encounter these warnings during a real implementation.

Configuring Storage Replica

Now that our servers are prepped and tested, it's time to build the real deal! Since we have met all of our prerequisites and built out servers with SR in mind, all it takes is one PowerShell command to get this Storage Replica partnership started. I will list the command below, which is pretty self-explanatory. The only piece that may be slightly unfamiliar is `SourceRGName` and `DestinationRGName`. The "RG" stands for "Replication Group," which is simply a name you must define for the replication group on each server:

```
New-SRPartnership -SourceComputerName FS01 -SourceRGName RepGroup1
-SourceVolumeName S: -SourceLogVolumeName L: -DestinationComputerName
FS02 -DestinationRGName RepGroup2 -DestinationVolumeName S:
-DestinationLogVolumeName L:
```

Boom! Just like that, Storage Replica is configured with FS01's S: drive being primary storage, automatically and synchronously replicated to FS02's S: drive. Depending on performance and networking specs, the initial sync between volumes can take a bit of time, during which you will see **ReplicationState = InitialBlockCopy** in the results of the Get-SRGroup command, as you can see in *Figure 12.28*. Once the initial sync has completed, that field will instead show **ReplicationState = ContinuouslyReplicating**. Any data that is stored on FS01's S: drive is automatically replicated over to FS02:

```
PS C:\Users\administrator.CONTOSO> get-srgroup


AllowVolumeResize   : False
AsyncRPO            :
ComputerName        : FS01
Description         :
Id                  : 6acd8be2-6638-4008-9c02-2f1dbfbe32e7
IsAutoFailover      :
IsCluster           : False
IsEncrypted         : False
IsInPartnership     : True
IsMounted           : False
IsPrimary           : True
IsSuspended         : False
IsWriteConsistency  : False
LastInSyncTime      :
LogSizeInBytes      : 8589934592
LogVolume           : L:\
Name                : RepGroup1
NumOfReplicas       : 1
Partitions          : {d2d6afbc-3417-47c9-8421-7275dbf5eccb}
Replicas            : {MSFT_WvrReplica (PartitionId = "d2d6afbc-3417-47c9-8421-7275dbf5eccb")}
ReplicationMode     : Synchronous
ReplicationStatus   : InitialBlockCopy
TemporaryPath       :
PSComputerName      :
```

Figure 12.28: Details of our Storage Replica group

Shifting the primary server to FS02

After poking around on the file servers, you'll notice that you can see data on FS01's S: drive, but if you try to browse FS02's S: drive you are met with an error message. This is by design. You are unable to browse and see data on the destination SR server, unless you run another command to make it primary, such as in the event of a disaster recovery scenario. To prove that SR is really working, let's follow that step to make sure data is automatically replicating from FS01 to FS02.

I have created some sample text files on FS01's S: drive, but I am unable to verify that they exist on FS02. Let's pretend that FS01 has gone offline or is having some other kind of issue, and I need to make FS02 my new primary file server. All I need to do is run the following PowerShell command to flip roles, turning FS02 into the new primary SR partner:

```
Set-SRPartnership -NewSourceComputerName FS02 -SourceRGName RepGroup2
-DestinationComputerName FS01 -DestinationRGName RepGroup1
```

Immediately after running this command, I can now see and browse through the data on FS02's S: drive, which means that it is now the primary SR member, and also proves to me that SR was working in the first place:

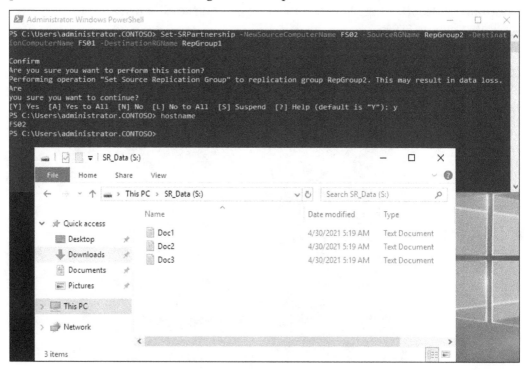

Figure 12.29: We have shifted the primary drive access to FS02

Storage Spaces Direct (S2D)

S2D is a clustering technology, but I list it here separate from general failover clustering because S2D is a core component of the **software-defined data center** (**SDDC**) and has had so much focus on improvements over the past few years that it really is in a category of its own.

In a nutshell, S2D is a way to build an extremely efficient and redundant centralized, network-based storage platform entirely from Windows Server. While serving the same general purpose (file storage) as a traditional NAS or SAN device, S2D takes an entirely different approach in that it does not require specialized hardware, nor special cables or connectivity between the nodes of the S2D cluster.

To build S2D, all you need are Windows Servers; the faster, the better, but they could be normal, everyday servers. These servers must be connected through networking, but there are no special requirements here; they simply all get connected to a network, just like any other server in your environment. Even more interesting, your servers don't even have to be exactly the same. You can mix servers from different manufacturers if you so desire! Once you have these servers running, you can utilize clustering technologies or WAC to bind these servers together into S2D arrays.

S2D is part of the overall **Hyper-Converged Infrastructure** (**HCI**) story and is a wonderful way to provide extremely fast and protected storage for anything, but especially for workloads such as clusters of Hyper-V servers. As you already know, when building a Hyper-V Server cluster, the nodes of that cluster must have access to shared storage upon which the virtual machine hard disk files will reside. S2D is the best way to provide that centralized storage.

S2D will take the hard drives inside your S2D cluster node servers and combine all of their space together into software-defined pools of storage. These storage pools are configured with caching capabilities, and even built-in fault tolerance. You obviously wouldn't want a single S2D node, or even a single hard drive going offline, to cause a hiccup in your S2D solution, and of course, Microsoft doesn't want that to happen either. So when you group servers and all of their hard drives together into these large pools of S2D storage, they are automatically configured with parity among those drives so that particular components going offline does not result in lost data or even the slowdown of the system.

S2D is the best storage platform for both SOFS and Hyper-V clusters.

While Server 2016-based S2D was configured mostly through PowerShell (which unfortunately means that a lot of administrators haven't tried it yet), Windows Server 2019 brings us the updated WAC toolset, which now includes built-in options for configuring an S2D environment:

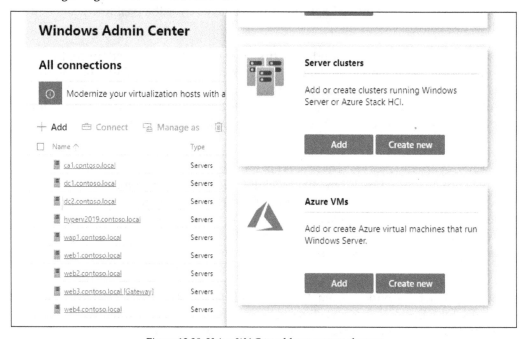

Windows Admin Center

All connections

ⓘ Modernize your virtualization hosts with a

╋ **Add**   Connect   Manage as   🗑

☐ Name ⌃   Type

🖥 ca1.contoso.local   Servers
🖥 dc1.contoso.local   Servers
🖥 dc2.contoso.local   Servers
🖥 hyperv2019.contoso.local   Servers
🖥 wap1.contoso.local   Servers
🖥 web1.contoso.local   Servers
🖥 web2.contoso.local   Servers
🖥 web3.contoso.local [Gateway]   Servers
🖥 web4.contoso.local   Servers

Server clusters

Add or create clusters running Windows Server or Azure Stack HCI.

[Add]   [Create new]

Azure VMs

Add or create Azure virtual machines that run Windows Server.

[Add]   [Create new]

Figure 12.30: Using WAC to add new server clusters

S2D is one of those technologies that warrants its own book, but anyone looking to try out or get started with this amazing storage technology should start at https://docs.microsoft.com/en-us/windows-server/storage/storage-spaces/storage-spaces-direct-overview.

New in Server 2019

For those of you already familiar with the concept of S2D who want to know what is new or different in the Server 2019 flavor, here are some of the improvements that have come with this latest version of the operating system:

- **Improved use of Resilient File System (ReFS) volumes**: We now have deduplication and compression functions on ReFS volumes hosted by S2D.

- **USB witness**: We already discussed this one. When using a witness to oversee an S2D cluster that is only two nodes, you can now utilize a USB key plugged into a piece of networking equipment, rather than running a third server for this witnessing purpose.

- **WAC**: WAC now includes tools and functionality for defining and managing S2D clusters. This will make adoption much easier for folks who are not overly familiar with PowerShell.

- **Improved capability**: We can now host four petabytes per cluster, compared to one petabyte in Server 2016. Keep in mind, though, that it is recommended to maintain a maximum of 400TB per server within the cluster.

- **Improved speed**: While S2D has been fast since the very first version, we have some efficiency improvements in Server 2019. At last year's Ignite conference, Microsoft showcased an 8-node S2D cluster that was capable of achieving 13,000,000 IOPS. Holy moly!

Summary

Redundancy is a critical component in the way that we plan infrastructure and build servers in today's world. Windows Server 2019 has some powerful capabilities built right into it that you can utilize in your own environments, starting today! I hope that by gleaning a little more information about both NLB and failover clustering, you will be able to expand the capabilities of your organization by employing these techniques and stretching the limits of your service uptime. Even for a small-medium business, there are some great replication options in Windows Server, made possible with a limited set of servers. You could use Storage Replica to replace many other third-party options that currently exist in these environments, giving you redundant file servers in a quick-and-easy fashion. For any enterprise-class organization that hasn't tested the waters with S2D yet, what's stopping you? Let's get serious about resiliency for your Hyper-V infrastructure. HCI will change the way that you work and give you some peace of mind that you didn't think was possible in a world aiming for 99.999% uptime.

Questions

1. Which technology is more appropriate for making web server traffic redundant – Network Load Balancing or failover clustering?

2. In Network Load Balancing, what do the acronyms DIP and VIP stand for?

3. What are the three NLB modes?

4. In Windows Server 2019, is Network Load Balancing a role or a feature?

5. What roles are most often used with failover clustering?

6. What type of small device can now be used as a cluster quorum witness (this is brand new as of Server 2019)?

7. True or False—Storage Spaces Direct requires the use of SSD hard drives.

13
Containers and Nano Server

Many of the new technologies included in Windows Server 2019 are designed to reflect capabilities provided by cloud computing, bringing your private clouds to life and granting you the ability to produce the same solutions given to you by public cloud providers within your physical infrastructure. The last few iterations of the Server operating system have also revolved around virtualization, and the idea of application containers is something that taps into both of these mindsets. Application containers will make the deployment of applications more streamlined, more secure, and more efficient. Containers are a relatively new idea in the Microsoft world, and outside of conversations about DevOps, I haven't heard many IT admins talking about them yet. This is something that has been enhancing Linux computing for a while now, and this newest Windows Server operating system brings it a little bit closer to home for us Microsoft-centric shops.

Application developers will be very interested in the application containers provided by Windows Server 2019, and in truth, they probably understand the concepts behind containers much better than a traditional server administrator. While the premise of this book is not focused on development opportunities and is clearly not focused on Linux, we are going to discuss containers because the benefits provided are not only for developers. We, as system operations, will also benefit from using containers, and if nothing else it is going to be important for us to know and understand how to conceptualize and how to spin up containers so that we can provide the infrastructure that our developers are going to require as they begin to build modern applications.

In this chapter, we will cover some topics dealing with application containers; specifically, the new capabilities that are available in Windows Server 2019 to bring this technology into our data centers:

- Understanding application containers
- Containers and Nano Server
- Windows Server containers versus Hyper-V containers
- Docker and Kubernetes
- Working with containers

Understanding application containers

What does it mean to *contain* an application? We have a pretty good concept these days of containing servers through virtualization. Taking physical hardware, turning it into a virtualization host-like Hyper-V, and then running many **virtual machines** (**VMs**) on top of it is a form of containment for those VMs. We are essentially tricking them into believing that they are their own entity, completely unaware that they are sharing resources and hardware with other VMs running on that host. Although we are sharing hardware resources, we can provide strong layers of isolation between VMs, because we need to make sure that access and permissions cannot bleed across VMs – particularly in a cloud provider scenario, as that would spell disaster.

Application containers are the same idea, at a different level. While VMs are all about virtualizing hardware, containers are more like virtualizing the operating system. Rather than creating VMs to host our applications, we can create containers, which are much smaller. We then run applications inside those containers, and the applications are tricked into thinking that they are running on top of a dedicated instance of the operating system.

A huge advantage of using containers is the unity that they bring to the development and operations teams. We hear the term DevOps all the time these days, which is a combination of development and operation processes working together to make the entire application rollout process more efficient. The utilization of containers is core to creating a successful DevOps mentality since developers can now do their job (developing applications) without needing to accommodate for the operations and infrastructure side of things. When the application is built, operations can take the container within which the application resides, and simply spin it up inside their container infrastructure, without any worries that the application is going to break servers or have compatibility problems.

I foresee containers taking the place of many virtual machines, but this will only happen if admins jump in and try it out for themselves. Let's discuss a few particular benefits that containers bring to the table.

Sharing resources

Just like when we are talking about hardware being split up among VMs, application containers mean that we are taking physical chunks of hardware and dividing them up among containers. This allows us to run many containers from the same server, be it a physical or virtual server.

However, in that alone, there is no benefit over VMs, because they simply share hardware as well. Where we really start to see benefits of using containers rather than separate VMs for all of our applications is that all of our containers can share the same base operating system. Not only are they spun up from the same base set, which makes it extremely fast to bring new containers online, it also means that they are sharing the same kernel resources. Every instance of an operating system has its own set of user processes. Often, it is a tricky business to run multiple applications together on servers because those applications traditionally have access to the same set of processes and have the potential to be negatively affected by those processes. In other words, it's the reason that we tend to spin up so many servers these days, keeping each application on its own server so that they can't negatively impact each other. Sometimes apps simply do not like to mix. The kernel in Windows Server 2019 has been enhanced so that it can handle multiple copies of the user-mode processes. This means you not only have the ability to run instances of the same application over many different servers but can also run many different applications, even if they don't typically like to coexist, on the same server.

Isolation

One of the huge benefits of application containers is that developers can build their applications within a container running on their own workstation! A host machine for hosting containers can be a Windows Server instance, or it can be a Windows 10 workstation. When built within this container sandbox, developers will know that their application contains all of the parts, pieces, and dependencies that it needs to run properly and that it runs in a way that doesn't require extra components from the underlying operating system. This means the developer can build the application, make sure it works in their local environment, and then easily slide that application container over to the hosting servers, where it will be spun up and ready for production use. That production server might be an on-premise container server that an IT admin has built, or it could even be a cloud-provided resource – the application doesn't care. The isolation of the container from the operating system helps to keep the application standardized in a way that it is easily mobile and movable, saving the developer time and headaches since they don't have to accommodate differences in underlying operating systems during the development process.

The other aspect of isolation is the security aspect. This is the same story as multiple virtual machines running on the same host, particularly in a cloud environment. You want security boundaries to exist between those machines, in fact, most of the time you do not want them to be aware of each other in any way. You even want isolation and separation between the virtual machines and the host operating system because you sure don't want your public cloud service provider snooping around inside your VMs. The same idea applies to application containers.

The processes running inside a container are not visible to the hosting operating system, even though you are consuming resources from that operating system. Containers maintain two different forms of isolation. There is namespace isolation, which means the containers are confined to their own filesystem and registry. Then there is also resource isolation, meaning that we can define what specific hardware resources are available to the different containers, and they are not able to steal from each other. Shortly, we will discuss two different categories of containers, Windows Server containers and Hyper-V containers. These two types of containers handle isolation in different ways, so stay tuned for more info on that topic.

We know that containers share resources and are spun up from the same base image, while still keeping their processes separated so that the underlying operating system can't negatively affect the application and also so that the application can't tank the host operating system. But how is the isolation handled from a networking aspect? Well, in the Windows Server world, application containers utilize technology from the Hyper-V virtual switch to keep everything straight on the networking side. In fact, as you start to use containers, you will quickly see that each container has a unique IP address assigned to it, helping to maintain network isolation.

Scalability

The combination of spinning up from the same base image and the isolation of the container makes a very compelling scalability and growth story. Think about a web application you host whose use might fluctuate greatly from day to day. Providing enough resources to sustain this application during busy times has traditionally meant overpaying for compute resources when that application is not being heavily used. Cloud technologies provide dynamic scaling for these modern kinds of applications, but they often do so by spinning up or down entire virtual machines. There are three common struggles with dynamically scaling applications like this. First is the time that it takes to produce additional virtual machines; even if that process is automated, your application may be overwhelmed for a period of time while additional resources are brought online. Our second challenge is the struggle that the developer needs to go through to make that application so agnostic that it doesn't care if there are inconsistencies between the different machines upon which their application might be running.

The third is cost – not only a hardware resource cost, as new VMs coming online will each be consuming an entire set of kernel resources, but monetary costs as well. Spinning virtual machines up and down in your cloud environment can quickly get expensive. These are all hurdles that do not exist when you utilize containers as your method for deploying applications.

Since application containers use the same underlying kernel and the same base image, their time to live is extremely fast. New containers can be spun up or down very quickly and in batches without having to wait for the boot and kernel mode processes to start. Also, since we have provided the developer this isolated container structure within which to build the application, we know that our application is going to be able to run successfully anywhere that we spin up one of these containers. No more worries about whether or not the new VM that is coming online will be standardized correctly, because containers for a particular application are always the same and contain all of the important dependencies that the application needs, right inside that container.

Containers and Nano Server

This topic wraps us back around to our discussion about Nano Server and why it has partially disappeared as a Windows Server installation option. Before discussing the purpose that Nano Server now serves, let's take a quick look at the structure of a Windows-based container. Here is a graphic similar to one from a public slide deck that was part of a Microsoft Ignite presentation:

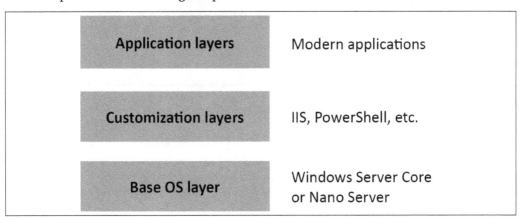

Figure 13.1: Layers of a Windows container

The lowest layer of a container is the base operating system. When spinning up a container, you need a base set of code and a kernel from which to build upon. This base operating system can be either Server Core or Nano Server.

The next layer of a container is the customization layer. This is where the technologies that will ultimately be used by your application reside. For example, our containers may include IIS for hosting a website, PowerShell, or even something such as .NET. Any of these toolsets reside in this layer.

Finally, the top slice of the container cake is the application layer. This, of course, is the specific app that you plan to host inside this container, which your users are accessing.

While Server Core is a great operating system for building small and efficient servers, it is still a heavyweight compared to Nano Server. Nano is so incredibly different, and so incredibly tiny, that it really isn't a comparison. You probably remember earlier where we installed Server Core and came out with a hard drive size of around 6 GB. While that is much smaller than a Desktop Experience version of Windows Server, think about this. A Nano Server base image can be less than 500 MB!

That is amazingly small. Additionally, updates to Nano Server are expected to be few and far between. This means you won't have to deal with monthly patching and updates on your application containers. In fact, since containers include all that they need to run the applications hosted on them, it is generally expected that when you need to update something about a container, you'll just go ahead and build out a new container image, rather than update existing ones. If Nano Server receives an update, just build out a new container, install and test the application on it, and roll out container instances based on the new image. Need to make some changes to the application itself? Rather than figuring out how to update the existing container image, it's quick and easy to build a new one, test it outside of your production environment, and once it is ready, simply start deploying and spinning up the new container image into production, letting the old version fall away.

Nano Server is now only used as a base operating system for containers. This is a major change since the release of Server 2016, when the scope that Nano was expected to provide was much larger. If you are utilizing Nano Server for workloads outside of container images, you need to start working on moving those workloads into more traditional servers, such as Server Core.

You may be wondering, "Why would anybody use Server Core as the base for a container image if Nano Server is available?" The easiest answer to that question is application compatibility. Nano Server is incredibly small, and as such it is obviously lacking much of the code that exists inside Server Core. When you start looking into utilizing containers to host your applications, it's a great idea to utilize the smaller Nano Server as a base *if possible*, but often your applications simply won't be able to run on that platform and in these cases, you will be using Server Core as the base operating system.

.NET applications can help to portray scenarios when one type of container may be used over another. If the app you are building is based on .NET Core, a Nano Server container image likely includes all of the needed dependencies to run that application. This will provide you the smallest possible footprint for your container and will run most efficiently. However, if you find yourself building an app that requires the full .NET framework, Nano Server won't cut it. You will have to change gears and utilize a Server Core container to bring your application to life.

Windows Server containers versus Hyper-V containers

When spinning up your containers, it is important to know that there are two categories of containers that you can run in Windows Server 2019. All aspects of application containers that we have been talking about so far apply to either Windows Server containers or to Hyper-V containers. Hyper-V containers can run the same code or images as Windows Server containers, while keeping their strong isolation guarantees to make sure the important stuff stays separated. The decision between using Windows Server containers or Hyper-V containers will likely boil down to what level of security you need your containers to maintain. Let's discuss the differences between the two so that you can better understand the choice you are facing.

Windows Server containers

In the same way that Linux containers share the host operating system kernel files, Windows Server containers make use of this sharing in order to make the containers efficient. What this means, however, is that while namespace, filesystem, and network isolation is in place to keep the containers separated from each other, there is some potential for vulnerability between the different Windows Server containers running on a host server. For example, if you were to log into the host operating system on your container server, you would be able to see the running processes of each container.

The container cannot see the host or other containers and is still isolated from the host in various ways, but knowing that the host can view the processes within the container shows us that some interaction does exist with this level of sharing. Windows Server containers are going to be most useful in circumstances where your container host server and the containers themselves are within the same *trust boundary*. In most cases, this means that Windows Server containers are going to be most useful for company-owned servers that only run containers owned and trusted by the company. If you trust both your host server and your containers and are okay with those entities trusting each other, deploying regular Windows Server containers is the most efficient use of your hardware resources.

Hyper-V containers

If you're looking for an increased amount of isolation and stronger boundaries, that is where you will foray into Hyper-V containers. Hyper-V containers are more like a super-optimized version of a VM. While kernel resources are still shared by Hyper-V containers, making them still much more performant than full VMs, each Hyper-V container gets its own dedicated Windows shell within which a single container can run. This means you have isolation between Hyper-V containers that is more on par with isolation between VMs, and yet are still able to spin up new containers at will and very quickly because the container infrastructure is still in place underneath. Hyper-V containers are going to be more useful in multi-tenant infrastructures, where you want to make sure no code or activity can be leaked between the container and host, or between two different containers that might be owned by different entities. Earlier, we discussed how the host operating system can see into the processes running within a Windows Server container, but this is not the case with Hyper-V containers. The host operating system is completely unaware of, and unable to tap into, those services running within the Hyper-V containers themselves. These processes are now invisible.

The availability of Hyper-V containers means that even if you have an application that must be strongly isolated, you no longer need to dedicate a full Hyper-V VM to this application. You can now spin up a Hyper-V container, run the application in that container, and have full isolation for the application, while continuing to share resources and provide a better, more scalable experience for that application.

Docker and Kubernetes

Docker is an open source project – a toolset, really – that was originally designed to assist with the running of containers on Linux operating systems. Wait a minute, what? The words **Linux** and **open source** written once again inside a Microsoft book! What is this world coming to? You see, containers are quickly becoming a big deal, and rightfully so. In Server 2016, Microsoft took some steps to start reinventing the container wheel, with the inclusion of PowerShell cmdlets that could be used to spin up and control containers running on your Windows Server, but the Docker platform has been growing at such a fast rate that Microsoft now expects that anyone who wants to run containers on their Windows machines is going to do so via the Docker toolset. If you want to utilize or even test containers in your environment, you'll need to get Docker for Windows to get started.

Docker is a container *platform*. This means that it provides the commands and tools needed to download, create, package, distribute, and run containers. Docker for Windows is fully supported to run on both Windows 10 and Windows Server 2019. By installing Docker for Windows, you acquire all of the tools needed to begin using containers to enhance your application's isolation and scalability.

Developers can use Docker to create an environment on their local workstation that mirrors a live server environment, so that they can develop applications within containers and be assured that they will actually run once those applications are moved to the server. Docker is the platform that provides pack, ship, and run capabilities for your developers. Once finished with development, the container package can be handed over to the system administrator, who spins up the container(s) that will be running the application, and deploys it accordingly. The developer doesn't know or care about the container host infrastructure, and the admin doesn't know or care about the development process or compatibility with their servers, because the application's dependencies live within the container.

Linux containers

There is a major update that is in ongoing development when discussing the capabilities that Windows Server 2019 possesses to interact with different kinds of containers. Earlier, in Server 2016, a Windows container host server could only run Windows-based containers because Windows Server containers share the kernel with the host operating system, so there was no way that you could spin up a Linux container on a Windows host.

Times are a-changin', and we now have some creative new capabilities in Server 2019 to handle scenarios such as Linux containers. While these features are still partly in preview and are being polished, there are some new options, called **Moby VM** and **LCOW**, that are going to enable Linux containers to run on a Windows Server container host, even running side by side with Windows containers!

One catch to running Linux containers on your Windows Server container host is that you must update to Docker Enterprise Edition Preview to do it. The Community Edition of Docker on Windows is currently unable to run Linux containers.

This is all new enough and still being built that more details are forthcoming, but visit this link to check the current status on these new capabilities if you're interested in running Linux containers: `https://docs.microsoft.com/en-us/virtualization/windowscontainers/deploy-containers/linux-containers`.

Docker Hub

When you work with containers, you are building container images that are usable on any server instance running the same host operating system – that is the essence of what containers enable you to do. When you spin up new instances of containers, you are just pulling new copies of that exact image, which is all-inclusive. This kind of standardized imaging mentality lends well to a shared community of images; a repository, so to speak, of images that people have built that might benefit others. Docker is open source, after all. Does such a sharing resource exist, one you can visit to grab container image files for testing, or even to upload images that you have created and share them with the world? Absolutely! It is called **Docker Hub** and is available at `https://hub.docker.com`.

Visit this site and create a login, and you immediately have access to thousands of container base images that the community has created and uploaded. This can be a quick way to get a lab up and running with containers, and many of these container images could even be used for production systems, running the applications that the folks here have pre-installed for you inside these container images. Or you can use Docker Hub to upload and store your own container images:

Figure 13.2: Docker Hub

You really should go ahead and create an account for Docker Hub now because if you want to follow along later in the chapter and try out implementing a container with Docker, you'll need a login to do it.

Docker Trusted Registry

If you're anything like me, you think the idea of Docker Hub is a great one: a neat place to store images and even to share them among the community. However, my next inclination is to look at this through an enterprise spyglass, which quickly turns my perspective from *neat* to *unsecured*. In other words, you may not be comfortable placing images in this public repository. Certainly not images that contain anything sensitive to your organization, anyway:

Figure 13.3: Docker Trusted Registry

Here is where **Docker Trusted Registry** may be something to look into. Docker Trusted Registry is a container image repository system, similar to Docker Hub, but it's something that you can contain within your network, behind your firewalls and security systems. This gives you a container-image repository system without the risk of sharing sensitive information with the rest of the world.

Kubernetes

While Docker is our primary interface for building and hosting containers, allowing us to create platforms within which we can host applications in this new and exciting way, the real magic comes after we are finished with the container's setup. Let's peek into the future a little and assume that you have an application now successfully hosted inside a container. This container can be spun up on a container host server in your environment or even slid over to an Azure container host very easily. This provides easy interaction with the infrastructure needed to seamlessly scale this application up or down, but there is a missing piece to this scalability: **orchestration**.

Kubernetes is a container orchestration solution. This means that Kubernetes orchestrates, or facilitates, how the containers run. It is the tool that enables many containers to run together, in harmony, as if they were one big application. If you intend to use containers to create scaling applications that can spin up new containers whenever additional resources are needed, you will absolutely need to have a container orchestrator, and Kubernetes is currently the best and most popular.

Microsoft recognized this popularity and has taken steps to ensure that Kubernetes is fully supported on Windows Server 2019.

As with any software, Kubernetes is not the only name in the game. Docker has its own orchestration platform, called Docker Swarm. While it might make sense that Docker and Docker Swarm would work together better than Docker and any other orchestrator, the numbers don't lie. A recent report shows that 82% of companies using scaling applications in the cloud are utilizing Kubernetes for their container orchestration.

As I mentioned earlier, tools such as containers, Docker, and Kubernetes are part of a cloud-first vision. While the use of containers for most companies is going to start onsite, using their own servers and infrastructure for the hosting of containers, this is a technology that is already capable of extending to the cloud. Because the containers themselves are so standardized and fluid – making them easy to expand and move around – sliding them into a cloud environment is easily done.

Working with containers

There are a lot of moving pieces that work together to make containers a reality in your environment, but it's not too difficult to get started. Let's walk through the initial setup of turning Windows Server 2019 into a container-running mega machine.

Installing the role and feature

The amount of work that you need to accomplish here depends on whether you want to run Windows Server containers, Hyper-V containers, or both. The primary feature that you need to make sure that you install is **Containers**, which can be installed by using either the **Add roles and features** link from inside Server Manager, or by issuing the following PowerShell command:

```
Add-WindowsFeature Containers
```

```
Administrator: Windows PowerShell                                    —    □    ×
Windows PowerShell
Copyright (C) Microsoft Corporation. All rights reserved.

PS C:\Users\Administrator> Add-WindowsFeature Containers

Success Restart Needed Exit Code        Feature Result
------- -------------- ---------        --------------
True    Yes            SuccessRest...   {Containers}
WARNING: You must restart this server to finish the installation process.


PS C:\Users\Administrator> _
```

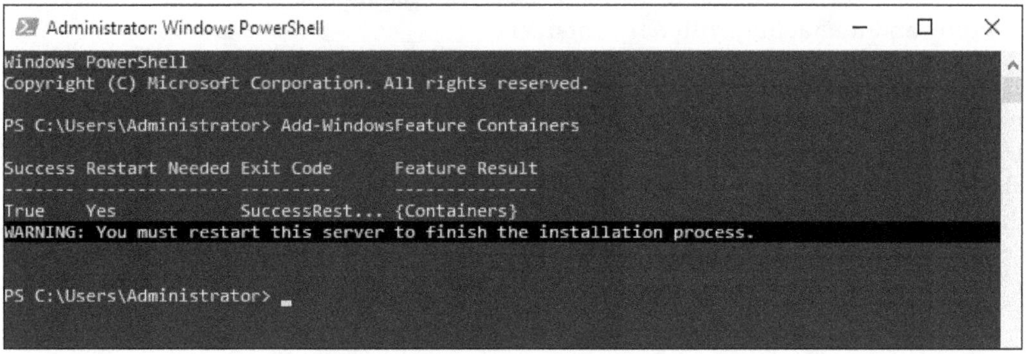

Figure 13.4: Installing the Containers feature

Additionally, if you intend to run Hyper-V containers, you need to ensure that the underlying Hyper-V components are also installed on your container host server. To do that, install the **Hyper-V role** and accompanying management tools onto this same server.

As indicated following the role and feature installation, make sure to restart your server after these changes.

At this point, you may be wondering, "If my container host server needs to have the Hyper-V role installed, doesn't that mean it must be a physical server? You can't install the Hyper-V role on a virtual machine, right?" *Wrong*. Windows Server 2019 supports something called **nested virtualization**, which was added for containers. You see, requiring physical hardware is becoming a limiting factor for IT departments these days, as almost everything is done from virtual machines. It makes sense that companies would want to deploy containers, but they may also want their container host servers to be VMs, with multiple containers being run within that VM. Therefore, nested virtualization was required to make this possible. If you are running a Windows Server 2019 physical hypervisor server and a Windows Server 2019 VM inside that server, you will now find that you can successfully install the Hyper-V role right onto that VM. I told you VMs were popular, so much so that they are now being used to run other VMs!

Remember that we can also host and run containers on our Windows 10 machines! To prep a Windows 10 client for this purpose, simply add the Windows feature called Containers, just like on the server operating system.

Installing Docker for Windows

Now that our container host server is prepped with the necessary Windows components, we need to grab Docker for Windows from the internet. The Docker interface is going to provide us with all of the commands that are needed to start building and interacting with our containers.

This is the point where that Docker Hub login becomes important. If you are working through this to test containers on your own workstation and need to install Docker Desktop for Windows on your Windows 10 *client*, the easiest way is to visit Docker Hub, log in, and search for the Docker client software. Here is a link to that software (this is the tool you need to use if you are installing on Windows 10): https://hub.docker.com/editions/community/docker-ce-desktop-windows.

However, since I am sitting on Windows Server 2019, my license for the server also includes licensing for Docker Enterprise, which can be pulled down without having to visit Docker Hub. If I open an elevated PowerShell prompt and run the following two commands, my server will reach out and grab Docker Enterprise, and install it onto my server:

```
Install-Module -Name DockerMsftProvider -Repository PSGallery -Force
Install-Package -Name docker -ProviderName DockerMsftProvider -Force
```

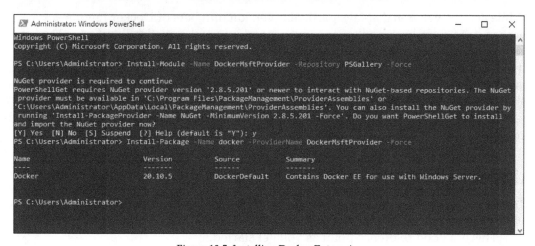

Figure 13.5: Installing Docker Enterprise

After package installation has finished, Docker is now configured on your server as a service, but that service needs to be started with the following command:

```
Start-Service docker
```

Docker commands

Once Docker is installed on your system, whether you are working with a Windows Server 2019 or a Windows 10 machine, you now have Docker Engine running on your machine, and it is ready to accept some commands to begin working with containers. If there is a single word to remember when it comes to working with containers, it is **Docker**. That is because every command that you issue to interact with containers will begin with the word *docker*. Let's have a look are some of the common commands that you will be working with.

docker version

Certain container images that you want to run may require particular versions of Docker Engine to be successful. When in doubt of what your current Docker environment is running, you can easily check over version numbers anytime by running `docker version`.

docker info

While `docker version` displays particular version numbers of Docker Engine, `docker info` steps back and gives some general info and statistics about your Docker container host server. Here you can see a Docker versioning number as well as the current Windows operating system version numbers, along with stats about the server itself such as allocated memory. Probably the most interesting numbers shown in the `docker info` output are counters for how many containers are on this server, with breakdowns as to how many of those containers are running, paused, or stopped.

docker --help

This is sort of like issuing *docker /?*, if that were a real command. The `help` function of Docker will generate a list of the possible Docker commands that are available to run. This is a good reference point as you get started.

docker images

After downloading some container images from a repository (we will do this for ourselves in the next section of this chapter), you can use the `docker images` command to view all of the images that are available on your local system.

docker search

Utilizing the `search` function allows you to search the container repositories (such as Docker Hub) for base container images that you might want to utilize in your environment. For example, to search and find images provided from inside Microsoft's Docker Hub repository, issue the following:

```
docker search Microsoft
```

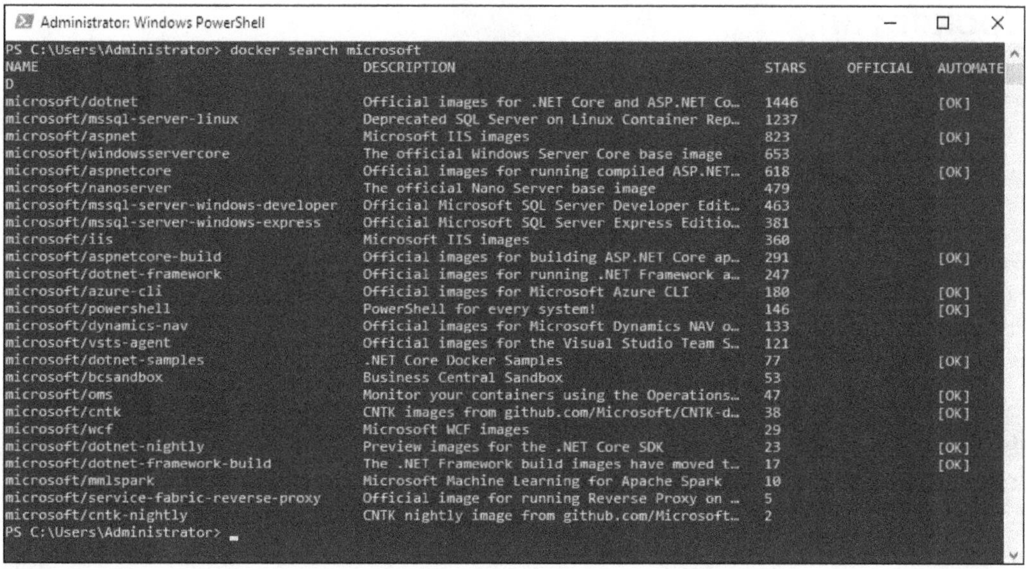

Figure 13.6: Searching the container repository

docker pull

We can use docker pull to pull down container images from online repositories. There are multiple repositories from which you can get container images. Most often, you will be working with images from Docker Hub, which is where we will pull a container image from shortly. However, there are other online repositories from which you can get container images, such as Microsoft's public container registry, known as MCR.

Here are some sample docker pull commands showing how to pull container images from Docker Hub, as well as MCR:

```
docker pull Microsoft/nanoserver
docker pull Microsoft/windowsservercore
docker image pull mcr.microsoft.com/windows/servercore:1809
docker image pull mcr.microsoft.com/windows/nanoserver:1809
```

docker run

This is the command for starting a new container from a base image. You will find that you can retain multiple container images in your local repository that are all based off the same container image. For example, as you add new things into your containers or update the application inside your containers, you may be building new container images that are now a subset of an existing container image. You may have numerous container images that are all named windowsservercore, for example. In this case, container tags become very important, as tags help you to distinguish between different versions of those container images. As an example, here is a command that would start a container based on a windowsservercore image for which I had associated the ltsc2019 tag:

```
docker run -it --rm Microsoft\windowsservercore:ltsc2019
```

In the preceding command, the -it switch creates a shell from which we can interact with a container, which is useful for building and testing containers, but you generally wouldn't need that switch for launching production containers that were 100% ready to serve up applications. --rm is a cleanup switch, meaning that once this particular container exits, the container and its filesystem will be automatically deleted.

docker ps -a

You utilize docker ps when you want to view the containers that are currently running on your system.

Downloading a container image

The first command we will run on our newly created container host is docker images, which shows us all of the container images that currently reside on our system; there are none:

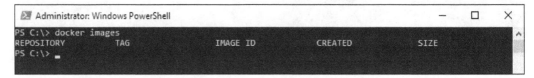

Figure 13.7: No current container images on our system

Of course there are no container images yet, as we haven't downloaded any. Let's grab a couple so that we can test this out. There is a sample container image file provided by the .NET team that showcases running a .NET application inside a Nano Server container—that one sounds like a fun way to get started with verifying that I can successfully run containers on this new host server.

First, we can use docker search to check the current container images that reside inside Microsoft's Docker Hub repository. Once we find the image that we want to download, we use docker pull to download it onto our server:

```
docker search microsoft
docker image pull microsoft/nanoserver
```

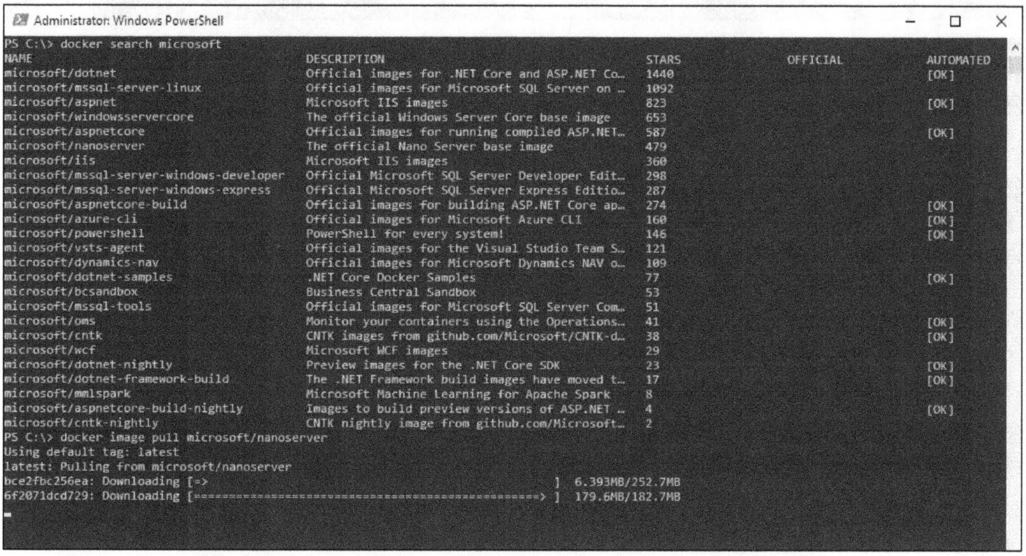

Figure 13.8: Using docker pull to grab a Nano Server container image

The preceding command downloaded a copy of the standard Nano Server base image, but we want to make our container do something in the end, so here is a command that will download that .NET sample image as well:

```
docker image pull microsoft/dotnet-samples:dotnetapp-nanoserver-1809
```

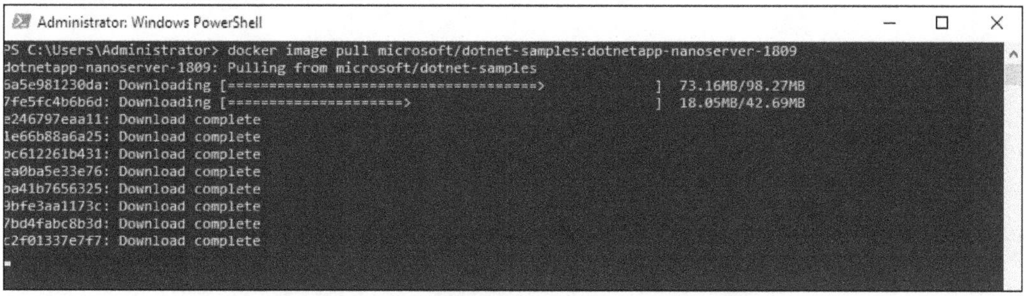

Figure 13.9: Downloading the .NET sample container image

After the downloads are finished, running docker images once again now shows us the newly available Nano Server container image, as well as the .NET sample image:

Figure 13.10: Local container image repository

From these base images, we are now able to launch and run a real container.

Running a container

We are so close to having a container running on our host! Now that we have installed the service, implemented Docker, imported the Docker module into our PowerShell prompt, and downloaded a base container image, we can finally issue a command to launch a container from that image. Let's run the .NET container that we downloaded before, with the following command:

```
docker run microsoft/dotnet-samples:dotnetapp-nanoserver-1809
```

The container starts and runs through its included code, and we see some fun output:

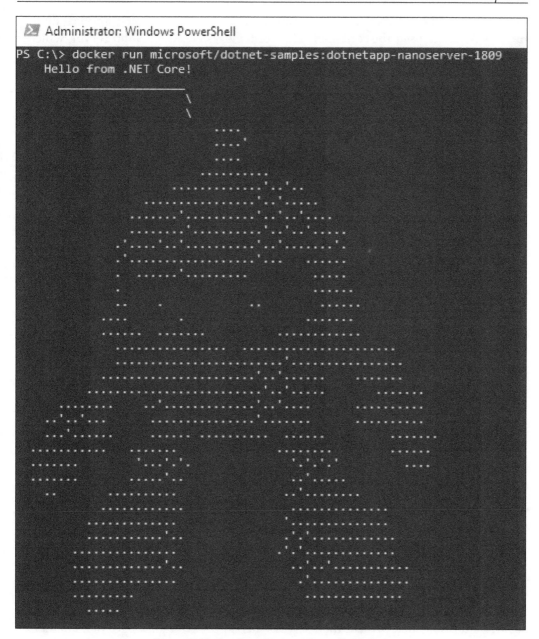

Figure 13.11: Our first container is up and running!

This container showcases that *all* components necessary for this .NET application to run are included *inside* the container. This container is based on Nano Server, which means it has an incredibly small footprint. In fact, looking back a few pages at the last docker images command that we ran, I can see that this container image is only 417 MB! What a resource saver, when compared with running this application on a traditional IIS web server.

The main resource for Microsoft documentation on containers is https://aka. ms/windowscontainers. The tools used to interact with containers are constantly changing, including changes to Docker and Kubernetes. Make sure to check over the Microsoft Docs site to find the latest best practices and approved installation path for preparing your container host servers.

Summary

Containers are revolutionizing the way that we build and host modern applications. By containerizing apps, we can run many more applications on each physical server, because they are capable of being fully isolated away from each other. Additionally, the container mentality allows the development of applications to happen in a much more fluid fashion. App developers can build their applications inside containers running on their own laptops, and once finished, simply hand them over to the infrastructure team to slide that container image onto a production container host server. That host server could be on premises, or even in the cloud. Orchestration tools such as Kubernetes can then be leveraged to scale that application, increasing or decreasing resource capacity and the number of necessary containers based on load or other factors. Usability of containers in the real world has been expanded greatly by the Docker project. The folks at Docker are clearly the front-runners in this space, enough that Microsoft has decided to incorporate the use of Docker – an open-source project developed by Linux! – straight into Windows Server 2019. We can now utilize both Docker Engine to run containers on our Windows servers, and the Docker client toolset to manage and manipulate containers inside Windows in the same way we work with containers in the Linux world.

Linux containers and Windows Server containers have a lot in common, and function in essentially the same way. Microsoft's ingenious idea to create an additional scope of container, the Hyper-V container, brings a solid answer to a lot of common security questions that present themselves when approaching the idea of containers in general. Everyone uses virtual machines heavily these days; I don't think anybody can disagree with that. Assuming the use of containers evolves into something that is easy to implement and administer, I foresee Hyper-V containers replacing many of our existing Hyper-V virtual machines in the coming years. This will save time, money, and server space.

Speaking of Hyper-V, it has become such an integral part of so many of our corporate networks today. In the next chapter, we will learn more about this amazing virtualization technology.

Questions

1. A Windows Server container can run a base OS that is one of two different types. What are they?

2. Compared to a Windows Server container, what type of container provides even greater levels of isolation?

3. True or False—In Windows Server 2016, you could run both Windows and Linux containers on the same Windows Server host platform.

4. What is the Docker command to see a list of container images on your local system?

5. What is currently the most popular container orchestration software that integrates with Windows Server 2019?

6. True or False—Developers can install Docker onto their Windows 10 workstations to start building applications inside containers.

14

Hyper-V

I've always been a country boy. Driving along dirt roads, working on cars, and hunting tend to fill my free time. Traveling to cities, and particularly a recent trip to Hong Kong, always hits me with a bit of culture shock. All those skyscrapers and tall apartment buildings serve an important purpose though, and serve to fulfill my metaphor: if there isn't enough land to grow outward, you have to build up. The vertical ascension of large cities is similar to what we have seen happening in our datacenters over the past decade. Cities need more and more places for people and businesses, just like we need to house more and more servers every year. Rather than horizontal expansion, with enormous server rooms filled with racks and racks of hardware, we are embracing the skyscraper mentality and virtualizing everything. We build considerably fewer servers but make them incredibly powerful. Then, on top of these supercomputers, we can run dozens, if not hundreds, of virtual servers. The technology that provides this hypervisor layer, the ability to run **Virtual Machines (VMs)** in Microsoft-centric shops, is the **Hyper-V** role in Windows Server. This is one of the most critical roles to understand as a server administrator because if your organization is not yet making use of server virtualization, then trust me when I say that it will be soon. Virtualization is the way of the future. The following are some topics we are going to explore so that you can become familiar with the virtualization capabilities provided by Microsoft in Windows Server 2019:

- Designing and implementing your Hyper-V Server
- Using virtual switches
- Implementing a new virtual server
- Managing a virtual server
- Shielded VMs

- Integrating with Linux
- **Resilient Filesystem (ReFS)** deduplication
- Hyper-V Server 2019

Designing and implementing your Hyper-V Server

Creating your own Hyper-V Server is usually pretty simple: build a server, install the Hyper-V role, and you're ready to get started. In fact, you can even install the Hyper-V role on a Windows 10 Pro or Enterprise computer, if you need to run some virtual machines from your own desktop. While most hardware that is being created these days fully supports the idea of being a hypervisor provider, some of you may try installing the Hyper-V role only to end up with the following error message:

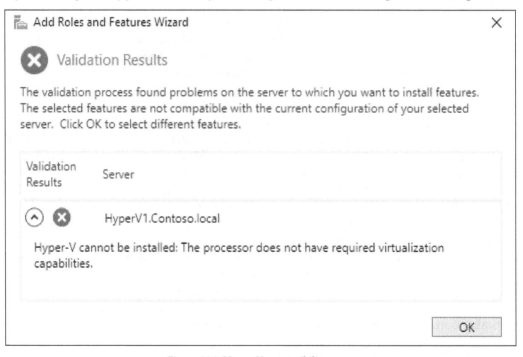

Figure 14.1: Hyper-V compatibility error

Uh oh, that's not good. This means one of two things: either my CPU really doesn't support virtualization, or I simply have some settings turned off inside the BIOS on my server that prevent this from working. There are three considerations you should check on your server to make sure it is ready to run Hyper-V. First, you need to be running an x64-based processor. This is kind of a given since Windows Server 2019 only comes in 64-bit anyway. If you don't have an x64 processor, you're not going to be able to install the operating system in the first place. Second, your CPUs need to be capable of hardware-assisted virtualization. This is typically called either **Intel Virtualization Technology (Intel VT)** or **AMD Virtualization (AMD-V)**. And last but not least, you must have **Data Execution Prevention (DEP)** available and enabled on your system. If you have investigated the hardware itself and it seems to be virtualization-capable, but it's still not working, it is likely that you have DEP currently disabled inside the BIOS of that system. Boot into the BIOS settings and enable DEP along with any other more-user-friendly-named settings that might indicate they are currently blocking your ability to run virtual machines.

As long as your processors are happy to run virtual machines, you can turn just about any size of hardware into a hypervisor by installing the Hyper-V role. It is not important to think about *minimum* system requirements because you want your system hardware to be as large as possible in a Hyper-V Server. The more CPU cores, RAM, and hard drive space you can provide, the more VMs you will be able to run. Even the smallest Hyper-V Servers I have seen in production environments are running hardware such as dual Xeon processors, 96 GB of RAM, and many terabytes of storage space. While 96 GB of RAM may seem like a lot for a single system, if your standard workload server build includes 8 GB of RAM, which is a pretty low number, and you want to run 12 servers on your Hyper-V Server, you are already beyond the capabilities of a Hyper-V Server with only 96 GB of RAM. 8 times 12 is 96, and you haven't left any memory for the host operating system to use! So *the moral of the story?* Go big or go home!

Installing the Hyper-V role

Hyper-V is just another role in Windows Server 2019, but during the installation of that role, you will be asked a few questions and it is important to understand what they are asking so that you can be sure your new Hyper-V Server is built to last and to work in an efficient manner. First of all, you will need to have Windows Server 2019 already installed, and use the **Add roles and features** function in order to install the role called **Hyper-V**:

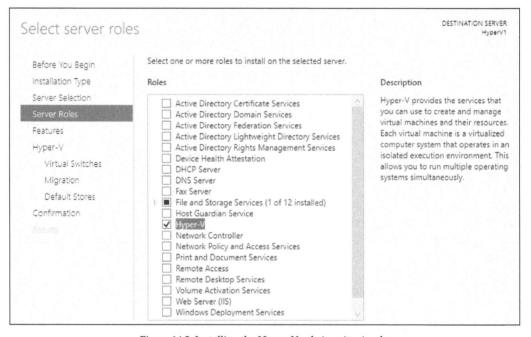

Figure 14.2: Installing the Hyper-V role is quite simple

As you continue working through the wizard to install the role, you'll come across a screen labeled **Create Virtual Switches**. We will discuss networking in Hyper-V a little bit more in the next section, but what is important here is that you get to define which of your server's physical NICs will be tied into Hyper-V and available for your virtual machines to use. It is a good idea for each Hyper-V Server to have multiple NICs. You want one NIC dedicated to the host itself, which you would not select on this screen. Leave that one alone for the hypervisor's own communications. In addition to that NIC, you will want at least one network card that can bridge the VMs into the corporate network. This one you would select, as you can see in *Figure 14.3*. If you will be hosting many different VMs on this server, and they need to be connected to different physical networks, you might have to install many different NICs on your Hyper-V Server:

Figure 14.3: Selecting the physical NICs that will be available for VMs to use

After defining NICs, we get to decide whether this Hyper-V Server will handle the live migration of VMs. Live VM migration is the ability to move a VM from one Hyper-V host to another without any interruption of service on that VM. As you can see in *Figure 14.4*, there are a couple of different ways you can set up the server to prepare it for handling live migrations, and take note of the text at the bottom that is telling you to leave this option alone for now if you plan to make this Hyper-V Server part of a cluster. In clustered environments, these settings are handled at a different layer:

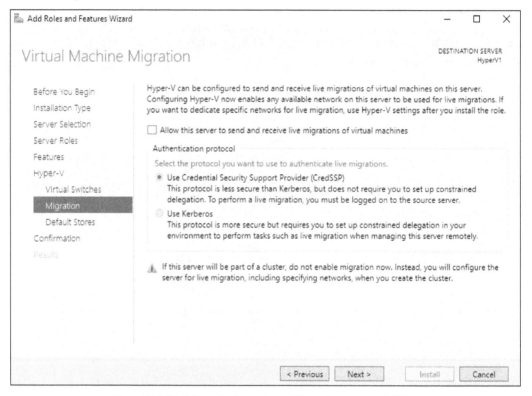

Figure 14.4: Deciding whether you need live migration capabilities

The last screen that I want to point out is the definition of storage locations for your VM data. After creating VMs and digging into what they look like at the hard-disk level (looking at the actual files that are created per VM), you will see that there are two key aspects to a VM: the virtual hard-disk file (**VHD** or VHDX) and a folder that contains the configuration files for that VM.

As you can see in *Figure 14.5*, the default locations for storing these items are something you would expect to see in a client application you were installing on a laptop, but you wouldn't expect something as heavy as Hyper-V to be storing its core files in a shared-user Documents folder. I suppose since Microsoft doesn't know the configuration of your server, it can't make any real guesses as to where you want to really store that data, and so it sets the default to be something that would work technically but should probably be changed as a matter of best practice. Many Hyper-V Servers will have dedicated storage, even if only a separate hard disk, on which these files are planned to be stored. Make sure you take a minute on this screen and change the default storage locations of your VM files:

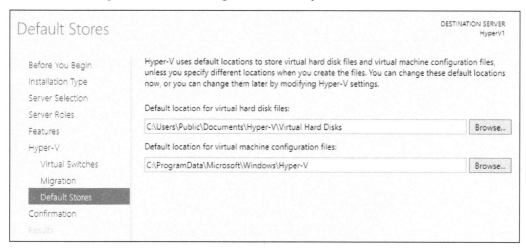

Figure 14.5: Defining default storage locations for VM files

 Remember that the version of Windows Server 2019 you are running determines how many VMs you will be able to run on top of this host. Server 2019 Standard limits you to running two VMs, while the Datacenter edition gives you access to launch as many as you can fit on the hardware.

Using virtual switches

Upon completion of the Hyper-V role installation, your first inclination may be to jump right in and start creating VMs, but you should really take a minute to make sure that the networking capabilities of your Hyper-V Server are adequate to meet your needs. During the role-installation process, we selected the physical NICs that are to be passed through into Hyper-V, and that screen told us it was going to establish a virtual switch for each of these NICs. But *what does that look like inside the console?* And *what options do we have for establishing networking between our virtual machines?*

To answer these questions, we need to open up the management interface for Hyper-V. As with any administrative tool of a Windows role, check inside the **Tools** menu of Server Manager, and now that the role has been installed, you will see a new listing for **Hyper-V Manager**. Launch that, and we are now looking at the primary platform from which you will be managing and manipulating every aspect of your Hyper-V environment:

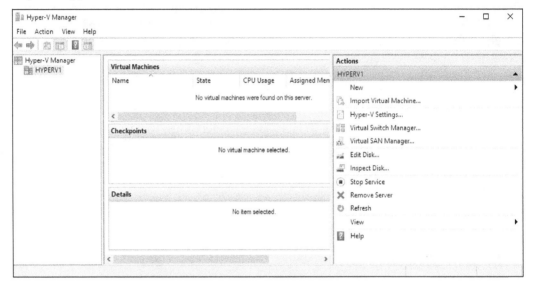

Figure 14.6: First look at Hyper-V Manager

We currently have a lot of blank space in this console because we don't have any VMs running yet. Over on the right side of **Hyper-V Manager**, you can see a link that says **Virtual Switch Manager...**. Go ahead and click on that link to be taken into the settings for our virtual switches and networking:

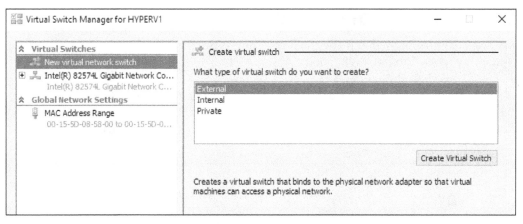

Figure 14.7: Managing virtual switches inside Hyper-V

Toward the left, you see a list of current **Virtual Switches**. On my server, there is only one switch listed there at the moment, which is named after the physical NIC to which it is connected. This is the virtual switch that the role-installation process created for us when we selected the NIC to be included with Hyper-V. If you selected multiple NICs during the role installation, you will have multiple virtual switches available here, each corresponding to a single physical NIC. Every VM you create will have one or more virtual NICs, and you will see shortly that you can choose where each of those virtual NICs gets connected. If there are five different physical networks that your VMs might need to contact, you can use five physical NICs in the Hyper-V Server, plug each one into a different network, and then have five virtual switches here in the console your VM NICs can be *plugged* into.

As you can see in *Figure 14.7*, we have a button named **Create Virtual Switch**, which is self-explanatory. Obviously, this is where we go to create new switches, but there are three different types of switches that you can create. Let's take just a minute to discuss the differences between them.

External virtual switch

The external virtual switch is the most common type to use for any VMs that need to contact a production network. Each external virtual switch binds to a physical NIC that is installed on the Hyper-V Server. If you click on an external virtual switch, you can see that you have some options for configuring this switch and that you can even change a switch type. In the following screenshot, I have renamed my external virtual switch so that it is easier to identify when I decide to add additional NICs to this server in the future:

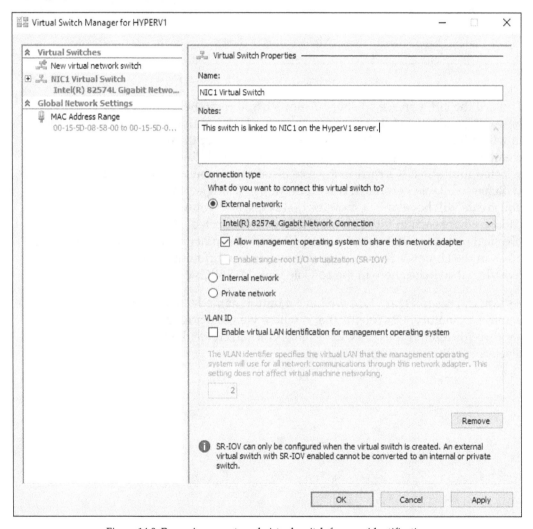

Figure 14.8: Renaming an external virtual switch for easy identification

Internal virtual switch

Internal virtual switches are not bound to a physical NIC, and so if you create an internal virtual switch and connect a VM to it, that virtual machine will not be able to contact a physical network outside the Hyper-V Server itself. It's sort of a middleman between the other two types of switches; using an internal virtual switch is useful when you want the VM traffic to remain within the Hyper-V environment but still provide network connectivity between the VMs and the Hyper-V host itself. In other words, VMs connected to an internal virtual switch can talk to each other and talk to the Hyper-V Server, but not beyond.

Private virtual switch

The private virtual switch is just what the name implies: private. VMs plugged into the same private virtual switch can communicate with each other, but not beyond. Even the Hyper-V host server does not have network connectivity to a private virtual switch. Test labs are a great example of a use case for private virtual switches, which we will discuss immediately following this section when we create a new virtual switch of our own.

Creating a new virtual switch

The following is an example I use often. I am running a new Hyper-V Server, which is connected physically to my corporate network, and so I can spin up new VMs, connect them to my external virtual switch, and have them communicate directly to the corporate network. This allows me to domain-join them and interact with them like I would any server on my network. Maybe I need to create some VMs that I want to talk with each other, but I do *not* want them to communicate with my production network. A good example of this scenario in the real world is when building a test lab. In fact, I am taking this exact approach for all of the servers that we have used throughout this book. My physical Hyper-V Server is on my production network, yet my entire Contoso.local network and all of the VMs running within it are on their own separate network, which is completely segregated from my real network. I did this by creating a new private virtual switch. Remember from the description that when you plug VMs into this kind of switch, they can communicate with other VMs that are plugged into that same virtual switch, but they cannot communicate beyond that switch.

Inside the **Virtual Switch Manager**, all I must do is choose the kind of virtual switch that I want to create, **Private** in this case, and click on that **Create Virtual Switch** button. I can then provide a name for my new switch, and I am immediately able to connect VMs to this switch. You can see in *Figure 14.9* that I have created two new private virtual switches: one to plug my test lab VM's internal NICs into and another switch that will act as my test lab's DMZ network:

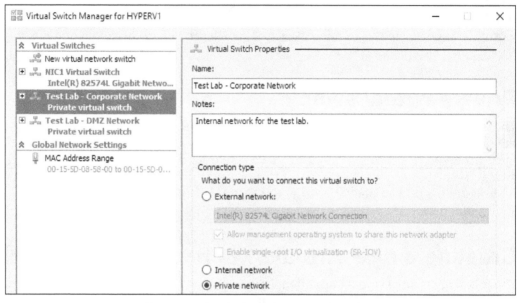

Figure 14.9: Creating new private virtual switches

Implementing a new virtual server

Now we are ready to spin up our first virtual server! Similar to creating new virtual switches, the process for creating a new VM is fairly straightforward, but there are some steps along the way that might need some explanation if you haven't been through this process before. We start in the same management interface from which we do everything in the Hyper-V world. Open up **Hyper-V Manager** and right-click on the name of your Hyper-V Server. Navigate to **New** | **Virtual Machine...** to launch the wizard:

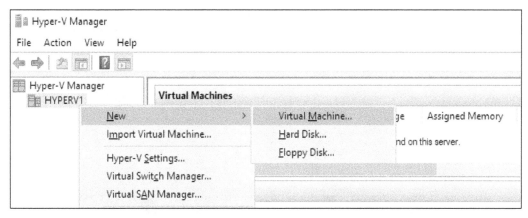

Figure 14.10: Creating a new Virtual Machine (VM)

The first screen where we need to make some decisions is **Specify Name and Location**. Create a name for your new VM, which is easy enough. Then you also have the chance to store your VM in a new location. If you set a good default location for your virtual machines during Hyper-V role installation, chances are that you won't have to modify this field. But in my case, I chose the default options when I installed the role, and so this wizard was going to place my VM somewhere inside C:\ProgramData, and I didn't like the look of that. So I selected the checkbox and chose a location that I like for my VM. You can see that I am using a dedicated disk to store my VMs, which is generally a good practice. An even better practice in a larger network would be to utilize resilient disk space that was accessed through the network, such as a Storage Spaces Direct infrastructure:

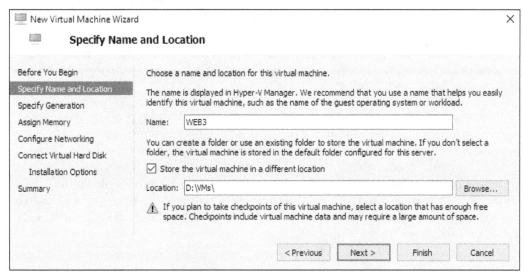

Figure 14.11: Specifying a storage location for a new VM

Next, you have to decide whether you are creating a **Generation 1** or **Generation 2** VM. We don't need to discuss this in very much detail, because explanations of the two are clearly stated on the page and in *Figure 14.12*. If your VM is going to be running an older operating system, you should likely go with **Generation 1** to ensure compatibility. Alternatively, if you are planning for a recent operating system to be installed on this new VM, selecting **Generation 2** is probably in your best interests from a new features and security perspective:

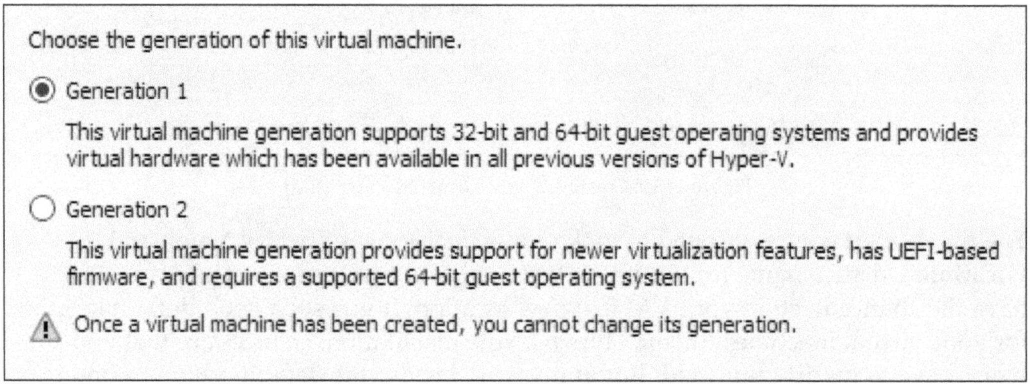

Choose the generation of this virtual machine.

⦿ Generation 1

This virtual machine generation supports 32-bit and 64-bit guest operating systems and provides virtual hardware which has been available in all previous versions of Hyper-V.

◯ Generation 2

This virtual machine generation provides support for newer virtualization features, has UEFI-based firmware, and requires a supported 64-bit guest operating system.

⚠ Once a virtual machine has been created, you cannot change its generation.

Figure 14.12: Each VM can be either Generation 1 or Generation 2

Now, define how much memory you want to assign to this particular VM. Keep in mind that this setting is adjustable in the future, so you don't have to plan too hard for this. The amount of RAM you dedicate to this virtual machine will depend on how much RAM you have available in the Hyper-V host system, and on how much memory is required to run whatever roles and services you plan to install on this VM. You can specify any amount of memory in this field. For example, if I wanted roughly 2 GB, I could type in 2,000 MB. However, what I find in the field is that most people still stick with the actual amount of MB, because that is what we have always done with hardware. So instead of rounding to 2,000, I am going to set my 2 GB VM to an actual 2 GB—or 2,048 MB.

Leaving the box unchecked for dynamic memory means that Hyper-V will dedicate 2,048 MB of its physically available RAM to this specific VM. Whether the VM is using 2,048 MB or 256 MB at any given time, the full 2,048 MB will be dedicated to the VM and will be unusable by the rest of the Hyper-V Server. If you select **Use Dynamic Memory for this virtual machine**, the VM only takes away from the Hyper-V host what it is actually using at any given moment. If you set it to 2,048 MB, but the VM is sitting idle and only consuming 256 MB, it will only tax Hyper-V with a 256 MB load:

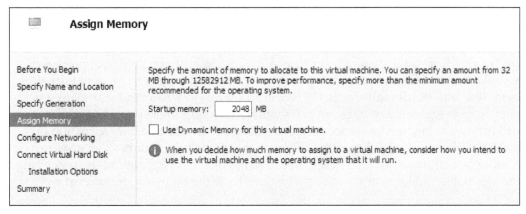

Figure 14.13: Defining memory allocation for the new VM

Configure Networking is the next screen we are presented with, and here we simply choose which virtual switch our VM's NIC gets plugged into. We do have the ability to add additional NICs to this VM later, but for now, we get a standard single NIC during the creation of our new VM, and we simply need to choose where it needs to be connected. For the time being, this new web server I am building will be connected to my Test Lab internal corporate network, so that I can build my web app and test it out, before introducing it into a real production network. If I drop down a list of available connections here, you will see that my original external virtual switch, as well as the two new private virtual switches that I created, are available to choose from:

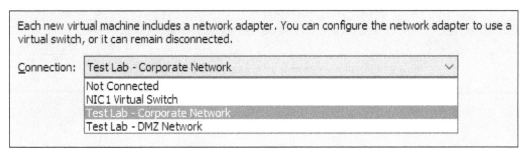

Figure 14.14: "Plug" the new VM into a virtual switch

A few details are also needed so that this new VM can have a hard drive. Most commonly, you will utilize the top option here so that the new VM gets a brand new hard drive. There are also options for using an existing virtual hard disk if you are booting from an existing file, or to attach a disk later if you aren't yet prepared to make this decision. We are going to allow the wizard to generate a new virtual hard disk, and the default size is 127 GB. I can set this to whatever I want, but it is important to know that it does not consume the full 127 GB of space. The disk size will only be as big as what is actually being used on the disk, so only a fraction of that 127 GB will be used. I mention this to point out that the number you specify here is more of a *maximum* size, so make sure to plan your disks appropriately, specifying enough size so that you and your applications have the necessary room to grow:

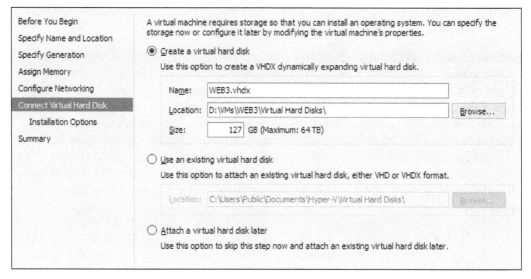

Figure 14.15: Allowing the wizard to create a new virtual hard disk

Our last screen of options in the wizard allows us to define the specifics of the operating system our new VM is going to run on. Or rather, where that operating system will be installed from. We are going to purposefully leave this set to **Install an operating system later**, because that is the default option, and it will give us the chance to see what happens when you do not specify any settings on this screen:

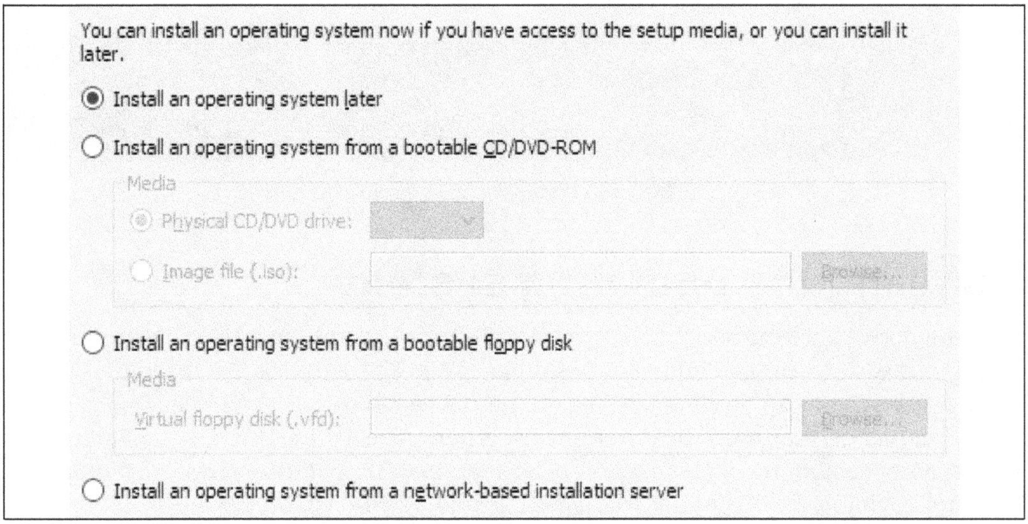

You can install an operating system now if you have access to the setup media, or you can install it later.

⦿ Install an operating system later

◯ Install an operating system from a bootable CD/DVD-ROM

   Media

   ⦿ Physical CD/DVD drive:

   ◯ Image file (.iso):   Browse...

◯ Install an operating system from a bootable floppy disk

   Media

   Virtual floppy disk (.vfd):   Browse...

◯ Install an operating system from a network-based installation server

Figure 14.16: Decisions to be made regarding operating system installation

Starting and connecting to the VM

We have now created a VM, which you can see inside the **Hyper-V Manager** console. Starting the VM is as simple as right-clicking on it, and then selecting **Start**. After selecting the option to start the VM, right-click on it again and click on **Connect....** This will open a console window from which you can watch the boot process of your new server:

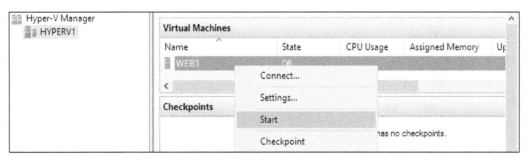

Figure 14.17: Starting our new virtual machine

Now that our new VM has been started, *what can we expect to see inside the console window?* A boot failure error, of course:

Figure 14.18: The initial start of this VM was not so successful

Installing the operating system

We get a boot failure message because we didn't specify any operating system media during our wizard, and so Hyper-V has created our VM and our new hard disk, but just like when you build a new server out of fresh hardware, you need software to be installed on that hard disk in order for it to do something. Luckily, installing an operating system on a VM is even easier than installing it on a physical server. Heading back into the **Hyper-V Manager** console, right-click on the name of your new VM and go to **Settings....**

Inside **Settings**, you will see that this VM has a **DVD Drive** automatically listed in **IDE Controller 1**. If you click on **DVD Drive**, you can easily tell it to mount any ISO to that drive. Copy the ISO file of the operating system installer you wish to run onto the hard drive of your Hyper-V Server.

I typically place all of my ISOs inside a dedicated folder called ISOs, right alongside my VMs folder, and then **Browse...** to it from this screen. Connecting an ISO to your VM is the same as if you were plugging a physical installation DVD into a physical server:

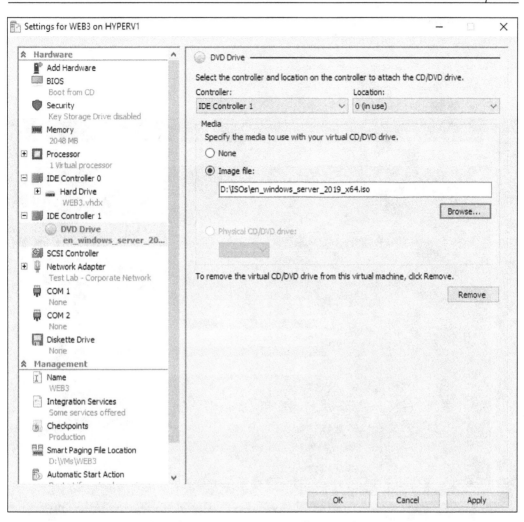

Figure 14.19: Providing operating system installation media to our new VM

After mounting the media, restart the VM and you will see that our operating system installer kicks off automatically:

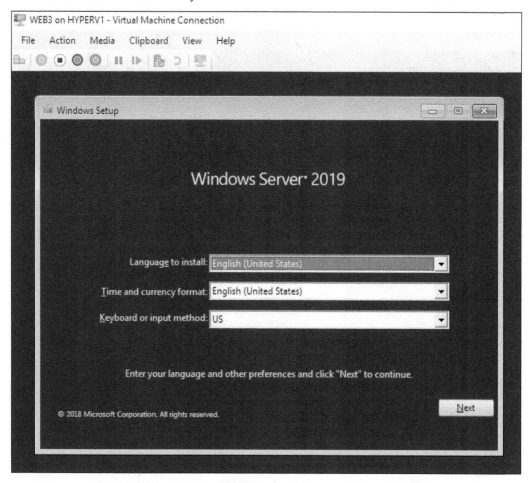

Figure 14.20: The VM is now booting to the installation ISO

Managing a virtual server

We have made use of **Hyper-V Manager** to manage our virtual switches and to create a virtual machine. This tool is all-powerful when it comes to manipulating your VMs, and I find myself accessing it frequently in my daily job. Let's take a look at a few of the other things you can do from inside **Hyper-V Manager**, as well as discussing other methods that can be used to work with the new virtual machines that are being created on your Hyper-V Server.

Hyper-V Manager

As you know, Hyper-V Manager is the primary tool for managing a Hyper-V Server. It is a nice console that gives you a quick status of your virtual machines and allows you to manage those VMs in a variety of ways. Something we did not cover – because I only have one Hyper-V Server running – is that you can manage multiple Hyper-V Servers from a single **Hyper-V Manager** console. Just like any MMC-style console in the Microsoft world, you can right-click on the words **Hyper-V Manager** near the top-left corner of the screen and select an option that says **Connect to Server...**. By using this function, you can pull information from other Hyper-V Servers into this same Hyper-V Manager console:

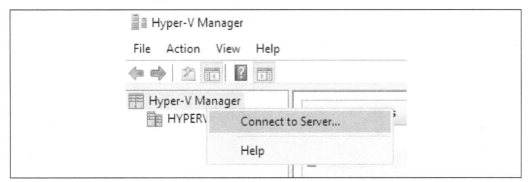

Figure 14.21: Connecting Hyper-V Manager to remote Hyper-V hosts

Furthermore, this enables you to run **Hyper-V Manager** software on a client computer. You can install the Hyper-V role on a Windows 10 machine, which will also install this console, and then use that local copy of Hyper-V Manager running on your Windows 10 desktop to manage your Hyper-V Servers, without needing to log in to those servers directly.

Some of the most useful actions inside **Hyper-V Manager** are listed along the right side of the console in the **Actions** pane – features such as **Virtual Switch Manager** and the ability to create a new VM. Once you have VMs up and running, you will find a lot of useful functions listed inside the context menu that appears when you right-click on a VM, as you can see in *Figure 14.22*:

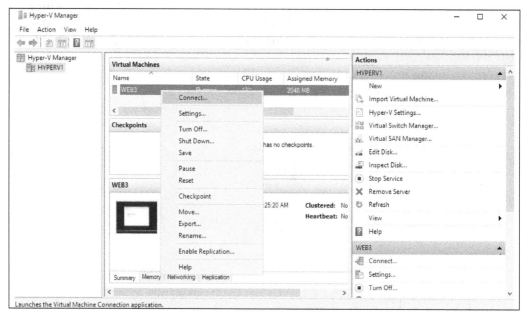

Figure 14.22: Available options in the Actions pane for managing a virtual machine

Some of these are self-explanatory, and some are worth playing around with. We have already used **Connect...** to connect to our VM's console. **Settings...** opens up a ton of possibilities, and we will take a look further inside the **Settings** menu immediately following this section. One of the most common reasons I open this right-click menu is for power functions on my VMs. You can see that you have the ability to **Turn Off...** or **Shut Down...** your VM. Turning it off is like pressing the power button on a server: it cuts off the power immediately to that server and will cause Windows some grief when doing so. The shutdown function, on the other hand, initiates a clean shutdown, at least when you are using Microsoft operating systems on the VMs. Shutting down a server is no big deal, but the real power here comes from the fact that you can shut down multiple VMs at the same time. For example, if I were running a dozen different VMs all for my test labs, and I decided that my lab was taking up too many resources and causing problems on my Hyper-V Server, I could select all of my VMs at the same time, right-click on them, then click on **Shut Down...** just once, and it would immediately kick off the shutdown process on all of the VMs that I had selected. Once a VM is shut down or turned off, right-clicking on that VM will give you a **Start** function; you can also select many servers and start them all at once by using this right-click menu.

The Settings menu

Making in-depth modifications to any of your VMs typically means right-clicking on that VM, and then navigating to **Settings...** for that particular VM. Inside **Settings**, you can adjust any aspect of your VM's hardware, which is the most common reason to visit this screen. Immediately upon opening **Settings**, you have the option to **Add Hardware** to your VM. This is the place you would visit to add more hard drive controllers or NICs to your virtual server:

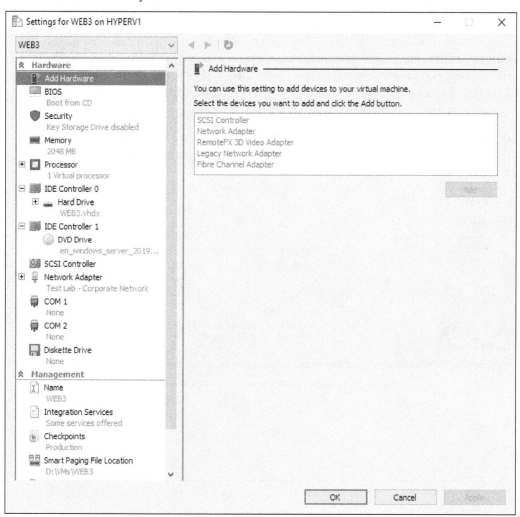

Figure 14.23: Adding new hardware to an existing VM

I don't know if you can tell from the preceding screenshot, but the **Add** button is currently grayed out. This is important. Many functions inside **Settings** can be manipulated on the fly, while the VM is running. Some functions cannot be accomplished unless the VM is turned off. Adding hardware is one of those functions. If you want to add a new hard drive or NIC to your VM, you will need to shut down that server before you are able to do it.

Next, we should talk about the **Memory** screen. This one is fairly simple, *right?* Simply input the amount of RAM that you want this VM to have available. The reason that I want to point it out is that a major improvement has been made in this functionality. Starting with Windows Server 2016 Hyper-V, you can now adjust the amount of RAM that a VM has allocated while it is running! In previous versions of Hyper-V, you were required to shut down the VMs to change their memory allocation, but even though my WEB3 server is currently running and servicing users, I can pop in here and increase RAM at will.

Let's say my 2 GB isn't keeping up with the task load, and I want to increase it to 4 GB. I leave the server running, open **Hyper-V Manager** settings for the VM, and adjust the relevant setting to 4,096 MB:

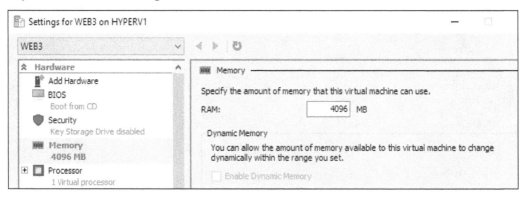

Figure 14.24: Increasing memory while the VM is running

The amount of memory immediately adjusts, and if I open up system properties inside the WEB3 server, I can see that the operating system has updated to reflect the 4 GB of RAM now installed:

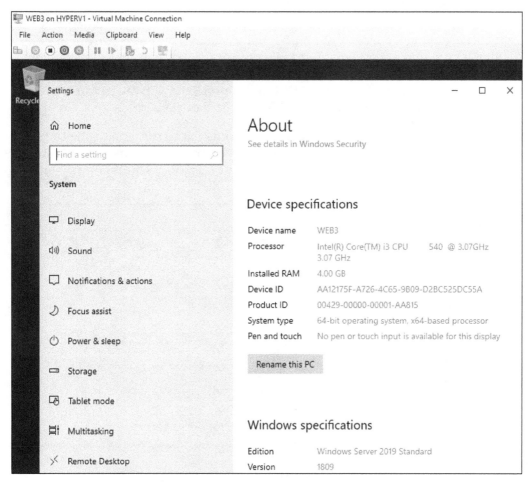

Figure 14.25: WEB3 is immediately increased to 4 GB of memory

Other useful settings screens are the **Processor** and **Network Adapter** sections. Here you define the number of virtual processors currently assigned to the VM, and performance weights associated with these processors. In the **Network Adapter** screen, you can change which virtual switch your virtual NICs are plugged into. I find myself accessing this section often as I move servers from one location to another.

Checkpoints

Another important function inside the **Settings** menu is called **checkpoints**. These were formerly called snapshots, which I think makes a little more sense to most of us. Checkpoints are a function that you can invoke from **Hyper-V Manager** by right-clicking on one or more VMs. It essentially creates a *snapshot in time* of the VM. Another way to look at checkpoints is that they are creating rollback points for your servers. If you create a checkpoint on Tuesday, and on Wednesday somebody makes a configuration change on that server that causes problems, you can restore the checkpoint from Tuesday and bring the VM back to that day's status.

There are a couple of different ways that checkpoints can be run, and the **Settings** menu is where we define those particulars. Simply right-click on any VM, visit the **Settings** screen, and then click on the management task called **Checkpoints**. You can see the options in *Figure 14.26*:

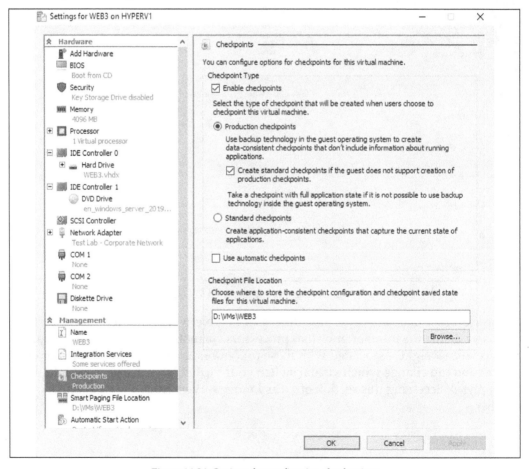

Figure 14.26: Options for configuring checkpoints

These settings are individual for each VM you are running; you could treat checkpoints for WEB1 differently than WEB2, for example. The default way to handle these snapshots in time is called **Production checkpoints**. This is generally the preferred method for creating these quick images of your servers, as it is the cleanest method. When choosing to generate a production checkpoint, Hyper-V invokes Windows backup functions inside the VM's own operating system, in order to create a backup of that server. This would be similar to you logging into that VM and manually launching an operating system backup task. Keep in mind that, when you do this, and therefore when Hyper-V does this for you, it is not a block-by-block identical backup of the VM, but rather a backup file that can then be restored in the future to bring the operating system files back to this point in time. In other words, a production checkpoint brings Windows back to the previous state, but any applications and data that are constantly changing on the server are not captured in the checkpoint, nor restored when the checkpoint is rolled back into place.

Alternatively, the **Standard checkpoints** option does just that. This takes more of a quick-and-dirty capture of the VM, kind of like right-clicking on the VHDX hard drive file and choosing to copy and then paste it somewhere else. Restoring standard checkpoints can be a messier process. Suppose your checkpoint was created while an application on the server was in the middle of an important function, such as a database write. Restoring that checkpoint would bring the server right back to the moment in time that the application was in the middle of that database write. This has the potential to cause issues inside that database.

Once you have made the decision on which kind of checkpoint is best for your VM, invoking checkpoints is very simple. Back at the main screen in Hyper-V Manager, simply right-click on your VM and select **Checkpoint**. After performing this task, you will see the middle pane of Hyper-V Manager receive some new information in a section you may not have even noticed earlier: **Checkpoints**.

The new checkpoint that we just created is now sitting here, waiting to be restored if the need arises. In the future, right-clicking on this checkpoint and choosing **Apply...** will initiate the restoration process:

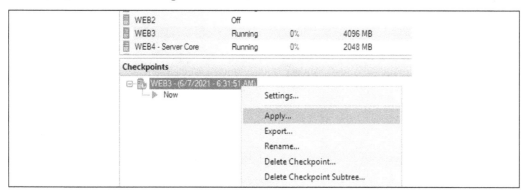

Figure 14.27: Viewing and recovering from a previous checkpoint

Configuring auto stop and start

VMware is another very popular hypervisor host platform (competing with Hyper-V in the space), and while this chapter is not in any way a comparison of VMware and Hyper-V, I mention it here to point out a common issue that I encounter in the VMware world. What happens to your virtual machines when the physical host server is shut down, restarted, or even loses power temporarily?

While a sudden loss of power is going to be an interruption to both physical host and virtual machines no matter what platform you are running, hopefully, you have spent some money on a smart UPS system to keep your host server running during a power outage and it is perhaps even capable of cleanly shutting down that physical host if the power remains offline for an extended period of time.

Assuming a clean shutdown of the physical host occurs, what happens to your VMs? Do they all need to be individually shut down prior to shutting down the physical host? That may take a long time, yet I see many IT admins do exactly this because they think it is necessary and are worried about messing up the operating systems of their VMs by initiating a shutdown of the host server. Fortunately, you do not have to worry about shutting down VMs in this scenario, and there are options inside Hyper-V Manager to declare what happens with each VM when the host is shutting down.

Inside **Settings** for any VM, scroll down to the bottom option called **Automatic Stop Action**. Here you can see that there are three options available to declare what happens with a VM when the host shuts down. The VM can be cleanly shut down by Hyper-V, the VM can simply be turned off (which may impact Windows on the VM), or Hyper-V can **Save the virtual machine state**. You'll notice the save option is the default for every new VM and is likely the option you want to leave selected. With this option in place, when your Hyper-V host server shuts down, the VMs are saved (another way to think about it is that they are being paused) so that when they are turned back on they will resume from exactly where they were prior to the host shutdown:

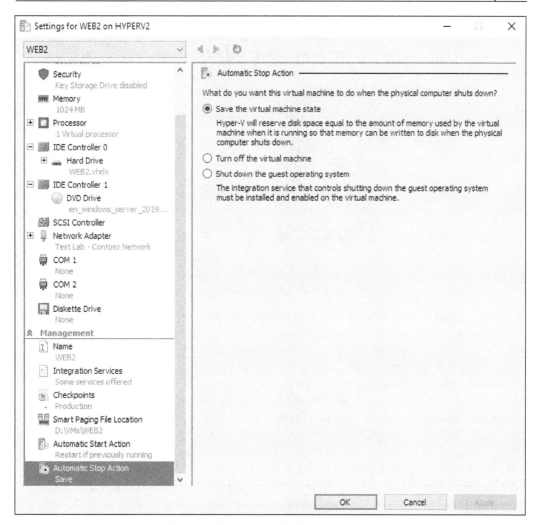

Figure 14.28: Automatic Stop Action settings

Clicking just one option higher inside the **Settings** screen for any VM, you will also find **Automatic Start Action** options. As you have likely surmised, here are your options for handling each VM when a Hyper-V host server resumes power after having been powered off. Here you can instruct Hyper-V to leave the VM powered off, to always start this VM when the host starts, or for Hyper-V to decide itself whether or not the VM was running prior to the host shutdown and to start up the VM only if it was previously running. This is the default option for each VM.

Also available on this screen is a **Startup delay** selection. This is useful when you need certain servers (VMs) to boot before others. For example, wanting your domain controller to be online before any domain member servers attempt to boot. You could configure a startup delay of 30 or 60 seconds for any member servers, which would cause them to start after the DC starts:

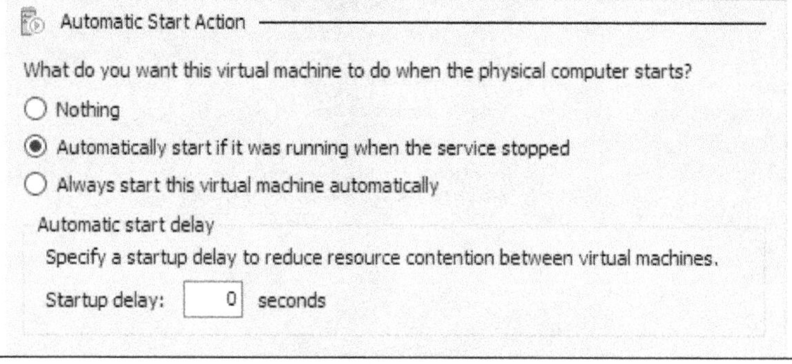

> Automatic Start Action ──────────────────────────────────────
>
> What do you want this virtual machine to do when the physical computer starts?
>
> ○ Nothing
>
> ◉ Automatically start if it was running when the service stopped
>
> ○ Always start this virtual machine automatically
>
> Automatic start delay
>
> Specify a startup delay to reduce resource contention between virtual machines.
>
> Startup delay: [0] seconds

Figure 14.29: VM auto start settings

Now you know where options live for configuring auto stop and auto start settings on each virtual machine, and it would seem that retaining the default settings and never even visiting these options would produce VM shutdown and startup procedures that fit most environments. Wrapping this topic back to my opening statement about a common problem in VMware, what I find in the wild is that VMware host systems are rarely configured with correct auto start settings. It is a rare occurrence that host servers go offline. I have seen hosts with uptimes longer than 1,000 days. Someday, however, you will encounter a situation where your host shuts down unexpectedly, and when that happens do you know with certainty what your hypervisor is going to do with its VMs? Most of the VMware environments I encounter do not have auto start settings configured for VMs, and so when the power goes off and comes back online, servers remain offline until you give them some manual attention.

No matter your hypervisor platform, spend a few minutes reviewing your VM auto stop and auto start procedures to ensure they fall in line with your expectations!

 Check the host BIOS! It's easy enough to check over VM settings to make sure they auto start following a power outage but do you know whether or not the host server itself is going to auto power on? This option is typically configured inside the BIOS on the physical server.

Expanding a virtual disk

Hardware changes to virtual machines are quick and easy, due to the nature of VMs and using all virtual resources that can be expanded or condensed with simple clicks of the mouse. Increasing or decreasing CPU cores and RAM resources is very self-explanatory and happens from inside the **VM Settings** menu. One other specific task that is a very normal procedure, but is not quite so straightforward, is the expansion of a virtual hard disk upon which a VM is running.

You can see in the following screenshot that my WEB3 server has a D: volume, but some yahoo (me) only allocated 5 GB initially, and it's almost full.

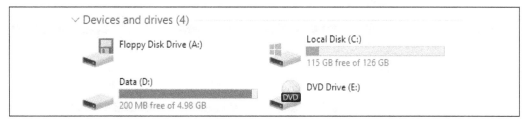

Figure 14.30: My data drive needs more room

On a physical server, this could be complicated, installing a newer and bigger drive and then needing to migrate everything to it. Since this is a VM, could we make things easier by adding a new disk that is larger and then copying everything over, saving us the step of dealing with hardware? Certainly. But there is a much simpler way even than that to deal with disks running out of space. Let's expand the existing data disk! The best part is that this only takes a few minutes:

Open Hyper-V Manager, and under **Actions** on the right side of the screen, select **Edit Disk...**.

Run through the Edit Disk wizard, specifying the **virtual hard disk file (VHDX file)** that you want to manipulate, and on the third screen of the wizard, select the option to **Expand** this disk. Following the **Expand** selection, you will be presented with the current size of the disk, and a field where you can populate the new size. I'll go ahead and quadruple the size of this disk from 5 GB to 20 GB:

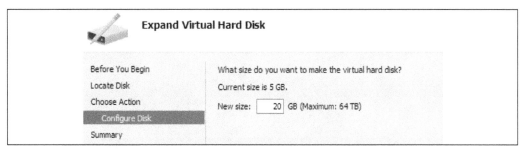

Figure 14.31: Expanding my data disk on the fly

After finishing that wizard, I revisit WEB3 and, low and behold… my D: volume is still sitting at 5 GB. What gives? Even though we have now successfully expanded the virtual disk to 20 GB, the D: volume inside Windows has only ever been configured for 5 GB, and the Windows instance inside the VM has no idea what you want to accomplish with this extra free space. Perhaps we intend to expand the D: volume, or we could even use this new space to create a new E: volume should we have the need.

Right-click on the **Start** menu and open **Disk Management**. Inside you will see the status of disks plugged into the VM, where it is clear the second disk has now been expanded to the larger size:

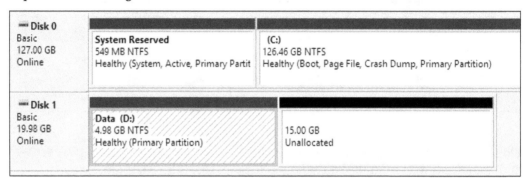

Figure 14.32: Disk 1 has now been expanded

Simply right-clicking on the D: volume and choosing **Extend Volume…** will walk through a very short wizard, after which the D: drive will have been extended to consume the entirety of our newly expanded disk:

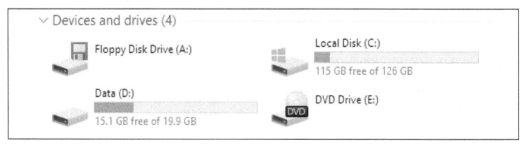

Figure 14.33: The data volume is now expanded as well

Hyper-V console, Remote Desktop Protocol (RDP), or PowerShell

While hardware adjustments to VMs need to be made through Hyper-V Manager, your daily interaction with these VMs running as servers in your environment does not necessarily mean you have to log in to your Hyper-V Server. If you happen to be inside Hyper-V Manager anyway, you can quickly and easily use that **Connect** function to interact with the console of your servers, through the use of the Hyper-V console tool. Accessing your servers this way is beneficial if you need to see something in the BIOS, or otherwise outside of the Windows operating system that is running on that VM, but it's not often that you require this level of console access.

When you have Windows Servers running as VMs, it is much more common to interact with these servers in the same way that you would interact with physical servers on your network. While I have been accessing my WEB3 server through the Hyper-V console in this chapter, now that I have Windows Server 2019 installed on WEB3 and I have enabled the RDP capabilities on it, there is no reason why I couldn't just pop open MSTSC and log into WEB3 that way, straight from my desktop:

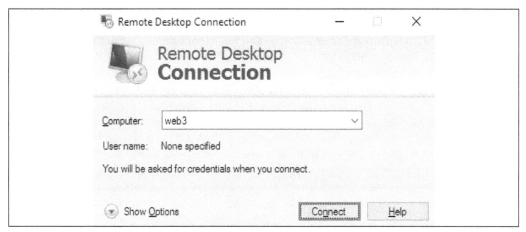

Figure 14.34: Using normal support tools to connect to VMs

The same is true for PowerShell or any other traditional way of remotely accessing services on any other server. Since this VM is fully online and has the server operating system installed, I can use PowerShell remoting to manipulate my WEB3 server as well, from another server or from my desktop computer. Once you are finished building out the hardware and installing the operating system on a VM, it's rare that you actually need to use the Hyper-V console to interact with that server. The primary reasons for opening up Hyper-V Manager to reach a VM are to make hardware-level changes on that server, such as adding a hard drive, adjusting RAM, or moving a network connection from one switch to another.

Windows Admin Center (WAC)

We have seen WAC scattered throughout this book, and for good reason. WAC is the new super-tool that Microsoft wants server administrators to start using to interact with and manage almost every single one of their servers. VM servers hosted in Hyper-V are no exception; you can make use of the WAC toolset to administer servers running on your Hyper-V hosts, and use WAC to manage the host servers themselves.

Shielded VMs

If your day job doesn't include work with Hyper-V, it's possible that you have never heard of shielded VMs. The name does a pretty good job of explaining this technology at a basic level. If a VM is a virtual machine, then a shielded VM must be a virtual machine that is *shielded* or protected in some way, *right?*

A shielded VM is essentially a VM that is encrypted. Rather, the hard drive file itself (the VHDX) is encrypted, using BitLocker. It sounds simple, but there are some decent requirements for making this happen. For the BitLocker encryption to work properly, the VM is injected with a virtual **Trusted Platform Module** (**TPM**) chip. TPMs are quickly becoming commonplace at a hardware level, but actually using them is still a mysterious black box to most administrators. Shielded VMs can also be locked down so that they can only run on healthy and approved host servers, which is an amazing advantage to the security-conscious among us. This capability is provided by a couple of different attestation options, which we will discuss shortly.

To explain the benefits that shielded VMs bring to the table, we are going to look at an example of what happens when VMs are *not* shielded. Keep in mind that the idea of shielded VMs is quite a bit more important when you think in the context of servers being hosted in the cloud where you don't have any access to the backend, or hosted by some other division inside your company, such as inside a private cloud. Unless you have already taken the time to roll out all shielded VMs in your environment, what I am about to show you is currently possible on *any* of your existing VMs.

You already know that I am running a Hyper-V host server, and on that host, I have a virtual machine called WEB3. Now, let's pretend that I am a cloud-hosting provider and that WEB3 is a web server that belongs to one of my tenants. I have provided my tenant with a private virtual switch for networking so that they can manage the networking of that server, and I don't have access to that VM at the networking level. Also, it is a fact that this WEB3 server is joined to my tenant's domain and network, and I, as the cloud host, have absolutely no access to domain credentials, or any other means that I can utilize to actually log in to that server.

Sounds pretty good so far, *right?* You, as a tenant, certainly wouldn't want your cloud provider to be able to snoop around inside your virtual machines that are being hosted on that cloud. You also wouldn't want any other tenants who might have VMs running on the same cloud host to be able to see your servers in any way. This same mentality holds true in private clouds as well. If you are hosting a private cloud and are allowing various companies or divisions of a company to have segregated VMs running in the same fabric, you will want to ensure those divisions have real security layers between the VMs, and between the VMs and the host.

Now, let's have a little fun and turn villain. I am a rogue cloud-host employee, and I decide that I'm going to do some damage before I walk out the door. It would be easy for me to kill off that WEB3 server completely since I have access to the host administrative console. However, that would probably throw a flag somewhere, and the tenant would just spin up a new web server or restore it from backup. So, even better than breaking the VM, I'm going to leave it running and then change the content of the website itself. Let's give this company's clients something to talk about!

To manipulate my tenant's website running on WEB3, I don't need any real access to the VM itself, because I have direct access to the virtual hard drive file. All I need to do is tap into that virtual hard disk file, modify the website, and I can make the website display whatever information I want.

First, I log into the Hyper-V Server (remember, this is owned by me since I am the host), and browse to the location of the VHD file that WEB3 is using. This is all on the backend, so I don't need any tenant credentials to get here. Furthermore, nothing is logged with these actions and the tenant will have no way of knowing that I am doing this. I simply right-click on that VHD and select **Mount**:

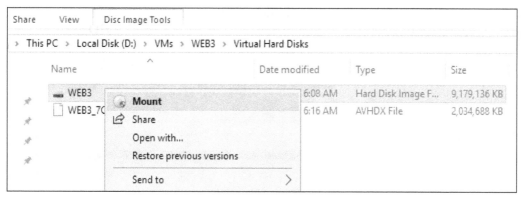

Figure 14.35: Silently mounting a connection to this virtual hard disk file

Now that the VHD has been mounted to the host server's operating system directly, I can browse that VM's hard drive as if it were one of my own drives. Navigate to the wwwroot folder to find the website files, and change the default page to display whatever you want:

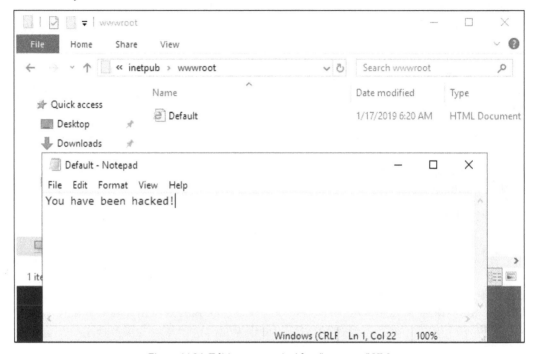

Figure 14.36: Editing content inside a "customer" VM

When I'm finished playing around with the website, I can open up **Disk Management**, right-click on that mounted disk, and select **Detach VHD** to cover my tracks:

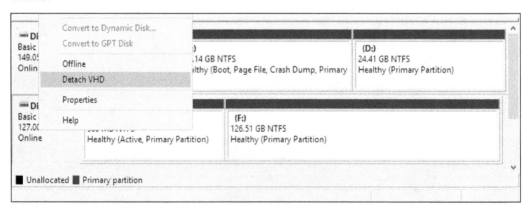

Figure 14.37: Removing the connection to this VHD, my work here is done

And then, just for the fun of it, I copy the entire VHD file onto a USB stick so that I can take it with me and mess around with it more later.

How do you feel about hosting virtual machines in the cloud now? This example cuts to the core of why so many companies are scared to take that initial step into cloud hosting—there is an unknown level of security for those environments. Thankfully, Microsoft is taking steps to alleviate this security loophole with a new technology called **shielded VMs**.

Encrypting VHDs

The idea behind shielded VMs is quite simple. Microsoft already has a great drive-encryption technology, called BitLocker. Shielded VMs are Hyper-V VMs that have BitLocker drive encryption enabled. When your entire VHD file is protected and encrypted with BitLocker, nobody is going to be able to gain backdoor access to that drive. Attempting to mount the VHD as we just did would result in an error message, and nothing more:

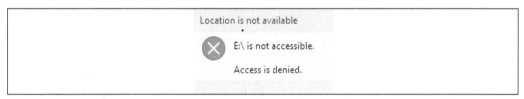

Figure 14.38: Access denied!

Even better is that when you set up your infrastructure to support shielded VMs, you also block Hyper-V console access to the VMs that are shielded. While this in itself isn't as big a deal as drive encryption, it's still important enough to point out. If someone has access to the Hyper-V host server and opens up **Hyper-V Manager**, they will generally have the ability to use the **Connect** function on the tenant VMs in order to view whatever was currently on the console. More than likely, this would leave them staring at a login screen that they, hopefully, would not be able to breach. But if that VM's console had somehow been left in a logged-in state, they would have immediate access to manipulating the VM, even if the drive was encrypted. So when you create a shielded VM, it not only encrypts the VHD using BitLocker technology, it also blocks all access to the VM's console from Hyper-V Manager.

Does this hardcore blocking have the potential to cause you problems when you are trying to legitimately troubleshoot a VM? What if you need to use the Hyper-V console to figure out *why a VM won't boot or something like that?* Yes, that is a valid point and one that you need to consider. Shielded VMs make the security of your VMs much higher. So much so that you could, in fact, lock yourself out from being able to troubleshoot issues on that server. As is often the case with everything in the IT world, we are trading usability for security.

Infrastructure requirements for shielded VMs

There are a couple of important pieces in this puzzle that you need to be aware of if you are interested in running shielded VMs.

Guarded hosts

You will need to run one or more guarded host servers to house your shielded VMs. Guarded hosts are essentially Hyper-V Servers on steroids. They will host VMs like any other Hyper-V Server, but they are specially crafted and configured to host these encrypted shielded VMs and to attest their own health as part of this overall security strategy.

Guarded hosts must be running Server 2016 Datacenter or Server 2019 Datacenter, and generally, you want them to boot using UEFI, and to contain a TPM 2.0 chip. While TPM 2.0 is not a firm requirement, it is certainly recommended.

These guarded host servers then take the place of your traditional Hyper-V Servers. It is their job to host your VMs.

Host Guardian Service (HGS)

HGS is a service that runs on a server, or more commonly a cluster of three servers, and handles the attestation of guarded hosts. When a shielded VM attempts to start on a guarded host server, that host must reach over to HGS and attest that it is safe and secure. Only once the host has passed the HGS attestation and health checks will the shielded VM be allowed to start.

HGS is *critical* to making a guarded fabric work. If HGS goes down, *none* of your shielded VMs will be able to start!

There are different requirements for HGS, depending on what attestation mode your guarded hosts are going to utilize. We will learn about those modes in the next section of this chapter. HGS will have to be running Server 2016 or Server 2019, and most commonly, you want to use physical servers running in a three-node cluster for this service.

I also want to point out a capability related to HGS that is brand new in Windows Server 2019: **HGS cache**. A previous limitation of Server 2016 shielded VMs was that HGS needed to be contacted every time *any* guarded host wanted to spin up *any* shielded VM. This can become problematic if HGS is unavailable for some temporary reason. New in Server 2019 is HGS cache for VM keys so that a guarded host is able to start up approved VMs based on keys in the cache, rather than always having to check in with a live HGS.

This can be helpful if HGS is offline (although HGS being completely offline probably means that you have big problems), but the HGS cache has a more valid use case in branch-office scenarios where a guarded host might have a poor network connection to HGS.

Host attestations

Attestation of the guarded hosts is the secret to using shielded VMs. This is the basis of security in wanting to move forward with such a solution in your own environment. The ability of your hosts to attest their health and identity gives you peace of mind in knowing that those hosts are not being modified or manipulated without your knowledge, and it ensures that a malicious host employee cannot copy all of your VM hard drive files onto a USB, bring them home, and boot them up. Those shielded VMs are only ever going to start on the guarded hosts in your environment, nowhere else.

There are two different modes that guarded hosts can use to pass attestation with HGS. Well, actually there are three, but one has already been deprecated. Let's take a minute to detail the different modes that can be used between your guarded hosts and your HGS.

TPM-trusted attestations

This is the best way! TPM chips are physical chips installed on your server's motherboards that contain unique information. Most importantly, this information cannot be modified or hacked from within the Windows operating system. When your guarded host servers are equipped with TPM 2.0 chips, this opens the door to do some incredibly powerful host attestation. The host utilizes Secure Boot and some code-integrity checks that are stored inside the TPM to verify that it is healthy and has not been modified. HGS then crosschecks the information being submitted from the TPM with the information that it knows about when the guarded host was initially configured, to ensure that the requesting host is really one of your approved guarded hosts and that it has not been tampered with. If you are configuring new Hyper-V Servers, make sure they contain TPM 2.0 chips so that you can utilize these features.

Host key attestations

If TPMs aren't your thing or are beyond your hardware abilities, we can do a simpler host key attestation. The ability of your guarded hosts to generate a host key that can be known and verified by HGS is new with Windows Server 2019. This uses asymmetric key-pair technology to validate the guarded hosts. Basically, you will either create a new host-key pair or use an existing certificate and then send the public portion of that key or certificate over to HGS. When guarded hosts want to spin up a shielded VM, they reach out to attest with HGS, and that attestation is approved or denied based on this key pair.

This is certainly a faster and easier way to make shielded VMs a reality in your network but is not as secure as a TPM-trusted attestation.

Admin-trusted attestation – deprecated in 2019

If your environment is new and based on Server 2019, don't pay any attention to this one. However, there are folks who are running shielded VMs within a Windows Server 2016 infrastructure, and in that case, there was an additional option for attestation. Commonly known as admin-trusted attestation, this was a very simple (and not very secure) way for your hosts to attest to HGS that they were approved. Basically, you created an **Active Directory** (**AD**) security group, added your guarded hosts into that group, and then HGS considered any host that was part of that group to be guarded and approved to run shielded VMs.

Integrating with Linux

Many companies utilize Linux in some capacity or another. The use of Linux may actually be poised to make a grander entrance into the Windows Server world now that we have this higher level of integration possible inside Windows Server 2019. There are ways in which your Server 2019 can now be used to interact with Linux VMs:

- **Running in Hyper-V**: VMs hosted on a Hyper-V Server used to be limited to Windows-based operating systems. This is no longer the case. The scope of the Hyper-V virtualization host has now been expanded to accommodate running Linux-based VMs in Hyper-V Manager. There is even good integration with the keyboard and mouse!

- **Linux shielded VMs**: You now know about running shielded VMs in Hyper-V, and you also know about running Linux-based VMs inside Hyper-V. *Does this mean we can combine those two ideas and run a Linux VM that is also shielded?* Why yes, we certainly can. This capability was introduced in Windows Server 1709, and also exists in the newest LTSC release of Windows Server 2019.

- **Running in containers**: While most server and Hyper-V administrators won't be chomping at the bit to install Linux on their systems because they simply have no reason to do so, there will definitely be a lot more Linux-y talk coming from anyone on the DevOps side of the IT house. When building scalable applications that are destined for the cloud, we often talk about running these applications inside containers. In the past, hosting containers on a Windows Server meant that the container itself had to be running Windows, but no more. You can now host Linux-based containers on top of Windows Server 2019. This allows great flexibility in the application development process and will be an important consideration for the future of containers.

ReFS deduplication

While filesystems and deduplication features are technologies that you may not expect to be discussed when it comes to Hyper-V, the improvements in Server 2019 related to ReFS and the deduplication of data carry some huge advantages for Hyper-V Servers. In case these are unfamiliar terms, let's take a minute and define ReFS and deduplication.

ReFS

Anyone who has worked on computers for a while will recognize FAT, FAT32, and NTFS. These are filesystems that can be used when formatting hard drives. The different versions of filesystems translate into different capabilities of how you can utilize that hard drive. For a number of years, NTFS has been the *de facto* standard for all hard disks connected to Windows machines.

That is until Windows Server 2016 came along. We now have a new filesystem option called ReFS. Even if you work in an IT department every day, you may have never heard of ReFS because so far, it isn't getting used all that much. It is primarily used in servers that are involved with **Storage Spaces Direct (S2D)**. If it's the latest and greatest filesystem from Microsoft, *why isn't it being used as the default option on any new system?* Primarily because ReFS is not a bootable filesystem. That immediately cancels out the capability of systems with a single hard disk to be running ReFS on the whole drive. What that implies is that ReFS is for secondary volumes on servers, perhaps volumes intended to hold large amounts of data.

In those instances where you do format a second volume to be ReFS and store data on it, there are some great resiliency and performance advantages to using ReFS instead of NTFS. These advantages were designed to make S2D implementations work better.

Data deduplication

Data deduplication is simply the ability of a computing system to discover multiple bits of data on a drive that are identical and *clean them up*. If there were six copies of the exact same file on a system, deduplication could delete five of them, retaining one for the purposes of all six locations. This idea enables some major space-saving. Data deduplication itself is not new; we had some capabilities introduced way back in Server 2012 regarding this.

Windows Server 2019 is the first platform where it is possible to enable data deduplication on a volume that is formatted via ReFS.

Why is this important to Hyper-V?

Data deduplication can be incredibly advantageous to run on a volume that stores Hyper-V VM hard drive files because, as you can imagine, there will be a ton of information that is duplicated over and over and over again when you are running dozens of VMs. Think about all of those Windows operating system files that will be identical among all of your VMs running on the Hyper-V host. It's pretty obvious why it would be beneficial to enable data deduplication on a volume that stored VHDX files.

ReFS has some big resiliency and performance advantages over NTFS, and so it is also obvious that VHDX files would be best served by being stored on an ReFS volume.

Windows Server 2019 is the first platform where you can have your cake and eat it too. We now have the ability to create an ReFS volume for storing virtual machine hard drives, and also enable data deduplication on that same volume.

Hyper-V Server 2019

It's very easy to get excited about virtualization. Build some hardware, install Windows Server 2019, implement the Hyper-V role, and bam! You're ready to start rolling out hundreds and hundreds of VMs in your environment... *right?*

Not necessarily. We haven't talked about licensing yet, and too often our technological prowess is limited by licensing requirements. The same is true with Hyper-V. Every VM that you spin up needs to have its own operating system license, of course. That requirement makes sense. What isn't as obvious, however, is the fact that you can only run a certain number of VMs on your Hyper-V Server, depending on what SKU you use for the host operating system itself.

The biggest *gotcha* is that using Windows Server 2019 Standard edition as your Hyper-V Server will result in the ability to run two VMs. Two! That's it, no more. You will be able to launch a couple of virtual machines and will then be prevented from running anymore. Clearly, the Standard edition SKU isn't designed to be used as a Hyper-V Server.

That leaves you with Windows Server 2019 Datacenter edition. Fortunately, Datacenter allows you to run *unlimited* VMs! This is great news! Except for one thing—Datacenter edition usually costs many thousands of dollars. This is a very limiting factor for deployments of Hyper-V Servers.

All of this talk about licensing and how messy or expensive it can be leads to one point: **Hyper-V Server 2019**. Wait a minute, *isn't that what this whole chapter has been about? Isn't that just Windows Server 2019 with the Hyper-V role installed?* No, not at all.

Hyper-V Server 2019 is its own animal. It has its own installer, and a whole different user interface from a traditional server. Installing Hyper-V Server 2019 onto a piece of hardware will result in a server that can host an unlimited number of Hyper-V VMs, but nothing else. You cannot use this as a general-purpose server to host other roles or services. Hyper-V Server also does not have a graphical user interface.

Hyper-V Server 2019 has one *huge* benefit: it's *FREE*. You are still responsible for licenses on each of the VMs themselves, of course, but to have a free host operating system that can run an unlimited number of VMs, now that is something my wallet can really get behind.

I have burned the ISO installer for Hyper-V Server 2019 onto a DVD (thankfully this one is small enough to actually fit!), and just finished installing it onto my hardware. The installation of the operating system itself was completely familiar: all of the installation screens and options were the same as if I were installing the full version of Windows Server 2019. However, now that the installer has finished and I have booted into the operating system of my Hyper-V Server 2019, everything looks completely different:

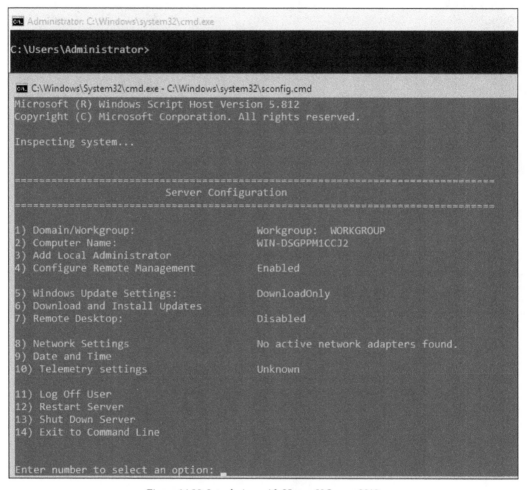

Figure 14.39: Interfacing with Hyper-V Server 2019

We are presented with only a Command Prompt, and inside that prompt, it has auto-launched a configuration utility called **SConfig**. By using the keyboard here, I can do things such as set the hostname of this server, join it to a domain, and change networking settings. Once you have finished using this CLI interface to set the basic requirements on the server and get it communicating with the network, you really don't need to access the console of this Hyper-V Server again, unless you need to backtrack and revisit this configuration screen to change something. Instead, after configuring the Hyper-V Server, you simply utilize **Hyper-V Manager**, or PowerShell, on another server or desktop inside your network, to tap remotely into the management of VMs that are running on this Hyper-V Server.

In *Figure 14.40*, you can see that I have launched Hyper-V Manager. I am running this instance of Hyper-V Manager from my Windows 10 machine where I have the Hyper-V role installed. From here, I right-click on **Hyper-V Manager** and choose **Connect to Server....** I then input the name of my new Hyper-V Server, and the console creates a remote connection. From this remote connection, I can now utilize all functionality inside my Window 10 Hyper-V Manager as if I were logged straight into the new Hyper-V Server:

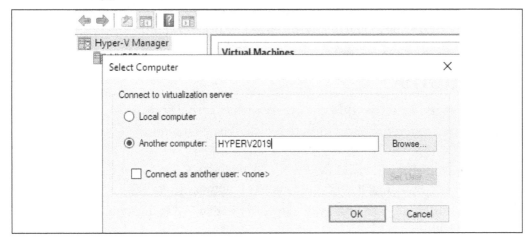

Figure 14.40: Remotely connecting to a Hyper-V Server

Similar to the way that most tasks performed on Server Core or Nano Server are handled remotely—through the use of remote consoles or PowerShell—we make all ongoing maintenance and administration of this Hyper-V Server happen from a remote Hyper-V Manager console.

Hyper-V Server gives you the security benefits of a GUI-less interface, combined with the flexibility benefits of hosting an unlimited number of virtual machines, at a price point that nobody can argue with!

Summary

I don't have official numbers, but I will take a risk and say that today there are already more virtual servers running than physical servers to keep our world online. While the battle continues to rage about which hypervisor platform is the best—typically the argument is split between either Hyper-V or VMware—you cannot ignore the fact that virtualization is the way of the future. Microsoft puts great quantities of time and resources into making sure that Hyper-V always stays ahead of the competition and introduces more and more features with every release so that you can keep your virtualized infrastructure up and running perfectly, all the time. *Is the capacity for cloud virtualization even more powerful than on-premise Hyper-V Server?* I would say yes, because the infrastructure that is in place at a cloud service provider is going to be the all-powerful Oz compared to what a single company can provide in their own datacenter. *Does this mean you can forget about Hyper-V altogether and just use cloud-provided servers?* Maybe someday, but most aren't ready to take that leap just yet. The need for on-premise servers and services is still immense, and some industries are simply never going to permit their data and applications to be hosted by a third party. Understanding the capabilities of Hyper-V and being able to build this infrastructure from the ground up will give you a major advantage when looking for a technology job in a Microsoft-centric organization.

Questions

1. What are the three types of virtual switches inside Hyper-V?

2. If you needed to build a virtual machine that booted using UEFI, which generation of VM would you need to create?

3. True or False—In Windows Server 2019 Hyper-V, you must shut down a VM in order to change its allocated about of memory (RAM).

4. True or False—The only way to interact with a VM is through the Hyper-V console.

5. What is the name of the technology inside Hyper-V that allows you to take snapshot images of virtual machines that can later be restored?

6. When running shielded VMs in your environment, what is the name of the role that handles the attestation of your Hyper-V host servers?

7. Which is the most comprehensive attestation method for shielded VMs—host key attestation, TPM trusted attestation, or admin trusted attestation?

15
Troubleshooting Windows Server 2019

When thinking of a position in server or system administration, we often recall images of designing infrastructure, spinning up new servers, and implementing new technology. The truth can reflect those items, but it can just as easily include 3 A.M. wakeup calls to deal with a system being down, poring over event and diagnostic logs, and living on Google and Bing when your acquired knowledge and wisdom just isn't cutting the mustard. Sometimes, hardware breaks. Other times, software freaks out. Certificates expire, internet connections fail, and occasionally, you work on an issue from a certain angle all day only to discover in the end that it was being caused by something entirely different. Working in IT can bring with it great mysteries every single day, which is one of the reasons I love it. This final chapter uncovers some of the tools available in Windows Server 2019 that can assist with troubleshooting and repair:

- Backup and Restore
- Task Manager
- Resource Monitor
- Performance Monitor
- Windows Firewall with Advanced Security
- System Insights
- Remote toolsets
- Event Logs
- MMC and MSC shortcuts

Backup and Restore

The need to back up and occasionally restore your servers is, unfortunately, still present in Windows Server 2019. I dream of a day when servers are 100 percent reliable and stable throughout their lifetimes, unaffected by viruses and rogue software, but today is not that day. While there are many third-party tools available on the market that can improve and automate your backup experience when managing many servers, we do have these capabilities baked right into our own Server 2019 operating system, and we should all be familiar with how to utilize them. Maintaining good backups should be priority number one for any business and is the most important troubleshooting component that exists. There is a myriad of reasons why you may fail to repair a server that is having a problem, and sometimes, your only two options are to build from scratch or restore from backup. Ransomware attacks are on the increase, and attackers are targeting companies of all sizes. If you have one bad firewall rule in place, it's only a matter of time before they find their way into your network, and before you know it, every single one of your servers will be encrypted and held for ransom. If you don't have a solid backup system and a restore plan that spells out exactly how you recover from those backups should the need arise, then you had better have a very deep wallet for paying the ransom because that is your only option.

For clarity, of course, you should never pay the ransom! If you pay, the hackers who locked down your system in the first place will release your files (if they didn't, they would immediately kick themselves out of the ransom business), but they are also going to build as many backdoors in your network as they possibly can before they do release your data, so that down the road, they can simply reconnect and do it again. Unfortunately, as we have seen recently in the news, failing to keep good backups results in being stuck between a rock and a hard place, where paying the ransom is the only available course of action. Don't let that be *your* story.

Schedule regular backups

Logging into your servers and launching a manual backup task every day is obviously not feasible for most of our organizations, as the process of running backups would turn into our full-time job. Thankfully, the Windows Server Backup feature gives us the option to create a backup schedule. This way, we can define what we want to back up, where we want to back it up to, and how often this backup should run. Then, we can sit back, relax, and know that our systems are performing this task on their own.

Before we can do anything with backups, we need to install the appropriate feature inside Windows. Using the **Add roles and features** link, go ahead and install the feature called **Windows Server Backup**. Remember that I said *feature* – you won't find Windows Server Backup on the primary **Server Roles** selection screen; you need to move ahead one screen further in the wizard to find **Features**. Once the feature has finished installing, you can launch the **Windows Server Backup** console that is available inside the **Tools** menu of Server Manager. Once inside, click on **Local Backup** in the left-hand side window; you will see some **Actions** appear on the right-hand side of your screen.

As you can see, there is an option listed here called **Backup Once...** that, as the name implies, performs an ad hoc backup job. While this is a nice feature, there is no way that any server administrator is going to log into all their servers and do this every day. Instead, clicking on the **Backup Schedule...** action will launch a configuration wizard for creating a scheduled, recurring backup job:

Figure 15.1 The Windows Server Backup console

The first option you come across is for deciding what it is that you want to back up. The default option is set to **Full server**, which will take a backup of everything in the operating system. If you want to customize the amount of data that is being backed up, you can choose the **Custom** option and proceed from there. Since I have lots of disk space available to me, I am going to stick with the recommended path of creating full server backups.

Next, we get to the real advantage of using the scheduling concept: choosing how often we run our backup. The most common way is to choose a particular time of day and then let the backup run every day at that allotted time. If you have a server whose data is being updated regularly throughout the days and you want to shorten your window of lost information in the event of needing to perform a restore, you can also specify to back up multiple times per day:

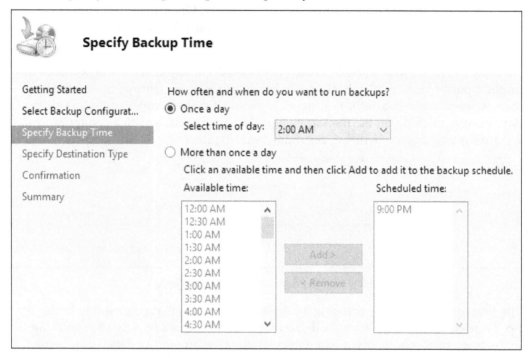

Figure 15.2: Setting a backup schedule

The last screen where we need to make a decision for our scheduled backups is the **Specify Destination Type** screen, where we set the location for our backup files. You can see that there are a couple of different options for storing the backup locally on the physical hard disks of the same server where you are configuring the backups. Storing backup files on a local, dedicated disk or volume can be advantageous because the speed of the backup process will be increased compared to network storage. For servers that you are trying to back up continually during workdays, this can decrease the resources being used by the backup and increase the number of backups that can be squeezed into a day. Another advantage of using a locally connected disk for backups is that you can create multiple rollback points within your backup schema, keeping multiple days' worth of backup information in case you need to roll back to a particular point in time.

There are also downsides to retaining backups on locally attached storage. One potential showstopper is a ransomware attack. If you have never been part of clean-up efforts following such an attack, you may not realize that ransomware locks down and encrypts all the files it can get its hands on. This almost always means that it encrypts the operating system volume, and any other volume (drive letter) that it can find attached to the system. Additional hard disks and USB drives where you might store backups will almost certainly be pulverized, along with your server in a ransomware attack.

> This brings up another good point – keeping offsite copies of your backups. This is not a chapter about disaster recovery scenarios, but you should absolutely keep copies of your server backups in a second location, whether that be in cloud storage or in another physical building.

I find that most admins prefer to keep all their backup files in a centralized location, and that means choosing the third option on this screen, the one entitled **Back up to a shared network folder**. By choosing this option, we can specify a network location, such as a file server or drive mapping to a NAS, and we can set all our different servers to back up to this same location. That way, we have a central, standardized location where we know that all our backup files are going to be sitting, if we need to pull one out and use it for restoration.

I cannot tell you which option is best, because it depends on how you are planning to utilize backups in your own environment. The screen where we choose which destination type we want for our backups includes some good text to read over related to these options, such as the important note that when using a shared network folder for backups, only one backup file can be stored at a time for your server. This is because the process of creating a new backup on the following day will overwrite the previous backup:

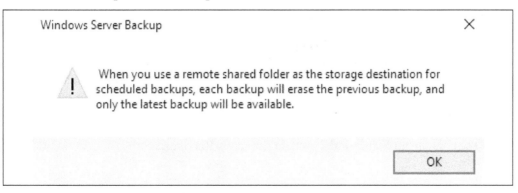

Figure 15.3: A warning about backups stored remotely

Once you have chosen a destination for your backups and specified a network share location, if that is the option you have chosen, you are finished in the wizard. Your backup jobs will automatically kick off at the allocated time that you specified during the wizard, and tomorrow, you will see a new backup file for your server. If you are impatient, like me, and want to see the backup job run right now, you can walk through the other **Action** that's available in the **Windows Server Backup** console, called **Backup Once...**, to run a manual backup right away:

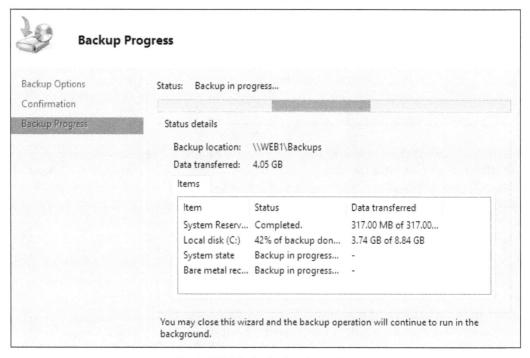

Figure 15.4: My first backup is running

Restoring from Windows

Since you are being diligent and keeping good backups of your servers, the hope is that you will never have to utilize those backup files to restore a server. But, alas, the time *will* come when you have a server that goes sideways, or some data is accidentally deleted, and you must revisit the process of restoring data or an entire server in your infrastructure. If your server is still online and running, the restore process is quite easy to invoke from the same **Windows Server Backup** console. Open the console and choose the **Action** that says **Recover...**.

This invokes another wizard that walks us through the recovery process. First, we specify the location of our backup file. If you have a dedicated backup location on the local server, it is pretty simple to find; otherwise, like in my example, where we specified a network location, you should choose **A backup stored on another location**, and then choose **Remote shared folder** to tell it where to find that backup file:

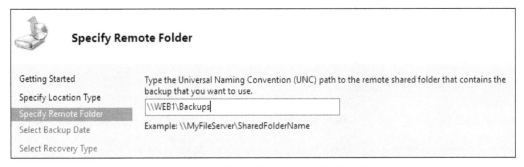

Figure 15.5: Specifying the location of backup files

Based on your chosen backup location, the wizard will now identify all the rollback dates that are available within the backup files. If you have stored your backup files on a local disk so that multiple days' worth of rollback points are available, then you will see numerous dates available to click on. For me, since I chose to store my backups on a network location, that means only one days' worth of backup information is available, and yesterday's date is the only one that I can choose. So, I will choose to restore yesterday's backup and continue working through the wizard.

Now that we have identified the specific backup file that is going to be used for recovery, we get to choose what information from that backup is going to be restored. This is a nice piece of the recovery platform because, often, when we need to restore from backup, it is only for specific files and folders that may have been deleted or corrupted. If that is the case, choose the top option, **Files and folders**. In other cases, you may want to roll the entire server back to a certain date, and for that functionality, you should choose to recover an entire **Volume**. Right now, I am only missing a few files that somehow disappeared between yesterday and today, so I am going to choose the default **Files and folders** option.

The **Select Items to Recover** screen is now presented, which polls the backup file and displays the entire list of files and folders within the backup file. Here, I simply choose which ones I want to restore. This kind of recovery can be critical to your daily management of a file server, where the potential is high for users to accidentally delete information:

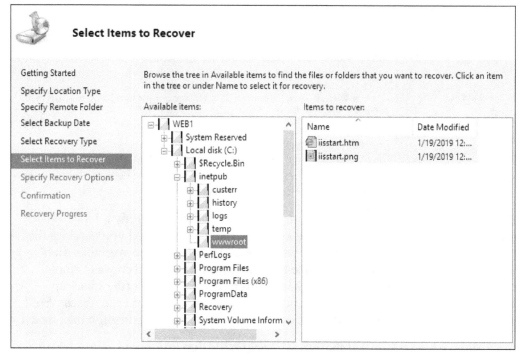

Figure 15.6: Restoring individual files

All that remains is to specify where you want these recovered files to be restored. You can choose for the recovered files to be placed back in their original location, or if you are running this recovery process on a different machine, you can choose to restore the files to a new location that you can grab them from and place them manually, wherever they now need to reside.

Restoring from the installer disk

Recovery from the console inside Windows is a nice wizard-driven experience, but what if your server has crashed hard? If you cannot get into Windows on your server, you cannot run the Windows Server Backup console to initiate your recovery process. In this case, we can still utilize our backup file that has been created, but we need to use it in combination with a Windows Server 2019 installation disk, from which we can invoke the recovery process.

It is important to note that this recovery process cannot access locations on the network, and your backup file will have to be stored on a disk attached to your server. You can utilize a USB drive for this purpose during the recovery process, if you did not originally set up your backup job to be stored on an existing locally attached disk.

To make things interesting, I'm going to crash my own server. This is the server that we took a backup of a few minutes ago. I accidentally deleted some very important files in my C:\Windows directory. Whoops! Now, this is all I see when I try to boot my server:

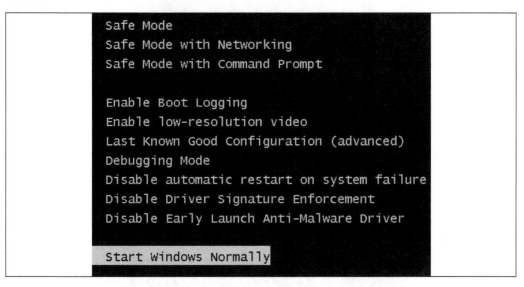

Figure 15.7: The C:\Windows folder is important – don't delete files from it!

That's not a very friendly screen to see first thing in the morning! Since I seem to be stuck here and unable to boot into Windows, my chances of running the recovery wizard are nil. What to do? Boot to the Windows Server 2019 installer DVD? That is really my only option, but I want to be careful that I don't simply install Windows afresh, as all of my programs and data could be overwritten in that scenario. Rather, once I get into the Windows Server installer screen, you will notice that there is an option down in the corner for **Repair your computer**. Choose this option to open the recovery options that are available on the installation DVD.

Now, you see the screen adjust to a new blue hue, indicating that we have entered a special portion of the installer disk, from which there are a few options:

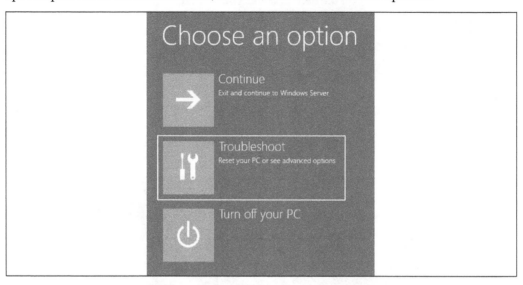

Figure 15.8: Recovery options on the Windows Server install disk

Clicking on **Troubleshoot**, you'll find a subset of advanced options that can be used to troubleshoot the operating system from this console outside of the OS itself. If you think you can fix whatever the issue is from **Command Prompt**, choose that option, as shown in *Figure 15.9*, and try to fix it yourself. For our example, I am pretty sure that I significantly hosed the operating system, so I am going to do a full **System Image Recovery** and click on that button:

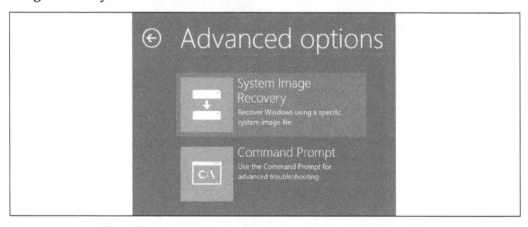

Figure 15.9: Running a System Image Recovery from installation media

As long as you have a hard drive connected that contains a Windows Server Backup file, the wizard will launch and pull in the information about the backup. Since I had originally chosen to store my backup file on a network location, I copied the backup files onto a disk and connected it as a second disk to my server. The wizard automatically recognizes that backup file and displays it in the **Select a system image backup** screen:

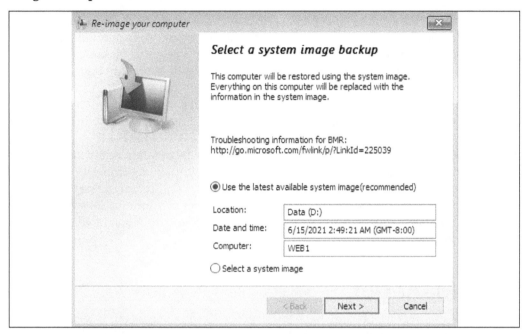

Figure 15.10: The recovery process recognizes backup files on attached storage

Now, by simply clicking on **Next** a few times to progress through the wizard, my backup image is restoring on my server:

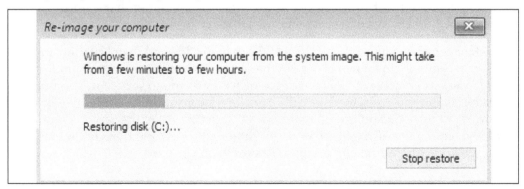

Figure 15.11: Restoring the server via advanced recovery options

Once the restore process has completed, the system reboots and launches itself right back into Windows, where it is fully functional back to the restore point. My test server doesn't have much of anything running on it, so the time that it took to restore was pretty minimal. A production box may take a little longer, but I'd say that 20 minutes from blowing up the server to being fully recovered is a pretty awesome length of time!

Keeping good and recent backup files is critical to your operation's sustainability. I have worked on quite a few systems where the admins took some manual backups after initially configuring their servers but never set up a regular schedule. Even if the data on the server never changes, if you are part of a domain, you never want to rely on old backup files. If a server fails, and you need to recover it, restoring a backup that is only a few days old will generally recover well. But if you restore an image that is six months old, Windows itself will come back online with no problems, and all of your data will exist. However, in that amount of time, your computer account for that server would most certainly have fallen out of sync with the domain, causing authentication errors against the domain controllers. In some cases, you may even have to do goofy things like disjoin and rejoin the server to the domain while following the image restoration to recover communications to the domain. If you have kept regular backups to restore from, you won't have to deal with those issues.

Task Manager

If you can remember all the way back to *Chapter 1, Getting Started with Windows Server 2019*, you'll know that we already discussed Task Manager. There, we described how to launch it and took a quick look at the different tabs available inside Task Manager. While there is no need to re-hash the same information here, it is important to note Task Manager in this chapter regarding troubleshooting, because it is one of the first places you should visit on any server that is portraying performance problems or otherwise strange symptoms.

Task Manager gives you a quick glance at the overall CPU and memory utilization on a server, letting you know how taxed the server is. One of the most common tabs to review on any server is **Processes**, which allows you to sort all the running applications and processes by their CPU or memory consumption, which can quickly identify a problematic application that may be hindering the entire server. Once identified, you can easily right-click on any running process and quickly **End task**, killing that process and freeing up those resources on your server.

When administering RDS servers, you will find yourself often visiting Task Manager to troubleshoot the slowness of one particular session host server. Sometimes, you can identify individual applications that are soaking resources in the **Processes** or **Details** tabs, while other times, you may want to go even further and review the **Users** tab to see status information about every user who is logged into that RDSH server. Oftentimes, this is the fastest way to find out how many users are logged into a particular server, and to quickly identify which user session might be causing grief for the others by consuming an extraordinary amount of server resources:

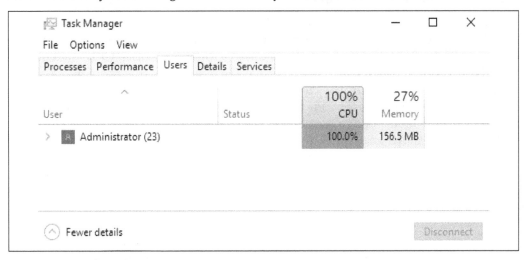

Figure 15.12: The Administrator user is consuming all available CPU

One of the most common reasons I open Task Manager is to visit the **Performance** tab and view system uptime information. While generally more stable than workstation computers, Windows Servers do need to be restarted occasionally, and uptime is a good indicator as to whether you should attempt a restart as a first form of troubleshooting. If your server has only been running for two days, you may want to focus your efforts elsewhere and not cause anyone a service interruption by rebooting in the middle of the day. On the other hand, if your server is really crawling and causing slowness, and it has a reported uptime of 120 days, you may want to go ahead and just reboot the thing to see if it resolves the issue.

 Another easy way to view system uptime is by typing **systeminfo** into a Command Prompt or PowerShell window! And taking it one step further, if your server rebooted unexpectedly and you want to find out how long it had been running prior to the restart, visit the System Event Logs and search for Event ID 6013. You'll have to calculate seconds into minutes/hours/days, but this event is logged at noon every day, so you always have an ongoing record of system uptime.

In cases where you find Task Manager to be lacking and want to dig a little bit deeper, go ahead and launch the newer **Resource Monitor**. This can be invoked by using the **Start** menu search function, but if you have Task Manager open anyway, visit the **Performance** tab. Way down at the bottom, look for a link called **Open Resource Monitor**.

Resource Monitor

Like Task Manager on steroids, Resource Monitor can take system monitoring and troubleshooting even further. There is plenty of the same information that we just experienced inside Task Manager but laid out in a different format. CPU, memory, and disk utilization metrics are present, as well as monitoring of your network interfaces. There are various ways to sort the items utilizing resources, quickly identifying the high hitters for CPU and memory, and there are also right-click functions to end or suspend processes. On the **Overview** tab, as shown in *Figure 15.13*, you can see that I can quickly identify the reason for my high CPU utilization – PowerShell is consuming almost 100% of available CPU resources:

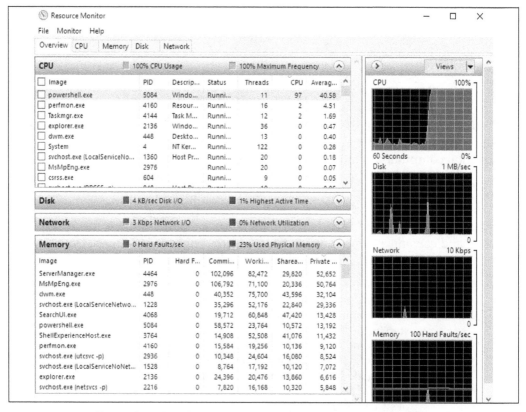

Figure 15.13: Using Resource Monitor to investigate high CPU utilization

Exploring the different tabs inside Resource Monitor will show you more detailed information about CPU, memory, and even disk resource consumption. This is particularly cool because you can see disk storage stats and available disk space right alongside metrics such as Disk Queue Length, which is an important indicator to monitor when hard disk performance may be a bottleneck.

The only tab I haven't mentioned yet is **Network**, which is my favorite place to visit inside Resource Monitor. A fairly common client/server troubleshooting task is to track down what a particular application may be calling for at a network level, and this can be a difficult thing to ascertain. For example, I have installed an application onto a client or server, and this application makes calls to another server to grab information or to interact with it in some way. Let's pretend the application isn't working correctly. First, you do some basic network troubleshooting and verify that the two machines can communicate with each other, by pinging back and forth. This means network traffic is flowing, but the application still won't connect. Your next thought is the firewall – what if the firewall on the receiving server is not allowing the traffic, or perhaps there is even a physical firewall device somewhere in-between that is restricting the ports being used by the application? You are unsure of what ports the app may be trying to use, and it's too late in the day to call the software vendor (if one exists).

Resource Monitor to the rescue! Now, if you've been around the block once or twice, you may be thinking, "Couldn't I just install Wireshark and use it to review network traffic leaving my machine?" The answer would be yes, but this information is to portray a similar capability baked right into Windows.

Inside the **Network** tab of Resource Monitor, you can see the applications and **Process IDs (PIDs)** that are currently generating network traffic on this computer or server. Keep in mind that Resource Monitor is available inside Windows Server, and it is also available inside Windows 10! Launch your application, look for the PID, and check the box next to it. Then, drop down the **TCP Connection** section, and if that application is utilizing a TCP traffic stream (or attempting to), as most applications do, you will see right here exactly what server name or IP address the application is calling for, and what ports it is using to attempt connection. The interesting columns here are **Remote Address** and **Remote Port**:

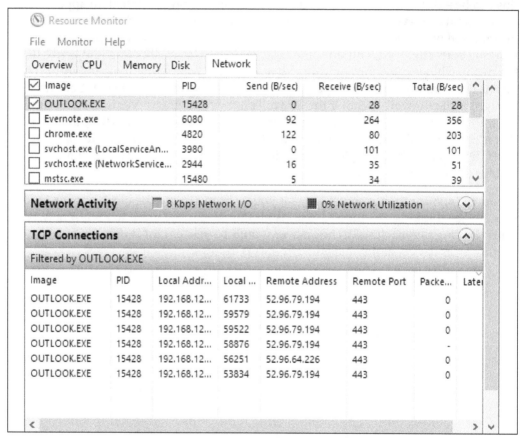

Figure 15.14: Using Resource Monitor for network troubleshooting

It is easy to see that my Outlook.exe application is reaching out to a couple of different IP addresses, using TCP port 443. If this information were from your own application, you could now use this information to verify that the application is calling for the IP or server that you expect, and that the port being used is accessible, listening, and not being blocked on the receiving server.

Performance Monitor

Another built-in monitoring tool is called Performance Monitor, commonly referred to as **Perfmon**. Almost every component inside Windows Server has predefined performance monitor counters, and Perfmon taps into those counters to display extremely in-depth information about what is happening with those components, but only when you specifically set up reporting to see it. Perfmon does not log anything by default, because to do so would consume plenty of server resources, so this tool is generally only to be used temporarily during troubleshooting or for a specific reason, and then disabled again when you are finished.

The easiest way to launch Perfmon is to **Start** | **Run** or open a Command Prompt or PowerShell, simply type Perfmon, and then press *Enter*. This launches the interface and by default, you can see that it has plugged in a counter for % **Processor Time**. You can obviously find CPU percentage information in much easier and better-looking places than Perfmon, so this is displayed simply as a sample of data:

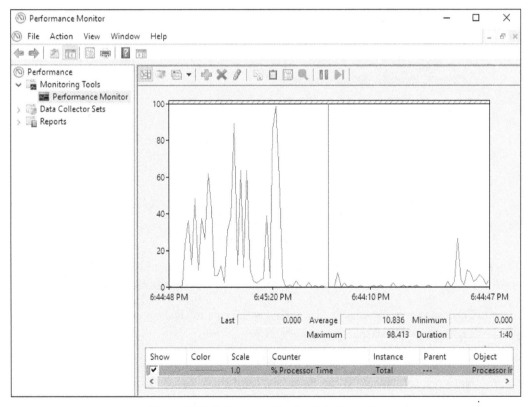

Figure 15.15: Performance Monitor default counter

What is very interesting here is that you can quickly see the **Average, Minimum,** and **Maximum** data fields. You will find that these fields exist with most counters, and this is some of the most useful information that I have pulled using Perfmon during real-life troubleshooting scenarios.

Right-click anywhere inside that graph and select **Add Counters...**. Here, we can discover the incredible breadth of data counters that are available to monitor with Perfmon:

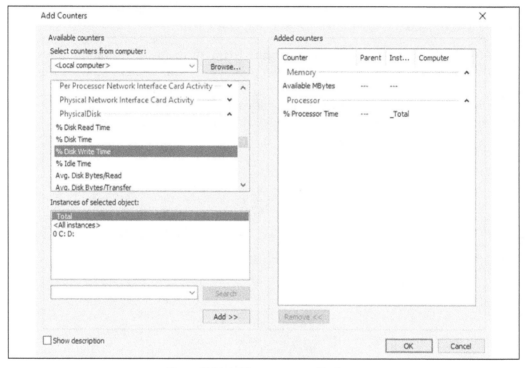

Figure 15.16: Adding counters to Perfmon

There is no way we can cover everything here, so I'll list out a few examples of counters that are useful in most server performance troubleshooting scenarios:

- Processor > % Processor Time (this is the one added by default)
- Memory > Available MBytes
- Network Interface > Bytes Received/sec
- Network Interface > Bytes Sent/sec (and these can be further defined per-NIC)
- PhysicalDisk > % Disk Time
- PhysicalDisk > Current Disk Queue Length

Many counters are role-specific. Things like Terminal Services > Total Sessions can give you counters on how many users you have logged into your RDSH hosts. Or you can use Print Queue > Total Jobs Printed when trying to gain an idea of how busy or overworked your print server might be. In a previous job, I often utilized IP-HTTPS, DNS64, and IPsec counters to keep tabs on under the hood components within the Microsoft Remote Access technologies. I have gone ahead and added all the performance-related counters that I specified previously (there are many, many more options available), and the Perfmon data graph has become a mess of multiple colors and overlapping line graphs. While the default graph view is interesting, it's not very easy to follow. Instead, if you drop down the toolbar icon that looks like a little graph, you'll find three options for how to display this data: Line, Histogram bar, and Report. I prefer looking at numbers, but the Report view does not display the Average-Minimum-Maximum, and those are really useful. So, you may find yourself utilizing a combination of all three views on a regular basis:

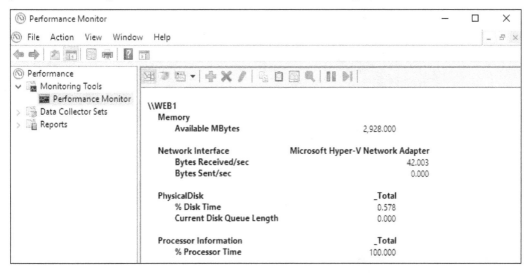

Figure 15.17: Performance metrics in the Report view

This is cool real-time information, but how often are you really digging in and troubleshooting a real-time problem with this much depth? Let's be honest; if you have a server tanking performance during working hours, you are probably going to restart the entire server to get things normalized before using Perfmon for a hardware review. Instead, what I have always found Perfmon to be most useful for is gathering statistics over a certain period. A great example is repeated reports of slowness on a particular server. Perhaps an RDSH or Remote Access server where users are interacting with it every day, and every few days, you receive support tickets indicating that the system was running slowly or wouldn't allow anyone new to log in. By the time that ticket crosses your desk and you hop into the server, whatever the problem was has disappeared, and the server is running happily again.

This is where Perfmon can shine. After defining the performance counters that you are interested in monitoring, you can create your own **Data Collector Set** (which is a collection of counters) and configure it to run on a schedule. Expand **Data Collector Sets**, then right-click on **User Defined** and select **New > Data Collector Set**. Walking through this wizard, you can use some predefined templates to gather common metrics, or you can define your data collector set manually. Pick and choose which performance counters you would like to include and how often the data collector set will log data for each counter (every 15 seconds by default). You can see in *Figure 15.18* that I am working my way through defining a manual list of counters, and I have added some of the classic hardware utilization metrics to my collection list:

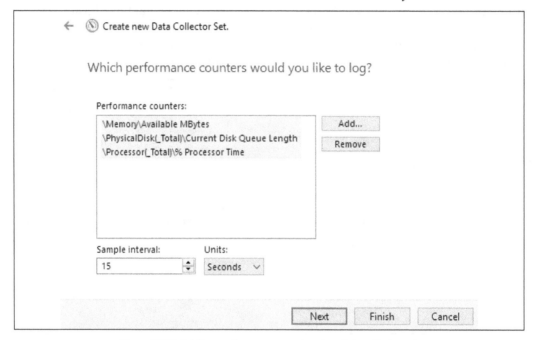

Figure 15.18: Adding performance counters to a data collector set

After defining your counters and specifying a location for this data to be saved, the last screen of the wizard provides the option to **Run as**. In many cases, you can leave **<Default>** configured here and your dataset will work just fine, but if any of your counters are struggling to gather data, you could alternatively specify a different account here, such as an administrator account. Leave the option selected for **Save and close** and click **Finish**. I want to use this option, rather than one of the others that invokes immediate action, so that we can see where it is inside the Perfmon console that our new data collector set is stored.

Back inside the Perfmon console, looking under the **User Defined** folder, you will see a **New Data Collector Set** that didn't exist previously. This is our new set of counters, ready to be run at any time. This is a nice way to save common sets of performance counters for easy running and reference later, and if you right-click on **New Data Collector Set** and head into **Properties**, you will also find a **Schedule** tab, which allows you to set this data collector up to start on a particular date and time. Then, inside the **Stop Condition** tab, you can define how long you would like these metrics to be gathered for. Remember that we set the interval to 15 seconds, so this data collector set will start at the time you specify and will log data from the included counters every 15 seconds for as long as you determine the data collector set should run, stopping the data collection as specified in the **Stop Condition** tab:

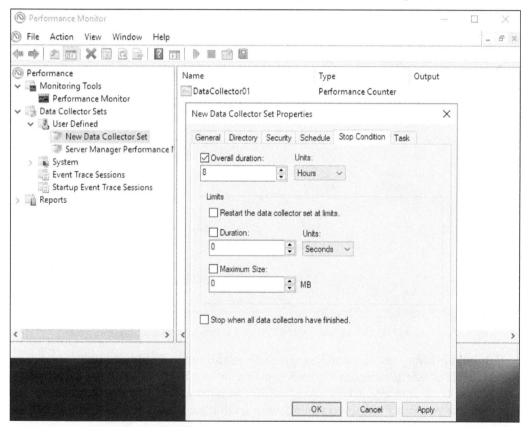

Figure 15.19: Configuring a scheduled runtime for the new data collector set

In the future, if I wanted to tweak which counters are included in this dataset, I can right-click on **DataCollector01**, shown in *Figure 15.19*, and visit **Properties** here to add new counters or remove existing ones.

I have allowed the new data collector set to run for a few minutes and gather some data. Now that I'm finished with the defined runtime, how do I find the data that was generated? Still inside the Perfmon console, look just a little further down the tree for **Reports**. Inside **User Defined** reports, you'll find a folder for your new data collector set. Each time that your collector set runs, it will generate a new file here with a date stamp. Clicking on today's file shows me all the data gathered, and I have the same options available for manipulating the data or changing how the graph looks as I did in the live data view:

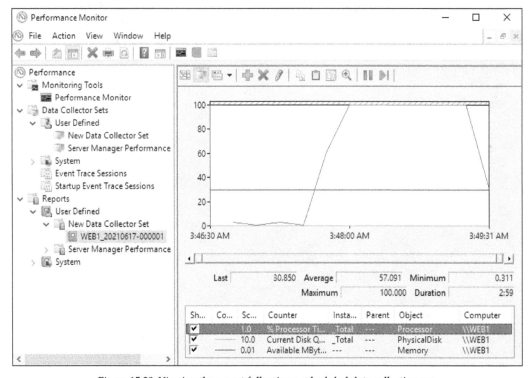

Figure 15.20: Viewing the report following a scheduled data collection run

Scheduled Perfmon datasets can be extremely useful when troubleshooting regularly occurring performance problems on a server. In the example of an RDSH server that we discussed earlier, when tackling reported slowness on that server, you could establish a Perfmon data collector set that took metrics surrounding hardware utilization. You could include session count metrics to see how many users are logged in during the same timestamps. This Perfmon report could then shed some very interesting and helpful light on the situation; perhaps you simply have too many people connected during the times that hardware is taxed. Or maybe, you'll find that the server slows down at the top of every hour and then use that information to realize that you have backups running at the top of every hour, which leads you in the direction of problem resolution.

Windows Firewall with Advanced Security

When thinking about Windows Server troubleshooting, the firewall is probably not one of the first things that comes to mind. However, the Windows Firewall with Advanced Security console can be a very friendly tool for identifying and resolving issues that crop up related to networking on our servers. While reading this book, you have already been given instructions on some of the most important things that you can do within WFAS. We discussed the three different firewall profiles and the fact that each individual NIC on a server could be utilizing a different firewall profile. This knowledge really comes into play within a corporate domain environment. When servers are running inside your network and can contact a domain controller, their NICs that are connected to that network should always self-assign the Domain firewall profile. This is important because the firewall rules you expect to be in place while that server is inside the network (which is probably at all times) are only in effect when the Domain profile is active. Even if you choose to have the Windows Firewall turned off when inside the network, most companies set up those policies so that ONLY if the Domain profile is active will the firewall be turned off. This implies that if a different profile gets assigned to a NIC, the Private or Public profile, then the firewall could indeed be turned on and block traffic flow.

If the server is inside the network, why would it ever self-assign the Public or Private profiles? If a domain controller is not available when the server boots, it won't grab the Domain profile. Sometimes, it won't grab the Domain profiles just because sometimes Windows goofs when it boots. It is actually a very regular ticket that I see at work where a server is not communicating properly and, after a little bit of discovery, we find that the NIC for that server reports it is using the Public or Private profile, even though it is on the same LAN as a DC. The three firewall profiles have potentially very different firewall rules and can even turn the firewall on or off, depending on how each profile is configured.

Another scenario is a server with multiple NICs, which increases the chances that one of those NICs may grab the wrong firewall profile upon boot. A common issue I had to face with deploying DirectAccess in many enterprise environments is that we would almost always be using two NICs, one on the internal network and one inside a DMZ. While deploying the server, we would expect that the internal NIC would use the Domain profile, but the DMZ NIC would use the Public or Private profile, as you *should never* be able to loop back inside the network and contact a DC from inside a DMZ network, right? You would be amazed at the number of times the installation of our DirectAccess server brought to light major security holes that existed in these enterprise-class DMZ networks. It is a very common thing to have that DMZ External NIC receive a Domain profile classification inside the firewall, which definitely means that the NIC was able to successfully contact a domain controller.

The moral of the story with this section is not to re-hash the WFAS tool that you have already seen and experienced, but to shed a little more light on how it can be used for troubleshooting purposes. If a server is having trouble communicating with something, or something with that server, take five seconds to pop open WF.MSC and verify that the correct firewall profiles are active. If you have booted a domain-joined server and expect that it be running the Domain firewall profile but find that it is not, you can visit SERVICES.MSC and restart the **Network Location Awareness (NLA)** service, and that will usually clear up the behavior. Following the service restart, the Domain profile should then be active on the NIC, assuming, of course, that it can successfully contact a domain controller.

System Insights

We summarized System Insights in *Chapter 1, Getting Started with Windows Server 2019*, but we definitely want to revisit it here in our chapter on troubleshooting. This is because this tool gathers all the right parts and pieces to help us build a comprehensive story about what is going on with our servers, and to help predict critical points at which servers may run out of resources and need to be upgraded or expanded.

System Insights is all about predictive analytics. It is available on any Windows Server 2019 (you just need to enable it) and utilizes performance counters to monitor the system and record data. This data is stored on the local server, which is important because it means you do not have to go through a bunch of work and hoops to implement some kind of centralized database for retaining the data, nor do any cloud work to maintain these metrics. The information collected by System Insights is individual per server and is retained on each server for up to a year.

Once System Insights is up and running, you can tap into the data it is collecting via PowerShell or Windows Admin Center. Let's flip the switch to enable System Insights on my WEB1 server and see what it looks like.

All we need to do on WEB1 is install the Windows Feature called… you guessed it… **System Insights**! This can be installed using the **Add Roles and Features** wizard in Server Manager, or by running the following PowerShell command:

```
Add-WindowsFeature System-Insights -IncludeManagementTools
```

Bonus feature! You can even install System Insights by pulling up Windows Admin Center, selecting a server, and then visiting the System Insights tool on the left-hand side of the screen. Here, you will find a simple **Install** button, which will roll System Insights to the server with one click!

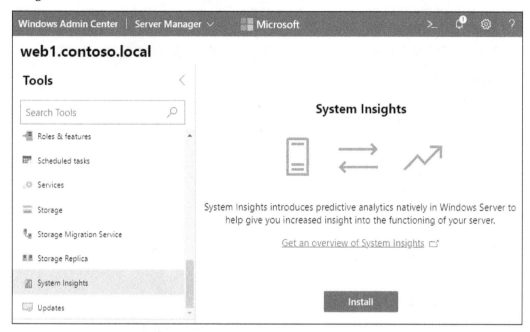

Figure 15.21: Installing System Insights from WAC with a single click

Once the feature is installed, revisit the System Insights screen inside WAC and you will see four different insight options available. These are the four predictive items that System Insights can help plan and forecast:

- CPU capacity forecasting
- Networking capacity forecasting
- Total storage consumption forecasting
- Volume consumption forecasting

Depending on what stats and hardware you are interested in monitoring, select the appropriate capability and click the **Invoke** button, or select them all just to see what System Insights comes back with. As you can see in *Figure 15.22*, I invoked all four, and currently, they are all reporting green. System Insights has determined that these components of my WEB1 virtual server are in good shape and are forecasted to remain that way:

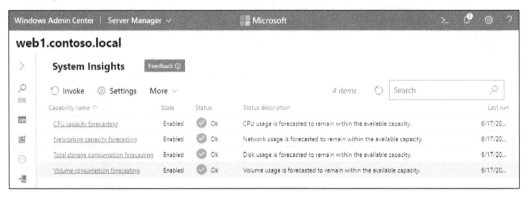

Figure 15.22: System Insights data displayed inside Windows Admin Center

Remote toolsets

Here is another section where you already have the information you need if you have been working through this book from start to finish, but it never hurts to receive a gentle reminder on taking what you have learned and putting it into practice.

Remote Desktop, Hyper-V Console, PowerShell, Sconfig, Windows Admin Center, MMC consoles, Server Manager. These are all different tools, any of which could be used to accomplish similar tasks on your servers. I love training new IT staff into our service desk and working alongside them on tickets, especially in areas where they have limited experience and are hesitant to dive in. Using the Remote Desktop client to RDP into servers is still by far the most common way that administrators log into their servers to make changes or for any reason, and when you do that all day every day, it is easy to forget about all the other ways that you can interact with those servers. RDP is one of the first things that will quit working when a server is under heavy load or struggling to breathe.

I have watched many an admin attempt to RDP to a server that is having trouble, be unsuccessful at making the RDP connection, and sit for a while at a roadblock, not knowing what to do next. There are so many ways that you can check the status of that server remotely or even reboot it remotely, but these options seem like distant memories when you're on the phone with an angry CEO who just wants their stuff to work *right now*.

Incorporate these remote administration tools into your daily workflow. Some are more efficient than others but continue to utilize them all at various times. That way, when you're in the heat of the moment and facing a difficult situation, muscle memory will take over, and you'll soon become the quickest draw in the West – for tapping into server administration toolsets, anyway.

Event Logs

Any investigatory work on a server is well-complimented by Windows Event Logs. Sometimes you catch a server in the act of misbehaving and can utilize all the tools we have discussed so far to figure out, in real time, what is happening and how to remediate it. Other times, you may have experienced a problem – an unexpected restart of a server is a prime example – and even though things are running smoothly again, you are now tasked with answering that enormous question, "What happened?"

The Windows operating system logs a lot of data, all the time. These logs can answer questions when nothing else in the system can, as it provides a historical roadmap of wins and challenges happening within the OS, visible in static text where patterns emerge and details are given.

The tool that is home to Windows Event Logs is called **Event Viewer**. Opening Event Viewer can be accomplished in a few ways. You could seek out Event Viewer in the **Start** search function, but there is also a quick link to open Event Viewer when right-clicking on the **Start** button. A third option is to call EVENTVWR.MSC from **Start | Run**, Command Prompt, or PowerShell. When you open this tool, you will see that your most common places to go are inside the folder called **Windows Logs.** Here, you will find **Application, Security**, and **System** event logs. For most log review tasks, these are the three most common sets of logs to visit for seeking out information related to diagnosing a problem that occurred:

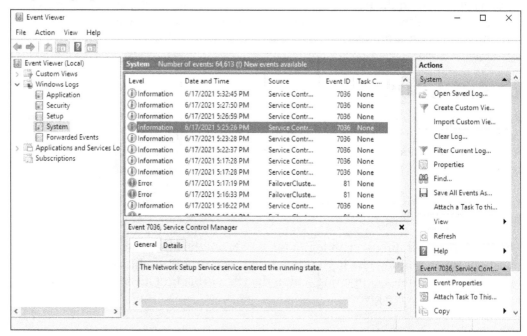

Figure 15.23: Event Viewer

I find myself spending most of my time inside **Application** and **System** event logs. As you can tell by the names of these logs, Application logs will contain information about the applications running on the server, while System logs pertain to the system itself. However, there is definitely some crossover, as "applications" in Windows could also relate to roles, and so you will find some information related to the operating system inside the Application event logs. For Security logs, the most common reason that the average server administrator would visit here would be to dig into authentication issues, such as a locked user account. The Security logs are also useful when you're investigating a security breach. Spending any amount of time in the Security logs will quickly overwhelm you because there is a *lot* of information in there, and much of it is ambiguous. Boy, I wish there was a way to filter out some of the noise here…

Filtering event logs

Oh yeah, there *is* a way to filter these logs! I rarely visit event logs *without* filtering in some way, lest I find myself lost in a sea of information for the entire day. While inside any log file, you can right-click on the name of the log (such as **Application** or **System**) and choose **Filter Current Log…**. There are many ways that filtering can be accomplished here, but one of the most common is to hide away all informational events. If you find yourself reviewing Windows log files just to peruse information events, you, without a doubt, have too much time on your hands. I'm kidding, of course, but seriously – when you're looking inside event logs, you are likely looking for a cause to a problem. Informational event logs will rarely be helpful in this scenario. Instead, selecting the following checkboxes will rid your Event Viewer view of all informational logs, focusing on all the warnings and errors that are present:

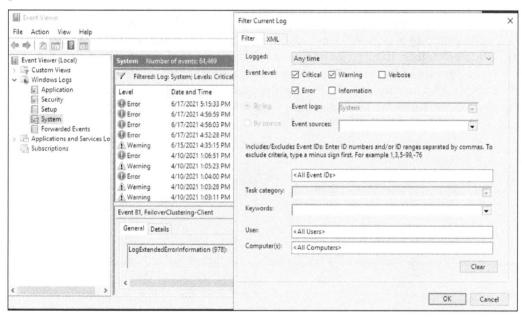

Figure 15.24: Filtering event logs to only display warnings and errors

Once filtered, you can easily scroll through all the errors and warnings listed in this event log and search for clues to help identify whatever issues you are trying to solve. If you identify something interesting, you could note the date and timestamp of that log entry and then reinclude informational events and search through everything that was being logged during that timeframe. This often helps tell a server's story as it approaches some form of trouble. In many cases, using a combination of Application and System event logs is going to give you a well-rounded picture of what was happening on the system during that time.

Looking at *Figure 15.24*, you can also see a filter option right in the middle for including or excluding Event IDs. Each event type has an identifier number. Once you've latched onto a particular event as being related to a problem that you are troubleshooting, a common question that comes up is "How often has this issue occurred?" To answer this, you can filter the logs to a particular Event ID simply by typing that ID number into this field. Event Viewer will then show you only instances of that Event ID. You can comma-separate multiple Event IDs to include more information in the log view, while maintaining a view only containing data that you are actually interested in seeing.

An alternative feature that I absolutely love and use all the time is to exclude particular Event IDs. As an example, my System event log is filled with informational events from Service Control Manager, which is just noise that I generally don't care about. I can see that these events have an Event ID number 7036. In *Figure 15.25*, I have two instances of Event Viewer side by side – one showing the System event log and the other showing the same log but with Event 7036 excluded. This really helps cut the noise and shows me more interesting events that actually pertain to my troubleshooting. In fact, not only was 7036 getting annoying to sift through, but I was seeing a lot of Event ID 81 as well, so I have excluded (hidden) those as well. In *Figure 15.25*, you can also see the method I used to exclude those two Event IDs. Simply use the **Includes/Excludes** field to input particular Event ID numbers, but place a minus (-) in front of each number:

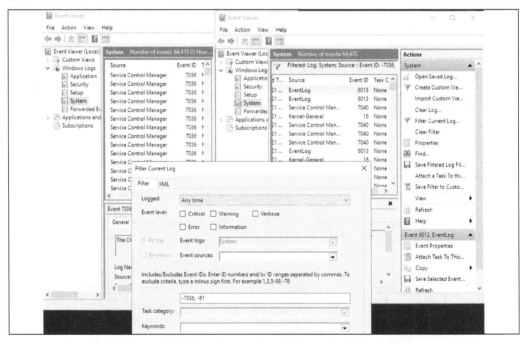

Figure 15.25: Using filters to exclude Event IDs 7036 and 81

When you've finished filtering the logs, to get back to the default view, there is no need to reverse all the filtering settings that you have put into place. Simply right-click on the log file and choose **Clear Filter**. This will immediately set that log file back to showing all events.

> You'll notice options in the right-click menu to save log files, save filtered log files, and even to save filters to views for later use. There is a lot of power available inside event log filtering!

Exporting Windows event logs with PowerShell

While using the Event Viewer console is the most common way to review and parse through log files, sometimes, you may wish for a way to easily export all this data and do some other types of manipulation on it, perhaps through Excel spreadsheets or something similar. To make this happen, we would need a way to export the information in these logs into something like a CSV file. Is this possible? You bet!

PowerShell can tap into anything inside Windows, including event logs. PowerShell also has a built-in function for exporting data into a CSV file, so let's combine those two capabilities and build out some commands that will suck Windows event logs out of Windows, directly into a CSV file. Here are some examples:

```
Get-EventLog -LogName Application | Export-CSV C:\Logs\Application_
Logs.csv
```

This command exports the entire contents of the Application event logs to a CSV file:

```
Get-EventLog -LogName System -Newest 100 | Export-CSV C:\Logs\System_
Logs_Newest.csv
```

Here, we are exporting the System event logs, but you'll notice an extra parameter in there. This time, we are only grabbing the newest 100 events from the log, and throwing them into a CSV file:

```
Get-EventLog -LogName Security -Newest 50 -ComputerName WEB1 | Export-
CSV C:\Logs\WEB1_Security_Logs.csv
```

As our commands get larger, they are doing more comprehensive things. This one grabs the latest 50 events from the Security logs but is specifying the WEB1 server. This is a good example to show that I don't even have to be logged into the server to pull logs from it. Instead, I can run these PowerShell commands from my workstation, against my servers, pulling log information remotely. You could then take this information and apply it to scheduled scripts, perhaps if you wanted to maintain long-term storage of event log data for particular systems:

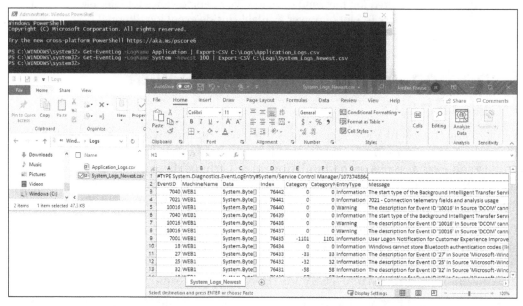

Figure 15.26: Exporting logs to CSV for easy searching and sorting

As you begin working with Windows log files, you will find that Event Viewer does a fantastic job of sorting by log type, and that using Event ID inclusions and exclusions will often find you the information that you are looking for. The one thing that is majorly lacking inside Event Viewer is the ability to easily search for text that exists inside events. When clicking on any event, you can see all the descriptive text that is included inside that log event, but there is not a good way to search within that text across all of your event logs. This is where exporting to CSV can be especially handy. Throw those commands in PowerShell to export the log, open the CSV file, and use Excel's search function to find what you are looking for.

Common Event IDs

Exploring event logs on a regular basis will start to form patterns in your brain about what types of events to look for, where to find them, and even which particular Event IDs are commonly searched for in daily troubleshooting and investigations. Here is a quick listing of some Event ID numbers that I keep in a list near my desk, at all times, as I often search for them:

- **4740 (Security log) – User account locked**. This is the first event to search for when investigating a user account lockout issue. Oftentimes, 4740 will show you a "Source computer name," which steers you toward which device in the network is causing the lockout.

- **4625 (Security log) – Account failed to log on**. I often search for 4625 alongside 4740. While 4740 will hopefully tell you which device to review, 4625 will give a reason as to why the account locked out; for example, if a bad username or password were given.

- **4767 (Security log) – User account unlocked**. Corresponding logs related to user account lockouts. Check these to find unlock events.

- **6013 (System log) – System uptime**. Every day at noon, every Windows computer and server logs this event. It shows, in seconds, the amount of uptime that the system has been running for. This can be useful for figuring out, historically, how long a server has been running, for example, by following an unexpected restart and if you want to know how long the server had been running prior to that restart.

- **6008 (System log) – Unexpected shutdown**. Many times, if a server unexpectedly restarts, it's not too concerning. All computers do that occasionally. If, however, you are investigating a server because it has unexpectedly restarted numerous times, you'll want to start searching for patterns about what is happening surrounding each of those unexpected restarts. Event 6008 is the event that is logged, and it will show you the exact timestamp of the unexpected shutdown event. Filtering for 6008 will give you a quick way to see all the instances of the unexpected shutdown. You can then document and dig into the logs surrounding each of those timestamps to gain further information.

While this is simply a short list of common events I search for, I'm sure that, depending on your role in IT, you will add many more Event IDs to your own "Common Event ID" lists.

MMC and MSC shortcuts

You have probably noticed that many of the management consoles that we utilize to configure components inside Windows Server 2019 look pretty similar. What happens under the hood with a number of these consoles is that you are actually looking at a snap-in function, a specific set of tools that are snapped into a generic console tool called the **Microsoft Management Console**, more commonly referred to as **MMC**. In fact, rather than opening all these management functions from inside Server Manager, for many of them, you could simply type MMC by navigating to **Start | Run** or Command Prompt and invoke the generic MMC console. From here, you can click on the **File** menu and choose **Add or Remove Snap-ins**:

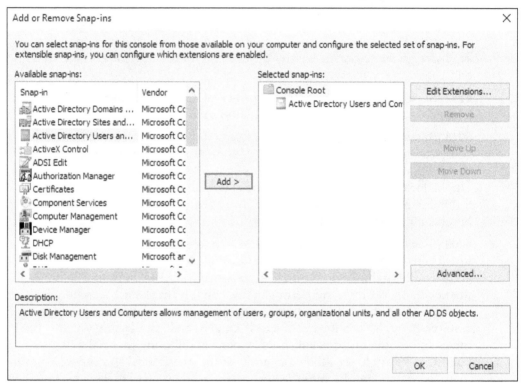

Figure 15.27: Using MMC to snap in management consoles

Choose the management snap-in that you would like to work in and add it to the console. There are a large number of management functions that can be accessed through the standard MMC console, and even some functions where MMC is the preferred, or perhaps the only method for interacting with some components of Windows. For example, when we utilized MMC to review certificates installed on the local computer back in *Chapter 6, Certificates in Windows Server 2019*.

Another interesting way to open many of the management consoles is by using their direct **MSC** tool name. An MSC file is simply a saved configuration of an MMC console session. There are many MSC shortcuts stored in Windows Server 2019 out of the box. If a given management console can be launched by an MSC, all you need to do is type in the name of the MSC by navigating to either **Start | Run**, Command Prompt, or a PowerShell window, and it will immediately launch into that particular management console without needing to snap anything in, and without needing to open Server Manager whatsoever. Since I tend to prefer using a keyboard over a mouse, I always have a PowerShell window or Command Prompt open on each system I'm working with, and I can very quickly use that window to open any of my MSC administrative consoles. Let's show one example, so that you know exactly how to use this functionality, and then I will provide a list of the common MSCs that I find useful on a day-to-day basis.

Open an elevated PowerShell window, type WF.MSC, and press *Enter*:

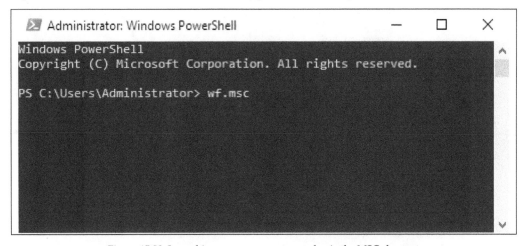

Figure 15.28: Launching a management console via the MSC shortcut

The **Windows Defender Firewall with Advanced Security** window will open and is ready to accept input from you. We didn't have to poke through **Control Panel** or open the regular **Windows Firewall** and then click on the **Advanced Settings** link, which are the common ways to get into this console by using a mouse. By knowing our MSC shortcut name, we were able to take a direct route to opening the full WFAS console, which is where I often go to check particular firewall rules or statuses:

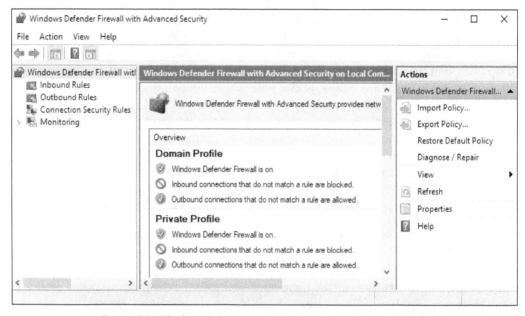

Figure 15.29: The fastest way to access Windows Firewall is via WF.MSC

Now that you've seen how an MSC command works, and again, there are many different places where you can type in the name of an MSC and invoke it, I want to leave you with a list of common MSC consoles that you can use to quickly gain access to many administrative consoles on your servers:

- DSA.MSC: Active Directory Users and Computers

- DSSITE.MSC: Active Directory Sites and Services

- DNSMGMT.MSC: DNS Manager

- GPEDIT.MSC: Local Group Policy Editor

- GPMC.MSC: Group Policy Management Console

- CERTSRV.MSC: Certification Authority Management

- CERTTMPL.MSC: Certificate Template Management

- CERTLM.MSC: Local Computer Certificates Store

- `CERTMGR.MSC`: Current User Certificates Store
- `COMPMGMT.MSC`: Computer Management
- `DEVMGMT.MSC`: Device Manager
- `DHCPMGMT.MSC`: DHCP Manager
- `DISKMGMT.MSC`: Disk Management
- `EVENTVWR.MSC`: Event Viewer
- `PERFMON.MSC`: Performance Monitor
- `SECPOL.MSC`: Local Security Policy Console
- `FSMGMT.MSC`: Shared Folders
- `WF.MSC`: Windows Defender Firewall with Advanced Security
- `shell:startup`: While not an MSC, this is a shortcut that opens the logged in user's `Start Menu\Programs\Startup` folder. This is a useful location to visit when looking for a program running on startup that you can't find elsewhere, or when you want to cause an application to start every time this user logs into the computer
- `shell:common startup`: Similar to `shell:startup`, but this launches into the Public User's Startup folder. Shortcuts added here will auto-launch whenever *any* user logs into the system

Summary

Designing and building brand new servers rarely presents challenges, and if they are encountered, those issues are typically low priority, since the new server won't yet be affecting a production workforce. Troubleshooting servers, on the other hand, can be very stressful and requires quick, on-the-fly recollection of tools and command sets available inside the operating system that can be used to identify issues and resolutions. I hope this chapter has given you the ammunition needed to feel more confident in those situations and to become the "go-to" person in your IT department when it comes to diagnosing server problems and digging deep into problems that arise.

This brings us to the end of our story on Windows Server 2019. Many of the topics we discussed could fill entire books, and I hope that the ideas provided in this volume are enough to prompt you to dig further into the technologies that you plan to work with. Microsoft technology reigns supreme in most data centers across the globe. The new and updated features inside Windows Server 2019 will ensure that this trend continues long into the future.

Questions

1. What is the MSC shortcut for opening Active Directory Users and Computers?

2. True or False – You should always store server backups on the same server that you are backing up for performance reasons.

3. Which Windows monitoring tool can be used to graph CPU utilization over a 24-hour period?

4. True or False – System Insights stores all data on a centralized RADIUS server.

5. What is the MSC shortcut for opening Windows Defender Firewall with Advanced Security?

6. Which PowerShell cmdlet can be used to gather Windows log files?

7. Which Event ID can be used to calculate system uptime?

Appendix: Answers to the end-of-chapter Questions

Chapter 1: Getting Started with Windows Server 2019

1. In Windows Server 2019, how can you launch an elevated PowerShell prompt with two mouse clicks?

   Answer: Right-click on the **Start** button and select **Windows PowerShell (Admin)** from the **Quick Admin Tasks** menu

2. What is the keyboard combination to open the **Quick Admin Tasks** menu?

   Answer: *WinKey+X*

3. What is the name of Microsoft's cloud service offering?

   Answer: Microsoft Azure

4. What are the two licensing versions of Windows Server 2019?

   Answer: Standard and Datacenter

5. How many virtual machines can run on top of a Windows Server 2019 Standard host?

   Answer: 2

6. What installation option for Windows Server 2019 does not have a graphical user interface?

   Answer: Server Core

7. Which is the correct verbiage for the latest release of Windows Server 2019, **Long-Term Servicing Branch (LTSB)** or **Long-Term Servicing Channel (LTSC)**?

   Answer: Long-Term Servicing Channel (LTSC)

8. What is the correct tool from which to change configurations on Windows Server 2019, **Windows Settings** or **Control Panel**?

   Answer: Both, although Windows Settings is the preferred method for most configuration options

Chapter 2: Installing and Managing Windows Server 2019

1. What is the name of the new web-based, centralized server management tool from Microsoft (fun fact, this toolset was formerly known as Project Honolulu)?

   Answer: Windows Admin Center (WAC)

2. True or False—Windows Server 2019 needs to be installed onto rack-mount server hardware.

   Answer: False. Windows Server 2019 can be installed onto physical hardware, or as a virtual machine instance.

3. True or False—By choosing the default installation option for Windows Server 2019, you will end up with a user interface that looks quite like Windows 10.

   Answer: False. The default option for Windows Server 2019 is Server Core, which does not have a graphical user interface.

4. What is the PowerShell cmdlet that displays currently installed roles and features in Windows Server 2019?

   Answer: `Get-WindowsFeature | Where Installed`.

5. True or False—Server Manager can be used to manage many different servers at the same time.

   Answer: True.

6. What is the name of the toolset that can be installed onto a Windows 10 computer in order to run Server Manager on that client workstation?

   Answer: Remote Server Administration Tools (RSAT).

7. What are the supported web browsers that can be used to interact with Windows Admin Center?

   Answer: As of this writing, Microsoft Edge and Google Chrome. Note that Internet Explorer is not supported.

Chapter 3: Active Directory

1. Inside Active Directory, a container (folder) that holds computer and user accounts is called a(n)...?

    Answer: Organizational Unit (OU)

2. What is the term for creating a computer account inside Active Directory prior to that computer being joined to your domain?

    Answer: Prestaging the account

3. Which management tool is used to specify that certain physical locations in your network are bound to particular IP subnets?

    Answer: Active Directory Sites and Services

4. What is the name of a special domain controller that cannot accept new information, only synchronize from an existing domain controller?

    Answer: Read-Only Domain Controller (RODC)

5. What tool is needed to create a fine-grained password policy?

    Answer: Active Directory Administrative Center

6. What must be configured inside DNS prior to establishing a forest trust?

    Answer: Conditional forwarder

Chapter 4: DNS and DHCP

1. What kind of DNS record directs email flow?

    Answer: MX record

2. Which type of DNS record resolves a name to an IPv6 address?

    Answer: AAAA record

3. Which DNS zone type resolves IP addresses backward into hostnames?

    Answer: Reverse Lookup Zone

4. What DHCP option is often used for VoIP phone provisioning?

    Answer: Option 66

5. Which mode of DHCP failover is often used between branch offices and a primary site?

    Answer: Hot standby mode

6. What is the standard recommendation and default setting for Maximum Client Lead Time when configuring Load balanced DHCP failover?

    Answer: One hour

7. Which Windows Server roles can IPAM tap into?

    Answer: Active Directory, DNS, DHCP, and NPS! We didn't talk about NPS in this chapter because we have not yet covered any NPS material, but it is a fourth role that can report data into IPAM.

Chapter 5: Group Policy

1. Are screensaver settings computer or user configuration?

    Answer: User configuration

2. Do domain-level or OU-level links process first?

    Answer: Domain-level links process before OU-level links, meaning that OU-level links will overwrite domain-level links when in conflict

3. What is the special GPO setting that forces user settings to apply to any user on a given computer?

    Answer: Group Policy loopback processing

4. What type of GPO filtering do you configure inside the GPO itself, such as with a mapped network drives policy?

    Answer: Item-level targeting

5. True or False— It is possible for a user to override a Group Policy preference.

    Answer: True

6. What is the default timer between Group Policy background refresh cycles?

    Answer: 90 minutes

Chapter 6: Certificates in Windows Server 2019

1. What is the name of the role inside Windows Server 2019 that allows you to issue certificates from your server?

    Answer: Certification Authority

2. What kind of CA server is typically installed first in a domain environment?

    Answer: Enterprise Root CA

3. Should you install the Certification Authority role onto a domain controller?

   Answer: No, this is not a recommended scenario

4. After creating a new certificate template, what next step needs to be taken before you can issue certificates to your computers or users from that new template?

   Answer: The new certificate template must be published

5. What is the general name of the GPO setting that forces certificates to be issued without manual intervention by an administrator?

   Answer: Certificate Auto-enrollment

6. An SSL certificate will only be able to validate traffic properly if it shares _____ key information with the webserver.

   Answer: Private key

7. What is the primary piece of information that a public certification authority needs in order to issue you a new SSL certificate (hint: you generate this from your webserver)?

   Answer: **Certificate Signing Request (CSR)**

Chapter 7: Networking with Windows Server 2019

1. How many bits in length is an IPv6 address?

   Answer: 128 bits.

2. Re-write the following IPv6 address in condensed form: `2001:ABCD:0001:0002:0000:0000:0000:0001`

   Answer: `2001:ABCD:1:2::1`

3. What is the name of the command that is similar to trace route, but displays the local NIC that traffic is flowing out of?

   Answer: `PATHPING`

4. True or False—On a server with multiple NICs, you can input a default gateway address onto each of those NICs.

   Answer: False. Doing so will cause routing issues. You should only ever have one Default Gateway address on a system, no matter how many NICs it has.

5. What is the PowerShell cmdlet that can be used to create new routes on a Windows Server?

   Answer: `New-NetRoute`

6. Which Windows Server operating systems can be used with an Azure Network Adapter in order to connect them straight to Azure virtual networks?

   Answer: Windows Server 2019, 2016, and 2012 R2

Chapter 8: Remote Access

1. What does AOVPN stand for?

   Answer: Always On VPN

2. What are the two primary protocols used for connecting AOVPN clients?

   Answer: IKEv2 and SSTP

3. In which version of Windows 10 was AOVPN released?

   Answer: Windows 10 1607

4. In what special instance would an AOVPN client be required to be joined to your domain?

   Answer: When you want to utilize the AOVPN Device Tunnel

5. Does DirectAccess require your corporate internal network to be running IPv6?

   Answer: No, your internal network can be completely IPv4

6. What is the name of the internal website that DirectAccess clients check in with in order to determine when they are inside the corporate network?

   Answer: **Network Location Server (NLS)**

7. What role does a Web Application Proxy server hold in a federation environment?

   Answer: WAP can be implemented as an ADFS proxy

Chapter 9: Hardening and Security

1. What is the name of the anti-malware product built into Windows Server 2019?

   Answer: Windows Defender Antivirus

2. When a domain-joined computer is sitting inside the corporate LAN, which Windows Defender Firewall profile should be active?

   Answer: The Domain profile

3. Other than the Domain profile, what are the other two possible firewall profiles inside Windows Defender Firewall?

   Answer: Public and Private

4. When creating a firewall rule to allow IPv4 ping replies, what protocol type must you specify inside your inbound rule?

   Answer: ICMPv4

5. What is the easiest way to push standardized Windows Defender Firewall rules to your entire workforce?

   Answer: Group Policy

6. A virtual machine whose virtual hard disk file is encrypted is called a...?

   Shielded VM

7. What is the name of the Microsoft technology that parses domain controller information in order to identify pass-the-hash and pass-the-ticket attacks?

   Answer: Advanced Threat Analytics

Chapter 10: Server Core

1. True or False—Server Core is the default installation option for Windows Server 2019.

   Answer: True

2. True or False—You can utilize PowerShell to change a Server 2019 instance from *Server Core* mode to *Desktop Experience* mode.

   Answer: False, switching back and forth is not possible in Windows Server 2019

3. When sitting at the console of a freshly booted Windows Server 2019 Server Core instance, what application do you see on the screen?

   Answer: Command Prompt

4. What cmdlet can be used to view the current networking configuration on a Server Core instance?

   Answer: `Get-NetIPConfiguration`

5. Which PowerShell cmdlet can be used to configure the hostname of a Server Core instance?

   Answer: `Rename-Computer`

6. Name some of the management tools that can be used to remotely interface with a Server Core instance.

   Answer: PowerShell, Server Manager, RSAT, and Windows Admin Center

7. What is the name of the utility built into Server Core that can be launched to provide quick task links for configuring IP addresses, hostnames, and domain membership?

   Answer: Sconfig.exe

Chapter 11: PowerShell

1. What is the fastest way to get from Command Prompt into PowerShell?

   Answer: Simply type the word powershell and press *Enter*

2. What is the cmdlet that will display all available PowerShell cmdlets?

   Answer: Get-Command

3. What PowerShell cmdlet can be used to connect your PowerShell prompt to a remote computer?

   Answer: Enter-PSSession

4. What file extension does a PowerShell scripting file have?

   Answer: .PS1

5. To which setting is the DEP configured on a fresh Windows Server 2019 instance?

   Answer: RemoteSigned

6. What key on your keyboard can be used to auto-populate the remainder of a cmdlet or filename when working in a PowerShell prompt?

   Answer: *Tab*

7. Which service must be running on a system before it can be connected to by a remote PowerShell connection?

   Answer: The WinRM service

Chapter 12: Redundancy in Windows Server 2019

1. Which technology is more appropriate for making web server traffic redundant – Network Load Balancing or failover clustering?

   Answer: Network Load Balancing

2. In Network Load Balancing, what do the acronyms DIP and VIP stand for?

   Answer: Dedicated IP address and virtual IP address

3. What are the three NLB modes?

   Answer: Unicast, Multicast, and Multicast IGMP

4. In Windows Server 2019, is Network Load Balancing a role or a feature?

   Answer: NLB is a feature

5. What roles are most often used with failover clustering?

   Answer: Hyper-V and file services

6. What type of small device can now be used as a cluster quorum witness (this is brand new as of Server 2019)?

   Answer: A USB memory stick

7. True or False—Storage Spaces Direct requires the use of SSD hard drives.

   Answer: False, you may use any type of hard drive with S2D

Chapter 13: Containers and Nano Server

1. A Windows Server container can run a base OS that is one of two different types: what are they?

   Answer: Server Core and Nano Server

2. Compared to a Windows Server container, what type of container provides even greater levels of isolation?

   Answer: Hyper-V container

3. True or False— In Windows Server 2016, you could run both Windows and Linux containers on the same Windows Server host platform.

   Answer: False, the ability to run Windows and Linux containers is new as of Windows Server 2019

4. What is the Docker command to see a list of container images on your local system?

   Answer: `docker images`

5. What is currently the most popular container orchestration software that integrates with Windows Server 2019?

   Answer: Kubernetes

6. True or False—Developers can install Docker onto their Windows 10 workstations to start building applications inside containers.

   Answer: True

Chapter 14: Hyper-V

1. What are the three types of virtual switches inside Hyper-V?

   Answer: External, Internal, and Private

2. If you needed to build a virtual machine that booted using UEFI, which generation of VM would you need to create?

   Answer: Generation 2

3. True or False—In Windows Server 2019 Hyper-V, you must shut down a VM in order to change its allocated amount of memory (RAM).

   Answer: False, you can adjust a VM's RAM count on the fly

4. True or False—The only way to interact with a VM is through the Hyper-V console.

   Answer: False, once your VM's operating system is installed, you can interact with it through any other traditional administration methods, such as RDP

5. What is the name of the technology inside Hyper-V that allows you to take snapshot images of virtual machines that can later be restored?

   Answer: Checkpoints

6. When running shielded VMs in your environment, what is the name of the role that handles the attestation of your Hyper-V host servers?

   Answer: Host Guardian Service

7. Which is the most comprehensive attestation method for shielded VMs—host key attestation, TPM trusted attestation, or admin trusted attestation?

   Answer: TPM trusted attestation

Chapter 15: Troubleshooting Windows Server 2019

1. What is the MSC shortcut for opening Active Directory Users and Computers?

   Answer: DSA.MSC

2. True or False – You should always store server backups on the same server that you are backing up for performance reasons.

   Answer: This is a trick question that is sort of true, sort of false. While it is true that backups will be most performant when kept on locally attached storage, you should store backups in a separate location in case the server completely dies or is taken by ransomware.

3. Which Windows monitoring tool can be used to graph CPU utilization over a 24-hour period?

   Answer: Performance Monitor

4. True or False – System Insights stores all data on a centralized RADIUS server.

   Answer: False – System Insights stores data on the local server where it is installed.

5. What is the MSC shortcut for opening Windows Defender Firewall with Advanced Security?

   Answer: WF.MSC

6. Which PowerShell cmdlet can be used to gather Windows log files?

   Answer: Get-EventLog

7. Which Event ID can be used to calculate system uptime?

   Answer: 6013

`packt.com`

Subscribe to our online digital library for full access to over 7,000 books and videos, as well as industry leading tools to help you plan your personal development and advance your career. For more information, please visit our website.

Why subscribe?

- Spend less time learning and more time coding with practical eBooks and Videos from over 4,000 industry professionals
- Learn better with Skill Plans built especially for you
- Get a free eBook or video every month
- Fully searchable for easy access to vital information
- Copy and paste, print, and bookmark content

Did you know that Packt offers eBook versions of every book published, with PDF and ePub files available? You can upgrade to the eBook version at www.Packt.com and as a print book customer, you are entitled to a discount on the eBook copy. Get in touch with us at customercare@packtpub.com for more details.

At www.Packt.com, you can also read a collection of free technical articles, sign up for a range of free newsletters, and receive exclusive discounts and offers on Packt books and eBooks.

Other Books You May Enjoy

If you enjoyed this book, you may be interested in these other books by Packt:

Mastering PowerShell Scripting - Fourth Edition

Chris Dent

ISBN: 9781800206540

- Optimize code with functions, switches, and looping structures
- Work with objects and operators to test and manipulate data
- Parse and manipulate different data types
- Create scripts and functions using PowerShell
- Use jobs, runspaces, and runspace pools to run code asynchronously
- Write .NET classes with ease within PowerShell
- Create and implement regular expressions in PowerShell scripts
- Make use of advanced techniques to define and restrict the behavior of parameters

Windows Server Automation with PowerShell Cookbook - Fourth Edition

Thomas Lee

ISBN: 9781800568457

- Perform key admin tasks on Windows Server 2022/2019
- Keep your organization secure with JEA, group policies, logs, and Windows Defender
- Use the .NET Framework for administrative scripting
- Manage data and storage on Windows, including disks, volumes, and filesystems
- Create and configure Hyper-V VMs, implementing storage replication and checkpoints
- Set up virtual machines, websites, and shared files on Azure
- Report system performance using built-in cmdlets and WMI to obtain single measurements
- Apply the right tools and modules to troubleshoot and debug Windows Serve

Packt is searching for authors like you

If you're interested in becoming an author for Packt, please visit authors.packtpub. com and apply today. We have worked with thousands of developers and tech professionals, just like you, to help them share their insight with the global tech community. You can make a general application, apply for a specific hot topic that we are recruiting an author for, or submit your own idea.

Share your thoughts

Now you've finished *Mastering Windows Server 2019, Third Edition*, we'd love to hear your thoughts! Scan the QR code below to go straight to the Amazon review page for this book and share your feedback or leave a review on the site that you purchased it from.

https://packt.link/r/1-801-07831-9

Your review is important to us and the tech community and will help us make sure we're delivering excellent quality content.

Index

Routing and Remote Access (RRAS) **316, 334**
routing table
  building 287
  default gateway 288, 289
  multi-homed servers 288

S

SAC releases 15
Scale-Out File Server (SOFS) 501
SConfig 593
Sconfig utility 428-431
SDN Gateway
  working with 303
secondary zones 153
Secure Server policy 384
security
  best practices 396-402
security identifier (SID) 82
Semi-Annual Channel (SAC) 10
Sender Policy Framework (SPF)
      record 143-145
  enforcement rule 145
server 91
  customizations and updates,
      configuring onto 83
  Windows Server 2019, installing onto 83
Server Core 8, 9, 48
  available roles 432
  interfacing with 409, 410
  managing, with Windows
      Admin Center 424-428
  need for 406, 407
  PowerShell, loading 411
  reference link 432
  servers, moving back and forth capability 408
Server Core domain controller
  AD DS role, installing 433, 434
  building 433
  server, promoting 434, 435
  verifying 435-437
Server Manager 52, 61-66, 419, 420
Server policy 384
servers
  adding, to Windows Admin Center (WAC) 76,
    77
  building 504, 505

building, with copies of master image 87, 88
managing, with Windows Admin Center (WAC)
  78
Settings menu 571-573
  used, for creating user account 32, 33
Shielded Virtual Machines 16
shielded VMs 582-585
  host attestations 587
  infrastructure requirements 586
  VHDs, encrypting 585
Shielded VMs 381
shielded VMs, host attestations
  admin-trusted attestation 588
  host key attestations 587
  TPM-trusted attestations 587
single-name certificates 226
single NIC mode 323
smart cards 223
soft restart 14
software-defined data center (SDDC) 12, 521
software-defined networking 297, 298
  Azure Network Adapter 305-307
  Generic Routing Encapsulation (GRE) 302
  hybrid clouds 300
  Hyper-V Network Virtualization 298
  Microsoft Azure 305
  Microsoft Azure Virtual Network 303
  Network Controller 301
  private clouds 298, 299
  RAS Gateway 303
  SDN Gateway 303
  System Center Virtual Machine Manager 301
  virtual network encryption 304
  working with 300
Software Defined Networking (SDN) 12, 382
split-brain DNS 95, 148, 149
SSL certificates 224-226, 318
  multi-domain certificates 227
  on DirectAccess server 329
  on NLS web server 329
  single-name certificates 226
  subject alternative name certificates 227
  wildcard certificates 227
SSTP 317
Standalone CA
  versus Enterprise CA 230, 231

CPSIA information can be obtained
at www.ICGtesting.com
Printed in the USA
LVHW021748060723
751728LV00006B/288

9 781801 078